A Secret Order

Investigating the High Strangeness and Synchronicity in the JFK Assassination

– VOLUME ONE –

H.P. Albarelli Jr.

A Secret Order: Investigating the High Strangeness and Synchronicity in the JFK Assassination

Copyright © 2013. H. P. Albarelli, Jr. All Rights Reserved.
Presentation Copyright © 2013 TrineDay

Published by:
Trine Day LLC
PO Box 577
Walterville, OR 97489
1-800-556-2012
www.TrineDay.com
publisher@trineday.net

Library of Congress Control Number: 2012936844

Albarelli, H.P. Jr.
A Secret Order: Investigating the High Strangeness and Synchronicity in the JFK Assassination—1st ed.
p. cm.
Includes bibliography.
Epub (ISBN-13) 978-1-936296-56-9 (ISBN-10) 1-936296-56-X
Kindle (ISBN-13) 978-1-936296-57-6 (ISBN-10) 1-936296-57-8
Print (ISBN-13) 978-1-936296-55-2 (ISBN-10) 1-936296-55-1
1. Kennedy, John F. – (John Fitzgerald), – 1917-1963 – Assassination. 2. Oswald, Lee Harvey 3. Central Intelligence Agency – United States – History – 20th century. 4. Organized crime – United States – History – 20th century. 5. Conspiracies – United States – History – 20th century. I. Title

First Edition
10 9 8 7 6 5 4 3 2 1

Printed in the USA
Distribution to the Trade by:
Independent Publishers Group (IPG)
814 North Franklin Street
Chicago, Illinois 60610
312.337.0747
www.ipgbook.com

*T*his book is for my extraordinary grandson, Dylan Jackson Albarelli Centellas, and for my very good friend Samantha Eagles Ryea. May their lives be replete with only those synchronicities, blessings, and wonders that come from the Creator of all that is Good and Forever shall be.

In all chaos there is a cosmos, in all disorder a secret order.

— Carl Jung

Even in this world more things exist without our knowledge than with it and the order in creation which you see is that which you have put there, like a string in a maze, so that you shall not lose your way. For existence has its own order and that no man's mind can compass, that mind itself being but a fact among others.

— Cormac McCarthy, *Blood Meridian*

The man who believes that the secrets of the world are forever hidden lives in mystery and fear. Superstition will drag him down. The rain will erode the deeds of his life. But that man who sets himself the task of singling out the thread of order from the tapestry will by the decision alone have taken charge of the world and it is only by such taking charge that he will effect a way to dictate the terms of his own fate.

— Cormac McCarthy, *Blood Meridian*

Anyone who looks at the rest of this is going to see that something happened. But no one is going to be able to figure it out. That's your objective. To make it so convoluted that anyone can have a theory. But no one's got the facts.

— Capt. Darius Jedburgh, *Edge of Darkness*, 2010

I suddenly had this feeling that everything was connected.

— Finch, *V for Vendetta*, 2005

I shouted out, "Who killed the Kennedys?" when after all it was you and me.

— Mick Jagger and Keith Richards

Big D. November '63. He was there that Big Weekend. He caught the Big Moment and took this Big Ride.... His father was a big Mormon fat cat. Wayne Senior was jungled up all over the nut Right. He did Klan ops for Mr. Hoover and Dwight Holly. He pushed the high-line hate tracts. He rode the far-Right zeitgeist and stayed in the know. He knew about the JFK hit. It was multi-faction: Cuban exiles, rogue CIA, mob.

– James Ellroy, *Blood's A Rover*, 2009

He thought he would go down to the lunch-room and have a Coke. They must be in the building by now. It was so easy to hide, with such confusion, so many stacks of crates here, there and everywhere. They might even be hiding in a crate, with the rifles. Including his Mannlicher-Carcano and three or four bullets they'd fired from it. He had no idea who "they" were, only that one of them looked like him, as it happened. "I don't know who'll do the actual shooting, Lee," Ferrie had said. "It's best we don't know. It's not a question of your courage, we know you'd shoot the fucker if we asked you to, but this really is going to take a crack-shot and you've had no practice."

– D.M. Thomas, *Flying In To Love*, 1992

They've taken me in because of the fact that I lived in the Soviet Union. I'm just a patsy!

– Lee Harvey Oswald, Dallas, Texas, November 22, 1963

Patsy: scapegoat. Red herring. Person accused of a something as a cover for a bigger more elaborate crime. The guy that always takes the fall. A loser. The nice guy that finishes last every time.

– Urban Dictionary: www.urbandictionary.com

The camp was Disneyland for killers. Six hundred Cubans. Fifty white men running herd.... Dig Nestor Chasco – staging mock-assassination maneuvers.... Dig the action in the barbed-wire enclosure – peons flying on a drug called LSD. Some of them screamed. Some wept. Some grinned like LSD was a blast ... let's flood Cuba with this shit before we invade. Langley co-signed the brainstorm. Langley embellished it: Let's induce mass hallucinations and stage the Second Coming of Christ!!!!!

– James Ellroy, *American Tabloid*, 1995

I knew something was happening, something big.... I'd been around New Orleans long enough to hear the rumblings, the rumors, the whispers, the warnings from people in the stream of things, the many bit players who only knew enough to carry out their roles in the manner assigned. Eventually, there came a time when you could smell it coming, a powerful stench all the way from Dallas...

– Jean Pierre Lafitte, March 1964

Table of Contents*

Foreword by Michael J. Petro...1

Introduction 5

1. Lee Harvey Oswald in New York City 9
   -with Rachael Sullivan

2. Almost: The Sad Ballad of Rose Cherami 91
   -with Steve Rosen, Esq.

3. Adele Edisen's Strange Encounter 125
   -with Steve Duffy

4. What Did Dimitre Dimitrov Know?.. 163

5. "Welcome Back to America, Mr. Oswald." 191

6. Who Was David Sanchez Morales?.. 217

7. The Strange & Somewhat Untimely Wisdom of Dale E. Basye 269

8. Oswald, Cuba and Other Places.. 287
   -with Ran Daniel

9. The Bizarre Diary of Eric Ritzek 327

10. The Strange and Sad Saga of Charles W. Thomas 341

11. Femme Fatale Enigma: Viola June Cobb 377

Notes.. 429

Acknowledgements 457

Index 459

*While writing *A Secret Order*, I asked a few good friends and excellent researchers, for whom I have great respect, to assist with supportive research for four sections of this book. Rachel Sullivan, who lives in New York, is an accomplished actor and singer, and a longtime expert assassination researcher. Steve Rosen is an attorney and an expert researcher on a number of subjects, including David Sanchez Morales and other CIA officials. Steve Duffy lives in Australia, is a very good friend, and is one of the best researchers I know. Ran Daniel lives in Haifa, Israel. He was a former IDF sergeant major, has a masters degree in philosophy, and is a highly skilled researcher of assassinations and intelligence matters. Last, I would like to extend my sincere and deep appreciation to Bruce Campbell Adamson, an amazing researcher, whose work will be prominently featured in Volume Two of this book.

From Here to ...

B ack in the days when the Earth was flat, the oceans that limned her single continent were populated by great beasts, creatures so terrifying and loathsome that their very constitutions required the avid and fearsome imagination of men.

They were quite real, as traveler after intrepid traveler returned to bear witness to the natures of those dark shapes that loomed, just barely visible. The terrors they evoked never failed to turn away those who would inspect the outer edges of the world – those who survived to return, anyway.

Eventually, there arrived the first man of uncanny character, one who ventured forth with an eye far steadier than those that preceded him. Setting aside all prior accounts, this man chose to inspect the beasts with a steady gaze. True natures thus revealed, the monsters melted away, and the Earth became round.

As far as our common understanding of the activities of our government is concerned, today the Earth is flat. The "continent" of the government's chartered activities is surrounded by apparitions variously and often incoherently ascribed to the CIA, the "shadow government," the Illuminati, the Bilderberg Group, New World Order, aliens, or the fevered dreams of Revelations. Whether they be ascribed to malice or to willful titillation, these apparitions take on fearsome dimensions in the popular imagination, a condition that serves these covert actors – whoever they may be – very well.

Our man of uncanny character is H.P. Albarelli Jr. While reading his work, his professionalism – a till far steadier than fear – is palpable. There is an uncompromising coldness in his gaze, and one imagines it can be quite withering for the wrong characters. Lest there be any misunderstanding, one should follow quickly with the other pillar of his character. This is a man in love.

It requires a great deal of love to navigate these waters. Others have tried without it, and the Internet is littered with these carnival barkers hawking stories and films of the beasts at the edges of the world – these souls lost or sold out, because they lack an essential love. A love for the truth, of course, is missing, but there is also a more important one that our author exemplifies: love for the innocents who have suffered harm in those waters. This confers a gravitas on Albarelli's work that distinguishes it from lesser efforts.

H.P. Albarelli Jr. and others like him are indispensable to understanding the totality of the truth of America, for she obscures her history in the service of an idealistic narrative that is becoming increasingly difficult to abide. Those who seriously challenge that narrative face not just the hard threats of possible harassment, but more poignantly the softer penalties that come from marginalization and ridicule. In these matters, it is all too easy to mistake the charlatan for the journalist. Do not make this mistake here.

A Secret Order: Investigating the High Strangeness and Synchronicity in the JFK Assassination is an exploration of the many curious scraps of information the author compiled while building his compelling case against our government in the murder of one of its own (*A Terrible Mistake: The Murder of Frank Olson and the CIA's Secret Cold War Experiments*). Readers of that book will be aware that many of the characters involved in Olson's murder had shockingly close connections with the events of November 22, 1963. Such is the nature of that shadowy world, to be sure, but as we learned from the Olson book, many such coincidences point to hard information that our government just frankly would rather not share. This book sets these before you. What will you see?

Innumerable interpretations and analyses are out there, and many are excellent. Our author has expounded, with his own sane prism, on some of these matters himself, in book and essay. But there is so much information! It should be digested anew by the "hive mind" of the public, with a cold gaze, and with love.

So let us go to the garden – perhaps to finally distinguish between the real, and the mythological.

– Michael J. Petro

DeconstructingTheManifest.blogspot.com

Young Lee Harvey Oswald at Bronx Zoo, 1954

Down The Rabbit Hole ...

This was the year he rode the subway to the ends of the city, two hundred miles of track. He liked to stand at the front of the first car, hands flat against the glass. The train smashed through the dark. People stood on local platforms staring nowhere, a look they'd been practicing for years. He kind of wondered, speeding past, who they really were.

This is how postmodern writer Don DeLillo describes young Lee Harvey Oswald at the start of his mesmerizing novel, *Libra*. He provides a striking image of Oswald jouncing along to the cacophony of steel wheels on steel tracks in a dimly lit subway car, perhaps images of sugarplums, Kremlin domes, and assassination in his head. Young Lee, a blooming juvenile delinquent, clad in a black leather jacket, blue jeans and white t-shirt, is a cultural harbinger of soon-to-arrive Jim Stark, a young rebel looking for a cause. Young Lee wanders along tony Park Avenue, trying to fathom where all the luxuries and wealth came from. Young Lee, sulking through the Lower East Side, is amazed at the conditions some workers and families occupied. Young Lee is speeding through time's dark tunnel toward a day of reckoning that will forever alter American history. In that rushing darkness, did he spot some specter of what was yet to come? Had he chosen to directly address us in order to share his fledging saga of rebellion, maybe he would have borrowed the introduction: "If you really want to hear about it ..."

But Lee, in his youth and later, was not one to bemoan his natural state, nor was he one to complain about his place in life. Life had not dealt him an easy or fair hand, but that was no cause for concern to him. The closest he ever came to expressing any form of complaint was in 1959, when he remarked that his father's death when he was quite young had left him with "a mean streak of independence brought on by neglect."

Wrote one JFK assassination chronicler in 1989: "Despite much later conjecture, there is little evidence that Lee's childhood was any better or any worse than others." However, one has to question this assessment. Before he was 13 years old, Lee had lived in three states, dwelled in more than a half dozen different homes, attended eleven different grade schools, spent several months in an orphanage, and skipped school for over 100 days.

In early 1942, Lee's mother, Marguerite, attempted to place Lee and his two brothers, Robert and John, in the Evangelical Lutheran Bethlehem Orphan Asylum. The orphanage accepted Robert and John, but refused to take Lee because he was only two years old, too young to be admitted. (Interestingly, Marguerite signed the January 3, 1942 orphanage admittance form with the name: "Mrs. Lee Oswald.")

Ten months later, Marguerite placed three-year-old Lee in the same orphanage as his two brothers, after leaving him in the care of her older sister, Lillian Murret, for about seven months. Marguerite dropped Lee off at the orphanage the day after Christmas, December 26, 1942. Marguerite removed him from the orphanage about a year later, but left his brothers there for another year.

That we know of, Lee never spoke about his days in the Bethlehem orphanage. However, his step-brother John Pic said in 1964: "Robert and I enjoyed Bethlehem. I mean we were kids with the same problems, same age group, and everything." Pic went on to remark that life in the orphanage became far less enjoyable after Lee arrived. Said Pic: "Things for myself became worse when Lee came there…. At Bethlehem they had a ruling that if you had a younger brother or sister there and they had bowel movements in their pants the older brothers would clean them up, and they would yank me out of classes in school to go do this and, of course, this peeved me very much …"

This, of course, hardly qualifies as "any better or any worse than others," yet Lee accepted the hand he had been dealt and did as he pleased with it, moving with an eclectic cadence, and with a solidly unconventional engine. At thirteen years of age, he is a tough youngster, insular and emotionally steeled. In 1959, he writes to his older brother, Robert, "Happiness is not based on oneself, it does not consist of a small home, of taking and getting. Happiness is taking part in the struggle, where there is no borderline between one's own personal world, and the world in general."

Young Lee speeding through time's dark tunnel ...

It is 1953, a year and an era framed in a spider web of contradictions. It is a time of post-war prosperity — if one conveniently overlooks the Korean "conflict," the ever-expanding Cold War, and the CIA's persistent covert plotting to assassinate annoying foreign leaders. Paranoia about Commies and Reds infiltrating the government, the military, science and the arts is rampant in some quarters. U.S. Senator Joe McCarthy warns and rants about communists infiltrating all levels, bottom to top, of the government and the military. There is a subtle and pervasive fear about nuclear annihilation, and children routinely practice civil defense drills by hiding under their school desks. The well-to-do build bomb shelters in their basements or backyards, and the burgeoning middle-class hopes for the best. Ayn Rand releases her superman manifesto, *Atlas Shrugged*, and "King Beat" Jack Kerouac begins paving the way for the Hippies and so-called Love Generation yet to come. Future Merry Prankster Neil Cassidy has yet to learn about the miraculous mind expanding merits of LSD. Tony Bennett and Perry Como top the charts with tunes like *Rags to Riches* and *Don't Let the Stars Get in Your Eyes*. Bill Haley, Elvis Presley and Buddy Holly keep feet tapping, while Nat King Cole and Frank Sinatra offer up soundtracks for lovers.

The fruits of capitalism seem to bless every table, except for those of an ever-growing number of poor families – soon to be christened "the other America." Economic opportunity, advancement and betterment seem available for all, except minorities, especially African-Americans who remain segregated from mainstream society, and subjected to heinous degradation and brutal lynchings.

It is an America where women are expected to be stay-at-home mothers, to stay out of the political realm, reserved for men, and not to enter the work force unless, of course, a woman's situation is much like that of Marguerite Oswald, a single-mother who has no choice but to work in order to take care of her family.

Organized crime in America is becoming evermore sophisticated, dividing up cities and regions into Mafia fiefdoms for the distribution of heroin, despite the fact that FBI director J. Edgar Hoover refuses to acknowledge the existence of any such organization.

Psychology is steadily working its way into the fabric of American society, with commerce and big business becoming well aware of the powers of mass marketing and consumer manipulation. The horrors of brainwashing and "enhanced interrogation" are becoming the vogue with the fellows in the intelligence community, and the high values of propaganda and media manipulation are skillfully molded into an art form and science within the same group.

Alienation and loneliness, steadily creeping into society as permanent fixtures, are artistically invoked in the works of artist Edward Hopper. It is the best of times and the worst of times – when a young boy named Lee Harvey Oswald and his mother Marguerite move to New York City.

Chapter One

Lee Harvey Oswald in New York City and Elsewhere

Oswald, NYC and the Shadow of MK/ULTRA

Often overlooked in the chronology of Lee Harvey Oswald's early years is that when he was 12 years old he lived in New York City for a period of about eighteen months, in 1952-1954. Astute readers will also recognize these as critical years in the development and operation of the CIA's MK/ULTRA safe house in the city's Greenwich Village, operated by Federal Bureau Narcotics agent and covert CIA consultant George Hunter White. The first-floor safe house was located at the corner of Bedford and Barrow streets. According to a 1978 CIA document, "an elusive Frenchman who was engaged in the import-export business" owned the two-story, brick apartment house, just a short walk away from Chumley's, one of agent White's favorite watering holes and perhaps a primary reason for its selection. The building that housed the safe house was torn down several decades ago, but Chumley's, with all its ambiance and ghosts, is still there.

Marguerite Oswald and Lee moved to New York City from Texas in early August 1952. For several weeks, Lee and Marguerite lived in a small, fifth-floor apartment located at 325 East 92nd Street, Brooklyn. The cramped unit was shared with Lee's half-brother John Edward Pic, his 18-year old wife Margaret, and their newborn child. Pic's mother-in-law, Mary Fuhrman, a Hungarian immigrant, owned the triplex building that housed the apartment, and while away from the city for about eight weeks she allowed Margaret's family use of the space. Marguerite Oswald enrolled Lee in a private school, the Trinity Evangelical Lutheran School in the Bronx. Within days, Lee became chronically truant. After Marguerite learned that he had skipped nearly two weeks of classes, she placed him in a public school.

John Pic was a Hospital Corpsman and Radioman with the United States Coast Guard. Beginning in early January 1952, and continuing for about four months, Corpsman Pic was assigned to assist with an outbreak of streptococcal infection at a U.S. Navy installation in Bainbridge, Maryland.

Bainbridge is about 170 miles away from Fort Detrick in Frederick, Maryland, the Army's chemical and biological warfare center and, at the time, Dr. Frank Olson's place of employment. The outbreak occurred not long after the CIA had initiated top-secret Project MK/NAOMI, a joint program with Fort Detrick's Special Operations (SO) Division, headed by Dr. Olson. Project MK/NAOMI's objective was to aggressively develop a cornucopia of lethal biochemical weapons that the CIA could use in targeting people – both individually and in groups – for incapacitation or death.

Said one SO Division bacteriologist about MK/NAOMI: "Our mission was pretty simple and to the point: to provide the CIA with every means possible to maim or kill targeted groups or individuals through the use of toxic and lethal biochemical agents. We worked hard at it and delivered." One of the CIA's earliest documents on the program's genesis uncharacteristically lists some of its objectives: "How to knock off key people ... knock off key guys ... make death look as if from natural causes ... [such as a] method to produce cancer ... and to make it appear as heart attack."

The same document cites the case of an imprisoned "Russian ... who had been subjected to the routine administration of intimidation, bright lights and more severe roughing, followed by insulin shock."

On site for the Bainbridge outbreak, along with Oswald's half-brother Pic, were bacteriologists from the U.S. Army's biological warfare center at Fort Detrick, as well as physicians from the Armed Forces Epidemiological branch. Dr. Charles H. Rammelkamp, Jr., a member of the Armed Forces Epidemiological Board (AFEB), was also present during the outbreak. Readers knowledgeable about the findings of the President's Advisory Committee on Human Radiation Experiments, appointed by President Bill Clinton in 1995, may recall that the committee took a cursory look at experiments approved, sponsored, and undertaken by the New York School of Medicine and AFEB on physically-healthy mentally retarded children at the Willowbrook State School in Staten Island, New York, done at the time of Rammelkamp's tenure.

The experiments centered on selected children being fed infected stool extracts obtained from individuals with hepatitis, thus infecting the children with the virus. Additionally, Dr. Rammelkamp was at the center of another controversial experiment conducted in the early 1950s. This experiment, conducted concurrently with the Bainbridge outbreak, involved American servicemen stricken with streptococcus, which can cause rheumatic fever and heart disease. The servicemen, hospitalized at Francis E. Warren Air Force Base in Wyoming, were intentionally not treated with penicillin, which at the time was still being investigated as an effective treatment for rheumatic fever.

In a 1966 *Time* magazine article, Harvard University's Dr. Henry K. Beecher (whose actual name was Henry K. Unangst), asked by the magazine to consider Dr. Rammelkamp's experiments, stated that he was "concerned about experiments that are designed for the ultimate good of society in general but may well do harm to the subject involved." Earlier Dr. Beecher had stated in the *New England Journal of Medicine* that since World War II, the numbers of patients used as unwitting experimental subjects was increasing at alarming rates. Beecher told *Time*'s editors that the increase was causing "grave consequences," but he declined to name any physicians, hospitals, or universities involved in such experiments. Beecher also did not reveal to *Time* or to anyone else that he, too, like other Harvard officials of his day and today, was involved in such experiments. Nor did Beecher disclose that for the previous thirteen years or more, he had served the CIA as a covert asset and consultant on interrogation and mind-control techniques, including the use of LSD, as well as his specialty – anesthesia. (See my book, *A Terrible Mistake: The Murder of Frank Olson and the CIA's Secret Cold War Experiments*, for details about Dr. Henry Beecher's work for the CIA overseas, which included several surreptitious meetings with Sandoz Chemical company officials. See NOTES section on Beecher's real name.)

We do not know if Dr. Frank Olson was among the Fort Detrick scientists who traveled to Bainbridge during the outbreak, but we do know that members of his Fort Detrick Special Operations (SO) Division were present, and that at the time, they were especially interested in creating a biological warfare weapon out of Group A streptococcus.

Group A streptococcus is a bacterium commonly found in the throat and skin. Infections can range from mild to life-threatening. Detrick's scientists wanted to deploy the bacterium through aerosol spraying, quite similar to what the SO Division had done earlier in an Eyes-Only, top-secret LSD experiment in Pont St. Esprit, a village in Southern France. That French experiment had produced better than expected results, an entire town was thrown into complete chaos and madness, but drew more scientific scrutiny than desired due to the unfortunate and unintended deaths of four townspeople. To circumvent this scrutiny, and to offer "viable" scientific explanations for the outbreak of insanity that took over the townspeople, the CIA and U.S. Army dispatched scientists from nearby Sandoz Chemical Company, the same company that had provided the CIA and U.S. Army with the LSD used in the experimental attack on the town.

As readers may suspect, the Sandoz scientists conjured up a seemingly viable medical explanation for the outbreak of insanity that was able to hold up until the incident became shrouded with time and largely forgotten. (Again, see *A Terrible Mistake* on the so-called Pont St. Esprit "ergot outbreak.")

From about 1948 through 1968, Fort Detrick scientists mounted a variety of plans that involved surreptitious bacterial and chemical spraying attacks in both domestic and foreign locations. Two of the very first plans considered, according to once-classified Army, FBI, and CIA documents, were a covert spraying in the New York subway system in 1949 and a simulated spraying attack through the Pentagon's ventilation system, also in 1949. Indeed, at the request of the CIA's Technical Services Section, George Hunter White himself, in 1952, detonated a small aerosol device that released a cloud of vaporized LSD in a New York City subway car. The reported results of this experiment were destroyed by the CIA in 1973.

Also in 1952, Dr. Olson's Fort Detrick SO Division undertook covert advance work, using Army microbiologists posing as state public health workers, in the Florida towns of Avon Park and Carver Park. The covert work was in preparation for secret experiments planned for 1956 through 1958 involving the release of infected mosquitoes into selected low-income African-American neighborhoods dense with public housing. As a result of the mosquitoes, many men, women and children became dreadfully ill, and some died.

According to one newspaper account of these secret experiments: "Within weeks of the first exposures, hundreds of men, women, and children became sickened with typhoid, mysterious fevers, chills, excruciating abdominal cramps, breathing problems including bronchitis, as well as neurological disorders such as encephalitis." (This author's 2002 FOIA request for documents regarding SO Division's Florida experiments was denied.)

Equally noteworthy is the fact that, not long after the Florida experiments, Fort Detrick's SO Division microbiologists assisted in several covert attacks against rural and agricultural areas in Cuba. These attacks involved aerial spraying with swine flu virus, dengue, and other lethal infectious agents. As a result, hundreds of farm animals and several humans died.

After his Bainbridge deployment, from April 1952 to February 1953, Lee Harvey Oswald's half-brother returned to New York City and was assigned to the Coast Guard's Port Security Unit at Ellis Island. The Security Unit, an outgrowth of the Espionage Act of 1950, was charged with identifying, investigating, and ridding New York harbor, the Longshoremen's union, and the maritime industry of communists and subversive elements.

John Pic's subsequent assignment is extremely interesting because earlier, in April 1951, one of Frank Olson's killers was being held, pending deportation, in a cell on Ellis Island. Later, at the same time that John Pic was assigned to duty on the island, several major drug traffickers from France and Corsica were also being held at Ellis Island. They had been apprehended in a major Federal Bureau of Narcotics (FBN) operation headed up by George Hunter White, acting as a dual narcotics-CIA operative.

Illicit drugs impounded from these arrests were transferred to a secret holding compound in New Jersey where, according to CIA documents, the drugs were disbursed to various researchers under contract with the CIA, and to other unknown places. One of the French traffickers apprehended by White would be sent to a federal prison in Atlanta, where he would be subjected to intense mind control experiments.

Multiple drugs were used during these experiments, including morphinum, dicain, and heroin. Readers may recall that some of these same drugs were discovered listed in John Pic's notebook in 1964. (Dicain, a strong local anesthetic, has never been available in the U.S. It can only be purchased overseas, and was used in Eastern Europe. In 1953-1956, the CIA experimented with the drug for possible mind-control uses.)

Of equal interest is that during World War II, George Hunter White and a number of other FBN agents assigned to the Office of Strategic Services (OSS), precursor to the CIA, worked very closely in New York City with Port Security and the Office of Naval Intelligence on what is now commonly called Operation Underworld. This was the top-secret project that involved freeing infamous gangster Charles "Lucky" Luciano from prison in return for his, and the Mafia's, assistance with security at America's ports and with the Allied invasion of Italy. All of the FBN agents assigned to work on Operation Underworld went on to become covert operatives for the CIA, and would become involved with Projects MK/ULTRA and MK/NAOMI.

Some of the drug traffickers and criminals held for deportation at Ellis Island were given the option of staying in the United States indefinitely if they "volunteered" for various secret government projects, including CIA-funded Project Artichoke experiments that were just beginning at the Atlanta Federal Penitentiary and various mental hospitals in Louisiana. At Tulane University in New Orleans, Dr. Russell R. Monroe was just beginning his research on neurological brain dysfunctions in the minds of criminals and psychopaths. The CIA and the military, which were quickly drawn to the program, were becoming intrigued with the possibilities of creating what were then referred to as "aggressive soldiers" and now are called "super soldiers."

Worth noting here is that adjunct to the Espionage Act of 1950 was the Emergency Detention Act of 1950, which created six large internment camps for thousands of persons who were to be apprehended and detained in the event of an internal security emergency. Among the six camps nationwide was the barbed wire-surrounded former Army installation in Avon Park, Florida.

After a few tumultuous weeks living with half brother Pic and his family in the late summer of 1952, Lee Harvey Oswald and his mother moved to a small, dank, basement apartment located at 1455 Sheridan Street in the Bronx. There, Lee complained of having to sleep on the living room couch. At the time, Marguerite worked at Lerners Dress Shop located at 45 East 42nd Street.

Interesting to note is that George Hunter White's wife, Albertine, called "Tine" by those closest to her, shopped at Lerners and had friends who worked there. Like Marguerite, Albertine White also worked in the clothing business as a buyer for the Abraham & Strauss Department Store in Brooklyn at 422 Fulton Street. After working at Lerners, Marguerite Oswald, in February 1953, went to work for Martin's Department Store in Brooklyn at 501 Fulton Street, a very short walk from where Albertine worked. Again, we find that Albertine had close friends who worked at Martin's.

Albertine and George White enjoyed living in New York City. Their apartment was at 59 West 12 Street in the Village. The Whites had many friends, although most of them were mainly attracted to the couple because of Albertine's vivacious personality and charming ways. George could be quite gruff and moody. His consumption of large quantities of alcohol, mainly Gibson's gin, didn't serve to enhance his social skills. His propensity to surreptitiously dose his guests with LSD, supplied to him by the CIA, also did not help matters much. During one of their many dinner parties George, much to Albertine's displeasure, secretly dosed a number of their friends with LSD, sending two women to the hospital in total panic and confusion at what was happening inside their heads.

FBN and CIA agent, George Hunter White

George White frequently used Central Park and the Bronx Zoo as rendezvous points for his meetings with criminals, confidential informers, intelligence agents and drug traffickers. White's alias for conducting business with and for the CIA was "Morgan Hall." Morgan Hall is also a section of the American Museum of Natural History in Central Park, opened in 1900 and named after magnate J.P. Morgan. It houses the minerals and gems collection. According to the Warren Commission Report, one of the first places John Pic took Lee Oswald to sightsee was the Natural History Museum.

George White's date book for 1953 contains numerous references to his meetings with unsavory characters at the Natural History Museum. It was a favorite rendezvous point for White. Several of White's date book notations cite a person referred to only as "Lee," but this Lee is thought to be much older than Oswald, and a close acquaintance of White's.

> *Okay, just a little pin prick,*
> *There'll be no more aaaaaaaah!*
>
> *-Comfortably Numb*
> Roger Waters and David Gilmour, 1979

Lee Oswald and School in New York

Lee Oswald greatly disliked attending school in New York. His attendance records, as provided to the Warren Commission, reveal that he was "excessively absent." By one authoritative count, Oswald missed over seventy-five days of school in a 12-month period. Teachers and school officials recalled that Lee was an extremely smart youngster, but that he "refused to salute the flag" and preferred to be alone. Oddly, some teachers recalled him to be "slight ... and thin" while others said he was "well built."

In the spring of 1953, Lee was picked up by a truant officer at the Bronx Zoo, a place he often visited when skipping school. Angry at being apprehended, Lee called the officer a "damned Yankee." This was reportedly the third time Lee had been picked up for being truant.

(The details about Lee Oswald's New York truancy problem are still quite clouded factually and seem to have been grossly manipulated in terms of numbers of school days missed. Reports by investigative journalists published just a few days after the assassination of JFK, stated that "teachers and principals in the Bronx" reported that "Oswald had spent only 15 days out of the entire school term at JHS [Junior High School] 117, and that later he was 'below par at JHS 44.'" Another report states that Oswald had been absent from JHS 44 and JHS 117 "for 47 days during October of 1952 through January 1953." Yet another report from 1963 states that Oswald "was not a truant from Beauregard JHS 44, missing only nine days."

Over time, and through today, reports in books and articles that Oswald missed between 90 and 120 days of school in a 2-year period are commonplace, but apparently far from accurate.)

Lee's biological father, Robert E. Lee Oswald, was named after the famous Confederate general. Lee Harvey Oswald, before entering the Marine Corps at the age of 17, had lived in 22 separate homes, including foster homes and an orphanage, and attended 12 schools.

In April 1953, reportedly following additional school absences, Oswald was sent to Youth House, located on 12th Street between 1st and 2nd Avenues in Manhattan. Here he was placed under psychiatric observation for three weeks, from April 16 to May 7, 1953. Observers termed him an "emotionally isolated boy ... who suffers under the impact of really existing emotional isolation and deprivation, lack of affection, absence of family life and rejection by a self-involved and conflicted mother." He was also described as having "superior mental resources and [he] functions only slightly below his capacity level in spite of chronic truancy from school which brought him into Youth House."

During his days at Youth House, Lee reportedly told Marguerite, "Mother, I want to get out of here. There are children in here who have killed people, and smoke. I want to get out."

Lee told a social worker at Youth House that he felt like "a veil" separated his life from those of others. He said he liked having the veil there.

Boys sent to Youth House who were deemed incorrigible were routinely sent to the nearby Bordentown Reformatory in New Jersey, a home away from home for what were then commonly called "juvenile delinquents." There is no known evidence that Oswald went to Bordertown, but several physicians who worked at the reformatory also performed work at Youth House.

The Bordertown facility is significant, because during World War II, and from 1951 to 1964, it was the site of secret CIA and U.S. Army behavior-modification and mind-control experiments. Dr. Carl C. Pfeiffer of Emory University in Atlanta and the University of Illinois Medical School oversaw some of these experiments, which were intended to both trigger and study "a model psychosis characterized by visual and auditory hallucinations." Pfeiffer later

17

refined his objectives with extensive experiments in Atlanta Federal Penitentiary. Questioned about these experiments in 1981, the CIA's Dr. Sidney Gottlieb said, "We learned a lot from the Atlanta experiments. The Agency learned that a person's psyche could be very disturbed by those means."

During World War II, the Bordentown Reformatory was used by the OSS, precursor to the CIA, for truth-drug experiments. These experiments included then OSS officer Capt. George Hunter White and psychiatrist Dr. Lawrence Kubie. In the late 1950s, Kubie wrote White a letter within which he "fondly" recalls their time together conducting drug experiments at Bordentown and a state prison in Baltimore, Maryland. Wrote Kubie: "I look back fondly on those days. What great fun we had." (As my Olson book details, Dr. Kubie had treated my friend, former Hollywood producer, Bill Hayward, when he was just a youth. This experience, Hayward said, was a psychological low point in his life, and I sadly believe it contributed greatly to Bill's eventual suicide.)

While at Youth House, three physicians examined Lee Oswald. They were Dr. Renatus Hartogs, chief psychiatrist at the facility; Dr. Milton Kurian, a psychiatrist working for the New York court system; and Dr. Irving Sokolow, a Youth House psychologist. Dr. Sokolow found Oswald "withdrawn" and "presumably disinterested in school subjects," but to have an intellectual functioning level "in the upper range of bright normal intelligence." (Oswald was also interviewed and observed at length by a Youth House social worker and a New York City probation officer. See NOTES for the results of their reports.)

Dr. Kurian, a former president of the American Psychiatric Association, an organization that has had a supportive and financially friendly relationship with the CIA for over 50 years, once allegedly wrote to Jacqueline Kennedy about Oswald after the assassination. Dr. Kurian apparently told Mrs. Kennedy that he examined young Oswald at the request of a New York probation officer assigned to Oswald's Domestic Relations Court case. Dr. Kurian says that he spoke with Oswald only once, and concluded that the youngster "was withdrawn from the real world and responded to outside pressures to a degree necessary to avoid the disturbance of his residence in a fantasy world." Kurian would later say that he felt Oswald was "mentally ill" and should have been hospitalized in a facility for children. (See John Armstrong's interview with Kurian in Armstrong's book, *Harvey & Lee*, page 58.)

For reasons unexplained, Dr. Kurian was never interviewed by the Warren Commission. Perhaps this was because no contemporaneous written report by Kurian concerning Oswald has ever been found. However, this does not explain why Dr. Kurian did not step forward in 1964 and offer himself as a witness to the Warren Commission. (This author was also unable to verify the existence of Kurian's letter to Jacqueline Kennedy.) Lastly, and most problematic, about Dr. Kurian's account of his interview of Lee Oswald is that he recounts that it took place on March 27, 1953, three weeks before young Oswald was sent to Youth House.

Youth House chief psychiatrist Dr. Renatus Hartogs examined Oswald on May 1, 1953. Hartogs was born into a Jewish family in Mainz, Germany in 1909. A brilliant student as a youth, he received a Ph.D. in psychology from the University of Frankfurt-am-Main in Germany and a medical degree from the University of Brussels Medical School in Belgium. Dr. Hartogs maintained a psychiatric practice in Belgium for three years and then, in early December 1940, he emigrated to the United States, where he became a citizen in 1945. After arriving in America, Hartogs studied medicine again in order to fulfill the requirements of the New York State Education Department.

In Montreal, Canada, Hartogs earned another medical degree from the University of Montreal Medical School and then an M.A. from New York University. In Montreal, Dr. Hartogs completed his internship and residency and then worked as a psychiatrist at the Allen Memorial Institute, which today is infamous in mind-control annals. It was the location where Dr. D. Ewen Cameron, beginning in the mid-1950s and under a covert MK/ULTRA contract with the CIA, conducted a series of horrific drug and sensory deprivation experiments on unwitting patients.

In 1951, after leaving Montreal and serving as a staff psychiatrist at the Sing Sing maximum-security prison outside of New York City, Dr. Hartogs became chief psychiatrist for the Youth House of New York City. In December 1963, Hartogs told the *New York Times* that "before joining Youth House, and since that time, he had tried to set up several research projects on potentially dangerous children but 'there never was enough money.'"

At Youth House, Dr. Hartogs oversaw a staff of three or four other psychiatrists. In 1953, the facility had a staff of over 250 employees. Hartogs' principle responsibility at the facility, as he testified before the Warren Commission in 1964, was to "examine all the children which have been remanded to Youth House on order of the court for the purpose of psychiatric examination ... [and to] submit to the court [a report] with recommendations and diagnosis."

Hartogs also routinely conducted workshops and seminars for Youth House staff to discuss the psychiatric aspects of social work and review particularly interesting cases that came before the psychiatric staff. Dr. Hartogs also testified before the Commission that he devoted about 30 hours per week to examining children in 1953, the same year Lee Harvey Oswald was his patient, and that on average he saw about 10 to 12 children a week, spending "about half an hour to an hour" with each child, and another half-hour studying his findings, and then dictating a report to the court.

Dr. Hartogs' Warren Commission testimony about his examination of Lee Harvey Oswald is very interesting for both what he said and what he did not say.

Asked by the Commission to relate his recollections about his interview with Lee Harvey Oswald, Hartogs said,

> That is tough. I remember that – actually I reconstructed this from the seminar. We gave a seminar on this boy [Oswald] in which we discussed him, because he came to us on a charge of truancy from school, and yet when I examined him, I found him to have definite traits of dangerousness. In other words, this child had a potential for explosive, aggressive, assaultive acting out which was rather unusual to find in a child who was sent to Youth House on such a mild charge as truancy from school.
>
> This is the reason why I remember this particular child, and that is the reason why we discussed him in the seminar.

Moments later, the Commission asked Dr. Hartogs if he could "recall: What recommendation you made to the court in respect to Oswald?"

Hartogs answered, "If I can recall correctly, I recommended that this youngster should be committed to an institution.... *I found him to have definite traits of dangerousness. In other words, this child had a potential for explosive, aggressive, assaultive acting out...."* [Emphasis added.]

This diagnosis and recommendation probably does not shock many readers; however, the point here is that Dr. Hartogs' actual report to the court, filed just days after examining Oswald, contained none of this seemingly prophetic language. Indeed, the closest Hartogs came to such a diagnosis in his report was:

> This 13-year-old, well-built boy, has superior mental resources and functions only slightly below his capacity level in spite of chronic truancy from school – which brought him into Youth House. No finding of neurological impairment or psychotic mental changes could be made.
>
> Lee has to be diagnosed as "personality pattern disturbance with schizoid features and passive-aggressive tendencies." Lee has to be seen as an emotionally, quite disturbed youngster who suffers under the impact of really existing emotional isolation and deprivation: lack of affection, absence of family life and rejection by a self-involved and conflicted mother.... We arrive therefore at the recommendation that he should be placed on probation under the condition that he seek help and guidance through contact with a child guidance clinic, where he should be treated preferably by a male psychiatrist who could substitute, to a certain degree at least, for the lack of a father figure.

In his testimony before the Warren Commission, Hartogs was asked about his dealings with the media immediately following JFK's assassination.

> **Mr. Wesley J. Liebeler** [for the Commission]: Did you make any statement to television people in connection with this at all?
>
> **Dr. Hartogs**: About Oswald?
>
> **Mr. Liebeler**: Yes.
>
> **Dr. Hartogs**: No; on the day after President Kennedy died, the television people asked me to make a statement on television in general about why somebody might kill the President. I did not mention any name. I did not refer to any individual. I just

made some general psychiatric remarks as to what kind of person would kill the President.

Mr. Liebeler: Do you recall approximately what you said?

Dr. Hartogs: That a person who would commit such an act has been very likely a mentally disturbed person, who has a personal grudge against persons in authority, and very likely is a person who in his search to overcome his own insignificance and helplessness will try to commit an act which will make others frightened, which will shatter the world, which will make other people insecure, as if he wanted to discharge his own insecurity through his own act, something like that in general terms.

Mr. Liebeler: Was it indicated by you at that time, or was it indicated on the television broadcast that you were the psychiatrist who had examined Lee Oswald?

Dr. Hartogs: No, no.

Mr. Liebeler: It was not?

Dr. Hartogs: No, no. They did not know. They called me because they call me very often to give some psychiatric explanation of murderers or something like that. They did not know, and I did not know for sure.

Mr. Liebeler: At that time neither one of you were ...

Dr. Hartogs: And they selected me. I mean it was a fantastic thing.

Mr. Liebeler: It was purely coincidence?

Dr. Hartogs: Coincidence that they selected me.

Dr. Hartogs was wrong. It was not mere coincidence that led television and newspaper reporters to him. Dr. Hartogs took great delight in dealing with the media, often initiating calls to reporters himself, going out of way day or night to meet with them to provide them with what he knew were enticing and provocative quotes. Not surprisingly, the diagnostic conclusions offered by Hartogs to the media often veered sharply from his actual 1953 findings regarding Lee Oswald.

Dr. Hartogs laid the groundwork for dispensing his revised diagnoses of Lee Oswald on December 2, 1963 when two FBI agents visited him at his New York City office at 7 East 86th Street. Hartogs told the agents, according to their report, dated the same day, that "upon reading a story in a New York newspaper concerning a psychiatric interview of Lee Harvey Oswald, *he realized that from the terminology used in the psychiatric report that he himself had conducted the interview of Oswald.* [Emphasis added.]

Hartogs, according to the FBI report, explained, "the specific phrases" used in the Oswald report of "potentially dangerous" and "incipient schizophrenia" were phrases that were *"peculiar to his type analysis, and he knows of no other psychiatrist who uses them."* [Emphasis added.]

Apparently, Dr. Hartogs had not actually gone back and read his 1953 Youth House report on Oswald, because that report does not anywhere contain the phrases "potentially dangerous" or "incipient schizophrenia." This discrepancy went unnoticed by the FBI agents because they did not yet have a copy of the 1953 report.

According to the FBI report, Hartogs additionally told the two agents that when he reflected on his examination of Lee Harvey Oswald, he recalled that "he was greatly impressed with Oswald in that the boy, who was 13 1/2 years old ... had extremely cold, steely eyes," and that "despite the fact that Oswald had no record of violence [*sic*], he recommended institutionalizing him as a result of his psychiatric examination, which indicated Oswald's potential dangerousness."

The FBI report goes on: "Dr. Hartogs again emphasized that despite the lack of violence in Oswald's past, he felt that he was potentially disturbed and dangerous, and that he should have institutional care."

Again, Dr. Hartogs was recalling observations and findings that allegedly had "greatly impressed" him ten years earlier, but, as reflected in his actual written findings above, they were not reflected in any way in his 1953 report on young Oswald.

The FBI report concerning Hartogs concludes by stating, "When questioned as to whether he [Hartogs] had retained a copy of the psychiatric report that he submitted following his interview with OSWALD, Dr. Hartogs stated that some years after his interview of OSWALD, he moved his office and destroyed all his old files, which included the OSWALD file. He advised that he was unable to re-call any further information at this time concerning OSWALD." (Although not at all clear, it is assumed that the copy of Hartogs' report on Oswald that soon emerged was taken from New York City Youth Court files, or from files of other Youth House em-ployees who had met with Oswald. See NOTES for details on these other employees.)

The day after his interview with the FBI, *New York Times* re-porter Martin Arnold interviewed Dr. Hartogs. Hartogs again stated that he had found young Oswald to be "potentially dan-gerous" and that he was a youth "given to violence." Pressed to say more, Hartogs told Arnold that he could say nothing else about Lee Oswald or his psychiatric report because Oswald's re-cords, compiled when he was a minor, were confidential under New York state law.

Judge Florence M. Kelley, administrative judge of the New York Family Court, had earlier used her allowed discretion to turn over Oswald's Youth House records to the FBI, but had or-dered "everyone involved" in the case "to refuse to comment to anyone except the FBI."

Said a very thoughtful Judge Kelley in December 1963 about Oswald's psychiatric report and Youth House files: "Our records are always confidential and we never reveal them to anyone. I did give some of the information to the FBI, as an exception, and contrary to our regular rules, for the simple reason that Oswald is dead, and if this kind of report could cast light on what kind of person he was, that would be in the national interest."

Undeterred by judicial orders, Dr. Hartogs spoke with at least two additional newspaper journalists over the next few days, of-ten talking in generalizations about his overall work with trou-bled youth and not mentioning Oswald's name specifically. In a December 6, 1963 article by reporter Lee Townsend of the *New York World Telegram*, entitled, "How Many Oswalds on Our Streets?" Hartogs said, "Over the years I have studied more than 10,000 youths. I estimate that about 13 percent of these are po-tentially dangerous – even in a homicidal fashion.... About 4 per-cent of those children in whom I found dangerous traits have returned to the Youth House within one to four years on a charge of assault or murder ... Only 1 or 2 percent of those children I have determined to be potentially dangerous were given the treatment they needed."

Dr. Hartogs, drawing on his days working at Sing Sing prison, added, "I found that practically 100 percent of the prisoners at Sing Sing ... had shown typical criteria of dangerous behaviors at the age of 10 or so."

A December 9, 1963 article in the *New York Journal-American* by Donald R. Flynn and Mike Pearl, "N.Y. Psychiatric Report Cited Oswald Violence," opened with the inciting sentence: "A 10-year old psychiatric report on Lee Harvey Oswald emerged today as a startlingly accurate blueprint for precisely the kind of violence that erupted last November 22 in the assassination of John F. Kennedy."

The article relied on a copy of Hartogs' 1953 report on Oswald and a brief interview with the psychiatrist. This time around, Hartogs, apparently, erroneously told the two reporters that his report was "based on three interviews [with young Oswald] during a five-week period in April and May of 1953 after Oswald had been referred from Bronx Children's Court."

The article also stated, without further details, that in January of 1953 Lee Oswald's mother, Marguerite, "telephoned the Bronx branch of the Community Service Society, and cried, 'He is driving me almost crazy.'"

When the two reporters attempted to verify this with Marguerite Oswald over the phone, she indignantly said, "He [Lee] caused me no trouble at all." She also told the two that she had "never called the Community Service Society." Said Marguerite, according to the subsequent article: "I don't remember that. I don't remember anything about being in New York."

In the same article, Milton Rosenberg, a health education teacher, who had Oswald as a student at JHS 44, told the two reporters, "He [Oswald] did what he was told. Tell him to turn right and he'd turn right. But the whole time his mind seemed to be wandering off somewhere." Hardly a "blueprint" characteristic for forthcoming violence.

"Whitewashed Zombie and Manchurian Candidate"

On December 14, 1963, Dr. Hartogs telephoned *New York Post* reporter Joseph Wershba to discuss his examination of Lee Oswald ten years earlier. Wershba had telephoned Hartogs the day before to inquire about Oswald's motive for killing President Kennedy. Wershba posed two questions to the psychiatrist that he included in his article published the next day.

"Could it have been political?" the reported asked.

Wershba also asked – in perhaps the very first print reference related to Oswald and the 1962 film, *The Manchurian Candidate* – "Is it possible Oswald was a 'Manchurian Candidate' – an indoctrinated and whitewashed zombie sent in by a conspiracy as a long-fused time bomb? And if Oswald was the assassin, why did he break the so-called assassin's pattern – by refusing to admit his act?"

Dr. Hartogs – in a reply to these questions that may have drawn on his full knowledge of the DSM Manual and then some, and may have caused Judge Kelley some consternation – answered,

I'm convinced there was no political motivation. The motive for people like Oswald is to avenge his grudge against the whole world. He picked the one symbol of power worthy of matching all his frustrations, the President. A person like Oswald – his early history, his conditioning, his behavior in later years – showed all the qualifications of a political murderer, even though politics had nothing to do with it.

The potentially dangerous child who later on actually becomes a killer may emerge in his final violent act as an unconscious means to forestall the total deterioration of his personality into psychosis. Such a person actually protects himself against total breakdown by committing murder.

A person like Oswald, with passive-aggressive tendencies – that is, suppressed feelings of great violence – resents a lifetime of being pushed to the sidelines. His dangerous tendencies may reflect early sexual conflicts. Most frequently, these conflicts are deep-seated fears of latent homosexual tendencies. He may fear impotence, he may fear inadequacies. He denies these fears by becoming power-thirsty and destructive. He culminates his career of injustice-collecting by committing a supreme, catastrophic act of violence and power. In this way, he denies his insufficiency, his impotence, his unimportance, and his fears of homosexuality. He has committed an act of power. He has shown his masculinity. Such a person would easily deny guilt in assassination. "I can get away with killing somebody – I can get away with denying it.

"I'm a bigger man than all of them put together – the President, the Secret Service, the FBI, the Dallas Police, and the whole country."

A person like Oswald has an all-devouring need to achieve and maintain a power position. He needs to display grandiose strength and social, as well as sexual adequacy. He didn't need any indoctrination. No one had sent him in. The violence came from within; he was his own best indoctrinator.

He was not a paranoid personality when I saw him 10 years ago. But failing treatment, he developed into a paranoid. Oswald is in the public eye because of the enormity of the act – but there are dozens and dozens of children with similar case histories who become murderers and rapists in later life.

Upon reading Hartogs' reply to reporter Wershba, this writer could not help but begin to see it as a Rosetta Stone for all arguments against the many soon-to-come alternative theories regarding Oswald as the assassin and the conventional story regarding his actions.

Within only three weeks of the murder of President John F. Kennedy, a psychiatrist, who spent little more than 30 minutes with a 13-year old boy 10 years previously, has unequivocally determined that Lee Oswald acted out of sheer madness to kill the President, and that he acted to commit that murder without any political motivation, indoctrination, or assistance from anyone or anything other than from his own paranoid and "power-thirsty" personality.

Fascinating to closely study and reflect on, is that Dr. Renatus Hartogs' lengthy, seemingly well-pondered, contemplated, rehearsed and, in some ways, seemingly convincing response to Wershba, is that it clearly served to lay a firm, sometimes unshakable, foundation for all those future debates to come on Lee Harvey Oswald's sanity, motivations, sexuality, and the argument that he acted alone as the sole assassin of President Kennedy.

Dr. Hartogs told the Warren Commission in 1964 that he had been "impressed" by Oswald because the young boy "was in control of his emotions" and "showed a cold, detached outer attitude."

In reply to this observation, Hartogs was leadingly asked, "As you remember, what particular thing was it about Oswald that made you conclude that he had this severe personality disturbance?"

Replied Hartogs, "It was his suspiciousness against adults, as far as I recall, his exquisite sensitivity in dealing with others, their opinions on his behalf. That is as far as I recall it."

It is especially intriguing that Dr. Hartogs is reported to have attended some of the wild LSD parties that Dr. Harold A. Abramson held on his Long Island estate throughout the 1950s. Dr. Abramson was the "psychologist" to whom the CIA sent Frank Olson for treatment in New York City in November 1953, just days before his alleged "suicide" – which we now know to have been murder.

Dr. Abramson was also the linchpin for many of the CIA's MK/ULTRA and MK/NAOMI drug experiments, as was the much-overlooked Dr. Robert Hyde of the Boston Psychopathic Hospital, who continued his work throughout the 1970s at Vermont State Hospital, a facility with much less than a stellar record in the care of mentally ill patients. It is difficult to believe that JFK assassination investigators from both the FBI and CIA, and members of the Warren Commission, were not aware of these relationships, yet they are never mentioned in documents detailing investigations.

There is more about Drs. Hartogs and Kurian. Dr. Milton Kurian, in 1964-65, was president of the American Psychiatric Association (APA), a position that put him into frequent contact with Dr. Donald Ewen Cameron, perhaps the most notorious of all MK/ULTRA experimenters. Cameron, who had been APA president in 1952-53, was an earlier founder, along with French LSD researcher Dr. Jean Delay, of the World Psychiatric Association. Files from the early 1950s reveal that this fledging association received financial assistance from the CIA. Dr. Cameron's work with LSD and "psychic driving" at McGill University's Allan Memorial Institute in Montreal was the subject of a high-profile lawsuit brought in the late 1970s as a result of the 1975 Rockefeller Commission's revelations about Frank Olson.

Dr. Hartogs, meanwhile, also held himself out as an expert on the occult. In June 1969, Dr. Hartogs appeared on a popular NBC-TV program, *First Tuesday*. The program focused on the subject of "Witches and Warlocks," and explored the question of why young people were so interested in occultism. Explained Dr. Hartogs: "The occult holds promise that no one else in our society can give. It helps the young person in his hopelessness." Added Hartogs: "Black magic enables the young person to indulge in some form of aggression. It has a beneficial effect since it releases his pent-up hostilities and he can go on to maturity."

Over the years, there have been several reports that Dr. Hartogs was also an aficionado of magic and that he knew famous New York stage magician John Mulholland, who made a brief but notable appearance in the Frank Olson case, and was a covert contractor for the CIA for about twelve years in the early 1950s to mid-1960s. In 1953-55 Mulholland, whose real name was John Wickizer, wrote a detailed manual intended for use by CIA operatives. The manual provided instructions on how to surreptitiously dose unwitting people with drugs, and how to perform other feats of slight-of-hand.

Dr. Hartogs' book, *The Two Assassins*, co-authored with Lucy Freeman two years after JFK's assassination, goes well beyond his 1953 examination of Lee Harvey Oswald, offering self-serving and harmful (to Oswald) perspectives formulated after the murder of President Kennedy. It is essentially a rehash of the central findings contained in the report of the Warren Commission as it pertains to Lee Harvey Oswald and Jack Ruby, with occasional over-dramatizations: "Lee Harvey Oswald was born into a world haunted by the black shadow of death."

Moreover, for their rendering of Jack Ruby, the authors of *The Two Assassins* relied heavily on the analysis of Dr. Louis Jolyon West, then head of the Department of Psychiatry at the University of Oklahoma Medical Center, and a long time covert contractor and consultant for the CIA and the U.S. army on mind-control and behavior-modification programs. Dr. West gained wide notoriety in 1962 when he and two colleagues killed an elephant by dosing it with LSD in an allegedly controlled experiment that went awry. In one of his detailed reports on Ruby, Dr. West, also a highly skilled hypnotist, writes,

> The patient [Ruby] had become convinced that all the Jews in America were being slaughtered. This was in retaliation against

him, Jack Ruby, the Jew who was responsible for "all the trouble." Somehow, through an awful mistake, and the distortions and misunderstandings derived from his murder trial, the President's assassination and its aftermath were now being blamed on him. Thus, he himself was now also the cause of the massacre of "25 million innocent people."

He had seen (hallucinated) his own brother tortured, horribly mutilated, castrated, and burned in the street outside the jail; he could still hear the screams. He had seen and heard many other similar horrors. The orders for this terrible "pogrom" must have come from Washington, to permit the police to carry out the mass murders without federal troops being called out or involved.

Despite its shortcomings, however, the Hartogs-Freeman book is not without value in that it does offer a number of intriguing observations and accounts of Oswald's life.

The book recounts the Warren Commission testimony of Oswald's mother Marguerite about visiting with her son Lee and his new wife Marina shortly after their return from Russia, where Lee had defected in 1959 and met and married 19-year old pharmacology student Marina Nikolayevna Prusakova.

Lee and Marina, along with their first child June, were temporarily staying with Lee's brother Robert at his home in Fort Worth, Texas. They had just arrived in the United States, having returned from the USSR on the SS *Maasdam* on June 13, 1962. They then flew to Love Field in Fort Worth, where JFK would arrive seventeen months later on the day of his assassination.

When Marguerite first arrived at Robert's home, according to her Warren Commission testimony, cited by Hartogs and Freeman, she told Lee, "Marina is a beautiful girl." She snidely added, "Marina, she doesn't look Russian. She is beautiful."

"Of course not," replied Lee. "That is why I married her, because she looks like an American girl."

"You know, Lee," said Marguerite, "I am getting ready to write a book on your *so-called* defection." [Emphasis added.]

Explained Marguerite to the Commission: "I had researched it and came to Washington in 1961, and, by the way, asked to see

President Kennedy, because I had a lot of *extenuating circumstances* at the time because of the defection." [Emphasis added.]

Lee replied, "Mother, you are not going to write a book."

"Lee, don't tell me what to do," Marguerite shot back. "I cannot write the book now, because, Honey, you are alive and back. It has nothing to do with you and Marina. It's my life, because of your defection."

Replied Lee: "Mother, I tell you, you are not to write a book. *They could kill her and her family.*"

Later that same day, according to Hartogs and Freeman, drawing from Marguerite's Warren Commission testimony, Marguerite asked Lee a question:

"Why is it you decided to return back to the United States, when you had a job in Russia, and as far as I know you seemed to be pretty well off, because of the gifts you sent me? And you are married to a Russian girl, and she would be better off in her homeland than here. I want to know."

"Mother," replied Lee, "not even Marina knows why I have returned."

Observed Marguerite to the Warren Commission: "And that is all the information I ever got out of my son."

In 1971, Dr. Renatus Hartogs was again the subject of national attention, but this time the spotlight was less than welcomed by the psychiatrist. A 36-year old secretary at *Esquire* magazine, Julie Roy, who had been a patient of Dr. Hartogs, filed a $1.25 million lawsuit against him for "irreparable emotional discomfort and harm, which aggravated her psychiatric condition."

Julie Roy had initially gone to Dr. Hartogs for treatment for depression. After six weekly talk sessions, Hartogs recommended that, as part of her treatment, he and Ms. Roy become intimate in order to better address and dispel her feelings about a sexual encounter with a woman.

The intimacy between Hartogs and Roy, acted out over a period of about six months, gradually evolved from heavy petting to engaging in sexual intercourse on a regular basis. Julie Roy felt so demeaned and depressed about this that she contemplated suicide. To try and make her feel better, Hartogs told Ms. Roy he was going to waive his fees for sessions (which at that juncture had been re-

Julie Roy   Dr. R Renatus Hartogs

duced to $10 per session) and that he would hire her as a typist for his practice. The unique sexual sessions continued for another year, and sometimes, according to her, resulted in "three sex treatments in one day."

Finally, Julie Roy stopped seeing Hartogs, but after only a few days she asked him to begin treating her again. When he refused, she grew even more depressed and in 1970 was twice involuntarily placed in a mental institution.

Dr. Hartogs' defense against Julie Roy's lawsuit was to assert that Roy was schizophrenic, just as he had branded Lee Harvey Oswald. "I never had sex with this person," he claimed. "She does not know the difference between fantasy and reality." Roy's attorneys called three former female patients of Hartogs' who also claimed they had been lured by the physician into special carnal treatments.

In 1976, following a protracted and contentious trial, a New York jury convicted Dr. Renatus Hartogs of malpractice. The jury awarded $350,000 in damages to Julie Roy. At the time the suit was brought against him, Hartogs had been writing a widely read advice column for *Cosmopolitan* magazine. The magazine dropped the column. Dr. Hartogs appealed the court's decision and filed for bankruptcy.

In 1976 former *New York Times* journalist Lucy Freeman co-authored with Julie Roy a widely read book about Roy's case against Dr. Hartogs. The book, *Betrayal*, was quickly made into a popular television movie.

In her sensationally tinged book, Freeman recounts that during the malpractice trial, the plaintiff's counsel asked Dr. Hartogs if he had "a visible imperfection on your body which is clearly visible?"

Hartogs answered, "Yes," and the following exchange took place:

Counsel: What is it?

Hartogs: That's a tumor of the right testicle called a hydrocele.

Counsel: And how big is it?

Hartogs: It is five times as large as the left testicle, and it resulted from a kick of a Nazi guard ...

Counsel: Objection. Your Honor, there is no ...

Judge: Overruled.

Hartogs: It came from the kick of a Nazi guard. While I was in a concentration camp in 1940.

Here it is interesting to note that Canadian Dr. James Tyhurst, who worked with Dr. Hartogs at the Allen Memorial Institute in Montreal, was also charged and convicted in 1991 of sexual and indecent assault on four of his patients. Dr. Tyhurst was also closely associated with highly respected Canadian neuropsychologist Dr. Donald O. Hebb. Tyhurst and Hebb both attended a seminal 1951 meeting – which included participants from the CIA– to discuss early advancements in sensory deprivation and brainwashing.

There is also the matter of hypnotism to consider with Dr. Hartogs. Highly respected JFK assassination investigator and author, Dick Russell, in his masterful book, *On the Trail of the JFK Assassins*, revealed that Dr. Hartogs may have been adept at hypnotism, something never before reported anywhere. This information came to Russell from Dr. Milton V. Kline, a well-known authority on hypnotism, who had worked closely with the CIA on Project Artichoke and MK/ULTRA, its hypnosis-related interrogation and mind-control programs. In the early 1950s, hypnotist George

Estabrooks had written to CIA director Allen Dulles about the merits of hypnosis in covert operations. Stated Estabooks: "The hypnotic state places a veil of sorts between the subject and the real world."

Kline told Russell that Hartogs, after losing his license to practice psychiatry as a result of the Julie Roy case, "set up shop as a hypnotist in New York." According to Kline, Hartogs had been involved "in some kind of government consultation" and also may have been involved in the 1950s with Dr. Sidney Malitz, a psychiatrist at the New York State Psychiatric Institute (NYSPI), located about ten blocks from young Oswald's New York address.

Dr. Malitz worked under eugenicist Dr. Paul Hoch, NYSPI Research Director. Hoch, a German who came to the U.S. with generous assistance from the Dulles family, was appointed by Gov. Nelson Rockefeller as New York's Commissioner of Mental Health. In the early 1950s, Hoch was very much involved in experiments at the Bordentown Reformatory. As early as 1948, Hoch cited his Bordentown involvement in a book he edited, *Failures in Psychiatric Treatment*. Through Dr. Hoch, Malitz was involved in a number of covert contracts with the CIA and U.S. Army to perform experiments with psychosurgery, electroconvulsive therapy, LSD, mescaline, and other drugs. Kline told writer Russell that Hartogs worked alongside Malitz on some of these experiments.

Apparently, however, what both Kline and Russell did not know, or perhaps what Kline chose to not reveal to Russell, was that at least three of the covert contracts Dr. Malitz worked under were with Fort Detrick's Special Operations Division, the unit that Frank Olson headed up at that time. These contracts, carried out under the auspices of the CIA's project MK/NAOMI, according to former Fort Detrick scientists, involved experiments on unwitting hospital patients and, as I would later learn, children and teenagers.

Dr. Sidney Malitz also worked with a number of additional physicians who conducted an elaborate number of experiments involving children during the same years that Lee Oswald was in New York City and afterwards. The CIA, U.S. Army through Fort Detrick and Edgewood Arsenal, and the Office of Naval Intelligence (ONI) funded many of these contracts. Chief among these physicians were: Drs. Bernard Wilkens, Harold Esecover, and Harold A. Abramson.

As my Olson book details, months prior to Olson's murder, a NYS-PI patient named Harold Blauer died as a result of one of these Fort Detrick-funded experiments. Blauer was unwittingly injected with a massive dose of mescaline that immediately sent his body into violent shock. Later, one NYSPI physician involved in the experiment said the Institute knew so little about mescaline that "for all we knew it could have been dog piss we were injecting [Blauer] with." In early 1954, as documented in *A Terrible Mistake*, the Pentagon and CIA colluded to suppress the government's involvement in Blauer's death and strongly pressured one of the Blauer family's attorneys not to pursue any legal action.

Harold Blauer

Following Blauer's death, Dr. Malitz, who served as Chief of Psychiatric Research at the NYSPI, and Assistant Clinical Professor of Psychiatry at New York's Columbia University College of Physicians and Surgeons, conducted an experiment using LSD and mescaline "comparing the hallucinatory phenomena evoked by hallucinogenic agents with those seen in spontaneously occurring psychosis." For this experiment, Malitz, assisted by Drs. Bernard Wilkens and Harold Esecover, selected a group of 100 "severely ill chronic schizophrenic patients who had been transferred to the Psychiatric Institute from other state hospitals for psychosurgical consideration." These patients ranged in age from 21 to 58, with 41 males and 59 females. Funded by the CIA, the experiment received additional funding from the U.S. Public Health Service. Following the experiment, all 100 of the patients underwent lobotomies.

A Note of Caution and Sound Speculation

This author, who is not easily given to wild speculation or conspiracy theories, did not originally intend to offer the above chain of intriguing coincidences and high strangeness in an effort to induce readers to believe that Lee Harvey Oswald may have been the unwitting subject of some devious government sponsored mind-control scheme that eventually placed him on a path toward the murder of President John F. Kennedy. That, in my view would have been irresponsible and outlandish, but when most of these odd connections between young Oswald and the CIA's MK/ULTRA programs were first detected I was unaware that the CIA and U.S. Army had funded and engaged in substantial behavioral modification experiments involving children.

Months after my book on Dr. Frank Olson was published, through continued research (that resulted in a few published articles) I came to unfortunately learn and understand that such experiments on children were indeed conducted. Therefore, I no longer consider such speculation to be outside the realm of possibility. While there remains little direct evidence that Oswald was some sort of programmed assassin or covert operative, there certainly are enough circumstantial facts that nudge this possibility into areas for serious consideration.

Was there time in New York City to perform such scientific manipulation on Oswald? Without question there was. Lee Harvey Oswald was reportedly absent from school for at least 50 days while in New York City. Surely, he did not spend all these unaccounted for days at the Bronx Zoo or riding the subway.

Government Sponsored Experiments NYC, 1952-1969

Not a great deal is known about experimental activities conducted in New York on children because the CIA, in 1973, destroyed all of its files related to such experiments under the rational that "the public would be too outraged over such activities and would not appreciate the Agency's objectives behind such work," but what is known is shocking. Experiments appear to have initially started in New York City at Bellevue Hospital from early 1940 to 1956. There, Dr. Lauretta Bender, a highly respected child neuropsychiatrist, experimented extensively with electroshock therapy on children who had been diagnosed, some incorrectly, with "autistic schizophrenia."

In all, it has been reported in several medical journals, as well as in at least two medical texts written by Dr. Bender, that she administered electroconvulsive therapy to about 100 children ranging in age from 3 years old to 13 years, with additional reports indicating the total may be twice that number. One source reports that, inclusive of Dr. Bender's work, electroconvulsive treatment was used on more than 500 children at Bellevue Hospital from 1942 to 1956, and then at Creedmoor State Hospital Children's Service from 1956 to 1969.

Here it is interesting to note, Dr. Lauretta Bender is perhaps best known today for her development of the Bender-Gestalt Visual Motor Test, a neuropsychological examination still widely used today. In her electroshock experiments on children throughout the 1950s, Dr. Bender frequently used her Bender-Gestalt test, the Wechsler Intelligence Scale for Children, Monroe Silent Reading Test, and Human Figure Drawings as diagnostic tools in her work with children.

Interesting to note, is that Dr. Bender's work at Bellevue Hospital involving children followed earlier "depatterning" electroconvulsive experiments conducted at the hospital, then termed "annihilation" therapy. This so-called therapy began in the mid-1940s and followed earlier efforts using insulin and Metrazol shock therapy practiced on well over 500 adult patients and an undetermined number of children at several New York Hospitals. In January 1937, Dr. Bender as part of a large contingent of Bellevue Hospital physicians, including Drs. Joseph Wortis and Karl Bowman, accompanied by Dr. Harold E. Himwich from Albany Medical College, attended a joint meeting of the New York Neurological Society and the psychiatric branch of the New York Academy of Medicine. The gathering featured a virtual who's-who of practitioners of insulin and Metrazol shock therapy, supposed cures for mental illness that, following sound discrediting of both techniques triggered a stampede toward electroshock therapy as a credible technique.

Also attending this joint meeting as a presenter was Dr. D. Ewen Cameron, who, according to historian Dr. David Healy, "in March 1936, introduced insulin coma at Worcester State Hospital in Massachusetts." Cameron, who would eventually head up infamous MK/ULTRA Subproject 68 in Montreal, also conducted extensive experiments at Worcester Hospital with a seizure-inducing drug called Metrazol, as did physicians at Bellevue Hospital and the U.S. Army's Edgewood Arsenal, where Dr. Harold E. Himwich served as research director. It is unknown how many, if any, children were subjects in these experiments, but funding for Cameron's Worcester activities was provided by the Child Neurology Research, which was part of the Friedsam Foundation.

In 1952 and 1953, CIA Project ARTICHOKE administrators in the Agency's Security Research Service (SRS) expressed strong interest in the use of "depatterning" shock therapy, as well as Metrazol shock therapy, in their efforts toward developing enhanced interrogation techniques. In 1952, SRS physicians conducted several experiments with depatterning therapy on subjects who were patients at Veterans Administration medical facilities in the United States and in Panama at Fort Amador. Additional experiments at these locations were conducted with Metrazol therapy.

In at least three experiments, conducted at unnamed VA hospitals in Pennsylvania and Ohio, patients, who were former American POWs in Korea, were repeatedly shocked with Metrazol to see if physicians could render them without any memories of their activities in Korea. The results of these experiments are unknown, but CIA scientists within the Technical Service Division picked up where SRS left off when Agency psychologists enthusiastically read Dr. Ewen Cameron's medical paper on "psychic driving and depatterning shock therapy," in 1955, and decided to fund Cameron's work at the Allan Memorial Institute of Psychiatry at McGill University, Montreal, Quebec through the Society for the Investigation for Human Ecology. (CIA records reveal that the U.S. Air Force in August 1969 was considering co-sponsoring Cameron's research. Additionally, CIA officials decided in about 1951 that Metrazol shock therapy was better used and more effective in coercive interrogation sessions. See this book's chapter on Dimitre Dimitrov.)

In April 1953, at Youth House, young Lee Harvey Oswald was administered all of the neurological examinations mentioned above by various psychologists and staff. Some of these tests were possibly administered to Oswald at the Bellevue Hospital, but the FBI, in 1964, was unable to confirm this. (The Bender-Gestalt Test was a significant topic of discussion in the 1969 trial of accused Robert F. Kennedy murderer, Sirhan Sirhan.)

Dr. Bender – who had two children, a son and daughter, and three grandchildren at the time of her death in 1987 – was a confident and dogmatic woman, who bristled at criticism, and oftentimes refused to acknowledge reality even when it stood starkly before her.

Despite publicly claiming good results with electroshock treatment, privately Bender said she was seriously disappointed in the aftereffects and results shown by the subject children. Indeed, the condition of some of the children appeared to have only worsened. One six-year old boy, after being shocked several times, went from being a shy, withdrawn child to acting increasingly aggressive and violent. Another child, a seven-year-old girl, following five electroshock sessions administered by Dr. Bender, had become nearly catatonic.

Years later, another of Bender's young patients who became overly aggressive after an astounding 20 electroshock treatments, now grown, was convicted in court as a "multiple murderer." Others, in adulthood, reportedly were in and out of trouble and prison for committing batteries of petty and violent crimes.

A 1954 scientific study of about 50 of Bender's young electroshock patients, conducted by two psychologists, found that nearly all were worse off after the "therapy" and that some had become suicidal after treatment. One of the children studied in 1954 was the son of well-known writer Jacqueline Susann, author of the best-selling novel *Valley of the Dolls*. Susann's son, Guy, was diagnosed with autism shortly after birth and, when he was three years old, Dr. Bender convinced Susann and her husband that Guy could be successfully treated with electroshock therapy. Guy returned home from Dr. Bender's care a nearly lifeless child. Susann later told people that Bender had "destroyed" her son. Guy, born in 1946, has been confined to private institutions since his treatment.

To their credit, some of Dr. Bender's colleagues considered her use of electroshock on children "scandalous," but few colleagues spoke out against her, a situation still today common among those in the medical profession. In July 2010, a very prominent New York physician, who was still a proponent of electroshock therapy in patient care, told this author, "Nobody back in the days that Lauretta was doing all her work had a clue that the government, the CIA, army, or whoever, was involved in any of this work ... that these were experiments of some sort.... For what purpose, I have no idea. I clearly had no knowledge of that, but I don't think it would have altered much at all in the way of open criticism of her work. In fact, and I hate to say this, it might have served to put a complete damper on any criticism at all."

Said Dr. Leon Eisenberg, a widely respected physician and true pioneer in the study of autistic children, in 1998: "[Lauretta Bender] claimed that some of these children recovered [because of her shock treatment]. I once wrote a paper in which I referred to several studies by [Dr. E. R.] Clardy. He was at Rockwin State Hospital – the back-up to Bellevue – and he described the arrival of these children. He considered them psychotic and perhaps worse off than before the treatment."

(Additionally, this writer could find no instance where any of Bender's colleagues spoke out against her decidedly racist viewpoints. Dr. Bender made it quite clear that she felt that African Americans were best characterized by their "capacity for laziness" and "ability to dance," both features, Bender claimed, of the "specific brain impulses" of African Americans.)

About the same time Dr. Bender was conducting her electroshock experiments on children, she was also widely experimenting on autistic and schizophrenic children with what she termed other "treatment endeavors." These included use of a wide array of psycho-pharmaceutical agents, several provided to her by the Sandoz Chemical Company in Basel, Switzerland (which maintained a small, private office in Manhattan, sometimes manned by Aurelio Cerletti and Dr. Rudolph P. Bircher – both frequent visitors to CIA offices in Washington, D.C. – for discretely dispensing products and experimental drugs to selected physicians in the New York area), as well as Metrazol, a sub-shock insulin therapy, amphetamines, and anticonvulsants. Metrazol was a trade name for pentylenetetrazol, a drug used as a circulatory and respiratory stimulant. High doses of the drug cause convulsions, as discovered in 1934 by the Hungarian-American neurologist and psychiatrist Ladislas J. Meduna.

Metrazol had been used in convulsive therapy, but was never considered effective, and side effects such as seizures were difficult to avoid. The medical records of several young patients who were confined at the Vermont State Hospital, a public mental facility, reveal that Metrazol was administered to them by CIA contractor Dr. Robert Hyde on numerous occasions in order "to address overly aggressive behavior." One of these patients, Karen Wetmore, received the drug on a number of occasions for no discernible reason. During the same ten-year period in which Metrazol was used by the Vermont State Hospital, patient deaths skyrocketed. In 1982, the FDA revoked its approval of Metrazol.

In 1955 and 1956, Dr. Bender began hearing glowing accounts about the potential of LSD for producing remarkable results in children suffering mental disorders, including autism and schizophrenia. Bender's earlier work with electroshock therapy had brought her into contact with several other prominent physicians who, at the time, were also covert contractors with the CIA's MK/ULTRA and ARTICHOKE projects. Primary among these physicians were Drs. Harold A. Abramson, Paul Hoch, James B. Cattell, Joel Elkes,

Max Fink, Harris Isbell, Abraham Wikler, Alfred Hubbard, Seymour Kety, Mary A.B. Brazier, Robert G. Heath, Byron E. Leach, Amedeo Marrazzi, and Carl C. Pfeiffer. These physicians, plus about twenty others, were considered at the time to be the crème-de-la-crème of psychochemical researchers, and all were wittingly under contract with the CIA, U.S. Army, or U.S. Navy to perform extensive research for the government, often using unwitting subjects in highly abusive, sometimes barbaric situations.

Dr. Harold A. Abramson, the physician who "treated" Frank Olson in New York City in 1953, was, at the time, considered the informal godfather of LSD research. Drs. Hoch and Cattell were responsible, along with others, for injecting unwitting NYSPI patient Harold Blauer with a massive dose of mescaline that killed him. Dr. Elkes was one of the earliest physicians in Europe to experiment with LSD, having requested samples of the drug from Sandoz Chemical in 1949. Elkes was a very close associate of Dr. Abraham Wikler, who worked closely with Dr. Harris Isbell at the now-closed Lexington, Kentucky prison farm, where drug-addicted inmates, ostensibly being rehabilitated and treated for their addictions, were given heroin in exchange for their participation in LSD and mescaline experiments underwritten by the CIA and Pentagon. Dr. Elkes worked closely with the CIA, Pentagon and Britain's MI6 on drug experiments in England and the United States.

Shortly after deciding to initiate her own LSD experiments on children, Dr. Bender attended an informal conference held in early 1960 and sponsored by a CIA front group, the Josiah Macy Jr. Foundation. The conference focused on LSD research and featured Dr. Harold Abramson as a presenter. In 1959, Abramson had conducted LSD experiments on a group of six children ranging in age from 5 to 14 years of age. Abramson's earliest experiments with children and LSD originated in 1953 in New York City and at a small hospital in Long Island, with additional experiments conducted each year thereafter through about 1963.

A few months following the Macy Foundation gathering, Dr. Bender was notified that her proposed LSD experiments on children would be partially and surreptitiously funded by the Society for the Investigation of Human Ecology (SIHE), another CIA front group then located in Forest Hills, New York. Signing the grant approval document for Bender's project was CIA psychologist John

W. Gittinger. The Society, headed by Colonel James L. Monroe, a former U.S. Air Force officer who had worked on top-secret psychological warfare and propaganda projects with Gittinger, oversaw about 55 ultra-secret projects underwritten by the CIA. These projects involved LSD, hypnosis, interrogation, ESP, clairvoyance, telekinesis, black magic, astrology, psychological warfare, media manipulation, and other more mundane subjects.

Apparently, Dr. Bender's work with children and LSD raised some concerns within the CIA's Technical Services Division (TSD). A 1961 TSD memorandum written to Monroe questioned the "operational benefits of Dr. Bender's work as related to children and LSD," and requested that the Division be kept "closely appraised of the possible links between Dr. Bender's project and those being conducted under separate [MK/ULTRA] funding at designated prisons in New York and elsewhere."

Mystery within Mysteries ...

Mystery within mysteries, the issue raised by the vague TSD reference to "operational benefits" appears to have been related to another still very mysterious CIA project involving young people and women. This project, commencing in early 1953 and running until about 1963, involved the training of small cadres of women for work as Agency and military couriers, as well as young girls and teenagers for mostly unknown objectives apparently related to the CIA's interest in hypnosis, slight-of-hand, and telekinesis. Some of the best evidence of this project comes from the activities of CIA officer Robert Vern Lashbrook in November 1953, when he was in New York City with Dr. Frank Olson (for Olson's alleged psychiatric sessions with Dr. Harold Abramson), and shortly thereafter in December 1953 and January 1954. We are fortunate to have this evidence from the assiduous research of writer and magician Ben Robinson, who reveals it in his book, *The Magician: John Mulholland's Secret Life*, the activities of Lashbrook concerning Dr. Andrija Puharich's research and projects.

Additionally, former CIA scientist John Gavin, who worked in the CIA's Technical Services Division under Gottlieb, said in 1979, "There was a project around the mid-1950s that involved children, covet operations and parapsychology of sorts. I didn't work on it, but I knew about it." Gavin, who resigned his CIA post in the late

1950s, also stated, "There was also one project I was aware of that trained women as couriers and covert operators. It made use of LSD and what was called "narco-hypnosis," a term devised by the Agency's Medical Office ... it was operated apart from Technical Services under the ARTICHOKE Project and involved the development of special interrogations techniques." A May 19, 1952 CIA document sent form the Agency's Medical Staff chief to the Assistant Director of Scientific Intelligence reads in part:

> Reference is made to the attached draft, subject "Special Interrogations." At the meeting of 14 May 1952 the Medical Office outlined its position regarding the Artichoke Project and requested that the term "Narco-hypnosis" be used to those responsibilities within the interim program that are basically medical.... It was also agreed at the meeting of 14 May 1952 that field activities would be under the command of the chief of field station concerned, provided that instances of this agreement would be referred back to headquarters for final decision.

In late 1998, when this author interviewed Dr. Sidney Gottlieb (see *A Terrible Mistake* on Dr. Frank Olson's murder), the former Technical Services Division chief said, "Yes, I have some trace memories of the project. I think it began before MK/ULTRA was approved ... with an unrelated program Morse Allen initiated around [Dr. Andrija] Puharich's work. It was never a formally sanctioned TSD program, but we were interested and [Dr. Henry] Bortner stayed with it for a while.... It was one of those projects that would be greatly misunderstood today."

Dr. Bender's LSD Experiments on Children

Dr. Bender conducted her first experiments with children and LSD in 1960 at the Children's Unit, Creedmoor State Hospital in Queens, New York. The LSD she used was supplied in carefully measured glass ampoules by Dr. Rudolph P. Bircher of the Sandoz Pharmaceutical Company. For the same experiments, Dr. Bircher also provided Bender with other Sandoz-produced products, UML-401 and UML-491, that the company described as being "very much like LSD but sometimes dreamier in effect and longer lasting." Bender's initial group of young subjects consisted of

14 children diagnosed "schizophrenic," all under the age if 11 years old. There were 11 boys and 3 girls, ranging in age from six to ten years old. (Because diagnostic criteria for schizophrenia, autism, Asperger's, and other disorders have changed over the years, today one cannot assess what actual conditions these children really had.)

Over the years, there have been multiple reports that many of Dr. Bender's subject children were either "wards of the State" or orphans, but the available records and literature on her LSD experiments reveals nothing on this. The same literature makes it obvious that the children had been confined to the Creedmoor State Hospital for long periods of time, some for several years or more, and that many, if discharged, needed suitable homes or placements in the community." There is also no evidence that any follow-up studies were conducted on any of the children experimented upon by Bender.

On Bender's use of LSD on children, Dr. Leon Eisenberg said years later, "She did all sorts of things. Lauretta Bender reached success in her career long before randomized controlled trials had even been heard of. She didn't see the need for trials of drugs because she was convinced she knew what worked." Many other physicians speaking privately were far less diplomatic in condemning Bender's LSD work, but were also concerned about speaking on the record because of CIA funding for the experiments. At the same time, many of the aging stalwarts of the arguable "virtues" and "potential" of LSD continue to cite her work as groundbreaking science.

Said one former Fort Detrick scientist in 2001, insisting over the telephone on confidentially: "I'm not going to say a whole lot about what went on in New York at the Institute, Creedmoor, and elsewhere. I'm just not going to go into that … but what really got to me, what always amazed me was that the press at the time of Blauer's death [at the NYSPI] failed to probe any deeper into what was really going on. There's this line… there's this line that the press guys don't go across, no matter what they know… It's beyond typical blinders … it's just a simple case where nobody wants to believe or acknowledge certain things. You know, 'My government wouldn't do this; my government would never consider doing these sort of things'.… Everyone knows that where there is smoke there is fire. People think Blauer was the only death, the only subject that turned up dead, but that's plain foolishness. [Blauer] was the tip of the iceberg, one of many, including children, some not yet in their teens."

This same former Detrick scientist provided this author with an aged printed chart, presumably generated by the Special Operations Division (SOD) at Fort Detrick in 1954 or 1955, that provided certain details and numbers concerning experiments with psychochemicals on children by various approved Army and CIA physicians. The chart highlighted five children, between the ages of 12 and 15, that had been given LSD, two were also subject to hypnosis for undefined objectives. This same scientist also remarked that he recalled viewing a film that "graphically displayed the effects of psychochemicals on young subjects." He was not certain, but he "thought the film had been produced by Dr. Leon Roizin, a former Chief of Neuropathology at the NYSPI."

Besides the above despicable experiments, it has recently been revealed that the CIA also funded a rural-based summer camp for urban children (mostly from New York City, many of them racial minorities) in southern Vermont. The camp, which was located on the grounds of a large secluded estate, was composed of about a half-dozen cabins for lodging, a large mess hall, and several barns, one used for recreational purposes. One former camper, an immigrant from South America, who contacted this author under terms of anonymity, reports that he was "made to take part" in "weird, and sometimes painful, experiments" whereby "metal things" were implanted in his head through his nose and ears, but he recalls little more than the bizarre after-effects. The former camper, today nearing the age of 68, says that he was sent to the camp after he ran afoul of the law for minor offenses and spent two weeks, in May 1953, at New York's Youth House. Today, the Vermont camp is entirely gone, dismantled, carted away, vanished.

And the story continues.

The Rosenberg Case, Aline Mosby and Lee Oswald

It was a seminal event in young Lee Oswald's life: One day in New York City, by chance, an "old woman on the street," as he would later describe her, handed young Lee a pamphlet as he walked by. Lee, the rebel in progress, seething with pubertal turmoil and testosterone driven emotion, became outraged by what he saw and read in the pamphlet. The pamphlet concerned the case of Julius and Ethel Rosenberg, who would be executed on June 19, 1953 as Soviet spies. The Rosenbergs, both Jewish and Communist Party members, were convicted and sentenced to death for allegedly passing to the Soviets secret data about the atomic bomb and other information, some of which was used by the Soviets in shooting down Gary Powers' U-2 spy plane in 1960.

Lee would later say in a 1959 UPI interview conducted in the Soviet Union, where he had defected: "I'm a Marxist. I became interested about the age of 15. An old lady handed me a pamphlet about saving the Rosenbergs."

UPI reporter Aline Mosby conducted the interview with Oswald. Mosby was an attractive and highly talented and experienced 37-year old reporter (CIA files refer to her as a "newspaperman"), who had been born and raised in Montana. Not long after graduating from the University of Montana, Mosby became a well-connected and sought after Hollywood reporter. She was tenacious and never failed to get the story or interview she was after. Nearly every big-screen star sat with her and opened up. Howard Hughes called her a "bitch" for her tenacity and tough style. Actors like John Wayne, Marilyn Monroe, Hedy Lamarr, and Sammy Davis Jr. spoke with her on a regular basis. Mosby went on to become the first female news correspondent stationed in Moscow, and worked for UPI for twenty-five years in many prestigious posts, including Paris and China.

Mosby was new to Moscow, having arrived there only months before, and was looking for a good story to begin her time there. She later recalled that in late October 1959 she learned about a young American defector who wanted to renounce his American citizenship and stay in the Soviet Union. The young man, Lee Harvey Oswald, was staying at Moscow's Hotel Metropole. Mosby telephoned Oswald at the hotel. At first, Oswald refused to see her, but she slowly talked him into allowing her an interview. Oswald told her to come to Room 233 on November 13, 1959.

Mosby was prompt for the interview and Oswald, at first a little hesitant, opened up and spoke freely about his life and motives for coming to the Soviet Union. The results of Aline's interview appeared two days later in a UPI story headed, "*Fort Worth Defector Confirms Red Beliefs.*"

According to the article, Oswald told Mosby that leaving America for Russia was "like getting out of prison." Oswald also told Mos-

by that he had renounced his U.S. citizenship "for purely political reasons."

Wrote Mosby: "He said he told the U.S. embassy he was a devoted believer in communism and had read books on the subject since he was 13. Memories of a poverty-stricken childhood played a part in his decision, he said. His father, he said, died before he was born."

Oswald went on: "I saw my mother always as a worker, always with less than we could use." He told Mosby, his mother "would not understand why he had fled to Russia." However, Oswald "insisted his childhood was a happy one, despite poverty."

He told Mosby nothing of his days in an orphanage or of having moved from place to place. He did not complain about anything other than capitalism.

"I could not be happy living under capitalism," he told Mosby. "I would not want to live in the United States and be either a worker exploited by capitalists or a capitalist exploiting workers or become unemployed."

"During his hitch in the Marines," Aline wrote, "[Oswald] learned to be a specialist in radar and electronics."

Asked what he had done before coming to Moscow, Oswald said, "I was with occupation forces in Japan and occupation of a country is imperialistic." Asked how he managed to get to Moscow, Oswald said, "I saved my money – $1,600 – to come to the Soviet Union, and thought of nothing else."

"Many things bothered him in the United States, he said," Mosby concluded her article. "Race discrimination, 'harsh' treatment of 'underdog' communists and 'hate.'"

Mosby stated in 1978 that after her 1959 interview with Oswald, she saw him only once more – at a Moscow performance of the opera *The Queen of Spades*. The opera was Oswald's favorite dramatic stage production, and he had attended several productions during his time in Russia. Mosby did not approach Oswald at the performance. Indeed, she never heard about him again until after the assassination.

In the same 1978 interview, Mosby said she was "surprised by Oswald's lack of sophistication, his shallow knowledge of communism, and his arrogance." Oswald, she recalled, cockily told her that he "expected the Soviets to give him an important job." Mosby speculated that Oswald had "a mother complex or some sort of hangup about women" because he granted interviews only to her and one other female reporter, Priscilla Johnson McMillan, who interviewed Oswald only a day later, and because "during the interview he dwelt on the problems of his mother," who he believed "was being exploited by American capitalism." (See Notes for more on Priscilla Johnson.)

The day following the assassination of JFK, Aline Mosby pulled out her detailed notes from her 1959 Oswald interview and drafted another, more complete, account of her afternoon visit in Moscow with the young defector.

Apparently, Mosby's expanded, post-JFK assassination account, drafted in 1963, was never published anywhere. However, since Mosby was a journalist with hundreds of interviews to her credit, it is well worth examining here.

Mosby states that she first heard of Oswald "at the American embassy" in Moscow where she was told that "a young American named Lee Harvey Oswald, 20 [years old], had walked in [on October 31, 1959], slapped his passport on the consular officer's desk and announced he'd 'had enough of the United States'. ... On November 2, he had signed an affidavit saying, 'I affirm that my allegiance is to the Soviet Socialist Republics.'"

Intrigued with this report, journalist Mosby set out to find Oswald and quickly located him at a Moscow hotel called the Metropole. When Mosby knocked on the door of room 233, "An attractive fellow answered my knock ... 'I am Lee Oswald,' he said, with a hesitant smile."

Oswald told Mosby that other reporters had been attempting to interview him, but he had allowed her to come to his hotel room because, "I think you may understand and be friendly because you're a woman."

Mosby's interview with Oswald went on for two hours, from which she noted the following impressions:

> He talked almost non-stop like the type of semi-educated person of little experience who clutches what he regards as some sort of unique truth. Such a person often does not expect anyone else to believe him and is contemptuous of other people who cannot see his "truth." A zealot, he is not remotely touched by what anyone else says. In fact, at times in my two hours with Lee Harvey Oswald I felt we were not carrying out a conversation, but that two monologues were being delivered simultaneously.

On hearing Oswald's own account of his defection, Mosby was skeptical: "It sounded to me as if he had rehearsed these sentences, and they had a tone of childish defiance and pretentiousness." She was perhaps referring to his comment that, "Soviet officials have informed me that either in the event of rejection or acceptance of my first application [to stay in the Soviet Union], I won't have to leave. They are investigating the possibilities of finding me an occupation. They think it would be best to continue my higher education."

Mosby observed that as Oswald spoke, "he held his mouth stiffly and nearly closed. His jaw was rigid. Behind his brown eyes I felt a certain coldness. He displayed neither the impassioned fervor of a devout American communist who at least had reached the land of his dreams, nor the wise-cracking informality and friendliness of the average American. Sometimes he looked directly at me, other times at the plush furniture…. He was pleasant and well-mannered, but he sounded smug and self-important. And so often that small smile, more like a smirk …" [(Mosby recalled Oswald as having brown eyes, a subject of long dispute. Oswald himself described his eye color as "blue-gray" on November 22, 1963.)

Mosby asked Oswald about where he was born and his early years. Oswald said he had been born on October 18, 1939 in New Orleans, where, Mosby colorfully noted, "like most of the south and southwest of the United States, a tradition of violence runs through the town like the Mississippi River."

Oswald told the reporter, "I lived for two years in New York … where I saw the luxuries of Park Avenue and the workers' lives on the East Side." He recounted how his "widowed" mother "took him and his two brothers to Fort Worth, Texas, back to New Orleans and Fort Worth again."

Mosby observed, "Oswald painted a verbal picture of a boy who grew up with an 'old mother and without the discipline, love and care of a father.'"

Mosby asked Oswald if he had had many friends in school.

"Oh, I had a certain amount of friends," Oswald replied, revealing his lifelong penchant not to complain, "but I don't have many attachments now in the United States. I traveled a lot. We moved from one city to the next. Besides, I was a bookworm."

"What did you read?" Mosby asked.

"Marx," said Oswald. "I'm a Marxist," he said, ignoring a long list of other non-political books, as well as comic books, that he had devoured as a youth.

"I became interested about the age of 15," Oswald explained. "From an ideological standpoint. An old lady handed me a pamphlet about saving the Rosenbergs."

"I looked at that paper," Oswald said, "and I still remember it for some reason. I don't know why."

According to Mosby, Oswald said that when he discovered *Das Kapital* in the library, "It was like a very religious man opening the *Bible* for the first time." Mosby quotes Oswald, as follows:

> I would not care to live in the United States where being a work-
> er means you are exploited by the capitalists. If I would remain

in the United States, feeling as I do, under the capitalist system, I could never get ahead. I could not be happy. I could not live under a capitalistic system. I would have a choice of becoming a worker under the system I hate, or being unemployed.

Or I could have become a capitalist and derived my profit and my living under the exploitation of workers.

Oswald went on and on and on. Mosby wrote that she asked "if he [Oswald] were a member of the Communist party."

"Communist?" Oswald said, looking surprised. "I've never met a communist. I might have seen a communist once in New York, the old lady who gave me the pamphlet, save the Rosenbergs."

Surprised by this, Mosby asked Oswald "what he thought about Communist Party members in the United States or even socialists."

"I don't want any socialist people to act for me," Oswald replied, in "a voice heavy with scorn," observed Mosby.

"I disliked them as I know them in the United States," Oswald said. "You don't just sit around and talk about it. You go out and do it. I just haven't got out of university and read about Marx. I've seen all the workers on the East Side."

Oswald went on: "The Soviet Union has always been my ideal, as the bulwark of communism. The communists have been a minority in the United States, and have to rely on outside power and moral support from the Soviet Union. American communists can look to the Soviet Union as some sort of ideal. The Americans are right in assuming that communism all over the world has ties with the Soviet Union, like the Catholic Church has ties with the Pope."

At this juncture, Mosby, having become quite tired of the young defector's pontificating, tried to steer the conversation back to Oswald's mother and his childhood years.

"Did your early poverty influence your decision to come to Moscow?" she asked.

Oswald replied, "Well-lll, my childhood allowed me to have a few benefits of American society. I was not completely hamstrung in enjoying life. But seeing my mother always as a worker, always with less money than she could use ..."

Here, Mosby writes, Oswald stopped speaking for a moment, "and then leaned forward and spoke very slowly to emphasize his words."

"You see, my coming here, well, it was, uh, a matter of intelligence. I couldn't care to gamble. One way or another I'd lose in the United States. In my own mind, even if I'd be exploiting other workers. That's why I chose Marxist ideology."

It was a matter of intelligence ...

What exactly was Oswald attempting to convey to Mosby?

Moments after this, Mosby somehow got Oswald to talk about his time in the U.S. Marine Corps. Said Oswald: "After I finished high school, I joined the Marines Corps at 17. I was in Japan, Formosa, and the Philippines. I was discharged when I was 20, in Santa Ana, California. I was a radar operator." (Oswald quit high school after the tenth grade, when he was 17 years old.)

Oswald added, "I joined the Marines because I had a brother in the Marines. I had a good conduct medal."

In her 1963 redrafted article, Mosby here added: "American Embassy officials had said Oswald told them he would reveal to the Soviets all that he knew about American radar." Mosby, in 1963, does write, "Oswald did not have smooth relationships in the Marines, however. I later learned he had been tried twice before a military court for breaking regulations. At the end of his three years in uniform, he still was a private first class. But he was skilled with guns. In classes he qualified as a sharpshooter, which is the second of three gradings for shooting ability in the Marine Corps." (Oswald was the subject of military discipline on two occasions.)

Oswald's military records corroborate that he was "skilled with guns." During his enlistment, he was consistently considered a "better than average" to "excellent" marksman. He qualified at these levels by firing a "U.S. Rifle, Caliber .30, M1 and U.S. Carbine, Caliber .30, M1A1."

Oswald ended his interview with Mosby by explaining what things he thought about while in the Marine Corps, and how he made his plans to defect. According to Mosby, Oswald explained his process, as follows:

"In the Marines I believed American leaders in certain foreign countries. The Russians would say 'military imperialism.' Well, the occupation of one country is imperialistic. Like Formosa. The conduct of American technicians there, helping drag up guns for the Chinese. Watching American technicians show the Chinese how to use them – it's one thing to talk about communism and another thing to drag a gun up a mountainside.

"If you live with that for three years, you get the impression things aren't quite so right. I guess you could say I was influenced by what I read, and by observing that the material was correct in its thesis, both in civilian life and military."

Mosby found it difficult to follow Oswald's line of thinking, and asked him about his reading habits while in the Marines.

Oswald replied that while in the service he "continued to read Marxist books and laid careful plans to go to Russia." Oswald added, "I thought it would give me a chance to observe that which I had read."

Mosby wrote that he "intensely" added, "When I was working in the middle of the night on guard duty, I would think how long it would be and how much money I would have to have. It would be like being out of prison. I saved about $1,500.

"For two years I've had it in my mind, don't form any attachments, because I knew I was going away. I was planning to divest myself of everything to do with the United States. I've not just been thinking about it, but waiting to do it. For two years, saving my money. I'm sincere in my ideal. This is not something intangible. I'm going through pain and difficulty to do this."

Mosby asked Oswald if any of his friends in the Marines were aware of his plans "to give up his country."

"Nobody knew how I felt about things," Oswald replied. "I felt them very strongly. My superiors thought I was just interested in a foreign language. My commanding officer, a major, was studying Russian and we used to talk about it."

Mosby asked, "Now that you're in Moscow do you think Soviet society works as well in reality as Marx had it on paper?"

Oswald replied, "Considering Russia of 50 years ago, I can see the Soviet worker of today is remarkably well off. Now I personally would not say every person who thinks of himself as a communist should migrate to Russia. The drawbacks are many. But the basic ideas that brought me here are sound. The United States has more light bulbs and hot water heaters, but I don't feel that will be the case in 20 or 30 years. I would like to spend the rest of my life getting a normal life here, and if that means a marriage and so forth, okay."

"What does your mother think of your decision?" Mosby asked.

"She doesn't know," Oswald said. "She's rather old. I couldn't expect her to understand. I guess it wasn't fair of me not to say anything, but it's better that way. I don't want to involve my family in this. I think it would be best if they would forget about me. My brother might lose his job because of this."

Mosby asked, "How do you think you'll get along in a foreign country where you don't know the language?"

"Oh, I've been in a lot of classes in Russian," Oswald replied, without naming where or when he had attended those classes. He went on, "I want to expand my reading and writing. I can get along in restaurants but my Russian is very bad. The only barrier here is learning absolutely fluently the language." Oswald added, "I have Soviet friends. I've gone to museums and theaters. They are very sympathetic to me."

Mosby wrote that at this, Oswald "thought a moment and chuckled."

"I am in essence," he said, "an ignorant immigrant. I never thought I'd be an immigrant from the U.S. to some other country. Like a German living in America."

Mosby wrote that when Oswald started in again on "the ebb and flow of communism," she stood up and said that she had to go. She wrote that, "I was tired of listening to what sounded like recitations out of Pravda."

She pulled her coat on, thinking about "how Oswald appeared totally disinterested in anything but himself. He never once asked what I was doing in Moscow, or how we foreigners lived here."

Wrote Mosby: "I also thought about a boy trying to digest that Metropole hotel food every night, a stranger in a foreign land without family or close friends. Perhaps if he came to my apartment where he would see other westerners, he might think twice of his decision."

As she was leaving, Mosby told Oswald that he should come to her apartment for dinner some night. Clearly, the reporter felt sorry for the young defector. Mosby was nearly twenty years older that Oswald, and quite possibly her compassion for someone she saw as being very confused and lonely, was also mixed with motherly feelings for Oswald.

Wrote Mosby" "'Thank you,'" he said to my causal invitation to come to dinner some night. It was obvious he had no intention of seeing me again."

Mosby concluded her draft article by writing of her impressions on the day of Oswald's arrest after the assassination of President Kennedy:

> That same little smile was on his face when he walked out of his cell for the last time to face reporters and photographers, but the smile changed to the grimace of pain and death.
>
> If he was guilty, why did he not confess in jail? In my opinion he did not confess probably because he felt nobody would understand him. Nobody ever had.

Aline Mosby would later write a book about her years as a reporter, *The View From No. 13 People's Street*, but she did not mention a word about Lee Harvey Oswald or her interview with him in the book. Asked about this, she explained that she had "simply not thought about Oswald." Said Mosby: "He really didn't make much of an impression on me. I was not impressed with him one bit." There is little doubt that after she died in August 1998, Aline would have been disappointed to see that the *New York Times* highlighted her interview with Oswald in its published obituary.

Oswald's "Suicide" Attempt: October 21, 1959

Strangely, Aline Mosby mentions nothing in her articles about Lee Oswald's suicide attempt in Moscow three weeks before she sat down with him at the Metropole Hotel.

According to numerous CIA and Russian KGB documents, as well as Oswald's diary, on Wednesday, 21, 1959, at about 7:00 P.M., Lee Oswald decided to end his life by his own hand. After arriving in Moscow by train from Helsinki five days earlier, Oswald had grown increasingly frustrated by his inability to convince Soviet officials to allow him to remain in Russia.

Writes Oswald in his diary: "Eve. 6:00 – Receive word from police official. I must leave country tonight at 8:00 P.M. as visa expires. I am shocked! My dreams! I retire to my room. I have $100 left. I have waited for 2 years to be accepted. My fondest dreams are shattered because of a petty official; because of bad planning – I planned so much!"

Oswald's diary continues: "7:00 P.M. I decide to end it. Soak wrist in cold water to numb the pain. Then slash my wrist. Then plunge wrist into bathtub of hot water. I think 'when Rima [Oswald's assigned Soviet Intourist guide while in Moscow] comes at 8 to find me dead it will be a great shock.'"

Continues Oswald with a great flair for the dramatic: "Somewhere a violin plays as I watch my life whirl away. I think to myself, 'how easy to die' and 'a sweet death,' (to violins)."

Oswald was found as expected by his Intourist guide, Rimma Shirakova. Knowing that he was always very punctual and was to meet her in the lobby of the hotel, when he did not show up, she alerted the hotel duty person who discovered Oswald bleeding in the bathroom. He was rushed by ambulance to Botkinskaya Hospital, where his wound was treated, and his arm heavily bandaged and placed in a sling.

There are many discrepancies in the reports about this incident. According to one hospital report, the slash in Oswald's arm was only about 2 inches long and not that deep: "The injury did not reach the tendons."

Oswald was given a psychiatric examination at the hospital on his third day there. It reads, "A few days ago [the patient] arrived in the Soviet Union in order to apply for our citizenship. Today he was to have left the Soviet Union. In order to postpone his departure he inflicted the injury upon himself. The patient apparently understands the questions asked in Russian. Sometimes he answers correctly, but immediately states that he does not understand what he was asked.

"According to the interpreter, there were no mentally sick people in his family. He had no skull trauma, never before had he made attempts to commit suicide. He tried to commit suicide in order not to leave for America. He claims he regrets his action. After recovery he intends to return to his homeland. It was not possible to get more information from the patient."

Given that Aline Mosby was allegedly first alerted to the presence of Oswald in Russia by State Department officials, it seems that she should have known something about the attempted suicide. If he had slashed his wrist, it seems hard to imagine that Oswald did not at least have some bandages on it when she met him. This reasonably leads one to think that perhaps Oswald's alleged suicide did not take place, and that he was "hospitalized" by the Soviets

for a few days for other reasons. Amazingly, and without any explanation, many books on Oswald fail to even mention or discuss
his "suicide" attempt, an alleged occurrence that should have been
considered significant. It has been suggested that some writers ignore this alleged incident because it undermines arguments and
theories that Oswald was an American government agent or that
he had no role in the Dallas assassination. (Of course, arguing that
he had no role whatsoever makes it difficult to explain why Oswald
would claim to be a "patsy.")

What was the real nature of Oswald's alleged suicide attempt?
Was it merely a ploy for attention and an effort to gain approval to
remain in Russia, or was it an elaborate ruse designed for Oswald to
be admitted to the hospital for other reasons? Oswald remained at
the hospital for five days before he was released, and then allowed
to remain and work in Russia.

Lastly, it is intriguing to note that the CIA, following Oswald's
death, was most curious to learn if his autopsy report revealed any
signs of a scar on his left wrist. On February 17, 1964, CIA Deputy
Director for Plans, Richard Helms, wrote to J. Edgar Hoover, FBI
Director, and inquired about Oswald's attempted suicide. Helms
noted that a December 2, 1963 interview with Oswald's wife, Marina, produced the remark that she "never knew Oswald to speak of
or attempt suicide, that she did not think he was capable of suicide
and that she did not believe that he has ever attempted suicide." In
addition, Marina had told FBI interviewers "she recalled seeing a
scar on the inner left wrist of Oswald after they were married. This
scar she said was completely healed and she asked him about this
and he evaded answering her."

Helms told Hoover that the CIA felt that Marina Oswald's recollections were "not adequate and that independent corroborative
evidence on [Oswald's attempted suicide] should be obtained if it
is possible to do so." Helms then requested of Hoover: "We would
appreciate receiving any other information, such as statements of
observations by police or others, including the undertakers, copies
of any reports, such as autopsy or other, which may contain information to this point."

Helms continued, "The best evidence of a scar, or scars, on the
left wrist would of course be direct examination by a competent authority and we recommend that this be done and that a photograph

of the inner and outer surface of the left wrist be made if there has been no other evidence acceptable to the [Warren] Commission that he did in fact attempt suicide by cutting his wrist."

Aline Mosby is Drugged in Moscow

Two years after her Oswald interview, in the summer of 1961, a strange incident occurred in Moscow involving Aline Mosby. She was surreptitiously drugged with an unknown substance that caused her to behave strangely, and then pass out. The incident was first reported to the CIA by "a representative [reporter] of the *Baltimore Sun*," Peter J. Kumpa. Reads a November 30, 1961 CIA report marked SECRET:

> In the summer of 1961, an incident took place involving Aline Mosby, a UPI representative approximately 38-40 years of age. Miss Mosby is a US citizen and has been in Moscow for about two and a half years. She spoke Russian indifferently with an atrocious accent. She would often go out socially with Soviet men. One evening she went with one of them to the Arnyat, a well-known Armenian restaurant. Like most people who work for the wire services, she was in the habit of constantly calling her office to see if any important news or other matters needed her attention. When she came back from one such telephone call, she said that her escort had ordered cognac. She chided him somewhat saying, "You know I don't drink cognac. Please order some champagne." She went again to the telephone and when she came back the second time, she found the champagne there, but slightly discolored. Her escort explained that he had poured the cognac into the champagne.
>
> According to her own testimony, she drank the champagne and immediately began to get very warm and dizzy. Shortly afterwards she passed out and woke up in a sobering-up station, of which there are a number in Moscow. (In 20 or 30 degree temperature, a completely intoxicated person would die if exposed on the street throughout the night.) A week later *Isvestia* [Soviet publication] published some very uncomplimentary pictures of her [Mosby] in the sobering-up station – very unusual for a Soviet publication – and she was attacked personally as a degenerate capitalist with a shady past. The UPI was attacked as well. The

references to her past were to the circumstances of her employment by a U.S. magazine of doubtful reputation when they ran an exposé on the life and loves of Hollywood movie stars.

Medical evidence later verified that Miss Mosby had indeed been drugged. Despite the obvious attempt to discredit her, the Press Section of the Foreign Ministry interposed no objection when she asked that her visa be extended.

Aline Mosby's drugging was kept secret, and the drug used was not identified in any documents discovered to date. However, it is known from CIA documents that at this same time, and until at least 1975, the Soviets were secretly dosing U.S. State Department employees and suspected American intelligence agents with LSD and other hallucinogenic drugs. When this author interviewed CIA official Dr. Sidney Gottlieb, former chief of the Agency's Chemical Branch, Gottlieb recalled several instances in the 1960s when Americans in Moscow were surreptitiously drugged with LSD.

According to Gottlieb, "It took us by surprise, but that it happened there is no question. The first instance I can recall was with a person who worked with the U.S. embassy in Moscow. He was dosed with what was surely LSD one evening while drinking with friends in a restaurant. He ended up climbing out the men's room window to escape the place because he thought his companions had decided to murder him. He wandered the streets for hours, and then began knocking on doors telling anyone that answered that he was a messenger from God."

During an earlier conversation with this author, Gottlieb also described a number of odd drug-related incidents that occurred during President Richard Nixon's visit to Moscow.

Asked if Lee Harvey Oswald could have been drugged while in Russia, specifically around the time that he allegedly attempted to commit suicide, Gottlieb said, "It would not have been out of the realm of possibilities. A lot of Americans around that time were singled out for unwitting dosing."

I Led Three Lives, *The Manchurian Candidate* & Sinatra

During the early fifties, Lee's favorite television show, according to his brother Robert, was *I Led Three Lives*. Robert spoke several times about Lee's tendency toward a "fantasy life," saying that his brother was especially "engrossed" in "that particular show," and watched it "every week without fail." *I Led Three Lives* first aired in early October 1953 and ran until the start of 1956. The show was based on the life and activities of Herbert Philbrick, an advertising executive who infiltrated the U.S. Communist Party as a covert operative for the FBI. Based on a best selling book published in 1952, *I Led Three Lives: Citizen, "Cmmunist," Counterspy*, the series ran for 117 episodes.

Today, many researchers believe that Oswald's fondness for *I Led Three Lives* was a bellwether for his future as a secret agent working for the CIA and FBI, and perhaps as a double agent for the Russians or Cubans or both. Readers can find references to Lee being a loyal viewer of the program in well over one hundred books on the assassination.

Some researchers, however, scoff at Robert Oswald's recollection that his brother watched the show, and slyly imply that perhaps Robert had made the whole thing up. This author, one of countless youths who faithfully watched the show, would find it surprising if Lee Oswald had not watched the program. The minor controversy over it is worth mentioning.

Lee's faithful watching of *I Led Three Lives* is first mentioned in Robert Oswald's book, *Lee: A Portrait of Lee Harvey Oswald by His Brother*, published in 1967, and co-authored with Barbara and Myrick Land:

> All of us had our dreams and fantasies, but Lee's always lingered a little longer. The center of Lee's fantasy world shifted from radio to television when Mother bought a television set in 1948. When it was new, all of us spent far too much time watching variety shows, dramas, and old movies. Lee, particularly, was fascinated. One of his [Lee's] favorite [television] programs was *I Led Three Lives*, the story of Herbert Philbrick, the FBI informant who posed as a Communist spy. In the early 1950s, Lee watched that show every week without fail. When I left to join the Marines, he was still watching the reruns.

Later, in a 1993 *Frontline* interview, Robert said, "Lee's fantasy life, to me, became apparent in the 1948, 1949, 1950 period. Living in Fort Worth [Texas], TV was making its debut. We had an old black-and-white. He [Lee] seemed to really get involved with it and hang onto it after the programs were over. John [Pic] and I would be off doing other things. *I Led Three Lives* – he became really engrossed in that particular TV show, and he was still watching it when I left to go in the Marine Corps in 1952."

The problem with both of Robert Oswald's statements was that *I Led Three Lives* did not first air on television until October 1, 1953 in New York and elsewhere. As pointed out by several writers over the past decade, including John Armstrong, who may have been the first to notice the discrepancy, Robert Oswald "joined the Marines and left for San Diego on July 15, 1952," but *I Led Three Lives* first aired in "September, 1953, a year and two months after Robert Oswald left Fort Worth and joined the Marines." (Armstrong is off on the "first aired" date by one month.)

Writes Armstrong: "When Robert Oswald left home to join the Marines on July 15, 1952, Lee could not possibly have watched *I Led Three Lives*, and there are no other indications that he was living in a 'fantasy world.' These facts indicate that Robert invented this story in an attempt to malign his dead 'brother.'"

But, before any readers jump to conspiracy-related conclusions here, it should be noted that the TV show was a companion show "of sorts to the radio drama, *I Was a Communist for the FBI*, which dealt with a similar subject and [*I Led Three Lives*]was syndicated by Ziv Television Programs from 1952 to 1954."

Robert might have mixed up the TV show with the radio show in relation to the time he left for the Marines, or he could have simply mistaken the dates.

Further, every written report that relies on Robert's apparently mistaken statements overlooks Marguerite Oswald's testimony before the Warren Commission on February 12, 1964. Asked why she believed her son, Lee, was being formally trained to become a covert agent for the U.S. government, Marguerite replied,

> Many, many things. We always watched – it is *I Led Three Lives*
> – the program – Philbrick. We always watched that. And when
> Lee returned from the service and the Marines, the three days
> – that program was on, and he turned it off. He said, "Mother, don't watch that, that is a lot of propaganda." It has been
> stated publicly that the FBI did not know – didn't have Lee on

the subversive list – I am probably not saying this right, gentlemen – but the rightwing in Dallas. I don't know anything politically. The FBI and Secret Service had a list of names in Dallas of people that had to be watched, and Lee Harvey Oswald was not on that list. That would lead [people to] believe there was some reason he was not on the list.

Some readers may have noted the earlier reference to Lee's favorite opera, *The Queen of Spades* by Pyotr Ilyich Tchaikovsky. In the Soviet Union, Oswald attended several performances of this three-act production, based on a short story of the same name by Alexander Pushkin. Oswald was said to be obsessed with the opera, and on his 22nd birthday, October 18, 1961, he wrote in his diary that he was lonely: "I spend my birthday alone at the opera watching my favoriot [sic] 'Queen of Spades.'" The opera is about a man who wants to perform a heroic deed for the woman he loves, but the woman has grown to distrust him. The man becomes frantic and suicidal.

On returning home from the performance, Oswald jotted down a translated line from one scene: "I am ready right now to perform a heroic deed of unprecedented prowess for your sake." After Oswald and his Russian wife Marina returned home to the United States from the Soviet Union, the couple often listened to recordings of the opera.

Interestingly, a playing card on a par with the Queen of Spades shows up in both the novel and film, *The Manchurian Candidate* – published in 1959 by author Richard Condon, and released as a major feature film in 1962, during the Cuban Missile Crisis (and remade in 2004). In the novel and the films, the Queen of Diamonds playing card is used as a trigger for the lead character, former U.S. Army Sergeant Raymond Shaw. Played initially by Laurence Harvey, and in 2004 by Liev Schreiber, Sergeant Shaw is an unwitting sleeper agent and hypnosis-induced assassin who has been brainwashed by the communists during the Korean War to murder the U.S. President. As described on the book's cover, "Buried deep within the consciousness of Sergeant Raymond Shaw is the mechanism of an assassin – a time bomb ticking toward explosion, controlled by the delicate skill of its communist masters…. Raymond has been successfully brainwashed. His subconscious mind is controlled by a man in Red China who has primed him to become a deadly instrument of destruction." Every time Raymond sees the Queen of Diamonds playing card, his persona as an assassin takes over.

Frank Sinatra in *The Manchurian Candidate*

It has been reported that Frank Sinatra, whose company produced *The Manchurian Candidate*, withdrew the film from circulation after the JFK assassination because its story line was too close to Lee Harvey Oswald's actions. As reasonable and believable as this may seem, it is not true. According to Sinatra himself, and the film's director John Frankenheimer, the film was pulled back as a business decision because it had "played itself out," having been in circulation for a year. Moreover the film's distribution deal was not one that pleased Sinatra and Frankenheimer, so the decision was made to take the film back until a better deal was worked out.

Often overlooked in assassination lore is another film that featured Frank Sinatra and the subject of assassination. Indeed, this film, *Suddenly*, released in 1954, has some uncanny similarities to the JFK assassination. Its story line concerns a small band of assassins, led by a man named John Baron (played by Sinatra), posing as FBI agents. The group takes over the home of a family in Suddenly, California. The home is used as an outpost for an operation aimed at murdering the President of the United States, who is slated to soon pass through the town.

This is the film's basic story line, but to focus on Sinatra's character, John Baron, brings some very strange surprises. Baron is a former serviceman, who did not enjoy his military stint one bit. He is not respectful of military authority or willing to take command from officers he considers less intelligent than he is. He is belligerent and cocky and keeps mostly to himself.

Noted JFK researcher Martin Shackelford wrote about the film: "Baron is a skinny young ex-serviceman with ties to organized crime…. As a child, he was left for a time in an orphanage." To Baron, Shackelford wrote, "the President is 'just another man … I got no feeling against the President.'" Baron favors a high-powered rifle for assassinations, and plans to shoot the President from a window high above the Presidential limousine, which he calls "a lovely target." After he kills his target, he plans to jump into a plane and leave the country.

It has long been reported that Lee Oswald watched *Suddenly* on television just weeks before the Kennedy murder, but this is now called into question by some researchers. However, Oswald did see another feature film about presidential assassination in October 1963. The film was *We Were Strangers,* which some researchers claim Oswald watched twice on television. (Examining these three Hollywood films and their alleged influence over Oswald is instruc-

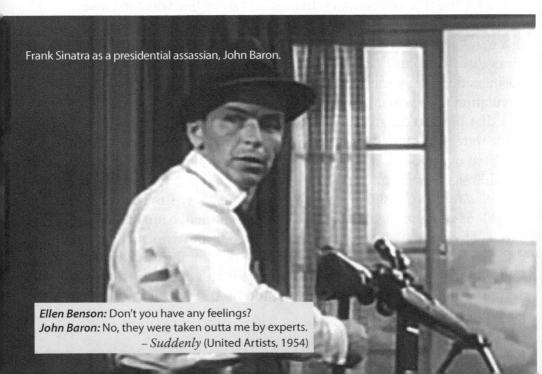

Frank Sinatra as a presidential assassin, John Baron.

Ellen Benson: Don't you have any feelings?
John Baron: No, they were taken outta me by experts.
– *Suddenly* (United Artists, 1954)

tive in many ways, especially as examples of speculation, misinformation and disinformation in various historical accounts that are presumed authoritative on Oswald and the assassination.)

Oswald and *We Were Strangers*

We Were Strangers, released in 1949, is a stereotypical B-grade film about an American leftist, Tony Fenner, played by actor John Garfield, who returns to his native Cuba to overthrow the island's repressive dictator named Gerardo Machado. (Gerardo Machado y Morales was president of Cuba until March 1933, when he was overthrown.) Fenner assembles a group of left-thinking rebels who are equally dedicated to ridding Cuba of Machado. Together, along with the obligatory love interest China Valdez, played by Jennifer Jones, Fenner plots to place a huge underground bomb in a location that will not only blow Machado sky high, but also his entire handpicked cabinet of evil doers. The plot goes wrong; the bomb kills nobody on the dictator's side, but Tony Fenner dies heroically amid the sound of dramatic music and an unexpected uprising of Cuba's oppressed people who overthrow Machado. Happy, democratic and dictator-free times are just around the corner. The end.

Marguerite's testimony before the Warren Commission included the following:

> **Mr. [J. Lee] Rankin**: Did he [Lee Oswald] discuss the television programs he saw that evening [November 21, 1963] with you?
>
> **Mrs. Oswald**: He was looking at TV by himself. I was busy in the kitchen. At one time when we were – when I was together with him they showed some sort of war films, from World War II. And he watched them with interest.
>
> **Mr. Rankin**: Do you recall films that he saw called *Suddenly*, and *We Were Strangers* that involved assassinations?
>
> **Mrs. Oswald**: I don't remember the names of these films. If you would remind me of the contents, perhaps I would know.
>
> **Mr. Rankin**: Well, "*Suddenly* was about the assassination of a president, and the other was about the assassination of a Cuban dictator.
>
> **Mrs. Oswald**: Yes, Lee saw those films.

Mr. Rankin: Did he tell you that he had seen them?

Mrs. Oswald: I was with him when he watched them.

Mr. Rankin: Do you recall about when this was with reference to the date of the assassination?

Mrs. Oswald: It seems that this was before Rachel's birth. [October 20, 1963.]

Mr. Rankin: Weeks or months? Can you recall that?

Mrs. Oswald: Several days. Some five days.

Marina also stated, in response to the Warren Commission asking if she had discussed the films *Suddenly* and *We Were Strangers* with her husband: "One film about the assassination of the president of Cuba [*We Were Strangers*], which I had seen together with him, he said that this was a fictitious situation, but that the content of the film was similar to the actual situation which existed in Cuba, meaning the revolution in Cuba." (Also worth noting here is that Robert Oswald would later write that Albert Jenner of the Warren Commission asked him if he had seen the films *Suddenly* and *The Manchurian Candidate*. He had not, but added, "When I did see *The Manchurian Candidate* on television later, it shocked me.")

Last, but far from least, it is worth noting the strange and coincidental connections between *Manchurian Candidate* director John Frankenheimer and the Kennedys. On the evening of June 4, 1968, Presidential candidate Senator Robert F. Kennedy enjoyed a fine dinner at the home of John Frankenheimer in Los Angeles. Also present were actress Sharon Tate and her husband, Roman Polanski. Later that evening, Frankenheimer drove Kennedy to the Ambassador Hotel, where Kennedy would be shot and killed minutes after midnight.

Marguerite and State Dept. Official Eugene Boster

Marguerite Oswald had been extremely concerned about her son immediately following his defection to Russia in October 1959. Indeed, Marguerite had no idea where Lee was for several weeks after his discharge from the Marine Corps. When she did learn that he was possibly in Russia, she had no idea why or where he was in the Soviet Union. Said Marguerite: "I didn't know wheth-er he was living or dead."

So concerned was she about his whereabouts that in January 1961 she borrowed money from an insurance policy, took $36 out of the bank, and boarded a train in Fort Worth, Texas to Washing-ton, D.C. The trip took nearly three days.

She arrived in Washington at 8:00 A.M., January 26, 1961, promptly located a pay phone, and telephoned the White House. Marguerite later testified before the Warren Commission: "A Negro man was on the switchboard, and he said the offices were not open yet, they did not open until 9 o'clock. He asked if I would leave my number. I asked to speak to President Kennedy. And he said the of-fices were not open yet. I said, 'Well, I just arrived here from Fort Worth, Texas … and I will call back at 9 o'clock.'"

The mother of the man who she strongly suspected was a govern-ment agent and who would be alleged to be JFK's assassin calling the White House and asking for President Kennedy three years before the fateful day in Dallas, Texas. Mere coincidence or the irrational act of a delusional mother?

Marguerite called back promptly at 9 o'clock, she recalled. "Ev-eryone was just gracious to me over the phone. Said that President Kennedy was in a conference, and they would be happy to take any message. I asked to speak to Secretary of State Dean Rusk, and they connected me with that office."

Marguerite was told that Secretary Rusk was also in a conference and unavailable to speak with her.

Undeterred, she explained, "I have come to town about a son of mine who is lost in Russia…. I would like personally to speak to Secretary Rusk."

Marguerite was placed on hold briefly and then told that Secre-tary Rusk had requested that she speak with Mr. Gene Boster, the State Department officer in charge of Soviet Union affairs. Boster came on the line and Marguerite introduced herself, and Boster

Marguerite Oswald
1907-1981

surprised her by saying, "Yes, I am familiar with the case of your son, Mrs. Oswald."

Gene Boster was quite familiar with cases of Americans defecting to the Soviet Union. Indeed, well before Marguerite Oswald's visit, Boster and Richard E. Snyder, the American Consul in Russia – who would first deal with Lee Harvey Oswald in Moscow – held ongoing discussions about how best to process and document what Snyder termed "defection cases." In a October 1959 follow-up letter to Boster, Snyder had raised the cases of two American defectors and how best to "leave ... avenues to repatriation ... open to future contingency."

Davis Eugene Boster, sometimes called David Boster, and called "Gene' by his friends, was a life-long Foreign Service Officer who, for decades before his death in 2005, was thought to be a covert CIA operative within the State Department – so covert that the Department itself did not know for sure. The State Department's Security Office, in the mid-1970s, secretly launched its own investigation into Boster's status, but found nothing.

During World War II, Boster had served in the Navy in the Atlantic and the Pacific, and was expertly trained in Russian near the end of his military service. He joined the Foreign Service in 1947 and was dispatched to the U.S. Embassy in Moscow, later serving as desk officer for the Soviet Union and liaison officer to the Soviet and Eastern European delegations at the Japanese Peace Conference in San Francisco in 1951. He was later a staff assistant to Secretary of State John Foster Dulles and officer in charge of Soviet Union affairs from 1959 to 1962. In 1962, not long after he met with Marguerite Oswald, he was assigned as political officer to the U.S. Embassy in Mexico City.

Is it mere coincidence that Boster was in Mexico City in 1963 at the same time as Lee Harvey Oswald's controversial visit there? Without doubt, Boster was alerted at the time to Oswald's presence in Mexico City. Thus, contrary to what the CIA has maintained for decades – that no one in the U.S. Embassy in Mexico City, prior to the assassination, was familiar with the name Lee Harvey Oswald – there *was* at least one person in the embassy who was amply familiar with Lee Harvey Oswald.

Gene Boster asked Marguerite on the telephone if she could come to his State Department office at 11:00 A.M. that day. Marguerite said, "Mr. Boster that would be fine, but I would rather talk with Secretary of State Rusk."

Boster told Marguerite he would see her at 11:00 o'clock. Marguerite asked, "Mr. Boster, would you please recommend a hotel that would be reasonable in costs?" He recommended the Washington Hotel, telling Marguerite it is near the State Department and convenient to where she is.

At the hotel Marguerite was asked if she has a reservation. She replied, "No, I don't, but Mr. Boster of the State Department recommended that I come here." After settling into her room, Marguerite took a taxi to the State Department, arriving at about 10:30 A.M.

Gene Boster greeted Marguerite and told her State Department employees Denman F. Stanfield and Edward J. Hickey would join them in their meeting. Stanfield was Acting Chief of Protection and Representation; Hickey was Deputy Director of the Passport Office. With everyone gathered in a large conference room, Marguerite told the three men, "Now I know you are not going to answer me, gentlemen, but I am under the impression that my son is an agent."

"Do you mean a Russian agent?" Boster asked.

"No," said Marguerite, "working for our Government, a U.S. agent."

The three men exchanged glances, and Marguerite boldly continued, "And I want to say this: That if he is, I don't appreciate it too much, because I am destitute, and just getting over a sickness."

Marguerite dismissed nothing and believed all her life that her son had been an agent of the U.S. Government. She testified before the Warren Commission that Boster gave her "the red carpet treatment" because Lee was an agent. When Commission members expressed doubts, she said, "Well, maybe you don't see why. But this is my son. And this is the way I think, because I happen to know all of the other things that you don't know — the life and everything. I happen to think this. And I can almost back it up with things.... Yes, sir, I think my son was an agent. I certainly do."

Oswald, the World's Future and LSD

On a humid afternoon in early October 1963, thirty-eight year old assistant district attorney, Juvenile Court, New Orleans, Louisiana, Edward G. Gillin looked up from his office desk to see a young man standing nervously before him. Fidgeting, the man asked Gillin if he could take a moment of his time. Gillin motioned to a chair in front of his desk, inviting the man to sit down. The young man ignored the invite and remained standing. Gillin later said the man's demeanor "gave every indication of emotional disturbance and lack of personal conviction or sense of security."

The young man told Gillin that the reason for his visit was to inquire about a fascinating drug he had just read about in a book. Gillin asked the man what his name was but the man replied it was unimportant. "He kept saying that he must determine the existence of such a drug, and whether it was legal or illegal," Gillin later recalled, unable to remember the name of the specific drug. "He said he was reading a book, and in the book the author stated that, if a reader could procure and use this particular drug, the reader would be able to see into the future as he, the author, had seen and envisioned it ... the subject matter of the book had to do with the socio-economic picture of the world 500 years in the future."

Gillin studied the man closely as he spoke, on that humid October 1963 afternoon. The man's delivery style was peculiar, recounted Gillin:

> He spoke so rapidly that I did not see any great content in what he was saying and I became disinterested ... however, what struck me the most, when he was "chattering" or "spieling," was that he was apparently emotionally detached from the subject matter itself ... he was demonstrating a super-imposed indoctrination in which he had no great self-identification. He was spouting words, phrases, and clichés without true comprehension, and without personal persuasiveness, as you might expect of someone who was a dedicated advocate of a cause.

"What did you say your name was again?" Gillin asked.

The man hesitated and then replied, but later Gillin could only recall that "Oswald" was part of the name given. Gillin said he only remembered this because when he heard the name "Oswald" he thought of a comedian on the Milton Berle radio show.

"What's the title of the book you're talking about? Gillin asked the young man.

"*Brave New World*," the man replied. "It's by Aldous Huxley."

"Well," said Gillin, "if a drug like the one you're describing could produce the kind of effects you've mentioned it would have to be a very strong narcotic, but I'm not by any means an expert on drugs."

The young man shifted his weight back and forth from one foot to the other.

"I suggest, since City Hall is only right next door," Gillin continued, "that you go there and consult with the City chemist. Maybe he would know."

The young man thanked Gillin for his help and departed the office.

About six weeks later, on the evening of JFK's assassination, assistant district attorney Gillin was startled to hear a voice coming from the television set in his living room. He stood at a kitchen counter and listened closely to the voice, hearing the very same "spiel and chatter-type expressions, which I had heard in my office before."

Before going to look at his television set, Gillin said he was "convinced" it was the very same voice. When he looked at the television screen he saw the very same "facial features" of the nervous young man who had visited his office. Gillin picked up the telephone and called the local FBI office. Years later, shortly before his death in 2007, Gillin, then a seated judge in Louisiana, recalled that nobody from the FBI ever called him back after he had made his statement over the telephone.

Judge Edward Gillin also recalled that on November 22, 1963, the day JFK was murdered, hundreds of miles away in California, writer Aldous Huxley died after a long bout with cancer. Hours before his death, Huxley's wife had given him a large dose of LSD to put his mind at ease.

Library records from the New Orleans public library reveal that Lee Harvey Oswald had checked out a copy of Aldous Huxley's book, *Brave New World*, on September 19, 1963.

Left unanswered is why Oswald would ever have approached Edward Gillin about LSD if he had had any experience with the drug while at the Atsugi base or in the Philippines. It is a good question. A possible answer is that Oswald was completely unaware of what specific drug he had been administered and was seeking to replicate the experience.

Lee Harvey Oswald's possible interest in and use of LSD is linked to the case of Dr. Frank Olson's murder in a peculiar sort of way. On December 1, 1953, two days after Olson's death, a CIA official, assisting in the cover-up of Olson's murder, wrote a memo to recently appointed CIA Inspector General Lyman Kirkpatrick, stating, "Only two (2) field stations, Manila and Atsugi, have LSD material."

Here, it should be noted that Lee Oswald, after quitting school in the tenth grade, enlisted, with his mother's required permission, in the U.S. Marine Corps. Following basic training, Oswald was stationed in 1957 and 1958 in Japan at Atsugi Naval Air Base. The Atsugi base, covering some 1,300 acres and located 37 miles from downtown Tokyo, had been used for kamikaze flights during World War II. After the war, it was taken over by the U.S. Navy, and a section of the base, including huge underground chambers, became a vast, 50-acre CIA field installation.

The December 1, 1953 memo was in response to Kirkpatrick's query about locations where the CIA kept supplies of the relatively new wonder drug, LSD. The same responding memo reads, "In summary, LSD material over which CIA has or had distributive responsibility is located in four places: (a) Dr. [Willis] Gibbons' safe [Gibbons was one of Sidney Gottlieb's superiors], (b) Manila, (c) Atsugi, and (d) that in the possession of George White. Exact amounts in each location are not yet available."

The memo, of course, does not mention Lee Harvey Oswald, or anyone else at the Atsugi base or in the Philippines. However, readers can easily imagine that these brief lines about locations, not long after their public release in 1976, would achieve interpretive elasticity to the point they would connect with Oswald. Eventually, it would be absurdly reported that Atsugi stored "over 100,000 dosages of LSD," an amount the Agency never came close to possessing simply because at the time there was not that much LSD in the world. Worse yet, several books and articles would claim that Atsugi, at the time Oswald was there, had become a Far East center for the CIA's MK/ULTRA project and that the center was routinely creating Manchurian Candidates through the use of LSD and other drugs. Some of these claims were carried to extreme and very creative lengths, yet none offered any supportive documentation.

However, it is important to note here that documents and several civil case legal depositions unearthed by this writer during his investigation of Frank Olson's death, clearly reveal that CIA officials, including Dr. Sidney Gottlieb, did travel during the mid-to-late 1950s to Japan for the purposes of conducting enhanced interrogations that included the use of LSD and other drugs. Additionally, and perhaps far more germane to possibilities concerning Oswald, several prominent American physicians under covert contracts with the CIA's ARTICHOKE Program, operated under the Agency's Security Research Service, traveled frequently to Japan's Atsugi base. Indeed, one very prominent physician (who can not be identified here because of possible legal implications) made over 15 trips to Atsugi, all related to the administration of LSD to unidentified subjects. However, it is known, through the same documents, that some of these subjects were U.S. servicemen. Indeed, one partial CIA document, dated 1957, the same time that Oswald was at Atsugi, places several ARTICHOKE physicians and technicians at the Naval base to conduct enhanced interrogations on several foreign nationals.

LSD, MK/ULTRA & Lee Harvey Oswald Redux

Lee Harvey Oswald's encounter with Edward Gillin did not end his interest or possible associations with LSD. Indeed, in the late summer of 1963, Oswald was reported to have visited the East Louisiana State Hospital, where experiments with LSD and other hallucinogenic drugs, with funding from the CIA, the Commonwealth Fund (a CIA front group; see Notes), and U.S. Army, had been ongoing since 1953.

In her 2005 book, *A Farewell to Justice*, Joan Mellen, a professor of English and creative writing at Temple University, Philadelphia, writes that Lee Harvey Oswald visited the East Louisiana State Hospital in Jackson, Louisiana ostensibly seeking employment. While there, Oswald, allegedly purely by chance, encountered Dr. Frank Silva, a psychiatrist, who served the hospital as director of medical services and also oversaw training for medical residents for work at Tulane University Hospital. Silva, whose given name was Francisco A. Silva Clarens, was born in Cuba in 1929 and graduated from the University of Havana Medical School in 1955. He then came to the United States and attended Tulane University School of Medicine, where he graduated in 1958. From 1959 to 1972, Dr. Silva was an associate professor of clinical psychiatry at the Tulane School of Medicine, and worked as medical services director at the state hospital.

The East Louisiana State Hospital, a state-operated mental institution, was founded in 1847 as the Louisiana State Insane Asylum. The facility was intended to primarily serve the city of New

Orleans and surrounding areas, but was placed in Jackson to escape the problem of disease-carrying mosquitoes that plagued the low-ground urban area. Initially, the hospital maintained about 170 psychiatric beds, but over the years grew to more than 600. In 1963, the same year Oswald visited the facility, renowned photographer, Richard Avedon, took a large series of photographs of the hospital's patients, which vividly depict the harsh, overcrowded, and seemingly primitive warehousing of its human population. The hospital is about 125 miles from New Orleans, where Oswald had been living, and is located less than a mile from the center of the small town Jackson, population about 4,000. Not surprisingly, the hospital serves as a major employer for the town.

Mellen writes that when Oswald first entered the hospital's main building, "Wearing a t-shirt, obstreperous and calling attention to himself," he "falls into conversation with some hospital attendants" he encounters in a hallway. Mellen states, "His subject is Cuba and what it would take to bring Fidel Castro down. His voice is loud."

As Oswald speaks, Mellen recounts, Dr. Frank Silva walked by and heard Oswald's comments about Cuba. "One of the attendants, who is from Texas, calls Dr. Silva over," Mellen writes. "Dr. Silva is from Cuba," the attendant informed Oswald.

Oswald turns his attention to Dr. Silva, states Mellen, and bragged to the psychiatrist "about how proficient he is with guns, how he served in the Marines, how he will go to Cuba."

"I'm involved with getting rid of Fidel Castro," Oswald tells Dr. Silva. "I'm using my skills as a Marine," Oswald tells Silva, according to Mellen.

Dr. Silva, well trained in listening and analyzing skills, takes in all that Oswald is saying, and according to Mellen's book, "concludes that this disrespectful, impolite man (who never introduces himself by name) ranting about killing Fidel Castro has no idea what he's talking about. He is a troubled man making a spectacle of himself while applying for a job at a mental hospital."

Dr. Silva politely bids the bragging man good day and goes about his daily rounds, and Lee Harvey Oswald goes on and applies for employment as intended.

The Oswald sighting at the East Louisiana State Hospital seems cut and dry, but as with most events concerning Oswald, the facts surrounding the visit dwell in an otherworldly realm of ambiguity and interconnectedness, an alternate universe clouded by high strangeness where everything has multi-dimensions of meaning and truth.

What Professor Joan Mellen does not mention in her book is that Dr. Frank Silva is also a highly-skilled research psychiatrist who co-authored at least two widely read medical papers with Dr. Robert G. Heath of Tulane Medical School, who readers will learn far more about in this book. The first paper Silva co-authored with Dr. Heath is entitled, "Administration of Taraxein in Humans," published in May 1959 in the medical journal, *Diseases of the Nervous System.*

The second paper Silva co-authored with Heath is entitled, "Comparative Effects of the Administration of Taraxein, d-LSD, Mescaline, and Psilocybin to Human Volunteers." It was published in 1960 in the journal, *Comprehensive Psychiatry.*

This seven-page paper – which when it was presented in June 1960 at a meeting of the Society of Biological Psychiatry in Miami Beach, Florida was accompanied by "a 16-mm sound movie film depicting brief excerpts of the reactions of the [experiment] subjects to each of four compounds" – concerned conducting experiments with LSD and other hallucinogens on "four volunteer subjects: one psychiatrist; and three prisoners at the Louisiana State Penitentiary at Angola [Louisiana]." The medical paper states: "Three of the subjects received taraxein, d-LSD, Mescaline, and Psilocybin. One subject received taraxein, Mescaline, and Psilocybin."

The paper also reveals that the prisoner subjects, at the time of the experiments, were "housed in a special Tulane University Research Unit at the East Louisiana State Hospital, Jackson, Louisiana."

What the paper does not specifically reveal is that the "one psychiatrist" who participated in the experiments as an actual subject was Dr. Frank Silva, then a psychiatrist at the state hospital. According to Silva and Heath's 1960 paper, Dr. Silva, identified as "VOLUNTEER 1 (F.S.)" was given an injection of taraxein, and within about ten minutes, he "was experiencing symptoms which he, as a psychiatrist, associated with the disease, schizophrenia." When he was given LSD [150 micrograms], assumably a day or more later, within about thirty minutes his "pupils were dilated" and he "commented that he was hungry and cold." According to the paper, he "described the situation as humorous and giggled in a silly manner."

The paper states that Silva "reported visual distortion: e.g. people seemed taller than their actual height; doors appeared oval instead of rectangular." Under Mescaline [administered orally in the amount of 750 milligrams] experienced some mild visual distortion and found "listening to music was enjoyable." Under Psilocybin [10 milligrams], Silva reported his experience as quite similar to "the feeling one has with a great amount of alcohol."

According to assiduous assassination researcher Bill Davey, writing in the essential James DiEugenio and Lisa Pease edited volume, *The Assassinations*, Dr. Alfred T. Butterworth, who arrived at East Louisiana State Hospital after Oswald's visit to the facility, also took part in the LSD experiments at the prison in Angola. Dr. Butterworth, who served as the state hospital's clinical director, had previously worked with the CIA's Dr. Sidney Gottlieb at Fort Detrick under Project MK/NAOMI, as well as with Drs. Harris Isbell and Abraham Wikler at the NIMH Kentucky Addiction Farm. Butterworth, who was interviewed by DiEugenio in August 1994, revealed that his "specialty" in his early years at the State Hospital was "instructing other doctors in the use of LSD for the treatment of mental disorders." Butterworth also told DiEugenio "the use of psychedelic drugs was apparently so pervasive at Jackson that the doctors nicknamed one of the department's the 'Magic Mushroom.'" Butterworth, however, apparently told DiEugenio nothing about other CIA-physicians dispatched to the Angola prison by the CIA-funded Human Ecology Fund to experiment with psychochemicals administered to prisoners in situations of solitary confinement and sensory deprivation.

Writer Bill Davey also briefly reveals in the same DiEugenio edited volume that in 1968, New Orleans District Attorney Jim Garrison "interviewed a witness" who attended a party at Dr. [Robert G.] Heath's New Orleans' home. "At the party Dr. Silva introduced [the unnamed witness] to New Orleans anti-Castro activist Sergio Arcacha Smith," Davey writes.

Arcacha Smith was closely connected to David Ferrie, who would emerge as a prime suspect in JFK's murder in District Attorney Jim Garrison's investigation. (Sergio Arcacha Smith's name would also come up in the strange story of Rose Cherami, as readers shall learn in this book's chapter devoted to Cherami.)

Adds Davey, "It appears Ferrie was also closely acquainted with one of the patients at the [East Louisiana State Hospital]." Davey goes no further with this and does not tell us why this chance encounter at a party in Dr. Heath's home was worth noting, nor does Davey tell us why Ferrie's acquaintance with the patient is important.

The unnamed witness and patient's name was Erick Crouchet. Crouchet, a former Civilian Air Patrol [CAP] cadet in a group overseen by David Ferrie from 1954 through to 1961, maintained, according to New Orleans Police Department records, a close relationship with Ferrie throughout the early 1960s. In August of 1963, according to Bill Davey, Crouchet was admitted to the East Louisiana State Hospital where he remained until late November of 1963, just after Kennedy's assassination. Additionally, not reported by Davey, was that Crouchet and a number of other youths, who had been members of Ferrie's CAP squad, were all briefly taken to the East Louisiana State Hospital in August 1961, at the same time as Rose Cherami's confinement there.

By supposed coincidence, in 1955-1956, Lee Harvey Oswald had also been a cadet in Ferrie's CAP group. [See Notes of this chapter for details on Oswald's CAP membership.] And, as readers shall learn, a woman named Rose Cherami was also a patient at the East Hospital less than 24-hours before Kennedy was murdered. Is it possible that Oswald's visit to the hospital was linked to Crouchet being a patient there? Oddly, nobody has ever raised this as a question or issue, but a close examination of Crouchet's history, along with that of others, as well as long overlooked New Orleans Police Department files, makes this question more intriguing.

Sexual Perversity in New Orleans ...

According to detailed documents obtained from the New Orleans Police Department, on Monday, August 21, 1961, Juvenile Bureau detectives paid a visit to 16-year old Erick Michael Crouchet, who was at work at a local grocery market. Detectives asked Crouchet if he would be willing to speak about his knowledge about David Ferrie. Crouchet, concerned about taking time away form his job, readily agreed and asked if detectives would pick him up at home the following morning.

The next morning, Crouchet was taken to the East Bank Juvenile Bureau headquarters of Jefferson Parish, where, according to Bureau documents, "[Crouchet] made a full, typewritten statement" concerning David Ferrie having had committed "acts of crimes against nature on him on two separate occasions." Crouchet also gave detectives crucial information on another case involving an acquaintance of his, who had run away from home about a year earlier after spending time with David Ferrie in his home at 331 Atherton Drive in Metairie, the largest metropolitan area around New Orleans. Young Crouchet also provided detectives with a great deal of information about other young boys, ranging in age from 15 to 17, that Ferrie had sexually molested at his Metairie home.

Earlier, in July 1961, New Orleans police detectives had begun an investigation into Ferrie's activities with young boys he had contact with through the Civil Air Patrol Squadron he operated. This investigation, apparently the second of several into Ferrie's activities, began after New Orleans police were assigned a case involving a 15-year old "runaway juvenile" named Alexander Landry, Jr. Young Landry, according to his parents and police reports, had run away from home, but was found 24-hours later "at the home of Capt. Dave Ferrie, a pilot with Eastern Air Lines."

Detectives who met with Landry's parents quickly discovered that Ferrie was not only sexually molesting young Landry, but also was allowing several other young boys, who were members of his CAP squad, to live in his home. Investigating officers visited the homes of these boys, and at least two of these young teens told police that Ferrie had sexually molested them. Additionally, both boys stated that Ferrie "was a hypnotist" and that they once "saw Ferrie put [another boy] under hypnosis and tell him that he should "forget his girlfriend." The two boys also told investigating detectives, "Ferrie hated women" and that he "could not stand being around them."

Investigators also learned that David Ferrie had an "untoward, crimes against nature" relationship with another boy named Layton Martens, who, according to police reports, was working in the Balter Building at 434 Camp Street in downtown New Orleans. There, Martens was employed by a "Cuban organization helping Cuban refugees" and headed up by Mr. [Sergio] Arcacha Smith." The same police reports state that both Ferrie and Layton Martens "had volunteered" their services to Arcacha Smith "after the Cuban situation broke."

Interesting to note here is that, perhaps by coincidence only, in addition to Arcacha Smith having an office in 1961 in the four-story Balter Building – owned by a wealthy businessman who had ties to the Ku Klux Klan and American Nazi movement – the building also had many of the same tenants, like Guy Bannister and Jack Martin (see below), who all relocated to the 544 Camp Street Newman Building, prior to the assassination of JFK. Lee Harvey Oswald would also claim on one pamphlet he distributed that he maintained the office for his Fair Play for Cuba New Orleans chapter in the 544 Camp Street building.

The investigation into David Ferrie's unlawful and perverse activities with young boys would quickly become extremely complex, involving well over 20 young boys, and Ferrie and Arcacha Smith, as well as several unidentified Cubans, making strong-arm efforts to suppress evidence and threatening bodily harm to several of the young boys interviewed by detectives. Indeed, Arcacha Smith and an unidentified Cuban, according to police files, visited at least one boy at his place of work telling the young teen that he would seriously regret talking any further to investigators about Ferrie. The convoluted case would also provoke a number of issues that, to date, remain unexplained and strange.

First, a number of the boys interviewed by New Orleans police stated that they had traveled to Cuba with Ferrie and others a number of times after the island's takeover by Fidel Castro. One youth, Al Landry, according to police reports, said, "that he had been to Cuba on several occasions since the revolution and stated that America should wake up because the Russians are 90 miles away." Unknown is why Ferrie took these youths to Cuba in 1960 and 1961, and what they did in Cuba while there.

Another youth told police that David Ferrie had taken several boys to Honduras "to do some mining" and that additional trips to Latin America were planned by Ferrie. When police officers executed a search warrant on Ferrie's residence on August 23, 1961, they discovered a passport "taken out in the name of Albert Paul Cheramie on August 2, 1960." (Cheramie is another of the boys Ferrie is believed to have sexually molested, and was reported to be a distant relative of Rose Cherami.) Why was Ferrie taking young boys to Honduras? What sort of "mining" were they doing there?

David Ferrie, when questioned by the police on August 21, 1961, said that he had "a degree in psychology, but only gave advice" to people and treated nobody. Neighbors who lived near Ferrie's home told detectives that they "understood that Ferrie was a psychologist" and that "a steady stream of boys were in and out of Ferrie's home" for what some thought was help with problems.

A number of the boys sexually molested by Ferrie were taken by law enforcement authorities to the Youth Study Center in New Orleans. The Center is a division of the city's Human Services Department, chartered "to provide secure detention to youth ages 8-16 that have been arrested and are in pre-trial status." The Center, which remains open today, also provides educational classes for housed youth. Since some of these boys molested by Ferrie had not been arrested, the reason for taking them to the Center is unclear and unexplained by police records.

According to a former New Orleans resident, who is closely related to two of the boys sexually molested by Ferrie and today lives in northern New York: "The Youth Study Center has been a hotbed of corruption, sexual abuse, police brutality, and God only knows what else for decades. I understand that it all still goes on today. [David] Ferrie used to go there posing as a doctor of some sort, some sort of sham, to recruit kids.... He [Ferrie] took a lot of kids to Cuba, Guatemala and Honduras. Why? I don't know... He was an amateur hypnotist, learned out of a book, I guess, and he practiced trance stuff on a lot of boys. I understand that, besides Youth Study Center visits he went to the East [Louisiana] State Hospital a lot, where some of his boys were taken for treatment. There were rumors and stories for years before I left [Louisiana] that Ferrie was in bed, no pun intended, with one of the doctors there, who was a drug addict.... Ferrie wanted the doctor to not treat the boys ... the crazy rumor was that the hospital was treating the boys with LSD to stop them from becoming homosexuals and Ferrie hated that."

Continued the former resident: "The Oswald kid, when he was young, was in Ferrie's [CAP] group for only a few months or so and then quit. It doesn't take a rocket scientist to know why. Everyone knew one or two kids who quit Ferrie's group because of his coming on to kids. A lot of people, parents, pulled their kids out when they found out he was molesting kids." (Volume Two of this work will include a detailed account of David Ferrie's life and his alleged participation in the assassination.)

The Mystery of David Ferrie's Library Card & LHO

Three days after the assassination of President Kennedy, one of David Ferrie's young friends and an employee of Sergio Arcacha Smith, Layton Martens, told FBI agents that when Lee Harvey Oswald was arrested in Dallas, police officers discovered David Ferrie's New Orleans library card in Oswald's wallet. Martens told FBI agents on November 25, 1963 that he had learned about the library card from G. Wray Gill, David Ferrie's attorney.

When Gill was questioned by the FBI the next day, he said he had been informed about the library card and Oswald by a man named Hardy Davis, who told Gill that he had been informed about the library card "through hearsay." William Hardy Davis was a prominent bail bondsman in New Orleans, who, according to FBI and New Orleans police documents, was "a homosexual like Ferrie who sometimes preyed on young boys." Davis was also a close associate of former FBI agent Guy Bannister.

According to intrepid researcher A.J. Weberman, Bannister was a notorious racist and anti-Semite, who once called on the services of Hardy Davis in May 1961 when American Nazi Party founder George Lincoln Rockwell was arrested in New Orleans for "illegally picketing the movie *Exodus*, which dealt with the Holocaust." Bannister, who put up his own funds for Rockwell's bail, had Davis arrange for Rockwell's release from jail.

When FBI agents questioned Hardy Davis, he informed them that he had heard the report about Ferrie's library card from a man named Jack S. Martin. Jack Martin, whose alleged real name was Edward S. Suggs, worked for Guy Bannister as a private investigator and had known Ferrie for at least several years. Davis said that Martin informed him that he had learned about the library card from a newscast on television by a New Orleans station. Said Martin to Davis, the report "mentioned the possibility that David Ferrie was associated with Lee Harvey Oswald in the Civil Air Patrol." Oddly, states the FBI report on Davis' questioning: "Martin and Davis may have come to the conclusion that Oswald had used or carried Ferrie's library card." The FBI report provides no explanation about how Martin or Davis came to this peculiar conclusion.

There has been much speculation over the past several decades, based on seemingly credible information, that Jack Martin greatly disliked David Ferrie and that he fabricated the story about Oswald having Ferrie's library card. However, the alleged fabrication seems strange, as it could be so easily disproved by Ferrie producing his library card, which indeed Ferrie did with FBI agents on November

27, 1963. Martin was clearly aware that Ferrie had known Oswald from as far back as 1954-1955 and had also informed FBI agents that on one of his visits to Ferrie's home years before, he had seen CAP group photographs on the wall that included Oswald in some of them, so why not simply emphasize that relationship if Martin's objective had been to tie Ferrie to Oswald and JFK's murder.

There is also the overlooked issue that Martin may not have been who he claimed to be. In 1963 and beyond, Jean Pierre Lafitte, an asset and sometimes contractor for the CIA and FBI since 1952, often frequented and worked in New Orleans using the aliases "Jean Martin," "Jack Martin," and "John Martin." Additionally, Lafitte had mysterious dealings with Guy Banister and Clay Shaw. This intriguing connection will be taken up fully in Volume Two of this work. Not to complicate matters, it should be noted that Jack S. Martin had in early 1957 spent time in the psychiatric ward at New Orleans' Charity Hospital, where some patients from the East Louisiana State Hospital were transferred after they had been used as subjects in LSD and other experiments.

According to an FBI report dated November 27, 1963, on that same day David Ferrie had telephoned Roy McCoy, a former member of Ferrie's CAP squad in the early 1950s, to inquire about any CAP photographs McCoy might still have. Roy was not in at the time of the call, but his wife took the call, taking Ferrie's message as to why he was calling. Ferrie also requested that Mrs. McCoy ask her husband if he recalled the name of Lee Harvey Oswald. Roy McCoy told the FBI he had no recollection of Oswald's coming to any CAP meetings.

According to Mrs. Jesse Garner, Oswald's former landlady in New Orleans, David Ferrie visited her home soon after the assassination asking about Oswald's library card. (Garner was confused about the exact date of the visit.) Apparently, nobody has questioned the logic of this report given that if the library card had been discovered in Oswald's possession upon his arrest, the card would have been in the hands of law enforcement officers and not in Oswald's room or with his landlady.

In December 1967, a Washington, D.C. newspaper would report that when New Orleans district attorney investigators searched David Ferrie's apartment in New Orleans they "shook Oswald's library card out of one of Ferrie's 3,000 books." (The report, nor anything else about it, ever appeared again.) In 1968, Mrs. Doris Eames told New Orleans district attorney investigators that "Ferrie had come by her house after the assassination, inquiring if Mr. Eames had any information regarding Oswald's library card."

Ozzie, Library Books, and *The Shark and the Sardines* ...

On December 10, 1963, about three weeks after the assassination, FBI Special Agent Roger D. Counts reported to FBI Special Agent in Charge John W. Rice, New Orleans, Louisiana that he had followed up on an earlier Bureau report dated November 27, 1963. According to Counts, the 1963 FBI report "mentioned that Lee Harvey Oswald had among his belongings [when arrested in Dallas] a New Orleans Public Library card No. 8460," and that Oswald may have checked out several books "pertaining to the U.S. Secret Service." On November 29, 1963, Counts interviewed New Orleans Head Librarian, Jerome Cushman. Cushman "advised [Counts] that the library card Lee Harvey Oswald had had been issued by the Napoleon Branch Library, 913 Napoleon Avenue, New Orleans, and that the original of this card had been picked up by the FBI along with all available books which had been checked out by Oswald."

Cushman advised Counts that "it would be extremely difficult to determine if Oswald had obtained books from the Main Library, as this would require examination of the microfilm of all transactions since Oswald obtained his card." Cushman added that, "it would also be quite possible that Oswald could have any number of cards issued to him."

According to the December 10 report, FBI agent Steve Callender "obtained the list of books checked out by Oswald. This list consisted of 34 books." The report also stated that an FBI Special Agent (last name Bouck), had "requested that an inquiry be made to determine if Oswald had obtained any of the four books written by the following authors: U.E. Baughman, Harry Neal, Edward Starling, or Michael Reilly." It was soon determined that Oswald had checked out no books by any of these authors. While the report does not include any information about the Bureau's interest in these particular authors, this author identified all four as having written books about the Secret Service.

Interestingly, among the 34 books checked out by Oswald were: *Profiles in Courage* by John F. Kennedy; *Portrait of a Presi-*

dent [JFK] by William Manchester; *The Huey Long Murder Case* by Hermann B. Deutsch; *One Day in the Life of Ivan Denisovich* by Alexander Solzhenitsyn; *Brave New World* by Aldous Huxley; four James Bond novels by Ian Fleming; and at least five science fiction titles that deal with various subjects concerning mind control and behavior modification.

On February 25, 1964, about three months after the assassination, the FBI conducted an inquiry into the books taken out of the Dallas Public Library by Lee Harvey Oswald. During the inquiry, according to a February 25, 1964 FBI report, the Bureau was informed by Lillian Bradshaw, Director of the Dallas Public Library, that "the only records maintained by the Library are keyed to delinquencies; therefore it would not be possible to determine a listing of the books read by Oswald."

However, Bradshaw gave the FBI "two copies of a Dallas Public Library delinquency notice which reflects LEE HARVEY OSWALD, 602 Elsbeth, Dallas, was delinquent on a book entitled, *The Shark and the Sardines*, by JUAN JOSE AREVALO." Stated the report: "The book was due on November 13, 1963, and, according to Mrs. Bradshaw, it would have been charged out on November 6, 1963. The delinquency notice was never mailed. According to library records, the book was never returned." Bradshaw told the FBI that library records indicated no other delinquencies for Oswald.

At the request of FBI SA Raymond P. Yelchak, Dallas, Mrs. Bradshaw provided the FBI with another copy of the book, which the FBI noted in its reports as having been "authored by a former President of Guatemala, JUAN JOSE AREVALO, translated from the Spanish by JUNE COBB and DR. RAUL OSEGUEDA and published by LYLE STUART, 225 Lafayette Street, New York 12, New York."

The FBI's February 25 report on Bradshaw's delinquency information stated, "The [book's] Introduction to the American Reader by the Author, in part, reads as follows:

> In your hands you hold a controversial book – a book that speaks out against your State Department's dealings with the peoples of Latin America during the Twentieth Century. In it is intended no insult to, nor offense to, the United States as a nation. The future of your country is identified with the future of contemporary democracy. Neither does this book seek to cast

blame on the North American people – who, like us, are victims of an imperialist policy of promoting business, multiplying markets and hoarding money.

Within a matter of days, the FBI's February 25, 1964 report on Lee Harvey Oswald's delinquent book, *The Shark and the Sardines*, was forwarded to FBI headquarters in Washington, D.C. and to CIA headquarters in Langley, Virginia. There is no indication in any available FBI records that the Bureau made any special note of the name "June Cobb" in the report. Nor are there any available CIA records sent to the FBI, or anyone else, concerning the fact that June Cobb, at the time of the FBI's Dallas investigation and thereafter, and months before the assassination, was employed as a contract CIA asset in Mexico City, Mexico, a position she had held there and elsewhere since at least 1960.

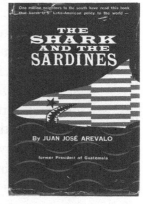

Readers thinking that June Cobb may have been in Mexico City during the time Lee Harvey Oswald paid his infamous visit there (September-October, 1963) would be correct. Readers now thinking that perhaps Lee Oswald, while in Mexico City, had "contact" with June Cobb would also be correct, in a sense. Indeed, following his return from Mexico City to Dallas, Texas, *The Shark and the Sardines,* translated by June Cobb, is the only known book that Lee Harvey Oswald withdrew from the public library before he was arrested for the murder of President Kennedy. (For more on June Cobb see the last chapter in this book.)

According to numerous books and articles that mention Oswald's delinquent book, *The Shark and the Sardines* was never returned to the library and remains missing and unaccounted for to this day.

This is not true.

Indeed, the book was returned at some point following the assassination, but by whom, and exactly when, we do not know. This overlooked fact was revealed in 1970 by author Albert H. Newman in his equally overlooked and excellent book, *The Assassination of John F. Kennedy: The Reasons Why.*

Newman reveals that, "as of the summer of 1966, when I visited Dallas and inquired into the matter with Mrs. Bradshaw's office

A Secret Order

by telephone, the volume had been mysteriously returned." Writes Newman: "Before arriving in Dallas, I assumed that whoever possessed the book had destroyed it because of its association with Oswald. Therefore my telephone call to Mrs. Bradshaw's office in the main library downtown on Commerce Street was in the nature of a routine check: had the book by any chance been returned? After half an hour an assistant to Mrs. Bradshaw called back: the book had been returned. But when, and by whom? I asked. The library kept no such records."

Newman, who was convinced that Oswald had shot JFK, speculates about why Lee Harvey Oswald was reading *The Shark and the Sardines*: "It may be noted that Oswald's selection of this volume (almost surely the last book he ever read) was entirely consonant with what we know of his ideological bent and corroborates his continuing interest in Latin American affairs.... I leafed through the book page by page and discovered no telltale marks to indicate who had read it or where it had been. Yet, what a story it might tell, and how unfortunate it is at times that books can speak only with the voices of their authors, I reflected, noting what Arevalo had said about the man who was fated to become the victim of one of his readers:

> Let us mention a phrase that crops up in the United States during election campaigns – "to buy the President." It seems that the Presidential candidacy is just one of so many businesses on the New York Stock Exchange. People better informed than I (those privileged to eat hot dogs within the United States) will be able to furnish documents to round out this list of Presidents "elected" by radar, from Wall Street.
>
> As far as I am concerned, it is hard for me to believe that a man of the military glory and natural bonhommerie [sic] of Eisenhower should have been negotiated and bought by Wall Street and the Republican Party. But this does not authorize us to forget that his successor John Kennedy is the son of the number one landlord in the United States or that Calvin Coolidge was President thanks to the ringing and ready money of the House of Morgan, in which Coolidge was a powerful stockholder.

Newman writes that the words on the dust jacket of the book "may well have held a certain appeal for Oswald." These words

86

resonate strongly when one considers the CIA's overall approach toward other countries and the roles of many of the players in the overall JFK assassination annals:

> *Dr. Arevalo's program so infuriated the United Fruit Company (which considers Guatemala its private plantation) and the other lords and masters of Central America that they tried thirty-one times to overthrow him. All the conspiracies – one of which employed tanks and heavy ammunition to shell the Presidential Palace – were defeated by the Guatemalan people's overwhelming defense of their government. Time after time the civilian population rallied to the defense of the pacifist educator who was their chosen President.*
>
> *In 1951, having completed his term of office, Arevalo stepped down and was replaced by young Jacopo Arbenz. Arevalo became a voluntary exile and resumed his service to Latin America as a university professor and writer.*
>
> *He was not in Guatemala when the Guatemalan revolution's enemies – armed, financed, and directed by the Central Intelligence Agency of the United States Government – attacked the lawful authority, invaded and bombed Ciudad Guatemala, and ousted the elected government. There followed shortly a series of reprisals, suspension of civil liberties, political persecution and assassination.*

At the time that Newman wrote his book, he had no idea, or even a clue, that Dr. Arevalo's translator, June Cobb, was a paid contract agent and asset for the CIA. In 1970, and for years past that date, the CIA did not release any records or documents pertaining to Cobb's covert work for the Agency. Indeed, while some documents are now available that very sketchily portray Cobb's work and activities for the CIA, it is estimated that well over 2,000 pages on Cobb remain classified for "national security reasons."

A Mysterious Listing in Oswald's Address Book

The address "1318 1/2 Garfield, Norman Oklahoma" was discovered in Oswald's address book after his death. For decades, it has remained unexplained. Intrepid assassination researcher A.J. Weberman has reported, "Mae Logan, who owned this property from 1961 to 1967, was contacted [by Weberman] in August 1993. She stated that several white teenagers along with one black lived in the top part of a rental unit she owned between 1962-1963: 'They quit payin' the rent, got into drugs and were arrested in Phoenix. There was a lady who lived up there to begin with. She got cancer and went to the M.D. Anderson Hospital. Her father and mother died of cancer two years ago.' Logan was never questioned by the FBI."

Investigating the Garfield address further, this author observed that another character linked to the assassination, Thomas Eli Davis, Jr., also briefly lived in Norman, Oklahoma, before JFK's assassination, possibly in the very same neighborhood. (Readers shall learn more about Davis in this book.) Compounding matters, and perhaps simply coincidentally, yet another assassination-related character, Loran Eugene Hall, lived briefly in Norman before the assassination. People that closely knew Thomas Davis have stated that he and Loran Hall together conducted gunrunning operations with Jack Ruby in 1962-1963, but these same people have consistently refused to speak publicly about the Davis-Hall-Ruby relationship, or about any possibility that Davis and Hall were involved with or were one and the same as the group that Ms. Logan reported occupying the 1318 1/2 Garfield apartment. Additionally, and very intriguing is that at least two elderly residents of the Garfield neighborhood, not wanting to "get involved in any way with anything to do with that Oswald character," reported that the "Black man" that lived with the group at the address "stood out some" because "he had reddish hair."

Astute assassination researchers will take note of this because, as readers shall see in this book's section on June Cobb, while in Mexico City Lee Oswald was reported to have been seen with a "tall, thin Negro with reddish hair." This man, according to a witness that contacted the CIA at the U.S. Embassy in Mexico City on November 26, 1963, allegedly told Oswald, "I want to kill the man," to which Oswald allegedly replied, "You're not man enough. I can do it." The witness also reported that the "Negro man" gave Oswald "$6,500 in large denomination U.S. bills."

Further still, this author has been able to confirm that at least one person who knew Lee Harvey Oswald well did live at the Garfield address in 1963. This was Paul Roderick Gregory, who testified before the Warren Commission in 1964, and who was never specifically asked for his address of residence in 1963, the year of the assassination. When asked where he lived, he only mentioned the University of Oklahoma in Norman, where he was reportedly a student. Gregory's father, Peter Paul Gregory, a petroleum engineer, born in 1929 in Siberia, taught Russian at the Fort Worth, Texas library, where he was once approached by Lee Oswald for assistance in obtaining employment as a Russian translator or interpreter. At about the same time, Paul Gregory arranged to obtain Russian language lessons from Oswald's wife, Marina. Gregory visited the Oswald's home for the lessons, from August to early September 1963, and often spoke with Lee Harvey Oswald while there. After the assassination, he told the FBI that he and Oswald had "general conversations, dealing with political matters."

According to the FBI, Gregory said Oswald "expressed his dissatisfaction with both the American system and the Russian system of government but at no time did [Lee Oswald] indicate any particular dislike for President Kennedy." Gregory also told the FBI, "I was completely shocked when I learned that Oswald was implicated in the assassination of the President." Thus, the mystery of the Garfield address only deepens.

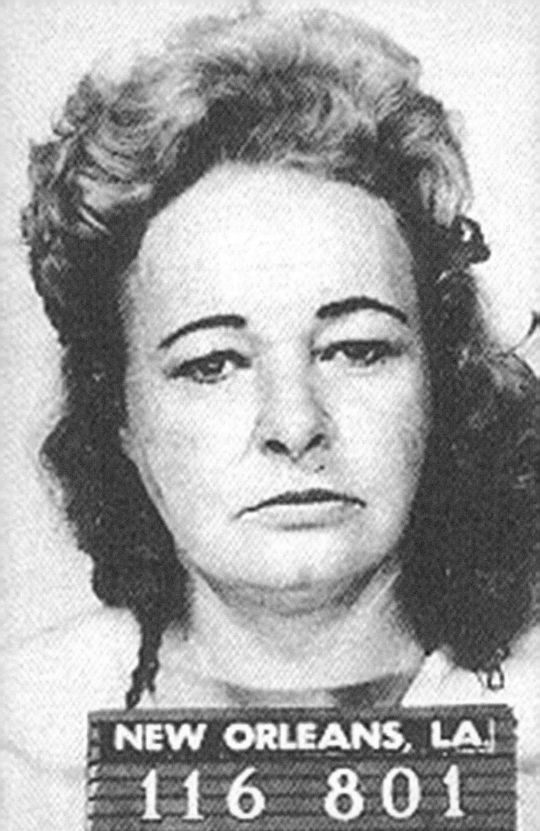

NEW ORLEANS, LA.
116 801
10   21   64

Chapter Two

Almost: The Sad Ballad of Rose

Sweet dreams of you
Things I know can't come true.
Why can't I forget the past,
Start loving someone new
Instead of having sweet dreams of you.

-Patsy Cline

Rose Cherami's face is a fleshy, haggard roadmap of hard-earned despair and disappointment. Her hollow eyes, shadowed by criminality and violence, betray her pain and lost hopes. Her gaze into the camera gives strong hints of broken dreams and heartache. At the age of forty, Rose, once remarkably attractive with near-movie-star looks, is prematurely aged, ravaged by alcohol and pharmaceutical overindulgence. Yet her appearance still evokes a certain air of grace and comfort. No one who knew her would dispute her hard edges and tone, but most would also remark on her insightful knowledge of things generally unknown to her peers. Those few who knew her well would recall her rare ability to silently communicate with dogs and cats, to somehow tame and befriend the meanest of canines, to cause timid felines to roll over and purr contentedly. Her acquaintances would also recall her passion for music and her devotion to the sad, haunting laments of her favorites, Patsy Cline and Johnny Cash.

One can only wonder how Rose Cherami would feel about her place today as an iconic prophet of the murder of President Kennedy. Always portrayed as an unfortunate junkie, prostitute and former stripper, Rose has become the quintessential victim of circumstance and coincidence, the epitome of being in the wrong place at the wrong time. Her mythical portrayal in the Oliver Stone film,

JFK, by Sally Kirkland, has made her a vital linchpin for conspiracy theories and speculation about Kennedy's assassination. Her oft-noted reputation as an addict and hooker has made her an easy target for mockery and dismissal by anti-conspiracy advocates, yet her serendipitous story is undeniably intriguing. Here, along with much new and never before revealed information, are the facts of Rose's incredible story. Readers are encouraged to form their own opinions and to draw their own conclusions.

Law enforcement reports on two accidents — the one minor and the other fatal — suffered by Rose Cherami, as well as her copious criminal file, are notable for what they do not reveal. They are scant, short on details, and incomplete, with no hope for resurrection because some files have gone missing, and some were destroyed shortly after JFK's assassination, and others about ten years later. Nonetheless, Melba Christine Marcades, alias Rose Cherami (usually and erroneously spelled "Cheramie") has assumed a rightful, however small, place in the annals of assassination literature.

On November 20, 1963, Rose Cherami, 40-years old, was hit by a car while hitchhiking along Highway 190 outside Eunice, Louisiana. The car's shaken driver, Frank Odom, a longtime Eunice resident, recounted years later, "After I hit her, she jumped up and said, 'Jesus

Melba Christine Marcades

Christ, you son-of-a-bitch, you hit me.'" Odom, who apologized profusely and explained that he simply had not seen her, transported Rose to the emergency room at nearby Moosa Memorial Hospital in Eunice.

Said Odom: "Most of the way she cursed me out something fierce, and then just about there, she asked me for a cigarette."

At the hospital, Rose was treated for several minor abrasions. Discovering that Rose had no health insurance, seemed to be without funds and appeared to be a drug addict, hospital administrator Louise Guillory telephoned Lt. Francis Paul Fruge, a seasoned Louisiana State Police trooper who sometimes worked the narcotics division. Guillory told Lt. Fruge that the hospital had no reason to hold Rose, but that she seemed intoxicated and had a serious drug problem. Lt. Fruge later said, "I did what I routinely did in such instances." He drove to the hospital, picked up Rose and transported her to a local Eunice jail cell, where she was to stay until she sobered up.

Rose was not locked-up for more than an hour before she began displaying symptoms of serious heroin withdrawal. Fruge, who had left the jail for a social event, was summoned back to observe Rose's signs of distress. Lt. Fruge was familiar with the symptoms of withdrawal. On observing Rose, he called in local physician Dr. F.J. DeRouen, who gave Rose a sedative to lessen her discomfort. The sedative had little effect. Rose thrashed about, pulling off her clothes, sweating profusely and complaining of chills. Dr. DeRouen would later say, "The woman was in a horrible way. She had scratched her nails bloody on the cell walls." Rose told Dr. DeRouen and Lt. Fruge she had been addicted to heroin for over nine years.

Upon hearing this, Dr. DeRouen, who also served as the area's assistant coroner, told Lt. Fruge he was going to commit Rose for treatment at East Louisiana State Hospital in Jackson, a facility that some readers may note comes up again and again in Kennedy assassination chronicles.

Dr. DeRouen telephoned the state hospital that night around midnight, alerting them to Rose's impending arrival, and then he summoned an ambulance from Charity Hospital in Lafayette to transport her. Lt. Fruge agreed to accompany Rose to the hospital. When Dr. DeRouen spoke with admitting personnel he was informed that Rose had once before been confined at the hospital, having been sent there by the criminal court of New Orleans about a year earlier. (Worth noting here is that there are credible reports that Rose may have been confined twice at the Jackson facility. Also, Rose was once a patient in 1956-1957, at St. Elizabeth's in Washington, D.C., during the same years that the CIA, through its Human Ecology Fund, operated a "behavior modification" project at the Washington facility involving CIA physicians Drs. John Gittinger and Louis Jolyon West. See Notes for more on Dr. Louis West.)

East Louisiana State Hospital was about 100 miles from Eunice, allowing time for Lt. Fruge to have a conversation with Rose en route. One of Fruge's first questions was how she had come to be struck by a car on Highway 190. Fruge, later, in 1979, appearing before the Select Committee on Assassinations, U.S. House of Representatives, recounted Rose's explanation:

> She related to me that she was coming from Florida to Dallas with two men who were Italians or resembled Italians. They had stopped at this lounge [outside of Eunice] and they'd had a few drinks and had gotten into an argument or something. The manager of the lounge threw her out and she got on the road and hitchhiked to catch a ride, and this is when she got hit by a vehicle.

Lt. Fruge explained to the Select Committee that the lounge where the three had stopped was actually "a house of prostitution called the Silver Slipper." Fruge also said that while at the lounge, the two Italian-looking men had met with another man named John Paul Jennette, who Fruge thought had been Rose's pimp.

When Rose had first related this to Fruge, he had asked her, "What were you going to do once you got to Dallas?"

Answered Rose: "Number one, pick up some money, pick up my baby, and kill Kennedy."

Fruge had asked what her baby's name was and she said, "Michael, my baby Michael."

Lt. Fruge had given Rose a look, shaking his head.

Rose, drifting in and out of a sedative-fueled stupor, had mumbled, "We're going to kill President Kennedy when he comes to Dallas in a few days."

Lt. Fruge later said he wrote off Rose's remarks about Kennedy as withdrawal-induced stupidity or gallows humor, but on November 22, after hearing that the President had been assassinated, he immediately called the State Hospital and told one of Rose's attending physicians, Dr. Charles Armistead, "By no way in the world should you turn her loose until I could get my hands on her." Dr. Armistead told Fruge there was no problem holding Rose, and she most likely would not be well enough to speak with the police officer until the following Monday.

That Monday, November 25, the day after Jack Ruby had shot and killed Lee Harvey Oswald, Lt. Fruge arrived at the hospital early in the morning and interrogated Rose at length. The story Rose told the officer amazed him. Rose explained again that she and her two male companions had been traveling from Miami to Dallas. Asked about the two men, Rose identified them only as "Osanto" and "Sergio," and mentioned a third man, John Jennette, who had joined the group at the Silver Slipper lounge.

According to Rose, the men were going to Dallas to assassinate Kennedy. Rose said she had nothing to do with the assassination and had only heard the men discussing Kennedy's murder, but that she was supposed to pick up $8,000 from an unidentified person in Dallas and then pick up her little boy from friends who had been caring for him. Rose explained that the $8,000 was for a heroin deal that, after the assassination, was to go down in Houston, Texas, her hometown. (Other credible, but unconfirmed, reports concerning Rose's son and the money she was to pick up in Dallas suggest that an individual named "Leo Parker" was the person holding Rose's son, Michael. The same reports claim that Rose then picked up $29,000 in Houston from an individual named "Vallone" for purchase of heroin. This may have been Tony Vincent Vallone, a known heroin dealer and club owner who is alleged to have been associated with Jack Ruby.)

Rose told Fruge she had already made a reservation at the Rice Hotel in Houston under an assumed name and that she and the two men, Osanto and Sergio, were to rendezvous with a seaman who was bringing 8 kilos of heroin into Galveston by boat. Rose gave Lt. Fruge the names of the seaman and the boat. Once the deal with the seaman was complete, Rose told him, the plan was for her, her son Michael, and the two men to go to Mexico. (Some accounts of Rose's story have her taking the drugs to Mexico, but this is incorrect.)

As a result of interrogating Rose, Fruge learned that prior to his arrival at the State Hospital, Rose had been talking about the JFK assassination to a number of people on the medical staff and that she had made some incredible and intriguing statements in the process. For example, the day before the assassination, Rose had calmly told one of her physicians, Dr. Don Bowers, that Kennedy was going to be murdered in Dallas. Dr. Bowers was troubled by Rose's remarks and had asked another physician at the hospital, Dr.

Victor Weiss, to speak with Rose. (Dr. Bowers would deny this in 2002. See Notes on this chapter.)

According to Dr. Weiss, Rose told him she had once worked for Jack Ruby in Dallas as both a stripper and drug courier and that "word in the underworld" was that Kennedy was targeted for assassination. Rose also told Dr. Weiss that she had seen Lee Harvey Oswald meeting several times with Ruby at his club in Dallas. Another hospital physician, Dr. Wayne Owen, told Lt. Fruge that the day before the assassination, Rose had said that a man named "Jack Rubenstein" was involved in the planned assassination.

According to seasoned assassination investigator and writer Jim DiEugenio, on November 22, Rose and "several nurses" at the State Hospital were watching a television broadcast covering JFK's arrival in Dallas when, moments before his assassination, Rose told the nurses, "This is when it is going to happen." DiEugenio interviewed two of the nurses who confirmed the account.

After hearing Rose's story, Lt. Fruge notified his supervisor and requested instructions as to what to do next. Incredulous at what he was hearing, Louisiana State Police Capt. Ben Morgan journeyed to the hospital to hear Rose's story first hand. After hearing Rose's account, Capt. Morgan and Lt. Fruge drove to Baton Rouge where the two consulted with their supervisor at police headquarters, Col. Thomas D. Burbank. Burbank instructed Fruge and Morgan to take Rose into custody in order to have her complete cooperation and to investigate further. Lt. Fruge arranged for Rose's release from the state hospital through one of her treating physicians, Dr. Malcolm Pierson.

The next morning, Tuesday, November 26, Lt. Fruge, Capt. Morgan and another state trooper, Wayne Moran accompanied Rose in a small private jet from Baton Rouge to Houston, Texas. The day before, Fruge had telephoned Nathan Durham, chief U.S. Customs agent in Port Arthur, Texas, who told Fruge that the boat identified by Rose, the SS *Maturata*, was due to come into port soon. The SS *Maturata*, built in 1955, was a British-registered cargo ship that serviced ports from England to Colombo, Sri Lanka to Suez, Madras, and Calcutta, as well as Port Arthur, Texas. (Rose had identified the ship phonetically as the "Mary Etta," but Durham quickly was able to come up with the correct name.)

During the flight to Houston, Rose happened to notice a newspaper on the seat in front of her that bore a headline stating that

Dallas investigators had been unable to discover any relationship between Jack Ruby and Lee Harvey Oswald. Rose laughed out loud and said, "Them two queer son-of-bitches. They've been shacking up for years." Rose referred to Ruby by his nickname "Pinkie."

Questioned later about Rose's outburst and how she knew that Ruby and Oswald had a relationship, Fruge said, "She told me she used to work for Jack Ruby at the Pink Door. She used to strip for Jack Ruby at the Pink Door." (Some debunkers of Rose's account enjoy proclaiming that Ruby had "never owned" a club called the Pink Door, but fail to acknowledge that he was part owner of a Dallas club called the Pink Slipper.)

Fruge later said that after he and Capt. Morgan heard Rose talk about Ruby and Oswald, Morgan telephoned Capt. Will Fritz of the Dallas Police Department to pass on Rose's statements. Fruge recounted, "Capt. Morgan called Capt. Fritz from Dallas up and told him what we had, the information that we had, that we had a person that had given us this information. And, of course, there again it was an old friend [Fritz], and there was a little conversation. But anyway, when Capt. Morgan hung up, he turned around and told us, 'They don't want her. They're not interested.'"

Customs agent Nathan Durham met the group in Houston and assisted them in checking into a Holiday Inn. Fruge told Rose to go ahead and check into the Rice Hotel, where agent Durham had confirmed her reservation. Rose went to the hotel accompanied by another Customs agent named Bob Woody, who posed as Rose's "sugar daddy."

Lt. Fruge later recounted that the journey to Houston was less than fruitful. As the facts reveal, it was also quite convoluted. U.S. Customs agents, with help from detectives from the Houston Police department, had tailed the seaman – identified only as "Luther" by Rose – from Galveston, but had lost the man somewhere in Houston. Houston Police Department records from December 1963 suggest that "Luther" may have been Joseph P. Luke, nicknamed "Luther" and "Luke." Joseph Luke was a narcotics trafficker who was closely associated with Dallas-based Mafia member Joseph Francis Civello, a known associate of Jack Ruby.

For unexplained reasons, nobody contacted Rose at the Rice Hotel so that she could meet the seaman at the prearranged rendezvous spot, and identify him. According to Lt. Fruge, once Rose received the heroin from "Luther" she was suppose to deliver it to someone named "Leo Parker," an alias, some speculate, for a man named "Portillo." (Here it is worth noting that in October 1963 Jack Ruby employed a comedy team at his Dallas club of which one member was named Carme Petrillo.)

The Houston police never took the investigation seriously and resented Lt. Fruge's presence in their city. Additionally, some Houston officers were less than pleased to see Rose back in their jurisdiction, and did all that they could to harm her credibility and to discredit her claims about drug trafficking. When things began to unravel, Lt. Fruge suggested to Rose that she sit down with the FBI to discuss the case, but she adamantly refused. One can easily imagine that Rose, after only a few days of withdrawal and nine years of chasing the dragon of heroin, was more than anxious to get away from anyone having anything to do with law enforcement.

Once things were at an obvious end, and Fruge and Morgan were arranging to return to Louisiana, Fruge remarked, "Well, Rose, I guess we almost got there, didn't we."

To which Rose nodded, and said, "Almost. The story of my life."

Given the slim extant record concerning Lt. Fruge's investigation in Houston, we do not know if he was aware of the checkered reputation of the Houston Police Department or of Rose's past activities in Houston when she was a resident there. To put it mildly, the Houston Police Department historically has had a less than stellar record – given checkered drug investigations and corruption within its ranks. Without doubt, Rose Cherami was well aware of this, and more. The story of Rose's earlier Houston connections to yet another unsolved murder – that of Houston police detective Martin A. Billnitzer – and therefore to the Federal Bureau of Narcotics, George Hunter White, and the CIA, was almost completely unknown until now.

Rose Cherami and the Death of Detective Billnitzer

Rose, born Melba Christine Youngblood in 1923 in Houston, Texas, had spent most of her time there before moving sometime around 1955 to New Orleans, where she worked as a dancer-prostitute and drug courier. Rose's long battle with heroin addiction had begun in Houston at a time when the port city, with strong and well-concealed Mafia ties, was a major source for the drug.

Numerous documents generated by the Federal Bureau of Narcotics throughout the 1950s and 1960s reveal the Bureau's deep frustration with corruption inside the Houston Police Department, especially when it came to narcotics investigations involving organized crime. In 1954, things came to a head when Houston detective, Martin Billnitzer – who had arrested Rose at least once, and regularly used her as a trusted and reliable confidential informant – allegedly took his own life by shooting himself twice in his heart – a feat rarely, if ever, replicated.

Martin Billnitzer was the quintessential dedicated and honest public servant and police officer. After graduating from college and joining the Houston police force in 1942, by the 1950s, Billnitzer was conducting a relentless one-man crusade against dope trafficking in Houston. One of his surviving relatives – who out of fear declined to be identified in this book – says, "Nobody hated drugs more than Martin. He felt that his mission in life was to tell people how evil drugs are."

Det. Martin Billnitzer and wife, Marie, Houston, Texas, 1953

A May 1953 newspaper article about his efforts opens with words that could have easily been written today: "Out of the seemingly endless war that is constantly waged against the scourge of 'dope' there comes from a Houston detective something that may finally prove to be the answer to this rampant racket that cripples, demoralizes and denigrates our city's youth." Billnitzer's answer turned on educating the public about drugs. "They are the ones who must shoulder the biggest share of responsibility in licking this thing," said Billnitzer.

In the three years before his death, Billnitzer traveled all over Houston and its surrounding towns and counties speaking to over 500 business, civic, school, and church groups about the evils of drugs and what people could do about them. One would have been hard pressed to find a high school student or churchgoer who had not heard the detective speak at least once. "Ignorance, superstition, and totally inadequate laws," intoned Billnitzer to his rapt audiences. "These are the things that have us hamstrung. These are the biggest and most stubborn obstacles that we have to lick."

Billnitzer, promoted to detective after only fourteen months on the job, was also recognized as one the best "dopebusters" in the Southwest United States. By 1949, he had worked countless successful undercover operations and had been instrumental in the mass arrest of nearly forty heroin traffickers operating out of the port of Galveston and believed linked to Charles "Lucky" Luciano, Santo Trafficante, and Carlos Marcello.

Billnitzer was also recognized as a master at establishing and maintaining an extensive network of confidential informants who fed him a steady stream of reliable and critically needed information. One of Billnitzer's most trusted informants, according to notebooks he kept, was Rose Cherami who went by the names "Patsy Allen," "Christine Allen," "Zada Rodman" and "Christine Youngblood." (In 1941-1943, Rose had been married to an Army Air Force enlisted man named "Boy Bobby" [Robert] Rodman.) Billnitzer's police notepads were riddled with references to "Patsy" and "Christine," including meetings and safety concerns. A handwritten note in one of Billnitzer's notebooks written a few days before his death reads, "Patsy worried she has been compromised. Wants to leave city for Dallas. Has work there."

In 1954, during an investigation of a large heroin trafficking operation that involved information supplied by Rose Cherami, Martin Billnitzer was summoned to a meeting with his superior, police chief Lawrence D. Morrison in Morrison's headquarters office. Minutes after the meeting concluded, Billnitzer returned to his own office, reportedly alone, and shot himself twice in the heart.

Within hours of his death, and with no autopsy having been performed, Houston Justice of the Peace Thomas Maes issued an official cause of death as "suicide." Chief Morrison told skeptical reporters he was "more than satisfied with the verdict." Not everyone agreed with Morrison's sentiments or Maes' finding. Most vocal among those dissenting was a team of three special agents from the Federal Bureau of Narcotics, which had arrived in Houston three days before Billnitzer's death. Said George Hunter White, the Bureau supervisor who headed the team, "I think the man was murdered. If he killed himself, he is probably the first man who ever killed himself twice."

George White, unknown to anyone in Houston, Texas or anywhere else in the United States (apart from a handful of FBN and

CIA officials) was a covert CIA contract employee. White, as noted, was also no stranger to death or suicide, as best exemplified by his role in the bizarre death of Dr. Frank Olson. Also, as noted earlier, White operated a CIA-funded safe house in New York City from 1952 through 1954, where he experimented on unwitting victims to see the effects of various mind expanding drugs, including especially LSD. As we shall soon see, these safe house experiments would eventually become a strange feature of Martin Billnitzer's death.

That White and his team were in Houston made it more than obvious that Federal narcotics officials were particularly concerned about drug trafficking in the city and surrounding areas. It also made it quite apparent that Federal officials were not focusing on local penny-ante street dealers, but instead on major traffickers like Santo Trafficante and Carlos Marcello.

Trafficante and Marcello regularly used the ports of Galveston, Tampa, and New Orleans with virtual immunity from local law enforcement officers and U.S. Customs officials, who were well compensated under the table to look the other way.

Waiting to greet George White when he arrived in Houston on May 27, 1954 were narcotics agents Fred Douglas, out of the FBN's Washington, D.C. branch, and Henry Giordano, an agent out of FBN's Kansas City office. Agent Douglas had already been in Houston for close to four months conducting a low-profile investigation into corrupt local law enforcement officials and U.S. Customs agents, as well as Houston's serpentine trafficking connections with New Orleans and Tampa. The previous day, Douglas had telephoned White in New Orleans, where he was working on a case involving Columbian drug traffickers Rafael and Tomas Herran, their Cuban connections, and another character we shall meet in this book (see chapter on June Cobb).

"It's about to hit the fan here," Douglas told White. "Anslinger [director of the FBN] said I should get you here right away."

Several days prior to this phone exchange, all hell had broken loose in Houston when a low-level dealer named Earl Voice, owner of a notorious Houston nightclub who was arrested for possession of heroin, blurted to his arresting officer that he had been buying confiscated drugs "from the back door of the Houston police department for nearly three years." In statements made after he was taken into custody and booked, with a deal in place to be released in exchange for his evidence, Voice implicated several Houston police detectives, including the head of the local Vice Squad and an FBN agent out of the Bureau's Houston office who worked closely with the squad. Said Voice, a smooth talking beau brummel whose nightclub, the Mona Lisa, was commonly called a "blood bucket" by law enforcement officers, "I've been buying back my own dope from city detectives for years now." Police records also showed that besides being a known heroin dealer, Voice also dealt extensively in white slavery, prostitution and the sex trade in general, not only in Houston but also in Louisiana and Alabama. While it can not be established that Rose Cherami actually worked for Voice, Martin Billnitzer's surviving investigative notes clearly reveal that Rose served as his main informant on Earl Voice's prostitution, white slavery, and drug activities throughout the years 1952 and 1953.

George White and Fred Douglas met with Earl Voice at the Houston jail where he was being held. Voice told the two agents that in late summer 1953, a Houston police detective named Sidney Smith (nicknamed "Sid the Kid") had given him "three 50-gram packages" of police-seized heroin for resale. Voice said he immediately recognized the three packages, because of their distinctive wrapping, as having been part of a large bust conducted against several of his associates by three Houston narcotics detectives, including Martin Billnitzer.

White and Douglas interviewed Billnitzer on June 1, 1954 at Houston's William Penn Hotel, where they were staying. White noted in his report on the interview that Billnitzer was "a tall, thin man who speaks softly and deliberately, who is married to a school teacher who was his high school sweetheart." Wrote White: "The couple have no children and live quite modestly in a small home."

Following the interview, White was convinced that Billnitzer was not involved in any wrongdoing, but that the detective was not telling the full truth about his colleagues in order to avoid implicating them in the allegations made by Earl Voice. Later that same day, White and Douglas also became convinced that Billnitzer was being set up by his fellow officers to take the fall for supplying Voice with confiscated heroin. White would later write, "This fellow Billnitzer was so squeaky clean that I couldn't understand how he had survived so long in the cesspool department he worked for. His murder must have been a thing a long time in coming."

The next day, detective Billnitzer came back to the William Penn Hotel and asked to see George White. The detective had telephoned White two-hours earlier and said he wanted "to drop by to correct some things I had said yesterday."

According to White's subsequent report, Billnitzer sat across from him and said, "I'm going to get something off my chest. I didn't tell the whole truth yesterday, and it's been bothering me ever since."

Billnitzer then told White, with FBN agents Douglas and Giordano sitting in, that he was fully knowledgeable that other police officers were providing dealers' confiscated drugs to be resold, occasionally involving large amounts of heroin that had come into the port of Galveston. Billnitzer told the three FBN agents that two of his best informants had been feeding him information about heroin shipments into Houston from New Orleans, Tampa, and through Mexico City, and that much of it originated from processing plants in France. Often these shipments, when confiscated, were among the drugs put back on the street through the back door of the Houston police department, but Billnitzer explained his chief objective was to get these drugs off the street permanently, and he had qualms about turning on fellow officers.

"If I were to turn on my colleagues I would render myself completely ineffective," Billnitzer said. "I know it's wrong, but I'm between a rock and a hard place in terms of upholding the laws I've sworn to enforce."

When Billnitzer left his meeting with White, he said he felt like "a hundred pounds have been taken off my shoulders." According to his report, White told the detective that he "would like to meet with him at least once more" and "I thanked him for his cooperation and courage in what was really a bad situation."

The next day, June 3, 1954, at about noon, minutes after he heard the news about Billnitzer's death, White wrote in his diary: "Martin Albert Billnitzer commits suicide in Morals Squad office – possible murder." According to interviews with two of Rose Cherami's surviving relatives – who declined to be named in this book due to "concerns about the police in Houston" – Rose left Houston about four days after Billnitzer's death and "didn't come back for years." White told his wife, Albertine, over the telephone the evening of Billnitzer's death, "I can't believe they killed this guy and think they'll get away with it."

Three days after Billnitzer's death, George White was blindsided by a series of stories in Houston's newspapers. Houston City Attorney Will Sears had informed reporters that he believed Billnitzer's "suicide" had been caused because George White "used ruthless tactics" on the detective and "bullied him out of his mind." Said Sears: "The unscrupulous conduct of White defies proper description. I believe sincerely that this man used threats against an officer to the point of disturbing the balance of the officer's mind, leading to his suicide." Without providing any details, Sears charged further that White had made threats to other Houston officials and was guilty of "character assassination" of local officers who had no connections with drug and heroin trafficking.

Sears didn't stop short with his accusations against White. In the newspapers and in a flurry of letters and telegrams to FBN head Harry Anslinger, Secretary of the Treasury George Humphrey, FBI Director J. Edgar Hoover, and U.S. Attorney General Herbert Brownell, Sears demanded that White be removed from Houston. Underscoring his seriousness, Sears sent copies of everything to Texas' two senators, Price Daniel and Lyndon Baines Johnson, and also to Rep. Albert Thomas. Sen. Daniel promptly wired Sears back, stating he had requested that Secretary Humphrey "give full and impartial consideration to the charges outlined." White responded to Sears' accusations by saying they were "ridiculous" and that his investigation would continue. "My shoulders are broad and the facts will speak for themselves," said White.

If Sears was expecting support from Houston District Attorney Ewing Werlein in his attacks on George White, he must have been sorely disappointed. At the height of Sears' attack, Werlein disclosed that White, Douglas, and Giordano had invited him, along with Assistant District Attorney Morris and Grand Jury Foreman Henry Burkett, to the William Penn Hotel where White had them listen to a tape recording of his 45-minute interview with Detective Billnitzer made less than twelve hours before his death.

Werlein and Morris told reporters that they detected "no trace of browbeating" of Billnitzer in the recording. District Attorney Werlein went even further and stated, "I didn't see anything in the recording to indicate a distraught mind or the possibility of a suicide. Based on the recording, I wouldn't say Billnitzer had anything to lose by living. As far as the recording went, he shouldn't have had any fear of prosecution."

As might be expected, Police Chief Morrison was quick to align himself with City Attorney Sears and in a few short days Morrison was telling anyone who would listen that White was running around in his jurisdiction like a "visiting hatchetman" and "Gestapo agent."

Houston's controversial mayor, Roy Mark Hofheinz, a 42-year old millionaire and former county judge and state representative, jumped into the fray by staunchly backing Morrison and Sears. Hofheinz, who was prone to wearing collarless silk suits with enormous, gaudy cufflinks, hinted to reporters that the FBN's investigation was merely a ploy to open up what he maintained was a vice-free city to nefarious East Coast interests. "With all the fume and furor," the mayor announced, "Houston is still a closed town. It will stay closed as long as I am mayor."

George White, never one to shy away from controversy or a good fight, didn't help matters after he promptly went out with a few reporters in tow and picked up three pimps and five prostitutes working in the shadow of Houston's city hall building. "We were looking for narcotics suspects and just stumbled onto these creatures," deadpanned White. "I am deeply shocked. I had heard that Houston was a highly moral town."

The same week Sears launched his attack on White, pandemonium erupted at a Houston City Council meeting when Councilman Joe Resweber, a well-respected attorney, moved that City Attorney Sears draft a resolution commending White, Douglas, and Giordano and offering them the council's complete cooperation. Speaking in support of the resolution, Councilman George Marquette sharply criticized Sears for "acting as Chief Morrison's personal mouthpiece." Mayor Hofheinz – who had arrested four city council members that year for boycotting a meeting – argued that it wasn't Sears' job to draft any such resolution and then exploded at Resweber, shouting, "You've always wanted an open city!" When order had been partially restored, Councilman George Kesseler asked why, since it wasn't Sears' job to draft the resolution requested by Resweber, had the city attorney fired off a telegram to the Treasury Secretary in Washington demanding that George White be pulled out of Houston? A red-faced Sears indignantly denied that his telegram had asked that White be removed, saying that it had only asked that Secretary Humphrey send one of White's superiors to Houston to oversee the probe.

Relations between the FBN's George White and Houston Police Chief Morrison worsened on June 11, when the police chief called White "a liar" in the newspapers after White had remarked to reporters that Morrison was refusing to speak to White, and refusing to cooperate in the FBN's ongoing investigation into heroin trafficking. "The statement is a continuation of White's known practice of untruths and half-truths," Morrison told reporters. Morrison quickly realized he was in danger of losing local press support. He began cooperating with White, ostensibly, ordering his officers to assist the federal agents – but only after they first informed his office directly. Commented one reporter, "Morrison is cooperating like a jaguar being force-fed with a hot poker."

Things heated up further after FBN Agent Fred Douglas told White the next day that there was a plainclothes detective from Morrison's internal security squad sitting in the William Penn lobby taking notes on people coming and going from the hotel. "What does he look like?" White asked, referring to Morrison's detective.

"You can't miss him," Douglas replied. "He's big, real big, and has a red coat and cowboy hat on."

When White went down to the lobby, the man in the red coat was still there and, in addition, White saw a dark sedan parked outside the hotel with several more of Houston's finest plainclothes officers inside. Within hours White would realize that there was a 24-hour watch on his activities.

The next day, White received a telephone call from Rudolph Halley in New York. Halley, an attorney and close friend of White's who headed the New York City Council and had just lost a bid to become mayor of New York, informed White that Houston police officers were running checks on White in Manhattan and other parts of the country.

"Believe it or not," Halley told White, "they're attempting to tie you to subversive and communist elements."

Halley must have found this amusing, given that several months earlier, White had performed undercover investigative work for Senator Joseph McCarthy's ongoing Congressional hearings. White, however was not amused. In his day book White wrote, "These people are psychopaths." Then he telephoned his boss, Harry Anslinger, in Washington and requested additional agents to assist in his widening investigation. Anslinger promised White that

New York-based narcotics agents E.P. Gross and Vance Newman would be on the next flight to Houston.

Also dispatched to Houston to assist three days later was FBN and CIA contractor Jean Pierre Lafitte. Lafitte, as we know, was one of Frank Olson's killers, an agent who would go on to perform numerous additional "executive action" duties for the CIA. Throughout the years 1952-1963, Lafitte worked closely and regularly with White and an operative named Vance Newman on a litany of secret projects for the FBN and CIA. Newman had been cleared by the Agency to work on CIA projects in early 1953 and proved to be one of the Agency's most trusted as well as little known contractors. In 1963, FBN agent and CIA consultant Charles Siragusa wrote about Newman in a letter to White: "As usual, Vance is here with us. I should write as preferred because I can't imagine any of this work being any where near effective without his participation. He's like a benevolent ghost, always watching over things, making sure all goes as planned and anticipated."

Indeed, not long before traveling to Houston, both White and Newman took part in a covert three-day training session in New York City involving hypnotism and a CIA consultant. The session was held in the apartment of a "world famous stage hypnotist." (The hypnotist is not named in the CIA documents citing the session.) Also attending were CIA officials James Jesus Angleton and Donald N. Wilbur. Wilbur would later claim that, following the training, he could put people into a trance simply by engaging them in normal conversation.

The dark sedan parked round-the-clock outside White's hotel was soon supplemented by several plainclothes detectives who began trailing White and his agents when they left the hotel on foot. Early in the morning of June 9, trailing after White as he stepped from the William Penn and began walking down the sidewalk, was the red-coated detective, at a safe distance behind him. White picked up his pace for about a block, turned a corner, and ducked into the side entrance of the Greyhound Bus Depot. When the detective hurried to follow, he ran into White coming back outside. White grabbed the man by his coat collar and shoved his FBN identification and badge in the man's face.

"Federal agent," White said, "why are you tailing me?"

"What gives you that idea," the detective replied, "do you have a guilty conscience?"

As he spoke, FBN agent E.P. Gross, who had exited the hotel after White and followed the detective, tapped the man on the shoulder and held up his FBN credentials. White again asked the detective what he was doing.

"I'm looking for the toilet," the man replied.

"Let's see some identification," White demanded.

"Mr. White," said the detective smugly, "isn't that blood on your hands."

"Call the cops," White told Gross.

"Wait," said the man, "I'm a Houston detective with the Internal Security Squad." He fumbled for his wallet and flipped it open revealing his badge.

"Call them anyway," White told Gross.

The flustered detective, William R. McCafferty, didn't know how to respond when White and Gross hauled him to a phone booth. Gross telephoned police headquarters and reported that he had apprehended a suspicious character. When a squad car pulled up moments later, White tried to turn the detective over to the officers. "Careful, boys," White said, "he looks like a subversive to me."

Gross wrote in his report, "During the remainder of the afternoon, Detective McCafferty was observed seated in a 1954 Grey Ford Sedan, bearing Louisiana License No. 22506, which was parked in a position as to observe both entrances to our hotel."

Meanwhile, not finished showboating, White had walked back to the hotel and found that the sedan was still there. At this point, his sidewalk encounter had attracted two reporters with cameras, and White made the most of his resources. He calmly strolled across the street and climbed into the sedan. Good-naturedly, he asked to bum a cigarette while the reporters clicked away with their cameras. When White walked back into the hotel he was grinning broadly, but his expression changed quickly when he saw that another detective had taken up McAfferty's place in the lobby.

Weeks later, Malcolm R. Wilkey, the United States Attorney for the Southern District of Texas, would question James McAfferty's superior, Houston Police Lieutenant Larry Fultz, about why he had placed George White under such intense surveillance. Fultz's answers were so remarkable that some bear repeating.

"What was the reason that made you think [White] was engaged in subversive activities?" Wilkey, who would be nominated by Richard M. Nixon in 1970 to fill the U.S. Court of Appeals District of Columbia Circuit seat vacated by Warren E. Burger, asked Fultz.

"My reason is," replied Fultz, "that any person who seeks to attack an institution in the community, be it the police department, the educational system or anything else, is certainly worthy of some concern on the part of the security division of any police department."

"Then you have no evidence whatever of White's subversive activities except your interpretation of his activities in Houston as an attack on the Police Department, rather than an investigative procedure ordered by his superiors in Washington?" asked Wilkey.

"Let me state this," replied Fultz. "He was a member of the OSS. Many members of the OSS have been questioned and they have stood by the Fifth Amendment privilege and they have refused to testify." Fultz was referring to former OSS officers who were targeted by Sen. Joe McCarthy.

"This is a rather strange case of guilt by association in your mind," observed Wilkey. "Did you believe Mr. White had violated or was violating within the territorial limits of your jurisdiction any statute of the State of Texas or any ordinance of the City of Houston?"

"Yes, sir," Fultz said. "Recently in connection with the State Legislature, we had a state law to make it an offence to be a member of the Communist party, punishable by twenty years and a ten-thousand dollar fine."

"Do you feel that Mr. White probably violated this statute?' asked Wilkey.

"I had no idea that Mr. White was a subversive," replied Fultz. "Our investigation commenced as all investigations commence, with gathering facts here, there, and yonder."

The day after he spoke with Rudolph Halley, White telephoned Dr. Sidney Gottlieb in Washington, D.C. The head of the CIA's Chemical Branch, Technical Services Division, Gottlieb had been surreptitiously working with White for about two years after the narcotics agent agreed to become a special consultant to the CIA. White specialized in experimenting with LSD and other hallucinogenic drugs as interrogation tools. White had first encountered Gottlieb when he was employed by the U. S.

Department of Agriculture. At the time, Gottlieb had been a budding expert at identifying various illicit drugs seized by the FBN.

White's reason for calling Gottlieb at this point was to alert him to the Houston situation and any possible blowback that could come from the investigation. Unfortunately, it was coming on the heels of another serious development that deeply concerned both men. Just weeks earlier, White had been subpoenaed to appear before a special session of the New York State Investigations Commission headed by William B. Herlands. Commissioner Herlands was investigating allegations that New York Governor Thomas Dewey had secretly accepted a $375,000 payment from notorious gangster Lucky Luciano in return for granting Luciano parole on February 2, 1946 as part of Operation Underworld. During White's testimony before Herlands, the subject of the CIA's New York City safe house and White's LSD experiments there had come dangerously close to exposure.

On June 15, 1954 front-page headlines in all of Houston's newspapers boldly proclaimed that a federal grand jury, initially seated in February 1954, was being recalled to investigate the Bacchus Street case now widely known as the "Houston dope scandal." Prior to the announcement, White and his agents had huddled at length with U.S. Attorney Malcolm Wilkey and his two assistants, Brian S. Odem and John Snodgrass. After their last meeting together on June 14, White jotted in his diary, "Wilkey ready grand jury – bomb to drop on Morrison."

About a week earlier, White, Douglas, and Giordano, after conferring with Wilkey, had driven to the office of a Houston osteopath named Julius B. McBride. When McBride opened his door, the agents identified themselves and asked to examine his drug records. Nervously, McBride produced his files and White quickly pointed to a column that repeatedly contained the name, Billy Jackson. Jackson was a cancer patient, Dr. McBride explained, whom he was treating with powerful painkillers.

"That's a lot of pain medication," White remarked. "I don't see how one body could hold all that stuff."

"You're right," Dr. McBride replied. "It looks very odd, but there's an explanation."

"What's that, Doctor?" White asked.

"Well, Billy doesn't get all those drugs," said McBride.... When I write something down for Billy Jackson that he doesn't get, I put a little mark alongside it."

"Who gets the drugs with the mark, Doctor?" asked White.

White later recounted that McBride "giggled nervously," as he was prone to do, stating, "Well, I hope this won't cause any trouble. It's Chief of Police Morrison."

Houston's newspapers soon revealed that Dr. McBride had provided Morrison with "a startlingly large amount of narcotics." The amount, detailed in a 26-count indictment brought against McBride, was "800 grains of codeine and other unspecified narcotics" administered over a "134 day period" for what the doctor claimed was a slipped disc in Morrison's back. Morrison steadfastly refused to comment on the case, even after he was officially relieved of his duties as Chief of Police. Dr. McBride, who faced a possible maximum sentence of 150 years in prison plus $179,000 in fines, was sentenced to 30 months.

Another character in the Houston drama that surrounded Rose Cherami in Houston was Alvin F. Scharff, "Al" to his friends. According to Martin Billnitzer's surviving case notes, on at least two occasions he shared confidential informant Rose Cherami with Scharff – with less than enjoyable results. Wrote Billnitzer on one case "Patsy doesn't get along with Al at all. Says she can't trust him to honor our agreement." Two days later, Martin wrote, "Patsy won't meet with Al any longer. Won't change her mind on this."

With both of them long dead, it is difficult to determine how Al Scharff and George White regarded one another. Scharff, in 1954, was a well-established supervisor with the U.S. Customs Department in Houston, and similar to White in many important ways. Both men were confident, insufferable egotists rarely visited by self-doubt or indecision.

Scharff is briefly mentioned in one of White's reports to Harry Anslinger on the Houston dope scandal. The report reveals that Scharff was prepared to testify that on the morning of June 2, 1954, the day before Martin Billnitzer died, detectives Foy Melton and Billnitzer "appeared in [Scharff's] office to discuss a situation involving narcotics drugs seized at 3306 1/2 Bacchus Street, Houston, Texas, on August 11, 1953; that during the course of their conversation, defendant Melton inquired as to the law on conspiracy and what part a person would have to play in a situation to be considered a conspirator or a co-conspirator."

A book about Scharff's life reveals more about his role in the Houston case. Published in 1964, *The Coin of Contraband* contains a chapter entitled, "The Houston Narcotics Scandal." Written by Garland Roark, an obvious fan of Scharff's who had his subject's complete cooperation, the book describes an alleged meeting between Customs supervisor Scharff and Billnitzer in "early June." The Roark account does not mention Melton. Roark writes of Billnitzer's visit with Scharrf: "Appearing very nervous, he told [Scharrf] that he had been talking to George White, who had said he was going to send him [Billnitzer] to the penitentiary." Billnitzer allegedly then asked Scharrf if White could "do it or not." According to Roark's book, "Al looked to the handsome little officer whose record was good, and replied, 'Certainly he can if you've violated the law. What did he accuse you of?'"

Clearly, this account doesn't square with White's report and it could possibly lead one to conclude that given Scharff's love of the spotlight, he invented the meeting so as to insert himself into a highly visible case. Indeed, on the day that Billnitzer died, White's diary entry noting the death as "possibly murder" is followed by: "Al Scharff, Customs intrudes into picture."

Roark's book claims that "shortly after" his meeting with Billnitzer, Scharff "went to the police station on business" and found out that Billnitzer had been found dead just moments earlier. Roark writes that Scharff asked Chief Morrison why the detective had shot himself, and Morrison replied that Billnitzer "had been interviewed by George White and Fred Douglas." Then Roark recounts an incredible vignette in which Scharff, overcome with "compassion and then anger" that a man would "seek escape behind the final curtain," heads straight to the William Penn Hotel to inform Fred Douglas of Billnitzer's death.

At the hotel, according to Roark, Scharff found Douglas, Giordano and White in the coffee shop. Joining them at their table, Scharff blurted, "Billnitzer just shot himself. The chief is terribly upset."

As Scharff concluded his announcement, Roark writes, George White, "dressed in black stepped in front of Al and stood across the table with feet spread apart, a snub-nosed six shooter at his right hip."

Looking at Scharff, White asked, "What in the hell are you so nervous about?"

Roark writes that at first Scharff thought White "must be talking to someone else," but seeing "no one but the company at the table," he replied, "Are you talking to me?"

"Yes," replied White.

"Look here, you big so-and-so, you ain't talking to no hired hand when you talk to me," snapped Scharff. "Now if you don't like what I've just said, you've got a six-shooter on your hip. Now just reach for it."

Roark writes that a Western-style duel was avoided only by the intervention of Douglas and Giordano. Leaving the hubris aside, as well as the fact that White already had several notches on his gun, it is interesting to note that for the first time it is revealed that Scharff was in the Houston Police headquarters at the time that Billnitzer was shot, a fact never revealed in the cursory investigation done by the department. This is doubly interesting in light of what happened weeks later.

After being indicted by the grand jury, Foy Melton was on trial in federal district court in nearby Brownsville, Texas. He was charged with unlawful possession and concealment of heroin. At the trial, according to Roark's book, Melton's attorneys revealed two confidential memos written by Scharff to Melton in January 1954. Both memos related to a gang of heroin smugglers working for Earl Voice. The gang was preparing to move a large quantity of heroin from Mexico City through Laredo, San Antonio, and on to Houston by passenger bus. Scharff was acting on a tip from a confidential informer named Rose Cherami through Martin Billnitzer, and he requested that Melton assist the U.S. Customs Service. Melton dispatched two detectives in pursuit: J.T. Conley would travel by bus, with Martin Billnitzer following it by car to Houston. Billnitzer's task was to tail the bus closely enough so as to observe that nothing was thrown out along the route.

Before the bus pulled into Houston, Melton told Scharff that he wanted to let the gang disembark and to follow them "from the bus station in order to catch the delivery of the heroin to Voice." Because it was his case, Scharff overruled this and requested in a written memorandum that Melton arrest the gang at the station. Scharff told Melton to handle the case and make the arrests "personally and very discretely because I am informed that there is a leak from police circles to Earl Voice." When the gang was arrested at the station they had about $400,000 worth of heroin in their possession.

At Melton's trial, Scharff replied to a question about his request to Melton by stating he was referring to ex-detective Sidney Smith who, by this time, had been sentenced to prison for his illicit dealings with Voice. White was suspicious about the origin and veracity of the memos and he and Scharff had yet another near-violent confrontation about this in the courthouse lobby. Foy Melton was subsequently acquitted, and George White was outraged. Scharff had boldly taken credit for first uncovering the Houston drug scandal and in the process helped Melton win acquittal. But Scharff was only able to bask in the limelight briefly. Within weeks, Scharff found himself the target of a federal investigation.

There had always been whispers and rumors about Scharff's high-spending life style. Even laudatory biographer Roark wrote, "And Al Scharff, who lived in an expensive home and drove a Cadillac, supposedly on the modest salary of a customs agent, had some explaining to do." Scharff quickly found himself the subject of a formal internal departmental investigation conducted by a Supervisory Customs Agent from Miami and an Inspector of Internal Revenue out of Dallas. Their 53-page report was sent to Washington, where the decision was made not to bring any charges against Scharff. Not long after, Scharff retired.

White departed Houston the first week of July traveling alone to New York, leaving Vance Newman behind and in charge. Dr. Gottlieb, in Washington, according to White's diary, was becoming "antsy with Bedford St. delays" and White's wife, Albertine (his third), was complaining about George's extended absence.

Meanwhile the federal grand jury in Houston was going full steam ahead, turning its focus on fired detective Sidney Smith. On July 6, the *Houston Press* reported that a mystery witness had been temporarily released from federal prison to testify about Smith. She was identified as Lois Murphy, a 22-year old "former dope addict, shoplifter and informer who worked with Smith." Two years earlier Smith had told a *Press* reporter that Murphy was working with him to "get information on a big narcotics operation" in Houston. The *Press* article went on to state that at least one other "mystery witness had been subpoenaed from federal prison," but it did not name that witness. (According to two letters between Fred Douglas and George White, written in 1956, the witness was Rose Cherami, referred to as "Rose Rodman," who had been arrested for heroin possession and sentenced to two years in prison.) The article also noted that Piney Williams, the district supervisor of the FBN's Houston office, had been suddenly summoned to Washington, D.C. the day before "to explain why he praised the Houston police department for its work with dope while the department is under federal investigation." Williams had outraged White, Douglas, and Giordano when he addressed a convention of the Texas Police Association meeting in Houston, saying, "I have never worked in any city that has given us better cooperation than we have gotten from the Houston Police Department."

In the same speech, Williams called Martin Billnitzer a "loyal officer' whose "work will go on although he is gone himself." T.C. Brennan, the foreman of the grand jury, when asked about the investigation, said, "This has more angles than anyone could imagine. One witness often leads to several others who must be questioned." Later, foreman Brennan would comment, "It's like a kettle full of snakes and when you reach in you just never know what you're going to come up with." The following day, White remarked that his investigators were receiving a "flood of responses" from prisoners who wanted the opportunity to tell what they knew about the narcotics situation in Houston. "Many of them want a free ride," White said, "but we are certainly going to talk to any who seem to have anything that may be of value in this investigation."

In 1978 and 1979, CIA investigators wrote several secret reports that underscored the similarities between Dr. Frank Olson's and Billnitzer's alleged "suicides." Reads one report: "As a result of the allegations against [George] White (re drugs) and of the [Frank] Olson suicide, [George] Gaffney, [a former Federal Bureau of Narcotics officer] suggested we review White's diaries particularly closely during his 1954 sojourn in Houston, Texas. During that TDY he charged virtually the entire Houston Police Force with drug violations. Billnitzer apparently committed suicide (shot himself twice) in his office the morning after being interviewed by White and Giordano ... Gaffney remembered the LSD-provoked 'suicide' by

Olson and after the revelations put two and two together and suggested the possibility that White had used a drug, possibly LSD, on Billnitzer ... White suspected Billnitzer was murdered, The episode created a scandal which escalated to the Secretary of the Treasury, J. Edgar Hoover, and the Attorney General."

In 1996, Sidney Gottlieb told this writer that White's 1954 interrogation of Billnitzer had "generated some serious consternation on my part and that of others" about whether or not "George had used LSD in the [interrogation] process." Said Gottlieb, "When we were sure the drug, or any drug for that matter, had not been used there was a collective sigh of relief at the Agency."

The End of the Road for Rose

Unfortunately, Rose's story only worsens. In late April 1964, Rose was committed to yet another mental institution, this one in Norman, Oklahoma, where reportedly she had been committed at least twice before. No researcher, to date, has explained what Rose was doing in Oklahoma, but neither has anyone yet been able to explain why Lee Harvey Oswald had "1318 1/2 Garfield Ave., Norman, OK" written in his address book. [For discussion see Notes for this chapter.]

According to CIA documents, it turns out, most likely just by coincidence, that the Oklahoma facility where Rose was confined, Central State Mental Hospital, was being covertly used by the CIA's Project MK/ULTRA, the agency's behavior-modification or mind-control program, at the same time that Rose was confined there. CIA psychologist and Oklahoma native John Gittinger, who oversaw the MK/ULTRA contract with Dr. Ewen Cameron in Montreal, Canada, worked with the agency's Technical Services Section and also monitored the CIA's subproject with the Oklahoma facility, at the same time as Rose's last confinement there. Additionally, Dr. Louis Jolyon West, M.D., professor of psychiatry and head of the psychology department at the University of Oklahoma and a CIA consultant, most likely also saw Rose while she was confined in Oklahoma, but this remains to be verified. What is certain and well documented is that Dr. West, also a longtime CIA consultant and contractor, did professionally visit Lee Harvey Oswald's killer Jack Ruby on April 27, 1964 in Dallas, at the same time that Rose was confined. Of course, Dr. West never revealed to Ruby that he had strong ties to the CIA. Not long after Rose was released from the Oklahoma facility, she was back in the Texas, where she met her ultimate fate.

On September 4, 1965, at 2:10 in the morning, a car again hit Rose. This time she did not get up. The accident occurred on Highway 155 near Big Sandy, Texas. The man driving the car, Jerry Don Moore, was on his way home to Tyler, Texas, 20 miles away from Big Sandy. He was admittedly drunk and speeding. He spotted three suitcases in the middle of the road and swerved to avoid hitting them. As he did, he saw a body lying in his path and he swerved again, almost missing Rose.

Almost.

Like everything else in Rose's life, it came down to that again. Moore at the last moment hit the brakes and skidded to a stop about 25 yards past where Rose lay.

Jerry Moore jumped out of his car, ran to Rose, finding she was still breathing, but unconscious. The upper portion of her skull was severely damaged. "I started to get really sick looking at her head," said Moore later. He added, "I don't know exactly whether I hit her or not." Most likely, Moore sobered up quickly. Moore had no idea who the woman he had struck was.

As he knelt over Rose, he saw tire-tread patterns on her face, and very little blood on the road. A car was approaching and he stood and waved his arms, signaling the driver to stop. The car slowed and pulled up alongside Moore and stopped. Inside, Moore later recounted, was "a group of black men and women."

"I need help," Moore told the driver, asking if his companions could pick up the scattered suitcases while he and Moore carefully put Rose on the back seat of Moore's vehicle.

Moore drove as fast as he could to Big Sandy, where he was told there was a doctor in the town of Hawkins, five miles away. There, Moore found a policeman who escorted him to the doctor's home. The roused doctor took one look at Rose and summoned an ambulance to take her to Gladewater Hospital, 20 miles further. At the hospital, Rose was pronounced dead. Her death certificate reads: "DOA," although there is some reason to suspect she actually passed away a few hours after arriving at Gladewater.

According to officer J.A. Andrews of the Texas Highway Patrol, Rose died at the hospital "as a result of head injuries." Officer Andrews investigated Rose's death upon being notified by Jerry Moore after he had taken Rose to the hospital. Andrews would later tell people, "Although I had some doubts as to the authenticity of the information received, due to the fact that the relatives of the victim did not pursue the investigation, I closed it as 'accidental death.'"

Why was officer Andrews suspicious? It seems that a medical examination of Rose at the hospital revealed what could have been a bullet hole in the severely damaged section of her skull. Rose's death certificate reads, "Traumatic head wound with subdural and subarchnoid and petechial hemorrhage to the brain caused by being struck by auto."

British investigative journalist, Chris Mills, writes that Rose's hospital records reveal she had suffered "a deep punctate stellate wound above her right forehead." Mills states, "[T]his type of injury, according to medical textbooks, often occurs as the result of a contact gunshot wound. When a gun is fired touching flesh, the resultant gasses, trapped between a layer of skin and the underlying bone, can cause a bursting, tearing effect on the surrounding tissue leaving a star-shaped (punctate stellate meaning star-shaped punctate) wound."

Most likely, an autopsy would have revealed a gunshot wound, and we are informed that an autopsy was performed on Rose's body, but the report from the procedure, according to hospital officials, is now either missing or was somehow destroyed. (Most states, by law, require an autopsy in the case of any suspicious or sudden death, but they're only required to keep the records for a certain period of time, which varies from state to state.)

Not only was Andrews suspicious, but so too was Jerry Moore. Moore recounted years later that when he stopped for Rose he noticed "a late-model red Chevrolet parked by the side of the road nearby." Moore said that he thought "someone inside the car was watching me before it suddenly drove off."

A brief article on Rose's death appeared on September 9, 1965 in *The Gilmer Mirror*, the local newspaper that served the Big Sandy, Texas area. Its bold headline read: "Woman Lying on Highway Fatally Hurt." According to the article, Rose was living in Duncanville at the time. Duncanville is a small city 15 miles from Dallas. Rose's body had been identified by her sister, who gave Rose's name as Melba Christine Youngblood. Rose's sister told local police that

Rose had telephoned her the night before her death "to say she was going to hitchhike to New Orleans and had a ride with three sailors." The article noted that Rose had "no identification" with her other than "the letters found in her luggage."

Incredibly, the only reason we have any knowledge or facts about Rose Cherami and her remarkable story is that in 1966, New Orleans District Attorney Jim Garrison began his own investigation into the JFK assassination. One of the first tasks Garrison set out to accomplish was to find Rose Cherami as quickly as possible. Toward that end, Garrison requested that State trooper Lt. Francis Fruge be assigned to him for the purpose of finding Rose. Assisting Fruge in his assignment with Garrison was Anne Hundley Dischler, also detailed to Garrison from the Louisiana State Revenue Department and the State Sovereignty Commission.

After learning that Rose was dead, Fruge visited the Silver Slipper lounge and interviewed owner Mac Manual (misidentified in the 1979 Congressional reports on the assassination as "Mr. Mac-Manual.") Manual told Fruge that Rose came into his lounge on November 20, 1963 with two men who were both "pimps" known to be engaged in the "business of hauling prostitutes" from Florida to Louisiana and Texas. During the interview, Fruge showed Manual a stack of photographs and asked if he could identify the two men among them. According to Fruge, Manual selected photos of two Hispanic men, Sergio Arcacha Smith and Emilio Santana. (The 1979 Congressional report on Rose does not specifically name Santana, but instead states what is believed to be his occasional nickname, "Osanto.")

Not "Eyetalians" at all, as Rose had allegedly claimed, they were both Cuban exiles. Manual, who would be shot to death about six years later in Ville Platte, Louisiana, told Fruge that both Santana and Arcacha Smith had stopped a number of times at his establishment and that he knew both men as drug traffickers and white slavers. As it turns out, both men also had extraordinary ties to the CIA, Lee Harvey Oswald, and the assassination. Rose's story suddenly takes on deeper and more complex implications. (This author has deep reservations about Rose's alleged comment concerning "Eyetalians." At that time in her life, she had been exposed to people of all ethnic and racial groups, and it seems quite unlikely that she would have made the alleged "Eyetalians" distinction, unless it was to throw Fruge and others off the trail to identification.)

Garrison investigators knew Arcacha Smith to be a high-profile anti-Castro Cuban refugee, head of the New Orleans Cuban Revolutionary Front in 1961. At that time, he was close with David Ferrie, a commercial pilot, amateur hypnotist, gunrunner, and occasional cancer researcher, who was said to know Lee Harvey Oswald and later to have been a conspirator in the JFK assassination. Ferrie, one of the most bizarre and intriguing figures in the annals of the assassination, was also believed to have strong ties to New Orleans Mafia boss Carlos Marcello. Many researchers also claim Marcello was close to Lee Harvey Oswald through Oswald family ties, a relationship which others say is purely coincidental. Some researchers maintain that young Lee was a runner for Marcello, but evidence of this in virtually nil.

One piece of especially provocative evidence regarding Arcacha Smith is that his New Orleans office was located at 544 Camp Street, the infamous address where, as noted before, former FBI agent and David Ferrie associate Guy Bannister, perhaps coincidentally, maintained his own private investigation office. The same address was also used by Lee Harvey Oswald on the Fair Play for Cuba leaflets that he passed out in New Orleans.

Emilio Galindo Santana was a CIA contract employee. CIA documents reveal that Santana, who sometimes used the alias Jose Juarez, as well as at least four different dates of birth, was recruited by the agency's JM/WAVE program in December 1960 and terminated on October 15, 1963. JM/WAVE was an agency cryptonym and codename for the CIA's Miami-based secret operations to overthrow the Castro government of Cuba. Oddly, in 1967 the CIA altered its files on Santana and stated he had initially been hired in October 1962 and that the December 1960 date was incorrect. The agency also reported Santana had been terminated, partly because of his "untruthful reporting concerning certain aspects of the team [JM/WAVE] operations." FBI files on Santana reveal that he "was alleged to own a Manlicher-Carcano rifle like Oswald's and to have been in Dealy Plaza at time of assassination on orders of ... Sergio Arcacha Smith."

Given that Santana came to the U.S. from Cuba in the early 1960s, it appears somewhat doubtful that he had time to establish himself as a pimp of any consequence in the trade. Arcacha Smith, who arrived in the U.S. about the same time, also falls short of the typical pimp profile.

Arcacha Smith, born in Cuba in 1923, came to the U.S. after Castro's takeover. In Cuba, Arcacha Smith had been a diplomat under the corrupt Batista regime. In that role, he traveled extensively worldwide. In 1954, he served as Cuba's Consul in Bombay, India, a job that brought him into frequent contact with Federal Bureau of Narcotics agents. Curiously, neither the Warren Commission's nor the CIA's files on Arcacha Smith ever mention his diplomatic ties, or the fact that nearly all of his diplomatic posts were to locations where extensive Federal Bureau of Narcotics investigations were conducted. Several CIA documents state that "early background information" on Arcacha Smith is unavailable. However, the agency's Security Research Section has a thick file on him that has never been released for viewing.

In the United States, Arcacha Smith spent time in New York City and then became very active in the anti-Castro movement – along the way being arrested in Venezuela for conspiracy to assassinate that country's president, Ernesto Betancourt. Arcacha Smith departed Venezuela after the U.S. embassy there inexplicably, but quickly, came to his rescue with visas to the U.S.

In New Orleans, Arcacha Smith headed an anti Castro organization, the CIA-created and supported Cuban Revolutionary Front. In this capacity, he acted as an FBI and FBN informant, just as he had from 1954 to 1957 when he had lived and worked as a hotel manager in Venezuela. FBI and CIA documents reveal that Arcacha Smith dealt with David Ferrie on a number of occasions to purchase arms, explosives, aircraft, boats, blood plasma, and pharmaceutical drugs for use against Castro's forces. Despite numerous claims to the contrary, both the CIA and FBI maintained that there was no evidence linking Arcacha Smith to Lee Harvey Oswald, or showing that Arcacha Smith or Santana had anything to do with the JFK assassination. (Lt. Fruge once made the intriguing claim that a map of Dallas' Dealy Plaza sewer lines was discovered in Arcacha Smith's home, but this claim remains to this day unconfirmed.)

In summary, the only real evidence regarding Santana and Arcacha Smith being with Rose – apart from a constant retelling and occasional embellishment of the Fruge/Manual identification story

121

– is Fruge's interview of Manual. This writer could find nothing that connected Smith with Santana, an unlikely combination in this writer's view. In recent years Rose's history and her drug activities, according to some writers, have suggested she was closely connected to Mafia kingpin Carlos Marcello, but evidence of this is just as elusive as it is for some of Fruge's accounts. Examining Rose's saga closely produces the uncomfortable sense that perhaps only Rose herself was actually telling the truth about things, and that many people who drifted in and out of her sphere of influence acted to take advantage of that truth and to twist it in unintended and untruthful ways.

George Hunter White and fellow FBN agents, 1956.
[Photos: Compliments of Douglas Valentine.]

Chapter Three

Adele Edisen's Strange Encounter

But let me tell you, that to approach the stranger
Is to invite the unexpected, release a new force,
Or let the genie out of the bottle.
It is to start a train of events
Beyond your control.

-T.S. Eliot, 1950

Adele Edisen's involvement in the chronology of the JFK assassination is one of the strangest and most perplexing stories out there. Edisen's account calls into question nearly every aspect of the official findings about President Kennedy's murder. In 1994, Edisen testified before the Assassination Records Review Board and to date, nobody has challenged or attacked her credibility. I interviewed Adele on eleven occasions over an eight-month span and found her account thoroughly intriguing and believable. Since her highly strange encounter in 1963, Adele has steeped herself in the facts surrounding JFK's killing and has become an expert, as well as a respectful critic, on many aspects of the case. Adele is the author of numerous widely published medical papers (see Notes section on this chapter for a list) and has taught at Tulane University, Rockefeller University, Louisiana State University School of Medicine, St. Mary's Dominican College, Palo Alto College, and the University of Texas at San Antonio. Today, at the age of 84, she is remarkably active and lucid.

Adele's story begins in April 1963, seven months before the assassination of President Kennedy. Adele was 35 years old at the time, married and raising three children. She had recently decided to return to her work and research in neurophysiology by applying for a National Institutes of Health (NIH) post-doctoral fellowship at Louisiana State University School of Medicine. Before starting a family, Adele, who has a bachelor's degree in liberal arts and a PhD in physiology from the University of Chicago, had also accomplished two years of post-doctoral work at Tulane University

Adele Edisen

School of Medicine, with financial support from the National Institute of Neurological Diseases and Blindness (NINDB) at NIH. One of the main reasons for Adele's return to neurophysiology was her concern about her husband's health. About eight months earlier, Dr. Clayton Byron Edisen, a psychiatrist, had become seriously ill with what was eventually diagnosed as acute cholecystitis, inflammation of the gall bladder. Severe abdominal pain greatly impaired Dr. Edisen's ability to practice psychiatry.

Adele and Clayton had met in 1948 in a philosophy class at the University of Chicago. He had just returned from active duty with the U.S. Army Occupation Forces in Germany. Recalls Adele: "He copied my notes on Aristotle as he had missed part of the class. One thing led to another and we fell in love. We married before he had been admitted to medical school at the University, and we lived in pre-fabricated veterans' housing on campus all through our following years, he in medical school and internship at Billings Hospital, and I in the Department of Physiology. We both finished in 1954."

Adele remembers: "Dr. Ralph Gerard wanted me to stay with him at the University of Illinois Neuropsychiatric Institute where he was now Director of Research, but because the Department of Psychiatry at the Billings Hospital lost its chairman, my husband had to find another place to take his residency training. We both ended up in the Department of Psychiatry and Neurology, chaired by Dr. Robert Heath, at the Tulane University School of Medicine in New Orleans, Louisiana."

Adele recalls that Dr. Heath "was a rather charismatic type person who charmed a lot of people. Women compared him to Gregory Peck, the movie star. He seemed to have a lot of research funds and had been instrumental in getting the annex built onto the old Tulane University Medical School on Tulane Avenue in downtown New Orleans. The Department of Psychiatry and Neurology occupied a number of floors there and, since it was next to Charity

Hospital, psychiatric and neurological patients were housed there at Charity."

Asked what she recalled about Dr. Heath's work, Adele described it:

"Dr. Heath's main research, when I first visited there, involved putting deep electrodes in the brains of schizophrenic patients and recording from them. Dr. Walter Mickel, a neurologist, who was expected to direct my research, but didn't, assisted Heath in recording interpretations. Bill Miller was an EEG technician; Hal Becker, an engineer, aided with the electronic equipment; and Dr. Russ Monroe and Dr. Harold Lief, both psychiatrists, worked with the patients. Dr. [Raeburn C.] Llewellyn, a neurosurgeon, did the brain surgery.

"Sometime not long after I arrived, Dr. Heath became involved with chemicals found in the blood of schizophrenics, and isolated something they called Taraxein*. This project involved injecting this chemical into jailed prison inmates who were not psychotic, and observing the effects. I much later learned from Florence Strohmeyer, a lab technician doing biochemistry in the Department, that she thought LSD was being slipped into some batches of Taraxein, because it only produced effects when the batches were made by one certain lab technician, and she knew that LSD was in the cabinet drawers that this technician oversaw." (See notes for more on Strohmeyer.)

"Of course, I had no idea at the time that much of Dr. Heath's work was being funded by the CIA and perhaps through contracts with the military. I did know that he was receiving some funding from the Commonwealth Fund, which sent representatives to our Department on occasion.... It was many years after I left the Department that I learned Heath had worked with the CIA. Long after 1963."

---

* Taraxein, according to Merriam-Webster's Medical Dictionary, "is a substance originally reported to have been isolated from the blood of schizophrenics and to cause schizophrenic behavior but not chemically characterized or confirmed by later workers attempting to replicate the results." dr. Heath received support from the Commonwealth Fund, a private foundation founded in the 1920s that worked closely with the Rockefeller Foundation, acted as a cut-out for the CIA for about twenty years beginning in the 1950s, after CIA director Allen Dulles approached Fund board members that he knew well. There is also evidence that Dr. Heath received funding from the Human Ecology Fund, another CIA front organization, and that other Agency funds routed to him were passed through two Washington, D.C.-based front groups, the Morwede Company, located on New York Ave. and Chemrophyl Associates, with only a post office box in the city. See Notes for more on taraxein.

Here we should briefly explain Dr. Robert Galbraith Heath's CIA-funded work. Often overlooked by researchers, Heath's work at Tulane for the Agency and the U.S. Army is some of the most egregiously brutal in the area of behavior modification.

Tulane University professors and historians Clarence L. Mohr and Joseph E. Gordon report that at the height of the CIA's interest in mind-control research, "nearly every scientist on the frontiers of brain research found men from secret agencies looking over his shoulders and impinging on the research." Mohr and Gordon are correct about the omnipresent eyes of the intelligence community. They point out, for example, that Dr. Robert Heath gave the keynote address in 1954 at a seminar conducted by the Army Chemical Corps at Edgewood Arsenal, which was attended by a virtual who's-who of biological warfare experts from Fort Detrick and private institutions across the country. The focus of Heath's address was "electrical stimulation and recording in the brain of man."

Dr. Heath at this point in his career was a widely recognized expert on the subject of brain manipulation, especially after several years of human experiments on prisoners at Louisiana State Penitentiary at Angola, nicknamed the "Alcatraz of the South," a facility made notorious to many Americans in 1971 when the American Bar Association described conditions at the prison as "medieval, squalid and horrifying." (Angola was also the setting of the film, *"Dead Man Walking,"* based on a book about one of Angola's death row inmates, played by Sean Penn, and the nun, played by Susan Sarandon, who visits him.)

A major component of Dr. Heath's experiments involved implanting painful electrodes into the brains of human subjects. As Australian psychiatrist Dr. Harry Bailey, one of Heath's associates on the experiments, noted years later, "It was cheaper to use niggers than cats because they were everywhere, and cheap experimental animals." (All of Heath's selected prison subjects were African-American males.)

Dr. Heath's belief in the benefits of electrical stimulation of the brain was so strong that he even believed homosexuality could be "cured" through its use. In one related experiment, Heath placed electrodes on the "pleasure centers" of the brain of a gay prisoner, codenamed "B-19," who "electrically self-stimulated his reward circuitry some 1,500 times." Wrote Heath in a medical journal on the experiment: "During these sessions, B-19 stimulated himself to a point that he was experiencing an almost overwhelming euphoria and elation, and had to be disconnected, despite his vigorous protests."

Heath also conducted a series of electrode stimulation experiments with the objective of bringing women to a high state of arousal and orgasm. Heath touted his work with one female patient by claiming he was able to bring her to "repetitive orgasms." He had no doubts about this, he writes, because "her sensuous appearance and movements offered confirmation."

In 2004, a special report compiled by the Citizens' Commission on Human Rights detailed that beginning in 1950, Drs. Heath, Bailey, and several other physicians operated on more than 60 human subjects, implanting in the skull of a single subject upwards of 125 electrodes that were allowed to stay in the skull for more than four years.

Subsequently, Heath worked with yet another team of physicians, experimenting extensively on prisoners by dosing them with LSD, mescaline and psilocybin. These prisoners, according to Heath's reports, were "housed in a special Tulane University Research Unit at the East Louisiana State Hospital in Jackson – the same location where Rose Cherami was confined and Lee Harvey Oswald had visited. Dr. Heath's experiments at the State Hospital also involved the participation of medical director Dr. Francisco ("Frank") Silva, who co-wrote with Heath a number of medical papers on the human experiments conducted at Tulane University.

There is evidence in CIA documents that some of Heath's drug experiments on human subjects involved hypnosis and that the ultra-secret CIA Office of Security's Unit B participated in these experiments during the years 1956 through at least 1959. (Unit B was initiated as a secret branch of the Agency's IS & O division [precursor to the Office of Security] in the early 1950s to explore and experiment with hypnotism. According to former Agency employees, the most extensive of Unit B's experiments were conducted in Mexico City.)

At Tulane University, meanwhile, the NINDB awarded Adele a two-year Postdoctoral Fellowship, enabling her to pursue her work. As Adele recalled: "I continued my research on monosynaptic excitation and inhibition and was published in two medical journals. My husband began his private practice of psychiatry, and we began our family of three children. I stayed home for several years to take care of our children. When Clayton became ill, I began searching for a position in teaching and research, and through the Department of Physiology at the Louisiana State University School of Medicine, I was able to apply to the NINDB for a third-year level Postdoctoral Fellowship."

While awaiting word on her second fellowship, Adele began conducting research on a volunteer basis at the Department of Physiology. In December 1962, Dr. Sidney Harris, chairman of the department, notified Adele that he had received a telephone call from a Dr. Jose Rivera of the NINDB informing him that Adele had been awarded a one-year fellowship beginning January 1, 1963. Adele's award included a salary and a small equipment grant for use in her on-going research on synaptic inhibition and excitation in the cat spinal cord.

In April 1963, Adele traveled to Atlantic City, New Jersey to attend meetings sponsored by the Federation of American Societies for Experimental Biology (FASEB), an umbrella organization for six biological societies, including the American Physiological Society. The dark-haired, attractive woman arrived at the Atlantic City Convention Hall on April 14. On April 17, as scheduled, she presented her paper describing her ongoing research with the LSU Department of Physiology. Adele's presentation went very well. She lunched with a group of former graduate school classmates, and then wandered through the scientific equipment exhibits at the Convention Hall.

Recounted Adele: "I was really pleased to find that there were also booths of various scientific foundations because I had just read of a new research award to be offered by the National Institutes of Health, which seemed to be perfect for me. I stopped at the NIH booth to ask about it and I was referred to the NINDB booth on the mezzanine floor above. I was excited to learn that NINDB had their own booth and went to the mezzanine right away." At the NINDB booth, Adele found that it was staffed by a man whose name tag read, "Dr. Jose A. Rivera," the man who had called to announce her fellowship. "He was quite short," Adele recalled, "at least an inch shorter than I am, and I'm 5 feet 4 inches tall. He was dressed in a brown suit. The buttoned jacket was tight because he was obese. He had intense dark brown eyes, which were magnified by the glasses he wore. His hair was jet black, thinning, and had some gray in it. His skin was noticeably dark and his face was pockmarked, as if from a bad case of past acne."

When Adele arrived at the booth, Rivera was speaking with someone else. While Adele waited for Rivera to be free, he glanced at her name tag, kindly acknowledged her presence and extended a roll of Life Savers to her, inviting her to take one. Adele took one from the pack, handed it back, and sat down to wait in a vacant chair off to the side of the booth.

With the presentation behind her, it felt good to simply relax, she remembered. A few days before traveling to Atlantic City, Adele had contracted what she recalled as "a bad upper respiratory infection" and had been running a slight fever. "Before I departed for the meetings, my physician prescribed an antibiotic, oxacillin, a semi-synthetic penicillin, to take for about ten days. By the time my presentation was over I was feeling better."

When Rivera finished his conversation, he turned his undivided attention to Adele. He connected her name right away to the call to Dr. Harris months earlier about her fellowship. Rivera told Adele he was delighted to finally meet her and that he had high expectations for her work under the NINDB award.

"I've heard wonderful things about your research," he told Adele, in what she later recalled as a "guttural voice, with a very heavy Hispanic accent." Rivera flattered Adele with his remarks, yet she felt uneasy about the way Rivera intently stared at her.

"His dark eyes held mine in an odd and challenging way," she recalled. "His face was also odd in the way that the sides seemed mismatched. His right side looked as if he had had Bell's palsy with a slightly drooping mouth."

Adele asked about the new NIH research award she had heard about, and any other support NIH might offer. "Rivera said he thought there were additional programs, but he didn't have any printed information or brochures with him. He promised to mail those available to me in New Orleans."

Dr. Jose A. Rivera

Rivera again handed Adele the Life Saver pack and she took another, and he suggested they walk downstairs to get a Coca Cola. Downstairs, the two sat drinking soda and talking. Years later, Adele recalled their conversation in detail:

"He said he would help me continue with my research. He was supportive. He spoke fondly about the time he had spent in New Orleans working at Loyola University, where he taught chemistry or biochemistry. It turned out we had mutual friends and acquaintances in New Orleans. He knew Dr. Fred Brazda, chairman of the Biochemistry Department at the LSU School of Medicine. I think he mentioned people that worked under Robert Heath. He also mentioned a few people and doctors at Ochsner Hospital and the new clinic opening there."

Rivera had asked Adele about her upbringing and Adele explained that she was born in New York City, the daughter of immigrants from Finland. Her birth name was Adele Elvira Uskali Edisen. Adele's father, before coming to America in 1917, had been a soldier in Finland's war for independence from Russia. Captured and imprisoned, he escaped and made his way to New York. There he soon met his future wife, a professional singer who had also emigrated from Finland. Adele's father became a merchant seaman and spoke several languages, including Russian and Spanish.

"Rivera continued to stare at me in his odd way," Adele remembered. "I kept talking, telling him things because he made me so uncomfortable. I told him that I planned to visit the NIH and NINDB in Bethesda after going by train to Philadelphia for the weekend to see friends there. He told me to call him as soon as I got to Washington, D.C., and that he would have his secretary make motel reservations for me. He then told me that on my return, I would have to come to his home for dinner and meet his wife and family. I thought his invite was most gracious and I accepted, telling him I'd be delighted to be his guest."

When Adele arrived in Washington, D.C. on Monday, April 22, seven months before Kennedy's assassination, she telephoned Rivera at his NINDB office. Rivera gave Adele the address of a Bethesda motel, the Kenwood Country Club Motel, where his secretary had booked a room for Adele. He explained that his wife, who was a nurse, had unexpectedly been called to work that night at the hospital where she was employed, but that he would pick Adele up that evening at the motel and they would go to a restaurant for dinner.

Rivera arrived at the motel around 7:00 P.M. and drove Adele to a well-known Washington, D.C. restaurant, Blackie's House of Beef, on the edge of Georgetown. On the way, Rivera again offered

Adele a Life Saver, which she accepted. While waiting for their table at Blackie's, Adele recalled, Rivera began telling her about his recent travels to Dallas, Texas.

"He said if I ever went to Dallas I should go to a nice nightclub called the Carousel Club," says Adele. "I told him I'd be sure to go there, and then he asked if I knew Lee Oswald."

"Who?" Adele asked.

"Lee Oswald," Rivera said.

"No, I don't know him," Adele answered, thinking of a boy she had known in high school named Fred Oswald.

"Oh, you really should get to know him," Rivera said, explaining that Oswald had lived in the Soviet Union, was married to a Russian woman and they had a child together. The Oswalds were planning to move to New Orleans soon, Rivera had said. Adele made a mental note of the name Lee Harvey Oswald, assuming he was an associate of Rivera's or a fellow medical researcher. Once seated for dinner, Adele remembered, their conversation turned to work-related subjects. "I was mostly talking about my research and plans for research, just babbling on about that. At some point, I asked him what he was interested in, what research he did. It was then that I learned that he was a bacteriologist. I had not known that. Later I found out he had been in the Army, but he didn't mention it. I asked what interested him in bacteriological work and he said hemorrhagic fevers. That, I remember. I knew very little, if anything, about hemorrhagic fevers in 1963. It was only later that we learned about Ebola, Lassa, and Marburg fevers which were hemorrhagic fevers. He didn't say anything to me about being involved in biochemical warfare research with the Army. He didn't mention Fort Detrick or anything about the Army."

After they had finished dinner and were about to leave the restaurant, Adele recalled, "Rivera spoke about a recent shooting at General Edwin Walker in Dallas. Then he said, 'You know, they think Oswald did it.'"

They think Oswald did it.

Adele says she had no idea what to think when Rivera said this. *The man named Lee Oswald – the person whom Rivera said she should go out of her way to meet – had shot at a general?*

"I didn't know if he was joking or what," recounts Adele. "I didn't ask. I kept quiet, not knowing what to say."

Adele recalled that she felt strange, almost otherworldly, walking out of the restaurant, asking herself who really was this peculiar man beside her, talking to her about so many odd things.

Rivera drove Adele back to her motel in Bethesda. The two made small talk along the way and Rivera commented that he had earlier heard on the radio that there was going to be a very severe rainstorm that night in the area. Adele recalls him telling her, "You'll probably be kept awake because of the storm and the other partying guests." Adele was not sure what he meant about the other guests, but had noted when she checked in that the motel was quite busy.

That night, Adele hardly slept at all. Indeed, there was a driving rainstorm, as Rivera had predicted. Adele's room was next to the motel's swimming pool and she listened to the hard rain striking the pool's surface. She fell asleep for about two hours before getting up with what she describes as a "distinct déjà vu feeling."

"Everything I was doing, I had done before, like checking out of the motel, getting into the taxi to go to NIH, watching the scenery and the buildings passing by as I rode along. That was very strange for me, along with the fact that before I got into the taxi I noticed that the ground outside was completely dry. Even the grass, short and tall, and shrubbery and furniture around the pool, were completely dry, as if there had been no rain at all."

That morning, Tuesday, April 23, 1963, Adele checked out of the motel because it had been completely booked except for the one-night she stayed there. Rivera had told her the day before that his secretary would arrange separate accommodations for Adele for her second night. Adele took a taxi to the NIH complex, where she spent the morning meeting with Dr. Karl Frank, a neurophysiologist who had attended the University of Chicago and studied under Dr. Ralph Gerard, along with Adele. Dr. Frank gave Adele a guided tour of his laboratory and told her of his work developing a way of measuring membrane electrical resistance, which excited Adele because it was closely related to her own research. Adele then had lunch with several former Chicago classmates.

Later that afternoon, Rivera met with Adele and drove her to the Victorian-style Hotel Raleigh on Pennsylvania Avenue in Washington, D.C. (The Hotel Raleigh was used often by the CIA because of the ease with which Agency security operatives could wire rooms there for covert eavesdropping and monitoring, as well as perform black bag jobs within. The hotel was razed in 1964 for redevelopment.) Adele went to her room to freshen up while Rivera waited for her in the hotel's expansive main lobby. They were to go to Rivera's home for dinner, but when Adele came back downstairs, Rivera explained that his wife had again been called in to work, so they would again go to a restaurant for dinner.

As the couple approached the hotel's main doors to the street, Adele recalled, "A tall, sharp-faced man called out to Rivera, addressing him as 'Colonel.' Rivera excused himself for a moment and walked over to the man. They stood a few feet away speaking to one another for a few minutes. I was able to catch some of the gist of the conversation and it seemed to be about their times together in the Army and work with telemetry and telephoto lenses."

Upon concluding this conversation, Rivera told Adele that they would have dinner at the Key Bridge Marriott Hotel on Lee Highway in Arlington, Virginia, just across the historic Key Bridge connecting Georgetown and Virginia. In his car, Rivera explained to Adele that when he was in the Army – the first time he had mentioned his military service to her – he had been involved in "photographing demonstrators with telephoto cameras from rooftops." He said, "We'd identify individual demonstrators and put their names in files. We've started this on the West Coast."

Adele recollected that just as she began to wonder how this covert surveillance work related to Rivera's NINDB duties, he mentioned having "another office on the hill," and one in "Foggy Bottom." Unfamiliar to Adele at the time, "Foggy Bottom" is the term for that area of the District of Columbia where the U.S. State Department is located, as well as George Washington University and Hospital.

After this, Rivera extended his ever-present roll of Life Savers to Adele, saying, "Here, take one; please help yourself." Adele recalled that she took only one.

Before driving to the Marriott, Rivera gave Adele a windshield tour of a number of nearby sites, including the Library of Congress, the Capitol building, the cherry blossoms along the Potomac River, the Armed Forces Institute of Pathology, and the White House.

"We passed the White House a number of times," Adele said. "The first time we approached it, he asked, 'I wonder what Jackie will do when her husband dies?'"

The question shocked Adele. "What?" she had blurted, thinking she may have misheard Rivera.

"Oh, no," he said, "I meant the baby. She might lose the baby."

Adele was still perplexed and had no idea what Rivera was talking about. She was also becoming very nervous and frightened. "This was the first time, the first inkling I had that he might be implying something sinister concerning President Kennedy."

During the strange ride through Washington with Rivera that night, Adele became increasingly nervous. "Every time we passed the White House, which was three times, Rivera would ask me if I saw Caroline on her pony Macaroni, and say other silly, crazy things like that. I was beginning to think that he was insane. For a minute or so I thought about somehow getting out of his car."

Adele added, "Not everything he said was nonsensical or bizarre. He was very critical of President Kennedy's position on civil rights. He made some really disparaging remarks about black people and the civil rights movement." Adele also recalls that Rivera made several remarks about NIH. "He referred to it as 'the Reservation' because there were so many 'chiefs' and no 'Indians.' He repeated this several times. Then out of the blue he asked me if I knew John Abt." (John Abt was the attorney Oswald asked for shortly after the assassination of JFK.)

"John who?" she asked.

"Abt. John Abt."

"No," Adele replied. "I don't know who he is."

Rivera then explained who Abt was. "He said Abt was a New York lawyer who defended communists against the Smith-McCarran Act. This was a law that forbade someone from being a member of the Communist Party, he said. He explained all of this to me as we rode along in his car."

Eventually, Rivera drove Adele to the Marriott in Arlington where they had dinner. Towards the end of the meal, Rivera asked Adele if she would mind doing him a favor when she got back to New Orleans. Adele agreed, and he said, "Well, it's detailed so you should write it down."

Adele took a small memo book and pencil from her purse. "Rivera asked me to call Winston de Monsabert, with whom he had worked at Loyola, and to tell him to call Rivera when he was leaving New Orleans." Adele wrote this down. (See Notes for more on de Monsabert.)

Rivera then began to talk about Dallas and how much he enjoyed the city. Adele vividly remembered that he pointed toward her memo book, and stared very intently at her, saying, "Pretend you're in a phone booth and you're very, very nervous and upset. Your handwriting is very shaky. Now write down this telephone number: 899-4244."

Adele says she wrote the number down and was surprised to see that her hand was shaking.

At that moment, Adele recalls, "Rivera said, 'Write down this name: Lee Harvey Oswald. Tell him to kill the chief.'"

Adele obeyed. "I wrote the name Lee Harvey Oswald and then under it wrote in quotation marks: 'kill the chief.' When he saw me writing down those three words, he said, 'No, no. Don't write that down. You will remember it when you get to New Orleans. We're playing a little joke on him.'"

Adele recalls looking at the name Lee Harvey Oswald and thinking that perhaps Oswald was an African American "because I knew in New Orleans African Americans often used three names, inclusive of their middle names. I thought the word 'chief' might have had something to do with Rivera's earlier joke about NIH. I thought that maybe Oswald was an NIH scientist married to a Russian scientist, the woman Rivera had said he married. I was trying to make sense out of everything he was saying."

Adele was becoming quite uncomfortable. She picked up her memo book and tore out the page she had written on, putting it in her purse. As she did this, Rivera said, "I'll show you where it will happen."

"Where what will happen?" she asked.

Rivera did not answer, "but he took my memo book and with a pen he took from his pocket he drew a square, and then a double line on top and on the right-hand side of the square. He said something like 'these are the windows and this is on the fifth floor,' and then he drew a little circle and said 'there will be some men up there.' Then he said, 'I'll show you where it will happen.'"

"Where *what* will happen?" Adele asked. "What are you trying to tell me?"

Adele was becoming increasingly alarmed with Rivera's words, as well as his appearance. She says, "He looked like he was having some sort of seizure, his face was puffy and red, and he was very excited."

Rivera did not respond to Adele's questions, but instead went on talking in bursts. She recalled him saying, "Oswald is not what he seems ... we're going to send him to the library to read about great assassinations in history ... after it's over, he will call Abt to defend him ... after it happens, the President's best friend will commit suicide ...the director of the International Trade Mart is involved in this ... it will happen after the Shriners' Circus comes to New Orleans.... After it's over, the men will be out of the country, but someone will kill Oswald, maybe his best friend... remember, the first time it happens won't be real." (See this chapter's Notes for more on Rivera's statement about the "President's best friend" committing suicide.)

Adele told Rivera she wanted to leave. Rivera walked with her out of the restaurant toward the elevators. Adele planned to hail a taxi as soon as she was outside, but there were none in sight. When she went to get into Rivera's car, Adele found that his passenger side door would not open from the outside; Rivera got into the car on the driver's side and opened the door from inside.

She recalls, "After I got into his car, I leaned over to shut the open door, and I heard him rustling through my purse, presumably looking for the notebook page. That made me quite angry, and I yanked my purse away from him. I had no idea then, of course, how important that page was, but I simply did not want him going through my purse. I was offended and frightened at once."

Adele said that Rivera told her, "Look, I really don't want to have to hurt you."

"Why in God's name would you want to hurt me?" Adele asked.

"If you go to anyone about this you'll be very sorry."

"I don't know what you're talking about. 'This' what?" Adele asked.

"The authorities, the FBI, or anyone. Don't go to anyone or we will hurt you. We will be watching you."

By this time, Rivera was driving Adele back to her hotel in Washington, D.C. Adele told Rivera, "I don't want any trouble with you or anyone. I really don't understand what this is all about."

"Don't worry," said Rivera. "Just don't go to anyone if you know what's good for you."

Adele continued, "We got back to the Hotel Raleigh and I thanked him for dinner and apologized for any misunderstanding. He told me that he would pick me up in the morning as planned and to get a good night's sleep. I got up to my room and again I couldn't sleep at all. By morning I was exhausted and confused and scared."

Said Adele: "I kept thinking about the things Rivera had said to me. And his threats. My hands were shaking and I was having trouble focusing my eyesight. I felt flushed.... I had no idea what was going on. When I looked at the wallpaper and the carpet in my room it looked like it was undulating.... The more I thought, the angrier I became. I looked up Rivera's home telephone number and called him even though it was late. A woman answered, his wife I assumed. I asked to speak with him, and when he came to the phone, I asked him what was going on and what were all the things he had talked about. He said that I was upset and that he should not have left me alone. He said that he should have stayed with me, which really scared me. I said that I wanted to talk with him the next morning, as he had promised to drive me to the laboratory of Dr. Ichiji Tasaki. I had an appointment with Tasaki. I really didn't want to see Rivera again, but I had to try to bring things to some sort of closure, to try to understand what was really going on." (See Notes for more on Dr. Ichiji Tasaki. Adele eventually became convinced that Rivera had dosed her with LSD or possibly another similar mind altering drug.)

The next morning, Wednesday, April 24, 1963, Adele took a taxi to NIH, where she met Rivera in a conference room in the NINDB building. "I was really mad at this point," Adele says. "I worked myself up to it, to being able to confront him. I asked him about what he had said and I threatened to go to the FBI."

Says Adele: "I wanted to see what he would do and he threatened me again. He said if I went to anyone, the FBI or anyone else, I would be very, very sorry."

"Don't be stupid about this," Rivera warned Adele. "We just played a little joke on you."

Adele went to her meeting with Dr. Tasaki and Rivera waited to drive her back to the hotel, where she was to check out around noon.

On the way back to the hotel, Adele recalls, Rivera made small talk and acted as if nothing out of the ordinary had happened between them. He suggested that he and Adele have lunch since Adele still had a few hours before her flight left for New Orleans.

Adele recounts, "At lunch he showed me a photograph of his wife and daughter from his wallet, and I spoke of my future research plans, asking him to be sure to send the application for the five-year research award, which he had promised to do."

Adele says that things briefly turned strange and frightening once more, "when Rivera talked about Jackie on Air Force One and about the plane catching on fire. He asked me, 'What would Jackie do?' And then he said, 'What would you do?' He looked at my stunned face, and said, 'We will be watching you, Adele. We will know what you are doing.'"

After lunch, Rivera walked Adele back to the hotel to say good bye, but not before he asked, "Adele, what did you do with the page you wrote on from the notepad last night?"

"I threw it away," Adele lied.

Rivera looked at her and said, "You're sure?"

"Yes," she lied again.

"Forget what happened here," said Rivera.

About a week after Adele returned to New Orleans, she thought to call the telephone number for Lee Harvey Oswald that Rivera had given her. However, Adele told the author, "My husband said, 'don't ever call that number.' I had told him about the strange happenings with Rivera, and he said it was all too bizarre to get involved in and that I was lucky to be okay. I told him that I thought I should go to the FBI or Secret Service, and he said, 'No, we'll end up getting investigated ourselves and we will never hear the end of it.' However, Clayton did try to look into it himself. He called people about Rivera, and he consulted a couple of attorneys, one in Chicago and another in New Orleans. Like he had predicted, everyone felt the story was bizarre."

Adele continued: "I called the phone number Rivera had given me for Oswald. It was around the first few days of May [1963]. A man answered who identified himself as Jesse Garner. I asked for Lee Harvey Oswald and he said there was nobody there by that name. I thanked him and hung up."

For about a week Adele tried to fathom why Rivera had given her a number and name that amounted to a dead end. She wondered if perhaps she had dialed the wrong number. About a week after her first attempt, Adele called the number once more. The same man answered again, but when she asked for Lee Harvey Oswald, he said, 'Oh, they've just arrived. Lee isn't here right now, but Mrs. Oswald is. Would you like to speak with her?'

Adele said she would. "She answers, it takes time for her to come to the phone, and she spoke Russian, which surprised me even though Rivera had told me she was Russian. I spoke to her in English, even though I knew a little Russian from what my father had taught me as a child. I asked her if it would be okay to call back in a few days to speak to her husband, that I wanted to ask him about someone who had asked me to call him. She said, 'Da', and I thanked her. And I did call back a few days later."

Adele said she called the Oswald number again at mid-day about five days later, and again Jesse Garner answered. Adele asked for Lee Harvey Oswald, and Garner told her to hold on and he would go and get him. When Oswald came on the line, Adele said, she introduced herself and asked him if he knew Dr. Jose Rivera, a research scientist at NIH in Bethesda, Maryland.

"No, I'm sorry, I don't know him," replied Oswald.

"Well, that's odd," Adele said, "because he seems to know you and your wife."

Adele said Oswald did not respond right away, so she apologized for asking him such a seemingly strange question, and then she asked him, "Would you mind telling me where your phone is located?"

Oswald gave Adele Garner's street address, 4909 Magazine Street. (Adele says she made her call to Oswald no later than May 20, 1963. According to the Warren Commission and the FBI, no government authority at this time knew the Oswalds had moved to Magazine Street.)

Adele then thanked Oswald for speaking with her and apologized for having bothered him. She also recalled that when she hung up she wondered how Rivera knew that Oswald, who she still assumed was a research scientist, would be moving to Magazine Street weeks before he actually did. She guessed that, most likely, the move had been planned well in advance, yet she also wondered why the Oswalds had selected "a rather run down section of the city" to live in.

"Needless to say," says Adele, "I didn't deliver Rivera's message to 'kill the chief' to Oswald."

As seasoned and respected JFK researcher William E. Kelly Jr. has astutely pointed out, "What is really strange is that Dr. Jose Rivera [while in Washington, D.C. with Adele] knew Oswald's New Orleans phone number on Tuesday, April 23, 1963, before Oswald himself knew where he was moving to in New Orleans."

A short while after this, Adele read a news account about the Secret Service that made her think that she should call them to report her experience with Rivera. She told Clayton she was going to make the call, and he strenuously argued against it. "We'll look like crazy people," he told her. "People will think we are out of our minds."

Adele made the call anyway. She recalls only that the date of her call was "a few days after July 4, 1963." She asked for an appointment in person at the local Secret Service office to speak to an official about what she knew. She recalled later: "A man identified himself as Special Agent J. Calvin Rice. I explained to him that I wanted to come down to his office and speak to the Secret Service about an experience I had had in April when I met a man in Washington, D.C. who said some very strange things about the President that I felt they should know about. Special Agent Rice said that would be fine and he gave me directions to his office." Adele was anxious and ambivalent. "I was going to go down the next day, but I got cold feet. I thought Clayton would get angry, and I was very scared. I had the note with Lee Harvey Oswald's name on it, and the words 'kill the chief.' Those words made me especially nervous."

The next day Adele phoned Special Agent Rice again. "I called yesterday and I wanted to come down to talk with you, but I can't do that right now."

Agent Rice replied, "Fine, we'll be here anytime you decide to come in." (Interestingly, J. Calvin Rice, an FBI agent who shared offices with the Secret Service in New Orleans, transferred to the FBI's Dallas, Texas office shortly after Adele's call and before the assassination of JFK.)

About two months later, in August 1963, Adele and her husband Clayton were watching television, she told this author, when they saw a local CBS evening news account about a man named "Leon Oswald" who had been handing out Fair Play for Cuba Committee leaflets in front of the International Trade Mart. Adele wondered if the leafleting man, shown on the account, could be the same Oswald that she had called. However, she soon forgot about it.

A few days after Labor Day, September 1963, while at work, Adele was surprised to briefly spot Dr. Jose Rivera coming out of an elevator at LSU Medical School. Adele stood in the hallway staring at him, not knowing what to do for a moment. Adele says, "When he looked up and saw me staring at him, he did a double take and literally tripped backwards, looking like he had seen a ghost."

Adele walked away briskly and called her husband, asking what he thought she should do. Clayton told her to stay calm and to avoid Rivera without being obvious or rude. Clayton then called a friend whom he asked to keep an eye out for Adele's safety. Adele did not see Rivera again.

On the day President Kennedy was killed, Adele had gone to a meeting with one of her children's teachers before reaching her office, and she had not heard any news. "I went to work and got there about a half hour past noon. When I walked into my section, everyone was listening to the radio. President Kennedy had just been shot while riding through the streets of Dallas. We also learned that Governor Connally had been shot, and he and the President were being taken to Parkland Hospital. Listening to the radio reports was otherworldly. It was hard to believe. When I learned later that day that the man who had shot Kennedy was Lee Harvey Oswald, I was shocked. I felt like I had been kicked in the stomach, my knees buckled. I thought about Rivera and all the strange things he had said to me."

Kill the chief. Tell him to kill the chief.

Adele went over and over the conversations with Rivera. "The more I thought, the more I felt that I was involved in all that had happened. I had thought that Rivera was most likely a cruel practical joker or worse, a psychotic, but not a conspirator in the murder of the President of the United States."

We are playing a little joke on Oswald.

On November 24, the Sunday after the assassination, Adele took a chance and called Special Agent Rice again at his office number. He answered the phone and Adele told him she had some information related to the assassination that he needed to hear right away. Rice told her to go right away to the Federal Building at 600 South Street in downtown New Orleans, where he would meet her in the main lobby. When Adele arrived, Rice was waiting and he took her to an office on the fifth floor. On the way to his office, Rice stunned Adele by informing her that Oswald had moments before been shot in Dallas.

In his office, Special Agent Rice identified himself this time as Secret Service Agent John W. Rice, in charge of the Secret Service's New Orleans office. He asked Adele to sit down.

Adele noted later, "Rice was a thin and short man, not much taller than I am. Later, I learned that FBI agent J. Calvin Rice was over 6 feet tall and quite husky."

Adele continued, "After I sat down, agent Rice introduced me to a tall, heavy set, balding man with wire-rimmed eyeglasses. This was FBI Special Agent Oren Bartlett. He was FBI liaison with the Secret Service. There was no one else in the office with us that I saw. They interviewed me for about four hours, and I think the interview was tape-recorded. Agent Rice sat at his desk and I sat to his right, and FBI agent Bartlett stayed standing most of the time. Several times, agent Rice got up and went behind a partition to check something, I think. I assumed this was a tape recorder."

Adele provided the two agents detailed background on herself, and then told them how she had come to meet Dr. Jose Rivera in Atlantic City, and about her two days in Bethesda and Washington, D.C. She showed the agents her airline tickets, hotel receipts, and the notes she had kept, including the notebook page with Lee Harvey Oswald's name on it.

"When I showed them all of this," Adele says, "their questions became more intense, and they asked me more about Rivera, his work at NIH, and his physical description. I answered all of their questions and gave them Rivera's home and office telephone numbers."

Adele recalls, "The FBI man, Oren Bartlett, went behind the partition in the office and called someone from a phone back there. I could hear him passing information on to someone about Rivera. I assumed they were going to bring Rivera in for questioning somewhere."

When Bartlett came back from behind the partition, he asked Adele if he and Rice could have the page from my notebook. Adele handed it over, realizing that her interview was over at this point.

However, as Special Agent Rice walked her toward the office door, he asked her to call if she remembered anything else she had not told them. Rice also requested that she not speak to anyone else about Rivera or the incidents in Bethesda and Washington, D.C.

"I understood this to be for my own protection as well as for their investigation," Adele recalled. She fully expected that she would soon hear news reports concerning the apprehension or questioning of Dr. Rivera. After a few days of hearing nothing, Adele called Rice and told him she was concerned about her safety. Adele says agent Rice told her, "Don't worry about anything. That man can't hurt you." Adele says that she took this to mean that either Rivera "had been apprehended or was being held for questioning." Adele never spoke again with agents Rice or Bartlett, and neither man ever contacted her.

Not long after Adele returned home from the meeting, and while she was still under the impression that Rivera was perhaps being held by the FBI or Secret Service, she received a form letter bearing Rivera's signature and acknowledging receipt of her routinely filed work-progress reports. The report had been requested by another official at NINDB who routinely signed them, and Adele was frightened and confused to see Rivera's signature.

The more she thought about the letter the more frightened she became. Within days, she says, "I became terrified. I assumed that the Secret Service and FBI agents did not believe me, although they had asked me to call them if I remembered anything else. They also had told me not to speak to anyone about my being there with them, as a protection for myself. I expected to be called before the Warren Commission, but I never was."

Adele recounted, "My husband suggested that I consult Dr. Milton Erickson, a widely known and respected medical hypnotist, to confirm my experiences and memories. I tried to make contact with Erickson several times, but each time he had some medical emergency of his own and I was never able to see him. I suffered through fearful times, depressions and anxieties. For many years I did not speak of these things and would not read anything about the assassination." (Adele, of course, had no idea that Dr. Erickson was covertly consulting with the CIA through the auspices of Project Artichoke, ZR/ALERT and Unit B, and other Agency programs. See the chapter 7 on Dale E. Basye.)

Adele continued to be surprised and perplexed that no one ever followed up on her November 1963 interview, and that she was never contacted by any investigators from the subsequent Warren Commission established by President Lyndon B. Johnson to investigate the assassination of JFK. After the Commission released its findings in 26 thick volumes, Adele was puzzled and disappointed to find nothing in it about Dr. Rivera. She contacted a New Orleans attorney, Jack Peebles, who filed a Freedom of Information Act request with the government for any files and documents related to Rivera and Adele, but the request produced nothing.

In 1975, after the U.S. Senate committee (known as the Church Committee) was formed and had begun its investigation into illegal intelligence community activities, Adele wrote to Sen. Frank Church about her experience. She was informed that the matter was "outside the purview of the committee's work."

On Adele's behalf, Attorney Peebles sent a letter dated December 13, 1976 to U.S. Rep. Thomas Downing of the Church Committee. The letter stated that Rivera, who Adele now believed might have been connected to covert research activities for the CIA, might have attempted to drug or hypnotize her in 1963. In his letter, Peebles made it clear that Adele did not want publicity, or her name used by the Church Committee, unless investigators were able to verify her statements.

Attorney Peebles wrote a second letter on May 2, 1977 to U.S. Congressman Louis Stokes, Chairman of the House Select Committee on Assassinations. On December 23, 1978, Adele wrote to U.S. Rep. Richardson Preyer asking for a formal response to one of Peebles letters. No response was received from anyone. Another letter by Peebles to Sen. Daniel Inouye brought a response of interest in her case, but Inouye's staff aide was reluctant to subpoena Rivera, and nothing further happened.

Adele was becoming increasingly concerned by the lack of follow-up of any kind with respect to her interview with agents Rice and Bartlett. "If my information was not considered to be relevant and pertinent, there should be some record of the fact that the interview took place. The fact that there is no record is odd and suspicious. I know what I know and what happened to me, and I think others have a right to know also."

In 1991, Adele wrote an account of her meetings and conversations with Rivera, and published it in the November 1999 issue of

The Third Decade, an obscure journal devoted to the JFK assassination. She wrote the article under the pseudonym K.S. Turner because she did not want to draw any attention to herself. The article drew a large amount of attention and interest among the publication's small readership, but attracted no mainstream media attention.

In the article Adele wrote, "Whatever forces were operating to assassinate President Kennedy may never be revealed, but this should not deter anyone from seeking the truth. If our system of government, its laws, and our civil rights are to survive, we need to know the truth, no matter how convoluted and strange it may be."

On November 18, 1994, Adele Edisen testified before an Assassination Records Review Board hearing held in Dallas, Texas. The Board heard the basics of Adele's strange encounter, but oddly, perhaps due to a very tight schedule, seemed to give it short shrift and had very few questions for her. The Assassination Records Review Board was created as a result of an act passed by the U.S. Congress in 1992. The act mandated the gathering and release of all U.S. Government records related to JFK's assassination. Many people claim that Congress passed the act because of a public outcry about the assassination after watching the 1991 Oliver Stone film *JFK*, which portrayed theories about the assassination that had not been thoroughly explored, or had been ignored, by the Warren Commission.

Who Was Dr. Jose Albert Rivera?

Jose Albert Rivera passed away on August 16, 1989. He had been hospitalized with pancreatic cancer at the Naval Medicine Center in Bethesda, Maryland several weeks earlier. He was 78 years old. According to his obituary, he had retired sixteen years earlier, in 1973, from his job as a "medical research analyst" at NIH's Institute of Neurological Diseases and Blindness, where he had worked full-time after retiring from the U.S. Army in 1965. This, of course, means that Rivera was an active duty military officer in 1963 when he encountered Adele Edisen. His military records reveal that in 1958 he was assigned "as an Army pathologist" to the Reserve Training Center in Washington, D.C., where he remained until his retirement in 1965.

There is confusion about when and where Jose Rivera was born. Some of his military records state he was born in Lima, Peru in 1911. Others give the year as 1905 or 1908 and state that he was born in Puerto Rico. Several people who knew Rivera well, but who declined to speak on the record for this book, say he was born and raised in Peru and came to the United States in 1930 to study at Johns Hopkins University in Baltimore. There, according to his military records, he earned an undergraduate degree, and then went on to earn his MD in 1939 from Georgetown University. He did his medical internship at Providence Hospital in Washington, D.C. (Here it should be noted that this author was unable to verify that Rivera earned an MD at Georgetown or performed an internship anywhere. Several people who knew Rivera personally maintained that he only had an advanced degree in chemistry.) Rivera's military records show that following his internship, he joined the war effort in 1942 as a commissioned first lieutenant in the Army Medical Corps. First stationed at Walter Reed Army Hospital, in 1944 he became "acting chief of pathology" at Halloran General Army Hospital on Staten Island, New York, a medical facility that also held a number of German POWs. Subsequently, Rivera was promoted to the rank of captain, served in Italy and France, and then in Germany with the 198th Army Hospital in Berlin.

In Berlin, the U.S. Army Chemical Corps recruited Rivera after he had ably assisted a Camp Detrick (today Fort Detrick) team with interviews of captured Nazi scientists who were in the pipeline of Project Paperclip – headed for the United States to work for the American government and private industries. Rivera returned to the States after the war and worked at Camp Detrick in Frederick, Maryland, where researchers were just beginning to contribute their chemical warfare expertise to enable the US to develop biological weapons.

It is highly likely that Rivera encountered Dr. Frank Olson at Camp Detrick, because Rivera worked there for two years under the supervision of Dr. Carl Lamanna. Several former Detrick scientists are on record as stating that Olson was friends with Lamanna. During the years 1946-48, according to declassified Army documents, Dr. Lamanna was Detrick's leading expert on biological warfare research with botulism, a rare but lethal illness caused by Clostridium botulinum bacteria. Botulinum toxin has been used in warfare at least since the 1930s, when the Japanese intentionally fed their POWs C botulinum cultures. In the early 1990s and later, UN inspection teams claimed that Iraq had missiles and bombs filled with the toxin, but this has never been verified. In the 1960s and

1970s, the CIA used botulinum toxins produced at Fort Detrick for assassination objectives. In September 1960, CIA official Dr. Sidney Gottlieb hand-carried, on a commercial flight to the Congo, a tube of botulinum laced toothpaste to be used by Jean Pierre Lafitte (Frank Olson's assassin) for the assassination of Patrice Lumumba, then-Prime Minister of the Congo.

Indeed, Capt. Rivera went on to work with Lamanna on several highly classified projects at locations other than Detrick, including the Naval Biological Laboratory, University of California, Berkeley, from 1959 to 1961.

Earlier Rivera had served in the Korean War from 1950 to 1953, earning a battlefield promotion to the rank of major. Following Korea, he was chief of laboratory services and pathology at the U.S. Army Hospital in Tokyo, Japan. Concluding his time overseas, Rivera was stationed at Brooke Army Medical Center at Fort Sam Houston in San Antonio, Texas until early 1958, when he spent several months at Georgia State University in Atlanta. Rivera's work at Brooke Army Medical Center deserves exploring here.

Following the end of World War II, as documented by numerous historians, the U.S. Army and intelligence agencies secretly recruited and dispatched to the United States a large number of former Nazi scientists. These scientists, targeted because of their specific scientific skills, were employed by various agencies of the U.S. government, as well as a number of private businesses. The primary areas of research assigned to these former Nazis were chemical and biological warfare, space medicine, and high-altitude heat and cold research.

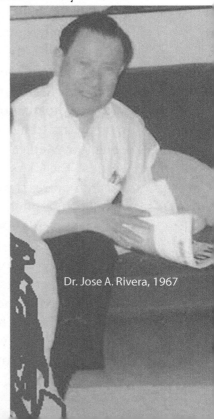

Dr. Jose A. Rivera, 1967

One of the estimated 3,000 former Nazis brought to America was Dr. Konrad J.K. Buettner, an expert in bioclimatology, who arrived in 1947 at the Brooke Army Medical Center in Texas. Buettner's research for the Air Force focused on the effects of extreme heat and burns on humans. This research led Buettner to consult closely with Maj. Jose Rivera who, with colleague Lt. Col. John A. Moncrief, had conducted a five-year study of "more than 1,000 burn cases" focusing on the mortality rate from septicemia (infection). In 1957, Rivera, still stationed at Brooke Army Medical Center, firmly established his credentials as an expert in the treatment of burn infections when he co-authored with Lt. Col. Moncrief a widely circulated and praised medical paper entitled, "The Problem of Infections in Burns by Resistant Micro-organisms with a Note on the Use of Bacitaracin."

This author found Dr. Buettner's work for the U.S. government particularly intriguing. Buettner had been brought to the United States in 1947 by Project Paperclip. In April 1952, Buettner made minor headlines when he announced the findings of a study he conducted in conjunction with the UCLA engineering department: "[That] Negroes would be in special danger of heat from an atomic explosion" due to their "heavily-pigmented skin."

In addition to working closely with Buettner, Rivera also worked at the Brooke Center with former Nazi, Dr. Ulrich Cameron Lutz. Lutz, who was recruited in 1947, worked from 1948 to 1963 as a consultant on high altitude acclimatization for both the Air Force and the CIA. Lutz's research included the ultra-secret development of the CIA's U-2 spy plane. The son of a Scottish mother and a German father, Lutz was born in Berlin in 1910, and schooled as a research physiologist and physician. By 1938 he was considered an authority in the fields of lung physiology and the physiological effects of oxygen deprivation.

In 1954, William Randolph Lovelace, II, a prominent American scientist who maintained a long-standing relationship with the CIA, invited Lutz to head the Department of Physiology at the Lovelace Clinic for Medical Education and research in Albuquerque, New Mexico. The CIA's Project Oxcart made extensive use of the clinic's research on respiratory problems and inhalation in the training of high altitude pilots. (Oxcart, the A-12 Lockheed project, was the CIA's secret successor/sequel program to the U-2 aircraft.)

During this period Rivera, following a three-year membership in the Texas Section of the American Association for Clinical Chemistry, was elected its chairman in 1956. The AACC was a group that Rivera helped found and that frequently met at Parkland Hospital in Dallas, where JFK was taken after he was shot.

In 1958, Rivera was assigned by the Army to the Reserve Training Center in Washington, D.C., where he officially remained until his retirement from the Army in 1965. Apparently, although nobody at NIH will confirm it, Rivera also worked part-time at the Institute of Neurological Diseases and Blindness [NINDB] for about three years beginning in 1962 until early 1965, when he was hired full-time by NIH. While some writers seem to go out of their ways to portray Rivera as a high-level NIH researcher and administrator (one writer erroneously states that Rivera was on the NIH Board) this could not be further from the truth. Rivera was one of many NIH employees "who performed routine laboratory work," said one NIH public affairs spokesperson, who seemed well aware of Rivera's notoriety and was less than inclined to discuss the former employee. A concentrated review of NIH and NINDB medical literature from 1962 through to 1975 reveals no published scientific papers by Rivera. He retired from NIH in 1973. (See Notes for more on NINDB.) Rivera was buried at Arlington National Cemetery.

Rivera's Varied and Strange Associates

Rivera's investigations into the effects of extreme heat and burns also led him to interact with yet another physician whose name frequently comes up in articles and books about the assassination of Robert Kennedy: Dr. William Joseph Bryan, Jr.

Bryan was an elusive and enigmatic character who introduced Rivera to the merits of hypnotism. Rivera first met Bryan in 1956, when Rivera's work with burn victims came to Bryan's attention. Interesting to note is that during this time, Rivera and his wife often socialized with Charles Cabell, the CIA's deputy director who regularly visited Texas where his brother, Earle Cabell, a prominent politician, served as mayor of Dallas from May 1961 to February 1964. Charles and Earle were the sons of former Dallas mayor Ben E. Cabell and the grandsons of William L. Cabell, who had also been mayor of Dallas. There are some indications that Charles Cabell may have introduced Rivera to Bryan.

William Bryan was prone to occasionally boast to friends and associates that he consulted covertly for the CIA in matters related to hypnotism. It has long been reported that Bryan was a technical consultant on the 1962 film, *The Manchurian Candidate*, as well as several other lesser-known films. Bryan first achieved national attention in 1965 when he induced, through hypnosis, a confession from serial killer Albert DeSalvo. Throughout the 1950s and early

1960s, Bryan was associated with several ultra-conservative right wing groups and through these associations came to the attention of the CIA's Morse Allen, a staunch proponent of the use of hypnotism in intelligence activities. One CIA Security Office document, from the early 1950s, details a lengthy meeting in New York City between Allen and Bryan, during which Allen sought assurances that Bryan could employ hypnosis in order to control selected, unwitting subjects. Reads the memorandum in part:

> We explored the issue of moral inhibitions blocking or preventing the effects of hypnosis and [Bryan] said as far as he was concerned there were no problems in this area at all.... With the task of inducing through trance a mental state whereby a subject would do harm to or kill another person, he said the task, although never attempted by himself or anyone he knows, would not be any more difficult than inducing a subject to drink a glass of water.

In May 1955, Bryan founded the American Institute of Hypnosis and served as the group's first president. Bryan believed strongly in the therapeutic use of hypnosis in the treatment of burn victims, a fact that drew the attention of Jose Rivera who, according to former associates, "dabbled in hypnosis sometimes himself." A former colleague of Rivera's, Dr. Louis K. Jordan, states that Rivera and Bryan "greatly admired each other's work." Jordan refers to a 1964 medical paper in which Bryan wrote,

> Hypnosis can be utilized in the control of infections by increasing the blood supply to the infected areas by hypnotic suggestion. Naturally, it is assumed that all the other normal measures that are utilized in medical practice will also be used in this case for the prevention and treatment of infection when it occurs. Naturally, the liberal use of the correct antibiotics is standard operating procedure, and many other medical drugs and compounds have been utilized within the past ten years based on burn research carried on at Brooke Army Medical Center.

Other strong evidence concerning Bryan's possible links to the CIA in the late 1950s and early 1960s centers on the now defunct

Granger Research Company, formerly based in Washington, D.C. In several obscure publications from 1959 and 1961 found among Bryan's Institute of Hypnosis library, the Granger Company is referred to as a provider of "technical assistance" to "agencies of the U.S. government" in the areas of "hypnosis and information gathering." According to declassified CIA documents, Granger Research was a CIA front operation created in early 1954 by Drs. Sidney Gottlieb and Robert Vern Lashbrook, who are listed on Granger Company stationary by their Agency pseudonyms, Samuel A. Granger (Gottlieb) and Robert V. Wittstock (Lashbrook). Ralph J. Labough is listed as Treasurer of the company. This was an alias for Dr. Henry Bortner, another CIA employee in the Agency's Technical Services Section. Granger Research Company succeeded another CIA front company, listed at the same Washington, D.C. address, with a different post office box number. This was Chemrophyl Associates, which was headed by Dr. Gottlieb operating under the alias Sherman C. Grifford. Chemrophyl Associates was dissolved about five weeks after Frank Olson's death in November 1953.

The CIA's Sidney Gottlieb traveled often under the name Granger, including at least seven trips to Chicago and New York City to meet with CIA contract magician John Mulholland and Dr. Harold Abramson, a CIA contractor researching LSD and other drugs. Abramson, readers may recall, was the New York physician who "treated" Fort Detrick biochemist Frank Olson during the last several days before his murder in Manhattan. Gottlieb, traveling under the name Grifford also made several trips in 1955 and 1956, accompanied by CIA psychologist John Gittinger, to meet with another CIA contractor, Dr. Louis Jolyon West. Gottlieb and Bortner, under their Granger aliases, also traveled on several occasions to meet with Dr. Paul Hoch at the New York Sate Psychiatric Institute and to the Lexington, Kentucky Federal Prison Farm to meet with Dr. Harris Isbell and other physicians concerning their CIA-funded LSD experiments on prison inmates.

As revealed in this author's book on Frank Olson's murder, prior to Olson's death, according to the notes and letters of CIA contractor and Federal Bureau of Narcotics agent George Hunter White, in June 1953, White, accompanied by fellow narcotics agents Vance Newman (also a CIA employee) and Arthur Giuliani, and special FBN and CIA employee Pierre Lafitte, crossed Manhattan from

FBN headquarters to the Statler Hotel on West 34th Street and Seventh Avenue. In a third floor Statler conference room, a highly specialized group awaited them: CIA officers Sidney Gottlieb, Robert Lashbrook, Henry Bortner, and Ray Treichler, a TSS chemist and newly appointed liaison to Camp Detrick's SOD, along with one of the nation's most renowned magicians, John Mulholland. The reason for the gathering was that Mulholland had been retained by the Agency weeks earlier to train selected persons in the arts of trickery and sleight-of-hand. Reads Mulholland's initial contract with the CIA's TSS:

> Mr. Mulholland will broaden the scope [of his work under MK/ULTRA subproject 4] to include services in connection with consultation, inclusive of training in CD/TSS [Chemical Division/TSS] selected areas. These expanded services will also include travel and operations supplies, including those necessitated by training sessions.

Said Dr. Sidney Gottlieb on the origins of John Mulholland's entry into the world of clandestine affairs:

> We were casting about for a trustworthy person expert in magic, someone who knew sleight-of-hand well and who was well-grounded, that was professional and was skeptical of the more bizarre trends in magic, someone who could interface well with our people and the narcotics officials working with us.... We interviewed a number of people around the country, finding nobody really satisfactory, and then Dr. S.L. Quimby at Columbia, who was already working with the Agency on another project, suggested to Bortner [TSS Chemical Division employee] we speak with Mulholland. Dr. Quimby knew that Mulholland had performed before a number of American troops on USO tours and was pretty patriotic ... And, to make a long story short, we eventually contracted with Mulholland.

William Bryan, as some readers may be aware, has long been suspected of having played a role in the assassination of Robert Kennedy through his hypnotic programming of assassin Sirhan Sirhan. Yet, despite this widely reported speculation, little serious research effort has been devoted to the dimensions of Bryan's role with the CIA, and possibly the Federal Bureau of Narcotics and the U.S. military. This author has long been fascinated by reports that Bryan was utilized by Federal Narcotics agent and CIA consultant George Hunter White, and White's FBN assistant, Ira "Ike" Feldman, for experiments that were conducted in a number of the CIA's MK/ ULTRA safe houses in California.

Indeed, in 2010, writer David M. Silvey, in his book, *Project Artichoke*, provided some very provocative leads on hypnotist William Bryan and FBN agents George White and Ira Feldman. The latter owned property near Silvey's family home and knew Silvey's mother. Incredibly, Silvey's book links one of the victims of the infamous Zodiac Killer with Bryan, the CIA, and the assassination of Robert Kennedy. When this author read Silvey's book, it brought to mind my conversation about George Hunter White with *San Francisco Chronicle* crime reporter Paul Avery, who had closely covered the Zodiac story – as depicted in the film, *Zodiac*, starring Robert Downey, Jr. (who played Avery). Having also written an excellent article on George White, Avery remarked to this author that he had long been suspicious of White's possible connections to the brutal Zodiac killings. Avery, now deceased, remarked that there had been other incidents of violence connected to White and Feldman that "troubled" him, and that the activities of the two MK/ ULTRA operatives "nagged" at him, as if they were "trying to tell me something."

Unfortunately, both Avery and Silvey are now deceased, as is William Bryan. Silvey passed away in late 2009 just before his book was published, but without doubt, William Bryan's life and its myriad intriguing connections, as explored by intrepid JFK researchers Greg Parker and Steven Duffy, deserve further, intense examination. (See Notes on Duffy's and Parker's research on Bryan.)

Another prominent and intriguing scientist at NIH with whom Rivera often associated has, until now, been completely overlooked. This is Dr. DeWitt Stetten, who passed away in 1990. Stetten, born in New York City in 1909, first joined the NIH staff in 1954 when he became associate director of the research program for the National Institute of Arthritis and Metabolic Diseases (NIAMD), a position that brought him into regular contact with Rivera. In his first nine years at NIH, Dr. Stetten successfully recruited a number of prominent scientists to the NIAMD program, including Dr. Marshall W. Nirenberg, a biochemist and geneticist who went on to become a Nobel laureate for his identification of the DNA code for specific amino acids. In many of his recruitment efforts, Stetten would consult Dr. Frank Fremont-Smith, who headed the Macy Foundation throughout the 1950s. The foundation funded a number of annual scientific gatherings and conferences underwritten by the CIA, and involving numerous scientists and researchers covertly funded by the Agency and U.S. military.

Dr. Stetten, educated at Harvard and Columbia University, was a lifelong, strong advocate for promotion of the sciences among young people. He worked tirelessly toward the establishment of the Foundation for Education in the Sciences, a nongovernmental teaching institution located adjacent to the NIH campus, that frequently brought Stetten and Rivera together.

Dr. Stetten left NIH in 1962 to serve as the founding dean of Rutgers University School of Medicine, but returned to Bethesda, Maryland in 1970 to serve as director of the National Institute of General Medical Sciences. From 1974 to 1979, Stetten was NIH's deputy director for science. Today, the NIH Museum of Medical Research is named after Dr. Stetten.

As a young boy in New York City, Stetten attended the Horace Mann School, an experimental facility associated with Columbia University. Because young Stetten was extremely shy and withdrawn, his parents asked one of his teachers at Horace Mann, who was also a skilled amateur magician, to provide DeWitt with individualized schooling in magic. The thinking was that training as a performing magician would help young DeWitt become more outgoing. It worked.

DeWitt's instructor's name was John Wickizer, who later, as a prominent stage magician, adopted the stage name John Mulholland. Mulholland maintained a lifelong friendship with Dr. Stetten and the two often met at various scientific and magic-related gatherings in the U.S. and abroad. On several occasions these gatherings included Dr. Frank Fremont-Smith, who by this time was neck-deep in working with the CIA's Technical Services Section's Chemical Branch. At some of these gatherings, Mulholland and Stetten were joined by Drs. Sidney Gottlieb and Robert Vern Lashbrook, respective director and assistant director of the CIA's Chemical Branch. In an interview with this author, Gottlieb recalled that Drs. DeWitt Stetten and S.L. Quimby were "two American scientists I admired tremendously." (At the time, this writer had no knowledge concerning DeWitt Stetten.)

Who was Dr. S.L. Quimby? I asked Gottlieb.

"A former Naval commander, I think … and a physicist at Columbia University. Very well known, as a matter of fact. He was a friend with [Dr.] Harris Isbell, another Agency contractor, and [Dr.] Harold Abramson."

Did Quimby work for the CIA as a contractor?

"I think … I believe that he did. I think he's already been identified, sometime in the Seventies hearings, in that role."

What did he do for the Agency?

"I don't recall specifically what he did … something related to his field of study, I'm sure."

Can you be more specific on Dr. Quimby?

"I don't really recall all that much about him."

Did Dr. Quimby have anything to do with John Mulholland?

"He may have, possibly. I think it was possible that they knew one another."

What do you recall about stage magician Mulholland?

"It was so long ago … not much, unfortunately. I liked him. He was easy to work with…. He was well to do, I think, or seemed to be. A folksy looking fellow, tall, very tall, always well dressed…. We knew that his real name wasn't Mulholland. We knew there was a dispute over that before I interviewed him in New York. I attended one of his shows before that. I don't recall his real name any longer."

In addition to Dr. Stetten, Rivera also had frequent professional and social contact with Dr. Stephen Szara, who served as director of the Biomedical Branch of the U.S. National Institute on Drug Abuse and worked closely with the NIH's Foundations of Neuroscience and Behavioral Research. Indeed, if Rivera had easy access to any ready supply of LSD, or any other mind-altering drug, it may well have been through Dr. Szara.

Dr. Szara, a chemist and psychiatrist, was born in 1923 in Hungary and moved to the United States after the 1956 Hungarian Revolution. Once here in the U.S., Szara was wooed by Dr. Joel Elkes, who sponsored his entry into the United States and was then Chairman of Psychiatry at Johns Hopkins University School of Medicine in Baltimore, Maryland. Dr. Szara is considered the foremost research pioneer in the study of the psychotropic effects of the drug DMT (dimethyltryptamine), a drug that intrigued CIA scientists for years, beginning in 1951. Szara was the first person to scientifically study the psychotropic effects of DMT on human subjects in the mid-1950s. Interestingly, Szara focused on DMT after he was refused any amount of research LSD from Sandoz Laboratories in Switzerland. Szara was still living in Hungary at the time of his request. Sandoz officials told Szara that any amount of LSD could be "dangerous in the hands of a communist country." Without doubt, this was a CIA reply parroted by the chemical company, which was the Agency's chief LSD supplier from 1950 through to late 1953. Partially declassified but heavily redacted CIA documents from the 1950s and 1960s indicate that Dr. Szara may have conducted experiments on unwitting human subjects at Washington, D.C.'s St. Elizabeth's Hospital, since closed and demolished.

Another scientist who knew Rivera professionally was Dr. Joel Elkes, a figure who has nearly escaped scrutiny in terms of the abusive and horrific features of LSD and psychedelic research and human experiments. Dr. Elkes emigrated to the United Kingdom in 1931 from Lithuania. Beginning in the early 1950s, after training in medicine at London's St. Mary's Hospital, and then moving on to the University of Birmingham, Elkes was regarded as "a leading exponent of the view that neurochemical transmission was important in the central nervous system, a view he and Phillip Bradley developed into a distinctively modern vision of neurotransmitters and receptors before the end of the 1950s," a view that (initially) "met considerable skepticism and disbelief." (Dr. David Healy, see notes.)

Dr. Elkes first became knowledgeable about the drug LSD sometime in 1950, however concerted efforts have been made over the past decades to make it appear that Elkes' LSD awareness postdated 1951. It is this writer's belief that these efforts were generated due to Elkes' possible knowledge about – and perhaps even involvement in – the U.S. Army's covert LSD experiment in Pont St. Esprit, France in late summer 1951. Ongoing research in France, the U.K. and the United States has recently revealed that Dr. Elkes, in the early 1950s, was close to French Drs. Jean Delay, Pierre Pichot, Therese Lemperiere, and others – all of whom may have had advance knowledge of the experiment at Pont St. Esprit that tragically resulted in at least five deaths.

Dr. Elkes is also known to have gone to great lengths to conceal from colleagues and historians another key activity in his professional career. This was his ultra-secret LSD work with the British Ministry of Defense beginning about 1952 or 1953 through to about 1964. Spurred aggressively forward by British military scientists visiting Camp Detrick in the U.S. and by U.S. scientists, including Dr. Frank Olson visiting the British chemical and biological warfare center, Porton Down, the English government jumped on the LSD-as-a-weapon bandwagon simply because it did not want to be left in the psychedelic dust by the Americans or Russians.

Although the Porton Down LSD experiments, including those involving Dr. Joel Elkes, are not as well known as those of the CIA and U.S. Army, it does seem clear that the British were no better than their American counterparts at setting up any modicum of safeguards for their many unwitting human subjects dosed with LSD. However, unlike the CIA, the British appeared to have steered clear of involving universities in the U.K. experiments. Under terms of anonymity, said one former CIA-contracted scientist in the U.S. about the Agency's use of American universities:

> It was easy money doing the [CIA's] experiments with LSD, mescaline and psilocybin. I don't have any idea how many students we messed up, some most likely seriously. I do know that we kept no records of names, nor did we do any follow-up of any sort. There was never any consideration given to follow-up. For all we knew, every one of these kids could have gone on to commit suicide, became a mass murderer, or ran for public office somewhere.

While at Birmingham University, Dr. Elkes created the school's first Department of Experimental Psychiatry. Researcher and writer David Healy states, "[Elkes] established a department whose range of research interests extended across clinical trials, neuroanatomy, neurophysiology, neurochemistry and animal behavior."

At about the same time, Elkes became aware of the work of British physician Ronald Sandison. In September 1951, Dr. Sandison was appointed Consultant Psychiatrist at England's Worcester Powick Hospital, formerly the Worcestershire County Pauper and Lunatic Asylum. A year later, in September 1952, Sandison, as part of an international study tour, visited the Sandoz laboratories in Basel, Switzerland. There he met Albert Hoffman who told him about a remarkable new drug called LSD and its "effects" on "the small group of people [unwitting human subjects] who had experimented [*sic*] with it so far." Presumably, Hofmann said nothing to Sandison about the events a year earlier in Pont St. Esprit, France.

Sandison later recalled, "It surprised me, because none of the other members of our party showed much interest in [Sandoz's] work." He goes on: "I, however, made a point of returning to Sandoz two months later, in November 1952, and this time came away with 100 vials of Delysid [Sandoz's brand name for LSD]. I brought them back to England and began using LSD as part of the psychotherapy programs [at Powick Hospital]."

Dr. Elkes, who had been aware of LSD about a year earlier than Sandison, hearing of the latter's work, attended a lecture on LSD given by the English physician and immediately became convinced that LSD was an extremely important drug.

Historian David Healy reveals "Elkes' achievements were recognized in the United States by Seymour Kety and others, who lured him across the Atlantic to the NIMH Institute at St. Elizabeth's Hospital in Washington, D.C." According to one of his former colleagues, Jose Rivera visited St. Elizabeth's regularly in the early 1960s and on several occasions spoke candidly about "experiments being conducted there on supposed hopelessly schizophrenic patients with various hallucinogenic drugs, including LSD and DMT." The colleague, a histologist at NIH for nearly 27 years, recalled:

> It would be a real understatement to say that Jose was really interested in some of the crazier drugs that were being used experimentally in the late 1950s and 1960s. Army and intelligence officials were in and out of his lab often on matters related to these drugs ... and you have to keep in mind that his ostensible work at Bethesda really had nothing to do with such matters.

Elkes was subsequently appointed Chairman of Psychiatry at Johns Hopkins University, again with the strong support of Seymour Kety. Some readers may recall from this author's work on Frank Olson, that Dr. Seymour Kety was a renowned American neuroscientist who briefly served as Hopkins' Psychiatry Department Chair. Kety covertly worked quite closely with the CIA on a number of its more abusive programs involving unwitting human subjects, including providing rivea corymbosa seeds, a natural drug that produces a hypnotic, trance-like state, to Drs. Harris Isbell and Abraham Wikler for experiments on unwitting federal prison inmates in Kentucky.

On July 24, 2011, Adele sent a letter to President Barack Obama at the White House. She began by stating, "I am writing to you for help with an important problem which I cannot solve by myself, despite all the Freedom of Information/Privacy letters I have written over the years, and those by my attorney, to various congressional investigative bodies."

Adele then provided the President with highlights of her career and provided a summary of her encounter with Jose Rivera, and her meetings with the FBI, including a late 1984 meeting with an FBI Special Agent "who asked me to write a very brief account of my experience in 1963 which he was to send to FBI Headquarters with his cover letter and a copy of my curriculum vitae." Nothing further was heard from the FBI, Adele explained. Her letter continued:

> I believe Jose A. Rivera, a former US Army Colonel, was one of the traitors and conspirators who plotted and murdered President John F. Kennedy. These traitors, in government positions in the military and intelligence and their financial backers, wanted to destroy Kennedy and his administration because he was working for economic improvements for all peoples, for Democracy, and for worldwide peace and harmony. These were not the goals of his murderers and War profiteers. Many of them can be linked to the conspiracy to overthrow President Roosevelt and our system of government in order to establish a fascistic dictatorship in 1933-1934, just thirty years before 1963.
>
> What I wish to ask is that you, with your Executive authority and power, ask the relevant agencies, the National Archives, and the National Declassification Center to release FBI, Secret Service, and CIA and Congressional documents, audio tapes,

film/video recordings, in their possession which relate to me, Adele E. Uskali Edisen, and to Attorney Jack Peebles, and to Jose Alberto Rivera, and Winston de Monsabert, and Grant Stockdale (friend of John Kennedy, whose death after the assassination was predicted by Rivera in April of 1963.)

Adele concluded her letter with the words: "November 22, 2013, about two years from now, will be the 50th Year Anniversary of the death of President Kennedy, and all documents and records currently withheld from the public's access should be made available to the American people. We have a right to know our true history."

Adele, as of this book's publication, was still waiting for a reply from President Obama.

Chapter Four

What Did Dimitre Dimitrov Know?

I know who killed President Kennedy, and I know why he was killed. I know who these men are that ambushed the President.... I met them while I was imprisoned and tortured by the United States.

> – Dimitre Dimitrov, Washington, D.C., 1976

The CIA has no idea what type relationship exists between Oltmans and Dimitrov, but is certain that that relationship is not advantageous to the United States Intelligence Community.

> – Stansfield Turner, CIA Director, Oct. 28, 1977

On January 25, 1952, Morse Allen, a CIA Security Office official who fancied himself a burgeoning practitioner of hypnosis and mind-control techniques, was summoned to the office of his superior, Security Office deputy chief Robert L. Bannerman, where he met with another agency official to discuss what Bannerman initially introduced as "the Kelly case."

In a subsequent memorandum for his files, Morse Allen wrote that the official, Joseph Pritchett, had been dispatched to Bannerman's office from the Eastern European Division of the Office of Policy Coordination (OPC). At the time, the OPC was CIA's covert action arm, overseen by Frank Wisner, a former Wall Street attorney and wartime OSS officer. According to Allen's memorandum:

Mr. Pritchett explained in substance the Kelly case as follows: Kelly, (whose real name is Dimitre Dimitrov), is a 29-year-old

Bulgarian and was the head of a small political party based in Greece and ostentively [*sic*] working for Bulgarian independence. [Dimitrov] was described by Pritchett as being young, ambitious, bright (elementary college education), a sort of a "man-on-a-horse" type but a typical Balkan politician. (See Notes for information on political situation in Bulgaria in the early 1950s.)

Pritchett further explained to Allen that several months earlier, CIA field operatives "had discovered that that the French Intelligence Service was attempting to bribe Dimitrov and make him a double agent, and Dimitrov was looking with favor upon the French offer." As a result, continued the memorandum, "a plot was rigged in which [Dimitrov] was told he was going to be assassinated and as a protective he was placed in custody of the Greek Police."

Successfully duped, Dimitrov was then thrown into a Greek prison. (At this point in time, Dimitrov was given the pseudonym "Lyle O. Kelly" by the CIA's Office of Security.) In prison he was subjected to intensive interrogation and torture. He was also forced to watch the brutal torture of other persons the CIA had induced Greek authorities to imprison. Greek intelligence and law enforcement agencies were especially barbaric in their methods. Highly respected Operation Gladio historian, Daniele Ganser, describes the treatment of prisoners held in Greece at this time:

> Their toes and fingernails were torn out. Their feet were beaten with sticks, until the skin came off and their bones were broken. Sharp objects were shoved into their vaginas. Filthy rags, often soaked in urine, and sometimes excrement, were pushed down their throats to throttle them, tubes were inserted into their anus and water driven in under very high pressure, and electro shocks were applied to their heads.

According to Allen's memo, after holding Dimitrov for six months Greek authorities decided he was no more than "a nuisance" and they told the CIA "to take him back." Because the CIA was unable "to dispose of Dimitrov" in Greece, Allen's memorandum states, the CIA flew him to a secret military interrogation center housed in an American military hospital in Panama. There, Dimitrov was admitted, according to Allen's memo, "as a psychopathic patient."

Morse Allen's memo and, perhaps, Pritchett's presentation were silent on Dimitrov's background. However, other CIA documents reveal that Dimitre Andropov Dimitrov, up until the time he was imprisoned in Greece, had played a strong leadership role in efforts directed against the communist dominated Bulgarian government, Soviet occupying troops in Bulgaria, and the Soviet NKVD. Dimitrov, who spoke Bulgarian, Greek, Russian, and German, was widely recognized and respected as a resistance leader extending back to early post-World War II days when the CIA launched operations QK/STAIRS, BG/SHAM, and BG/CONVOY – covert psychological warfare programs against the communists in Bulgaria.

DIMITROV IN PANAMA

The hospital and interrogation center where Dimitre Dimitrov was placed were on the grounds of the U.S. Army's Fort Clayton in Panama. In the 1950s, Fort Clayton, along with nearby sister installations, Fort Amador and Fort Gulick, both in Panama, were the original sites of the Army's notorious School of the Americas which, among other activities, trained the world's most notorious foreign secret police units – including DINA (Chile), SAVAK (Iran), BOSS (South Africa) and KCIA (South Korea) – in interrogation techniques and torture. Throughout the 1950s and 1960s, and beyond, all three army forts also served as secret prison compounds and interrogation centers for double agents, defectors and others kidnapped by American intelligence agents and spirited out of Europe and elsewhere. Additionally, Fort Gulick was extensively used as a training facility for paramilitary and guerrilla fighters who were covertly dispatched to Cuba before and after the Bay of Pigs invasion. Fort Gulick also served as a secure depository for a number of biological warfare substances sent from Fort Detrick and used in Cuba, including the Swine Flu virus that was covertly introduced by the U.S. military into Cuba's pig population.

Indeed, after leaving Panama, Dimitrov would say that while being held on the isthmus, he encountered several people who have emerged over the past fifty years as possible key players in the JFK murder. One of these people was David Sanchez Morales, who later briefly returned to Panama as a trainer for the ultra-secret Project Cobra. As some readers are aware, Morales, aka "El Indio" and "Didi," worked for the CIA from 1951 to 1975 under cover as an

Army enlisted man, U.S. State Department Foreign Service Officer, and AID (Agency for International Development) advisor. A close friend and business associate of Morales told a Congressional investigator in 1978, three years after Morales' death by heart attack, that Morales said that he was in Dallas on November 22, 1963, and that Morales also said about President Kennedy, "Well, we took care of that son of a bitch, didn't we?" Dimitrov first encountered David Morales in early 1951 in Frankfurt, Germany, where Morales was stationed near the CIA holding facility where Dimitrov had been sent from Athens. Entirely coincidentally, Dimitrov encountered Morales again in Panama about eight months later. [See Notes and Chapter 6 for more on David Morales.]

Beginning in 1951, Fort Amador and Fort Gulick were used extensively by the Army and the CIA as secret experimental sites for developing "behavior modification" using a wide range of techniques, including "truth drugs," mescaline, LSD and heroin. Former CIA officials have also long claimed that in the 1950s and later, Fort Clayton and Fort Amador housed and trained a number of Army assassination teams that operated throughout North and South America, Europe and Southeast Asia.

There in Panama, Allen's memo explains, Dimitrov was aggressively interrogated and then confined as "a psychopathic patient" to a high-security hospital ward at Fort Clayton. Allen's memo makes a point of stating, "[Dimitrov] is not a psychopathic personality."

Unbeknownst to many Americans is that for more than a century and a half, beginning about 1856 to the present day, Panama has served without interruption as a host country for U.S. military bases, and for covert training and experimental projects. Ideally situated as a connecting bridge, and gateway to Central America and South America, and a short distance from major U.S.-based military and political centers, the isthmus has also serves as a much overlooked point-of-departure for huge shipments of illicit drugs. Panama has long been a point-of-entry for a myriad of American pharmaceutical companies conducting untold numbers of unregulated human experiments with a virtual cornucopia of chemical and biological substances, as well as callous and secret experiments with carcinogens and radiation.

Military documents produced by Fort Detrick Special Operations scientists, as well as secret reports obtained through the Freedom of Information Act (FOIA) by John Lindsay-Poland, and interviews with former Fort Detrick physicians, reveal that experiments with radioactive-laced milk and other liquids were conducted in Panama, inducing cancer and death among untold numbers of Panamanians in the 1950s and 1960s.

Said one former Fort Detrick researcher in a 2001 interview: "Under our [Special Operations Division] agreements with the Pentagon and CIA, we were forbidden to record in writing, or to produce written reports on, any of the results of our cancer experiments, but I can assure you that people died as a result of these [experiments]. Death was an intended by-product of experiments, deaths marked success and desired results be they among humans used or the hordes of other animals targeted."

Another former Fort Detrick researcher, who went on to work at Vanderbilt University, recalls: "It was beyond any measure of inhumanity or disregard for human dignity. The scenes haunt me … I still have nightmares, and what I witnessed was mild compared to those [experiments] others more regularly were involved with."

Were there experiments with behavior-modification or mind-control techniques?

This same researcher replies,

> Yes, on a smaller scale in terms of the number of [human] subjects. Experiments generally were divided between activities conducted with pre-approved pharmaceutical company products and substances, and those that originated with the military or CIA themselves. These CIA projects sometimes employed known products, as well as all sorts of esoteric mind-altering substances.... Some very exotic, natural substances brought in from other locations were frequently used.

CIA records reveal that Panama, as well as Mexico City, Mexico, were so frequently used as sites for drug experiments on human subjects that the agency's Technical Services Division (TSD) opened sophisticated branch offices in both countries. Former CIA technical officers are on record reporting that TSD contractors, in addition to conducting a wide range of drug experiments, also experimented with hypnotism as an interrogation technique, using sites in both Panama and Mexico. CIA psychologist John Gittinger, in a legal deposition taken in the 1980s, explained that "projects involving hypnotism carried out in Panama" were "mostly of an experimental nature," while those in Mexico City were "nearly always of an operational nature." Said Gittinger, "In Mexico City there was more emphasis on the esoteric elements of behavior manipulation, on things like hypnosis and other such matters left outside the MK/ULTRA sphere."

THE ARTICHOKE TREATMENT

The remarkable summary concerning Dimitre Dimitrov given to Morse Allen by Joseph Pritchett prefaced Pritchett's main purpose for wanting Allen to join the meeting. After months of confinement in Panama, Pritchett explained, Dimitrov had become a serious problem for the CIA and the military officials holding him in the hospital. Dimitrov had become increasingly angry and bitter about his treatment, and he was relentlessly insisting that he be released immediately. Dimitrov, noted by his captors for his strong intellect and powers of observation, was also of great concern to the CIA because he was witnessing a great deal of Project Artichoke activity at both the interrogation center and the hospital.

Project Artichoke was an ultra-secret program initiated in August 1951 upon the approval of CIA director Walter Bedell Smith and the Agency's Scientific Intelligence Director, Dr. H. Marshall Chadwell. The code name "Artichoke" was selected with sardonic humor from the street appendage given to New York gangster Ciro Terranova, who was referred to as the "Artichoke King." (The first organization meeting for the project was held at the Statler Hotel in Manhattan.) Following a brief period of bureaucratic, intra-Agency infighting over which CIA department would have jurisdiction over Artichoke, it was decided that the project would be overseen and directed by the Agency's Security Research Service (SRS), a component of the Office of Security headed by former Army Brigadier General Paul F. Gaynor, who had extensive experience in wartime interrogations. (See Notes for more on Gaynor and SRS.)

Here it is important to note that the Artichoke Project originated from the CIA's short-lived Project Bluebird, which operated for about two years, 1949 through the summer of 1951, and primarily concentrated its efforts on former American POWs returned from the Korean War. These servicemen were placed as patients in several Army hospitals, including Valley Forge Hospital in Pennsylvania and the Walter Reed facility in Washington, D.C. There, former POWs were subjected to various "behavioral modification" programs involving the use of experimental drugs, hypnosis, and special interrogation methods, all for what the CIA deemed "offensive objectives." Joining the CIA in Project Bluebird as formal partners were the Army, Navy and Air Force. The FBI declined to participate in Bluebird.

Reads one April 1951 Bluebird Project report:

> The Navy's research efforts in regards to Bluebird objectives had actually begun in 1947 at Bethesda Naval Hospital. There, according to the Navy's Bluebird designees, J.H. Alberti and Lt. Cmdr. Hardenburg, extensive experiments had been conducted using both drugs and medical aids (polygraph machines, surgical means, hypnotism). Besides Bethesda hospital, the Office of Naval Research conducted a project in partnership with the University of Indiana, which in essence [was] a search for valid indications of deception other than the mechanical indicators now being used.

In 1951, just weeks before Bluebird was renamed Artichoke, officials within the CIA's Security Office – working in tandem with cleared scientists from Camp Detrick's Special Operations Division, who in turn worked closely with a select group of scientists from Edgewood Arsenal in Maryland – began a series of ultra-secret experiments with LSD, mescaline, peyote, and a synthesized substance (sometimes nicknamed "Smasher") which combined an "LSD-like drug with pharmaceutical amphetamines and other enhancers." Former Detrick scientist, Dr. Gerald Yonetz, described the substance: "It was like a rocket ship to Mars."

From its inception, Project Artichoke needed a steady supply of experimental subjects. Wrote CIA SRS chief Paul Gaynor in a never-before-revealed February 1953 memo: *"It is imperative that we move forward more aggressively on identifying and securing a more reliable, ready group, or groups, of human research subjects for ongoing Artichoke experimentation. There can be no delays in this extremely important work."* [Emphasis added]

Other CIA reports reveal that the CIA's SRS was not sitting idly by while awaiting the recruitment of groups of human subjects.

Teams of Agency officials and contract physicians were traveling frequently to locations in Europe and the Far East, including Atsugi, Japan, where in the isolation of CIA and military safe houses and installations, enhanced interrogations and mind-control experiments were being conducted on defectors, double-agents, and kidnapped foreign agents. Reads a November 1956 Artichoke team report that could have easily been written today at Guantanamo, Cuba: "The team physician administered a suppository containing a small amount of heroin to the subject so as to increase subject's pain threshold." (The Artichoke physician referred to in this report, a well-known Washington, D.C. psychologist, made over 90 Artichoke-related trips abroad.)

In September 1953, Artichoke Project director Morse Allen, Paul Gaynor's deputy and a former Naval intelligence officer and State Department employee, hand-carried a two-page memorandum to SRS chief Gaynor. The memo bears the subject: "Artichoke Research Program." It reads in part:

> [T]here are some four thousand (4,000) American military men who are serving court martial sentences in the federal prisons at the present time. These men are scattered through the federal institutions according to their age – some being at reformatories, others at prisons. It is administratively possible that the sentences of these men can be reduced by direction of the Adjutant General's office. Therefore, if these men should be wanted for work on a dangerous research project, it might be possible to motivate their interest by promising that recommendations would be made to the Adjutant General's office to have their sentences appropriately reduced if they co-operated in the experimentation. Also, many offenses of military men were committed in circumstances which might tend to lessen the feeling of guilt on the part of the individual and such cases might reveal interesting information.

Allen next suggested that federal prisons "that have hospital set-ups with doctors on the permanent staff" be used for experiments. Wrote Allen: "Such things as the size of the institution and current population would have to be considered but it is a fact that the federal prisons are not overcrowded as is the case with many state prisons, thus it would be much easier to obtain working space in a federal institution." Proposed Allen: "Artichoke teams secretly working in the prisons could be passed off as coming from nearby universities or research institutions." About a week later, Allen amended his proposal to include "federal hospitals and institutions under the control of the [U.S.] Public Health Service."

Paul Gaynor promptly approved Allen's recommendations, ordering that immediate efforts be made to implement them. Within a few weeks, progress reports concerning the conduct of experiments at three federal prisons, as well as extended work at a reformatory in Bordentown, New Jersey, were submitted to Gaynor and the Artichoke Committee. Experiments were also conducted at St. Elizabeth's Hospital in Washington, D.C., a Veterans Administration hospital in Detroit, Michigan, and at the Federal Narcotics Farm in Lexington, Kentucky. Experiments at the Narcotics Farm, somewhat romanticized in some current publications, were specifically targeted at African-American inmates, who were considered by the program's director to be inferior to white inmates at the facility.

From 1951 to about 1963, when the Artichoke Project was revamped and renamed, a primary project objective, according to several Artichoke documents, centered on: "…. *ascertaining whether effective and practical techniques exist, or could be developed, which could be utilized to render an individual subservient to an imposed will or control, thereby posing a potential threat to National Security.*" [Emphasis added]

The same documents explain that the CIA also wanted to put the same techniques to their own effective uses in the field offensively. Reads one document: "We need to also explore the 'subtle' means of making an individual say or do things he would normally not consider through the use of covertly administered drugs, 'Black Psychiatry', hypnosis, and brain damaging processes. Dr. Chadwell feels these processes may be tried but they are 'elaborate, impractical and unnecessary.' (Dr. Chadwell was H. Marshall Chadwell, the CIA's director of Scientific Intelligence. See Notes for definition of "Black Psychiatry.")

Dimitrov and the Artichoke Treatment

On occasion, while at Fort Clayton, Dimitre Dimitrov would engage military and CIA officials in unauthorized conversations concerning the Artichoke Project activities. Pritchett explained to Allen that the CIA could release Dimitrov to the custody of a friend of his in Venezuela, but they recommended against it because Dimitrov had witnessed a large number of highly sensitive and secret activities and was also now judged to have become extremely hostile toward the CIA.

"Hence," explained Pritchett, according to Allen's memo, "[CIA] is considering an 'Artichoke' approach to Dimitrov to see if it would be possible to reorient him favorably toward us." Explained Pritchett: "This [Artichoke] operation, which will necessarily involve the use of drugs, is being considered by OPC with a possibility that Dr. Ecke and Mike Gladych will carry out the operation presumably at the military hospital in Panama. Also involved in this would be a Bulgarian interpreter who is a consultant to this Agency since neither Ecke nor Gladych speak Bulgarian."

Allen noted in his memo that security chief Bannerman "pointed out" that this type of Artichoke operation could "only be carried out" with his authorization or that of his superior, Office of Security chief Sheffield Edwards, and "that under no circumstances whatsoever, could anyone but an authorized M.D. administer drugs to any subject of this Agency of any type."

The "Dr. Ecke" named in Allen's memorandum was Dr. Robert S. Ecke of Brooklyn, New York and Eliot, Maine (where he died in 2001). "Mike Gladych," according to former CIA officials, was a decorated wartime pilot who became, after the war, "deeply involved in black market trafficking in Europe and the US." In the early 1950s, Gladych was recruited into a newly constituted Artichoke Team operating out of Washington, D.C., Mexico City and Panama.

Following the end of World War II, Dr. Ecke, assigned to the Supreme Headquarters Allied Expeditionary Force, participated in the interrogation of high-level Nazi POWs confined within secret holding areas outside of Frankfurt, Germany near Oberursel. Oberursel was a former Nazi interrogation center taken over by the U.S. Dr. Ecke worked closely with a special interrogation unit run by Capt. Malcolm S. Hilty, Maj. Mose Hart and Capt. Herbert Sensenig. The unit was especially notorious in its applications of harsh interrogation methods, including electroshock, Metrazol, mescaline, amphetamines, morphine and heroin. Said former army Counterintelligence Corps officer, Miles Hunt: "The unit took great pride in their nicknames, the 'Rough Boys' and the 'Kraut Gauntlet,' and didn't hold back with any drug or technique … you name it, they used it." Added Hunt: "Sensenig was really disappointed when it was found that nothing had to be used on [former Reichsmarschall] Herman Goering, who was processed through the camp. Goering needed no inducement to talk."

Allen also wrote that Bannerman was concerned that the military hospital at Fort Clayton might not approve or permit an Artichoke operation to be conducted on the ward where Dimitrov was being held, thus necessitating the transfer of Dimitrov to another location in Panama. Lastly, Bannerman stated to the official and to Morse Allen that "[the CIA's Office of] Security [through its Artichoke Committee] would have to be cognizant" of the operation, and might even want to "run the operation themselves since this type of work is one which Security handles for the Agency." Here it is interesting to note that among the specially selected members of the Agency's Artichoke Committee in 1952 was Dr. Frank Olson who, about a year later, after being subjected to Artichoke treatment himself, would be murdered in New York City. Morse Allen concluded his memo:

> While the [Artichoke] technique that Ecke and Gladych are considering for use in this case is not known to the writer [Allen], the writer believes the approach will be made through the standard narco-hypnosis technique. Re-conditioning and re-orientating an individual in such a matter, in the opinion of the writer, cannot be accomplished easily and will require a great deal of time…. It is also believed that with our present knowledge, we would have no absolute guarantee that the subject in this case would maintain a positive friendly attitude toward us even though there is apparently a successful response to the treatment. The writer did not suggest to [Bannerman and Pritchett] that *perhaps a total amnesia could be created by a series of electro shocks, but merely indicated that amnesia under drug treatments was not certain.* [Emphasis added.]

Interestingly, Allen noted in his memo that, about thirty days prior to his meeting with Bannerman and Pritchett, he had been approached by Walter G. Driscoll, a former FBI employee, who was then working with the CIA's Technical Services Division, and who had discussed "the Dimitrov case" with him. No details of that discussion were provided in Allen's memo or in available files. Driscoll served as a covert liaison between the Federal Bureau of Narcotics and the CIA on its New York City safe houses overseen by narcotics agent George White. Other documents from the FBN indicate that Driscoll and White had been approached to discuss supplying Artichoke operatives Ecke and Gladych with two drugs, datura and psilocybin, that the CIA desired to use in conducting interrogations in Panama, and presumably on Dimitrov.

About a month later, according to former CIA officials, after seeking and eventually gaining Artichoke Committee approval to subject Dimitrov to Artichoke techniques, an unidentified, high-ranking CIA official objected to treating Dimitrov in such a manner. That objection delayed application of the techniques for about "three weeks." In March 1952, however, according to the same former officials, Dimitrov was "successfully given the Artichoke treatment in Panama for a period of about five weeks." While specific details of the techniques applied to Dimitrov remain unavailable, subsequent statements made by Dimitrov himself make it clear that he was subjected to intense and repeated interrogation using an array of drugs, including LSD, heroin, and barbiturates, and "near weekly hypnosis sessions," that also made use of an array of drugs. Dimitrov further stated that he was subjected to electro-shock treatments used in combination with LSD "so as to jumble my thoughts and memories" and "to try to create a total amnesia" in his mind of all events that occurred in Greece and Panama.

In late 1956, the CIA brought Dimitrov, at his request, to the United States. Apparently, the Agency felt comfortable enough with Dimitrov's presumed diminished hostility and anger to agree to bring him to America from Athens, where he had returned for undetermined reasons. CIA files state, "The Agency made no further operation use of Dimitrov after he came to the United States." However, former CIA officials dispute this, stating that "[Dimitrov] was later used on a few occasions for sensitive jobs."

This, however, was far from the end of Dimitre Dimitrov's story, and in many ways was only the beginning of an even more bizarre saga.

DIMITROV IN THE UNITED STATES

Dimitre Dimitrov came to the United States in 1956 with his daughter, Daphne, and his Greek wife, Flora (Vavanos) Dimitrov. According to FBI files, the Dimitrovs flew into New York from Athens, Greece on November 26, 1956. One of Dimitre's first visits in New York was to the CIA's Domestic Contact Division office, where he requested financial assistance for the resettlement of his family. Dimitrov told the interviewing Agency officials that he was virtually without any funds, having spent the last five years imprisoned in Greece and Panama. CIA records seem to indicate that the Agency gave Dimitrov two $500 payments, the last one in May 1960. Following this, it appears that Dimitrov was given no additional financial assistance from the CIA or the Federal Government. CIA documents produced much later indicate that Dimitrov remained quite bitter about his experience at the hands of the CIA, and that he reminded the Agency of this whenever he had contact with them. Some Agency documents maintain that Dimitrov "resumed his bitterness toward the CIA" after the Agency refused to grant him what he thought was fair compensation for his imprisonment. Additional CIA records also reveal that Dimitrov asked the Agency on a number of occasions for assistance and support in resuming his opposition to the communists in Eastern Europe, but there is no indication that the CIA provided any such help.

From this point forward, Dimitrov's activities in the United States are sketchy and are only traceable through FBI documents and Dimitre's letters to friends. It appears that the Dimitrovs stayed in New York's legendary Chelsea Hotel in December 1956 and January 1957, with Dimitre attempting to make contact with several former Bulgarian opposition colleagues. By 1961, FBI records show that he traveled about four times to Ontario, Canada, where on one visit he was issued a Canadian driver's license.

In 1958, Dimitrov began to make contacts with various individuals connected with the Hollywood film industry, including a woman named Carol Jean Andren, who lived for about five months in New York's Hotel St. Moritz and was, for a period of time in 1958, an acquaintance of June Viola Cobb, whose story appears later in this book. (Very little is known about Andren.)

In 1961, at the urgings of family and friends, Dimitrov contacted an editor at *Parade*, a Sunday newspaper magazine that, at the time, and unknown to Dimitrov, had strong, informal ties to the CIA. Dimitrov's intention was to have the magazine publish an account of his story. He had been discussing his story as an opposition leader in Bulgaria and his time in a Greek prison and in Panama with a number of Hollywood movie producers, who had suggested that he first get some publicity about his experiences in order to gear the market for such a film. A *Parade* editor, who was initially very interested in what he learned from Dimitrov, contacted the CIA and was informed, according to CIA documents, that Dimitrov was "an imposter" who was "disreputable, unreliable, and full of wild stories about the CIA." The Agency told the editor he would be foolish to believe or to publish anything that Dimitrov claimed. Without doubt, this added to Dimitrov's bitterness toward the CIA.

In 1962 and 1963, Dimitrov was nearly destitute, with his wife working a full-time job in a factory. He was becoming increasingly frustrated with his efforts to create a lucrative endeavor in the film industry and to sell his story to either the publishing industry or Hollywood. At about this time, he attempted to generate income by producing other films. FBI records reveal that in 1963 he became associated with Orion Enterprises Cinematographiques, apparently a film production company that he organized and claimed was headquartered in Athens, Greece. The same year, he was using a business card that claimed he was associated with Diko Productions, Inc., a production company also located in Greece. Dimitrov told people that he had two feature films in production at the time, *The Loves of the Greek Gods* and *One Dark Night*.

On April 3, 1964, not long after he separated from his wife, Dimitrov was arrested in Los Angeles. Booking papers state that Dimitrov, born in Sofia, Bulgaria in 1924, was 5 feet 7 inches tall, weighted about 135 pounds, and had dark hair and brown eyes. One LA police department detective later described Dimitrov: "He was a good looking guy. Very smooth and cordial ... with his accent and movie star looks I could easily see how he could have conned anyone. Everything about him seemed real, genuine."

According to a draft FBI press release, he was charged with extortion and having "swindled at least $20,000 from people in the LA area while he periodically resided there from 1956 to 1961." Another FBI document, dated April 29, 1964, reads: "Dimitrov [then spelling his surname as Dimitroff] made claims that he knew prominent people in the movie industry and political circles as well as being personally acquainted with the Queen of Greece. He also claimed the Greek Government was backing his movie to be filmed in Greece." Los Angeles police and FBI officials, noted the document, were also aware that Dimitrov was wanted in Colorado for "obtaining $10,000 from a Colorado resident by means of a confidence game."

Little is known about what happened following Dimitrov's arrest. Apparently the charges went away, and while some people suspected that the U.S. government stepped in to protect Dimitrov, there is no evidence of that whatsoever. It is much more likely that Dimitrov, with assistance from a number of women friends, was able to obtain a good attorney who plea bargained his cases and was able to get key plaintiffs to withdraw their charges against Dimitrov. By all available accounts, from about 1964 to 1976, Dimitrov was able to survive on his intellect, wits, good looks, and the largesse of several wealthy women friends.

DIMITROV AND THE ASSASSINATION OF JFK

About ten years after Kennedy's assassination, Dimitrov – operating sometimes under the aliases James Adams, General Dimitre Dimitroff and Donald A. Donaldson – revealed to a number of people that he had information about "who had ordered the murder of JFK" and "who had committed the act." Dimitrov also said that he had encountered two of the assassins while he had been confined to the hospital in Panama. He also told several people that he had detailed information about military snipers who had murdered Martin Luther King, Jr..

On September 15, 1975, Dimitrov sent a confidential, registered letter to Senator Frank Church (D-ID), chairman of the Senate Select Committee to Study Governmental Operations with Respect to Intelligence Activities. Church's committee was investigating the illegal activities of the CIA and FBI, including CIA assassination programs and drug testing and human experiments, as well as projects MK/ULTRA and MK/NAOMI. The committee interviewed over 800 individuals, and conducted about 20 public hearings and 250 executive-session hearings. Dimitrov wrote that he had been following Church's committee work very closely and he had "decided to come forward and volunteer an appearance before your respectful committee." Promised Dimitrov: "I assure you that I am holding the answers to some very important questions.... One of the answers that I know is who gave the order to assassinate President John F. Kennedy. The President knew who gave the order, and he told me about it as he had received a warning. He asked me to look for prospective assassins among groups and people your Committee is now investigating. This means there was a well-organized conspiracy to assassinate the President. And the President was extremely puzzled about the man who gave the order to kill him."

It is uncertain if Sen. Church, anyone one on his committee, or any staff for the committee, ever responded to Dimitrov. A search of available Church Committee files reveals no documents pertaining to Dimitrov. In early 1977, Dimitrov told several people that he was unable to arrange an appearance before Church's committee because the committee staff "would not agree to my terms." This writer has been unable to locate the details of those terms.

About the same time that Dimitrov spoke of his failed appearance before the committee, he also made the startling revelation that he had met privately with President Gerald Ford at the White House in February 1976. According to Dimitrov, he met with the President for a few hours, and afterwards Ford had asked him to keep the meeting confidential until he had the opportunity to explore Dimitrov's information more fully and to consult with a number of people. Asked to comment on the meeting months later, reportedly a spokesman for the former President would say only, "No comment." (This author was unable to find any evidence of the meeting in Ford's official White House papers held in the Gerald Ford Library.)

Not long after the alleged Ford meeting, Dimitrov also reported to at least two newspaper journalists that JFK's widow, Jacqueline Kennedy, was holding a "top secret report" concerning her husband's assassination "that quoted Dimitrov on the key evidence of who killed Kennedy and why he was targeted for murder." Further, Dimitrov told the same two journalists that JFK's former close advisor and speechwriter, Theodore Sorenson, had seen the report and had also seen detailed information supplementing the report that had come from Dimitrov. Dimitrov maintained that it was because of this information seen by Sorenson, who Dimitrov said had promised to "flush all the murder and Mafia connections out of the CIA," that the former JFK aide had been aggressively opposed by the CIA after President Jimmy Carter nominated him for director of the Agency. (Sorenson withdrew his name due to opposition, and Stansfield Turner was named DCI. Sorenson later said, "I've always thought that the CIA's motto ought to be 'Often Wrong, But Never in Doubt.'")

If that were not enough, Dimitrov also maintained that the CIA had murdered Aristotle Onassis' 24-year old son, Alexander, on January 23, 1973, because the Agency wanted "to scare the hell out of [Jackie's then husband] Aristotle so that he would stay away from looking into the [Kennedy] assassination." Claimed Dimitrov: "I know who kill Alexandros and that he was killed only to send a message of what could happen to others in the families." (Reportedly, Dimitrov, without offering any evidence, fingered David Sanchez Morales as Alexander's killer, saying that Morales, who worked for the CIA undercover with AID and the U.S. Air Force, arranged to have Alexander's Piaggio seaplane crash on takeoff. Alexander died in the crash. Aristotle Onassis had married Jackie Kennedy on October 20, 1968.)

Without doubt, Dimitrov's activities, as only outlined above, had caught the serious attention of the CIA. Knowing this, Dimitrov, beginning in 1976, began predicting his own imminent death. He wrote in summer 1977, "Don't bet on me being alive much longer. I know they are coming for me. I know they can't let me live much longer. I only hope I don't end up like this Rosselli person. That was not pretty at all." Rosselli was Johnny Rosselli, a dapper, urbane Mafia member used extensively by the CIA as a covert operative. He disappeared in Florida in 1976 and died sometime in early August 1976. His dismembered body was found inside an oil drum in Miami's Dumfoundling Bay. He had appeared before the Church Committee as a witness, and was about to be called before the committee again just days before he vanished. Right before his death, he allegedly told columnist Jack Anderson that Oswald was killed by Ruby because the Mafia feared that he would crack and inform on them. Rosselli was close with a number of people who have long been suspected as having killed JFK, including not only mobsters Santo Trafficante, Sam Giancana and Meyer Lansky, but also the above-mentioned notorious CIA assassin David Sanchez Morales, and a number of lethal Cuban and American soldiers of fortune who constantly remained in Morales' sphere of influence and control. (See Notes for more on Rosselli.)

Dimitrov could not have been closer to the truth. When he met a Dutch journalist in May 1977, it marked the beginning of the end he had predicted for himself.

DIMITROV MEETS WILLEM OLTMANS

Frustrated that he was unable to testify before Sen. Church's committee, Dimitrov contacted George De Mohrenschildt sometime during the later part of 1976. Like many people, Dimitrov was aware of De Mohrenschildt's peculiar relationship with Lee Harvey Oswald. Dimitrov later wrote to a girlfriend, "One of my contacts at the Pentagon told me I should talk to this man [De Mohrenschildt]. He said this man had survived the publicity of the assassination and might be a good person to suggest to me what best to do." Dimitrov and De Mohrenschildt spoke at least once on the telephone and Dimitrov later said, "[De Mohrenschildt] told me I would serve myself well by going to the press ... finding someone who I could trust and telling my story."

On March 29, 1977, Dimitre Dimitrov, after recovering from his shock at having learned that George De Mohrenschildt had allegedly killed himself that same day, telephoned a Dutch writer and

Willem Oltmans

television correspondent named Willem Leonard Oltmans. Perhaps it was De Mohrenschildt who suggested Dimitrov contact Oltmans, since Oltmans was well acquainted with De Mohrenschildt, but we do not know for sure.

Oltmans was in Amsterdam when Dimitrov called and told the Dutchman that his name was "Jim Adams" and that he was interested in Oltmans' assistance in producing a big budget Hollywood film about JFK's assassination. Oltmans later said, "Since he had seen on television that I had been involved in investigative reporting of the Dallas murder, he felt we should get together." Dimitrov and Oltmans agreed to meet on May 31, 1977 at the Amsterdam Marriott Hotel. When Dimitrov appeared he told Oltmans that his real name was Dimitrov and that he was now known as General Donald A. Donaldson.

Now somewhat leery of Oltmans because of De Mohrenschildt's sudden death and the fact that he had no idea what the

Dutchman's true relationship had been with De Mohrenschildt, Dimitrov was cagey with Oltmans, but remained optimistic that he could gain some benefit through the journalist. As time went on, however, Dimitrov found ample cause to distrust Oltmans and to fear his tendency toward grandstanding and blatant opportunism. Dimitre would later tell a friend that he had been led to believe from his conversation with De Mohrenschildt that Oltmans was a respected and widely published journalist. Now that Dimitrov had been exposed to Oltmans, and had been able to check him out with other journalists, he was beginning to have serious doubts about the Dutchman's journalistic credentials and abilities.

Within weeks of their first meeting, Oltmans was attempting to convince Dimitrov to provide him with exclusive information about who had killed Kennedy and why, so that he could broker a deal for Dimitrov with then-President Jimmy Carter. Oltmans was vague about what actual benefit Dimitrov would derive from the arrangement, but consistently implied that Dimitrov would no longer have to worry about making financial ends meet for himself and his family. Dimitrov told Oltmans he needed time to think about any arrangement, but insisted that only he would verbally deliver to President Carter what he knew about JFK's murder. He also told Oltmans that he was overwhelmed at the time with efforts to get a feature film production off the ground in order to pay back his investors and realize a long sought dream. (Presumably, Dimitrov was also attempting to pay off those persons who had claimed he had swindled them.)

According to a letter he later wrote, Dimitrov told Oltmans, "I have to carefully think things through…. [You] don't know the danger I am in. [You have] no idea what could happen to me if I talk about certain people. I've seen firsthand what these people can do, what they are capable of, and you would not believe what I've seen."

In the same letter, Dimitrov also wrote, "It is very uncomfortable for me to be caught where I am … between journalists, who have their own objectives, and politicians with other objectives, all opposite in many ways my own. My dear, it is like when I was [in prison] in Greece and my fingers were placed in a vise and squeezed until my skin broke and blood came…. I feel like that again, helpless, caught in the middle."

181

Caught in the Middle ...

A round June 15, 1977, Willem Oltmans sent a letter to President Carter stating that he would appreciate meeting with the President as soon as possible so that he could "pass on to you some new and vital information on the JFK assassination." As noted earlier, Oltmans and Dimitrov had discussed the possibility of Dimitrov meeting with Carter and Dimitrov had said he was open to such a meeting, but would have to think about it before agreeing. Having never heard back from President Ford, Dimitrov recounted later, he had become very skeptical of following "the unpredictable way of politics," as he described it. Additionally, Dimitrov was becoming increasingly frustrated with Oltmans' handling of the overall situation.

"Why can't you just publish a big article that will capture all the attention necessary?" Dimitre asked Oltmans.

"I'm working on it," replied Oltmans. "But first I need to know everything that you know."

Dimitrov told Oltmans that when he was assured that an article was ready to be published in a major newspaper or magazine, he would allow Oltmans to interview him and ask any questions he wanted.

On July 15 Oltmans, having received no response from the White House, impatiently sent another written request to President Carter, by way of his Chief of Staff Hamilton Jordan, with a copy to White House attorney Robert J. Lipshutz. Oltmans' message, unseen by Dimitrov, displayed the Dutchman's political naiveté and lack of professionalism. The letter took a demanding tone underscored by Oltmans, implying that the President could find himself in a most embarrassing position if the White House continued to ignore the Dutchman's requests for a meeting.

In mid-August, Oltmans received a telephone call from the U.S. Department of Justice advising him that Robert Keuch, a deputy assistant Attorney General, would meet with him on the morning of August 29 at the Department of Justice. (Oltmans would later boast that Keuch was "a White House attorney" and "a Presidential lawyer" and that his meeting had been at the White House not the Department of Justice.) At their 10:00 A.M. meeting, Robert Keuch, Deputy Assistant Attorney General of the Criminal Division, told Oltmans that if he had any viable, previously unknown information about the Kennedy assassination, he should turn it over immediately. Oltmans, to whom Dimitrov had still not given the names of Kennedy's assassins nor their motive, told Keuch that he and his source would only turn their information over to President Carter in a face-to-face meeting. Keuch, mindful that Oltmans was a step or two short of being a bona fide journalist, attempted to explain to the Dutchman that the White House and Justice Department simply did not deal with information, however important, in the fashion that Oltmans desired. Oltmans boldly told Keuch that he would have to consult with his source before any decision was made as to how to proceed, and that he would get back to the Justice Department. Keuch would later agree with the CIA's assessment of Oltmans as merely one "of a myriad of 'assassination buffs,' although of questionable veracity."

Again, revealing his reckless lack of professionalism, and now in a highly visible manner, Oltmans called a press conference the next day at the Washington Hilton Hotel and, as he later wrote, "drew the attention of the press corps to the existence of a new witness in the JFK assassination who maintained he knew who ordered the assassination of the President."

When Dimitrov, the following day, learned of Oltmans' meeting with the Department of Justice and of his press conference, he flew into a rage, screaming that if he were not killed first, he would murder Oltmans "with my bare hands." Dimitrov, in London raising funds for one of his films, telephoned Oltmans and angrily told the Dutchman how he felt about his deception. Oltmans flew to London the next day to try to calm Dimitrov down and to ensure that he would not destroy all chances of gaining access to the vital information Dimitrov claimed to have.

Oltmans met with Dimitrov at the Holiday Inn near London's Heathrow Airport where Dimitrov was sharing a room with a close woman friend. When Oltmans arrived and asked to speak to Dimitrov alone, the Bulgarian told him that the woman would remain in the room. Oltmans stayed and listened as Dimitrov ranted, claiming Oltmans had ensured that he, Dimitrov, would soon be a dead man.

Oltmans argued, "I didn't give your name to anyone. I've never mentioned your name to anyone."

Dimitrov laughed at this and told Oltmans he was stupid and had no inkling of how easy it was to discover whom Oltmans was dealing with. When Oltmans scoffed at that, Dimitrov asked him if he had taken any precautions in telephoning him over the past several days or in coming to his Holiday Inn room. Oltmans countered that Dimitrov was being paranoid, and Dimitrov merely shook his head in resignation and sadness.

On the issue of precautions and personal safety concerns, Oltmans later wrote, seemingly without any regard for the possible danger Dimitrov could have been in:

> [Following the Washington Hilton Hotel press conference] I could not, at that point, release the name of Donaldson [Dimitrov], and this obviously irritated a number of writers and journalists, and I can hardly blame them for that. In some respects the press conference was premature. But on the other hand, *I needed the publicity to exert pressure on the authorities and, at the same time, protect myself in more than one way. For instance, I remembered what had happened to Dorothy Kilgallen after she had spoken for half an hour with Jack Ruby, the assassin of Oswald. She was found dead. [Dimitrov] himself had showered a series of warnings upon me to be extremely careful if I returned to the United States, because the Kennedy assassins would not hesitate to bump me off as well."* [Emphasis added. See Notes for Dorothy Kilgallen.]

Dimitrov finally told Oltmans to leave his room, yet the Dutchman continued to try to convince Dimitre that he was his best bet to financial reward and that he should give him all the information on Kennedy's murder that he had.

Dimitrov said, "I should kill you right here before they come to kill me."

Oltmans, knowing that all was lost and that no information would be forthcoming, told Dimitrov "that he was in my view an accomplice of the assassins by withholding that information for fourteen years."

Dimitrov lunged for the Dutchman, but the woman stepped between the two men and told Dimitrov that they should leave London right away. Replied Dimitrov, "It's too late. You should go right now and save yourself before they come for me."

Oltmans only made matters worse when, on his way out the door, he told Dimitrov that he was "not prepared to wait any longer."

Oltmans then offered "to arrange a television interview through [Netherlands] NOS-TV" for Dimitrov.

"They'll pay you $100,000," Oltmans said, most likely lying, and trying one last time to obtain Dimitrov's information.

Dimitrov laughed at the offer and shut the door in Oltmans' face, once again telling Oltmans to go away before he killed him.

Oltmans later wrote, "I ignored his threats, flew back to New York, and on September 8, 1977 I went before the cameras of ABC-TV in New York for fourteen minutes. On *Good Morning, America* I showed [Dimitrov's] picture and parts of his letter to Senator Church, and I gave the fullest information possible at the time, about this mysterious Bulgarian-turned-American general, and later, Hollywood producer."

Oltmans provided this account:

> I carefully stated during this ABC interview on David Hartman's show that my investigation into the data offered by [Dimitrov] had reached an end for me, that I had no way of further discovering whether he was speaking the truth and to what extent his statements could be corroborated by facts.
>
> I said that I had turned my notes over to both the Justice Department in Washington, D.C. and the Select Committee on Assassinations for further study and examination. In my opinion, the crime to kill the President of the United States justified my position, and it was no longer permissible for me as a journalist to withhold from the House Committee or the Justice Department any information I had obtained in the course of my own investigation, information that might assist other investigators to unravel the murder of the century.

Here it must be noted that Oltmans never informed Dimitrov that he was going to reveal his identity on national television in the United States. Further, the notes Oltmans turned over to the Justice Department and the Select Committee, according to both, were essentially worthless – as they contained no information whatsoever about what Dimitrov knew about the assassination. Lastly, Oltmans' testimony before the Select Committee (see section on Oltmans and De Mohrenschildt below), which almost exclusively concerned George De Mohrenschildt, was deemed basically worthless, and even laughable in places, by the Committee.

Several days after Oltmans' ABC-TV appearance, Dimitre Dimitrov vanished from the London Holiday Inn room where he was reportedly still staying. He has never been seen or heard from since. Former CIA officials, who declined to be identified here, say privately, "Dimitrov was murdered" and "his body will never be found." To date, nobody who knew Dimitrov has come forward publicly with any information regarding what he knew about the assassination of President Kennedy.

In October 1977, Americo R. Cinquegrana, an attorney in the CIA's General Counsel's office dispatched a priority memorandum to his superior, CIA General Counsel Anthony A. Lapham. Cinquegrana, while reviewing Project Bluebird/Artichoke files, had come across a January 27, 1952 memorandum about Dimitre Dimitrov that concerned him. Cinquegrana, who would go on to become the Agency's Inspector General for Investigations, provided Lapham with a written overview of Dimitrov's situation in Greece and Panama, noting that the Bulgarian had "been imprisoned in Greece on false pretenses" and flown to Panama where he "was misrepresented as a psychopath."

Cinquegrana alerted Lapham, "As you will note from the attached transcript of a 8 September interview on *Good Morning America*, Mr. Dimitrov (now General Dimitrov and known as General Donald A. Donaldson) apparently is alive and alleging that he knows who ordered the assassination of President Kennedy."

Cinquegrana continued: "Based solely upon the soft file summary, and prior to reviewing the official security file from which I extracted the additional details, it appeared to me that the nature of the Agency's treatment of Dimitrov *might be something which should be brought to the attention of appropriate officials within and outside the Agency. The fact that he is still active and is making allegations connected with the Kennedy assassination may add yet another dimension to this story.*"[emphasis added.]

Cinquegrana's memorandum to Lapham also indicated his understanding that Artichoke techniques were "never consummated" on Dimitrov. Possibly, Cinquegrana had not yet seen the complete hard file on Dimitrov, or perhaps Cinquegrana was laying the initial basis and trail for the CIA to attempt to plausibly deny that Dimitrov had been severely mistreated, tortured, and subjected to Artichoke techniques in Greece and Panama due to actions on the part of the CIA. (See Notes for more on plausible denial.)

Several hours later, General Counsel Lapham returned the memorandum to Cinquegrana with a pithy note written at the bottom: "See me ASAP about this." In addition, the same day, Lapham routed a copy of Cinquegrana's memo to the Agency's Inspector General and to Richard H. Lansdale, CIA Associate General Counsel, asking for "any thoughts on whether any action or further investigation needs to be undertaken with respect to this information."

On November 22, 1977, B. Hugh Tovar, the CIA's Chief, Counterintelligence Staff, at the direction of the Agency's Deputy Director for Operations, William W. Wells, sent a detailed memorandum to the Director of the FBI, Clarence M. Kelley, concerning the "Assassination of President John Fitzgerald Kennedy – Willem Leonard Oltmans, and Dimitur Adamov Dimitrov," as well as four sub-subjects, all of which reference previous memos on Oltmans to the FBI from the CIA.

The four-page memo, which makes no mention of Dimitrov's disappearance or murder, leads off with a paragraph on Willem Oltmans that reads:

> Since March 1977 of this year, [Oltmans] has appeared before the House Select Committee on Assassinations (on at least two occasions – 15 March and 1 April 1977), talked to the press, and appeared on television, claiming knowledge of conspiracies against the life of President John F. Kennedy.
>
> One of his prime sources, according to Oltmans, was George de Mohrenschildt. Oltmans claimed de Mohrenschildt has said "he had been the middleman in a conspiracy of rich Texas oilmen, headed by the late H.L. Hunt, and anti-Castro Cubans to kill Kennedy." (*Time*, 11 April 1977, p. 20). According to the same article, de Mohrenschildt "had been hospitalized as a psychiatric patient for two months at the end of last year, and he had twice attempted suicide." Oltmans is also quoted as saying that "de Mohrenschildt would vacillate between claiming his conspiracy tale was a hoax and asserting it was true."
>
> On 29 March 1977, de Mohrenschildt apparently committed suicide by placing a 20-gauge shotgun in his mouth and pulling the trigger. [See section on Oltmans and De Mohrenschildt below.]

On 28 August 1977, Oltmans told a UPI correspondent that he would meet with a Justice Department official the following day (29 August) to discuss safety guarantees for a person he said was "a CIA go-between in the John F. Kennedy assassination." According to the UPI release, the alleged go-between was the second of two men whom Oltmans said were involved in a conspiracy to kill Kennedy. The first man had been George de Mohrenschildt; the second, Oltmans declined to identify.

The remainder of the memo, initially issued publicly in a heavily redacted format that excluded all details about Dimitrov, focuses briefly on Oltmans' *Good Morning, America* appearance and his public identification of Dimitre Dimitrov. The following three pages focus on Dimitrov and seem to go out of their way in portraying the Bulgarian in a bad light, however, the memo nowhere mentions Dimitrov being tortured in Greece and being an Artichoke subject in Panama, despite that it does provide further intriguing information about his life prior to his coming to the United States.

The sections dealing with Dimitrov lead off with the ominous words, "[T]his Agency believes that Oltmans' 'new source' is one Dimitur Adamov Dimitrov, a Bulgarian born on 7 May 1924 in Medkovets, District of Lom, Bulgaria, in whom this Agency had an official interest from October 1950 to April 1951."

The memo, often oddly worded and without any explanation or details in places, goes on to state that Dimitrov, during the war, "worked illegally in Greek Macedonia and Vardar, Macedonia, to escape authorities," and that he returned after the war and "soon [became] disillusioned by [*sic*] the communists." Soon thereafter, Dimitrov "made a clandestine tour of Bulgaria towns and cities urging agrarians to take positive action against communism."

"Finally captured in Sofia," the memo states, "he [Dimitrov] stated his life was spared because he was groomed as a witness against Nikola Petkov." (Petkov, an opposition party leader, who attempted to overthrow the Bulgarian government, was hanged in Sofia's central prison.) In 1947, [Dimitrov] escaped to Greece, where he worked in propaganda projects, which the memo fails to mention as CIA-sponsored programs.

"In 1950," the memo continues, sometimes reading as if a first-year psychology major had drafted it, "the American Embassy evaluated Dimitrov as having a very great deal of the charlatan about him, and was considered a 'phony'. However, notwithstanding his superficiality and the exaggeration to which he was prone, Dimitrov had an intuitive grasp of the rudiments of political deportment and showmanship and he was so devoted to his self-appointed task of organizing his 'democratic block' that it was thought he might become an important Bulgarian figure. Dimitrov was then very active among Bulgarian refugees in Greece. Early in October 1950 he visited the Lavrion Camp where he spoke to the Bulgarian refugees and outlined the tasks that he was to assume, which included intelligence activities in Bulgaria, and organizing sabotage activity against Bulgaria. In April 1951, Dimitrov was in contact with the French Vice Consul and his wife, a French diplomat stationed in Athens, an elderly Greek who worked and otherwise had close connections with the French, and other Greek personalities. He also had several bed partners besides his wife.

"Observers in Athens consider Dimitrov to be too dictatorial and self-important, and if he was not actually insane, he appeared to be suffering from delusions of grandeur. Dimitrov felt that he could cause the downfall of the communist government of Bulgaria and would become prime minister of the country thereafter.

"In early 1951, various operational and administrative difficulties began to appear, and in April 1951 it came to the Agency's attention that Dimitrov intended to sell his operational knowledge to a foreign intelligence service. Because of operational security considerations stemming from Dimitrov's duplicity and personal makeup, it was decided to transfer him to a holding facility in the Western Hemisphere. He was flown from Athens to a Frankfurt hospital where he underwent four days of observation. [It was here that Dimitrov first encountered David Morales, when Morales was an enlisted man with the Army's 82nd Airborne assigned to the 7821st Composite Group, European Command.] Dimitrov was then flown to a CIA holding facility at Fort Clayton in Panama, arriving on 4 September 1951. Dimitrov remained there until January 1954 at which time the facility was to be closed down. Inasmuch as there were no immediate possibilities of resettling Dimitrov, he was moved from the holding facility to a refugee detention camp on the Greek island of Syros. Efforts were made to resettle Dimitrov in Canada, New Zealand, Australia, and elsewhere, but to no avail. It was finally decided that the best solution was to let him immigrate to the United States on his own under the auspices of the Refugee Relief Program. In October 1955, Dimitrov sought admission to the united States under that program."

There is little need to point out to readers that Dimitre Dimitrov's treatment and handling by the CIA during the years from 1950 forward was deceptive, brutal, inhuman, and quite illegal under international law. Nowhere in the above CIA summary of Dimitrov's life from 1945 to his coming to the United States, are we provided even a glimmer of the brutal torture he was subjected to in several Greek holding facilities and detention camps, nor are we told anything about his being an unwilling and unwitting enhanced-interrogation and Artichoke-techniques subject for at least three years in Panama. One can only marvel that he was able to survive his years in CIA hands and that he did not completely lose any semblance of sanity. That he was sent to the United States after years of brutal mistreatment and then abandoned to his own devices in a strange land amounts to little more than inexcusable inhuman treatment.

Dimitre Dimitrov never revealed what he knew about the assassination of John F. Kennedy to Willem Oltmans because he simply never trusted the Dutch journalist. Fortunately, we have a few glimmers of what he did know through a number of letters and remarks he made to friends during his final years in the U.S. and England. As already noted, Dimitrov encountered David Sanchez Morales at least twice in his lifetime under less than ideal circumstances. It is safe to assume that both times Morales played a domineering role in his exposure to Dimitrov.

In his communication to friends about Morales and the assassination, Dimitrov clearly connected Morales, whom Dimitrov was terrified of, to what he knew and what Oltmans so coveted. In one of his letters to a close friend, Marie Tosev, Dimitrov wrote: "[Y]ou have no idea how frightned [sic] I am of this man and his kind ... and I fear few men, dear.... It is of little hope or expectation that I would gain by telling what I know of Moreles [sic] and the others. In my lifetime I have seen too many times that standing up for what is right and truthful brings nothing more that misery and a quick death. For once, I would like to live a happy, carefree life before I go to death."

Chapter Five

"Welcome Back to America, Mr. Oswald."

In view of Mr. Oswald's extreme anxiety to not use the money sent him by his brother, we telephoned Miss Elliott of the State Department and informed her of Mr. Oswald's request.

– FBI Report, New York City, December 13, 1963

In one of the many "coincidental" happenings in the long and twisted saga of Lee Harvey Oswald, revealed here for the first time, is that Dimitre Dimitrov was held for four months in 1951 in the same refugee compound in Lavrion, Greece, as another Bulgarian named Spas T. Raikin.

This coincidence could perhaps be viewed as completely inconsequential were it not for the additional fact that in 1962 Spas Raikin earned a small and permanent spot in history when he was employed as a "case worker" for Travelers Aid Society in New York City. The Travelers Aid Society was a philanthropic service group that was under contract with the U.S. Department of Health, Education, and Welfare to assist repatriation cases assigned to HEW by the U.S. State Department. According to HEW records issued in 1963, Lee Harvey Oswald and his wife and daughter were "three of 42,891 persons helped by the New York [Travelers Aid] in 1962."

On June 13, 1962, the Society dispatched Bulgaria-born Spas Raikin to meet the SS *Maasdam* of the Holland-America Line when it arrived from Rotterdam and docked at Hoboken, New Jersey. Raikin's specific assignment, according to FBI documents, was to "assist LEE OSWALD and his

Spas Raikin 1951 or 1952

family who were arriving from Russia." According to all available records regarding Raikin's assignment, the fact that he had been born in Bulgaria and spoke Russian fluently, as well as three other languages, had nothing whatsoever to do with his being assigned to meet the Oswald family.

In summer 1962, Oswald had reportedly grown tired of living in Russia and with a $435.71 loan from the United States State Department, brokered for him by U.S. Senator John Tower, he returned to America with his 20-year-old wife, Marina, and their four-month-old daughter, June.

Over a year later, several days after the assassination of President Kennedy, the *New York Times* interviewed Spas Raikin about his 1962 encounter with the Oswald family in New Jersey. The subsequent article, published on November 26, 1963, makes no mention of how the newspaper became aware of Raikin or his work with Travelers Aid, but states that the *Times* contacted Raikin in Rio Grande, Ohio, where he was working as "an assistant professor of Western civilization at Rio Grande College."

Raikin told *Times* reporter Peter Kihss, "It was like pulling teeth to get information out of him," meaning Oswald. Explained Raikin: "I was under obligation to contact this man. I had been paging him three or four times for one hour on the ship, because the people were not allowed to disembark. For one hour apparently this man was hiding. He did not respond to the paging. Finally, when the people were let down on the pier, I waited for his luggage, so I caught him there. One thing that impressed me was that he was trying to avoid contact with anybody."

Raikin said that he found Oswald "extremely reserved in revealing any kind of information," yet, according to the article, he was able to elicit from Oswald what reporter Kihss dubbed "Oswald's considerably inventive version of his life in the Soviet Union." According to Raikin, Oswald's version of his life, without any direct quotes from him, was, as follows:

> Oswald had been a member of the Marine Corps on duty with the United States Embassy in Moscow; he had become acquainted with a Russian girl, married her and renounced his citizenship; he worked as a specialist electro technician in Minsk, but found things were not as rosy as Soviet propaganda promised;

it took him more than two and a half years to get exist [*sic*] visas for himself, his wife and child.

Worth noting is that while Raikin apparently recalled nothing more specific that Oswald had said to him about his time in Russia, Raikin did tell reporter Kihss that "Oswald was a man 5 feet 6 inches tall, slim. He wore a gray suit and a light blue tie," and the Oswalds "had six suitcases and one bag" with them when they came off the ship.

First FBI Interview with Spas Raikin

On November 27, 1963, the day after Peter Khiss' *New York Times* article was published, FBI agent Wilfred Goodwin sat down with Spas Raikin at the Bulgarian's home in Ohio. It is unclear what specifically prompted Goodwin's visit to Raikin, since it appears from his subsequent report, dated the same day, that Raikin may have telephoned the FBI on the day of Kennedy's assassination. However, Goodwin may have acted in response to the *New York Times* article.

Evidence that Raikin may have actually telephoned the FBI on the day of the assassination is in a FBI Airtel sent to the Dallas FBI office from its Cincinnati office dated November 27, 1963. The Airtel, bearing the subject "Spas T. Raikin," states, "RAIKIN advised that he telephoned SA [John James] Broderick, NYO [New York Office], on November 22, 1963, after he recognized OSWALD from television program." Further evidence is a June 21, 1964 "URGENT" teletype to FBI director J. Edgar Hoover stating that Raikin "verified information set forth in referenced teletype which he [Raikin] said he previously furnished to SA John Broderick of NYO."

Seven months later, however, a brief follow-up teletype, dated June 24, 1964 states, "No reference found in BUFILES [FBI files] to Broderick interview with Raikin and New York office should advise on this matter." The following day, June 25, 1964, an FBI Airtel to Hoover from the Bureau's New York Office also referred to information furnished to agent Broderick by Raikin: "NYO should advise regarding this matter inasmuch as no reference was found in Bureau files to such an interview." The Airtel further informs Hoover, "Raikin came to this country originally from Bulgaria and formerly lived in the New York City area."

Following this are two redacted lines of text that are unreadable, but may refer to either Raikin's CIA or ultra-right anti-communist associations, or both. The Airtel concludes: "RAIKIN telephonically contacted SA Broderick, at which time he advised of the above [his recognition of Oswald on November 22, 1963] and agreed to make himself available for a detailed interview by agents of the Cincinnati Office."

According to FBI agent Goodwin's report, on Friday, November 22, 1963, Spas Raikin "saw a television program concerning the assassination of the late President Kennedy and during the program, observed a picture of Lee Harvey Oswald and recalled that he [Raikin] had talked with OSWALD when he, RAIKIN, worked as a case worker [for Travelers Aid Society in New York City]." Goodwin interviewed Raikin in Rio Grande, Ohio where Raikin was an assistant professor of social sciences at Rio Grande College. Raikin recounted that he had been assigned by Mrs. Edna Norman, his supervisor at Travelers Aid, "to meet the Holland-American ship *Maasdam*, which docked at Hoboken, New Jersey." According to Goodwin's report: "In his capacity as a case worker, [Raikin] regularly met persons arriving on ships who needed financial assistance and OSWALD was in this category. It is his [Raikin's] recollection that OSWALD came to the attention of Travelers Aid from the Health, Education, and Welfare Department, who probably learned of OSWALD through the State Department of the United States."

Goodwin's report repeats what Raikin had told reporter Khiss about attempting to locate the Oswald family at the port. Raikin now added, however, that "his custom" in meeting people at the port was to go "immediately" to the Immigration and Naturalization Service office there to ask for assistance, and that he did so on June 13, 1962, requesting INS officials "to refer Oswald to him." At that point, according to Goodwin, Raikin "learned that OSWALD had already been cleared [for entry into the country] since he was a citizen of the United States." Goodwin's report states,

> [Raikin] next attempted to contact OSWALD by having him paged some three or four times over a period of approximately one hour over the ship's paging system. He [Raikin] feels confident that OSWALD heard the paging but OSWALD did not respond and he does not know why. Being unsuccessful in locat-

ing OSWALD through this medium, [RAIKIN] next went to the Customs baggage collection point, where baggage is assembled alphabetically, and located OSWALD's baggage, where he waited until OSWALD arrived with his wife and child. Mr. RAIKIN said that he spoke to OSWALD's wife in Russian, which language Raikin speaks, and that she greeted him, but that she stayed in the background and did not speak further. He then talked with OSWALD and recalls asking him why he returned to the United States and OSWALD replied in general terms something that now Mr. RAIKIN recalls as having to do with OSWALD being disillusioned with life in Russia. This point was not pursued further. Mr. RAIKIN said he was primarily concerned with furnishing OSWALD financial assistance to his destination, which he now recalls to have been Ft. Worth, Texas, where he was to live with his mother or brother. OSWALD told RAIKIN that he had some money, but not sufficient to get to their destination. Mr. RAIKIN did not recall the amount, but said that a reporter from the *New York Times* had suggested to him the amount of $46.00, which he feels is possibly accurate.

Raikin explained to Goodwin that he assisted the Oswald family "to board the Holland-America Bus, which took them from the Pier in Hoboken to the Port Authority Building in New York City, where they were met by his fellow case worker, Mr. F'PIERRE."

Raikin further explained to Goodwin that "he made a complete report at the time" and "that this report would be on file at the Travelers Aid office," but that "the reports are normally destroyed after one-year except in special cases." Raikin believed, according to Goodwin, "that this report was that type of case since it was referred to Travelers Aid by the Health, Education, and Welfare Department." (Raikin's report was never located and was presumed destroyed.)

Goodwin concluded:

Mr. RAIKIN never met or heard of OSWALD prior to the date on which he met him at the Hoboken, New Jersey Pier, never saw him or heard of or from him since that time. He does not know any members of his [Oswald's] family or any of his associates, nor does he have any further information concerning the political affiliations or philosophy of OSWALD.

Apparently, FBI Special Agent Wilber Goodwin was confident enough about what Raikin told him in his interview that he believed the above declaration to be true. However, Spas Raikin would soon magically recall several new and seemingly bizarre pieces of information about Oswald.

Raikin is Interviewed Again by FBI

Oddly, despite the published *Times* article about Spas Raikin on November 26, 1963 and the subsequent FBI interview with Raikin the following day, the Bureau did not interview Raikin again until about seven months later. This time, Raikin's recollections would set off a flurry of Bureau investigative activities.

An FBI report dated June 24, 1964, written by special agent John J. Connolly, Jr. gives an account of the FBI's second interview four days earlier, June 20, with Spas Raikin, after locating him in New Jersey, and reads in part:

> Mr. RAIKIN advised that while he was with OSWALD during the above period of time, OSWALD was very reticent to do any talking, but he [Oswald] did state he had been a guard at the American Embassy in Moscow, Russia, and had been kidnapped by communists agents. Mr. RAIKIN could not recall any further statements by OSWALD concerning this situation and he did not ask OSWALD any questions since he did not believe what OSWALD was telling him.

Apparently, agent Connolly did not ask Raikin why he did not believe what Oswald had told him or what knowledge Raikin had about Oswald before meeting him at the Hoboken harbor.

Hoover Orders Interview of Raikin Again

On June 24, 1964, a teletype marked "URGENT" was sent from FBI director J. Edgar Hoover's office to FBI agents in New York and New Jersey. The teletype contained Hoover's order that Newark, New Jersey agents "should re-interview Spas Theodore Raikin and specifically question him re allegation that Oswald claimed to have served as guard at the American Embassy, Moscow, and to have been kidnapped by communist agents."

For reasons that remain unclear, it seems that Hoover's directive was provoked by the FBI's serious concern that a book published earlier in 1964 in Europe, *The Red Roses of Dallas* by Nerin E. Gun, was connected to Raikin's statement.

Nerin Gun was a writer and free-lance journalist, born in Rome, Italy. Educated in France and Germany, he worked for a newspaper in Berlin at the start of World War II and was quickly arrested by the Nazis for his reporting on the Warsaw ghetto and the situation with Jews in Germany. Gun was held in several Gestapo prisons and then sent by the Nazi SS to three concentration camps, ending up in Dachau. Gun's book on the JFK assassination, published in Europe, contained a number of claims about Oswald – including that Oswald had traveled to Cuba, and had been an active duty Marine in Moscow who had been kidnapped by the Soviets – that drew the CIA's serious attention.

Several sources who declined to speak on the record, maintain that Gun's book was blocked by the CIA for publication in the United States and that the Agency's Security Research Service, on instructions from its director Paul F. Gaynor, made concerted efforts in 1964 and 1965 to destroy any copies it could lay its hand on in the United States, France and England. An August 18, 1964 FBI memorandum to William. C. Sullivan reads: "In both versions of his book [English and French] Gun attempts to cast doubt on the so-called 'official version' of the assassination and the evidence which points to Oswald's guilt as a lone assassin. The English version of the book, as the French version previously published, contains no factual information that would cause the Bureau to alter its conclusion that Oswald acted alone in the assassination of President Kennedy." (See Notes for more on Gun's book.)

Spas Raikin was interviewed again, as ordered, by telephone on June 25, 1964. According to the FBI's report on the call, Raikin again recalled that Oswald "stated he was with U.S. Marine Corps, and a guard at the U.S. Embassy in Moscow." Raikin also recalled "that Oswald may have said he deserted U.S. Marines rather than having been kidnapped." Raikin explained, according to a report of the telephone interview, that due to the "lapse of time" he could not "completely vouch for his recollection of Oswald's statements." Raikin also said, according to the report, that he "did not believe [Oswald's] allegations were true and felt Oswald made up the story to cover his defection to USSR."

A report by FBI agent John J. Connolly, Jr. dated June 26, 1964, two days after his earlier report and based on the additional interview with Raikin, reads:

> SPAS THEODORE RAIKIN advised OSWALD told him he was with the United Sates Marine Guard at the United States Embassy, Moscow, USSR, and on further recollection, Mr. RAIKIN recalls OSWALD may have said he deserted from the Marines rather than that he was kidnapped by communists agents. However, due to the lapse of time and the fact he handled so many other cases for Travelers Aid, he would not want to completely vouch for an accurate recollection of statements made by OSWALD. He stated the reason he did not go into detail with OSWALD regarding the statements he made was because he did not believe them to be true and felt that OSWALD made up the story to cover up the fact he had defected to the USSR which was known to Mr. RAIKIN.

Agent Connolly's report provides no explanation as to how or when Raikin became aware that Lee Oswald had defected to Russia, or how presumably Raikin had known that Oswald was no longer a Marine when he did so. Apparently, Connolly also did not inquire of Raikin how many other similar cases Raikin could have handled for Travelers Aid that would have caused him to question his recollections about Oswald. Nor did Connolly ask Raikin why he assumed Oswald had made his account up. Oswald's defection to Russia drew extremely little media attention at the time, and there is no evidence that people at Travelers Aid were informed about anything to do with Oswald's situation in the Soviet Union, or his circumstances before traveling there.

A summary report by agent Connolly, dated June 29, 1964, states:

> SPAS THEODORE RAIKIN, employed by the Travelers Aid, New York City, on 6/13/62 assisted OSWALD and family at Hoboken, N.J. During conversation [with Raikin] OSWALD declared he had been U.S. Marine Guard at U.S. Embassy, Moscow, USSR. [Raikin recalled] OSWALD may have said he deserted U.S. Marines rather than he was kidnapped by communist agents. However, lapse of time cannot guarantee accu-

rate recollection. Further, he [Raikin] believed statements made to cover fact OSWALD defected USSR. RAIKIN reported this matter to Travelers Aid at the time. [Author's note: There is no evidence that Raikin reported any of this information to Travelers Aid.]

The FBI's concerted attempts, and eventual success, at having alterations made in Raikin's account of his time and brief conversation with Oswald are odd and suggestive of something significant motivating the Bureau's efforts. But what? Was it to deflect any attention or credibility that might have been drawn toward Nerin Gun's book, which seems apparent, or was there a more complex reason?

LEE HARVEY OSWALD AND CLEARY F'PIERRE

A June 19, 1964 teletype to FBI director Hoover marked URGENT reveals that on that date FBI agent Emil E. Hopkins interviewed former Travelers Aid employee Cleary F'Pierre. F'Pierre, a Haitian who had come to America years earlier, told Hopkins that in 1962 he had been employed "as a professor at Elizabeth City State College in Elizabeth City, North Carolina, but had previously been employed by Travelers Aid in New York City from 1959 to September 1960. F'Pierre explained that he "was visiting New York City in June 1962 and stopped by Travelers Aid headquarters to visit with employees there."

According to Hopkins' report: "While there [at Travelers Aid], at about 1 P.M., Mrs. Edna Norman, supervisor, asked if he [F'Pierre] would assist her, since no one else was available to help." Mrs. Norman asked F'Pierre to take a man, his wife, and baby, according to Hopkins' report, from the Travelers Aid office to the Immigration and Naturalization Service office, located in downtown New York City.

The report continues: "This man was Lee Harvey Oswald. Mr. F'Pierre noted that Oswald's wife could not speak English and spoke only Russian. Oswald seemed able to speak Russian very well. Mr. F'Pierre stated he spent more time with Oswald than did anyone else at Travelers Aid and since he was with Oswald and Oswald's wife and child from about one P.M. until four-thirty P.M. he engaged in conversation with Oswald. They went from Travelers Aid office to INS by taxicab and after Oswald completed his business at INS, F'Pierre took Oswald and family back to Travelers Aid by taxicab."

199

Hopkins' report further states that F'Pierre commented that his conversations with Oswald were "primarily of a philosophical nature and he [F'Pierre] did most of the talking."

F'Pierre asked Oswald why he married a Russian girl and Oswald shot back by asking why F'Pierre had married his wife. F'Pierre asked Oswald how he was "able to marry a Russian girl and get out of Russia since he had heard that Russians were not allowed to leave Russia." Hopkins' report states that Oswald told F'Pierre that, *"he [Oswald] had to stay in Russia for about two years before he was allowed to bring his wife out of the country."* Oswald also told F'Pierre that he *"was returning to the United States to remain here permanently."* [Emphasis added.]

Apparently, quite curious, F'Pierre pressed Oswald and asked, "How he was able, as a citizen of the United States, to travel to Russia, saying he understood the United States Government did not allow such travel."

Oswald, according to Hopkins' report, told F'Pierre *"that he was serving in the U.S. Army* [sic] *in Europe and receiving his discharge while in Europe, Oswald stated, he traveled to Russia from where he was stationed in Europe after his discharge."* [Emphasis added.]

F'Pierre told Hopkins that "at no time" during the conversations "did Oswald mention that he had served as a guard at the American Embassy in Russia, or that he had been kidnapped by communist agents."

Hopkins' report continues: "F'Pierre stated he asked Oswald how he could, after having been raised in the United States, believe in the ideologies of communism. He [F'Pierre] recalled that, in answer to this query, Oswald mentioned that upon arriving in the United States he had to worry about such things as taxi fare and high rent, whereas while in Russia he did not have to pay high rent."

Hopkins' report states that F'Pierre challenged Oswald in a sense: "F'Pierre pointed out to Oswald that the theories of communism sounded good on paper but were not workable in practice, but Oswald indicated he felt they were workable."

F'Pierre at this juncture in the interview, told agent Hopkins that he thought, "Oswald did not know what to think, and was 'lost', that is, did not know in what direction he was headed in life."

When agent Hopkins finally got around to asking F'Pierre about what had transpired at the INS, after the Oswalds arrived there,

F'Pierre said he "did not know what transpired there." However, F'Pierre recalled "that a man, who had the features of a native of the Philippine Islands, whose name F'Pierre does not recall, if he ever knew it, took Oswald into an office at INS, and F'Pierre waited in the waiting room area until Oswald returned." (F'Pierre makes no mention of Marina Oswald or the Oswald baby, June, during this alleged waiting period at INS, nor does it seem that agent Hopkins asked anything about them.)

In response to Hopkins' last question to F'Pierre, "F'Pierre re-iterated that Oswald never mentioned having served as a guard at the U.S. Embassy in Russia and never mentioned having been kid-napped by communist agents. Mr. F'Pierre does not know Nerin E. Gun and is not familiar with the book, *The Red Roses of Dallas*."

When Hopkins concluded the interview, F'Pierre told the agent that following the assassination and after Oswald's arrest, he "felt somewhat guilty because [he felt] he had assisted Oswald in a small way."

In the teletype summary of Hopkins' report sent to FBI director Hoover, the Bureau's Cincinnati office dutifully wrote, "New York [Office], if not already done, will interview official at INS, New York City who handled Lee Harvey Oswald on June thirteen, Nineteen Sixty-Two, when he arrived in New York from Russia."

Apparently, the INS interview never happened. Subsequent FBI re-ports indicate that either Cleary F'Pierre was mistaken about where he took Oswald from Travelers Aid, or agent Hopkins misunder-stood F'Pierre's explanation about where he took Oswald from the Travelers Aid office on June 13, 1962. Another URGENT FBI tele-type dated June 22, 1964, three days after F'Pierre's interview, states in part: "[It would appear that F'Pierre was mistaken in stating he escorted Oswald and family to INS office, NYC."

The teletype also reveals additional information on Lee Harvey Oswald's first day back in the United States. The report reveals that an FBI review of the INS, NYC manifest indicates that the Oswald fam-ily, upon arrival at Hoboken were processed by INS inspector Fred-erick Wiedersheim and that "no unusual notations were disclosed on the manifest" regarding the family's entry into the United States. In-terviewed by the FBI on the same date as the teletype, Wiedersheim stated that he "did not specifically recall processing [Oswald] and family in view of large number of individuals processed daily." The INS inspector also stated that he recalled no statements made by Oswald upon entry. Wiedersheim told interviewing FBI agents that had Oswald made any statement about having been a guard at the American Embassy in Moscow and having been kidnapped, he "would have made a record of same and notified the proper authorities."

Further, and directly contradictory to F'Pierre's statement, Wiedersheim "advised the FBI that here would have been no reason to have brought Oswald, as a U.S. citizen, to the INS office in downtown New York City unless there was a warrant outstanding for his arrest, nor would there have been any reason to have brought his wife to INS as long as her papers were in order."

Equally confusing matters and contradictory to F'Pierre's interview statement is that on the same day Wiedersheim was interviewed, FBI agents interviewed Filemon Villareal, a social investigator for the NYC Department of Welfare who, according the FBI's report, had been "acting as a receptionist" at the Welfare Department on June 13, 1962, when the Oswalds reportedly visited there. Villareal told the FBI that an employee from Travelers Aid, whose name he did not recall, but assumed to be F'Pierre, brought Oswald to the Welfare Office on June 13, 1963, but the employee "did not wait for Oswald and family but left shortly after accompanying them to the office." Obviously, Villareal's account does not agree with F'Pierre's, who told the FBI he was with the Oswalds for three-and-a-half hours during the afternoon of June 13, 1962. Villareal explained that the Oswalds came to the Welfare Office for the express reason of obtaining $200 so that they could continue their journey by air to Forth Worth, Texas, where they were to live with Oswald's brother, Robert, until they could find a place of their own.

Lastly, and further confusing matters is that the June 22, 1964 FBI teletype states, "It is to be noted that Villareal is a Filipino and is probably the individual referred to by former TAS employee Cleary F'Pierre." The teletype also makes no mention of who it was that met privately with Oswald in the Welfare Department office, nor does it indicate that Villareal was questioned about whether or not he met privately with Oswald, as F'Pierre had stated.

This author could locate no other files or documents concerning F'Pierre's alleged mistake about where he took the Oswalds and there are reportedly no other documents in the FBI's files concerning any additional interviews or telephone calls to F'Pierre to gain his reaction or response to his alleged mistake. This author will observe that it seems peculiar that F'Pierre would confuse the New York City Welfare Office with that of the INS. This author also observes that the FBI's report on Oswald's return to America seemed almost solely directed at his alleged statements about being an Embassy guard and having been kidnapped and appear to have no investigative interest in any other details regarding Oswald's return. Given that Oswald was a defector, who had renounced his American citizenship in Russia, had threatened to give the Soviets top-secret information regarding his military work, and had married a Russian citizen, this may appear odd to a reasonable person.

That apparently nobody from the FBI, CIA, or any other Federal entity had any interest in promptly interviewing Oswald upon entry seems, at the very least, peculiar behavior for agencies charged with protecting the security of the United States and its citizens. Lastly, by some accounts, unverified by this author, F'Pierre dropped out of sight sometime in 1965 or 1966.

Interesting to note here is that in 1978, assassination investigator and writer Edward Jay Epstein maintained in his book, *Legend: The Secret World of Lee Harvey Oswald*, that assassination researcher Jones Harris had interviewed Cleary F'Pierre at an ungiven date and place after the FBI had spoken with the Haitian. Epstein writes, "F'Pierre told Harris that he left the Oswalds at the railroad station, assuming that they would soon be departing by train." Epstein continues: "These details were not included in FBI Agent Hopkin's [*sic*] report of this interview. It is possible that Oswald took a train to Washington, D.C. that evening. A psychologist code-named Cato on assignment for the CIA claimed to have interviewed a Russian defector at the Roger Smith Hotel who resembled Oswald. Oswald could then have returned in time to visit the Welfare Department the following morning. This, of course, would be inconsistent with Marina's testimony that she and Oswald spent the evening in New York." Given that train schedules in 1962 between New York and Washington, D.C. would not have allowed for this alleged trip, this claim seems highly doubtful. This also author seriously questions the results of Jones Harris' interview with Clear F'Pierre.

Epstein also included in his book that Spas Raikin had been instructed by his Travelers Aid Supervisor to "find out as much as he could about Oswald" but Epstein cites no source for this and, as can be imagined, Raikin has never made any such statement to anyone much less the FBI.

OTHERS WHO DEALT AND SPOKE WITH OSWALD IN NYC

Perhaps clarifying some of the confusion and questions about Oswald's time in New York City, and perhaps compounding it in other ways, are two 1964 FBI reports concerning interviews with James M. Josoff, Public Affairs Director of the Travelers Aid Society of New York, and several other Travelers Aid and Welfare Department employees. James Josoff told the FBI that the Oswald family left the Welfare Department office on their own and took a taxicab to the Times Square Motor Hotel at 8th Avenue and 43rd Street, with Oswald paying the fare of $1.50, which amount Josoff verified with a local cab company. Josoff also told the FBI, according to two Bureau reports dated April 10, 1964 and a May 3, 1964, that "it appeared from the Travelers Aid record" that "Oswald and his family stayed at the Times Square Motor Hotel" on the night of June 13, 1962. On April 9, 1964, according to the reports, John Huber, Jr., the manager of the hotel told the FBI that his files showed that an "L. Oswald" registered at the hotel on June 13, 1962, and checked out the next day, June 14, 1962.

"Huber stated," reads the reports, "that Oswald's bill, totaling $15.21, included $10 for the room, $.50 tax and $4.71 for telephone calls." Huber also told investigating agents that the hotel's telephone toll cards were destroyed after six months and the only information available regarding the calls "is that one long distance call amounting to $2.31 was placed on June 13, 1962 and one long distance call amounting to $2.20 and one local call amounting to $.20, were placed on June 14, 1962." The FBI attempted to find out more about Oswald's calls, and on April 10, 1964, Edward L. Braune, a Security Supervisor for the NYC Telephone Company, told agents that the company's records had been routinely destroyed for those dates. (Interestingly, an FBI report dated 1969, reveals that John Huber, Jr. in his capacity as manager of the Times Square Motor Hotel, was mentioned in a criminal investigation regarding the murder of Michael Granello in New York City. Huber, misidentified in several FBI documents as "John Hauber, Manager, Times Square Hotel," according to the FBI, associated with a number of the persons involved in the murder. The House Select Committee on Assassinations files, for unexplained reasons, contain reports regarding the Granello murder.)

FBI investigators, on April 8, 1964, spoke with Dorothy Downing, Supervisor, Special Investigations, New York City Welfare Department, who also informed them that after Oswald left the Special Services office, he and his family registered at the Times Square Motor Hotel. Downing explained that the Oswalds returned early the next morning, June 14, 1962, "at which time he [Lee Oswald] was accompanied to the Western Union office at 428 Broadway, which is only a few blocks from the Special Services office, where he obtained $200 sent by his brother from Texas."

Earlier FBI reports, from December 1963 are far more revealing of Oswald's time in New York City, as well as very revealing of Oswald's overall character and concern for his family. The same December 1963 Bureau reports reveal previously unpublished details about Oswald's time in 1962 in New York City. These details, in summary form, follow below.

Prior to the arrival of the Oswald family in New York City, in early June 1962, Lulu Jean Elliot, a Senior Consultant to the NYC Welfare Department informed Janet F. Ruscoll, Administrative Supervisor, NYC Welfare Department, that if the Oswalds needed any financial help upon their arrival, such help was available through HEW's Repatriation Program, for which the Oswalds were eligible. Elliot said that this information was relayed to her from a "Miss Chodia" of U.S. Department of Health, Education and Welfare. Chodia told Elliot that the Oswalds were "considered destitute." Oswald upon arrival in New York had only about $63, and needed additional funds to take his family on to Texas.

For reasons not fully explained in the handful of documents concerning Oswald's visit the NYC Welfare Department, but perhaps because of bureaucratic processes and entanglements, Oswald was unable to obtain $200 from the Welfare Department and instead received these funds from his brother Robert through a Western Union cash transfer to New York. The wire transfer was arranged by the Welfare Department telephonically with Robert Oswald on June 13, 1962. Evidence of this is found in the notes contained in the Welfare Department's June 1962 "History Sheet" on the Oswald family which reads: "[The Oswalds] had only $63 upon their arrival. They were brought to our office upon their arrival by a worker from Travelers Aid. They were referred overnight to the Times Square Hotel and Mr. Oswald returned to our office the following morning. Before leaving our office on 6/13, a long distance call was placed [by a Welfare Department employee] to client's brother, Robert Oswald, 7313 Davenport St., Ft. Worth, Texas. Mr. [Robert] Oswald informed us that he would take out a mortgage on his car for $200 and send this money to us the following day."

The "History Sheet" continues: "[The next day] June 14, 1962, client [Lee Harvey Oswald] was seen in this office, and at first balked at using the money sent by his brother. He preferred that this money be returned to his brother, and that we advance the money for transportation expenses, and he would repay us when he is able." (The previous day, Oswald had thought he was applying for a loan of $200 from the Special Services office of the Welfare Department and had no idea that his brother was telephoned and asked to wire the funds.)

According to the History Sheet, when Oswald made this request he had become agitated. Oswald then insisted on speaking with a person in a position of authority with the Welfare Department. A supervisor, Janet Ruscoll, sat down with Oswald. Oswald, according to supervisor Ruscoll's subsequent report, "urgently requested" that the $200 be sent back to his brother. Oswald told Ruscoll "that his brother is a dairy deliveryman and that it had been a great hardship upon his brother to advance the money."

According to a subsequent FBI report dated December 1963 that quotes from the Welfare Department's History Sheet: "Mr. Oswald said [to Ruscoff] that he telephoned his brother this morning [June 14, 1962 from the Times Square Motor Hotel] and was informed by his brother, Robert, that the money was raised by placing a mortgage on his car." The report continues: "Mr. Oswald was so anxious that he not use the money sent by his brother that he stated he was considering returning the money and using the small portion of his own funds remaining to carry the family as far as these monies would permit, and then requesting the local authorities to transport him the balance of the way to Texas. We [Ruscoll and Welfare Department] discussed with Mr. Oswald that that would be poor planning on his part, that it was urgent that he reach his destination in Texas for the benefit of his family group, that any locality in which he stopped off might contact us and that it would be obligatory for us to report about the fact he had the funds available to him here for his return to Texas."

Apparently, Oswald did not back down to this subtle threat, as the report continues: "In view of Mr. Oswald's extreme anxiety to not use money sent him by his brother, we telephoned Miss Elliott of the [U.S.] State Department and informed her of Mr. Oswald's request.

The report December 1963 continues: "Miss Elliott told us that she would discuss the matter with the New York City office of the Department of Health, Education and Welfare and call back. She called back later and requested additional information regarding the man's relatives. She was informed that Mr. Oswald has told us that Robert is his only full sibling. He has one half-brother, who is a sergeant stationed in Japan, who has a wife and two children. His only other relative is his widowed mother who has no home establishment of her own and who makes her home with the persons for whom she works, moving from job to job as a practical nurse for elderly patients. We gave Miss Elliott the information regarding the flight and departure time, and arrival time in Texas, obtained from the [Welfare] Unit. Miss Elliott said that [HEW] is wiring ahead to the local public assistance agency [in Texas] informing them that should Mr. Oswald apply for assistance, any funds expended [on] his case are federally reimbursable under the Repatriation Program. Any assistance extended will not create difficulties for his wife with the Immigration authorities. It will be necessary for Mr. Oswald to use his brother's funds for his return transportation. This information was shared with Mr. Oswald. He was not completely satisfied with the decision but accepted it and accepted the fact that on this point the wisest course he could pursue was to prepare himself and his family for the return flight today."

The report then concludes with an explanation of Oswald's final activity in New York: "We escorted Mr. Oswald to the Western Union office 428 Broadway, who issued $150 and gave client a check made out for $50, to be cashed at the 1st National Bank on Broadway and Canal. We then escorted client to the 1st National Bank, where after first being told that they could not cash the check eventually agreed at the bank manager's insistence that they would cash it. [Oswald] was issued $50. [No reason is given as to why this problem was encountered with the check.]

"[A Welfare Department employee] then went with [Oswald] to the West Side Airlines Terminal and bought two tickets previously reserved for flight 821, Delta Airlines, to Ft. Worth, Texas.... [The employee] and [Oswald] then went to Times Square Hotel where client paid his bill, went to his room to pick up his wife and baggage and infant, and met [department employee] in the lobby. At this point, he had 5 pieces of luggage. [Employee], who had seen client with 7 pieces the day before, asked [Oswald] what had happened to the other two pieces, and he informed us that he had sent them on ahead, railway express. [Employee] helped client and his family and his baggage to the street where [they] took a taxi to ESAL [East Side Air Lines: baggage check-in], and checked [Oswald's] luggage and then escorted [Oswald family] to the Delta Airlines building at Idlewild, remaining with Mr. Oswald until he boarded his plane at 4:15 P.M." It is not known when, how, or why Oswald went about placing two pieces of luggage on railway express, or what was in these pieces of luggage.

Of course, at this juncture, readers may be seriously wondering and asking themselves why it was at all necessary for the Oswalds to have visited the Welfare Office to begin with had Lee Harvey Oswald known all along that his brother was sending money for his trip to Texas. The short answer appears to be that, while not clearly indicated in any documents, Lee Oswald had expected that the needed funds were to be provided directly by the NYC Welfare Department and was unaware that his brother had been telephoned until it was too late to receive the funds any other way. Additionally, as some readers may think, it does not seem at all out of the realm of possibilities that the entire matter regarding the $200, was a classic case of bureaucratic red tape, and not some sort of contrived ruse to delay Oswald's return to Texas for reasons unknown. Anyone who scoffs at this, should first consider the true nature of Spas Raikin in 1962.

Nobody Reveals Raikin was a CIA Employee

Neither the FBI nor U.S. Department of Justice, nor any other federal group, including the Warren Commission, made any mention that Spas Raikin was a contract employee for the CIA. Raikin's covert employment by the CIA would remain a closely held secret for decades.

According to CIA documents dated 1957, some by CIA Security Officer Robert Cunningham – who participated in the post-murder cover-up of Dr. Frank Olson's death in New York City– Spas Raikin was first cleared and approved for hire by the Agency on August 22, 1957. W.M. Knott of the Agency's Personnel Security Division, Office of Security, issued Raikin's final clearance for CIA employment with Project USJPRS in New York City on December 13, 1957. Project USJPRS was a just organized program within the United States Joint Publication Research Service, whereby mostly unwitting CIA contractors reviewed foreign language technical and defense-related publications for the Agency. The USJPRS was created within the U.S. Commerce Department's Office of Technical Services in March 1957 "to provide government agencies with translations of unclassified foreign documents and publications worldwide.

This would be the beginning of a somewhat mysterious professional relationship lasting at least fifteen years between Raikin and the Agency. Here, however, it is important to note that the *initial* CIA Request for Clearance for Contract Personnel, listing Spas Raikin and seven others to become contract employees with the Agency, specifically stated that all names on the list "will not be made witting of true employer [CIA]." It would be another two years, in 1960, before Raikin would become fully aware he was working for the CIA.

Additionally, a FBI document dated November 20, 1957, designated "SUBJECT: RAIKIN, Spas T" and sent by courier to the CIA, reveals a deeper interest in Raikin. The two-page document details Raikin's life, family background, and military activities in Bulgaria, as well as his coming to America in 1954, where he quickly became Secretary of the Bulgarian Escapee Program of the Church World Service in New York City. Shortly after, he became Secretary-General of the right-wing, anti-communist Bulgarian National Council headquartered in New York City, a position he held when he encountered Oswald in New York.

One of Raikin's first acts in this position, as revealed by Raikin's CIA 201 file, was to send a letter on September 19, 1962 to CIA director John McCone. The letter invited the DCI to come to New York City to take part in a memorial event honoring "the fifteenth anniversary of the tragic death of Nikola Patkov, leader of the Bul-

garian parliamentary opposition to the communist regime in Sofia." Raikin's letter to McCone also states: "The Bulgarian National
Council is greatly honored to announce that the official Proclama-
tion issued by Governor Nelson A. Rockefeller declaring September
23rd, 1962 the NIKOLA PETKOV DAY will be read at the celebra-
tion." [Raikin misspelled McCone's name on the letter, "MacCone."]
Raikin also sent a steady stream of ingratiating letters to the House
Un-American Activities Committee, frequently forwarding carbon
copies to the White House, U.S. State Department and CIA. At the
same time, according to a number of declassified "SECRET" CIA
personnel 201 assignment forms, Raikin was "sponsoring" a long
line of Bulgarian refugees for work assignments with the Agency.

At least 100 pages of CIA documents concerning Spas Raikin
remain classified "SECRET." However, a declassified CIA "Confidential Notice of Security Action" reveals that in January 1967, four
years after the JFK assassination, Spas Raikin applied for full-time
employment with the CIA. Following at least one Agency polygraph session, Raikin was cleared by the CIA's Office of Security for
several possibly sensitive positions in Washington, D.C. and Langley, Virginia: "at the headquarters building;" "at building #213 Naval
Weapons Plant," "as a GSI employee in the headquarters building,"
"as a C. and P. Telephone Co. employee in Agency buildings," and
"as an independent contractor of US/JPHS."

HOW SPAS RAIKIN CAME TO THE UNITED STATES

According to several CIA documents generated in 1957, while
Spas Raikin was being considered for additional assignments
with the CIA, Raikin and two other Bulgarians, on May 6, 1951, deserted their Trudovaks (Bulgarian Labor Corps) military unit "and
made their way to Plovdiv [city in Bulgaria] and then to Greece."

A November 1957 FBI report, in response to the CIA's request to
the Bureau for any information it had on Raikin, reads: "The reason
for [Raikin's] desertion was to join an alleged illegal group working
in the mountains south of Plovdiv. Unable to make contact with the
group [Raikin and his two fellow deserters] wandered around the
mountains obtaining provisions from relatives and friends. Unable
to hold out any longer they entered Greece on June 19, 1951."

The report elaborates on Raikin's desertion: "Subject's [Raikin's]
desire to desert was to join in the fight against communism in the

name of the Bulgarian Orthodox Church. When he found it would be impossible to do so inside Bulgaria, he decided to escape to Greece and join such a church group there, if such existed. If none existed, he desired to form a militant illegal church group to fight communism inside Bulgaria."

The 1957 FBI report cites an earlier FBI report dated November 21, 1956, concerning Vladimir Tyekoff Metchkarski, identified as "a Bulgarian political exile who became disgruntled in the U.S. and sought to return to Turkey." The FBI report states, "A Mr. Raikin [Marginal note spells name Spas Raykin] was sent to Chicago by the World Council of Churches in New York to assist Metchkarski."

The same FBI report also cites a September 12, 1951 CIA report "concerning the Bulgarian Orthodox Church prepared from information furnished by Raikin *who considers himself an ordained priest in the Bulgarian Church. In preparing the information [Raikin] used the nom de plume Prezviter KOSMA. The FBI field station comments that [Raikin] was brought to Athens from Salonika [a major port in Greece] on 19 July 1951 to work for CIA LKB... GASP/10."* [Emphasis added. The letters "CIA LKB... GASP/10" are handwritten, presumably by a CIA or government official, on the document copy provided this author.] GASP and GASP/8 were elite, ultra-secret CIA interrogation teams.

The FBI report briefly noted that the CIA already knew from Raikin's GASP interrogation in the Greek refugee camp that he was born on October 26, 1922 in Zelenikovo, Bulgaria. It stated: "He is single and has two brothers, Petur and Stoyu, who are farmers in Zelenikovo. His father, Todor Petrov RAIKIN, is living and is also a farmer. Subject [Raikin] finished the Theological Seminary in Plovdiv and the Theological Faculty in Sofia. He then taught for one year on the Sofia Faculty. On 5 April 1950 he was called up for military service and was assigned to Bezmer airfield until 22 December 1950 when his unit was transferred to Balchik airfield."

A CIA memorandum written on November 26, 1951 and sent by air pouch the same day to the CIA FDP chief provides a wider look at Spas Raikin's first encounter with the CIA in Greece, following his interrogation. Chief of Station Lloyd K. Desmond, a CIA official who would play a still-unexplained role in the CIA's hasty post-assassination investigation into Lee Harvey Oswald's Mexico City phone communications, signed the document. ("Lloyd K. Desmond" was a pseudonym for an unidentified high-ranking CIA official. See Notes on this section for Desmond's Mexico City role.) The 1951 memorandum reveals events that occurred after Raikin's interrogation.

In his memorandum, Desmond notes that Spas Raikin, along with six other Bulgarian men who had escaped to Greece, had been interrogated by both GASP and GASP/8 "in order to get an organized report on their situation and to check their individual statements against each other in an effort to find out if any of the individuals may be a Bulgarian agent." Desmond also noted that Raikin and the other escapees had been interrogated "to ascertain their future possible operational use."

Desmond's memorandum, using CIA parlance, refers to the escapees as "bodies," requesting that his superiors in CIA headquarters place the seven Bulgarians as quickly as possible in Greek safe houses "in order to properly evaluate their operational potentials" and to "prevent them from getting contaminated in the Lavrion Camp." Writes Desmond: "In the meantime the bodies will be individually evaluated and every effort will be made to pick up any additional information bearing on the security factor.... If a sound operational plan [after the men are divided into two groups and placed in safe houses] is formulated for each group, a project outline will be forwarded soonest, bearing in mind that we can hold one member of each group here as a hostage in order to be reasonably sure that the men who go on a mission will not double-cross us."

Other FBI and CIA documents reveal that Raikin came to the United States in late 1954 and became a United States citizen in 1959, as noted in a July 15, 1960 handwritten CIA memorandum that reads: "Raikin's resume seemed so interesting, I thought someone might have an interest.... How about McPherson's staff?" ["McPherson" is thought to be a reference to Fort McPherson in Georgia, where in the late 1950s the CIA, Army G-2 intelligence and the Office of Naval Intelligence maintained a contingent of intelligence operators interacting with other units in Florida.]

"OVER AMBITIOUS MERCENARY, MEGALOMANIAC ..."

A fascinating and once-stamped "SECRET" September 9, 1960 CIA memorandum on Spas Todorov Raikin reveals that some CIA officials had deep concerns and suspicions that Raikin was "a 'sleeper' type agent" for the communist-controlled Bulgarian Intelligence Service (BIS). The document, written by Donald M. Allen (most likely a pseudonym for a CIA security official) states that when the Agency initially reviewed and approved Raikin for CIA employment, "many reports emanating from [name redacted] are missing or rather had never been included in the [CIA's 201 file on Raikin] and that subsequent activities of his [Raikin's] in Switzerland and the United States had never been reported."

Donald Allen reveals early in his memorandum that he was amply familiar with Spas Raikin because he "was directly involved with Raikin's initial refuge in Greece." Allen states that he "participated in the interrogation of Raikin and others who defected with him due to the suspicious nature of their escape story." Allen does not mention it, but earlier CIA documents reveal that he was a member of the elite, ultra-secret CIA interrogation team known only as GASP and GASP/8.

Allen's memo reveals that during Raikin's time "in the DP [displaced persons] camp in Athens [Lavrion], Raikin became actively involved in political discussions and at the time claimed to be an adherent "of a right wing faction that had been outlawed" after the communist takeover of Bulgaria. States Allen: "[Raikin's] political machinations caused splitting of the refugees into splinter groups and rather than succeeding in affecting unity, it caused disunity. Again, the thought came up as to whether Raikin was a provocation agent or not. However, no evidence was uncovered to substantiate this theory."

Allen's three-page document emphasizes that four CIA covert operatives in various locations in Europe and the United States had shared with him their serious suspicions about Raikin possibly being an undercover agent for the Bulgarian intelligence service. Included among these operatives was a woman codenamed GOLONESOME in Switzerland, where Raikin traveled after leaving Greece, according to Allen, to "study in a theological seminary under the World Council of Churches (WCC)."

Also casting suspicions on Raikin, after the Bulgarian arrived in the United States in July 1954, was Boris Clark, whom Allen identified as "a former contract employee of the Agency who was stationed in Greece as an interrogator." Earlier, following the end of the war, Clark had worked with the Office of Naval Intelligence and CIA in Germany. Clark told Allen that both he and his wife, who apparently also had contact with Raikin, "complained bitterly" to Dean Woodruff, then Chief of the CIA's Bulgarian Branch, about Raikin's presence and activities in the United States. Interesting to note here is that Woodruff earlier had dealings with David Sanchez Morales and Lucien Conien when all three men were involved in intelligence matters in Germany.

Allen writes, "According to the Clarks, Raikin's activities could indicate that his job was to create chaos and division among Bulgarian émigrés and which could logically be a requirement of the BIS."

Another person, identified by Allen only by the codename DILABBIO, a consultant to the CIA who had been very much involved in the activities of the Bulgarian Church in America, had more to say about Raikin. DILABBIO said that Raikin, after arriving in the U.S., had been a divisive force aggressively campaigning throughout the United States Bulgarian community to be appointed a Bishop with the Church, which the Church leaders opposed. DILABBIO explained that when the matter of Raikin's appointment "came to a vote [and it was decided that Raikin] would not get the job, but would be offered a priesthood, he [Raikin] suddenly decided, despite the years and money spent on him by WCC in theological training, that he did not want to be a priest anyway and, a few weeks later, turned around and married a girl in New York."

After the sudden reversal, Allen states that on "numerous occasions" Raikin, "using his offices in WCC as a cover, has sent denunciatory letters concerning other Bulgarians to various U.S. Government agencies if these Bulgarians happened to have crossed him or if he has taken a dislike to them."

Concludes Allen's memorandum: "The undersigned, like all other sources involved, cannot offer any evidence that [Raikin] is an agent of the Bulgarian communist regime, but feels that his activities have certainly played into their hands and have been such as they would have conducted through a provocation or sleeper type agent. To be frank, the undersigned feels that perhaps [Raikin] is an over ambitious, mercenary, megalomaniac, who is not content unless he is stirring up things in which his name will appear in prominence and from which he can derive some benefit."

David Sanchez Morales (Photo compliments of James Richards)

Chapter Six

Who Was David Sanchez Morales?

"'El Indio', for one," Mark said. "Otherwise known as Emilio Gonzales. Best dark alley operative I ever worked with while in the military. He retired recently when the Pentagon abolished his task force created to handle really sensitive intelligence operations....In the sixties he trained counterinsurgency forces in three or four Latin American countries under the A.I.D. public safety program."

– David Atlee Phillips
The Carlos Contract, 1978

A former grade school classmate of David Morales' provides a telling anecdote about Morales' toughness and tenacity as a youth. "David never gave up on anything he set his mind to.... He got into a fight one day with another kid, who was a grade ahead of him. The kid was much bigger, but David kicked his ass royally. The scary thing is that David never let up, even once he knew he had the kid beat. He got a bunch of extra licks in just to drive his point home. He was that way with a lot of things."

In this same vein, years after Morales' death, one of his best friends and a business associate, Ruben "Rocky" Carbajal, says, "David could kill your ass countless different ways." Says former CIA operator Robert N. Wall, who worked with Morales: "He was a rough-neck. He was a bully, a hard drinker and big enough to get away with a lot of stuff other people couldn't get away with." Said top-flight, ultra-shadowy CIA covert operations official Anthony "Tony" Sforza (alias Henry "Hank" Sloman) who had worked with Morales beginning in the early  1950s in Panama, Guatemala, Cuba, Mexico City, South America and Latin America: "You did not mess with David in any way, shape or form unless you were stupid and had no regard for living."

David Sanchez Morales was born in Phoenix, Arizona on August 26, 1925 to Mexican-American parents. David was the youngest of five children. Raised in Phoenix, Morales and his life-long friend Ruben Carbajal attended St. Mary's Monroe grammar school, where Morales was sometimes called "Davey" and "Didi," a nickname that stuck. In later years, Morales was referred to as "El Indio," not always lovingly, and never to his face. (Here it should be noted that there were at least three other people who worked with David Morales in Guatemala and Cuba, or were involved in the Cuban revolution, and were also sometimes referred to as "El Indio." One was a Dominican named Armentino Feria Perez. Another was a Castro rebel remembered by American soldier of fortune Neill Macaulay as "El Indio." And even pre-Castro dictator Batista was called "El Indio" because of his facial features.) Investigator and writer Gaeton Fonzi states that Morales was also known as "Mikoyan," "El Gordo," and "Hector Aguero." (Fonzi does not mention that, according to some Kennedy assassination researchers, Aguero was also an actual person.)

Joseph Morales, David's father, was a Mexican national and Yaqui Indian ten years older than his wife, Rose. Following David's birth, the couple began having marital problems. After the divorce of his parents, David Morales, according to Ruben Carbajal, was "all but formally adopted" by the Carbajal family. "No, he [Morales] wasn't happy about it [the divorce] at all, but he didn't show it ever. He toughed it out on the surface, like he did everything. But, yeah, it had a big hand in shaping who he was." When David graduated high school, he weighed about 145 pounds and was sinewy and hard muscled.

Morales attended Arizona State College in Tempe for about nine months in 1944-45, and then moved to Los Angeles where, in the summer of 1945, he enrolled at the University of Southern California. From October 1945 to February 1946, in order to support himself, he worked as a physical education instructor at Soledad Catholic Grammar School in Los Angeles. His salary was $35 a week. In 1946, bored by university life and classes, Morales enlisted in the U.S. Army. He went through basic training at Fort Bragg, North Carolina, and then completed jump school (parachutist training) at Fort Benning, Georgia. Following additional advanced infantry training in Georgia with the 82nd Airborne Division, Morales was sent to Germany to serve with the Allied Occupation Forces. Two of David's older brothers were fighter pilots for the U.S. Air Force.

In Germany, Morales was recruited by the Army Counter-Intelligence Corps in 1947 to work on highly classified projects in Frankfort, Berlin, and Munich. While in Germany, Morales, in mid-1949, also caught the attention of the CIA, which was interested in him as a prospective employee, but was not formally contracted by the Agency until late 1951. On August 11, 1949, Morales signed and submitted a lengthy "personal history statement" to the CIA's office in Munich, Germany.

Morales' "personal history," heavily redacted, stated that he was a "moderate" user of "intoxicants," and that he was "fluent" in Spanish, "fair" in Portuguese, and "slight" in German. He described himself as an "average" participant in football, basketball, baseball, track, and boxing. Asked if any governmental agency had ever investigated him, Morales stated he had been subject to a "complete background investigation" in July 1947 for a "sensitive [U.S. Army] position handling classified material" and "cryptography." At the time he completed this statement, Morales was 23 years old, stood 5 feet 10 inches tall, and weighed 190 pounds.

On October 10, 1949, CIA Personnel Security Branch chief, Ermal P. Geiss, issued a cover sheet to Morales' file indicating: "Subject [Morales] will be assigned to CIA in military capacity. It is requested that a seven-day name check be conducted relative to [Morales]."

A review of Morales' "Army Service Record," wrote Geiss, was to include "all data that might aid this branch in evaluating, from a security standpoint, the desirability of [Morales'] use by this Agency." Chief Geiss informed the Research Division that Morales was "one of several men from the same Army group [7821 Composite Group, European Command, Germany] about whom a similar request is being or will be made," and that CIA investigators should exercise their efforts to "best avoid drawing undue attention to these inquiries."

The CIA security chief who guided Morales' personnel investigations, security clearances and approvals, Ermal P. Geiss, remarked that he recalled meeting Morales on at least one occasion in the early 1960s in Washington, D.C. Geiss, however, stated that he had "no recollection that [Morales] made any marked impression on

David Sanchez Morales (Photo compliments of James Richards).

him." Given Geiss' position with the CIA, it is quite doubtful that he would have made any other type of comment. Ermal Geiss has a colorful and intriguing biography. His initial investigative training came under the tutelage of former FBI agent Donald Nicholson, a member of the Bureau's squad that had captured John Dillinger. During World War II, Geiss served as Chief of Counter Intelligence in the U.S. Army's Counter Intelligence Corps [CIC]. After the end of World War II, he spent at least six months at Atsugi airbase on the staff in the office of Assistant Chief of Staff G-2 General Charles Willoughby. Geiss joined the CIA as a charter member in 1947 and was the Agency's first Chief of Personnel Security. He eventually became the Deputy Director of the Agency's Office of Security.

A January 18, 1950 CIA Security Division memorandum bearing the subject: "MORALES, David Sanchez, Cpl. −39418" reveals that while still assigned to the 7821 Composite Group in Germany, Morales was being considered for a "provisional cryptographic clearance ... upon a priority basis." The memo states that military intelligence files "reveal that the subject [Morales] was investigated in 1947 due to his assignment to CIC [Army Counterintelligence Corps]. At least 10 informants were contacted and favorable information was obtained. A police department file checked during the course of this investigation disclosed a report that the subject was AWOL in November 1946 from a camp in California. Records at this camp were checked and revealed no record of the subject."

The memo, written by CIA Special Security Branch chief George P. Loker, Jr. to CIA Security chief Sheffield Edwards, elaborates: "The records of CIC reveal that a waiver was granted the subject [Morales], whose education qualifications were not up to par in that he only had one year of college but had a real knowledge of Spanish. It is noted that the subject [Morales] claims two years of college on his current Personal History Statement. The subject [Morales] was removed from training at the CIC school in June of 1947 because of academic deficiencies. However, CIC records reveal that three student evaluations reports for [Morales] in non-academic matters such as attention to duty, cooperation, discretion, etc., rated him very satisfactory and excellent. The subject's [Morales] Army Service Record revealed no derogatory information." The document concludes by making the recommendation that Morales "be granted provisional cryptographic clearance and that his case be forwarded to the FBI in order that a determination may be made relative to full security and cryptographic clearance for the subject [Morales]."

In 1950, while in Munich, David met 24-year old Joan Kerrigan, a very attractive and brilliant historian from Brookline, Massachusetts. Joan (nicknamed "JoAnn") was a contract employee for the CIA, initially helping assess, research, and catalogue various art and artifacts looted by the Nazis. Joan would later say, "David and I were assigned to the same special project for several weeks. When he wasn't around, I was unable to stop thinking about him." Joan and David fell in love and were married in late 1951, over the strong objections of Joan's father who believed that "mixed race" marriages were wrong. Joan and David eventually had eight children, ten grandchildren, and two great grandchildren.

Joan and the children frequently moved with David on his tours of duty for the Army and CIA, and Joan became an expert on Asian art and history, which she formally studied at Boston College in the early 1980s. Tony Sforza described Joan Morales as "an incredibly smart, strong, and tolerant woman. She embraced other cultures and people with enthusiasm and intellect. Over time it was obvious that Joan was the glue that held David from coming apart when things became really rough. She fiercely loved her family and David, and allowed nothing to harm them." Within ten years of marriage, David would put on about 30 pounds, becoming much more muscular from routine weight-lifting and physical exercise, combined with the sometimes heavy ingestion of alcohol and poor eating habits while in the field. Joan would often tell David that he had to pay better attention to his nutrition, but for the most part he ignored her until he began to experience some health issues.

According to declassified CIA documents, on July 9, 1952, Morales signed off on the CIA's Security Regulations Manual stating that he had "read and understood" the terms of the manual. However, a former CIA contract physician who knew Morales, speaking confidentially, reports that David was formally hired by the Agency in 1951, but had been "detailed" beforehand by the Army to "at least" two CIA projects during the same year. Both projects were related to the behavior-modification and interrogation program called "Artichoke." Beginning about mid-1951, the CIA had begun assembling Artichoke teams for eventual permanent stationing in Japan [Atsugi], Korea, Germany and France. Postwar Germany was an incredibly deadly place that was dubbed "kidnap central" by many of its resident spies.

In Germany, Morales first met CIA officials William King Harvey and Theodore Shackley, the two men with whom he would work closely for the next two decades. Morales also briefly encountered OSS veteran Henry Hecksher in Germany. Hecksher, in early 1952, was the CIA's chief, East European Division. Beginning in 1946, the German-born Hecksher had handled double-agent cases, and in 1953, Hecksher became William Harvey's deputy in Berlin. Before Harvey's arrival in Germany, Hecksher had been acting chief of the Berlin base of operations, perhaps contributing greatly to his clashing often with his new boss.

Nicknamed "Fat Henry," Hecksher worked for Harvey for "less than a year" before being reassigned to Guatemala for the overthrow of Arbenz. CIA historian Joseph J. Trento writes that Hecksher's work in Guatemala "became the template for future covert operations." (This is also said about players in the coup against Mohammad Mossadeq in Iran in 1953, which preceded the coup against Arbenz. They were all practicing apparently. In Iran, it was Halliburton that supplied the CIA with transport, weapons, cover, and more.)

In 1953-54, after returning to the United States for specialized training under cover as a University of Maryland student, Morales became a central player in the more brutal aspects of the CIA-sponsored coup d'etat to violently overthrow the Guatemalan government led by Jacobo Arbenz. Arbenz had greatly angered American corporations and businessmen engaged in commerce in Central America, especially the United Fruit Company, a corporation that maintained close ties to the CIA, when he proposed grand agrarian reforms that included the expropriation and redistribution of much of the land controlled by United Fruit. Indeed, when the overthrow of Arbenz began, the CIA employed United Fruit cargo ships to transport arms and supplies into the small country. Working with Morales on the Guatemala project, dubbed PB/SUCCESS, were David Atlee Phillips, another newcomer to the CIA, and former OSS officer and old Agency hand, E. Howard Hunt.

The Guatemala project was directed on the ground by Albert "Al" Haney. In Korea, Haney had played a critical role in evacuating Allen Dulles' wounded son, Sonny, and Dulles was forever grateful to him. The CIA's Tracey Barnes, who backed Haney's appointment by DCI Allen Dulles in December 1953, was named chief of political warfare. *New York Times* reporter Tim Weiner writes that Al Haney, who was resented by scores of CIA operatives for "coming in from the outside," was "one of the loosest cannons in the CIA's arsenal." Haney may have also been one of the CIA's oddest officers. He recommended, for example, that the Agency's psychological warfare branch attempt to distract Guatemalan citizens from his operation to overthrow Arbenz by fabricating a "big human interest story, like flying saucers," or by telling them that Arbenz was "forcing all Catholic troops to join a new church that worshipped Stalin," and that Soviet submarines were delivering arms to Guatemala.

Former Agency PB/SUCCESS participants report that Al Haney was less than fond of David Morales, that the two men frequently clashed on proposed plans, but that "David was ever the loyalist and did as he was told regardless his personal feelings." According to one former PB/SUCCESS communications officer, Charles Frances Gilroy, "Morales had his crafty ways of putting his own stamp on things. He had a temper, sure, but in his early years he knew when not to sound off, and to act responsibly to get his way."

As noter earlier, also dispatched to Guatemala by Dulles and Frank Wisner was Henry Hecksher, who had been chief of the CIA's Berlin Station and, as mentioned above, had had some minor dealings with Morales in Germany. In Guatemala, Hecksher was involved in tracking the alarming flow of cargo ships filled with arms from Czechoslovakia for Arbenz's troops.

While Al Haney was Morales' ultimate superior on the ground in Guatemala, Morales also reported to CIA officer Enno Hobbing, another greatly overlooked character in the Oswald saga. Morales may have met Hobbing earlier in post-war Germany, where Hobbing worked for the Agency undercover as a journalist. Hobbing, before joining the CIA and again in post-war Germany, served as a U.S. Army officer and was deeply involved with Project Paperclip, as well as its earlier incarnations.

In 2006 writer Thomas Bass, a professor at the University of Albany, stated in a radio interview, "Many spies have worked for *Time* magazine. Of course, most of the spies who've worked for *Time* Magazine, at least the spies that we know of, were, in fact, working for the Central Intelligence Agency. There's that very famous example of *Time* magazine Bureau Chief, Mr. Enno Hobbing, who was, in 1954, moved from Paris to Guatemala where he led the coup d'etat while working out of the offices of *Time*."

Indeed, Department of State and U.S. Army Project Paperclip files reveal that First Lieutenant Enno Hobbing escorted former Nazi scientist Alexander Lippisch, designer of prototype German jet fighter planes, including the deadly Messerschmitt ME-163 jet fighter, to America's Wright Field in Ohio. Hobbing was also involved, along with Boris Pash, in the transport of former Nazi Werner von Braun to the United States.

On his experiences with Hobbing, Morales would later tell a close colleague that he had "a deeper respect" for Hobbing [over Haney] because "Enno had some real experience in dicey situations." David reportedly added, "But I always felt like he looked down on me like I was not up to his place in life."

The CIA has consistently claimed that Hobbing resigned from the Agency around 1955, but it also declines to explain why Enno Hobbing's name appears on several CIA reports and cables from 1962 and 1963. Some of the Hobbing cable traffic is found in the file of Agency asset June Cobb, without explanation. Cobb was working for the CIA in Mexico City in 1962 and in 1963, at the time of Lee Harvey Oswald's visit there. (We shall examine June Cobb later in this book.)

HANNA YAZBECK AND HAROLD "HAPPY" MELTZER: ASSASSINS

Special markings and coding on the Hobbing cables reveal that his involvement in the Mexico City activities was connected to Project ZR/AWARD, a top-secret operation the Agency refuses to define, but that may have been connected to the Agency's ongoing hypnosis and behavior-modification activities, Project ZR/ALERT, in Mexico and possibly New Orleans. Additionally, ZR/ALERT appears to have had an undefined operational connection with CIA assassination projects QJ/WIN and ZR/RIFLE. These connections involved two CIA assassins, Harold Meltzer and Hanna Yazbeck, recruited by the CIA through the efforts of William Harvey and David Morales. (Some FBI files state that Meltzer's real name was Harold Fried.)

Both Meltzer and Yazbeck were recruited initially for the Agency's QJ/WIN assassination program. (QJ/WIN is often cited by researchers as the codename for an individual CIA assassin, but the cryptonym also referred to a CIA program under which other assassins were recruited by the Agency. This author has been able to identify twelve such individuals recruited by the CIA under the QJ/WIN moniker.)

An October 1976 CIA memorandum concerning a "review of the ZR/RIFLE file" reveals the following:

> In 1959, [Harold Meltzer] furnished information to our QJ/WIN California office but has not since cooperated with us. N.B. he has the background and talent for the matter we discussed but it is not known whether he would be receptive. [This from a partial 1960 CIA document.]
>
> YAZBECK lived in Beirut and worked for QJ/WIN's office intermittently during the past 10 years (dates not given-possibly during 51-61.) YAZBECK's chief bodyguard from 50-58 (not named) was a convicted murderer. The bodyguard was murdered. States that YAZBECK has an available pool of assassins....
>
> As far as ZR/RIFLE aspects this op, which have been covered under the QJ/WIN authorization for security reasons and with which Fletcher Knight [CIA alias] is fully familiar, except for one precautionary "life line," aspects of this case have been terminated and need no longer be considered part of the project.

As some readers are aware, Harold Meltzer – who interacted with David Morales from 1960 through to about 1963 primarily through his CIA "control" mobster Johnny Rosselli, another close associate of Morales – was a character well-known to the FBI. A former FBI special agent, Ted Meacham, reports that Meltzer, nicknamed "Happy" by his friends, had an extensive criminal history associated to Rosselli "going back to the early 1950s in Los Angeles and Las Vegas, with some minor dealings in New York." Rosselli, who replaced Jack Dragna as "West Coast boss of the Mafia," near exclusively directed Meltzer's substantial underworld activities in California. Meltzer was born in New Jersey in 1908 and, according to 1964 FBI files, his arrest record "dates back to May 1926 and includes arrests for assault with a deadly weapon, smuggling, robbery and Federal Narcotics Act violations."

A December 1960 Federal Bureau of Narcotics report (forwarded to the CIA) on Meltzer reads: "He owns and operates the Fried Sportswear Company, 843 South Los Angeles Street, Los Angeles, California. On August 3, 1959 he was convicted in Federal Court at Los Angeles for failure to register as a previously convicted narcotic law violator at the time of his travel abroad. He was fined $1,000 and placed on three years probation, which is still in effect. Meltzer appeared before a Federal grand Jury at Los Angeles on March 24, 1966, under subpoena, but invoked the Fifth Amendment throughout questioning. Although he was threatened with contempt proceedings this action never materialized."

Meltzer first came to the attention of the CIA after Johnny Rosselli had a conversation about him in 1959 with Agency Security Office chief Sheffield Edwards. Earlier the same year, according to a letter from FBN agent and CIA contractor, George Hunter White to Garland Williams, White and Charles Siragusa had recommended Meltzer to Rosselli in a meeting in Miami that included two attendees identified only by the initials "D.M." and "J.E.," thought to be David Morales and Jake Esterline. It is believed that Meltzer was not recruited by the CIA to perform assassinations, but instead was slated to help spot and recruit potential candidates for the Agency's ZR/RIFLE and QJ/WIN programs. However, Meltzer's skills as a hit-man for Rosselli were notorious in mob circles. That the Agency, as exposed in the above quoted memorandum, maintained a "QJ/WIN California office" is beyond intriguing and, of course, summons up all sorts of theories about the assassination of Robert Kennedy.

Worth noting is Harold Meltzer's deep involvement in drug trafficking, especially through illicit routes originating in Mexico City, which extended back to the mid-1940s when Meltzer was protected by close and high-ranking associates in the U.S. embassy in Mexico City. By the 1950s, Meltzer's extensive trafficking involved two wealthy young South American brothers, one of whom was madly in love with young June Cobb, an eventual Federal Bureau of Narcotics confidential informer and CIA asset.

Meltzer and his trafficking associates, according to FBI and FBN documents, would sometimes fly to and from Mexico City in private, charter flights on Tri-Cities Flying Service, owned by Evelyn "Pinky" Brier, a former wartime Women's Auxiliary Air Force pilot. Included among Pinky Brier's flying clients were CIA DCI John McCone and U.S. Supreme Court Chief Justice Earl Warren.

Worth serious consideration is the strong possibility that if the CIA had recruited Happy Meltzer for its QJ/WIN potential assassins spotting team, then surely the Agency's stable of galloping seasoned killers was replete with qualified domestic personnel. Which, of course, begs the question: Whom were they targeting? Additionally, that Meltzer was well-known for operating out of the lounge of L.A.'s Ambassador Hotel during his tenure with the QJ/WIN program is also intriguing, given Robert Kennedy's murder.

A revealing December 19, 1960 CIA bio-sheet contained in Hanna Yazbeck's CIA 201 file, most likely written by Garland Williams, a Federal Bureau of Narcotics supervisor, who worked for the CIA as a contract employee, reads: "Yazbeck lives in Beirut, Lebanon and worked for my office intermittently during the past ten years. I have often visited his home but I cannot now remember the address. However, he is quite well known in Beirut as the leader of a gambling syndicate. He often heads up a hatchet squad when disputes arise between the Moslem and Christian underworld factions in Beirut. Yazbeck is of the Christian faith. During the period I was in Europe (1950-1958), his chief bodyguard was a convicted murderer who owed his release from prison to Yazbeck's power. This bodyguard has since been murdered but Yazbeck has an available pool of assassins. He has been convicted in an Egyptian Court at Cairo or Alexandria on a charge of smuggling hashish. Since then, he has had a passionate hatred for Egyptians and Arabs in that order. In addition to his very wide circle of criminal friends in Lebanon, Syria, Turkey and Egypt, he also has many friends in high political positions in these countries. YAZBECK lives ostentatiously. He has a beautiful home and both he and his wife are loaded with jewelry. He has a stable of girls for his own private enjoyment. I suspect that during the summer holiday season he is a procurer for wealthy Arabs in various Middle Eastern countries who visit the mountain resorts adjoining Beirut. Rumors were constantly received regarding his importance as a narcotic trafficker but we have been unable to develop a successful narcotic case against him. I have always strongly suspected he has been, and will continue to be, engaged in any criminal activity that is profitable."

An undated typed CIA document (perhaps in follow-up to the above) on Hanna Yazbeck reads in part: "YAZBECK is well known to Garland Williams [FBN official, who worked on occasion for the CIA] as a major drug trafficker operating in Turkey, Syria, and Egypt, according to FBN official Charles Siragusa.... Siragusa says that if anyone could assemble a reliable team of murderers, Yazbeck is the man. Obviously, there is need for close coordination with other agencies here and abroad, if Yazbeck, as assumed, is to continue his narcotics and sex-trafficking activities. Siragusa says it may be necessary to brief, to whatever extent needed, [FBN supervisor and CIA contractor] George [Hunter] White, now in San Francisco. White once conducted an investigation targeting Yazbeck and others and developed a deep dislike for the man. Siragusa can handle the appropriate people within the Narcotics Bureau without drawing any attention to our use of Yazbeck."

Several former associates of David Sanchez Morales, who refused to be identified in this book, remarked to this author that they were familiar with both Yazbeck and Meltzer, but none had ever met Yazbeck. Said one, "Meltzer was sometimes a fixture with Rosselli in some of the Florida training operations, but I think he stood out to an extent that made Rosselli uncomfortable. I think Harold hated the bugs down there anyway, being from the West Coast."

Said former CIA operative and Morales associate Charles F. Gilroy, "I was never aware of Yazbeck. I guess he was beyond my pay-grade contact wise. I knew Meltzer, but never had to deal with him on any level. I had no awareness of the QJ/WIN program until years later, after it was exposed in the papers or by Congress ... but that doesn't mean I wasn't aware of some of the other contractors who operated under the [QJ/WIN] program. I was. [William] Harvey made me pretty uneasy about things. You know all the stories about his drinking and craziness, none of which can be overly exaggerated. He'd show up places and would be practically staggering around sometimes. Rosselli was incredibly patient and kind to him no matter how drunk he was. There was an assuredness, a calmness, about Rosselli that was infectious in ways. I mean, you could tell he'd been around, if you know what I mean, and that he's probably seen and done it all. He had a certain wisdom about him, not that he was smarter than David [Morales]. He wasn't, but his character was the antithesis of David's character.... Anyway, there were a few others that Harvey and David [Morales] handled who fell into the 'executive action' mechanic category. Besides a slew of Cubans, all hot to kill at the drop of a hat, I know there were a few Italians, recruits from Italy and Sicily, who David spoke of, and at least one guy from Canada, who was recruited through [George] White or Charlie Siragusa in New York City. David dealt with this guy a lot it seems. His name was Layton Smith or something close to that.... He might have been set up by [Pierre] Lafitte and then approached, which was the standard ploy back then. There was never any shortage of candidates for assassination programs. The supply seemed endless.... I always wondered what happened to these guys after they were used by the Agency."

Gilroy is most likely referring to Edward Lawton Smith, a Canadian mobster who has long been rumored to have been in Dallas, Texas, after a quick trip to Mexico City, Mexico, on November 22, 1963. The same rumors have Harold Meltzer in Dallas alongside Edward Smith as well as at least two Cuban snipers, one of whom who is consistently identified as Nestor Izquierdo, a Cuban veteran of the ill-fated Bay of Pigs invasion. Says Gilroy cautiously on this: "I know Tony [Izquierdo] worked with David [Morales] for a while but I'm not sure of the details. I know when he [Izquierdo] went to Latin America, David mentioned it, and I'm almost certain that Harvey and David [Morales] first recruited Tony in Cuba for work with ZR/RIFLE." (Gilroy also remarked that he was aware that Izquierdo had been identified as having taken part in the JFK assassination by former soldier of fortune Gerry Hemming. See Notes for this author's 1999-2001 interviews with Hemming in North Carolina. At that time, I only asked Hemming about Lee Harvey Oswald and Jean Pierre Lafitte, but Izquierdo's name came up and, being unaware of anything about him or his possible involvement in Dallas in 1963, I made notes that unfortunately were not reviewed until after Hemming's death.]

Interesting to note here is that Edward Lawton Smith, who came to the United States sometime in the early 1950s, was reported to look similar to Lee Harvey Oswald. Smith, who frequently traveled to Mexico City in the early 1960s, had been in the Canadian army during World War II, serving in Germany, France and Belgium. Smith was recruited in 1953 by Jean Pierre Lafitte, a "special employee" of the Federal Bureau of Narcotics and contractor for the CIA, to be an undercover, paid informer reporting to the Bureau's George White and Garland Williams. In 1959, Smith had mysterious dealings with June Cobb and Warren Broglie in New York City, thought perhaps to have been related to a drug trafficking ring in New Orleans that both Smith and Cobb were knowledgeable about.

MORALES AND NAPOLEON VALERIANO

It appears that David Morales first encountered the enigmatic and ultra-deadly Napoleon D. Valeriano, sometimes referred to as "El Ulupong" [Cobra], in Guatemala during his brief stint in Panama. According to former CIA operative Charles Gilroy, "Dave [Morales] ... worked with Valeriano on some levels during the pre-Bay of Pigs training phase when Valeriano came in as lead guerilla instructor ... There was some friction there between the two ... Dave resented that Lansdale inserted [Valeriano] into that slot as lead guy."

Gilroy noted, "The friction, while legitimate, was not without respect from either man. I know that Valeriano was eventually let go [removed from Bay of Pigs planning], but it had nothing to do with Dave.... What I mean is that Dave and Val [Valeriano's nickname] respected one another but there's this natural, instinctive jealousy between highly skilled guys like these two. It's unavoidable ... you're a member of a small elite cadre of the very best but you can't say a word to anyone about what [you] do ... to want to be the very best among that group is only natural."

Napoleon Valeriano, much overlooked and ignored by many historians and researchers, remains an enigma in terms of his sig-nificant involvement with, and influence upon, not only Morales but also the CIA's concentrated training of the forces that participated in the Bay of Pigs invasion. Valeriano was widely dubbed a "hunter-killer" who "relished stalking his human prey and then slowly killing them for the sheer pleasure of the act." He was born in the Philippines and was a highly deco-rated World War II veteran who had ac-complished an incredibly daring escape from captivity by the Japanese.

After the war, former OSS officer and now Air Force Lt. Col. and CIA officer Edward G. Lansdale was appointed in

Napoleon D. Valeriano

231

the late 1940s as the Agency's lead officer in Manila. In 1950, he was handed $5 million in Agency funds to quell a growing opposition force of dirt-poor Philippine farmers fighting for land reforms. Lansdale selected Valeriano as his right-hand man in eliminating these farmers, commonly called communist Hukbalahap (Huk) rebels. Not only was Valeriano a cold, calculating and brutal enforcer but he also became, under Lansdale's tutelage, an expert in combining murderous force with psychological warfare. Valeriano organized, trained and supervised a number of death squads that slashed and burned their way through the Huk rebels. Writer Michael McClintock reveals that the Huks greatly feared Valeriano's death squads (dubbed the Nenita Death Squads, named after Valeriano's then girlfriend), which became widely notorious for killing Huks and then systematically draining their bodies of all blood and placing bite marks on their necks so as to capitalize on the Philippine belief in "aswangs" – shape-shifting, night vampires.

Lansdale described Valeriano's tactics in his personal journal: "All this killing during a peace is getting rather sickening.... Cruelty and lust for murder are commonplace."

Working closely with Valeriano was a key member of Lansdale's advisory team, U.S. Army Captain Charles Bohannan, an expert in guerilla warfare and terrorism tactics. In 1959 and 1960, Bohannan would meet with David Morales several times in Colombia, South America to discuss and plan U.S. sponsored "counterterrorism" activities there. Also attending these same meetings were CIA officials Hans Tofte and Lucien Conein. (Bohannan and Valeriano would write a book together in 1962, entitled, *Counter-Guerilla Operations, The Philippine Experience.* The book is widely used today by the U.S. Army and CIA in training courses.)

Gilroy recounts, "I know that Dave [Morales], like most of us, was at the start taken aback, maybe even shocked, if he was capable of that, by the soulless viciousness of Valeriano's tactics.... I also know that Dave went to Colombia sometime in 1959 on a trip that involved Valeriano, Charlie Bohannan – he [Bohannan] was a major then – and a few others ... [Lucien] Conein may have also gone ..."

Charles T.R. Bohannan, who died in 1982, was an American army officer, who, as noted, worked very closely with Napoleon Valeriano in the Philippines and elsewhere. Today, he is considered to have been one of the U.S. Army's foremost experts on guerilla warfare. He and Valeriano are also widely regarded as experts on the techniques of enhanced interrogation and torture as exercised during unconventional warfare. Former Navy Seals and Army Rangers have reported that "special techniques" developed by Valeriano and Bohannan in the Philippines and later in Vietnam are today taught in advanced interrogation courses.

In World War II, Bohannan fought in the Philippines and survived the infamous Bataan Death March. He was educated as an anthropologist and geologist, and served with Valeriano in both Vietnam and Latin America, two locations where he would again encounter and work with David Morales. In Vietnam, Bohannan and Valeriano were special advisors working under Edward Lansdale. Both men also worked quite closely with Morales in training anti-Castro forces in the Florida swamps in the early 1960s.

Gilroy explained the purpose of Morales' trip to Colombia, as follows: "There was some trouble there in Colombia then. There was a series of meetings, two with Dr. Otto Morales Benitez, the Labor Minister, who made a long presentation to the group about communist generated violence…. Later on, I think, Valeriano and Morales went back, the same year, for additional meetings. Bohannan and Joe Koontz went with them. The objective was to plan counter moves against rebel groups. Koontz had worked with us in Guatemala and Miami … David [Morales] and Koontz, who spoke Spanish as well as David, got on pretty well." Gilroy noted, "Of course, [Morales] would again encounter Lansdale, Bohannan and Valeriano, and Shackley and Conein in Vietnam, along with William Colby, when all of them were there for that war."

LUCIEN E. CONEIN & MORALES

In 1971, Lucien Conein turned down an offer from "former" CIA officials James McCord and E. Howard Hunt to join the ill-fated Watergate burglars. Conein later said, "If I'd been involved, we would have done it right."

Conein, who passed away in 1998, is a legend in the annals of intelligence and covert operations, with much of his exploits still unknown. Indeed, Conein's life story appears torn from the pages of a 1950s men's adventure magazine. Additionally, Conein's professional life closely tracks that of David Sanchez Morales in numerous ways. While some of Conein's more sensational activities for the CIA and Drug Enforcement Administration (DEA) in the 1960s were exposed through media revelations concerning the Watergate crimes and scandals, those of Morales near exclusively escaped notice and journalistic investigation.

Says one of Morales' former associates who insisted on confidentiality, "David's work intersected so often and so closely with Conein's that sometimes it's hard to separate the two. David was just a lot better at maintaining a low profile ... he was invisible to the press and others ... he relished his privacy. He never once showed any interest whatsoever in sharing his secrets and demons with anyone."

Charles Gilroy says on Morales and Conein: "He [Morales] couldn't help but respect and admire Luigi [Conein's nickname for himself] but David was always extra careful, maybe *vigilant* is more appropriate, around Conein. It was that kind of respect that bordered on a well-founded fear that if somebody like Conein decided you were a serious liability to any operation you were dead, meaning really dead. And I'm sure Conein felt the same way about David."

Lucien Emile Philippe Conein was born in Paris, France and grew up in Kansas City, Missouri. In 1939, at the age of 17, he enlisted in the French army and was sent to France to fight. When France fell to the Germans in 1940, he returned to the United States and quickly joined the U.S. Army. Because of his combat experience in France, and his fluency in the French language, he was assigned to the OSS, precursor to the CIA. The OSS sent Conein to stateside parachute training and counter-insurgency school, where he encountered Garland Williams as one of his trainers, and then dropped him by parachute behind enemy lines in Vichy France, with orders to assist the French Resistance launch covert and sabotage operations against the Nazi occupiers. It was in France that Conein first encountered Jean Pierre Lafitte and Francois Spiritto, Frank Olson's future killers. Through Lafitte, then operating sometimes under the names Jean Pierre Voyatzis, Conein was introduced to key members of the Corsican Brotherhood, a highly secret criminal cabal that worked closely with elements of the French Resistance. Conein would later proudly reveal that he was made an honorary member of the Corsican Brotherhood.

Following the 1945 surrender of Germany, Conein parachuted into Vietnam where he organized attacks against the Japanese Army. At the conclusion of World War II, Conein in 1947 joined the staff of the CIA, on the recommendation of former OSS officer Richard Helms. As a covert Agency employee, he worked in Eastern Europe, Southeast Asia, South America, and Panama. According to CIA documents, Conein became a U.S. citizen on August 11, 1942, when he was 22 years of age. He maintained his French citizenship and thus was a dual citizen of France and the United Sates.

In 1954, when Conein returned to Vietnam as a CIA covert operative, he became one of the most important members of Gen. Edward Lansdale's special team. Much to Lansdale's chagrin, the CIA, for unknown reasons – perhaps because Conein was too chummy with the Vietnamese high command, or that some CIA officials in Vietnam thought he was a bit crazy – pulled Conein from Vietnam. However, Conein soon found his way back to the land he loved, and he again became a crucial member of what *Washington Post* reporter George Crile III called, "an elite 10-man counterinsurgency team under Gen. Lansdale, which included Daniel Ellsberg, then still a war hawk."

Conein maintained his military rank as cover, and continued to plan and mount extraordinarily dangerous missions and covert operations into areas selected by the CIA, becoming "the indispensable man" for Henry Cabot Lodge, President Kennedy's ambassador to Vietnam, "who appointed Conein as his liaison with the generals plotting to assassinate President Ngo Dinh Diem in 1963."

Historian Douglas Valentine, in his masterful history of the Federal Bureau of Narcotics, declares Conein Edward Lansdale's *"consigliere*, the most adept member of Lansdale's team" in Vietnam. Adds Valentine: "Conein's [he had married a Vietnamese woman after the war] knowledge and contacts [in Vietnam] were invaluable to Lansdale."

British historian John Simkin writes, "In 1951, Gordon Stewart, the CIA chief of espionage in West Germany, sent Conein to establish a base in Nuremberg. The following year Ted Shackley arrived to help Conein with his work. The main purpose of this base was to send agents into Warsaw Pact countries to gather information needed to fight the Soviet Union during the Cold War. The venture was not a great success, and the governments in both Poland

and Czechoslovakia announced that they had smashed several CIA espionage rings. Later, [Conein] worked with William Harvey in Berlin. In 1954, Conein was sent to work under Gen. Edward Lansdale in a covert operation against the government of Ho Chi Minh in North Vietnam. The plan was to mount a propaganda campaign to persuade the Vietnamese people in the south not to vote for the communists in the forthcoming elections. In the months that followed they distributed targeted documents that claimed the Vietminh had entered South Vietnam and were killing innocent civilians…. In the late 1950s, Conein worked closely with William Colby, the CIA station chief in Saigon. Conein helped to arm and train local tribesmen, mostly the Montagnards, who carried out attacks on the Vietminh. These men also guided Vietnamese Special Forces units who made commando raids into Laos and North Vietnam."

In July 1973, Conein allegedly resigned from the CIA to join the Drug Enforcement Administration (DEA), where he oversaw a series of secret operations, many of which involved commanding small, elite assassination teams sent to foreign countries to murder targeted drug cartel overlords. Conein's DEA title was Director of the Special Operations Branch, and his mandate came straight from the Nixon White House which recruited him: stop the flow of illicit drugs into the United States through any means necessary.

Says Gilroy on Conein's new assignment: "I'm not so sure that Lucien ever left the Agency entirely…. I have my doubts. I was still active then, and it was no secret that the crossover and exchange of CIA and DEA staff was significant … no different then when the DEA was the Narcotics Bureau and nearly every Bureau supervisor or agent worth his weight in salt also worked for the CIA in one capacity or another." Added Gilroy: "It's also no secret that the DEA's Secret Group One [an assassination group commanded by Conein] was closely coordinated between Conein and Richard Helms. David [Morales] knew all about the group's activities mostly out of necessity, but he was also consulted frequently on DEA targeting."

Were others besides high-profile drug traffickers targeted by Secret Group One?

"What do you think?" replies Gilroy.

Gilroy also recalls that a lot of Conein's former CIA supervisors were more than surprised by Lucien's new assignment. Said Peer Da Silva, Conein's supervisor and the CIA's Saigon chief of station:

"God save us all. You've got to start with the premise that Lou Conein is crazy. He worked for me in Vietnam, if work is the word. He was certifiable at that point, I think."

Some writers and JFK conspiracy theorists have written that Conein was involved in the assassination of JFK. This is far from certain and is based on highly circumstantial evidence at best. First and foremost in the accusations about Conein are claims that he was photographed standing on a sidewalk in Dallas as JFK's open car passed by him. While the man in the photograph in question does look like Conein, it is not him. Indeed, the man in question has been identified by his wife, family, and friends as Robert H. Adams, a Dallas postal worker on his lunch break to watch the President's motorcade.

LANSDALE AND DALLAS 1963

Some readers may be familiar with reports that Edward Lansdale was in Dallas on November 22, 1963, heading up a small team of snipers, highly skilled in assassination techniques. The reports about Lansdale originated with L. Fletcher Prouty, former OSS and U.S. Air Force officer. Prouty, who worked for years at the Pentagon, frequently interacting with the CIA, said that one day he looked at a photograph taken on November 22, 1963 in Dallas and realized that he was gazing at Lansdale.

Prouty, who knew Lansdale from the early 1950s in Manila, was so convinced that the photo is of Edward G. Lansdale that he wrote a letter to New Orleans District Attorney Jim Garrison in March 1990. (Why he waited until then to write is uncertain. Perhaps he had not seen the photograph until then.) Prouty informs Garrison that he had known Lansdale "since 1952 in the Philippines" and that he had met Col. Valeriano, among others, in Manila with Lansdale.

Prouty also speculates about Lansdale's possible connection to the 1963 events in Dallas, although without offering any real evidence: *"I am positive that he [Lansdale] got collateral orders to manage the Dallas event under the guise of 'getting' Castro.... The 'hit' is the easy part. The 'escape' must be quick and professional. The cover-up and the scenario*

are the big jobs. They more than anything else prove the Lansdale mastery. Lansdale was a master writer and planner. He was a great 'scenario' guy. I still have a lot of his personally typed material in my files. I am certain that he was behind the elaborate plan and mostly the intricate and enduring cover-up.... The 'hit men' were from CIA overseas sources, for instance, from the Camp near Athens, Greece.'' [The same compound where Dimitrov had been held by the CIA.]

Prouty describes the assassins: *"[The hit men] are trained, stateless, and ready to go at any time. They ask no questions: speak to no one. They are simply told what to do, when and where. Then they are told how they will be removed and protected. After all, they work for the U.S. Government. The 'Tramps' were actors doing the job of cover-up. The hit men are just pros. They do the job for the CIA anywhere. They are impersonal. They get paid. They get protected, and they have enough experience to 'blackmail' anyone, if anyone ever turns on them ... just like Drug agents. The job was clean, quick and neat. No ripples."* [Emphasis added.]

On the Internet today, it is widely reported that there is "no uncertainty that the photograph is of Lansdale," but the photo is only a side view of a man walking with his face turned from the camera. Nonetheless, as some of us know, certainty is measured in many ways in cyberspace.

JAKE ESTERLINE & MORALES

Another former OSS official, Jacob Donald ("Jake") Esterline, ran the Guatemala operation from a command post in Washington, D.C., making regular excursions to Guatemala. When the coup against Arbenz succeeded, Esterline wrote a glowing report on Morales' involvement, citing his work as "excellent." Esterline would also send a handwritten note to William Harvey and Allen Dulles stating that David Morales "is one of the bravest men I've worked with ... including [my] service in China and elsewhere."

Like Morales, Esterline took his advanced infantry and parachuting training at Fort Benning, Georgia, before serving in World War II. He was recruited into the OSS and stationed in India in 1943, and then was sent to Burma. Following this, he ran a number of fierce guerilla bands against the People's Republic of China, where he encountered fellow Americans and cold warriors E. Howard Hunt, Paul Helliwell, Robert Emmett Johnson, and Lucien Conein.

At the outbreak of the Korean War, Jacob Esterline was recruited by the CIA, trained at its rural compounds outside Front Royal, Virginia and in the Maryland mountains, and then appointed chief of guerilla training at the CIA's Virginia school, "the Farm."

In 1954, Esterline assumed control of the Agency's coordinating group for the overthrow of Jacobo Arbenz. Following this, he was appointed CIA station chief in Guatemala, Venezuela (1957-60), Panama, and Cuba (1960-61). There is ample evidence that during this time, Morales sometimes worked closely with Esterline, performing sensitive assignments for Esterline in all of these locations. In December 1965, he was appointed deputy chief of the CIA's Western Hemisphere Division, under J.C. King.

Well worth recounting is that Esterline, a man of high integrity and a soldier's sense of honor, frequently butted heads with J.C. King and David Morales over the issue of the CIA's use of mobsters and Mafia members. Initially, Esterline was outraged when he learned that Agency higher-ups, as well as Morales, were dealing closely behind the scenes with the Mafia, and on at least six occasions he and Morales vigorously argued about the involvement of mobsters in anything related to Cuba, the planned invasion at the Bay of Pigs, or the Agency in general. Morales consistently took the "whatever-it-takes" stance, while Esterline took the position that "getting into bed with the devil is wrong no matter what."

The 1954 overthrow of Arbenz was quick and extremely brutal. The CIA was upset when photographs depicting atrocities turned up soon after the completion of PB/SUCCESS. Many of the photos revealed that castration, mutilation, torture and rape had been committed by foes of Arbenz and presumably supporters of the CIA operation.

In addition to the rampant violence surrounding the coup, and perhaps spurring it along, the CIA had initially launched in 1952 a pre-PB/SUCCESS assassination program in Guatemala codenamed PB/FORTUNE. Under this program, CIA planners drew up extensive lists of Guatemalans targeted for assassination by specially trained murder squads, or "K squads" (K for "kill"), as they were called by the Agency. In late 1953, PB/FORTUNE was replaced by PB/SUCCESS, after CIA director Walter Smith terminated the assassination program because its cover had been blown through sloppy field work. However, the assassination features of PB/FORTUNE were incorporated into PB/SUCCESS.

Assassination was an overly played CIA calling card in Guatemala. Agency documents from 1952 to 1954 starkly reveal that the CIA routinely composed detailed lists of Guatemalan civilians and politicians targeted for murder. One undated memorandum, believed to have been written in 1953, bears the subject: "Guatemalan Communist Personnel to be disposed of during Military Operations of Calligenis." (Calligenis was the code name for Carlos Castillo Armas, slated by the CIA to assume power after Arbenz was deposed.) The list, covering two pages attached to the memorandum, contains the single-spaced names of over 100 people, separated into two categories.

"Category I" includes "persons to be disposed of through Executive Action" [assassination]. "Category II" lists "persons to be disposed of through imprisonment or exile." The document states that the two lists were revised from original lists "prepared by Headquarters in February 1952."

DAVID ATLEE PHILLIPS AND MORALES

In his book, *The Night Watch*, David Atlee Phillips, one of the CIA's coup organizers, recalls that following the overthrow, Arbenz fled, along with "six hundred of his supporters," to the Mexican embassy in Guatemala City to seek asylum. Subsequently Phillips, along with Albert Haney, Rip Robertson [whom Phillips only referred to as "Hector"], Henry Hecksher, Howard Hunt, and David Morales flew to Washington, D.C. to report on their successful coup to President Dwight Eisenhower at the White House.

Phillips identifies Morales in his book only as "'El Indio,' a massive American of Mexican and Indian extraction I had seen only briefly during the revolt but who was to work with in other operations over the years." Phillips, who sometimes used the alias "Paul D. Langevin," explained that Guatemalan and Salvadoran guerillas under Morales' command gave David the nickname "El Indio." (Morales also used the alias "Jose Calderon" in Guatemala.)

When Phillips' group arrived at the White House, each man was allowed ten minutes to brief the President. Also in attendance for the presentations were DCI Dulles, his brother John Foster Dulles, Secretary of State, the U.S. Attorney General, the Joint Chiefs of Staff, and Vice President Richard Nixon. Haney's presentation, recalls Phillips, was "confused" and concentrated on "his role in Korean operations several years before." Following the White House presentation, Phillips writes that "El Indio," who apparently made a favorable impression on Eisenhower and the others, "received a promotion and new assignment."

David Sanchez Morales, 29-years old, only about ten years past being a dirt poor, Hispanic kid from Arizona in search of a future, now standing before the President of the United States, explaining his role in assisting a CIA-sponsored coup in Central America. Later that week, he and JoAnn went out to celebrate. JoAnn was enormously proud of David, but was constantly worried that he had become addicted to the dangers of his work. The wife of another Agency man who worked with Morales told JoAnn, "They get hooked on courting death and coming away alive. The more it happens, the more they mock their mortality."

According to one former close associate of David Morales, following the Guatemala operation, David was near exhaustion, fighting flu-like symptoms for several weeks. "For a while," says the former associate, "we thought maybe Dave had picked up something serious, but he was just completely run down. Eventually, Shackley told him to go home to his wife and to relax for a few days…. Ted told him not to take it all so serious or he'd end up killing himself one way or another."

According to an autobiography written by Morales sometime in the 1970s, David explained his CIA years from 1953 through 1955 with the brief line: "I was with the Department of the Army as a civilian training advisor to several Central American governments."

One of the most overlooked of Morales' associates in Guatemala was Hans Tofte. Several people who knew Morales well while he was in Guatemala and later Cuba have candidly remarked that Tofte had a great influence over young David, especially in the areas of organizing "covert paramilitary groups and counter-insurgency activities."

Tofte was one of the chief planners of the Guatemala operation, appointed by CIA senior staffer and Special Assistant for Paramilitary Psychological Operations Tracy Barnes. A superb executor of guerilla operations, Tofte has been given short shrift by some historians who neglect to consider that the Agency ran a concerted disinformation campaign against him following the 1960s, when he clashed with CIA executives.

Tofte, like William Harvey, would often be found deep in his cups in his later years. Tofte had worked with Al Haney in Korea in 1951, commanding three brigades and forty-four guerrilla teams to serve as "intelligence-gathering infiltrators, as guerilla-warfare squads, and as escape-and-evasion crews to rescue downed American pilots and crews." Tofte, who had been the CIA's senior officer in Japan, described his guerillas as North Korean "refugees [who were] down-in-the-mouth, bored with nothing to do. Joining the guerillas would give them a chance to get out, to eat three meals a day, to have something to do. They would be buddies with a purpose, rather than shuffle around the [refugee] camp."

New York Times reporter Tim Weiner writes that before Tofte left Korea, most of his brigade members and guerillas had been either captured or slaughtered by the North Koreans. Writer Evan Thomas adds that most of Tofte's guerilla infiltration agents "had been 'doubled' by the communists [in Korea] and fed disinformation, which they duly relayed to their unsuspecting masters at the CIA."

Tofte, who followed his Guatemala stint with several years in South America for the Agency, became a major embarrassment to the CIA in 1966 after his expense accounts were questioned, and Agency Security Office investigators broke into his Virginia home, finding "secret documents that were not supposed to leave Langley."

Following the disposal of Arbenz, Morales was assigned by the CIA, from 1955 through to 1958, to the staff of the U.S. Embassy in Caracas, Venezuela. According to several researchers, it was while in Caracas that David Morales "became known as the CIA's top assassin in Latin America." The answers to the questions about what David did in Caracas, whom he did it to, where and how he did it, have yet to be provided publicly by anyone, and we are left to our own imaginations.

One thing that appears quite certain is that David Morales first met David Atlee Phillips, his case officer, in Caracas. In 1958, the CIA moved Morales from Caracas to the U.S. Embassy in Havana, Cuba. Fulgencio Batista was still the head of state in Cuba, but Fidel Castro's relentless rebels, expertly trained and assisted by a cadre of independent American soldiers of fortune, were steadily chipping away at Batista's foundation. Morales was perhaps pleased to find that in Havana he would sometimes work closely with Tony Sforza, whom he encountered earlier in Venezuela. By this time,

Morales had heard all the stories connecting Sforza to the Mafia, Corsican Brotherhood, French assassins, and elusive drug traffickers and smugglers awash in cash. Sforza was a classic shape-shifter able to maneuver any situation or environment with finesse and sophistication. He was also expert in small arms, and hand-to-hand, in-close fighting, but as he repeatedly told Morales, "Using your brain in tough situations always beats having to use violence."

Indeed, every whispered story or rumor about Sforza drew Morales ever closer to wanting to befriend and learn from Tony. David and Tony had hit it off right from the start, and Morales must have known instinctively that the multi-lingual Sforza was a wealth of information and experience that could only benefit an ambitious man with a growing – some would say insatiable – need for adventure and danger.

According to researcher and writer A.J. Weberman, Wayne S. Smith, a State Department officer in the U.S. Embassy in Havana, claimed that Morales could be very indiscrete when he was heavily drinking, which he increasingly did. On one occasion, Smith recounted that a drunk Morales began blabbing in a Havana bar about a top secret CIA operation involving Navy Seals operating out of Guantanamo. Other CIA, army and FBI officials working with Morales out of the U.S. Embassy in Havana included Robert Van Horn, Sam Kail, Hugh Kessler, and Edwin Sweet. Cuban military intelligence official Fabian Escalante reveals that in Havana, David Morales used the "nom de guerre Moraima," among other aliases, including surnames "Garrison," "Martinez," and "Morrison."

Morales also met surreptitiously at least twice with covert CIA asset and operative June Cobb at Geraldine Shamma's house in Havana. Cobb, within about two years, would begin reporting to David Atlee Phillips in Mexico City. The ever insightful and sharp-tongued Cobb later remarked, "There was something distinctly animal-like about [Morales]. He was young, handsome [and] quite friendly, but when facing him I always felt like I was confronting a poised cobra about to strike. His black eyes didn't help dispel the feeling any.... Later on, I heard his deadly airs held a lot of real punch." Geraldine Shamma was more charitable about Morales: "I always trusted him. He was tough and honest, and those were rare qualities in embassy people back then."

Morales' cover employment was U.S. State Department Attaché, and he lived openly in Havana with his wife, according to local Havana listings at the time, which read: "David S. Morales, wife: Joann Kerrigan, and children: Juanita, Martha, James, David, Anthony."

In Havana, David Morales also encountered John Martino, an American who spent 40 months in Castro's dreaded Cabana prison, and later was suspected of having critical and unrevealed information about JFK's assassination. We are unsure as to how Martino first became aware of Morales, but in his 1963 book, *I Was Castro's Prisoner*, published before the assassination, Martino writes that Morales replaced CIA man Earl Williamson in the U.S. Embassy in Cuba after Williamson was "quietly withdrawn" from Havana for having made unapproved promises of recognition to Castro's rebels.

A heavy drinker, not prone to deep thinking, Williamson, in an unauthorized 1959 meeting, informed a group of Castro's "agents and supporters … that the United States would recognize the Castro Government as soon as the Rebels overthrew Batista." Martino, who apparently had some very good sources for information, writes: "Williamson [was] replaced by David Morales, an American of Mexican descent and an intelligent and patriotic public servant. Morales sent voluminous reports to Washington concerning the communist affiliations of Fidel Castro and his henchman, which apparently had no effect."

Writer Larry Hancock speculates that Morales was well connected "early on to the Havana casino crowd and revealed himself as a CIA officer there," but there is little evidence that Morales had any dealings with Cuba's mobbed-up casino crowd. Indeed, given Morales' doings in the embassy it seems hard to imagine when he had time to rub elbows with the Mafia in Havana. A far safer speculation, in this writer's view, is that Morales perhaps began socializing with Cuba's more unsavory and Mafia-related characters after William Harvey joined JM/WAVE.

David Morales, while operating out of the Havana embassy, certainly had the means of easy access to Havana's mobbed-up casino crowd through Frank Brandstetter. Frank Brandstetter (called "Brandy" by his friends), ostensibly an employee of Hilton International corporation and manager of the Havana Hilton hotel at the time of Castro's takeover of Cuba, was a colonel with the Office of the U.S. Army Chief of Staff for Intelligence. Morales met often with Brandstetter, sometimes with June Cobb, who was then working as a public relations aide to Castro, or with Geraldine Shamma. Brandstetter was especially close to the CIA's Sam Kail, who worked in the U.S. embassy in Havana with Morales. Indeed, Brandstetter and Kail were longtime friends, as was Brandstetter with U.S. Army Intelligence officer Colonel George Lumpkin, who would go on to become deputy chief of police in Dallas, Texas at the time of the murder of President Kennedy. Brandstetter was also very close to David Atlee Phillips, and to fellow hotelier, Warren Broglie. After departing Cuba, both Broglie and Brandstetter worked at the same time in the hotel business in Mexico, as well as several other foreign countries. (One former intelligence operative told this writer in 2002, "It's pretty common to find intelligence people operating under cover as hotel employees at all levels of work ... it's the perfect cover for moving around and foreign assignments.")

Brandstetter, in addition to his intelligence role with the military, would also serve as a very reliable confidential informant for the FBI and CIA. Records from both agencies reveal that the hotelier routinely supplied the government with information on the activities of Frank Sinatra, Jimmy Hoffa, Sam Giancana, Morris Dalitz, Roy Cohn, and others.

MORALES AND JM/WAVE

After Fidel Castro assumed control of Cuba, David Morales was moved in late November 1961 from his CIA base of operations in the American Embassy in Mexico City, Mexico to the huge JM/WAVE CIA station in Miami, Florida. There he assumed the position of Chief of Operations, overseeing several cadres of covert paramilitary and elite assassination teams trained to infiltrate Cuba and wreak deadly havoc on Castro's fledgling government. Here, Morales' pseudonym was Stanley R. Zamka. Some writers have claimed that William Harvey had a large hand in Morales' posting to JM/WAVE, and indeed a November 19, 1961 priority cable from William Harvey to Mexico City CIA Station Chief Winston Scott requesting that Morales be sent to Florida appears to confirm this. Morales' old friend Ted Shackley was the CIA's Miami JM/WAVE station chief and Morales reported directly to him. The JM/WAVE station was a huge operation involving over 50 front corporations and 300 CIA case officers, with each directing about 7 to 10 Cuban agents who in turn were responsible for about 10 to 25 regular Cuban agents on the ground in Cuba. The JM/WAVE station occupied over 1,500 acres of land and some 90 buildings, some very large, able to store thousands of weapons – including tanks, amphibious assault craft, and aircraft of all sorts.

Besides working nearly 12-15 hours a day in Miami, Morales often traveled to Mexico City, Panama, Nicaragua, the Dominican Republic, and to Georgia, where at Fort Benning, his old stomping ground, hundreds of Cubans were being trained in advanced infantry techniques and guerilla operations.

David Morales also worked closely with future Watergate burglar Bernard Leon Barker, nicknamed "Macho" and code-named "AM/CLATTER-1" by the CIA. Born in Cuba to a Russian father and Cuban mother, Barker served in the U.S. Air Force during World War II, and was shot down during a bombing raid in Germany, where he was held as a POW until the Russians liberated the Stalag compound in 1945 and freed him. Not long afterwards, Barker returned to Cuba, and went to work for Fulgencio Batista's brutal secret police force. After the revolution, he was hired by the FBI to be an undercover operative, and also continued as a CIA asset.

On June 21, 1972, Morales was questioned about Barker by the CIA's Chris Hopkins of the Agency's Latin American division. Morales told Hopkins that Barker was recruited in Havana in 1959 as a "support agent" by "Woodrow C. Olien" (a pseudonym for Henry Hecksher). Morales told Ms. Hopkins that Barker "provided Havana Station information on police and political matters. He was also used to transport our agents to the harbor(s) for exfiltration."

Morales continued: "The Agency exfiltrated [Barker] to Tampa in 1959, and put him in touch with the FRD [Frente Revolucionaio Democratio] in Miami. He had a job in the FRD recruiting candidates for the invasion. He worked with CARDONA on propaganda. Howard Hunt became [Barker's] case officer on CA matters at JM/WAVE Station."

Clearly, Morales had little regard for Barker. We are not told in the memo why Hopkins is inquiring about Barker, although given that the Watergate break-in had occurred less than a week earlier, it is safe to assume Barker's arrest and the CIA's efforts at damage control provoked Hopkins' questions. Nonetheless, Morales told Hopkins that Barker "tells the authorities anything he knows," adding, "He tells all to everyone." According to CIA's Hopkins, "Because he [Barker] was such a loudmouth, Dave [Morales] recommended in 1962 that he be terminated."

Bernard Barker, as many readers are aware, was subsequently recruited by E. Howard Hunt, his former superior, to join the infamous "Plumbers" unit, Nixon's White House "Special Investigations Unit," still largely uninvestigated.

Several activities are well worth noting about Barker in his role as Watergate burglar. Underscored by Douglas Valentine in his masterful book on the Federal Bureau of Narcotics, *The Strength of the Pack*, is that Barker was part and parcel of an elaborate effort to blackmail the Nixon White House. Writes Valentine: "Backed into a corner, Nixon turned to the faithful 'mob,' and as author Dan Moldea writes, 'the mob came through in January 1973 with a million dollars in hush money.'"

Valentine reveals, "The finance chairman [of Nixon's re-election committee in Texas] had laundered money through a Mexican bank account belonging to Watergate burglar Bernard Barker...." Valentine explains that Myles Ambrose [U.S. Customs Commissioner, former U.S. Treasury Department Assistant Secretary for Law Enforcement and representative to the National Security Council] told him that "public knowledge" of a "CIA operation in Mexico" involving "CIA assets and channels for handling money" could have "saved Nixon."

Ambrose would not reveal what the actual CIA operation was, Valentine writes, but Ambrose felt that Nixon had no reason to worry about it. As Valentine notes, "This raises the question: what ongoing CIA operation in Mexico could have been so important that Nixon risked his presidency to protect it?"

Valentine speculates further: "A connection to the Kennedy assassination is a possibility. The money the Watergate burglars carried at the time of their arrest was part of an $89,000 donation from four Texas businessmen that had been laundered through Barker's account in a Mexican bank. The FBI was investigating the deposits into Barker's account until [CIA director Richard] Helms and Nixon intervened; then, according to author Peter Dale Scott, the FBI 'called off a proposed interview in Mexico City with CIA officer George Munro, the CIA official in charge of the electronic intercept program which allegedly overheard Lee Harvey Oswald [while Oswald was in Mexico City before the Kennedy assassination].'" Very

247

interesting to note in this convoluted saga is that George Munro, according to two confidential sources, had "extensive dealings" with David Sanchez Morales, of which "the nature was highly guarded and secret."

MORALES, JM/WAVE AND JOHNNY ROSSELLI

When David Morales arrived in Miami at JM/WAVE headquarters he discovered Johnny Rosselli anxiously awaiting him. Morales and Rosselli in many ways were complete opposites, yet the two men, perhaps for this very reason, generally liked one another and always got along well. Several observers who knew both men well have reported, "Rosselli was the one person who could put David at ease and actually make him laugh."

It has been written that Rosselli had no military training or experience, but FBI files reveal this for the lie that it is. Rosselli was inducted into the U.S. Army on December 4, 1942, at Fort MacArthur, California. Reads one FBI document: "At the time of induction Rosselli stated he was born on June 4, 1905, in Chicago and was a U.S. citizen; that he was married, and his occupation in civilian life was insurance man; that he attended six years grammar school and no other school; that he had worked six years as an insurance and public relations man prior to his induction; that his home address was 1705 Chevy Chase Drive, Beverly Hills, and his nearest relative was his own wife, Winifred, who resided at 222 North La Peer, Beverly Hills; that the person to be notified was a friend, Isadore Ruman, 215 West Fifth Street, Los Angeles, and his beneficiaries were his wife and a cousin, Salvatore Piscopu."

Isadore A. Ruman is a much overlooked figure in Rosselli's story. Ruman, often alleged by the FBI to be of Russian decent, was both an investor and the office manager of the insurance firm Rosselli worked for. The firm was owned by Herman Spitzel and did substantial business with Hollywood studios and producers. Other reports maintain that Ruman was Rosselli's lover for several years. Ruman was also investigated by the FBI for over a decade as possibly being a Soviet spy, but the Bureau was never able to find any evidence of her possible espionage activities, but suspicions about her lingered for years.

Former friends and CIA associates of David Morales say that he may have first met Johnny Rosselli in Cuba in 1959 through his friendship with Joseph Fischetti, a gregarious gangster, whose gangster brother, Rocco, visited Cuba often in the years before 1960, twice with Frank Sinatra. The same Agency associates report that Morales enjoyed low-stakes gambling and would visit Las Vegas at least a few times a year. By other seemingly authoritative accounts, Morales never encountered Rosselli in Cuba prior to Castro's take-over of the island, however, the two men did work briefly together in Guatemala in 1955-1956, when Rosselli was asked to "do certain favors" for the CIA and the Standard Fruit Company. Addition-ally, one former Agency source reports that Morales and Rosselli has "also done some unsavory work in Mexico City" following "the 1957 murder of Castillo Armas in Guatemala."

Rosselli was brutally murdered and dismembered in summer of 1976, after he had testified before the U.S. Senate's Church Com-mittee investigating the CIA. Rosselli had leaked an allegedly false story to the committee that Fidel Castro had had JFK assassinated as "blowback" for attempting to murder Castro numerous times. Rosselli, months later, was strangled to death, shot several times in the chest and head, cut open from mid-chest to below his na-vel, and then stuffed into a 55-gallon steel drum wrapped in heavy chain and tied to a heavy cement block. Rosselli's penis and tes-ticles were also cut off and shoved into his mouth. Rosselli's murder remains unsolved. In 1976, some investigators said that Rosselli's murder was "an obvious case of overkill, made to look like a mob hit, but perhaps actually and methodically committed by a group other than organized crime or the Mafia." The Miami coroner's of-fice was especially troubled by the fact that Rosselli's grisly autopsy revealed that he had been drugged with a paralyzing chemical sub-stance before he was strangled.

MORALES AND WILLIAM "RIP" ROBERTSON

In this author's opinion, the most interesting operative who worked with David Morales was William "Rip" Robertson, known variously during his intelligence career as "Carlos," "Alligator" and "Tinka." Born in the Lone Star State, where rugged individualism is placed at a premium, Robertson served in the U.S. Marine Corps and saw extensive action in the Pacific theatre during World War II. Rip, as he was nicknamed from his early teen years, joined the

CIA as a contract employee after the war, and in 1953 and 1954 was responsible for organizing and training special groups of guerillas for the assassinations in Guatemala during the Arbenz overthrow. During the Bay of Pigs invasion, Robertson again oversaw special group training and covert operations, many related to naval and amphibious landings. He joined the staff of JM/WAVE in Miami, again training guerilla bands for special operations. On several occasions, Robertson traveled to Panama and the Guantanamo Naval Base to carry out top-secret missions.

Robertson was a paramilitary fighter of superior expertise at the time he joined the JM/WAVE operation. He was a thin, solidly built 50 year-old Texan who stood "about 6 feet two, with a perpetual slouch and wrinkled clothes," as a 1975 *Harpers* magazine article noted. "Everything about him was unconventional. He wore a baseball cap and glasses tied behind his head with a string, and always had a pulp novel stuffed in his back pocket. From the military point of view, nothing looked right about his appearance, but to the Cubans he was an idol who represented the best part of the American spirit and the hope of the secret war."

William "Rip" Robertson

In 1971, tenacious Washington, D.C. reporter Jack Anderson wrote an exposé about how the CIA plotted to kill Castro by dispatching "assassination teams and commando squads" to Cuba. Anderson wrote that the Agency's base of operations was "a columned building with the cover name of Zenith Technical Enterprises" and through "its doors passed some of the nation's most secret operators: the dapper John Rosselli, rugged Bill Harvey, 'Rip' Robertson and a huge New Mexican [sic] remembered only as 'The Big Indian.'"

While at JM/WAVE, Robertson helped organize several highly secret and dangerous missions, and again worked closely with David Morales, as well as William Pawley and Ted Shackley. According to Eddie Calderon Acosta, nicknamed "Nestor," who was trained by Robertson and today lives in Central Florida, in the early 1960s, "Morales, for the most part, steered clear of [Robertson]" because "Rip had been in the real deal in the South Pacific" and "knew and understood combat up close and personal." Explained Acosta: "[Morales] liked to brag a lot about his combat skills but that just didn't wash around Rip, who didn't have to fake or brag about anything. Even during the period Rip reported directly to David, the two men always did a delicate dance around one another."

In 1963, Robertson made several secret excursions into Cuba to carry out ultra-sensitive sabotage and "executive action" (assassination) jobs. In June 1963, Robertson joined a Morales-approved small group including John Martino, William Pawley, Eddie Bayo, and Richard Billings, a *Life* magazine journalist, which surreptitiously traveled to Cuba to try to smuggle two defecting Soviet army officers into the United States. Dubbed Operation Tilt, the highly dangerous mission failed, and reportedly resulted in Bayo's death, which remains unconfirmed.

In 1975, Ramon Orozco, one of Robertson's paramilitary fighters, said, "I loved Rip, but oh, my God! He was not the kind of man you want as an enemy. If the United States had just 200 Rips, it wouldn't have any problems in the world. He loved war, but it was very different for him to adjust to the kind of warfare we were making. He wanted an open war, and we were waging a silent one."

Years after the close of JM/WAVE station, Col. Richard Dale Drain, CIA Chief of Operations, Western Hemisphere Branch/4, and an expert in psychological operations, revealed his thoughts on the Agency's use of the Mafia. In a rambling interview with CIA historians documenting the history of the Bay of Pigs invasion, Drain revealed:

> Well, mind you, I am not saying what I've just said in any kind of pique; and I certainly don't want to leave you – or this tape recorder – with the impression that I had known about this [use of Mafia by CIA], I would have been opposed. I must say, I don't think I would have enjoyed the instrument very much – whereas we put out an awful lot of bullshit to the Cubans about the restoration of democracy and all that. Those Cubans that were working with us were not, I submit, working for the re-establishment of the Mafia as a controlling factor in Havana. I had a helluva lot rather, in contemplating the assassination of Castro, contemplated in the way that we were contemplating it – that is, can we get a Rip Robertson close to him? Can we get a really hairy Cuban – I mean a gutsy Cuban – to be infiltrated with this one thing in mind? We surveyed all of our agent material to see who could take a shot at him, but the assassination

of that charismatic guy, coincidental with the invasion, would have been a highly desirable thing. Whether the instrument to be picked should have included the Mafia, I think, I might have questioned at the time. It was part of my job ... to ask, "Now wait a minute...What are we doing here? ... If this comes out ... what will we look like? Not only to ourselves, which is important, but to the Cubans."

Eddie Acosta, when asked about the intra-Agency disagreement and dissent over using the Mafia remarked, "What's amazing to me is that it was only a couple of old Mafioso dons and Rosselli that get all the attention when at the time there were countless other low-level Mafia thugs and button-men running around the station all the time. To be honest, most of the people there [at JM/WAVE station] didn't have any idea who Rosselli was, and I'm not sure most of them would have cared any had they known."

Most likely, Rip Robertson would have been relegated to the dustbin of history had not many credible JFK assassination researchers advanced the theory that he was present in Dealey Plaza the day Kennedy was murdered. Today, many research-  ers, based solely on a photograph taken on November 22, 1963 of a man who they claim "looks identical" to Robertson, say that Robertson may have been part of an assassination team in Dallas. The photograph shows the man standing on the corner of Main and Houston in Dealey Plaza as JFK's limousine passes by. The man, dressed in a suit, has his right hand raised to the brim of his fedora.

DAVID MORALES AND NICHOLAS DEAK

Another intriguing character that Morales knew well was Nicholas Deak. Strangely murdered on November 18, 1985, Deak was perhaps the CIA's wealthiest covert intelligence operative. Known as "the James Bond of money," Deak with substantial CIA financial support in 1947 founded the Wall Street firm Deak-Perera, one of the nation's oldest and largest foreign money-exchange firms.

Nicholas Deak first encountered David Morales in Cuba prior to the Castro takeover and then again more extensively in Guatemala and South America. Deak has long been rumored to have had discussions, months before Morales' death in 1978, with Morales, and several of Morales associates, about a substantial investment the group was contemplating making in South America.

Nicholas Deak, born into a wealthy Hungarian family in 1905, moved to the United States in 1939 to escape Nazism. Eagar to perform his part in defeating the Axis powers, Deak joined the U.S. Army, became a paratrooper and was promptly recruited by the OSS. Interestingly, providing Deak's advanced basic training were OSS officers George Hunter White and Garland Williams. Following the end of the war, Deak was stationed in Hanoi, where he oversaw American intelligence operations in French Indochina. With special guidance from his close associates Allen Dulles, Frank Wisner, William Casey, William Colby and James Jesus Angleton, Deak began forming private corporate entities worldwide as well as global investment firms that served the CIA as front operations for covert channeling of substantial amounts of funds into whatever projects the Agency had at hand. Deak's front companies and financial network played crucial roles in CIA operations in Asia, Israel, Lebanon, Guatemala, Europe, Latin America, and Africa.

On November 18, 1985, an alleged homeless bag lady named Lois Lang murdered Nicholas Deak in his plush Wall Street office at 29 Broadway, New York City. Most intriguing about Deak's murder is its possible connections to two ultra-secret CIA behavior-modification and hypnosis programs conducted initially in Mexico City in 1962 and 1963, and continued well beyond these years under different cryptonyms. The programs initially called ZR/ALERT and ZR/AWAKE shared the objective of "creating hypnotically-controlled operatives to carry out Agency-directed tasks." Former CIA contractors, speaking under terms of anonymity, report that "the same and similar programs" were "operated in Cuba within the U.S. Embassy" there during Morales' tenure there, and then later "throughout 1961-1964" in Mexico City. [Volume Two of this work will cover these programs in detail.]

Deak's killer, Lois Lang, as early as 1975, was confined to the Santa Clara Valley Medical Center under the care of the late Dr. Frederick Melges, a psychiatrist associated with the Stanford Research Institute, a longtime facility used by the CIA and U.S. Army for behavioral modification experiments, many of which are still classified as top secret. According to numerous medical journal articles written by Dr. Melges, his specialty field was narco-hypnosis and the use of hypnosis to create dissociative states. Dr. Melges worked closely at Stanford with Dr. Leo Hollister, also deceased, who had been a CIA MK/ULTRA sub-contractor working with LSD and other drugs. Melges also worked with Dr. Donald Dudley. Dudley, in November 1992, told the mother of one of his patients that he "was working for the CIA, and if she told anybody about this, he'd kill her." Dr. Dudley, according to the patient's attorney, helped train CIA and military assassins.

Confidential sources, who knew Nicholas Deak well, report that he met "a few times around 1974-1975 in Washington, D.C. with [David] Morales," who was then "working as a consultant on Latin American and South American affairs with the Pentagon. Deak's meetings with Morales included several of Morales' CIA associates: Tony Sforza, Edwin Wilson, Ted Shackley, and a former CIA Technical Services Division employee who Morales had worked with in Mexico City in 1961. The former TSD employee, who sources declined to identify, operated a small "security firm" near Alexandria, Virginia dealing in high-tech security systems and devices and "small arms." The same sources say that Morales' business group, looking to make "some serious money in the private international market," went as far as forming "at least one corporation" with the objective of marketing and selling "security hardware" and "surplus arms" to countries in South America and Central America. "The plan was to set up two offices, one in Northern Virginia, another in Panama for marketing purposes," said one source. "I think they rented space in both locations."

The name of the corporate entity Morales' group organized?

"Oh, God, that was a while ago.... I remember it was a Spanish name, but I'm not sure now. I think Deak put some funds into it as an investment of his own."

Accounting for his time from 1960 through 1965, David Morales wrote in his biographical summary: "From 1960 through 1965, I advised the U.S.A.F. [U.S. Air Force], foreign governments and their military and police personnel on training techniques which included protection of personnel, installations and equipment, the use of investigation techniques, small unit tactics, and counter-guerrilla activities. I also helped to set up specialized schools and training cadres. This service was performed primarily in Florida and in Washington, D.C."

A CIA Office of Security document bearing the subject David S. Morales and dated October 24, 1960, confirms a verbal request from Agency security officer J.J. Mullane that "two backstopped residence addresses be provided for [David Morales] one in the Washington, D.C. area and one in the Los Angeles area." The document further states: "[Morales has] to be identified as a recently returned State Department employee who had secured a new position with the Department of the Army, since returning from overseas and resigning from the State Department.... [Morales'] family had not joined him in the Washington, D.C. area but were understood to be at the home of his wife's family somewhere in New England [Newton, Massachusetts].... It was explained to Mr. Lavery [CIA security officer] that this residence and cover was [*sic*] necessary to backstop [Morales] in the event of inquiry arising out of some private business ventures in which he is currently engaged in the Phoenix, Arizona area." The same document reveals that Morales under the CIA's backstopping efforts was also to be identified as a "local representative for a New York City concern doing economic research in Latin American trade."

A June 2, 1961 CIA memorandum provides insight into Morales' duties as Chief of Operations and Chief of Counter-Intelligence Section at the JM/WAVE base. (Morales used both titles interchangeably and concurrently.) The document tells us that Morales "arrived in Miami in October 1960 after spending two years at the Havana Station." The memorandum continues: "Morales appears to have done a unique CI [counter-intelligence] job in organizing within the Frente, the future intelligence service for the new government of Cuba that the invasion force is expected to install. He also organized two other groups. He did this with the help of a Chilean instructor that was supplied by headquarters, and with training materials that WH/4/CI Section, Mr. [name redacted] sent down to him."

According to the same CIA document, the "principle group" of the "two other groups" organized by Morales was comprised of "39 selected, highly educated Cubans, who were trained by Morales as case officers to form the future [Cuban] intelligence service. They are known as 'AMOTS'. After being trained they were employed by Morales in doing a series of highly important tasks for the good of the station."

These tasks involved "penetration of the local anti-Castro organizations"; penetration of the pro-Castro Miami-based group called the 26th of July organization; preparation of biographical dossiers "on all prominent persons in the Frente"; "carding some 200,000 Cubans in the period of three months; creation of a "special section of the AMOTS" to monitor all radio transmissions coming from Cuba, including "eight stations that were covered on a 24-hour a day basis"; screening all persons recruited as military trainees; censoring all mail coming from the CIA's military training camps in Guatemala; infiltrating four AMOTS into Cuba "with instructions to report on CI targets: chiefly the [Cuban] secret service and police.

The second group trained by Morales consisted of "100 selected Cubans who were given training as future CI [counter-intelligence] officials and civil government officials." Reads the memorandum: "Of the 100 thus trained, 61 were sent to the camp[s] in Guatemala for training with the brigade. They accompanied the brigade on the invasion, and of the 61 only two were lost, nine were caught and the rest got out, due to the circumstance that most of them were on the steamer *Lake Charles* which, owing to the developments at the beaches, did not land its troops."

The 1961 memorandum continues: "Morales accomplished all of the foregoing with the aid of only two girls, one a GS-9 analyst. He tried in vain for more than three months to get a junior case officer assigned, but in vain.... As a result of being short handed, Morales had to work about 14 hours a day, seven days a week."

MORALES AND E. HOWARD HUNT

E. Howard Hunt briefly mentions David Morales in his 2007 book, *American Spy*, published just before his death the same year. Hunt recalls that William Harvey "posted Morales to the CIA's Miami station in 1961, where he became chief of Covert Operations for JM/WAVE ..." Hunt writes, "Morales and Harvey could have been manufactured from the same cloth — both were hard-drinking, tough guys, possibly completely amoral."

Apparently wanting not to reveal complete knowledge of Morales' resume, Hunt states that "Morales was *rumored* to be a cold-blooded killer, the go-to-guy in black ops situations when the government needed to have someone neutralized." [Emphasis added.]

Quipped Hunt, "I tried to cut short any contact with him, as he wore thin very quickly."

Not long after E. Howard Hunt's death, his son, Saint John Hunt, publicly released details of his father's alleged deathbed confession concerning what he knew about the JFK assassination. Morales' name comes up again in the context of being a central member of a group plotting to kill the President.

According to an April 2007 article in *Rolling Stone* magazine by Erik Hedegaad, a very ill and near-death E. Howard Hunt "scribbled the initials 'LBJ'" on a piece of paper with lines connecting the President's initials to the names Cord Meyer and Bill Harvey, and a line connecting Meyer's name to that of David Morales. A line connects Morales' name to the words, "French Gunman Grassy Knoll."

Later still, according to the article and Saint John Hunt, E. Howard Hunt gave his son two sheets of handwritten paper "that contained a fuller narrative," starting with LBJ, that states, "Cord Meyer discusses a plot with [David Atlee] Phillips who brings in William Harvey and Antonio Veciana." Veciana was a Cuban exile leader of Alpha 66, who told a Congressional committee, following the assassination of JFK, that a man thought to be Phillips once pointed out Lee Harvey Oswald to him.

Hunt's written "narrative" continues: "He [Phillips] meets with Oswald in Mexico City [presumably in September or October of 1963].... Then Veciana meets with Frank Sturgis in Miami and enlists David Morales in anticipation of killing JFK there. But LBJ changes itinerary to Dallas, citing personal reasons."

On another sheet of paper, E. Howard Hunt explains that he was invited to a meeting with Sturgis and Morales in a Miami hotel room.

After Morales, for unexplained reasons, leaves the room, Sturgis asks Hunt, "Are you with us?"

Hunt asks, "What are you talking about?"

"Killing JFK," replies Sturgis.

Hunt's sheet of paper states he was "incredulous" about the brief exchange, but nonetheless he told Sturgis, "You seem to have everything you need. Why do you need me?"

Hunt also told Sturgis that he would not "get involved in anything involving Bill Harvey, who is an alcoholic psycho."

Saint John Hunt says he was stunned by his father's confession. Nobody says anything about why E. Howard Hunt did not alert the CIA, FBI, or Secret Service about the alleged plot to kill JFK.

The *Rolling Stone* article oddly states that, following the assassination, "like the rest of the country [E. Howard Hunt] is stunned by JFK's murder and realizes how lucky he is not to have had a direct role." (This author is unsure precisely what is meant by "stunned" and "direct" and the article does not clarify this.)

Does this mean that Hunt thought because he refused to take part in the murder that he simply assumed the plot had been cancelled? Was he refusing to take part in the murder only because Harvey was involved? Did Hunt feel no obligation to alert anyone about the plan he was privy to? Of course, Hunt writes nothing about any of this in his deathbed book, *American Spy*. What all of this means is anyone's guess, but Hunt's alleged confession in many ways makes far more sense than a lot of the assassination stories floating around out there.

GEORGE FREDERICK MUNRO & MORALES

Another close associate of Morales' in Mexico City was George Frederick Munro. Morales' family members and one friend recall that David was fond of George Munro, having first met him through CIA covert agents Tony Sforza and Bruce McMasters. Munro is often misidentified as Mexico City CIA Station Chief, perhaps because actual station chief Winston Scott considered him one of his most trusted aides, sometimes having Munro act in his place.

Munro, a former wartime OSS official and FBI special agent, knew James McCord and Robert Maheu from his Bureau time in New York City. Munro was widely regarded in intelligence circles as an expert in surreptitious electronics, a skill he developed as a youngster and then continued to refine for his adult life.

Writer Jefferson Morley describes Munro as the "son of a millionaire," who completed law school when he was only 21 years old. Munro's family maintained an expansive ranch in Cuernavaca, Mexico which CIA contract asset June Cobb claimed to have visited several times, as did a number of former CIA Technical Services Section employees. Munro may have first encountered Cobb in November 1961 when, according to CIA Mexico City cables, she was "deported from Guatemala with Achilles Centeno Perez." Centeno is believed to have been a CIA operative acting with Cobb. Cobb had been told by Guatemalan police and border officials that if she or Centeno returned to Guatemala, they "would be killed."

Munro assisted with Cobb's entry into Mexico, and against his better advice, Cobb told him she wanted to return to Guatemala to complete an undisclosed Agency task there. Also frequently visiting Munro's ranch were CIA officials E. Howard Hunt, David Atlee Phillips, and Ted Shackley.

Charles Gilroy says that Morales "had a deep respect for Munro as well as some jealousy over Munro's wealth. Dave was always struggling to support his family and really envied those without financial worries."

Writer John Armstrong, who misspells Munro's name "Monroe," reveals that Munro was the CIA's expert and go-to-guy on electronic surveillance for both the Cuban and Russian embassies in Mexico City.

George Munro was also close with Mexico City's Hotel Luma manager, Warren Broglie, with whom Munro often dined, along with June Cobb. Munro also knew Broglie's right hand man, Franz Waehauf, a Czech intelligence agent who served as a CIA informer and who posed as a bartender and headwaiter at Hotel Luma.

Worth noting is that Munro, on several occasions in Mexico City, used the electronic skills of Allan Hughes, a former military intelligence operative who, in 1953, was assigned to Dr. Sidney Gottlieb's Technical Services Section. Hughes attended the secret and infamous Deep Creek Lake meeting in Maryland in November 1953, where Dr. Frank Olson was dosed with LSD and then interrogated.

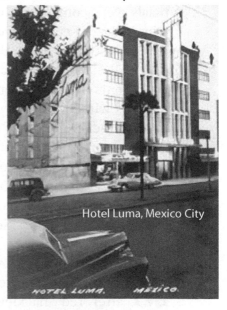

Hotel Luma, Mexico City

Hughes' task at that meeting was to covertly tape record the interrogation session. Interestingly, Hughes, after 1954, would work briefly for the Atlantic Research Corporation, where Ruth Paine's brother-in-law John Hoke also worked. (Ruth Paine's home is where Lee Harvey Oswald and his wife and child were living at the time of the assassination.)

Munro's primary CIA alias was Jeremy K. Benadum, and he spoke fluent Spanish and French. An August 1962 CIA "Career Assessment" on Munro reads: "Subject [Munro] maintains unofficial liaison between the [CIA Mexico City] Station and a Mexican Ministry. He also develops independent agents.... [Munro] is an experienced, well-trained, serious intelligence officer, capable of spotting, assessing, recruiting and handling agents.... [Munro's] cover is a natural one, which poses no difficulties. Since [Munro] has been in the intelligence field for over 20 years, he is psychologically prepared for his dual role in intelligence operations and is well qualified to operate without strong station support."

Following the assassination of JFK, staff investigators from the Congressional House Select Committee on Assassinations made concerted efforts to locate and interview George Munro. According to the Committee, Munro was then retired from the CIA and living in Mexico City. HSCA staff was especially interested in Munro's dealings for the CIA with certain members of the Fair Play for Cuba Committee.

At the top of the list of these members was Vincent Lee, FPCC Chairman, who had exchanged a number of letters with Lee Harvey Oswald. Next was Elizabeth Callett de Mora (aka Betty Mora), who the CIA described as an "American negress, commie" who became a "naturalized Mexican and wife of Francisco Mora." Some CIA officials were convinced that the Moras had information regarding trips Vincent Lee had made to Cuba in December 1962 and January 1963, and that Lee was also "in on planning the Oswald assassination of President Kennedy." Apparently, according to sketchy CIA documents, Munro, operating as Jeremy Benadum, somehow interacted with Vincent Lee and the Moras when all were in Mexico in 1962 and 1963.

Also worth mention about Munro is that following the death of station chief Winston Scott, the CIA stated in a rather cryptic classified cable, that it was maintaining concerted efforts "to keep in touch with [Munro] to have his help or, better yet, neutralize him as inimical factor in Mrs. [Scott's] affairs as they involve us."

MORALES AND VIETNAM

Morales was dispatched by the CIA to Vietnam in 1966, after Ted Shackley was assigned by the Agency to oversee its secret war in Laos. Shackley needed a fearless man willing to take on potentially dangerous and possibly deadly risks and tasks, and he thought right away of David Morales. Shackley assigned

Morales to head up the Pakse (or also called Pakxe) paramilitary and black operations base in Laos. The third most populous city in Laos, Pakse has a population of about 85,000, and is situated at the confluence of the Xe Don and Mekong Rivers in the southern province of Champasak. The city was founded in 1905 by the French as an administrative outpost.

The full history of the CIA's activities in Laos has yet to be told, but Shackley, with Morales often at his side, developed a chain of secret bases and outposts in Laos, including one infamous place called "Spook Heaven," according to writer David Corn. This site, Corn writes, was located south of the Plain of Jars and included a 3,000-foot runway and a tribal population (Hmong and Lao Theung) of 45,000. Morales, although often located elsewhere, is said to have loved Long Tieng, Spook Heaven's real name. Writes Corn: "Those who visited Long Tieng described it as Shangri-La."

Morales is Awarded CIA Medal of Merit

In 1978, David Sanchez Morales was awarded the CIA's Intelligence Medal of Merit "for his twenty-five years of dedicated service" with the CIA. A still partially redacted memorandum concerning his recommendation for the medal reads in part: "Mr. Morales spent more than twenty years in the field in several different installations in the areas of Europe, Latin America and East Asia. He held senior level positions engaged in FI, CI, CA and PM operations. His record includes such items as participation in key roles in both Latin America Division's two major PM/political action operations plus tours as [redacted] in Laos (supervised 45 employees); and Regional Officer in Charge, [redacted], Vietnam (supervised 60 employees). These assignments were carried out in war zones requiring considerable personal courage."

The recommendation continues: "During his Agency career Mr. Morales was constantly engaged in an exceptionally wide variety of activity in hazardous areas (Guatemala, Cuba, the Dominican Republic, Laos, Vietnam). He recruited countless assets and sources directed against a wide range of targets. In addition, he managed large installations and sizeable groups. He always shouldered heavy responsibilities and consistently demonstrated that he had the capacity, determination and necessary judgement to take on such jobs. After nearly thirty years of dedicated and productive service with the U.S. Government, Mr. Morales retired on 31 July 1975. Throughout his long career he was a dedicated, skillful and professional clandestine operator and unfailing in the pursuit of Agency objectives. His performance was of the highest caliber and unquestionably contributed significantly to the Agency's mission."

David Sanchez Morales died on May 8, 1978 in Arizona. He was 52 years old, a little over two years past his retirement from the CIA. His good friend Ruben Carbajal told investigative journalist Gaeton Fonzi that he saw Morales the day he died. Carbajal sensed from the moment he set eyes on Morales that day that something was wrong, something was weighing heavily on Morales' mind.

"Man, you don't look up-to-date," Carbajal told his friend.

"I don't know what's wrong with me," Morales replied. "Ever since I left Washington I haven't been felling very comfortable."

Morales also told Carbajal that he did not feel very well. Carbajal later said he had an odd feeling when Morales drove away from their meeting place.

Morales died of what Carbajal termed "a supposed heart attack" that night.

Later, Carbajal would say that Morales remarked a few times, "You know, Rocky, with what I know about things, things over the past twenty years, I should be worried about myself. I know too damn much."

Carbajal says there was no autopsy for David Morales. "JoAnn didn't want one done," he says. "Maybe she had a good reason for not wanting one." Carbajal also later said, "David said they [the CIA] is the most ruthless mother-fuckers there is, and if they want to get somebody they will. They will do their own people up."

On the day of Morales' funeral, the population of the same town he lived in nearly tripled with all the strange visitors that came to pay their respects. Says Gilroy, "I didn't think he had that many friends. I know I shouldn't say this, but I think half the people that came just wanted to make sure that David was really dead ... that he was really gone. I'm sure some of those people breathed a deep sigh of relief at his passing.... I was sad that he passed away so early. Beneath all the hard-shell, anger, tough-guy veneer there was a really good man there. He had a tough life growing up, really tough. A lot of men would have eventually overcome those early years of hurt, but David went in another direction not open to most people. That direction gave him no opportunity or chance to become the man that he really was."

DAVID MORALES AND THE JFK ASSASSINATION

Incredibly, most people today would know little or nothing about David Morales had not Gaeton Fonzi written about him in his must-read book, *The Last Investigation*, first published in 1993. Fonzi, who died at the age of 76 in September 2012, had been an award-winning investigative journalist and a relentless staff investigator for the House Select Committee on Assassination in the late 1970s. In his book, Fonzi reveals a number of explosive facts about Morales.

According to one account, told to Fonzi by Robert Walton, Morales' sometimes attorney, David was drinking with Walton and Reuben Carbajal at the Dupont Plaza Hotel, Washington, D.C. one evening when, at the mention of JFK's name, Morales jumped up and screamed, "That no good son of a bitch, motherfucker."

Fonzi additionally explains that, according to Walton, the three men had been drinking very heavily. "At one point, between the three of us we had gone through a fifth of Scotch and we had to re-order," recalled Walton. Walton was telling Morales and Carbajal about his early years, and he mentioned President Kennedy. At this, writes Fonzi:

> [Morales] flew off the bed, says Walton. I remember he was lying down and he jumped up screaming, "That no good son of a bitch, motherfucker!"
>
> He started yelling about what a wimp Kennedy was and talking about how he had worked on the Bay of Pigs and how he had watched all the men he had recruited and trained get wiped out because of Kennedy.
>
> Walton says Morales' tirade about Kennedy, fueled by righteous anger and high-proof booze, went on for minutes while he stomped around the room.
>
> Suddenly he stopped, sat back down on the bed and remained silent for a moment. Then, as if saying it only to himself, he added: "Well, we took care of that son of a bitch, didn't we?"

Following Fonzi's book was a magnum opus on the assassination by Noel Twyman, entitled *Bloody Treason*. Twyman's book went even further with revelations from Robert Walton and Ruben Carbajal. Twyman interviewed the two men in 1995. Following is a significant excerpt from that interview, which is also included, as presented here, in Douglas Horne's masterful book, *Assassination Review Board, Volume Five*:

Carbajal: [Referring to the 1973 statement by Morales that "Well, we took care of that son of s bitch, didn't we?"] Like I said, it could mean different things. But you know, you wouldn't make a statement like that unless you knew what was behind it or knew enough about it, you know, that you could put the finger on something, you know. That's my way of thinking because how in hell would you make a statement like that. "We took care of that son of a bitch." He said "we." That's a whole organization, it's plural, it's more than one.

Twyman: And that would mean the CIA.

Carbajal: God damn right that's what it means.

Twyman: Walton mentioned that Morales told him, he thinks it was on the same trip. Morales said to the effect, "Well, I was also in Los Angeles when Bobby Kennedy got his."

Carbajal: I don't remember that part right now.

Twyman: So Walton inferred that since he said he was in L.A. when Bobby Kennedy got his, that perhaps he was in Dallas when Jack Kennedy got his.

Carbajal: I don't remember that part.

Twyman: Walton was clear that Morales didn't say specifically that he was in Dallas.

Carbajal: Because he could have been there. He was there many times. Two sisters, you know, lived there and one of his daughters.

Twyman: Well, you know, there were 8 million people in Los Angeles at that time. I was in Los Angeles when Bobby Kennedy got his, so there may not be any significance to that.

Carbajal: I was in Guadalajara then, in my home resting; the hell with then goddamn Kennedys and their bullshit. See, I had forgotten when the goddamn, what was his name? The one that got knocked off over there in Los Angeles? Robert Kennedy. When his brother made him the general attorney of the goddamn nation, he had never had one court trial. And then, I haven't forgotten, when he said he told the blacks to take whatever you want, man, its yours. I haven't forgotten those words. They pissed me off that day.

Twyman: Well, Jack Kennedy put Bobby in unofficial charge of the CIA, too.

Carbajal: He was an asshole.

Twyman: He was 35 years old and had no experience in CIA operations.

Carbajal: Stupid asshole.

Twyman: Well, that covers the main key points. Let's see how this plays back now. When you write these books you've got to make sure. It's so easy to misrepresent what somebody says.

Walton [on the psychology of Morales]: He [Morales] was just ... he was very matter of fact. There wasn't that much passion.... What he talked about most of the time was very clinical.... At the time I had never met anybody quite like that ...

Twyman: He was cold blooded?

Walton: He really sounded an awful lot like Hemingway. I mean, Hemingway's short story "The Killers"... It was just "I eliminated this problem and took care of that problem" ... This man [Morales] ... really felt he was doing the right thing for his country, that there were all these bad guys out there. Not only the Castros but the Russians, the corrupt people within the turmoil in Vietnam and, in his own mind, he really thought that he was Zorro. That he was getting rid of the cancer within the organization and I don't think he ever considered himself to be a hit man. He was a surgeon.

Twyman: He was a what?

Walton: A surgeon.

***

Twyman: ... Do you have an opinion formed about whether or not he participated in the [President] Kennedy assassination?

Walton: I have no doubt. When he told me, "We got that son of a bitch," he told me he was in Dallas. He said, "I was in Dallas and I was in L.A. when we got that Bobby too."

Twyman: Oh, he said he was in Dallas, too?

Walton: No doubt in my mind he was there. I doubt very much that he personally pulled the trigger or anything else, but he was there, he helped organize it.

Twyman: Well, that's important that he mentioned he was in Dallas. He said he was in Dallas? Well, I'll be damned.

Walton: He said, "We got that son of a bitch and I was in Los Angeles also when we got Bobby."

Twyman: When "we" got Bobby?

Walton: "When we got Bobby." And when he said "also" I linked that back to Dallas. I'm not sure he ever said "I was in Dallas" but he did say "I was in Los Angeles when we got Bobby."

Twyman: I see. You can't specifically remember he said he was in Dallas?

Walton: No. Just the way he linked it on with "and I was also in Los Angeles."

Interviewing Charles Gilroy by phone, I asked what he knew about Dave Morales and his possible presence in Dallas and L.A. at the times of the murders of JFK and RFK. Earlier, I had shared [sent by mail] copies of the relevant pages dealing with Morales from the books of Gaeton Fonzi and Noel Twyman. Before I mailed these pages, Gilroy said that he had never read either book.

Gilroy was hesitant to answer at first, and then said: "Dave had family, a daughter, a couple sisters, in Dallas and he went there a lot to see them ... so *maybe* he was there around that time, but so what. A hell of a lot of people were there in Dallas that day. I guess what you're really trying to get at is what I think about the possibility of David having had a hand in the murder of JFK or RFK, or both. I doubt very much that he was in LA when Robert Kennedy was murdered.... My heart wants to say it's all rubbish, complete conspiracy rubbish, but my head at the same time draws on the anger he felt over certain things to do with Cuba. Going beyond that is a waste of time for me. I will never know, anymore than you or anyone else, about half the things David did, much less about anything possibly directed at the Kennedys. These aren't the kind of things people put in diaries, memos or policy papers, and dead men don't talk."

Dale E. Basye, Dallas, 1964
[Compliments of Dale E. Basye, Jr.]

Chapter Seven

The Strange & Somewhat Untimely Wisdom of Dale E. Basye

I finally asked him bluntly, "Lee, what the Sam Hill is going on?"

"I don't know," he said.

"You don't know? Look, they've got your pistol, they've got your rifle, they've got you charged with shooting the President and a police officer. And you tell me you don't know. Now I want to know just what's going on."

He stiffened and straightened up, and his facial expression was suddenly very tight.

"I just don't know what they're talking about," firmly and deliberately. "Don't believe all this so-called evidence."

I was studying his face closely, trying to find the answer to my question in his eyes or his expression. He realized that, and as I stared into his eyes, he said to me quietly, "Brother, you won't find anything there."

– Robert Oswald on his November 23, 1963 jail meeting with his brother, Lee Harvey Oswald

Can we create an individual who can be made to perform an act of assassination under the influence of Artichoke techniques?

– CIA official Morse Allen, 1954

I learned some time ago that when a writer focuses his or her attention on matters coincidental, then serendipitous happenstance becomes a regular visitor to that writer's life. Put another way, as my friend and fellow author Peter Janney put it: "Serendipity sometimes intertwines with providence." As a faithful reader of the works of Peter Levenda, also a good friend, as well as those of Colin Wilson and Robert Anton Wilson (no relation to Colin), I know the phenomenon often has the tendency to deliver stunning moments of synchronicity.

Recently, while discussing the subject of coincidence with another widely published writer and friend, Jack O'Connell, one of America's best authors of fiction, I related that working on this book had produced many odd moments of serendipity in my life. "Many quirks in time and place," I said to Jack. He responded that he was fascinated by the term "quirks in time" and asked for an example. I decided to provide him this one, but waited until now.

I became a grandfather recently, nine months ago to be precise, and my grandson Dylan has become the absolute light of my life, to use a tired but most appropriate cliché. Being a writer and, out of necessity and love, a lifelong and incessant reader, it has been sheer delight for me to see that Dylan, at such an early age, also loves to be read to. A few days before my conversation with O'Connell about coincidence, a friend had suggested I buy a few children's books by a writer with whom I was unfamiliar – Dale E. Basye, Jr., whose books had intriguing titles such as *Heck: Where the Bad Kids Go; Rapacia: The Second Circle of Heck*, and so on. I added a couple of his books to my list of titles to purchase for Dylan. Says Dale Basye Jr., "My books are basically a darkly comedic reworking of Dante's *Inferno* for kids."

Later that same day, I was going through about 300 pages of unread FBI and CIA documents dealing with Lee Harvey Oswald and I was stunned to see the name Dale E. Basye at the top of a December 24, 1963 FBI document. I blinked, looked again and the name was still there. I quickly realized, and later confirmed, that this Basye had to be the father of Dale E. Basye, Jr. On the FBI report, beneath the elder Basye's address and contact information in Dallas, appeared the line: "Basye's summary of the OSWALD case is quoted as follows."

What followed was Mr. Basye, Sr's firm conviction that Lee Harvey Oswald was possibly a psychologically disturbed man who had been placed under hypnotic control by Russian intelligence experts. Basye, a writer and editor for the *Dallas Morning News* at the time of the JFK assassination, had subsequently documented these thoughts and produced a detailed, typewritten summary that he mailed to Dr. Milton H. Erickson in Phoenix, Arizona. Erickson, a psychiatrist, was then considered one of the nation's leading experts on hypnosis. Basye had also forwarded his summary to the FBI office in Dallas. The Bureau then incorporated the summary into its official records, later declassified, concerning Kennedy's murder.

Basye introduces his eloquent hypothesis by posing what would later prove to be a series of uncanny questions:

> Was Lee Harvey Oswald under hypnosis when he shot President Kennedy? Was he subjected to intensive psychological brainwashing techniques in Russia, perfected even further than in Korean War days? Was he given a post-hypnotic suggestion that he would shoot the President at the first feasible opportunity and upon being given a certain signal, which would set him in motion? Was this suggestion periodically enforced by Red psychological experts working in this country, and did they lay the basic framework of planning which put Oswald in the Texas School Book Depository with a rifle in his hands at the time the presidential motorcade passed?

Unaware that his questions bore an ominous resemblance to – nearly replicating exactly – a set of questions posed earlier by others, Basye points out that Oswald's case "parallels the fictional case detailed in the novel and movie, *The Manchurian Candidate*." As mentioned before, that book and film, originally released in 1962 and then remade by Hollywood in 2004, is a fictionalized portrayal of a psychologically disturbed young soldier who has been brainwashed while being held as a POW during the Korean War. Hypnotically controlled, he has returned to the United States where his communist captors have planned to use him as an assassin to murder selected targets in America.

Basye then unfolds his central thesis, listing several reasons why Lee Harvey Oswald "would have made a good subject" for hypnotic control, and for carrying out assassinations. Oswald had defected and renounced his American citizenship, yet refused Russian citizenship, thus making it much easier to return to the U.S. Additionally, Basye writes, Oswald "had a deep hatred of authority, and the President represented the supreme U.S. authority." Moreover, as first demonstrated during his youth in New York City, Oswald "was a psychologically disturbed young man," an ideal subject for mind control.

Basye lists a series of "facts" that "seem to point toward the theory that Oswald was under hypnosis." Basye's observations, revealing a remarkable knowledge of the case so early on, are as follows:

Oswald seemed to have no set plan of escape. After carefully laid plans which put him in the Texas School Book Depository right on the motorcade route, he seemed to move aimlessly after the shooting. Being a fairly intelligent young man, Oswald must have known that without a silencer it would be known immediately which building the shots came from. And when he didn't return to his job that afternoon it would be reasonable to assume that he would be the number one suspect. Yet, he went back to his apartment, got a jacket and a revolver and set off on foot in a direction which led him deeper into a residential area – not a place where he could catch a train, plane or bus or even hitchhike a ride out of town. It seemed that he either was headed for a rendezvous with an accomplice or really did not have a plan of escape. Perhaps his Red bosses had planned it that way – so that he would be killed resisting arrest and his lips would be sealed and he wouldn't be subject to psychological examination.

1. When stopped by Officer Tippit, a woman eyewitness said Oswald first leaned inside the car and talked with him. It was only when the officer got out of the car to take him in that Oswald drew his pistol and shot him – as if Oswald had been preconditioned to resist apprehension by authority. The woman who saw him shoot the officer yelled at him, but Oswald just looked at her and fled. Why didn't he shoot her also? Obviously, she could later identify him to police. A witness reported seeing Oswald walking down a street openly reloading his gun after killing the officer. Later, he was seen fleeing from doorway to doorway, finally rushing into the Texas Theater on Jefferson Ave. This flight was more like the unplanned struggles of an animal to escape. It contrasts with the detailed planning of the cool, calculating killer who planned the assassination down to the last detail, even drawing a diagram of the motorcade route and the path of the bullets from the sixth-floor window to the presidential car. It also contrasts with the conduct of the cool assassin, which a witness described as a sniper who took his time, carefully scoring three hits with three shots. It was as if escape had never entered into the planning of the murder.

Yet, if Oswald had wanted to commit suicide, he could have done so easily by continuing to fire from the sixth-floor window at the police, which represented the authority he hated. It seemed that Oswald had been a puppet and someone, after they were finished with him, had cut the strings, hoping he would be killed in his feeble escape attempts.

2. When the Texas Theater was flooded with police and it was obvious that escape was impossible, Oswald put up a suicidal-type resistance. He leaped to his feet and shouted, 'It's all over!' Then he drew his pistol and would have shot it out with the officers had not the gun misfired. (This misfire could have been part of the plan to make sure Oswald would be shot in his escape attempt.)

3. After his apprehension, Oswald declined all knowledge of either the President's assassination or the police officer's death. (This was similar to the behavior of the assassin in 'The Manchurian Candidate' who, under hypnotic suggestion, forgot all the details of his crimes.) Why did Oswald leap up and shout something curious such as, 'It's all over!'? Had he been given a post-hypnotic suggestion that when his capture seemed *inevitable* he was to shout, 'It's all over,' and then forget all about his crimes? Despite overwhelming evidence against him and intense questioning, Oswald steadfastly maintained that he was innocent and knew nothing about either crime.

4. Oswald's behavior seemed strangely unlike the normal pattern of a fanatic who would shoot a President then brag, 'Yes I did it and I'm glad.' He seemed cool, composed in custody, and didn't give his interrogators any information at all. When his wife and mother visited him he told them not to worry, that it was all a mistake. He was concerned that his wife should buy some shoes for one of their children. His own mother was convinced of his innocence after her visit to the jail. It was as if Oswald's mind had been erased of all knowledge of the crimes. This cool attitude of innocence by a man of average intelligence in the face of overwhelming evidence that he murdered the President, together with

conclusive evidence including an eyewitness that he killed Officer Tippit, is unbelievable.

5. In New Orleans and at two Dallas addresses Oswald lived near public parks – a likely location to meet Red [Communist] agents who may have been controlling his actions.

6. Oswald was in Mexico from September 26 to October 3 of this year [1963]. Could this hypnotic suggestion have been given to him at that time – when he visited the Cuban embassy? It is a known fact that the Castro regime promulgates a theory of assassination of heads of state as part of their hemispheric revolution plan. And the Cuban regime's hatred of Kennedy was well-known.

If the hypnotic suggestion originated in Russia and was reinforced by Soviet agents in this country, what would the Russians hope to gain by Kennedy's death. There are several possibilities:

1. They may have figured that his successor would be less firm in opposing Red moves throughout the world.

2. The assassination may have been a subtle warning to any presidential successor that the Reds can murder our president any time they choose if his policies stir their wrath.

3. Perhaps Oswald had been instructed to kill both Kennedy and Vice-President Johnson to paralyze the country as a prelude to an all out attack. (At a distance, Gov. Connelly and Johnson look very much alike, and Oswald might have been thinking that both would likely be in the same car.)

Basye's speculation continues:

The actions of the Russians while Oswald was in the Soviet Union stir several questions. It seemed that something else – perhaps the psychological grooming of an assassin – was going on under the surface. Quoting from a column by Victor Riesel on December 6, 1963: "The Russians have said officially they denied Oswald Soviet citizenship because he was a 'Trotskyite.'

This means he was declared an enemy of the state – a few days ago. But why was he permitted, back in 1959, to travel freely inside the Soviet Union? This is a coveted privilege. Official permission is needed by foreigners for bus and train travel. Yet he went some 420 miles from Moscow to Minsk. Why did the Soviet employment services direct him to a job? This must have happened. He spoke no Russian then. He read no Russian.... Who vouched for his identity card? Who got him his work permit? Such documents are absolutely necessary – especially for foreign workers....Who approved Oswald's membership in a Russian union?.... If the Soviet authorities believed Oswald to be a 'Trotskyite' and an American spy, why did they permit him to associate freely with his fellow factory workers? Such activity might have eluded the secret police for a few weeks but not for more than two years. Why did the secret police permit him to marry a Russian girl? Why was he permitted to quit his job and then travel freely from Minsk to Moscow? Workers are not yet absolutely frozen to their jobs inside Russia. But few just pick themselves up and leave. How did Mrs. Oswald get permission to abandon her job in a land starved for workers? Finally, how did the alleged assassin get his wife and child out of the Soviet Union? Mighty few have accomplished this.... Why were the Russians so kind, and why did they offer so many privileges to a 'Trotskyite?'"

A final question: Was the wife of Oswald allowed to leave so readily by the Russians because she was the one who was to trigger the hypnotic suggestion and give Oswald his orders?

I have noticed a parallel between the Lee Harvey Oswald case and the fictional case detailed in the novel and movie, 'The Manchurian Candidate.' In 'The Manchurian Candidate,' a psychologically disturbed young man was brainwashed in a Manchurian POW camp to such an extent that he would obey unquestioningly any orders given him by the Reds. He was given a post-hypnotic suggestion that when he saw the card, the queen of hearts [sic], he was to carry out any orders given him immediately after viewing the card.

In many ways this disturbed young man was like Lee Oswald. He was disliked by most people, had few friends, was a loner, didn't talk much and was filled with hate for those in authority in particular and all the world in general. He had been dominated by a strong-willed mother.

Upon his return to the United States, the former POW was used by Red agents to assassinate. First it was minor officials that he murdered, but the Reds were grooming him to kill the man likely to win election as President of the United States. The agents would call the former POW on the phone when he was alone and tell him that it was time he played a game of solitaire. This triggered the post-hypnotic suggestion and he would play solitaire. When he had had time to view the queen of hearts [*sic*], the agents would call him again and give him his orders to kill. The man obeyed as if a zombie, having no memory of his crimes after they were committed.

Lastly, in his speculative summary, newspaperman Basye provided Dr. Erickson with "a few [*sic*] questions I would appreciate your views on:

> 1. Is it possible in theory to induce a person to kill under hypnosis?
>
> 2. Is it possible to have a person under hypnosis obey your every order by giving him a code word or some symbol to set him off, such as the playing card in 'The Manchurian Candidate'?
>
> 3. Could an individual of Oswald's type – said by psychiatrists to have had schizophrenic tendencies with deep feelings of hate – be given a post-hypnotic suggestion, then have it reinforced periodically so that he would kill?
>
> 4. Is it likely that a post-hypnotic suggestion could be kept alive by reinforcement over a period of 17 months?
>
> 5. How long would a hypnotic indoctrination take that would put Oswald completely under the power of agents so he would kill for them?
>
> 6. Would there be noticeable changes in a person's behavior if he were under such a post-hypnotic suggestion?
>
> 7. Could a person in such a state be made to forget all about a crime once it was committed?

8. If the plot of 'The Manchurian Candidate' is unrealistic, under what circumstances and through what means could a person be hypnotized to kill?

9. Do you know of a case where a person had been induced to crime through hypnosis? Or do you know of an experiment by scientists which would indicate that this might be feasible?

10. Do you know of a theory developed in the writings of an expert on hypnosis which holds that 'The Manchurian Candidate' type of case is possible? Can you give me any names or works of psychiatrists who have written on the subject?

11. From what you have read of Oswald's personality, what is your view of his psychological state?

12. Would drugs play a role in inducing such a hypnotic state where a person's will could be controlled?"

On or about December 17, 1963, Basye received a reply from Dr. Erickson in a letter dated December 13, 1963. Erickson opened his missive by assuring Basye that he had taken great care to "peruse his analysis" of the Oswald case. He then offered his professional opinion:

> ...[B]ased on 40 years experience in hypnosis at a professional level, the reading of practically every book and article on the possibilities of the use of hypnosis to instigate anti-social compulsions which are at a scientific level of approach, and many years' experience in connection with correctional institutions and psychological and psychiatric examination and treatment of criminals, I must express a complete disagreement with your theory from beginning to end. [Emphasis added.]

In what surely must have been very disappointing words for Basye, Erickson categorically stated that *The Manchurian Candidate*, both the book and the film, in his view, "are complete, utter, and pernicious nonsense from beginning to end." To drive his point home Erickson added, "If there is a single idea in it which reveals a grasp of the nature of hypnosis or of the psychopathic or socio-pathic type personality, I have not found it." Dr. Erickson's blunt dismissal of Basye's theory continued:

> In answer to your suggested questions the answers are completely in the negative. You have outlined a plot which, by the nature of the inter-personal relationship known as hypnosis, is impossible.
>
> In a protected laboratory situation, hypnotic subjects will perform acts that have the semblance of being anti-social. In experiments where wrongful acts are actually to be committed against others, the evidence is very much against such anti-social acts being induced by hypnosis. Cases which are cited as examples of anti-social behavior overlook the all-important factors of the demands of an experimental situation, the implicit agreement of a subject to carry out an experimental procedure, and the prestige and responsibility of the experimenter, all of which are as fully operative in experiments in which hypnosis has no place, as in those in which it is utilized.

Erickson's letter proceeded to systematically dismantle Basye's theory. The psychiatrist offered an obscure example illustrating his belief that hypnotized subject could not be induced to commit an anti-social act, stating, "I know of no genuine instance in which hypnosis has been used for anti-social purposes except news stories of questionable merit."   Regarding Basye's analysis of Lee Harvey Oswald's behavior, Erickson wrote,

> In the very detailed analysis of Oswald's behavior as a result of a supposed plot, rather than as the egotistical and deliberate act of a disturbed psychopathic personality, one tends to lose sight of a simple fact. This is a consideration which a more na-ïve viewpoint can sometimes set clear with a straight forward, simple, wondering comment. My daughter, aged 13, a typical teen-aged girl, saw an article which developed another theory about Oswald. It was based on the memory of several years back without notes, of a stenographer who typed out for Oswald an account of his sojourn in Russia. She recalled that he had carried off all her notes and copies, even her carbon paper,

but she was willing and eager to speculate that, because of his bitter criticism of every aspect of politics and life in Russia, he was probably functioning as an American spy sent by our own government. My daughter's horrified comment was, "Would we pick a person like that to spy for us?" I agree that it takes a far stretch of the imagination to see any government entrusting an important mission to an unreliable, unstable, egocentric, rebellious, disobedient, untruthful erratic character such as Oswald seems to have been since childhood.

Now regarding his disorganized behavior after the assassination; it is absolutely typical of the psychopathic personality. They will plan a course of action to the tiniest detail, rehearsing, checking, taking endless precautions, and the plan will end completely at a climactic point. The planner then proceeds to act at random and irrationally, exactly as Oswald did after the shots were fired. You could make a parallel with John Wilkes Booth, and you could make an informative and reliable instructive account that would do you more credit as a writer if you developed that story as the 'Climactic End of a Psychopathic Personality's Life Long Egocentric Career.'

Following his bold suggestion that Basye alter his theory and write up a comparison to Lincoln's assassin Booth, Dr. Erickson concluded his letter, with a brief postscript: *"That 'trigger one' or 'trigger word' is just as childish an idea as is the 'pass word' to the little boys' 'Secret Six Club.'"* [Emphasis added.]

There remained a substantial amount of information that Dr. Erickson did not relate to Basye. First and foremost was the fact that he, Erickson, had been a long-time covert CIA consultant on hypnotism. Furthermore, the primary objectives of the Agency's work with hypnosis, as Erickson was well aware, centered precisely on those issues raised by Basye: can a subject be induced to kill through hypnosis? Indeed, Dr. Erickson was there from the very start of the U.S. government's exploration of this provocative subject.

In 1945, a small novel was published which told the story of a group of diabolical Germans who secretly hypnotized selected Allied personnel in order to carry out a series of actions highly harmful to the United States and Britain. The novel's hero, Johnny Evans, must save the day and the Free World, but not before his love interest and the book's heroine is captured by a mad German scientist who strips her and brutally beats her in an attempt to force her to betray love and country. It is a lurid and sensational tableau recreated on countless pulp book and magazines covers throughout the 1940s and 1950s. *"She did not faint until they had beaten her, with their fists and a rubber hose, and mostly on her body, for several minutes ..."* [Emphasis added.]

The novel, *Death of the Mind,* was co-authored by G.H. "George" Estabrooks who included the following curious and intriguing introduction to the book aimed, perhaps, at certain careful readers: "This is a work of fiction and, as such, deals with imaginary persons and incidents.... It is also true that the authors have inserted no scientific theories for the purposes of fiction and have described no hypnotic phenomena which have not been observed during known experiments." Among those careful readers, as might be expected, were certain officials at the CIA.

George Hoban Estabrooks was a professor of psychology and chairman of the Department of Psychology at Colgate University in New York. He had been a Rhodes scholar and completed his Ph.D. at Harvard University in 1926. Most people who came into close contact with Estabrooks considered him to be brilliant, but overly egotistical when it came to his bold claims about hypnotism: "I can hypnotize a man, without his knowledge or consent, into committing treason against the United States."

Besides hypnotism, Estabrooks was very interested in telepathy, and early in his career he worked with Walter Franklin Prince and Gardner Murphy, who established the Boston Society of Psychical Research. In 1942, when Estabrooks was bragging the loudest – that he could turn any man into a traitor through hypnosis – the War Department, precursor to the Department of Defense, quickly took notice and summoned the proud professor to a meeting at the Pentagon.

Asked one general of Estabooks, "What is the likelihood that the Japanese would employ hypnosis against the United States?"

Replied Estabrooks, "Two hundred trained foreign operators working in the United States could develop a uniquely dangerous army of hypnotically controlled Sixth Columnists."

"You're kidding," said another general.

"No, I'm not," Estabrooks shot back, "besides, are you willing to take the chance?"

Apparently, the Pentagon was not willing to chance it, as evidenced in an article by Estabrooks that appeared in 1971 in *Science Digest*. In it, Estabrooks provides a glimpse into his work for the military on hypnosis:

> One of the most fascinating but dangerous applications of hypnosis is its use in military intelligence. This is a field with which I am familiar through formulating guidelines for the techniques used by the United States in two world wars.... The "hypnotic courier" ... provides a unique solution [to communication in war]. I was involved in preparing many subjects for this work during World War II.

Decades earlier, in 1939, Estabrooks and Dr. Milton H. Erickson, well before both men went to work for the CIA, had conducted an experiment for the FBI, which Erickson later recalled in fascinating detail:

> At the end of an hour they asked me to awaken Tommy, to bring him out of the trance, talk awhile, then put him back into the trance, and reorient him to that first trance. They had a program of exact movements, and they asked me ... to have him visualize the entire procedure. Tommy gave a blow-by-blow account of the first hour, including the exact time in which so-and-so uncrossed his legs, when he re-crossed them, when he shifted his hat to one side, when he lit the other fellow's cigarette, when the other fellow lit his cigarette.

As with many of the CIA's early operational activities, the Agency's interest in applying hypnosis to intelligence work originated primarily with its precursor, the Office of Strategic Services (OSS) during World War II. At the time, OSS and British intelligence operatives mounted a concerted effort, still largely unexamined, to use hypnotists and hypnotism in the war effort. One of the more detailed glimpses into these efforts comes from OSS research director Stanley Platt Lovell, a chemical plant owner summoned to war duty and dubbed "a devious little nihilist" by OSS director William "Wild Bill" Donovan.

During the war, Lovell had anxiously inquired of "two of the most famous psychiatrists in the country" about the possibility of hypnotizing "a German prisoner-of-war" and then smuggling "him into Berlin or Berchtesgaden where he would assassinate Hitler in that posthypnotic state, being under a compulsion that might not be denied."

One of the psychiatrists whom Lovell had consulted was Dr. Lawrence Kubie who, months earlier, had closely assisted OSS officer George Hunter White with truth-drug experiments, some notably at New Jersey's Bordertown Youth Reformatory – where, about nine years later, social workers would consider sending Lee Harvey Oswald. Lovell, who would go on after the war to work closely with the CIA and the U.S. Army's Fort Detrick, also consulted brothers Drs. Karl and William Menninger. None of these three shared Lovell's enthusiasm.

"There is no evidence," the Menningers said, according to Lovell, "that supports posthypnotic acts, especially when the individual's mores and morals produce the slightest conflict within him. A man to whom murder is repugnant and immoral cannot be made to override that personal tabu."

Kubie, who years later would go on to visit George White's CIA funded safe house in New York City, took a slightly different tack, pointing out, "If your German prisoner-of-war has adequate and logical reason to kill Hitler, Heydrich or anyone else, you don't need hypnotism to incite or motivate him. If he hasn't, I am skeptical that it will accomplish anything."

Days later, Lovell recounts, he was summoned to the office of OSS deputy director Col. G. Edward Buxton to meet a hypnotist "who alleged he was a master of post-hypnotic suggestion." While Lovell did not identify the hypnotist, it was most likely G.H. Estabrooks.

Unfortunately, other than providing us with a mostly silly account of what may or may not have occurred in Buxton's office, Lovell left behind nothing else about OSS use of hypnosis, despite the fact that numerous, completely unsupported claims have been made over the past decades about the OSS' use of posthypnotic couriers and assassins.

The CIA's interest in hypnotism developed primarily from Morse Allen's fascination with the subject and his review of surviving and classified OSS materials. Commencing in early 1951 Allen, who worked in the Agency's Security Research Section (SRS) and had had about four-months study and training in hypnosis, convinced his CIA superiors to cover the costs of his participation in a four-day course given by a well-known stage hypnotist in New York. According to Dr. Sidney Gottlieb:

> The origins of CIA interest in hypnosis began before I arrived at the Agency with [Morse] Allen and others in SRS who recognized the practice as a possible means for eliciting information. Apparently there was earlier interest in the subject with the OSS, but I'm unaware of the details or extent of that. [Morse] Allen, as I understand it, became deeply involved in conducting hypnosis experiments at headquarters and elsewhere…. I recall only one meeting with a hypnotist named [Milton] Erickson in New York around 1952 or 1953 …

With the advent of the CIA's Project Artichoke, developed and operated by the Agency's SRS to the near total exclusion of the Technical Services Division and Gottlieb's Chemical Branch, Morse Allen was easily able to incorporate hypnotism into many aspects of the program, including hiring hypnosis consultants Estabrooks and Erickson, among others. Incredibly, SRS' initial Artichoke objectives, listed as a series of questions, mirrored those posed by Dale Basye to Milton Erickson. Allen also recruited a cadre of volunteer Agency support staff, all of whom, not surprisingly – given the tenor of the times – were women. These women were used in an intensive series of hypnosis-related experiments, most of them conducted in CIA-owned buildings and Washington, D.C. hotel rooms. The experiments grew increasingly complex, as well as quite dangerous. Some "secretaries" were hypnotized to engage in sexual acts with complete strangers whom they would be induced to approach in bars and restaurants. One particularly appalling experiment is reported by researcher and author John Marks:

> On February 19, 1954, Morse Allen simulated the ultimate Experiment in hypnosis: the creation of a 'Manchurian Candidate', or programmed assassin. Allen's 'victim' was a secretary whom he put into a deep trance and told to keep sleeping until he ordered otherwise. He then hypnotized a second secretary and told her that if she could not wake up her friend, 'her rage would be so

great that she would not hesitate to kill.' Allen left a pistol nearby, which the secretary had no way of knowing was unloaded. Even though she had earlier expressed a fear of firearms of any kind, she picked up the gun and 'shot' her sleeping friend. After Allen brought the 'killer' out of her trance, she had apparent amnesia for the event, denying she would ever shoot anyone.

In July 1954, SRS Chief Paul Gaynor and Morse Allen met to discuss a proposal from George Estabrooks involving the "idea of the [Agency utilizing] couriers that had been hypnotized." According to several CIA documents about the meeting, Allen informed Gaynor that the idea "is not new and I am absolutely certain that Estabrooks did not invent the idea." When Gaynor questioned the viability of the concept, Allen explained, "We [CIA] ourselves have carried out much more complex problems than this and in a general sense I agree that it is feasible."

Gaynor also inquired about what he termed the "third-degree problem," meaning what would occur if a courier was subjected to third-degree interrogation tactics or given drugs. "We don't know at this point in time," answered Allen, "but we expect to have answers to this issue soon as a result of planned experiments that are soon to be carried out." Allen would later write in one SRS memorandum-for-the-record that hypnotized couriers and covert operatives had been used in the late 1950s in East Germany and in the Soviet Union.

Gaynor also questioned Allen at length about the likelihood of SRS being able to definitively determine whether or not an individual could be "made to commit murder" under hypnosis. Again, Allen responded that Agency experiments, already underway, had thus far shown "promising results" and that the "long ago raised problems of moral inhibitions blocking hypnosis" did not seem to be "that great a problem at all."

When Gaynor asked when an "actual demonstration" could be enacted, Allen replied, "[T]here have already been a number of successful tests with [name redacted, but believed to be Dr. Milton H. Erickson] that showed religious and moral inhibitions were not problematic." Allen explained that one subject, an Agency employee, had been induced to "commit harm to fellow employees on a number of occasions ... resulting in physical violence."

Because of Dale Basye, Sr.'s letter to Dr. Milton Erickson and the FBI, and at least one other such theory advanced to the FBI (see Notes at end of this chapter), the Warren Commission investigating Kennedy's assassination sought to "investigate" the possibility that Oswald, while in Russia, "may have received medical or psychological treatment or conditioning designed to reinforce or accentuate his apparent hostility to authority and thereby render him a disruptive factor in this country after his return."

On May 19, 1964, the general counsel for the Commission sent a letter to the CIA's Richard Helms, Deputy Director of Plans (DDP), stating, "We [the Commission] think that a study of the latest Soviet techniques in 'mind conditioning' and so-called 'brainwashing' would be helpful in that regard. We would greatly appreciate your making such materials as you may have on that subject available [to the Commission]. Perhaps a conference on this subject between appropriate members of your organization and members of our staff would be desirable."

One does not have to speculate at any great length to realize that the Warren Commission well understood that any "study" had been accomplished long before the Kennedy assassination and that the "techniques" it wished to examine had already been investigated by the CIA. Indeed, on June 19, a month later, DDP Helms advised the Commission that "a collection of classified and overt materials" on Soviet brainwashing techniques would be provided by the Agency to the Commission. On June 25, Helms forwarded to the Commission by courier "twenty-three unclassified items and one classified report which are relevant to the subject, although perhaps somewhat outdated in several instances."

The one classified report detailed programs and projects, as well as a number of human experiments, conducted by the Russians. None of the materials handed to the Commission mentioned in any manner any of the concerted projects, programs, and human experiments conducted by the CIA itself in the areas of behavior modification, enhanced interrogation, and hypnosis over the past thirteen years and ongoing. Nobody on the staff of the Warren Commission was appraised of or briefed about the Agency's Projects Bluebird, Artichoke, MK/NAOMI, or MK/ULTRA, or the specialized, and much overlooked, work of the CIA's Human Ecology Fund.

There is yet another coincidental connection between the JFK assassination, Oswald, and Dale E. Basye, Sr. To supplement his newspaper reporter's income, Basye sometimes pursued stories as a freelance journalist. In December 1962, he and *Dallas Morning News* staff photographer, Jack Beers, went to Jack Ruby's Carousel Club where they spent a long afternoon researching an article about the club. The article, entitled "Cool School," was published a few weeks later in the popular men's, or stag, magazine, *Adam*. It described an on-going amateur night Ruby held at his club – a contest for young women, non-professionals, who stripped. Any woman who won the contest stood a good chance of becoming a regular paid stripper at the Carousel.

One year later, in December 1963, Basye told FBI investigators who questioned him about the article that he knew of no connection between Jack Ruby and Lee Harvey Oswald, whom he had never heard of prior to the assassination. However, Basye told investigators that he did meet once again with Ruby at the Dallas Hotel, across the street from the *Dallas Morning News,* simply to give Ruby a copy of the *Adam* article.

Basye told the FBI that at the time of his December 1962 visit to Ruby's Club, Ruby had introduced him to two Dallas police officers who had arrived there shortly after Basye. According to the FBI report on this encounter, Basye recalled "that one of these policemen was said to be engaged to the woman who was with Ruby at the time, Kathy Kay." During his FBI interview about this encounter, Basye remarked that it was his impression that Ruby was a "scatterbrain" and an "overly emotional guy."

Jack Beers, the *Dallas Morning News* photographer who had worked on the "Cool School" story with Basye, went on to achieve minor fame as the photographer who took the infamous photo of Jack Ruby a split second before he murdered Lee Harvey Oswald.

Chapter Eight

Oswald, Cuba, and Other Places

*One thinks of history as fiction: it is designed to give the
shape and significance that the chaos and untutored raw
experience seems to need – mainly for institutional and so-
cietal indoctrination.
It is mostly false. The worst becomes doctrine.*

-Robert Taber, unpublished letter, 1992

A Strange Letter to Lee Harvey Oswald ...

On December 5, 1963, the U.S. Secret Service forwarded an
intercepted letter to the Dallas FBI office. The letter, dated
November 10, 1963, was written in Spanish and addressed
to Lee Harvey Oswald, "Mail Office," Dallas, Texas. It was postmarked La Habana, Cuba, November 28, 1963. The FBI laboratory
received the letter on December 9 for processing and translation,
describing it as "conspiratorial in content and implies a prior conspiracy between the writer and Lee Harvey Oswald to assassinate
the President." As translated, the letter reads:

La Habana
Nov. 10, 1963
Lee Harvey Oswald
Mail Office
Dallas, Texas
U.S.A.

Amigo Lee:
One time more I write you since the last time that we saw
each other in Miami. The Spanish books that you took from
the hotel and I have hardly anything. I told you of the man
who was thinking of visiting here shortly and you ought to
close the business as soon as possible, like I told you before
in Miami. I recommend much prudence and do not be fool-

ish with the money I gave you. So I hope you will not defraud me and that our dreams will be realized. After the affair, I am going to recommend much to the chief that he certainly will have much interest in knowing you, as they need men like you. I told him you could put out a candle at 50 meters and he did not want to believe me, but I made him believe it because I saw you with my own eyes and the chief was astonished. Good Lee, practice your Spanish for when you come to Habana for Habana is the land of the free, of the beautiful women and the rich Habana tobacco. Don't forget to do all I told you to the very letter and leave nothing that could lead to your trail and when you receive my letters destroy them as always. After the affair, I will send you the money and we will see each other in Miami as always.

Sincerely always,
Pedro Charles
[Signed by hand: "Peter"]

A second letter, dated November 27, 1963, also written in Spanish, was forwarded to the FBI laboratory on December 9, 1963. This letter also came from Havana, Cuba (postmarked November 28, 1963, 9:30 A.M.) and was addressed to JFK's brother, Robert Kennedy, wrongly identified as "Secretary of Justice"; he was U.S. Attorney General. The translated letter reads:

Havana, November 27, 1963
Mr. Robert Kennedy
Secretary of Justice
Washington, D.C.

Dear Mr. Kennedy:
This letter is to advise you that former Marine Lee Harvey Oswald was the man who assassinated your brother by the express order of a gentleman named Pedro Charles, residing in Miami, Florida. This gentleman had an interview with him in a Miami night club about two months ago. This Mr. Pedro Charles is an agent of Fidel Castro in the United States and uses other names. Young Lee Harvey Oswald received an advance payment of $5,000 which he spent in various night clubs, af-

ter which Pedro Charles advanced him another $2,000. The understanding was for Lee Harvey Oswald to go first to Houston and then to Dallas where President John F. Kennedy was scheduled to pay a visit. In fact, information was available at the Chamber of Commerce of Dallas that the President would visit Texas. Pedro Charles reached an understanding with Lee Harvey Oswald, an expert marksman, for the President to be killed and for an international scandal to be unleashed so that all the blame would fall on the racists and the extreme-rightists of the State of Texas. This is the truth about the assassination of President Kennedy. I was acquainted with these details, but I never gave them any credence. I learned of them through the words of a lady who lives with Pedro Charles, who is the man who uses several false names and passports to enter and leave the United States of America, Mexico and Cuba. The lady in question, whose name I cannot disclose, lives here in Havana and is very much affected by the lamentable happenings. She never thought of what might happen because they were in the habit of kidding about everything, but this joke was reality. If the accused Lee Harvey Oswald had not been assassinated at the hands of a gambler, there is no doubt that the accused would have told the whole truth as time went on, because the first thing that Pedro Charles told Oswald was for him to be wide awake in doing the job and, if possible, to erase all clues and not "get caught." In addition, he was not to carry anything compromising in his pockets; anything that might prevent him from achieving the objective of his mission.

We sincerely regret the loss of President Kennedy. He was a man of peace and I, myself, feel mortified and ashamed of being a communist and of knowing a little about this matter from my conversation with this lady who knew all the details and was not brave enough to report this monstrous crime. Right now, as I am writing this report, I am preparing my effects in order to embark for Venezuela clandestinely. In fact, if the political police of Castro should arrest me I would face the firing squad. Some day the lady in question will make very interesting statements about this crime; as soon as she recuperates from her nervous state and is able to point out the mastermind behind the assassination of President Kennedy who is none other than

Pedro Charles, agent of the State Security Department of Cuba and a fanatic of Fidel Castro.

Sincerely yours,
(Signed) Mario del Rosario Molina
Havana, Cuba

A third letter, dated November 27, 1963, postmarked Havana, Cuba on December 3, 1963, 6:00 P.M. and also written in Spanish, was sent by airmail to the "Directors of the Program 'The Voice of the United States of America'" in Washington, D.C. Signed by Miguel Galban Lopez, the letter reads:

November 27, 1963
To the Directors of the Program
"THE VOICE OF THE UNITED STATES OF AMERICA"
Washington, D.C.
United States of America

Gentlemen:
Hereby we are addressing ourselves to you to let you know that the assassination of the President of the United States, John F. Kennedy, is connected with the Revolutionary Government of Cuba. Approximately two months ago, the alleged assassin of the President, Lee Harvey Oswald, had an interview in the city of Miami with Pedro Charles, an agent of Fidel Castro in Mexico, who was in charge of delivering to the above-mentioned Lee Harvey Oswald the amount of seven thousand dollars. This source is official; every time that a certain lady went in the company of Pedro Charles to a night club in Miami, she saw both of them together in conference and this lady recognized him from the photographs published here in Havana. This lady resides in Havana, but her name cannot be disclosed because her escort, Pedro Charles, is currently in Mexico on a mission by the Castro Government for a cultural exchange. As soon as this lady leaves the country – in fact, she is suffering from a serious nervous breakdown – she will go to one of the countries of Central America clandestinely in order to avoid being detained by the Castro police. This is all I can inform for the time being and it is the truth; let us hope, then, that

the lady in question leaves Cuba in order to learn from her own voice everything connected with this monstrous event in which President Kennedy lost his life.

Sincerely yours,
Miguel Galban Lopez
(Typed and handwritten signature)

A fourth letter, dated November 27, 1963 and postmarked Havana on December 3, 1963 at 6:00 P.M. was addressed to: "The Director of the *Diario de New York*," a Spanish language newspaper published in New York City. This letter was also signed by Miguel Galban Lopez and beneath his signature was added: "Ex-Captain of the Rebel Army, Cuba Exile." The translated letter, originally written in Spanish, reads:

Havana, November 27, 1963
To the Director of the "Diario de New York"
New York, New York
United States of America

Dear Sir:
It is my pleasure to write this letter to inform you that the assassination of President John F. Kennedy was paid for by Mr. Pedro Charles, Fidel Castro's agent in Mexico. This man became a close friend of former marine and expert shooter Lee H. Oswald in Mexico. They were seen together frequenting various night clubs. The above-mentioned Mr. Pedro Charles had to deliver to Oswald $7,000 as a down payment. Later he was to deliver $10,000 upon completion of the work. In other words, the crime was agreed upon for $17,000.

Mr. Pedro Charles, who uses other fictitious names and a diplomatic passport to enter and leave Mexico and the United States, is at present in the residence of the Cuban Ambassador in Mexico, according to the latest information in my possession. I want you to know before anybody else the truth about the Dallas assassination of President Kennedy.

(Signed) Miguel Galban Lopez
Ex-Captain of the Rebel Army
Cuban Exile

All four letters were intercepted and analyzed by the FBI, and quickly forwarded to the Warren Commission. On January 17, 1964, FBI director J. Edgar Hoover informed the Commission's General Counsel, J. Lee Rankin, that the Bureau's laboratory found that all of the letters "were actually prepared on the same typewriter and that several of the envelopes used came from the same source." Concluded Hoover: "It is, therefore, clear that this [all four letters] represents some type of hoax, possibly on the part of some anti-Castro group seeking to discredit the Cuban Government."

In his letter to Rankin, Hoover did not address the identities of any of the signers of the letters, nor did he provide details of the FBI's investigation, if any, into the existence of Pedro Charles. Despite Hoover's seemingly cursory dismissal of the four letters, however, their existence provoked and fueled sustained discussion among Commission members about Lee Harvey Oswald's possible ties to Cuba as well as speculation that Oswald had visited Cuba several times. The Warren Commission's discussions about Oswald's visits to the island were significantly fueled by a comment made by J. Edgar Hoover to Attorney General Robert Kennedy on the afternoon of the assassination, that Oswald had "made several trips to Cuba."

Oswald Sighting in Cuba

On December 3, 1963, according to a U.S. Army Security Information Summary Report prepared by military intelligence officers with the 470th MI Detachment at Fort Amador, Panama, Dr. Enrique Lorenso-Luaces y Vilaseca had encountered Lee Harvey Oswald in Cuba in May 1961.

According to Dr. Luaces, he had met Oswald at a bar in Havana, Cuba called Sloppy Joe's "about three weeks after the Bay of Pigs invasion." Luaces told investigators that while he was at Sloppy Joe's, former CBS news correspondent Robert Taber entered the bar accompanied by a "young North American." Dr. Luaces had first met Taber in October 1960 when Taber was a reporter for *La Revolution,* a pro-Castro newspaper. At the time, Luaces was a correspondent for the Copley News Service in San Diego, California.

When Taber entered the bar, the report recounts, Luaces observed that, "his right leg was in a cast and he was using crutches." He asked Taber what had happened, and the newsman explained that he had been "wounded while covering the Bay of Pigs invasion as a reporter for the Castro-Cuban government." Following this, Taber "then turned to his young companion and introduced him to Luaces as Lieutenant Harvey Oswald, an arms expert."

Dr. Luaces, according to the Army intelligence Report, "not hearing the last name, asked Oswald if the name was spelled with a 't' or 'd,' to which the young man answered 'd.'" The Report continues: "Taber, who Luaces calls an 'egotistical show-off,' asked Oswald to open his briefcase and show Luaces what it contained." Luaces stated that the briefcase "held a series of folded charts, one of which Oswald extracted and unfolded. The chart was a cut-away training aid of the M-1 rifle."

According to the U.S. Army Report, Luaces left the bar shortly after this and said that he "never saw Oswald again until his [Oswald's] photograph appeared on television as the suspected assassin of the late John F. Kennedy."

Luaces told military investigators that "there was no doubt in his mind that the Harvey Oswald he met at Sloppy Joe's in 1961 and the Lee Harvey Oswald whose picture appeared on the television screen are one and the same." Luaces also said that besides himself, Taber, and Oswald, there was no one else in the bar, other than two Cuban bartenders, at the time that he met Oswald.

Again, about 1970, Luaces told a newspaper associate there was "no doubt" in his mind that the man he had met was Oswald, but that now he had no interest in discussing the encounter any longer. Reportedly, he cryptically said, "I am more interested in spending my remaining days alive."

WHO WAS ROBERT TABER?

Robert Bruce Taber, born in 1919 in Chicago, attended elementary school in Detroit, and went to boarding school in Dundee, Illinois, leaving his formal schooling after the seventh grade. He spent his early teen years traveling the country, working first as a farmhand in Greensboro, North Carolina at the age of thirteen, and then as a merchant seaman, tugboat fireman, and railroad worker. He landed his first job in journalism at age sixteen working for a newspaper in Kingsport, Tennessee. He moved to New York City when he was eighteen, hired as a reporter for the daily newspaper *Queens Evening News*. He remained there until he was drafted into the U.S. Army to serve in the infantry during

World War II. Reportedly, Taber saw a fair amount of combat, but was always reluctant to discuss the subject. Following his honorable discharge from the army, Taber took a job in 1945 with the New York-based wire service, the Standard News Association, followed by two years with the Newhouse newspapers in Queens, New York as a crime reporter.

In 1950, Taber went to work for CBS as a journalist, covering a number of heated political conflicts and revolutionary situations around the world. In Germany, Morocco, and Guatemala, he was arrested and detained by military forces for his aggressive reporting style. A 1964 CIA Security Office report states that Taber "was of operational interest" to the Agency in several countries where he covered news, "but was never used."

In March 1957, *New York Times* writer Herbert Matthews, like a number of CIA and American diplomats in Cuba at the time, was quite supportive of Castro's rebel forces. Matthews was also very close to CIA director Allen Dulles and his brother, Secretary of State John Foster Dulles. Matthews put Cuban Mario Llerena – who informally advised Fidel Castro on public relations – in touch with CBS in New York. Llerena had requested that Matthews arrange a meeting for him with CBS after he had convinced Castro that television, as opposed to the editorial pages of the *New York Times*, was the best vehicle for reaching the hearts and minds of the broader masses in America. CBS had been trying for weeks to gain an interview with Castro, who was still in the midst of his revolution to take control of Cuba. Llerena flew to New York and, as arranged by Matthews, met with Taber at the CBS offices. It was eventually arranged for the newsman to interview Castro. On April 23, Llerena, Taber and Taber's cameraman, Wendell Hoffman, flew to Havana where they told Cuban authorities they were researching a film about Presbyterian schools in Cuba.

Taber and Hoffman spent four days with Castro and his rebel forces at their camp in the Sierra Maestra Mountains, filming interviews. Included in the interviews were three young American soldiers of fortune who had run away from their U.S. Navy families and homes in Guantanamo to join the rebels. They were Charles Ryan, Victor J. Buehlman, and Michael L. Garvey. Said Ryan to Taber, "I figure the fight in Cuba is for the kind of ideals on which the U.S. was set up." (Taber talked Castro into allowing him to take

Robert Taber
[seated on ground],
Cuba, 1959.

runaways Buehlman and Garvey back to Havana to be reunited with their parents. Charles Ryan, the oldest of the three, choose to remain in the rebel camp.)

During Taber's interview with Castro, the rebel leader denied any interest in communism and any association with communists. At the close of the interview Taber handed Castro his microphone and allowed him to speak directly to the American public. The interview was nothing less than historic, and when Taber's half-hour documentary, "Rebels of the Sierra Maestra: The Story of Cuba's Jungle Fighters," aired on CBS on May 19, 1957, it far exceeded the expectations of Castro and Llerena in that it garnered tremendous American support for the Cuban rebel's cause. Parts of Taber's interview, along with Hoffman's photos, appeared in the May 27, 1957 issue of *Life* magazine, pleasing Castro even more. (Taber and Hoffman's documentary was edited by Don Hewitt, later editor of CBS' *60 Minutes*.)

In April 1960, Robert Taber along with another CBS newsman, Richard Gibson – the first African-American newsman hired by the corporation – purchased a full-page advertisement in the *New York Times*. The ad proclaimed their belief that the Cuban revolution was very important in offering freedom to the Cuban people and that the United States should cease its economic boycott of the island. The ad also announced the formation of the Fair Play for Cuba Committee (FPCC). The full-page ad bore the bold headline, "What Is Really Happening in Cuba." In January 1961, Dr. Charles

A. Santos-Buch, a Cuban teaching at an American university, revealed that he was also a founder of FPCC and that he and Taber had obtained the funds to pay for the advertisement from Castro's Government. Subsequent FBI and CIA documents state that both agencies traced $3,500 used to pay for the ad to Santos-Buch who had been given the money by a Cuban delegate to the United Nations.

From the start, FPCC was a highly controversial organization, and its history has never been completely told. It is estimated that nearly seventy percent of FPCC's files and records were destroyed following JFK's murder. Consequently, the best sources, however slanted and less than objective about FPCC, are CIA and FBI files – of which an estimated sixty-five percent remain classified and stamped "secret."

Within less than 48-hours after the Taber-Gibson ad appeared in the *Times*, more than two thousand people nationwide joined the FPCC and over a thousand letters of support were sent to the organization, including from Truman Capote, Norman Mailer, Linus Pauling, Jean-Paul Sartre and James Baldwin. By the end of 1960, FPCC had over 10,000 members organized into about 35 local FPCC chapters, along with 40 college FPCC councils.

No doubt the April 6, 1960 *New York Times* advertisement caught the serious attention of the CIA and FBI, and when yet another full-page FPCC advertisement appeared in the *Times* on April 21 containing what both agencies viewed as a very pro-communist slant, the government kicked its surveillance and covert infiltration activities into full gear. Within weeks, in May 1960, Paul Gaynor, CIA Security Research Section (SRS) chief, would tell Agency Office of Security chief Sheffield Edwards that the Agency "had sand to dirt and worse" on most of the FPCC leadership. Morse Allen, an SRS employee, told Gaynor in June 1960, "A good number of the Negroes drawn to this group appear to be either homosexuals or violent people for yet to be determined reasons." About a year later, a CIA official detailed to infiltrate the group complained, "Half the members I encounter are FBI informers, the other half our own guys going from meeting to meeting."

As some readers are well aware, in May 1963, Lee Harvey Oswald allegedly single-handedly formed the New Orleans chapter of the FPCC. Less well known are reports out of Cuba and Russia – beginning in 1963-64 and continuing to the present – that while in Russia, Oswald met with Cuba's Ambassador to the Soviet Union Faure Chomon, and Cuba's Minister of Foreign Affairs Carlos Olivares, and that Oswald was given funds by the Soviets, some of which he used in the U.S. for the New Orleans FPCC. Equally fascinating are related reports that Oswald visited Cuba, as well as Mexico, both prior to and after his return to the United States from the Soviet Union, and that in Mexico City he had encounters with CIA asset June Cobb (see this book's chapter on Cobb). It is well documented in CIA and FBI files that Cobb, working covertly for the CIA, was actively assisting FPCC in organizing trips to Cuba for its members and student groups while she was working for Castro in 1960 and 1961, and meeting with Richard Gibson on numerous occasions.

In April 1962, Robert Taber appeared as a witness before a closed session of a U.S. Senate Internal Security Subcommittee. It was Taber's third appearance before the committee, his first was in May 1960, his second in June 1961, and his reception at all three was less than cordial or civil. The open contempt and disrespect directed toward Taber throughout the lengthy session was remarkable. In particular, Sen. Thomas J. Dodd (D-Conn.), the subcommittee's vice chair, and a former FBI special agent and trial counsel at Nuremberg, seemed to go out of his way to vilify and slander Taber. A press release about Taber's testimony issued by the subcommittee, which quotes Dodd, underscores Dodd's demeanor and attitude toward Taber:

> It is something to ponder that a man like Taber would worm his way into a top position on the CBS staff, get himself assigned as CBS correspondent in Cuba in the period preceding the Castro takeover, and then have his totally pro-Castro presentations purveyed to the American public by one of our two great television networks.

In a caveat to his strong words, Dodd issued a clear nod and wink to the intelligence community and their ongoing infiltration into the American media in general with the words:

> It is my earnest hope that the story of Robert Taber, as here presented can do something to persuade our news media that

their correspondents can not be selected on the sole basis of their ability as newspapermen or cameramen or commentators – that it is their duty to the American public to conduct a somewhat closer check into character and basic loyalties than was conducted in the case of Robert Taber.

Robert Taber was grilled mercilessly by the Senate Subcommittee, which probed into virtually every part of his professional and personal life. Often his Senate inquisitors ran through topics so quickly that possible important connections were left unexplored and dangling for verification, explanation and closure. Several of these topics months later, following the assassination, could have possibly helped in better understanding Kennedy's murder, but as with most Congressional hearings the objectives turned primarily on political self-aggrandizement and character assassination, not real information, truth or fact gathering. A couple of examples may suffice here to illustrate this.

During the same session before the subcommittee in 1962, Taber was asked out of the blue about June Cobb by subcommittee chief counsel Julius Sourwine. (See Chapter 11 on Cobb, who was at the time a CIA asset, most likely unknown to Taber or anyone else in the FPCC.)

> **Mr. Sourwine:** I do not recall if I asked you this question. Do you know June Cobb?

> **Mr. Taber:** I have never met her. I have seen her.

Before Sourwine could respond to Taber's answer or follow-up, Sen. Dodd interrupted by changing the subject to Taber's arrest record as a youth. This was perhaps a deliberate ploy. Cobb's name did not come up again.

Another example was when Taber was questioned about a pistol he was carrying in April 1961 when he was seriously wounded while covering the disastrous CIA-backed Bay of Pigs invasion of Cuba.

> **Mr. Sourwine:** Mr. Taber, referring to the pistol which you were carrying at the time you were wounded last April, you bought this in Florida. Where in Florida did you buy it?

Mr. Taber: I didn't buy it personally. A friend bought it for me.

Mr. Sourwine: Who bought it for you?

Mr. Taber: A chap named Bradley. I have forgotten his first name.

Mr. Sourwine: His last name was Bradley?

Mr. Taber: Yes, sir.

Mr. Sourwine: Was he a member of the Fair Play for Cuba Committee?

Mr. Taber: No, sir.

Mr. Sourwine: Who is he? Who is Bradley?

Mr. Taber: He was a flyer that I knew by chance in Havana and, on one of his trips back in Havana, he brought along this pistol.

Mr. Sourwine: You were in Cuba?

Mr. Taber: Yes.

Mr. Sourwine: He was a flyer? Private or airline?

Mr. Taber: Private.

Mr. Sourwine: He had a plane of his own?

Mr. Taber: I believe so.

"Zombie Creation": Who Was Leslie Bradley?

Bradley was Leslie Norman Bradley, a skilled small plane and crop duster pilot, as well as a flight instructor. At the time that Taber dealt with Bradley, the pilot was about 32 years old. Bradley, a former resident of Minneapolis, Minnesota, was a man of many contradictory stripes, usually conservative, liberal on some issues, nearly anarchistic on others. He was a mystery to even his closest friends, all of whom said that he "was fiercely loyal in his relationships," but "not above ignoring rules and convention" or exercising a faint streak of larceny. Friends also said that Bradley "appeared to be very well educated" and "well read." According to Clayton Daniels, a former soldier of fortune who worked with Bradley in both Miami and Cuba, "When he wasn't in motion he was either reading or trying to learn all that he could about his surroundings. He knew more about Nicaragua then anyone I ever met."

While working in Florida in 1953 as a flight instructor, Bradley had been approved by the CIA for use as a contract pilot. In 1959-60, he was reportedly also working as an independent "soldier-of-fortune," flying guns from the United States to Cuba, Panama, Mexico City and Nicaragua. (Leslie Bradley should not be confused with Edgar Eugene Bradley, who will be discussed shortly.)

In the summer of 1960, Bradley, who spoke Spanish, was arrested in Havana for "plotting and participating in an invasion of Nicaragua that would embarrass Fidel Castro." According to FBI documents, "Cuban authorities charged that the plot was hatched on orders from the United States [CIA] to discredit the Castro regime." In advancing the Nicaraguan scheme, Bradley had dealings with a number of known mercenaries, including a fiercely independent soldier of fortune named Robert Emmett Johnson, as well as Nicaraguan Chester Lacayo, Cuban army officer Maj. Jesus Carreras, legendary American soldier of fortune William Alexander Morgan, Loran Hall and David Morales. In October 1960, a Cuban military court sentenced him to ten years in prison on charges that he "took part in a secret plot against the Castro regime." Thrown into one of Castro's worst prisons, Bradley later said that he experienced "barbaric treatment from guards" including "sexual abuse, and vile behavior."

William Morgan, who had fought valiantly alongside the Castro brothers and Che Guevara during the revolution, had turned against the Castro government after it had made a sharp turn toward communism. For months he worked surreptitiously for the overthrow of Castro, often using the American June Cobb, a secret CIA asset who had maneuvered her way into a job with Castro as a means of feeding information to the Agency.

On April 23, 1963, the *New York Times* reported that New York attorney James B. Donovan – who negotiated the release and trade of Soviet spy Col. Rudolf Abel for U-2 spy plane pilot Francis Gary Powers – had negotiated the release of 27 American prisoners held by Castro in Cuba. Among those released was Leslie Bradley. Far less fortunate was William Morgan who had been executed by a

Cuban firing squad on March 11, 1961. Then Cuban Defense Minister Raul Castro had ordered Morgan "executed as a traitor kneeling with his back to the firing squad," but Morgan, who had refused to kneel, was shot in both knees forcing him to the ground where he was then executed. Other Americans formally executed in Cuba were soldiers of fortune Anthony Zarba from Boston, Texan Allen Thompson, and Robert Otis Fuller of Miami.

While Donovan was negotiating the release of the 27 American prisoners in Cuba, the ultra-secret CIA Task Force W, working alongside Agency Technical Services scientists, was organizing two of the many plots to murder Fidel Castro.

The first plan centered on a rigged sea shell that was to be loaded with explosives and placed on the ocean floor where Castro regularly skin dived. Technical Services scientists were stumped about how they would induce Castro to pick up the shell – thus triggering an explosion. One staffer sarcastically suggested, "Should we put a neon sign on it?" CIA administrators were less than amused and responded that they were getting intense pressure from Attorney General Bobby Kennedy, appointed by JFK to oversee the task, to come up with a viable plan to kill Castro. Alternatively, Agency technicians devised a more realistic plan whereby they purchased an expensive diving suit that attorney Donovan would present to Castro as a gift at one of their negotiating sessions. Apparently, Donovan was not informed that the suit would be contaminated with debilitating fungus spores and tuberculosis bacilli. The CIA and Bobby Kennedy were disappointed to learn, therefore, that Donovan, on his own, had already given Castro a diving suit. (Some former Agency officials have remarked publicly that Bobby Kennedy was relentless in his determination to kill Castro, and that he frequently would threaten CIA administrators that if they did not perform more to his liking, he would "tell his big brother on them." Reports have it that the CIA attempted to kill Castro over 400 times during a twenty-year period, making Castro perhaps the luckiest man in the world.)

Bradley's story of intrigue and adventure did not cease with his release from a Cuban prison. Indeed, it accelerated, and Volume Two of this book shall examine Leslie Bradley in detail.

Meanwhile, the FBI was constantly tailing and watching Robert Taber. Propelling the FBI's intense interest in Taber was his alleged close association to Robert F. Williams, one of the FPCC founders. Indeed, Williams was at the top of the lengthy list of FPCC members who drew the constant surveillance and concern of the FBI and CIA. The notoriety of Williams was so intense among law enforcement officials in late 1963 that within minutes of JFK's assassination, FBI investigators were looking very closely at his every move and association. Williams was law enforcement's quintessential nightmare: a black man who stood up for his rights and was not afraid to say that he would defend himself to the extreme. FBI documents produced 48-hours after JFK's murder focused exclusively on William's perceived threat and likelihood that he could have shot the President. The FBI had quickly labeled Williams "dangerous" and "schizophrenic" – a term the government had recently discovered and was becoming overly and wrongly prone to apply to any person officials wanted to paint as a threat to society. Of course, the fact that Williams had written a book in 1962 entitled *Negroes With Guns* handed the FBI and CIA an extra weapon to use against him.

Robert Taber resigned from his post with the FPCC in February 1962. By this time the organization had become a hopeless muddle of government informers, psychopaths, communists, black militants, liberal social activists and socialists who carried with them agendas that clashed with the group's modest objectives.

As readers may expect, the FBI moved quickly to interview Robert Taber after learning of the Army's intelligence report concerning his alleged encounter with Lee Harvey Oswald. On January 28, 1964, FBI director J. Edgar Hoover sent an airtel message to the FBI's New York office. The message contained two copies of the 407th military intelligence report concerning Dr. Luaces, Robert Taber, and Harvey Oswald. Hoover's message also noted that FBI files "disclose that Taber went to Cuba in January 1961 in an apparent effort to avoid testifying before the U.S. Senate Internal Security Subcommittee concerning the Fair Play for Cuba Committee." The message went on:

> [Taber] reportedly fought with Cuba militia during April 1961 invasion at which time he was wounded. While in Cuba he was also employed as a writer for Cuban newspaper *La Revolution*,

however, he was later dropped for not using the proper propaganda line. He also contributed to other Cuban publications. Following the assassination of President Kennedy, Taber, who at the time was residing at 118 West 79th Street, Apt. 10B, New York City, twice contacted the New York [FBI] office apparently under the influence of alcohol indicating he was extremely sorry concerning assassination of President and wished he had never heard of FPCC. He denied knowledge of Oswald stating he had never heard the name prior to the assassination.

Director Hoover then reminded the Bureau's New York office, "Oswald reportedly was in the Soviet Union from late October 1959, until his return to the U.S. in June 1962, however, his exact whereabouts during this entire time is not known." Because of this, Hoover ordered, "New York office should, therefore, immediately interview Taber concerning the specific allegations re association with Oswald as set forth in the enclosed Army communication."

In response to Hoover's directive, on January 31, 1964 FBI Special Agents Francis I. Lundquist and John James O'Flaherty went to Robert Taber's apartment to interview him. Taber told the two agents, according to their subsequent report, that he had been "temporarily discharged from the military hospital in Cuba during the third week after the April 1961 [Bay of Pigs] invasion." He confirmed that he was using crutches at the time and that while recovering from his wounds, he had frequented a number of bars in Havana, including, in all probability, Sloppy Joe's.

However, Taber added, according to the report, "he had never been in the company of any individual known as Oswald" and "he had never heard of Lee Harvey Oswald prior to the assassination of President Kennedy and, furthermore, based on newspaper photos of Oswald which he has viewed since the assassination, he does not recall ever meeting any individual who resembles Oswald." The report concluded: "[Taber] stated that if he had ever met or seen Oswald he is certain that he would have recalled such an acquaintanceship. He stated that he was not acquainted with any individual known as Lieutenant Harvey Oswald."

It is frustrating to note that apparently the two FBI agents did not ask Taber if he knew Dr. Luaces, or if he had ever encountered Luaces in Cuba or in Sloppy Joe's or at any other place. Without this information we are left knowing nothing about Luaces or what exactly Taber thought about him.

As noted above, and according to another FBI document, Taber had already been interviewed at least twice by Bureau agents prior to the assassination. According to a December 5, 1963 Bureau report, on the evening of the Kennedy assassination at about 9:45 P.M., November 22, 1963, Taber had telephoned the FBI's New York office and asked to speak with either Special Agent James A. Day or Francis I. Lundquist, both of whom had previously interviewed Taber in Boston and New York. Neither agent was available, so Taber spoke with Special Agent Harold A. Hoeg.

Hoeg, as recorded in the report, noticed right away that Taber sounded as if he had been drinking heavily. Taber emotionally told Hoeg that he was upset and "extremely sorry concerning the assassination of President Kennedy.

"What do you think of your Fair Play for Cuba Committee now?" Hoeg taunted.

Taber replied, "I wish I'd never heard of the damned outfit."

"Tell me if you've ever known or heard of Lee Harvey Oswald," Hoeg asked, reminding Taber that Oswald was then under arrest in Dallas.

Taber "replied that he did not know him, nor ever heard the name," states the report.

"It was apparent that Taber was in a barroom of some type," the report continues, "by reason of the noise and music in the background, and his mumbling gave every indication of his degree of intoxication."

Taber told Hoeg that he "would like to buy either Special Agent Lundquist or Hoeg a drink some time."

Replied Hoeg, "Any time you want to clear your conscience and tell the truth concerning the formation of the Fair Play for Cuba Committee and other matters about which you've lied previously we would be most willing to talk to you."

According to the report, Taber "made some utterances to the effect that he would do just that, if it would do some good, but claimed the only good it would do would be to put him back in jail, and inasmuch as he had four years under his belt, he was not anxious to return."

This same December 5, 1963 report also revealed that on that same date Taber again called Hoeg "and again appeared, from his conversation, to have been drinking heavily." The report states that Taber told Hoeg, "this Kennedy thing was bothering him."

Hoeg reminded Taber, "The only way you can clear your conscious [*sic*] would be to come into the [FBI] office voluntarily and to set the record straight on the Cuban's [*sic*] Government's involvement in the formation of the FPCC." Following Taber's January 31, 1964 interview by Special Agents Lundquist and O'Flaherty, according to a subsequent memorandum to J. Edgar Hoover, Taber called Lundquist a third time and "volunteered some additional information concerning another Bureau case." We are not told anywhere what this case was, but it is thought to have concerned one of the several cases still open on members of the FPCC. Wrote Lundquist in the subsequent memorandum: "It is felt that Taber would not have done this unless he was sincere in his offer to assist…. Taber's offer of his services arose out of a general discussion of Cuba and queries as to Taber's present attitude toward the Castro Government."

According to his memorandum, Lundquist pointed out to Taber "that the FBI does not have primary responsibility in intelligence gathering abroad, and that this offer, on his part, would have to be conveyed to another governmental agency, not identified." Taber agreed with that, requesting that his offer be kept confidential by all involved. The report to Hoover concluded by explaining what Taber did next:

> Apparently, Taber assumed the other agency would be the CIA because on the afternoon of January 31 Lundquist was telephonically contacted by Harry Real of CIA, who said that Taber contacted him and said he had been interviewed by the FBI and that he wished to make some statements directly to the CIA. Real was advised of the offer made by Taber and Real said that when he personally contacted Taber in response to Taber's call, Taber, in effect, made the same offer to him. Real said that he felt quite sure CIA would be very interested and seriously consider Taber's offer and would be most anxious to receive the results of the Bureau's interview and the impressions and opinion of the interviewing agents.

On March 13, 1964, Leo J. Dunn, a special assistant in the CIA's Personnel Security Division, received the request from the Agency's New York office "to use Robert Taber as a cut-out for contacting an individual recently returned from Cuba." The request had come from Virginia Throne, a longtime CIA employee in the Agency's New York Contact Division office.

In responding to Throne's request to use Taber, Dunn forwarded to his superior a review of Taber's background, making no mention whatsoever of the alleged Taber-Oswald encounter in Cuba. He sent this along with his recommendation that, due to "serious questions [about] Taber's honesty, loyalty, integrity, and trustworthiness," the request "be disapproved."

Dunn's recommendation appears surprising in light of the fact that, as he noted in his disapproval memorandum, the New York Contact Division had already been using Taber for over a month, "without Headquarters authorization," and that the New York division had made it clear that it was "anxious to use Taber as a cutout." [In espionage parlance, a cut-out is a mutually trusted intermediary, method or channel of communication, facilitating the exchange of information between agents. Cut-outs usually only know the source and destination of the information to be transmitted, but are unaware of the identities of any other persons involved in the espionage process. Thus, a captured cut-out cannot be used to identify members of an espionage cell.]

Little is known of Robert Taber's years following the JFK assassination. He died in 1995, leaving behind two excellent books: *M-26, The Biography of a Revolution*, an up-close and detailed account of Castro's six-year struggle to gain control of Cuba, and *The War of the Flea*, considered by many the best book on rebel counter-insurgency and how small, organized guerrilla armies can defeat sophisticated, heavily armed governmental forces. The book has been widely cited as a brilliant analysis of precisely the types of wars that are fought all over the globe today, underscoring Taber's well-documented assertion that guerrillas cannot be overcome by sheer military means.

YET ANOTHER LEE HARVEY OSWALD SIGHTING ...

The main reason the CIA's New York office was anxious to use Robert Taber as a cutout operative was because of his past association through the FPCC with a man named Marc David Schleifer. An activist with the FPCC and described in CIA documents as "an American Marxist and journalist," Schleifer had traveled extensively overseas in support of FPCC, including trips to Cuba, Mexico, France, Morocco, and Tangier.

In February and March 1963, U.S. State Department memoranda to the FBI and CIA noted that Schleifer was the editor of a new, radical, Algerian-based magazine, *Revolutionary Africa.* Earlier in August 1961 and then later in September 1963, Schleifer, according to CIA officials, traveled to both Cuba and Mexico, causing considerable alarm and attention from both the Agency and FBI for his associations with then-notorious American black militants and counterculture figures. In 1965, prior to moving to the Middle East where he eventually went to work for NBC News, Schleifer converted from Judaism to Islam, changing his name to Sulayman Abdallah Schleifer.

In June 1964, alarm bells went off at the CIA after detailed reports came in from Tangier that a subject identified as "IDEN D" had been seen in Tangier in 1962 and 1963 in the company of Schleifer and several of his associates.

"IDEN D," according to declassified CIA documents, was Lee Harvey Oswald.

The CIA Chief of Station in Rabat, Morocco, based on accounts from several CIA sources and assets, reported that Oswald had attended a number of gatherings and parties at the Tangier home of a man named Narayan Kamalaker. An Indian by origin and sometimes an accountant for Coca Cola in Tangier, Kamalaker was married to a Russian woman named Sonya Dragadge, whose son reportedly worked for *Time* magazine in Rome.

The CIA also claimed that another Tangier resident named George Greaves had told one of their British sources – identified as Paul Gill – that he knew people who knew Oswald, but "they were not in Tangier." CIA internal files stated that Gill had been a smuggler and gunrunner whose boat had been blown up by French frogmen. According to the report, Paul Gill was associated with several Americans in Tangier. One of them was an American businessman named Winthrop Buckingham who managed a hotel in Tangier and was an associate of June Cobb's friend and CIA asset, Warren Broglie. Paul Gill was also closely connected to an American soldier of fortune, Thomas Eli Davis, III, who often roomed in Tangier with Buckingham and his wife. Davis, according to the CIA, often used the alias "Oswald" and was a gunrunner who reportedly had close ties to the infamous CIA assassin, QJ/WIN.

Lastly, the Rabat report mentions another American, Rev. Carl Ray Jackson, in connection with Oswald allegedly having attended social gatherings in Tangier with Schleifer. Additionally, Rev. Jackson's daughter, described "as being a little 'flitty,'" allegedly had seen Oswald several times in a Tangier "beatnik hangout."

The CIA Chief of Station in Rabat was skeptical about all of these reports of Oswald sightings, stating: "[It] would appear that the whole affair is a product of highly vivid imaginations brought to a simmer in a pot of kif, booze, beatnik poetry and stirred by the Tangier sea breeze."

However, CIA officials in Washington, D.C. remained concerned about the sightings at the time, and also about Schliefer's activities. Through extensive follow-up investigation, according to one former Agency official, some CIA analysts eventually determined that there "was a strong possibility" that "some of the Tangier reports had some validity," while others may have been "mixed up with other reports that came from Mexico City regarding Oswald's activities there with counterculture types."

Asked if this possibly meant there was a connection between the Tangier reports and that of Elena Garro having seen Oswald at a party in Mexico City in September 1963, the former official replied, "Absolutely." Almost as an afterthought the former official added, "A lot of that thinking turned on reports related to [Thomas] Davis and Ruby." Of paramount interest here, as noted above, is that Thomas Eli Davis, according to the CIA, often used the alias "Oswald." Incredibly, Davis, as shall be explained below, was also closely associated with Oswald assassin Jack Ruby, and infamous CIA contract assassin QJ/WIN.

Who Was Thomas Eli Davis, III?

Thomas Eli Davis, III, sometimes identified as Thomas Eli Davis, Jr., the name he preferred and used most often, is easily one of the most intriguing and mystifying victims of circumstance, if indeed that is what he was, in the annals of the JFK assassination. His story in relation to the Kennedy assassination has appeared in a number of books and articles in synopsis form over the past quarter decade, frequently with erroneous information included, as well as key associations and details excluded. What follows is based on the author's own research, careful scrutiny of existing accounts, interviews with people who knew Davis, and newly uncovered documents.

Davis was born on August 27, 1936 in McKinney, Texas. Next to nothing is known about his early years growing up in the Beaumont area of Texas, one of two children to a well established and highly respected ranching family. Following high school, Davis entered the U.S. Army at the age of eighteen. There are unconfirmed reports that he served in an intelligence-related military unit. Several FBI reports contain statements made by others that Davis was stationed in Korea during the war and was a POW there for about 8 to 12 months. The details of Davis' military service cannot be confirmed; according to Army officials, Davis' file "has been destroyed." However, this author was able to verify that Davis was honorably discharged from the U.S. Army in February 1957, having enlisted in early January 1955, thus making it impossible that he served during the Korean War (1950-1953) or was a POW.

Shortly after JFK's murder, on December 9, 1963 the U.S. State Department's consulate in Tangier, Morocco sent a "Priority" cable to Secretary of State Dean Rusk concerning Thomas Eli Davis, Jr. The next day copies of the cable were forwarded by Secretary Rusk's office to the top ranking officials at the CIA, with additional copies to the Office of Naval Intelligence (ONI). The cable related that Davis, carrying a U.S. passport issued in New Orleans on January 31, 1963, had been arrested in Tangier the day before, December 8, for "trying to sell two Walter pistols." At the time of his arrest, Davis was accompanied by Carolyn Hawley Davis, his third wife, who informed arresting officers that the couple's home was in Chico, Texas.

Moroccan National Security officers, after arresting Davis, contacted the U.S. Embassy in Tangier. Their cable stated that while the "sale of pistols" charge was "minor," they were still holding Davis "on the basis of a rambling, somewhat cryptic, unsigned letter in Davis' handwriting which refers in passing to "Oswald" and to the "Kennedy assassination." The cable also stated that the "intended addressee" of the Davis letter was attorney Thomas G. Proctor, "a political contributor" to President Lyndon Johnson. According to the cable, Thomas Proctor was the "legal agent for Morocco's World Fair exhibit in New York," and his address was the Hotel Iroquois in New York City, a favorite haunt of CIA and Federal Narcotics officials in the 1950s and 1960s. Worth noting is that subsequent State Department cables stated that Proctor had been "advised" by Davis to contribute to Lyndon Johnson's campaign.

Here we should briefly look at Thomas Proctor.

Proctor was an established attorney in New York City at the time. Nonetheless, U.S. State Department investigators attempting to follow up on Davis' letter reported that they were unable to locate Proctor. Later still, investigators with the House Select Committee on Assassinations (HSCA) reported that they, too, had failed to locate Proctor. Apparently the State Department, and later the HSCA, made no inquiry to the CIA about Proctor. Had they done so, and assuming that the CIA would have fully cooperated, the fact that Proctor was also associated with CIA assets June Cobb and Warren Broglie (Mexico City's Hotel Luma manager) might have come to light. Investigators might also have consulted Martindale-Hubbell Directory of Attorneys to track his legal career and current location, but apparently no one thought of this.

Thomas G. Proctor, according to former law practice colleagues – who declined to be identified in this book because of what they claimed could be "possible legal complications" – reported to the author that Proctor had known both Cobb and Broglie "since at least around 1959 ... in New York City ... maybe having met Cobb at the Hotel Iroquois, when she lived there briefly before going to Cuba." The same former colleagues also state that Proctor, during the "early 1960s," traveled several times to Mexico City, "reportedly for work related to the [United States] embassy there, and something to do with that country's Olympic bid." (Mexico City hosted the Summer Olympics in 1968. See more on Proctor and McNutt in Notes on this chapter.)

Several seasoned assassination researchers, including John Simkin and Tom Scully of the JFK Education Forum, discovered that Proctor practiced law in New York with Paul Vories McNutt. Proctor and McNutt both grew up in Indiana, where they were boyhood friends. While Proctor maintained a lifelong low profile, McNutt was constantly in the political limelight. During the Great Depression, McNutt served as Indiana's 34th State Governor. Under the New Deal, McNutt was President Roosevelt's director of the Federal Security Agency (FSA). During the war years, the FSA acted as "a cover agency" for the War Research Service. FDR's third-term vice presidential mate, McNutt was appointed by Roosevelt as chairman of the War Manpower Commission. McNutt caused a bit of a stir in this role when he proposed the "extermination of the Japanese in toto."

In 1946, President Harry Truman sent McNutt back to the Philippines to serve a second tour as high commissioner, a post he had held earlier in 1937 under Roosevelt. During his second tour, McNutt first encountered CIA official Edward Lansdale. Lansdale observed McNutt closely and was ever mindful of the commissioner's tremendous influence over the leadership of the Philippines.

McNutt went into private law practice with Thomas Proctor in New York City and Washington, D.C. in 1947 after resigning as America's first ambassador to the Philippines. McNutt died in 1955 at the age of 63 following a visit to Manila.

Worth noting is that prior to the assassination of JFK, Proctor had what former associates reported as "extensive legal dealings" with Alfonso Martin, a self-described "promoter of international finance and investments" who advised an extensive network of "business contacts in New York and Washington, D.C." Martin, it turns out, was also a resident of New York's Hotel Iroquois.

The U.S. consulate in Tangier, according to the State Department's December 9, 1963 Priority cable to Secretary of State Rusk, sent an official to interview Carolyn Davis. She informed the official that her husband was "a soldier of fortune," having served "with U.S. forces in Korea, where he spent a year as a POW." Mrs. Davis also reported that Thomas had worked in "Indochina, Indonesia, Algeria, and Cuba, 'always on the Western side, if there was one.'" Apparently, Carolyn Davis felt so comfortable speaking with the embassy official that she inquired if he could arrange for her husband to "get a similar job in Angola." The State Department cable also notes that Moroccan authorities questioned both Davises and the "consulate general office regarding knowledge about Howard Schulman who was allegedly in Tangier and peddling pro-communist propaganda." According to the cable, neither the Davises nor the embassy knew anything about Schulman. The cable concluded: "Request department advice if Davis or any associate has police or other record in the U.S.; if information may be supplied local authorities it may facilitate release."

On December 20, 1963, FBI director J. Edgar Hoover sent a special courier to the State Department, hand-carrying a memorandum to the Deputy Assistant Secretary of Security bearing the subject: "Lee Harvey Oswald, Internal Security." The two-page document made scant mention of Oswald and focused almost exclusively on Thomas Eli Davis, III, and one other American citizen.

Hoover was writing in reply to a telegram he had received from the State Department ten days earlier. The telegram had advised "that Thomas Eli Davis, Jr. was being held by the Moroccan National Security Police [in a Tangier jail] because of a letter in his handwriting which referred in passing to 'Oswald' and to the 'Kennedy assassination.'" Hoover's memorandum next made reference to yet another telegram the State Department had sent him on December 16, 1963 advising that, "Howard Loeb Schulman was arrested by the Moroccan Surete [police] after having reportedly stated that he was wanted by the United States authorities in connection with the assassination of President Kennedy."

Hoover then explained to the State Department that in May, June, and July 1963, he had furnished the department with several memoranda concerning Thomas Eli Davis, III and Davis' attempts during those months at "recruiting men for an invasion of Haiti." Hoover oddly, and without any details, claimed that this was actually a "scheme" on Davis' part "to become acquainted with the 'soldier of fortune' type of individual so that he might acquire background information for an article he planned to write." As far as anyone knew, Davis had never written any article of any type and was not known anywhere as a writer or journalist.

As to Howard Schulman, Hoover explained that since 1961 he had furnished the State Department with a good many reports concerning Schulman, "who has in the past expressed pro-Castro sympathies and made an unauthorized trip to Cuba." Added Hoover: "It has been revealed in these reports that this person possesses suicidal tendencies." Hoover concluded his memorandum by stating:

> It is requested that you expeditiously secure, if at all possible, the exact nature of [Thomas] Davis' reference to Oswald and the President's assassination. It is further requested that this Bureau be completely appraised of any oral statements he may have made concerning this matter to the Moroccan National Security Police or representatives of your Department in Tangier.

The story of Thomas Eli Davis, Jr. becomes stranger still. FBI director Hoover was soon made aware through Bureau records that years earlier, on June 18, 1958 at around noon, Thomas Davis, dressed in olive drab coveralls and an army fatigue cap, got into his 1957 Ford sedan with a loaded .38 automatic in his pocket and drove to a branch of the National Bank of Detroit. At the bank, Davis handed a teller a note that instructed, "Put the money on the counter. If you make one move other than for the money I'll shoot you on the spot." Davis then curtly explained, "I want a big pile of money, say about $2,000 will do it."

Thomas Davis: He Just Couldn't Do It

The frightened teller pushed a pile of about $1,000 in twenties toward Davis, who started to pick up the cash. He then hesitated and pushed the cash back at the teller and said, "I just can't do it. I just don't have the heart."

Davis turned and ran from the bank, but was followed by another teller who had pressed the alarm. This teller followed Davis down the street to an alley where he observed Davis begin to remove his coveralls. The teller ran back to the bank and directed a nearby squad car to the alley where Davis was arrested. When Davis' car was searched, officers found boxes of ammunition and two German-made rifles and a handgun. Initial arrest reports describe Davis as having light blond hair, blue eyes, standing 5 feet 11 inches tall, and weighing 150 pounds. Officers also found his threatening note to the bank teller in the pocket of his discarded overalls.

Davis told police officers at the Wayne County jail that he had never been in any previous trouble, had never before been arrested, and had just finished his first semester of college, flunking all of his subjects at the University of Michigan, where his wife Cora had just graduated. "It's been a rough few months for me," Davis said sheepishly, in his youthful and laconic, good-old-boy style.

He claimed that he had decided a year earlier, after realizing college did not suit him, to become a dealer in antique guns. To start

313

his business venture he had borrowed $500 from a Texas bank on the strength of his father's co-signature, but was now late on his payments. This, he insisted, had prompted him to make a spur of the moment decision to rob the branch bank – much like two other characters soon to be encountered in this book.

Davis pled guilty in U.S. District Court on July 10, 1958, after failing to make a bond of $50,000. A judge declared him guilty of attempted bank robbery but suspended his sentence and placed him on probation for five years. As a condition of his probation, he agreed to undergo psychiatric treatment verified by his probation officer.

THOMAS DAVIS AND PROJECT MK/ULTRA

According to FBI reports and Michigan probation records dated June 1963, Thomas Eli Davis, III was admitted for psychiatric treatment at Detroit's Lafayette Clinic, operated by the state of Michigan, beginning on July 16, 1958, and was formally discharged on October 1, 1958. One of the FBI reports states that Davis' physicians believed that he "displayed tendencies and symptoms of a 'schizo-phrenic' [sic] mental condition." Other psychologists on the clinic staff, according to Davis' medical reports, disagreed and felt that the young Texan was "suffering for a long time from a basic character disorder evidenced by severe emotional upsets," however, "it was generally agreed that this condition was related to the family situation wherein [Davis'] mother, who has many fine qualities and traits, is on the domineering side. [His] father is characterized as a passive, rather weak type of individual, who at times has been a heavy drinker." The reports could have quite easily applied to young Lee Harvey Oswald.

Psychiatric speculation and babble aside, here the reader should be reminded of this book's earlier revelation that beginning in 1954 several psychiatric facilities in Detroit, including the Lafayette Clinic, were being covertly used and funded by the CIA under cover of the Human Ecology Fund in its notorious MK/ULTRA mind-control program. Perhaps Davis' confinement to the Detroit clinic, like Lee Harvey Oswald's proximity to the Bordentown Reformatory in New Jersey – another CIA funded MK/ULTRA facility– was merely coincidental, but this seems a real stretch.

As previously underscored, human experiments on unwitting patients were conducted at the Lafayette Clinic, as well as at Michigan's Ionia State Hospital for the Criminally Insane. Ionia State Hospital was particularly abusive and cruel to African-American inmates, who were considered mere human fodder for any behavior-modification quackery that the CIA and U.S. Army thought might yield domination over the minds of others. As is well established, the vast majority of CIA files on the Lafayette Clinic project have been destroyed, but a few surviving Agency documents reveal that covert work at the clinic included electrical brain stimulation, induced psychosis through psychotropic drugs, and other "behavior modification techniques" [read: psychological torture].

Interviews with former CIA Chemical Branch and Technical Services Section staff, as well as legal depositions and files from the Agency's Artichoke Project, reveal that a number of MK/ULTRA luminaries made MK/ULTRA-related visits to the clinic. These "visitors" included Dr. Jolyson West (who would later "treat" Oswald assassin Jack Ruby.), and Dr. Amedeo Marrazzi (the Army Chemical Corps chief of clinical research). "Visitors" also included CIA officials such as chemist Robert Vern Lashbrook, psychologist John Gittinger (who treated Rose Cherami), and chemist Henry Bortner. At the time, all three scientists were working under the direction of the CIA's Dr. Sidney Gottlieb. In many quarters, particularly some highly respected medical institutions, the Lafayette Clinic has long been considered a place of dubious practices. Among other distinctions, the clinic's neurologist Dr. Ernst Rodin, achieved wide notoriety with recommendations that individuals who took part in Detroit's race riots in the 1960s should be physically castrated.

Following his discharge from the Detroit clinic, Davis was transferred from federal probation oversight in Michigan to supervision in Fort Worth, Texas, and then to the federal probation office in Beaumont, Texas. In Beaumont, between numerous trips to New Orleans, New York, and Mexico City, Mexico, according to CIA files and confidential interviews with former Davis associates, Davis was trained in deep sea diving and learned how to operate a boat in preparation for his gunrunning activities.

A June 1963 FBI document concerning Thomas Davis, copies of which were routed to the CIA, State Department, and Office of Naval Intelligence, reveals that on June 20, 1963, in follow-up to an alleged renewed interest in Davis because of his recruitment of soldiers of fortune, FBI field agents visited the Lafayette Clinic for

315

undisclosed reasons, but apparently to gather more information on Davis.

The brief report states that special agents of the Bureau met with clinic physician Dr. Elliot D. Luby, "a toxicologist." who carried out extensive experiments with sensory deprivation and LSD and other mind-altering drugs with Dr. Jacques Gottlieb (no relation to Sidney Gottlieb) and Dr. Rodin. Dr. Luby (who appears again in connection with Dr. Louis J. West) was able to provide the FBI with the needed information, but according to the report, "advised that he did not want his identity revealed in view of the fact that he or anyone else connected with the Lafayette Clinic are not authorized to divulge information concerning former or present patients without written consent of the former patient or present patient or by special authorization from a duly authorized court."

One would think at this juncture that Thomas Davis' story is nearly complete, but in fact, at this point his saga becomes even stranger.

One wonders how Davis, a convicted bank robber on probation, could have obtained a U.S. passport allowing him to travel to Algeria and Morocco, a feat highly unlikely without high-level governmental intervention. And what about the reports that Davis often used "Oswald" as an alias in his global travels? And what of the "Oswald" letter in Tangier? Plus, how did Davis accomplish his release from the Tangier jail – not revealed in any FBI, CIA, or State Department files – and what did he do after his release? Taking up the last of these issues first carries Davis' twisted saga into territory that is provocative and intriguing, madly so, due to a lack of specifics.

According to newsman and former White House correspondent of Scripps-Howard Newspapers, Seth Kantor, Thomas Davis was released from his Tangier jail cell through the intervention and assistance of the mysterious CIA contract assassin known only by his Agency cryptonym QJ/WIN. (See chapter in forthcoming volume two on QJ/WIN and other assassins for more on this specifically.) Unfortunately, Kantor provides no source for his information on QJ/WIN, and Kantor is now dead. However, as this author discovered, Kantor's account of Thomas Davis, QJ/WIN, and Jack Ruby (yes, the gods of coincidence thrust Ruby into Davis' life) follows the same twisted road as Davis' overall odyssey.

Well before Kantor wrote about Thomas Davis, *Dallas Morning News* reporter Earl Golz gained knowledge of Davis' links to Jack Ruby, as well as to a number of other unsavory Texas gunrunners. Together, they carry the mystery of Thomas Davis into the stratosphere of serpentine connections and coincidence. (Golz was a close associate of reporter Dale Basye.)

On July 10, 1976, Earl Golz wrote a much overlooked *Morning News* account concerning Jack Ruby's role in running guns to anti-Castro forces in Cuba. According to Golz's article, after Ruby's arrest for murdering Lee Harvey Oswald, Ruby "was concerned that the name of a gunrunner for anti-Castro Cubans might come up during his 1964 trial [in Dallas]." The name was Thomas Eli Davis, Jr.

Golz went on to state, "Both Davis and Ruby said they had met several times before the assassination and discussed gunrunning as a lucrative business, but each of them denied ever engaging in the business together."

This seems unlikely, and depends largely on their definition of "together." However, according to Golz, Ruby's attorney Tom Howard had stated that before Ruby's trial, when he had asked Ruby "if any surprise names might come up during the trial," the only name Ruby gave in reply was Thomas Eli Davis, Jr.

A year after the Golz article appeared, Seth Kantor wrote a similar article that appeared in the *Detroit News* in November 1977. The story echoed Golz's account but contained additional details about Davis, whom Kantor dubbed "a criminal and CIA operative." Kantor wrote that after Davis moved to Beaumont, he began running guns to CIA units training in Florida and Central America, adding that the Texan's trip to Morocco was for running guns to "secret army terrorists" attempting to kill French Premiere Charles de Gaulle, and that after Davis was arrested, QJ/WIN "sprung him from jail." As noted earlier, Kantor provided no source or evidence for this information about QJ/WIN.

Kantor's article went on to state that Davis first met Jack Ruby "when he walked into Ruby's downtown Dallas club with a plan to film a stag movie using Ruby's strippers" as performers. Kantor also claimed that Ruby and Davis together shipped arms to Cuba and that Warren Commission investigators knew all about it, but that they only had Davis' last name and could not fully identify him. Kantor quoted a Commission memorandum dated March 19,

1964: "Ruby has acknowledged independently that … he contacted a man in Beaumont, Texas, whose name he recalled was Davis. The FBI has been unable to identify anyone engaged in the sale of arms to Cuba who might be identical with the person named Davis."

Kantor's article continues with his observations: "When Ruby was questioned on June 7, 1964, by two commission members, then-Rep. Gerald Ford of Michigan and Chief Justice Earl Warren, he was not asked about any connection with Davis or with gun-running. The FBI pursued the subject, but interviewed the wrong Davis and got nowhere. Meanwhile, the CIA kept the identity of the real Davis a secret."

Apparently, Kantor was unaware of, or failed to dig into, declassified State Department files concerning the Tangier letter that mentioned "Oswald" and the JFK assassination. The letter appears reasonably explained and demystified in a December 30, 1963 State Department telegram from the U.S. embassy in Madrid, Spain, which had been requested to follow up on the department's investigation of Davis and his provocative letter.

Contrary to numerous published accounts, Davis' draft letter referred only to "Oswald" and not to "Lee Harvey Oswald." Indeed, as it turned out, explained the State Department cable, the coincidental "Oswald" referred to in Davis' letter was Swiss-born Victor Oswald, a former wartime OSS operative and now an extremely wealthy international weapons trafficker who often brokered multi-million dollar deals behind the scenes for the armed services of many countries, including the United States.

The December 30, 1963 State Department "priority" cable regarding Davis reveals that a Moroccan Security officer identified only as "Hussein" informed the U.S. embassy in Tangier that Davis' letter in question was "three or four pages" long and had indeed been addressed to attorney Thomas Proctor (whom FBI agents later claimed they could not locate). The letter contained a short sentence that read, "I've seen Oswald," and later the phase, "This is first Sunday AK (after Kennedy)."

According to the cable, as noted above, the "Oswald" was Victor Oswald (sometimes referred to as Viktor Oswald) with whom both the Tangier and Madrid authorities were amply familiar. The cable reads:

> Until today had no idea Davis oral comments either to police or others. Upon receipt reference telegram I asked him. He

said Oswald refers to Victor Oswald of Madrid to whom he had
Proctor's introduction. Reference to 'after Kennedy' was for
dating letter as he had forgotten date, and that he had told this
to Police. He offers to repeat full story to FBI when he returns
to U.S.

The cable concluded: "My opinion is Davis somewhat unstable
and entire matter given disproportionate importance by local authorities who fear any and all arms traffic in view local recent political events."

A follow-up cable from Madrid to Secretary of State Rusk, also
sent hours later on December 30, 1963, reads in its entirety:

> Victor Oswald, a businessman of Madrid, contacted this date,
> stated that Davis came to Madrid approximately six weeks ago
> with a letter of business introduction to Oswald from a friend of
> Oswald's, a New York lawyer named Thomas Proctor. Oswald
> said that he only talked with Davis 5-10 minutes since Davis was
> only interested in cattle and was headed for Morocco. Oswald
> stated that this was the extent of his contact with Davis.

While on the surface Davis' explanation concerning Victor Oswald makes some sense, other features of his explanation do not. For
example, his claim of not knowing the date in question is a bit hard
to swallow. Also troubling is that the FBI was never able to locate attorney Proctor in New York, and that nobody who questioned Davis
asked him about reports of his use of the alias "Oswald" in other
locations. This author, indeed, was not able to find any evidence at all
that Davis ever used the name Lee Harvey Oswald.

Thomas Eli Davis died in September 1973 in an abandoned Texas quarry while allegedly attempting to steal copper wire. He was
electrocuted when he cut through a high power line. Shortly after
his death, Carolyn Davis told reporters that she had no desire to
discuss her husband's death but that she thought it was highly suspicious. Some reporters, including Seth Kantor, would continue to
press Carolyn Davis, and eventually she made statements concerning her husband's use of the alias "Oswald," his gunrunning with
Ruby, which she confirmed, and his dealings with various CIA officials, but she refused to go on the record with anything.

Some readers may be curious to know where Tom Davis was on November 22, 1963. CIA and FBI documents and files are of no help in finding an answer to that questioned. For whatever reason, it seems that nobody ever questioned Davis' wife about his whereabouts during the assassination.

Thomas E. Davis Jr. Recruits Mercenaries for Haiti

In early June 1963, just prior to Davis' trip to Morocco, an FBI special agent interviewed Davis' third wife, Carolyn H. Davis, at her place of employment in Ventura, California, where the couple had apparently relocated. The special agent, John J. Schmitz, wanted to know why Carolyn's husband had placed an advertisement in the *Los Angeles Times* recruiting former Army paratroopers and rangers for "military-type work."

Carolyn Davis told Schmitz she had no idea why her husband had placed the ad. "I am only interested in my job and did not question him about it," she said.

Schmitz pressed her, asking why, if she knew nothing, did she attend a subsequent meeting at a motel where men who responded to the advertisement were present. Carolyn said, "I spent the entire time in my own room [in the motel] washing my hair and bathing." She added, "The only reason I made the trip to Los Angeles was [so] that Tom could charge the expenses for the meetings on my American Express charge account."

"You're sure of that?" special agent Schmitz asked.

Carolyn Davis was quiet for a moment and then said, "I can't be compelled to give testimony against my husband, anyway."

Schmitz smiled and said, "Mrs. Davis, I've already interviewed your husband. My contact with you was to have you corroborate his explanation of the entire meeting and how it came about."

Carolyn Davis grimaced. She said, "I'm sorry I can't be of more help." Pausing, she then said, "Can you tell me what Tom told you?"

"No, I can't," Schmitz replied.

Special Agent Schmitz had interviewed Thomas Davis about three hours earlier. According to Schmitz's report on the interview, he met with Davis at his apartment in Ventura. Prior to meeting with Davis, Schmitz compiled a partial Bureau bio sheet on the Texan, which he completed during his interview of Davis about his ad for mercenaries. Highlights of the sheet reveal that Davis, describe as having "a long handlebar mustache, light blond hair, blue eyes," informed Schmitz that he had been in the U.S. Army but had "no foreign service." Davis gave his occupation as "self-employed writer and field geology work" with prior employment as the operator of the "Republic of Texas Film Productions." Davis also told Schmitz that he and his wife had been living in Mexico since September 1962.

When Davis opened his door to Schmitz and the special agent identified himself, Davis said, "I've been expecting you."

"Why is that, Mr. Davis?" Schmitz asked.

Replied Davis, "From the first when I placed the ad I expected the FBI to take an interest and contact me. Matter of fact that was my second objective in placing the ad."

"Really," said Schmitz.

"I'm a freelance writer," Davis said, "and I'm doing an article on soldiers of fortune. That's why I ran the ad. I'm interested in what makes up such a man."

Davis handed Schmitz a copy of a book by Richard Harding Davis entitled *Real Soldiers of Fortune.*

"You wrote this?" Schmitz asked.

"No, no," Davis said, "same last name, but just a coincidence. It was written in 1912. It's a really great book."

Davis then explained to Schmitz that three months earlier, "I got an idea to write an article for possible sale. The article was to deal with soldiers of fortune and the methods used in organizing an army and the type of men employed in such an army, as well as the attitude of the U.S. Government concerning the type of laws violated and possible punishment for any such violations."

Davis explained that he had placed the ad in the *Los Angeles Times* on May 12, 1963 requesting that any former paratroopers and rangers interested in military type employment write to a blind box at the newspaper. Davis said he received 28 replies in response to the ad, and he then arranged a meeting with selected men to be held on May 18 at the Tahitian Village Motel in Downey, California. About twelve men showed up for the meeting. Davis said he told the group that "parties placed high in the Haitian government are backing me and I'll pay each man $300.00 a month along with looting privileges if you get on a plane for Haiti where we will take over the government there."

Special Agent Schmitz must have been amused when Davis added: "At this point I wish to state that in my opinion there was no one in this group who harbored socialistic or communistic tendencies."

Davis told Schmitz, "After I told the group that Haiti was to be the objective of the operation I felt like they all basically lost interest."

The FBI individually interviewed each and every man that attended Davis' Tahitian Village gathering. Detailed statements taken from each man reveal a number of interesting things said at the meeting. According to William Henry Wade, a Korean War veteran who had traveled from his home in Wilmington, North Carolina for the meeting, Davis said the group he was seeking to hire would "represent the U.S. government in Haiti" and that "either the U.S. government or CIA was not actually behind his movement to overthrow Duvalier in Haiti, but that they would turn their back until they saw how it turned out." Wade also told the FBI, "We were to be picked up to go to Haiti at the Los Angeles International Airport in a C-119 on or before Friday, May 24, 1963, and flown to some base in the United States where we would then leave for Haiti."

According to FBI reports, Davis told another former paratrooper and ranger who attended the meeting that "he had served in Korea and that he had already visited Haiti." Davis told him, that "he had met a man in Mexico who had given him $25,000.00 for this purpose [invasion of Haiti]. Another man who attended the meeting, John R. Pickett, told the FBI, "After being at this motel for just a short while I became more than ever convinced that Davis had no organizational ability and had no concrete plan whatsoever."

Despite all the FBI man-hours and investigation into Davis' convoluted activities in California, it appears that nothing came of it. As we are well aware, Davis was allowed to leave the U.S. for Morocco within weeks.

Through yet another serendipitous perusal of my extensive files related to QJ/WIN, it emerged that one of Frank Olson's murderers, Jean Pierre Lafitte, was also connected with Thomas Eli Davis, Jr. This connection appears to have started in New Orleans in 1961, about two years before Davis was issued a passport there. At this time, Lafitte was working covertly for the CIA, and sometimes the FBI, often traveling to Europe, the Middle East, and Africa where he performed duties that fell under the "executive action" (assassination) category. Lafitte, it should be noted, also worked for Clay

Shaw in New Orleans for at least a year. (See *A Terrible Mistake* for more on Frank Olson.)

Apparently, Davis first encountered Lafitte through Davis' previously unknown activities as an informer for the Federal Bureau of Narcotics, sometimes surreptitiously meeting with agent George Gaffney and at least once with Charles Siragusa. Davis, according to a letter from Siragusa to George White, once met with French drug traffickers in Algiers, including drug dealer and assassin Jean Souetre. Siragusa referred to Davis in his letter to White as "a galloping clod whose testicles are larger than his home state of Texas, but who lacks the adjoining brains ... however, he's more loyal and trustworthy than a blind sheep dog, and he does bring in some damn decent information."

Davis' Narcotics Bureau and QJ/WIN connections also brought the tall Texan into a still somewhat mysterious relationship with two men very much tied up in the illicit narcotics trade, Hanna Yazbeck and Edward Lawton Smith. Yazbeck, who occasionally teamed up with QJ/WIN for lucrative extortion schemes, was also involved in white slavery and prostitution, often traveling to Algiers and Morocco.

THOMAS DAVIS, LESTER L. LOGUE, LORAN HALL, & GEORGE DE MOHRENSCHILDT

Incredibly, Tom Davis' connections to people identified in JFK assassination lore do not end with Lee Harvey Oswald, Jack Ruby, and QJ/WIN. Indeed, completely overlooked by researchers is the Texan's connection to Lester L. Logue, Loran Hall, and George de Mohrenschildt.

Following his death in 1973, Davis' widow Carolyn was extremely reluctant, often totally refusing, to talk about her deceased husband. However, about eighteen months after Davis died, Carolyn Davis described Logue as "a wealthy guy Tom did some work for in Texas" and "a Cuban guy, I think, named Lauren, that Tom met in LA." It's safe to assume that "Lauren" is Loran Eugene Hall, like Davis, a soldier of fortune who was in California at the same time that Davis was recruiting for his invasion of Haiti.

Lester L. Logue, according to FBI documents, was a Dallas, Texas-based petroleum geologist who became a multi-millionaire in the oil business. That Tom Davis, who claimed to have performed "field geology work," would know Logue is not the least surprising. However, that Logue also had extensive dealings with other soldiers of fortune deeply enmeshed in today's accounts of JFK's assassination, and who were acquainted with Davis, tells an entirely different story. Significantly adding to this is that Davis himself knew several of these soldiers of fortune personally.

Lester Logue is perhaps best known to serious assassination researchers as the Texas oilman and arch-conservative who, in a pre-assassination meeting with several wealthy Texas businessmen, reacted very angrily when one of the men proposed, "Here's $50,000 and if the rest of you will match it we'll give it to this man to blow Kennedy's ass off."

Here another character from the Dr. Frank Olson murder story enters the picture. This is Logue's political associate U.S. Representative John Rousselot, an ardent member of the John Birch Society in the 1960s and 1970s, when he was serving in the U.S. Congress. (Rousselot was the lone Congressman who opposed the White House- and CIA-approved wrongful death settlement to the Olson family in 1976.)

Meanwhile in 1975, a man named Harry Dean, who claimed to have been a former undercover agent for the FBI and CIA, reported that in 1963 he had covertly infiltrated the John Birch Society, where he learned that Rousselot, in partnership with fellow arch conservative Army General Edwin Walker, had hired two assassins, Loran Hall and Eladio del Valle, to kill President Kennedy in Dallas, Texas. Dean had no evidence to back up his bold claim, but credible reports that both men had been in Dallas on the fateful day made easy dismissal difficult. Oswald, it may be recalled, allegedly had at one time attempted to murder General Walker.

Loran Hall, one of these hired assassins, was a self-made soldier of fortune with strong ties to the Mafia. The other one, Eladio del Valle, was a former Cuban police officer and elected official under the Batista regime overthrown by Castro. Unfortunately, del Valle, in February 1967, the day before David Ferrie died in New Orleans, was brutally murdered in Miami. His murder remains unsolved, although many people suspected the Mafia or CIA or both. Noteworthy is that del Valle was close to Mafia chieftain Santo Traffi-cante and reportedly had worked closely with David Ferrie in running guns and bombing raids against Castro's Cuba. Cuban intelligence officials in the Castro government to this day maintain that del Valle was in Dallas on November 22, 1963.

Soldier of fortune Loran Eugene Hall (also known as Lorenzo Hall, Lawrence Hall, and "Skip") first encountered Thomas Davis in New Orleans about two years before the assassination. Davis also had dealings with Hall in 1963 in Los Angeles when he [Davis] was recruiting for his Haitian operation. Hall, surely not coincidentally, was also recruiting for what was most likely the same operation. Indeed, there is serious speculation, according to one former CIA operative, that Davis' Los Angeles operation was deliberately slipshod and high-profile by design so as to throw off FBI investigators from Hall's concurrent recruitment activities. Said the same official, who declined to be named in this book, "It's a common ploy with CIA. Sometimes there can be 3 or 4 operations in play at one time but only one is actually fully planned and intended to go forward. It's similar to sophisticated drug traffickers sending out three or four large shipments of drugs with the objective that only one shipment will actually make it to its intended destination." There are indications that Loran Hall may have initially met Tom Davis through Davis' wife, who had briefly worked in Texas "doing accounting chores" for Haroldson L. Hunt (H.L. Hunt). Another arch-conservative multi-millionaire, H.L. Hunt knew Lester Logue, and has often been accused of having had JFK killed.

"Sept 20, 1963

"Charles was gone a few hours this morning. When
he returned to our hotel room he brought a chap of about
our age. After I had a chance to observe him I found
him to be likeable on the surface, but he really is a
despondent little worm. Professes to be a Communist
or some such thing. To induce a Communist to kill the
incumbant American president will be a real test of
my abilities. (Poor Charles how he envys my power over
little toys.) I found Lee Harvey Oswald to be an easy
subject. I do honestly believe he could be induced to
anything even his own destruction. Which will have to
be done.

"Lee Harvey Oswald, I feel it important to record
this tool's name in full. For he will be the
unwittenly tool in the hands of the skilled craftsman.
I am that skilled craftsman. Poor resourceful Charles.
The cunning planning Charles is also a tool of the
skilled craftsman. I worked with Lee H. Oswald several
hours today. I induced hynosis and brought him forth
several times. He is such an easy subject, busteth for
grandeur. That is his, as most men, Achilles Heel.

"The true craftsman remains in the shadows and
plys his tools.

"Sept 26, 1963

"I worked with Lee Harvey Oswald (I must record the
name, for he will prove history greatest tool) all this
week. He is aboard this very bus as we are travelling
through Mexico to Mexico City. He is not presently
in a trance. But he knows not why he travels thusly.
Nor does he remember Charles and myself. A well made
tool in our hands. Poor buy like fool. -- Evermore,

104
CS COPY

201-289248

Chapter 9

The Bizarre Diary of Eric Ritzek

I find Lee Harvey Oswald an intelligent person.

Surly, hateful and at odds with the universe — but not without a degree of undeveloped intelligence.

His thoughts are confused. I will put them in order to my satisfaction.... A glorious Frankenstein monster I have created.

— Eric Ritzek, September 29-October 1, 1963

On August 19, 1964, a man named G.C. Hoskins contacted FBI Special Agent Phillip B. Deily about a "strange diary" that had been found four days earlier at the ticket counter of the Continental Trailways bus station in Los Angeles, California. The diary's handwritten cover bore the odd inscription: "Diary of Impressions & Observations of Eric Ritzek Began September 5, 1963."

Hoskins, the Trailways Terminal Manager, told agent Deily that the diary had been discovered by ticket clerk Adrian Mount, who handed it over to Hoskins, who had thumbed through it. Hoskins said he had read several sections of the black-covered journal. In response to questions from Deily, Hoskins said that neither he nor Adrian Mount had any idea where the diary had come from or who Eric Ritzek was, and that he, Hoskins, had no interest in the diary.

Within a few days, the FBI's Los Angeles office forwarded the diary to their laboratory. After running a series of tests on the journal the laboratory concluded it "was not possible to determine if the diary was written at or about the same time" as opposed to over a period of time.

At the same time that the diary was forwarded to the FBI's laboratory, a copy of the small black journal was sent to CIA headquarters. The CIA quickly labeled the diary: "Alleged Diary of ERIC RITZEK Reflecting He Caused Lee Harvey Oswald to Commit Assassination and Oswald's Subsequent Murder by Jack L. Ruby by Hypnosis."

According to an August 31, 1964 FBI memorandum about the diary to Bureau director J. Edgar Hoover:

> Efforts by the Los Angeles Office to identify ERIC RITZEK have been negative. The contents of this alleged diary indicates that ERIC RITZEK and a companion, CHARLES (last name unknown), were attending a college in some foreign country in September 1963. Eric Ritzek was majoring in political science and was at least a Junior; his minor was human psychology. He had apparently been in attendance at summer classes and his roommate was his companion, Charles. This alleged diary indicates that Eric Ritzek was a hypnotist and used hypnotism on a girl named Carol, who was apparently known to both Charles and Ritzek, and Carol died in September 1963.

Not to cloud or complicate matters, here it should be pointed out that one of the diary copies provided this author had a brief handwritten note on its second page that read: "Ritzek – Albert Schweitzer College, Switzerland, enrolled/files." Readers familiar with Lee Harvey Oswald's life will recall instantly that Oswald applied to attend Albert Schweitzer College in March 1959. Whether Ritzek ever actually attended the college is presently unknown. The FBI memorandum continues:

> As of September 10, 1963, the alleged diary indicates that Eric Ritzek and Charles obtained visas to the United States and Mexico. An entry on September 11, 1963, indicated that the goal of Eric Ritzek and Charles was to kill President Kennedy.

The Ritzek diary describes an Odyssean-like journey of two individuals who are identified as friends, Eric Ritzek and Charles. Allegedly, in early September 1963, while attending an unidentified college or university located somewhere outside of North America, the two young men decide that Eric, in his own written words, should employ his "skills and powers as a hypnotist over this certain young lady. Formerly of high chastity and moral character."

Writes Eric Ritzek: "I managed to trigger the final destruction of the girl's will by a previous suggestion last week. I simply bit off the end of a cigar and spat it upon the floor, and Carol desired Charles and myself as her lover [sic]."

Eric states that, after Carol "accepted us both as her one husband in acts that defy description," he placed Carol "into a deep sleep, into a sleep so deep, so everlasting that her heart will beat ever slower, ever slower, until it stops. And she will awake – Nevermore."

Seemingly possessed of a seriously disturbed mind, Eric then writes in his diary that he and Charles, on September 10, 1963, "obtained our visas to the United States and Mexico. An awful lot of red tape to go through. I really consider myself and Charles citizens of the universe, personally, I owe no allegiance to no one but myself.... We leave on the 15th. Charles has arranged for us to meet a chap in about a fortnight [fourteen days]."

A few lines later, Eric writes, "Charles has received a letter today from America, Texas in fact. It contained thousands of dollars. Charles has declined to divulge the identity of our benefactor."

The next day, September 11, Eric states, "Charles plans to launch a great adventure purely in the interest of observing political science and human psychology. Our goal is to kill the American president John F. Kennedy."

On September 16, Eric writes, "We sailed for New Orleans yesterday before sunrise. That's [sic] a place called Louisiana which is in the southern extremitie [sic] of America." Three days later, in the afternoon, following "a ghastly trip," Eric and Charles arrive in New Orleans. There, on September 20, according to the diary, the two somehow link up with Lee Harvey Oswald, someone who Eric "honestly believes" can "be induced to anything even his own destruction. Which will have to be done."

Eric claims that he worked with Oswald for nearly a week, and on September 26 writes, "He is aboard this very bus as we are traveling through Mexico to Mexico City. He is not presently in a trance. But he knows not why he travels thusly. Nor does he remember Charles and myself. A well made tool in our hands. Poor bug like fool. Evermore."

On September 28, the day after arriving in Mexico City, Eric writes that he "summoned Lee Harvey Oswald to our hotel room by prearranged signal. To which he answered not knowing why. I worked all this day with him." The following day, September 29, Eric observes, "I find Lee Harvey Oswald an intelligent person. Surly, hateful and at odds with the universe – but not without a degree of undeveloped intelligence. His thoughts are confused. I will put them in order to my satisfaction. The American president will die in Dallas, Texas. That much has been decided. And Lee Harvey Oswald will be my weapon of destruction. He has no choice, I am his master, the skilled craftsman. He is my tool in the glorious experiment. Silly fool. Evermore."

On October 1, Eric's diary reads: "We released Lee H. Oswald from his willing prison. He is a fool, but with a keen mind that I properly arranged to my satisfaction. He will be a craftsman – for a while. He is able, and will think for himself, and bring about the end of President Kennedy's life. He, for a brief moment in time and space will hang suspended above all men and the great skilled craftsman, and function like a programmed computer. A glorious Frankenstein monster I have created. With his function performed, he will deteriorate. Become a scared running carnivorous animal. He will seek destruction by his actions. By a policeman's bullet. And he will remember nothing. Lee H. Oswald will serve his purpose and go the way of all tools discarded – Cast out. By the skilled craftsmen. – Evermore. Arise again? – Nevermore."

The next day, October 2, Eric writes "Oswald left at noon or shortly thereafter by bus for Laredo, Texas. He goes to America at my bidding, for a reason that is at this time vague to him."

On October 20, after traveling around Mexico for about 17 days, Eric and Charles arrived in Fort Worth, Texas. After checking into an unnamed hotel, the two spent time sightseeing throughout the city. On October 23, Charles reports that he returned to their hotel room, after having been out alone, carrying a package of "plain brown wrapping paper" containing $100,000 in cash. "Small bills, fives, tens, and twenty's." Eric writes that Charles "still refused to reveal the identity of our benefactor. But he affirmed the fact that it is the same individual that sent us money in the mail, and that this individual has everything, in fact very much to gain by the President Kennedy being slain."

Adds Eric, "Now he is insisting on how much this individual has to gain from the hands of his fallen chieftain."

Eric's diary entry for November 6 states, "I observed in the newspaper that President Kennedy plans to make a public spectacle of himself in the streets of Dallas, Texas the coming 22nd. He shall indeed."

And then on November 11, Eric writes: "We journeyed to Dallas and walked over President Kennedy's intended route. I have noticed everything, now I must place myself in Oswald's mind for a few minutes to ascertain the best location of the assassination."

After the two left Dallas on November 13, Eric records his impressions: "I observed that the townspeople are largely disenchanted with their President. In fact our deed may bring about widespread rejoicing. The innocent Oswald may be heralded in time to come as a great hero. But first he must pay for the guilty."

From November 14 to November 20, Eric and Charles spent their days in Juarez, Mexico, which Eric dubs "a dreadful place" that "hasn't enough dignity to be referred to as a city or even a hamlet."

The November 21 entry reveals Eric's state of mind: "We returned to Dallas, and are boarded in a hotel. Both Charles and I anxiously await the morrow's festivities. Behold the fruit of our labours. I am tired from the travel, but too excited and gleeful to sleep. On our way to this hotel we observed derogatory handmade signs posted against President Kennedy. I have heard his name taken in vain in the lobby of this hotel. I have even heard a fellow wish evil upon the President. If what we are about to achieve can possibly be defined as evil, that individual shall get his wish."

Eric provides a special heading for November 22, "*The Day of the Thump*." He writes, "The great and glorious day has transpired, and I Eric Ritzek was the master craftsman."

He continues: "I shall start a virgin page. A new book, a testament. Ring out the old, and herald the coming of the new."

Eric's "virgin" and egotistical page begins: "I Eric Ritzek the master craftsman was the designer, author, and witness of November the twenty-second, nineteen hundred and sixty-four." (The FBI and CIA do not comment on Eric's writing "sixty-four." Was this a mistake? It seems to suggest that the diary may have been written after the assassination, as a raging, schizophrenic delusion.) The diary continues: "I must write quickly weighing each precious thought. As the events of this day are hours old but still vivid in my marvelous mind. My beautiful wonderious [sic] brain. The brain and thoughts and mind and deeds of the Master Craftsman, I, Eric Ritzek – Evermore. Eric Ritzek, the Author of Destiny."

Ritzek's extraordinary, obsessive recollections are recorded in painstaking, if somewhat jumbled detail, as follows:

November 22, 1963

Today is Friday. It was warm and sunny. I had feared rain but it was naught.

At about 9:00 A.M. Charles and I managed to secure a picnic lunch box from the kitchen staff of the hotel in which we stayed. Under the guise that we wanted to eat our lunch in the park and get a chance to see the American President. Having obtained the desired lunch box we departed to our prearranged vantage point. The crowds en route were so dense it was eleven o'clock before we arrived at the small park. There were a few disconnected souls in the crowds lining both sides of the thoroughfare. Some bearing placards that expressed their ill feelings.... Arriving at the park we climbed a low hill. Seating ourselves, we were joyed [sic] at our vantage point....

At about 12:30 P.M. while we were still eating our lunch and finishing a thermos of coffee, the motorcade came into view. The crowds went mad with cheers. I glanced towards the School Book Depository and observed a figure crouched in the sixth floor. I couldn't see the face at that distance, but I assumed that it was Oswald. I assumed correct, as the coming events were to prove. In his hands a long metallic object glinted in the warm sunshine. Apparently that was his rifle.

The motorcade came closer. Oh – I wish I owned a camera. I could've owned one at the moment. Money certainly is no problem with me. The Master Craftsman. On came the motorcade. Past Oswald's vantage point. Closer they neared the network of bridges.

Why doesn't Oswald fire? Has he been discovered, have we failed? Damn Charles and his great plan. Soon the object of this mission will be safe beneath the bridge.

Hark – A shot. A shot was fired from the sixth floor of the School Book Depository. I saw the smoke. I saw Oswald reload. The President did a complete flip, his wife tried to flee on foot in panic. Another shot, still another. The President's car is racing away at a high speed. A bloody foot hangs over the side. The Secret Service men are trying to restrain the President's wife.

She is completely seized with panic as she tries to jump out of the car. One of them just struck her a blow with his fist knocking her down. The crowds are in a panic. People are screaming and running. Some are throwing themselves upon the ground as policemen run about with drawn guns.

Three motorcycle officers carrying shotguns are headed this way. Terror – fear. Have we been discovered? How could we? I do not see Oswald. They pass. Go right on by and do not even look at us. The police are everywhere. They seem confused. I now see them, several of them, enter the School Book Depository....

I have just seen Oswald leave the School Book Depository. He even held the door open for a hard running policeman with a machine gun in his hands to enter. Then he disappeared in the milling mob. Soon his coolly functioning mind will cease, and as the Great Craftsman had ordained, Lee Harvey Oswald the assassin will seek self destruction....

Charles and I now return to our hotel. Along the route I hear several persons say things like: 'I told you so.' 'I knew something like this would happen.' 'I'm glad, he needed killin'.'

Eric writes that once he and Charles return to their hotel, they immediately locked the door to their room and turned on the television.

We turned it up loud to drown out the sounds of any conversation between Charles and myself.

The police have announced that they have a prime suspect in custody. This isn't good, Oswald wasn't meant to be taken alive. They have not disclosed his identity.... The police released the identity of their suspected assassin. It is Lee Harvey Oswald that they lay hold to. This is not good, his being taken alive. He also killed a police officer in his thwarted fight to self-destruction. Something went wrong, I do not like this. Neither does Charles. The television cameras must be stationed in the police station itself.

Yes, they are. I have seen Oswald. He is smiling so smugly. I do not like this at all. He should be seeking death. Hark, a reporter hurridily [*sic*] questions him as the police push him into a room.

'Why did you kill the president?' asks a reporter.

'I never killed nobody,' was the reply, and Oswald has gone into the room. The door is closed. Policemen are shoving persons down the hallway from the room that contains Lee Harvey Oswald. I do not like this. Oswald *must* die. By all means he *must* die. Charles agrees.

We shall begin at once to arrange his execution.

For the innocent must pay for the crimes of the guilty. – Evermore.

Eric Ritzek's diary now moves to Saturday night, November 23, 1963. He notes that it is "very late" in the day. He and Charles have left their hotel room to go out. Eric states, "Charles and I met a tavern owner of very questionable character. He was truly mourning the death of the president. He was in the process of closing his place of endeavor when we happened to encounter him. I detected true grief and sincerity and I expressed likewise." Eric and Charles allegedly befriended the man who – it soon becomes obvious – is Jack Ruby. Eric claims that as he was having a drink and talking with Ruby, "with hardly any effort what-so-ever," he hypnotized Ruby. According to Eric's diary, he then planted a "hypnotic suggestion" in Ruby's mind "that he should avenge the President's death." Writes Eric: "Having completed our business I placed the man in a responsive trance to last until dawn, and Charles and I left to await the further results of our labours. Another innocent shall pay for the guilty."

The diary moves to Sunday, November 24, 1963: "We learned via the radio while breakfasting that Oswald is to be moved from the police station to the county jail. The police say he has not admitted anything but they possess an 'air tight case' against Oswald." Eric writes that he and Charles go to "the Dallas police station at around noon this day, to see what could be seen." He relates what happened:

It was most profitable. We could not gain entry because of the crush of people. But we observed our newly fashioned tool of our trade leave his parked car and shove his way inside the building. An armoured truck was parked in the car part [*sic*] and garage way. Our tool looked straight at me, but did not know me. He roughly shoved Charles aside and disappeared within.

A moment later that seemed like an eternity there was a clamour of voices. Then a shot resounded from within the tiled walled interior. There was a rattle and a clatter of running feet and horse [*sic*] frantic incoherent shouting from many throats. The armoured car was moved out of the car part [*sic*] after some frantic delay and shouting, and an ambulance arrived. Oswald, looking very poor was dumped upon a litter and roughly handled into the waiting ambulance, and hurried away still shackled to a policeman.

Then our tool was carried bodily away.... Upon returning to our hotel room and our television set, we discovered who our tool was: Leon Jack Rubinstein, known around this city of Dallas, Texas as one 'Jack Ruby.'

Monday, November 25, 1963
The new king, President Johnson has declared a period of national mourning. To last until December 22nd. Just in time for Christmas shopping. How very convenient. Everywhere institutions are closed while the workers take a holiday. How hypocritical....

December 24, 1963
I see everywhere, cheap-overpriced publications lamenting the death of President Kennedy. The public at large has fairly well recovered from the shock. In fact they never were shocked. From all the generated sorrow via publishing firms, and elaborate special 'Collector's Copy' magazines someone has made a greedy lucrative profit from all of this. Wherever money can be made – no matter how made – to hell with ethics – all men are corrupt – money shall be made.

DECEMBER 25, 1963

Eric Ritzek's diary now takes an even stranger track, and assumes a ranting quality and tone. Apparently, shortly after Ruby's murder of Oswald, the two men have returned to their college campus. Incredibly, Eric writes,

> Charles is dying. He is suffering from a rattlesnake bite. However, there are no rattlesnakes here at college. Charles' affliction was hypnotically induced by myself.... Charles and I had a falling out over who is the master craftsman. The true giant. Poor Charles could only place a poor second to the greatest. I am the greatest.

> Charles has stopped screaming. Yes – he is very stiff and dead. His body continues to swell and turn black and purple.... I shall return home before the expiration of the holidays, and report in full to our superiors. I regret having to report Charles' paramount weakness. But it must be reported to prevent such a recurrence, in future experiments with the people of the planet called Earth. In the ten years we have been stationed here, Charles showed an overwhelming weakness and desire to be a human being.

The diary of Eric Ritzek then moves to a strange, rambling rant, all written under the heading January 3, 1964:

> Alas enouch hynauch – Evermore.*
> I am very weary of my endeavors. I savor my homeland. – Evermore.

The diary continues for two pages with what appears to be a lengthy mathematical equation, and then resumes the bizarre narrative:

> Someday they will lower your stinking useless body into the moist dark earth. Merely to get you out of the way.... That stinking pile of human garbage, who walked for some three score and some odd years. That pile of rotting flesh and bones whose present value is now $1.98. A New York Jew will give you a $1.88.... $1.88 from a New York Jew, and linddy [sic] you won't keep. The maggots are now peeling back your skin and sucking out your juice. Getting drunk on it.... Guess what happens now? Oh boy, you'll never guess what your loved ones have gone and done now. They forgot all about you. You're gone and forgotten, and big daddy I do mean forgotten....

All men are fools. Good health is a luxury enjoyed by the rich. Are you rich? How is your health? Does the failing beat of your heart scare you at night, when you roll upon your left side and press your sweaty breast to the mattress? That is terror. Evermore....

(One full page consists of a drawing of a skull and crossbones.)

Death is in many forms. Dwells in all hearts. We all must go and we all will go. And all for the same purpose. *DEATH*. Ponder this thought a moment: You didn't exist *longer* than you existed. You will be dead *longer* than you've lived. Why bother?"

At the conclusion of the retyped diary, the CIA has inserted a number of its own comments, as well as the FBI's comments and observations. They read as follows:

The indices of the Los Angeles Office contain no information identifiable with ERIC RITZEK. A check of the telephone directory covering the Los Angeles Office on August 19, 1964, by Special Agent PHILLIP B. DEILY for this name was also negative.

On August 20, 1964, the records of the Retail Merchants Credit Association of Los Angeles were checked by Investigative Clerk PAUL H. CHAMBERLAIN, JR., and no record identifiable with ERIC RITZEK was located.

On August 20, 1964, the criminal records of the Los Angeles County Sheriff's Office were checked by Investigative Clerk MILLARD T. ANDERSON, and no record for ERIC RITZEK was located.

The indices of the Dallas Office contain no information identifiable with ERIC RITZEK.

On August 31, 1964, the above-described book bearing the written Notations set forth above was submitted to the FBI Laboratory for examination.

It should be noted that the name "ERIC RITZEK" did not appear on any passenger lists of buses in which OSWALD is known to have traveled, although the entry for September 26, 1963, in the alleged diary reflects RITZEK and CHARLES were on the same bus as OSWALD en route to Mexico City.

It is also noted that JACK L. RUBY'S places of business, the Carousel Club and the Vegas Club, were closed to the public on Saturday, November 23, 1963, although an entry in the alleged diary for November 23, 1963, states that CHARLES and ERIC RITZEK met a tavern owner, who was later identified as RUBY, as he was closing his place of business, and CHARLES and RITZEK were invited by this tavern owner into his place of business for a drink, at which time RITZEK claims to have hypnotized RUBY.

It is further noted that the alleged diary reflects on November 11, 1963, ERIC RITZEK and CHARLES walked over the route to be taken by President KENNEDY in Dallas, although such route had not been released as of November 11, 1963.

Eric Ritzek's strange diary certainly appears to be the obvious product of a confused and bizarre mind. But for what purpose? Was it written only to satisfy what some claim had to be insane urgings and fantasies? Is there any truth to it at all? What of the handwritten note about Albert Schweitzer College? Who was Eric Ritzek? Did he even exist? Why were the FBI and CIA unable to make any headway at all in identifying who authored the diary?

CENTRAL INTELLIGENCE AGENCY
WASHINGTON, D.C. 20505

APPROVED FOR RELEASE 1993
CIA HISTORICAL REVIEW PROGRAM
2A 8/3/93

1 6 SEP 1969

MEMORANDUM FOR: Deputy Assistant Secretary for Security
Department of State

SUBJECT : Charles William Thomas

Reference is made to your memorandum of 28 August 1969.
We have examined the attachments, and see no need for further
action. A copy of this reply has been sent to the Federal Bureau of
Investigation and the United States Secret Service.

FOR THE DEPUTY DIRECTOR FOR PLANS:

Signed: Raymond G. Rocca
James Angleton

CSCI-316/03323-69

cc: Federal Bureau of Investigation
cc: United States Secret Service

DECLASSIFIED BY SP6 - Bja/hal
ON 1/23/89 # 6451
Per CIA letter 9/23/88.

62 - 109060

Chapter 10

The Strange and Sad Saga of Charles William Thomas

We are condemned to kill time, thus we die bit by bit.

-Octavio Paz

Everything in my life had happened in the wrong way.

-Elena Garro

... but now I don't wish to be called, I fit in the voice of no one, do not call because now I'm descending to the depths of my meagerness to the satisfied roots of my shadows ...

-Eunice Odio

On September 26, 1963, fifty-nine days before the assassination of JFK, Lee Harvey Oswald traveled from Texas to Mexico City, Mexico, where he spent about 5 days. The evidence that Oswald journeyed to Mexico is substantial yet remains substantially unexamined and uninvestigated. In fairness, it should be noted that many conspiracy theorists steadfastly maintain that Oswald made no such trip. While Oswald's days in Mexico City are still shrouded in mystery and confusion, there can be no rational doubt that he was there. Additionally, those writers who discount, or write off, the claims of Elena Garro are simply ill informed, meaning they have not examined the full record, as well as all its complexities, or perhaps they hold biased agendas of their own. The story of Lee Harvey Oswald's time in Mexico, in this author's opinion, is the proverbial key to unlocking the mysteries surrounding JFK's assassination. Coupling what is known about Oswald's time in Mexico City with what Elena Garro and June Cobb tell us through their own words and activities make deciphering the overall Mexico City story a Herculean, but not impossible, task. What follows below, while detailed in places, is but an outline of that overall story with all its glorious mysteries and provocative questions.

A Secret Order

On July 25, 1969, U.S. Secretary of State William P. Rogers received a letter marked "CONFIDENTIAL," from a recently resigned State Department employee named Charles William Thomas. Thomas had served as the department's Political Officer in the U.S. Embassy in Mexico City from 1964 to 1967. Before that, from January 1961 to August 1963, he had been stationed in the U.S. Embassy in Port-au-Prince, Haiti.

Early on in his stint in Haiti, Thomas inadvertently ran slightly afoul of a team of three physicians working under contract with the CIA's MK/NAOMI project, according to at least one former Fort Detrick researcher. Beginning about 1954, both the CIA and U.S. Army, sometimes working in tandem, favored using Haiti – because of its complete lack of governmental regulatory authorities, as well as the ease with which any supposed concerned authorities could be bought to turn-a-blind eye toward questionable and unethical activities – for risky human experiments with psycho-chemicals and other more lethal drugs. Charles Thomas, according to a former Fort Detrick researcher, who declined to be identified herein, "was surprised at the conduct of the experiments, as well as their nature, and expressed innocent surprise and perhaps dismay" upon first learning about them.

As underscored in this author's book, *A Terrible Mistake,* on Fort Detrick researcher Dr. Frank Olson, and in several excellent articles by investigative journalists Dr. Jeffery Kaye and Jason Leopold on the Truthout.org website, the U.S. Army and CIA, under MK/ULTRA, MK/NAOMI, and MK/DELTA conducted extensive covert experiments with many "incapacitating agents" during the 1950s through to about 1970. Haiti was a favored location for some experiments. Dr. Kaye reveals that the military and CIA were especially interested in anti-malarial drugs derived from cichona bark. The curative and medicinal powers of cichona bark, sometimes referred to as chichona bark, have been known for hundreds of years in Haiti and elsewhere. During the 1977 Congressional hearings on the CIA's stockpiling of lethal and incapacitating drugs, it was revealed that the CIA and army were interested in anti-malarial drugs for more devious reasons. Writes Dr. Kaye: "CIA-linked researcher, Dr. Charles F. Geschickter told Sen. Edward Kennedy in 1977 hearings that the CIA was interested in anti-malarial drugs that 'had some, shall I say, disturbing effects on the nervous system of the patients.'"

At any rate, and even more intriguing, Charles Thomas made quick amends for his comments about the experiments he had witnessed, and before departing Haiti for his new assignment in Mexico City, he was invited to make some personal investments in private ventures being conducted in Haiti by a then obscure businessman, who would soon become a high-level source of mystery in the JFK assassination, George de Mohrenschildt. Adding significantly more intrigue and mystery to Thomas' experience in Haiti is that de Mohrenschildt's dealings in Haiti, as involving Thomas, also involved another covert CIA operative and a Harvard educated, high-profile Washington, D.C. attorney named Charles R. Norberg. During World War II, Norberg had served in the U.S. Army Air Force as an intelligence officer, and like many of the characters that appear in this book, encountered the ubiquitous George Hunter White in both Burma and India during the war. Following the war, Norberg worked for both the CIA and in the public affairs division of the State Department, then joined the prestigious international law firm of Morgon, Lewis, & Bockius, and then in 1956 went into private practice.

Norberg was more than simply a CIA operative and well-connected attorney. Norberg was George de Mohrenschildt's attorney, representing him in a series of complex Haiti-based oil and geological business ventures, some of which according to at least two former U.S. State Department officials, involved the "technical, in-country [Haiti] services of Thomas Eli Davis III, [as well as] two or three other American soldier-of-fortune-types who were in and out of Haiti, Guatemala, Panama, and the Dominican Republic on a regular basis … wearing enough hats to stock a tony haberdashery shop." (Some of these "technical" service soldier-of-fortune-types and contractors were also occasionally employed by the Schlumberger Wireline and Testing corporation, founded in Houston, Texas in 1935, and doing work in Latin America, the Belgium Congo, Haiti, South Africa, Serbia, Romania, and numerous other locations across the globe.)

Beginning in June 1951, Charles Norberg had also been an initial and key member of the United States Psychological Strategy Board created in 1951 by President Harry Truman through an executive order issued to the directors and secretaries of CIA, U.S. State Department, and U.S. Department of Defense. Norberg served for a number of years in the White House as the Psychological Strategy Board's assistant director. In the mid-1950s, when CIA director Allen Dulles and close associate Adolph Berle huddled with Cornell University physicians Harold G. Wolff and Lawrence Hinkle to create the Foundation for the Study of Human Ecology, Charles Norberg's name was at the top of their list for possible board of director members. Dr. Wolff especially admired Norberg's expertise in the burgeoning fields of enhanced interrogations and covert psychological operations. Dulles was continually impressed with Norberg's positions on biological warfare as a psychological weapon, as well as Norberg's proposal to establish within every U.S. embassy a psychological operations officer under the cover of working as a State Department political officer. Norberg also served as legal advisor for over a decade for the CIA-created front companies Morwede Associates and Mankind Research Unlimited.

Throwing additional light on the overall nature of Thomas' private business affairs in Haiti is Bruce Adamson's essential book, *Oswald's Closest Friend: The George de Mohrenschildt Story.* Adamson reveals: "After de Mohrenschildt's suicide on March 29, 1977, [former CIA director] George H.W. Bush acknowledged he knew the man [George de Mohrenschildt] as a relative of his Andover prepschool roommate, but had not "heard from him in many years." Adamson, however, goes on: "A recently declassified State Department document shows that Bush had heard from de Mohrenschildt in 1971. The document is a June 24, 1971 letter from Chief of Haitian Affairs, David R. Ross to Bush, who was the U.S. Ambassador to the United Nations at the time." The Ross letter to Bush reveals that de Mohrenschildt's "private attorney" for his Haitian affairs was Charles R. Norberg. In 1993, Norberg told Adamson he could not find his work files on his de Mohrenschildt's dealing, nor could he remember "the precise nature of his legal work on behalf of his former client." (In his book, Adamson also reproduces in its entirety a May 20, 1971 letter de Mohrenschildt wrote to Congressman Earle Cabell, former Mayor of Dallas when JFK was murdered and brother to Charles Cabell, who was deputy director of the CIA at the time of Kennedy's assassination in Dallas. The letter, which requests help on Haitian issues, also identifies Charles Robert Norberg as his then attorney.)

Thomas did not note in his July 1969 letter to Secretary of State Rogers concerning Elena Garro Paz and Lee Harvey Oswald that he was also an employee of the CIA's Branch 4, Covert Action Staff. Hired by the CIA in early 1952, following service in the U.S. Navy as an ensign assigned to still-secret intelligence matters, Thomas had already covertly served the Agency at several posts, including Monrovia, Liberia; Sierra Leone; Accra, Ghana; and Tangier, Morocco. We can only guess whether Secretary Rogers was aware of Thomas' dual employment and covert role with the CIA.

In his letter, Thomas informed Secretary Rogers that he was "winding up affairs at the Department of State" but wanted to draw Rogers' attention to "a pending matter which I believe merits your attention." Thomas did not explain to Secretary Rogers that he was "winding up affairs at the Department of State" because he had been "selected out" of the department. "Selected out" is a governmental euphemism for losing your job because of failure to move up in classification rank within a specified period. Charles Thomas, as readers shall learn, despite consistently superior evaluations with the Department of State, oddly was never advanced in his classification rank.

The "matter," explained Thomas in his letter, concerned "Lee Harvey Oswald, the presumed assassin of President Kennedy, [who was] allegedly present at a party given by a Mexican communist sympathizer and attended by the Cuban Consul, a veteran intelligence officer, when he was in Mexico shortly before the assassination."

Continued Thomas, "There are allegations that the Mexican Government may have been aware of Oswald's presence at that party and that the Cuban Government may have tried to intimidate others who saw him there."

Thomas' letter continued, informing Secretary Rogers that "public disclosure" of Oswald's presence at the Mexico party "could reopen the debate about the true nature of the Kennedy assassination and damage the credibility of the Warren Report."

Based on this concern, Thomas informed Rogers that since he had been the embassy officer in Mexico "who acquired this intelligence information, I feel a responsibility for seeing it through to its final evaluation."

"Accordingly," Thomas wrote, "I have prepared a memorandum (enclosed) explaining this information and its initial assessment, keyed to three memoranda of conversations with my Mexican informant."

Thomas concluded his letter in 1969 with this sentence: "I believe you would want to consider carefully whether to let well enough alone in this case, or whether the risks attending possible public disclosure of these allegations make further investigation warranted."

As readers may be concluding, nothing about Oswald's being "present at a party given by a Mexican communist sympathizer" or anyone else had been publicly revealed by the Warren Commission or any other Government entity, and would be unknown to the public and most researchers until 1978 when investigators for the House Select Committee on Assassinations (HSCA) stumbled over the story.

CHARLES THOMAS' "INVESTIGATION OF LEE HARVEY OSWALD IN MEXICO"

The first of Thomas' enclosed memoranda to Secretary Rogers, also dated July 25, 1969, bears the subject: "Investigation of Lee Harvey Oswald in Mexico." The memo details Thomas' involvement as embassy political officer with his friend and "informant," the well-known and respected Mexican playwright and novelist Elena Garro de Paz. Elena Garro spoke four languages fluently, including

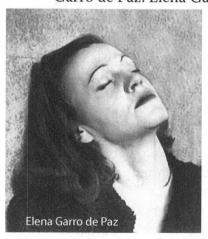

Elena Garro de Paz

English, and maintained significant social, literary, and political connections. She had one daughter, Elenita, who also lived in Mexico City. Elena Garro was also the former wife of Octavio Paz, one of Mexico's finest writers and leading intellectuals, as well as a career diplomat.

Charles Thomas recounted in his memo that he and his wife Cynthia, who lived with him in Mexico City, were good friends with Ms. Garro and found her to be "an intelligent, witty, and outspoken woman" and a "very useful if sometimes biased source of political gossip and personal history on significant Mexican personalities." Interestingly, Janet Leddy Scott, the wife of Winston Scott, Thomas' CIA superior at the embassy, was also a friend with Elena Garro.

Thomas' memorandum focused on a particular incident involving Elena Garro: While socializing on one occasion, *"Miss Garro inadvertently mentioned to me that she had been at a party with Lee Harvey Oswald and two American companions when Oswald was in Mexico just before the Kennedy assassination."* [Emphasis added.]

Thomas did not explain what he meant by "inadvertently," nor does he explain the context of his getting together with Garro, but he attached a two-page memo reporting his conversation with Garro on December 10, 1965. The memo/report bears the same date. It details Garro's remark about Lee Harvey Oswald and her answers to a number of questions Thomas posed to her about her encounter with Oswald on this first occasion and then questions that came later.

(Clearly, it would be helpful to know and understand what Charles Thomas' specific CIA job entailed at the embassy in Mexico City and whether or not that job involved keeping tabs on Elena Garro, but the CIA, to date, had refused to release any specifics on Thomas or Elena Garro. Indeed, it appears that there may be well over 150 pages dealing with the Thomas-Garro incident that are still withheld from public viewing.)

Thomas' December 10, 1965 Report on Garro & Lee Harvey Oswald

According to Thomas' December 10, 1965 report: "In September 1963, shortly after her return from abroad, [Elena Garro de Paz] went to a party at the home of Ruben Duran, who is married to her cousin. Her daughter, Elenita, accompanied her. There she met Oswald and two other young Americans who were with him. The three young Americans remained apart from the other guests. She expressed an interest in talking to them, but was discouraged from doing so by some of the other guests."

In response to Thomas' questions, Garro said, "Most of the guests at the party were communists or philo-communists." Thomas wrote that she recalled "seeing the Cuban Consul, Asquez (phonetic); General Clark Flores of the Mexican Olympic Committee; Sylvia Duran, who she later learned was Oswald's mistress while he was here; Emilio Carballidio, the writer, who she thinks is now in the United States; and a Latin American Negro man with red hair."

In November 1963, Thomas reported, "when the identity of Kennedy's assassin became known, Elena and her daughter went to the Cuban Embassy and, once admitted through the front gate, shouted 'assassin' and other insults at the staff there."

Shortly after Garro's shouting incident, Thomas explained, "she and her daughter were visited by a friend, Manual Carvillo, who was then an official in the Secretariat of Gobernacion [Mexican government internal affairs agency], and were told he had orders to escort them to a small and obscure hotel in the center of town. They were kept there for eight days under pretext that they were in danger." Most likely unknown to Garro, and perhaps also to Thomas, Carvillo was also a CIA asset who reported on a regular basis to CIA embassy personnel in Mexico, including Mexico City CIA station chief Winston Scott.

Thomas had given a copy of his December 10, 1965 report to his superior Winston Scott but, but as noted in his later July 25, 1969 memorandum, he did not send any copies to Washington. In his memorandum to Secretary of State Rogers, Thomas reports that a few days after having turned in his report to his boss, he was called to the office of Mr. Winston Scott, who headed the Embassy's Political Research Section (CIA). By including (CIA), Thomas was clearly identifying his boss as a covert agency operative. Scott was, in fact, CIA Chief of Station in Mexico City. Thomas went on to recount that when he met with Scott, Nathan Ferris, the Embassy's Legal Attaché was also present. After the word Attaché, Thomas added "(FBI)" indicating that Ferris was an FBI employee working undercover in the embassy.

Winston Scott told Thomas that he and Ferris were very interested in his December 10 report and he "pointed out" to Thomas "that there had been a great many rumors about Oswald at the time of the assassination and that some could not be verified and others had proved false." Scott then asked Thomas "to try and get a more detailed replay of Miss Garro's story." As Thomas explained in his 1969 memo to Rogers, "Mr. Scott made clear that the FBI had full responsibility for any further investigations of the Oswald Case."

Fifteen days later, on Christmas Day, Thomas provided Winston Scott with "a much more detailed and accurate restatement of Miss Garro's alleged encounter with Oswald and subsequent developments."

Thomas states in his new report, "Certain errors in my original presentation were corrected." He "fixes" the date of the party: "Miss Garro guessed that the date of the party at her cousin's was in early September 1963. She admitted that she had gone to the [American] embassy to report briefly about this matter on an earlier occasion."

In his July 25, 1969 memorandum to Secretary Rogers, Thomas writes that he "got no reaction" to his second report from Scott or Ferris, but he did hear from Clarence A. Boonstra, Embassy Deputy Chief of Mission in Mexico City, who "told me that Oswald had not been in Mexico on the date given for the party." Boonstra, a career Foreign Service officer who had served in Cuba when guerrilla fighters under Fidel Castro battled the Batista regime, charged that Ms. Garro had "changed her story," but Thomas countered, "that she hadn't changed her story but that rather I now had given a more accurate account of it." Boonstra again said the "date was wrong," and Thomas wrote, "[Boonstra] seemed to dismiss the whole affair." Thomas does not speculate in his report as to why Scott and Ferris did not respond to him, but he does seem to subtly imply that Boonstra acted either rashly or simply was seizing on a good excuse to brush the entire matter aside and not discuss it any further, perhaps acting on behalf of Scott or Ferris.

Apparently, nobody with the FBI ever questioned Clarence Boonstra about his certainty concerning Oswald not being at the party or Elena Garro, but over the years since, there have been credible reports that Boonstra, who has a degree in geology from Michigan State University, had more than a passing association with George de Mohrenschildt. Boonstra served as U.S. ambassador to Costa Rica in 1967 to 1969, and before that was Political Advisor to the Armed Forces in Panama, Caribbean Command, School of the Americas, a position that put him close to David Sanchez Morales on several occasions, according to private correspondence with Boonstra

In April 1964, Boonstra, along with newly arrived U.S. Ambassador to Mexico Fulton Freeman and Clark Anderson, lead FBI official in the embassy, met with a three-member team from the Warren Commission investigating Lee Harvey Oswald's time in Mexico. The team arrived in Mexico on April 8, 1964, and on April 9 and April 10 met with CIA Chief of Station Winston Scott. Ambassador Freeman had advised Scott that the team "had Top Secret clearances and that he [Freeman] felt we [FBI and CIA] should not try to be too secretive in talking to them."

Scott's April 11, 1964 report to CIA headquarters on his meetings with the team, also attended by deputy CIA chief of station, Alan White, reveals that he "threw all Station assets and sources into the job of trying to get all possible details of OSWALD's travel to and from Mexico, the place he had stayed, the contacts he had made and places he might have visited," however, there is scant evidence that this occurred.

Scott additionally, writes, "They said that Assistant Secretary Mann still has the 'feeling in his guts' that Castro hired OSWALD to kill Kennedy; they said, however, that the Commission has not been able to get any proof of this."

Scott lastly writes, "It is believed that all three of these visitors were pleased with this Station's work on the OSWALD case." While the subsequent Warren Commission team report, dated April 22, 1964 and written by team-member W. David Slawson, goes out of its way to praise the FBI agents on the ground in Mexico, it makes no comments on the quality of the CIA's assistance.

Thomas' report continues: "Some time later, Elena Garro told me she had found her old calendar and had reconstructed the date of the party at which she had seen Oswald. She stated it had been in late September rather than early September. (Oswald was in Mexico from September 26 to October 3, 1963.)"

Upon learning this, Thomas writes that he "accordingly went to Mr. Ferris' office and informed him of this." Ferris, the U.S. Embassy's FBI man, told Thomas that "[Garro] had given the late September date accurately when she had come to the Embassy and made her original report to the FBI." According to Thomas, "[Ferris] added, however, that someone who was at the party had stated that there were no Americans there."

Continues Thomas: "He did not reveal who had provided this information. I asked Mr. Ferris to tell me frankly if he thought I should continue pursuing this matter. *He advised me that it was not necessary since he considered the Oswald case closed, stating again that he had heard all the rumors before.*" [Emphasis added.]

Thomas does not note his reaction to Ferris' dismissal. He writes, "Although the date of the alleged party had been placed in the proper time frame, I was puzzled at the report that there had been no Americans at the party. I had assumed that Miss Garro could have clearly been mistaken about the identity of the Americans she saw there, but never doubted that she had seen some Americans. Although, I had met Elena Garro's sister, Deva Guerrera, I had never discussed the Oswald case with her. Mrs. Guerrera's grown son, however, told me that he was quite convinced that his mother had seen Oswald."

Based on the assurances of FBI official Ferris, Thomas backed off. He writes, "Although I pursued the matter no further, I felt obligated nevertheless to report in writing the developments described in the memorandum of conversation dated July 13, 1966. I thought it was particularly strange that the Cuban Government would carry as Miss Garro's address the small hotel where she was allegedly hidden away after the Kennedy assassination by a man identified with the Mexican Ministry of Interior. I should perhaps add that it was I, rather than Miss Garro, who first noticed the address. At the least, the letters lend some cross confirmation to her story about the small hotel. At the most, they provide a source of endless speculation about conspiracy and international intrigue."

Thomas goes on to note, "In early 1967, in the context of the Garrison investigation, Allen White, the number two in the CIA in Mexico, made an interesting comment to me about the investigation of Oswald's activities in Mexico. He stated that the DSF (the security police attached to Mexico's Ministry of Interior) had interrogated the Durans after the assassination about a party, which Oswald had reportedly attended, but that the transcript of the interrogation was entirely unsatisfactory by normal investigatory standards. Furthermore [according to Allen White], the party inquired about was not the one at Ruben Duran's house, reported by Elena Garro, but at an entirely different place. This transcript may well be the source of Mr. Ferris' belief that Elena Garro's story had been checked out and found to be untrue."

Observes Thomas: "It would appear that whereas the FBI has discounted the Elena Garro allegations, the CIA is still considerably disturbed by them. The CIA may not have pressed for further investigation, however, for a number of reasons: 1) considering the sensitive overlap and subtle competition between two intelligence collecting agencies, it had to yield to the FBI's clear jurisdiction; 2) there are obvious complications in conducting such an investigation in a foreign country; 3) there is a close and delicate relationship between CIA Station Chief and the former Minister of Interior – President Gustavo Diaz Ordaz; and 4) some of the people appearing in the Elena Garro scenario may well be agents of the CIA. Under the circumstances it is unlikely that any further investigation of this matter will ever take place unless it is ordered by a high official in Washington."

Thomas concludes: "If all the allegations in the attached memoranda were true, they would not, in themselves, prove that there was a conspiracy to assassinate President Kennedy. However, if they were ever made public, those who have tried to discredit the Warren Report could have a field day in speculating about their implications. The credibility of the Warren Report would be damaged all the more if it were learned that these allegations were known and never adequately investigated by the competent American authorities.

"Reference is again made to the biographic report on Elena Garro. She is hardly an ordinary or average person. Her strengths and weaknesses become exaggerated precisely because she is not. It would be easy and convenient to sweep this matter under the rug by claiming that Miss Garro is an unreliable informant since she is emotional, opinionated, and 'artistic.' I have been affected at times by that temptation myself. *No American official, however, knows her better than I do. On the basis of the facts that I have presented, I believe that, on balance, the matter warrants further investigation.* [Emphasis added.]

"Finally, the record should show that a representative of a major American publication has at least some knowledge of this story."

On December 25, 1965, as revealed in yet another of the memoranda Thomas attached to his letter to Secretary of State Rogers, Thomas again met with Garro to discuss at greater length "her alleged encounter with Oswald." Present for this discussion were Garro's daughter, Elenita, and Thomas' wife, both of whom had been present at the initial December 10 discussion.

Oddly, at the start of this four-page memorandum detailing this meeting and dated the same day (December 25), Thomas writes, "Some further information on this subject was given subsequently on January 9, 1966," leading one to easily presume that the memorandum had actually been written sometime after this later date.

Thomas writes, "During this latter conversation [of January 9, 1966], Sra. De Paz [Elena Garro] admitted that she had gone to the [United States] Embassy [in Mexico City] on an earlier occasion with her daughter and mother-in-law and had talked to two Embassy officers (presumably from the Legal Attaché's Office) about the matter [of seeing Lee Harvey Oswald at a party]. She said since the Embassy's officers did not give much credence to anything they said, they did not bother to give a very complete story."

Thomas goes on: "The following information supplements and in some instances corrects that given in the memorandum of December 10."

At this point in his writing, Thomas launches into a very detailed accounting of the Garros' encounter with Oswald. The party, Elena told Thomas, was held at the house of Ruben Duran, who was a cousin to Elena Garro. Elena explained, "Lydia, Horacio, and Ruben Duran are all cousins … [and] Silvia Duran [who worked in the Cuban Embassy in Mexico City and who spoke with Oswald when he visited that embassy in September 1963] is married to Horacio, who is a rather weak man … Sra. De Paz [Garro] had never had anything to do with Silvia, who [Garro] considers a communist and a whore. Ruben [Duran] was born in the United States and served in the U.S. Army during the war. He still goes to the U.S. from time to time but has no relatives or particular connections there…. The party in question was held at the home of Ruben Duran."

Elena Garro was unsure of the date of the party. She said that it had been held sometime in September 1963, and believed "it was on a Monday or Tuesday because it was an odd night to have a party."

Thomas' report goes on: "At the party, the man she assumes was Oswald wore a black sweater [maybe the same black sweater he wore in Dallas when he was shot by Jack Ruby]. He tended to be silent and stared a lot at the floor. Of his two young American companions, one was very tall and slender and had long blond hair which hung across his forehead. He had a gaunt face and a rather long protruding chin. [A near perfect description of Thomas Eli Davis III, in this author's estimation.] The other was also rather tall and had short, light brown hair, but he had no real distinguishing characteristics. All three were obviously Americans and did not dance or mix with the other people. The three were evidently friends, because she [Elena] saw them by chance the next day walking down the street together."

Thomas' report then includes a lengthy paragraph about Elena Garro's provocative encounters at other social gatherings she had recently attended. Writes Thomas: "Although Sra. De Paz had returned from an extended stay in Europe only in June or July, she had already met Eusebio Azcue and knows positively that he was at the party. [Azcue, at the time of Oswald's visit was Cuban Consul in Mexico.] On another occasion (it was not clear whether before or after the party in question), she attended a party where she saw, among others, Eusebio Azcue; Emilio Carballido, the pro-Castro writer; *and a Latin American Negro man with red hair.* (These last two were not at the Duran party as was mistakenly stated in the December 10 memorandum.) *Carballido and Azcue, along with a few others, got into a heated discussion on that occasion about President Kennedy, and they came to the conclusion that the only solution was to kill him.* Sra. de Paz said that Carballido is known as a Castro agent in Mexico. He has been to Red China, the Soviet Union, and many times to Cuba. [Emphasis added]

"Following the assassination of Kennedy, he spent about a year in Cuba. When he returned, he got a job teaching at Rutgers University through Dr. Jose Vasquez Amaral, who was formerly with the Rockefeller Foundation in New York and who is now a professor at Rutgers. Carballido is presumably still there. The day after the assassination, Elenita Paz encountered Sra. de Azcue [while out shopping in a store]. On seeing her, Sra. de Azcue turned and hurried out of the store. Azcue was immediately called back to Havana after the assassination, and his wife followed him shortly thereafter." [Emilio Carballido, according to CIA and FBI files generated in 1966, entered the U.S. on September 21, 1965. A 1966 FBI document reports that Carballido had a number of ties that the Bureau viewed as "Marxist" and "Communist," said information forwarded confidentially to the U.S. State Department.]

Thomas' memorandum continues: "Others present at the Duran party in addition to her and her daughter were Horacio and Silvia Duran; Lydia Duran; Sra. De Paz's philocommunist sister, Deba Guerrero; General Jose Jesus Clark Flores and his mistress, a Guatemalan woman; a medical doctor from Dalinde Hospital; a young American couple, both fat and blond, who were on their honeymoon in Mexico; a 40-year-old Mexican woman in a red dress; and a rather strange man who claimed to be a Mexican but did not look or talk like one. His first name was Alejandro and he subsequently wrote Elenita several love letters. She claims she turned these in to the American Embassy. Riccardo Guarre, a communist, and his wife, Rosario Cantellases, a writer, were both supposed to come to the party but declined to come, according to Sra. De Paz, when they learned that she would be there."

Thomas continues: "On Saturday, November 25, 1963, the day after the Kennedy assassination [*sic*], Sr. de Paz's brother drove her and her daughter at about 3:30 P.M. to the Cuban Embassy. Her brother was embarrassed by their behavior and drove a block up the street to wait for them after letting them out. The two women then went inside the gate and shouted 'assassin' and other insults."

Later that same day, Thomas continues, Elena and her daughter were visited by a close friend, Manuel Calvillo, who told the two women that they were "in serious danger from the communists and that he should take them to a small hotel where they would be safe for a few days." Elena told Thomas that it was unclear whether Calvillo was acting under orders or not. Wrote Thomas: "Calvillo was known around town to be an undercover agent for the Secretariat of Gobernacion ... among things he said was that Sylvia Duran had been arrested by [the Mexican authorities]."

Thomas goes on: "Since she could not remember the name of the hotel, Sra. de Paz took me to the part of town where she remembered it to be, and we found it. It is the Vermont Hotel, located at Calle Vermont 29.... She stated that the hotel is owned by someone from San Luis Potosi and is used by businessmen from the area. She and her daughter did not personally register at the hotel. She thinks Calvillo registered them as relatives or friends of his from San Luis Potosi. Although modest, it is a modern and comfortable-looking hotel. They stayed there until the following Friday and hardly left their room.

Elena Garro and her daughter Elenita

"It was not until after they were in the hotel and saw newspapers and the photographs of Oswald that she [Elena] and her daughter both came to the independent conclusion that he was one of the young Americans at the Duran party," continued Thomas. "*When Calvillo visited them at the hotel, she told him she wanted to report to the American Embassy what she knew about Oswald's connections with local communists and with Azcue. Calvillo said she shouldn't go because the American Embassy was full of communist spies. When she returned to her home the following week, guards were posted around it."* [Italics in Original]

Thomas went on and explained that when Garro returned home she found her sister Deva "terrified because of Oswald's presence at the Duran party." Wrote Thomas: "She [Deva] had come to the conclusion independently that it was Oswald who she had seen there. [Deva] was also very angry with the Durans because she thought they had become involved in the assassination plot for money. Despite being a philo-communist, she was an admirer of President Kennedy's because she is also a patrician and a monarchist. *About two months after the assassination, [Deva] was called in by two communists, whom she refuses to identify, and was warned with threats never to reveal to anyone that she had been to a party with Oswald. She remained so terrified that she would not accompany [Elena and her daughter] to the American Embassy to tell what she knew of Oswald. A short time after the assassination, Emilio Carbellido, the pro-Castro writer, took the Durans to Jalapa, Veracruz and kept them out of the way for a while until the initial shock of the Kennedy assassination wore off."* [Emphasis added.]

Interesting to note here, is that on February 23, 1966 FBI Legal Attaché Nathan Ferris sent a "confidential" memorandum to U.S. Ambassador [to Mexico] Fulton Freeman through Clarence Boonstra to be circulated to Mr. Wallace W. Stuart, Counselor for Political Affairs, concerning Lee Harvey Oswald and Elena Garro. Ferris references Charles Thomas' December 25, 1965 memorandum and writes: "Extensive investigation conducted in the United States and Mexico after the assassination of President Kennedy failed to disclose that Oswald traveled to Mexico prior to September 26, 1963. Oswald was residing in New Orleans, Louisiana, in early September 1963, and no information has been obtained to indicate that he was away from that area in early September 1963. In view of the fact that Mrs. Garro de Paz's allegations have been previously checked but without substantiation, no further action is being taken concerning her recent repetition of those allegations." Ferris' memorandum, as can be expected, was also sent to Winston Scott, as well as the CIA's Central Biographic Division.

THOMAS REPORTS ON JUNE COBB'S TIME WITH GARRO

Now, in his lengthy December 25, 1965 report, Thomas turns his attention to what Elena Garro told him about June Cobb. Thomas includes nothing in his report that indicates that he may have known that Cobb was a paid asset and operative for the CIA.

Writes Thomas: "Also shortly after the assassination, an American woman named June Cobb came and spent several days in Sra. de Paz's house. She [Cobb] was sent by their mutual friend, Eunice Odio, a Costa Rican who is now [December 1965] June Cobb's roommate and she was formerly the mistress of Vasquez Amaral when he was with the Rockefeller Foundation…. *June Cobb expressed great interest in the Kennedy assassination. She succeeded in getting Deva Guerrera drunk one night, and the latter told all she knew about Oswald and the party at the home of Ruben Duran. Miss Cobb then wanted them to tell what they knew to the American authorities. Claiming to be a CIA agent, she* [Cobb] *advised against going to the American Embassy and urged them to go to Texas to tell their story. Failing in this, she* [Cobb] *said she would arrange a meeting in a quiet café* [later revealed to be the café in the Hotel Luma] with the CIA Station chief [Winston Scott]. *The meeting did not materialize, however, because she* [Cobb] *was asked to leave the Paz house. Miss Cobb had kicked Sra. de Paz' cat.*" [Emphasis added.]

Charles Thomas' brief account about Cobb coming to stay with Elena and her daughter is revealing, but raises many issues, which remain unaddressed, uninvestigated and unanswered. Why did Eunice Odio send Cobb to Garro's home? Who was Eunice Odio? Was Cobb actually sent to Garro's home by the CIA? What "authorities" did Cobb want Elena and her daughter to speak with? Why did Cobb reveal to Elena, her daughter and Elena's sister that she was a CIA operative? Why did Cobb advise against going to the American Embassy? Where in Texas did Cobb want the Elena, her sister, and daughter to go? Who in Texas did she want Elena Garro to speak with? Some of these questions, and more, will be answered in the next chapter.

Charles Thomas' December 25, 1965 report concludes with several more intriguing revelations: "At the end of January, 1964,

Ruben Duran visited Sra. de Paz," he writes. "He [Duran] said he was going to visit the United States and wanted her to protect him as much as possible while he was away. *He feared it might be discovered that Oswald had been to his house. Since he [Duran] had been born in the United States, he knew it would be easy for the Mexican Government to divest him of his citizenship and deport him. They both agreed to say nothing about it. He said it was Silvia Duran who got him involved with Oswald. He added that he was not really a communist and was against the assassination [of JFK]."* [Emphasis added.]

State Department Alerts FBI & CIA About Thomas' Letter

We do not know if Secretary of State William Rogers ever responded to Charles Thomas' July 1969 letter (by all appearances he did not), but we are well aware that the State Department promptly alerted the FBI about the contents of Thomas' "confidential" letter.

On September 9, 1969, FBI official W.A. Branigan, one of the Bureau's top Soviet espionage experts – who often interacted with the CIA's George Joannides, who was chief of the Psychological Warfare branch of JM/WAVE in Miami – wrote a memorandum to William C. Sullivan, the Bureau's domestic intelligence division director, to alert Sullivan that the State Department had "furnished us a letter and accompanying documents which it received from a recently retired [*sic*] State Department employee, a Mr. Charles Thomas, in which Thomas relates information received by him as to an alleged party attended by Lee Harvey Oswald in Mexico." The memorandum goes on: "Thomas worked at the American Embassy, Mexico City, from 1964 to 1967, and the source of his information is one Elena Garro de Paz, a Mexican woman. State Department requested it be advised of any action initiated by the FBI in this matter and also advised it had notified the CIA and Secret Service about it."

Branigan, who may or may not have known that Thomas was a covert CIA operative, underscored his concerns with this paragraph: "Thomas points out to the State Department that if the allegations he has received from Mrs. Paz are true, although they would not prove a conspiracy to assassinate President Kennedy, they would, if made public, damage the credibility of the Warren

Commission Report. He notes that a representative of a major American publication has some knowledge of the story."

It appears that FBI official W.A. Branigan was writing to Sullivan on a follow-up to an earlier August 28, 1969 memorandum on Charles William Thomas to FBI director J. Edgar Hoover from Bert M. Bennington, the State Department's Acting Chief, Division of Protective Security. Bennington's memorandum stated in part, "Mr. Charles William Thomas, a former employee of the State Department, reported certain events and speculations, which tend to suggest that a conspiracy applicable to the assassination of former President John F. Kennedy may have existed involving representatives of the Cuban government."

> *How can it be ascertained that Oswald did not travel to Mexico prior to September 1963? There must be some basis for Elena's reporting.*
> — Handwritten note on Charles Thomas report, Dec. 1965

CHARLES WILLIAM THOMAS COMMITS "SUICIDE"

In April 1971, Charles William Thomas, according to *Time* magazine, "took up a gun and shot himself to death." Thomas was 45 years old, had a wife and two children, and had served both the State Department and CIA for nearly 20 years.

A November 15, 1971, *Time* magazine article on Thomas' death called him "a desperate man." Thomas, the article explained, "had been 'selected out' of the Foreign Service" because "he had not been promoted from Class 4 level to Class 3 within the mandatory eight years." In State Department parlance, "selected out" essentially means, "fired." The department gave Thomas one-year's salary, a $323 monthly retirement payment, which came out of money he had paid into a departmental fund, and said good bye to its former employee.

Before committing "suicide," Thomas spent nearly three years sending out resumes in hopes of gaining a new job. In all, according to the *Time* article, he "endured 2,000 job rejection letters; he was told 'too old' or 'too qualified,' and anyway, he had been fired by the State Department." Friends of Thomas' at the time of his death said he was depressed, but not suicidal, and that he "deeply loved his children and wife" and "would not do that to them."

Not surprisingly, *Time* magazine's article, as well as several other newspaper accounts of his death and battle with the U.S. State Department, made no mention that Charles William Thomas was also an employee of the CIA. Of course, doing that would have raised a completely new can of worms in regards to Thomas' issues and alleged depression over his unemployment. Incredibly, nobody to date has asked why the CIA did not act to assist Thomas with his "employment" problems; nor has anyone asked why the CIA did not simply reassign him after his time in Mexico, or was he also let go as a CIA employee, and if so, why?

FBI AND CIA ACT TO KILL MEDIA STORIES ABOUT THOMAS

Not long after Thomas' sudden death, the "representative of a major American publication" that Thomas referred to in his reports as being aware of the Elena Garro-Oswald story, was revealed to be well-known White House correspondent Sarah McClendon.

A May 6, 1971 memorandum to FBI Domestic Intelligence director, C.D. Brennan, from W.A. Branigan, FBI Soviet espionage expert, reads at its start: "Former Special Agent Nate Ferris informed Special Agent L. Whitson on 5/3/71 that he heard that the woman journalist, Sarah McClendon, plans to write a feature story on Charles William Thomas, a former State Department employee who recently committed suicide. According to Mrs. McClendon's daughter who lives next door to the Ferrises, Sarah McClendon is going to do the article because Charles Thomas, former Political Officer of the U.S. Embassy in Mexico, knew so much about the 'Oswald case.'"

The memorandum goes on and recounts the Garro de Paz-Oswald party account from the FBI's perspective, offering a number of erroneous observations. The document concludes by stating, "The Assistant Attorney General, Internal Security Division, and the Acting Chief, Division of Protective Security, Department of State, were furnished the result of the Bureau's 1964 investigation of the allegations of Mrs. Elena Garro de Paz. For information and for the assistance of Crime Records, Mrs. McClendon should contact Bureau in connection with the reported story." The memorandum was also sent to four of the Bureau's top COINTELPRO officials.

The McClendon feature story never appeared. As some readers may be aware, Sarah McClendon was long suspected of being an asset for the CIA. Researcher and writer John Bevilaqua provides some intriguing information on McClendon. Bevilaqua bluntly dubs McClendon a "right-wing wacko who had to be humored for decades by various Presidents." JFK especially disliked McClendon, Bevilaqua reveals, and often refused to call on her at White House press conferences. Pulling no punches, Bevilaqua writes, "McClendon was a member of Maj. Gen. Charles Willoughby's Anti-Communist Liaison-Committee of Correspondence which featured a handful of people closely associated with both the CIA or military intelligence and the JFK assassination by multiple independent researchers: Rev. Billy James Hargis, Alexander Rorke who died 2 months before the JFK assassination but was a constant associate of Frank Sturgis now definitively tied to the JFK ploy by E. Howard Hunt, his case officer, and Edward Hunter, the author [and CIA asset and contractor] of *Brainwashing*, which was published by Henry Regency Press (1952) one of the foremost Holocaust Denial and anti-Semitic publishers in existence. Regency's father William Regency headed up the pro-Fascist America First Committee, which was so isolationist before World War II that they were considered pro-Nazi. Rev. Gerald L.K. Smith, perhaps the most prominent clerical Fascist of the 20th Century also was a prominent leader in the America First movement and the Hollywood Blacklisting campaign, as well as William Dudley Pelley's Nazi-inspired and xenophobic Christian Nationalist Crusade. [Edward] Hunter was a self-described fascist and an anti-Semite who is considered to be the originator of the term 'mind control.' Willoughby himself was identified as a JFK plot conspirator in *The Man Who Knew Too Much* by Dick Russell [and] as Adolph Tscheppe-Weidenbach.... McClendon penetrated the Coalition on Political Assassinations as a founding member, in order to gather intelligence on the status of the JFK assassination investigation ostensibly to determine how close investigators were getting to implicating her cohorts like Willoughby, Sturgis, Hunter, Regency and Hargis in the events surrounding the JFK assassination conundrum. McClendon was a constant associate of McCarthyites, anti-Semites, dedicated xenophobics and pro-Fascists for most of her lifetime."

WHAT CIA STATION CHIEF WINSTON SCOTT KNEW: LET'S TWIST AGAIN ...

The very first CIA report concerning Elena Garro's sighting of Lee Harvey Oswald at the Duran party is dated October 5, 1964.

June Cobb wrote this two-page, typed report under her Agency alias, Joyce H. Pineinch. The report has been frequently miscited and misquoted in several key books on the CIA by writers who have confused it with other later reports due to the HSCA's often-confusing report on Oswald in Mexico City. (The HSCA states that the report was filed under Cobb's cryptonym, LI/COOKIE, but this is incorrect.) Cobb's report expresses no doubts about Elena Garro's report or truthfulness, nor about Oswald's visit to Mexico. Her matter-of-fact wording seems to convey that she well knew that Oswald had been in Mexico and at the party in question, and as readers shall soon see this appears to be precisely the case. Her report reads:

> Pineinch
> October 5, 1964
>
> Mexican communists who had contact with Oswald, as has not appeared in Warren Commission write-ups in press. All weekend, Elena Garro de Paz, Elena Paz, (the daughter) and Deba Garro de Guerrero Galvan sat around recalling details of having been in a group with Oswald here last fall during the days that he was in Mexico.
>
> The write-ups of the Warren Commission Report in the newspapers sparked this discussion, and they apparently had never really sat around determined to piece it all together, although all three were deeply affected by Kennedy's assassination, seemed literally to adore the Kennedy family image, still follow Robert Kennedy's career with great interest and admiration.
>
> The main points: Elena and Deba are first cousins of three young Mexicans named Duran: Ruben, Horacio, and Lynn. Horacio is the husband of Sylvia Duran, the Mexican girl who was arrested for questioning about Oswald because she had been in touch with him at the Cuban Embassy when he went there looking for a visa. (She is or was also a ringleader at the Cuban-Mexican Institute on Tokio, I remember).
>
> While Oswald was here last fall the Duran cousins invited the Garro sisters and young Elena Paz [Elena Garro's daughter] to a "twist party" at the home of Ruben Duran mid-week. A few communists they knew (Deba is a communist herself and

Elena has been in touch since she was a young girl and went to Republican Spain with Octavio Paz) and a number of people who struck them as very peculiar at the time, were there. AND OSWALD WAS THERE WITH TWO OTHER BEATNIK LOOKING BOYS, ONE OF WHOM WAS VERY TALL, AND ALL THREE OF WHOM THEY REMEMBER QUITE WELL. When they began asking questions about the Americans, who

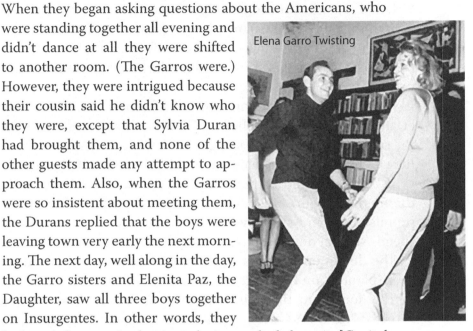

Elena Garro Twisting

were standing together all evening and didn't dance at all they were shifted to another room. (The Garros were.) However, they were intrigued because their cousin said he didn't know who they were, except that Sylvia Duran had brought them, and none of the other guests made any attempt to approach them. Also, when the Garros were so insistent about meeting them, the Durans replied that the boys were leaving town very early the next morning. The next day, well along in the day, the Garro sisters and Elenita Paz, the Daughter, saw all three boys together on Insurgentes. In other words, they had not left town. At the time, they remarked about it. [Capital letters in original.]

As soon as Oswald's picture was printed in the newspapers all three clearly remembered him. And of course the arrest of Sylvia Duran almost immediately afterward, underlined their certainty. They were so sickened (Elena and Elenita) that they broke off their relations with the Durans. However, their cousins very nervously looked them up later. Deba Garro de Guerrero Galvin says that Lynn Duran and one of the Duran boys have made trips to Texas, and that most conspicuously they have all prospered this last year. Always poor before, they now have an expensive car each.

Horacio Duran works at *El Dia* newspaper.

It is not at all clear that Winston Scott ever saw June Cobb's October 5, 1964 report, but on November 25, 1964, about a year before Charles William Thomas had his initial conversation with Elena Garro de Paz concerning Lee Harvey Oswald, CIA officer "Willard C. Curtis," a pseudonym used by CIA Chief of Station Winston Scott, wrote a memorandum for the files bearing the subject "June Cobb."

The memorandum explained that through two trusted covert sources –Manuel Alonzo Calvillo, a Mexican codenamed LI-CHANT/1, and Alfonso Rudolph Wichtrich, executive vice president of the American Chamber of Commerce in Mexico and codenamed LIHUFF/1 – Curtis had been informed that the former wife of Octavio Paz "rents a room to an American communist whose name is June Cobb."

Continued the memorandum: "The former Mrs. PAZ is, however, afraid of Miss COBB. She said COBB broke the legs and smashed the ribs of a pet cat when she got mad at the cat. Mrs. Paz is afraid June COBB will 'break her arms and legs' one day if she gets angry."

If Cobb's alleged animal cruelty was not enough, according to the memorandum the informants also reported, "June COBB is promiscuous and sleeps with a large number of men, sometimes spends several nights (consecutively) with a man in his apartment."

The document continues: "Mrs. PAZ believes COBB may have been 'planted' on her by communists."

The document then turns its attention to Lee Harvey Oswald. It reads: "Mrs. PAZ tried to talk to Robert Kennedy when he was here. She wanted to tell him that she had personally met Lee Harvey OSWALD when he was here in Mexico City. She said she met him and two friends (Cubans) at the home of Horacio (and Sylvia) DURAN. Mrs. PAZ says she is absolutely sure of this – and knows OSWALD was at the DURAN apartment for a party at which she was present."

Winston Scott's memorandum concludes: "Mrs. PAZ told LI-CHANT/1 that she had come to the U.S. Embassy and had told an American official of this story about OSWALD. She said the U.S. Embassy officer told her that he was the official representative of the Warren Commission. He also told her she should be afraid of June COBB. I asked LIHUFF/1 to get LICHANT/1 to pursue this story of OSWALD and to continue to report on both Mrs. PAZ and on June COBB." Below this last sentence, Curtis/Scott included a "Distribution" list for the document. Listed first to receive a copy was "LICOOKY/1," the CIA cryptonym for June Cobb.

"THREE BUMPS ON A LOG ... JUST PASSING THROUGH"

An apparently hastily typed and earlier Memorandum for the Record dated October 12, 1964 and sent to Winston Scott bearing the subject "Oswald case" reads: "Elena garro told Eunice Odio (who relayeds [*sic*] to June Cobb on 9 October) she and her daughter were invited to a party at the Cuban ezbsnsy [*sic*] during the period she now finds out that Oswald was here in Mexico city prior to the Kennedy assassination. She was invited by a Mexican secretary in the Cuban embassy whose husband is a cousin of the garro family. At the party, she saw three gringos, not drinking, not mixing, and more or less just standing around together like 'three bumps on a log.' They were so obviously out of place, she asked someone in the Cuban embassy about them and was told, 'They were just passing through.' She claims that on account of the way those three gringos stood out she took a good long look at them as did her daughter. When Kennedy's assassination occurred and Oswald's picture was spread into the newspapers, both Elena and her daughter immediately said that he was one of the three gringos 'without a doubt' at the party."

The memorandum bears the initials "JF." This was James E. Flannery, CIA Chief of Covert Action in the U.S. Embassy in Mexico City. However, there is reason to believe that the memorandum had originated with and actually been typed by June Cobb, who passed it on to Flannery, whom she reported to at the embassy. Flannery then initialed it and passed it on to Scott. (The typos in the memorandum and typing style, as well as the paper the memo was typed on, is all common to Cobb's reporting style.)

Readers may not be surprised to learn that Flannery, born in San Antonio, Texas, was a friend to David Sanchez Morales, and the two often worked together in 1963 through to about 1967, first in Bolivia and then in Mexico City, after Flannery took up his CIA post there in February 1964 under the cover of being a State Department political officer like Charles Thomas, whom he also knew well. (Flannery departed Mexico City in June 1965.) Former embassy officials say that Flannery was a "rough and tumble, hardscrabble kind of guy," who "got on well with June Cobb, who reported to both Flannery and David Atlee Phillips."

Following legendary exploits in the Army during World War II that resulted in his being awarded the Silver Star and two Bronze

Stars, James Flannery attended Georgetown University School of Foreign Service in the late 1940s and graduated in 1951. Recalled for active duty during the Korean War, he was assigned to duty with the CIA, and then in 1952 he became a full-time Agency employee stationed in Japan, often working out of the huge underground CIA compound at the Atsugi air base. In the late 1950s, Flannery worked at CIA headquarters as an assistant to Richard Bissell, who developed the U-2 spy plane operation. Writer David Corn writes that Ted Shackley later "inherited" Flannery as his deputy director of the CIA's Western Hemisphere Division, which had previously been headed up by William Broe. Broe is but another CIA official whose shadowy dealings related to the assassination have never been explained.

Contributing further toward Winston Scott's continuing knowledge concerning Garro's reports as expressed through Charles Thomas' memorandums to the CIA Station Chief, is an October 13, 1966 memo to Scott from embassy Legal Attaché Nathan L. Ferris. The brief memo makes reference to Thomas' July 13, 1966 report (cited above) and then states: "A confidential source who has furnished reliable information in the past advised on October 10, 1966, that a record had been located at the Hotel Vermont, Vermont #29, Mexico, D.F. disclosing that Elena Paz, housewife from San Luis Potosi, San Luis Potosi, Mexico, had registered at the Hotel Vermont on November 23, 1963, leaving November 24, 1963, again registering on November 25, 1963, leaving November 27, 1963, and again registering on November 28, 1963, leaving November 30, 1963." Ferris concludes his memo by stating, "The above individual may or may not be identical with Elena Garro de Paz referred to in referenced memorandum."

FBI INTERVIEWS ELENA GARRO AND HER DAUGHTER

On December 11, 1964, fifteen days after CIA Station Chief Winston Scott wrote his initial memorandum about Elena Garro, and a full year before Charles William Thomas interviewed Garro about her encounter with Oswald, FBI officials in the U.S. Embassy in Mexico City sent FBI director J. Edgar Hoover what the FBI terms an "LHM" [letterhead memorandum] concerning Elena Garro. The memorandum, which was attached to a cover memorandum that stated that Garro and her daughter, Elenita, "first came to the attention of this office on November 17, 1964 when they contacted Mr. Peter H. Jacoby, who is employed at the Office of the Regional Book Center in the Embassy. According to Jacobi [*sic*], Mrs. Paz's husband, Octavio Paz, had at one time been the Mexican Ambassador to India and had been known by Jacobi there."

The cover memorandum goes on to explain that Elena Garro was interviewed on November 17, 1964 by FBI agent Rolf L. Larson because it had come to the attention of the FBI that "she claimed to have seen Oswald at a party in the home of Ruben Duran, but was unable to specify the date." The memorandum then reads: "When asked by SA Larson as to why she had not come forward with the information sooner, she indicated that she had been afraid to do so. At that time [November 17, 1964], *she declined to furnish further information unless she could be assured that it would not be made public.* She also stated she wanted to do some further research in an effort to fix the date of the party." [Emphasis added.]

The FBI document then states that Elena and her daughter "were interviewed [again] in the Mexico City Office on 11/24/64 [seven days later] by Legat Clark D. Anderson and [FBI agent] Richard S. Clark." Reads the report: "The stories of both were inclined to be rambling and it was difficult to pin them down on details. From comments made during the course of the interview by Mrs. Paz, it was obvious that she was rather familiar with at least some of the details of the Warren Commission Report, particularly those concerning Oswald's activities while in Mexico City." Anderson and Clark offered no information on what Warren Commission details Garro was familiar with. Additionally, according to other FBI documents, only Anderson spoke Spanish and neither man was familiar with the culture of Mexico. Further, their report made no mention of any Government translator or assistant, male or female, being present for the interview.

The FBI interview report [of which no transcript or tape recording exists] continues:

> Mrs. Paz and her daughter readily identified photographs of the the members of the DURAN family and of EUSEBIO AZCUE. Photographs of OSWALD in different poses were exhibited to them along with photographs of several individuals completely unconnected with the OSWALD case. While they picked

out some of the photographs of OSWALD as resembling the American they saw at the party in the RUBEN DURAN home, they did not make a positive identification and it is to be noted it would have been quite easy to pick out the OSWALD photographs because of the numerous press photographs of him which appeared in Mexico City newspapers following the President's assassination.

Mrs. Paz and her daughter appeared to be somewhat Bohemian [sic]. Mrs. Paz, herself, while denying she was ever a Communist, stated that in former years she had taken an active part in promoting agrarian reform in the State of Morelos in order that poor peasants might be granted land. She mentioned the names of numerous Mexican liberals and leftists with whom she has been acquainted in the past.

As has been mentioned, Mrs. PAZ'S conversation during the interview was quite rambling and *the impression was gained by the interviewing agents that she might not be completely stable. Despite her request that her identity and that of her daughter be concealed, their names have been included in the letterhead memorandum since it is felt the memorandum would have no meaning if this were not done.* [Emphasis added.]

As noted above, the above quoted FBI cover memorandum was attached to a more detailed FBI LHM issued by Bureau agents in Mexico City. That letterhead memorandum provided a few more details about the interview with Elena Garro and her daughter on December 11, 1964. These details are as follows:

"According to Mrs. PAZ, she had infrequent contact with her cousins, the DURANS; however, on a date she fixed as Saturday, September 28, 1963, she received a telephone call from RUBEN DURAN, who invited her and her daughter to attend a party at his house during the first part of the following week. She was unable to fix the exact date of this party, but felt it had been held on Monday, Tuesday, or Wednesday, September 30, October 1, or October 2, 1963, respectively, with the most likely possibility that it was held on the evening of October 1 or October 2, 1963.

"Elena Garro estimated that some thirty people attended the party, described as a 'twist' party, at the home of Ruben Duran.... At about 10:30 P.M. three young, white Americans arrived at the party. They were greeted by SILVIA DURAN and spoke only to her. They more or less isolated themselves from the rest of the party and insofar as she [Garro] observed they had no conversation with anyone else at the party.

"The three Americans appeared to be between twenty-two and twenty-four years of age. One of them was dressed in a sweater and dark trousers and appeared to be about five feet nine inches in height. The second one was about six feet tall, had blond, straight hair, a long chin, and was a bit 'beatnik' in appearance although his dress included a coat. The third American wore no coat.

"Mrs. PAZ said the American dressed in the sweater and dark trousers resembled very much press photographs of LEE HARVEY OSWALD. Her daughter agreed with this observation. Photographs of OSWALD in various poses were exhibited to both Mrs. PAZ and her daughter at the time of the interview and they were unable to make a positive identification, but claimed he very much resembled the American at the party as they recall him.

"Mrs. PAZ could not state how long the three Americans remained at the party nor did she observe them when they departed. She questioned HORACIO DURAN as to the names of the Americans, and he told her they were friends of SILVIA DURAN. He did not give her their names, but did tell her they were supposed to depart Mexico City the following morning. She added that this latter was not correct inasmuch as she and her daughter, while driving in an automobile on Insurgentes Street the following morning, observed the three Americans walking near a furniture store on that street."

Sylvia Duran

Here the FBI report on the interview states: *"It is to be noted that investigation has established that LEE HARVEY OSWALD departed Mexico City by bus at 8:30 A.M. on October 2, 1963, and could not have been identical with the American allegedly observed by Mrs. PAZ at the party if this party were held on the evening of October 1 or October 2, 1963."* (As it turns out, there is credible evidence that Oswald departed Mexico by automobile, although nobody has a clue who provided him the automobile or if anyone accompanied him back to Texas.)

The FBI report provides no explanation as to why Oswald could not have attended a party on the evening of October 1, 1963, since he clearly was in Mexico City on that day and evening and there exists no other reported eyewitness account as to where Oswald was that evening. Was this a typographical error or was the FBI simply overly anxious to discount the Garro sighting?

The FBI report goes on and states, "Mrs. PAZ was questioned regarding the identity of other persons attending the party at the RUBEN DURAN home who might have been in a position to observe the three Americans. She said that in the course of the party her daughter met a young man named 'ALEJANDRO' at the party and danced with him. He was supposedly quite smitten with the daughter and tried to call her on several occasions after the party. The daughter did not take the calls and as a result 'ALEJANDRO' wrote several letters to the daughter. Mrs. PAZ exhibited two of these letters, as well as a business card with identified the young man as ARIO ALEJANDRO LAVAGNINI STENIUS."

The FBI report goes on to make a point that one of Alejando's letters to Garro's daughter was postmarked September 2, 1963, and that FBI agents had interviewed him on November 27, 1964, at which time Alejandro, an employee of General Electric de Mexico, told agents he "recalled attending a large party sometime in the latter half of 1963 at the apartment of RUBEN DURAN." He told interviewing Bureau agents "he was not a friend of the DURAN family, but had been invited to the party by Mrs. ISABEL NANSON, a divorcee who was formerly married to an American and a close friend of the wife of RUBEN DURAN. An Italian friend of his, MARCELLO FABRE, was also invited to the party by Mrs. NANSON. He, Mrs. NANSON, and FABRE went to the party together."

Alejandro Lavagnini told FBI agents he "was unable to fix the date of the party" and that he "noted no Americans present at the party." Reads the report: "He volunteered to consult his papers and attempt to fix the date of the party. On December 2, 1964, he advised that he recalled having been at two different parties at the DURAN home, one of these being the large party at which he had met the Mexican girl who had formerly lived in France [Elena Garro's daughter]. He was unable to fix the date of this party." The report's last sentence reads: "LAVAGNINI said he had questioned Mrs. NANSON and MARCELLO FABRE, and they were unable to recall the date of the party nor could they recall that any Americans had been present at the party."

370

Apparently, the FBI never choose to interview Nanson or Fabre, nor did Bureau agents ever inquire what Mrs. Nanson's relationship was with Sylvia Duran. Over the past twenty-five years there have been steady reports that Isabel Nanson was not only a friend of Sylvia Duran but also a friend to CIA Station Chief Winston Scott and his second wife.

Elena Garro Takes Her Story to Her Grave

Elena Garro passed away at the age of 82 in August 1998 at the Cuernavaca Hospital, south of Mexico City. Garro's lengthy *New York Times* obituary (which incorrectly stated her age as 78) extensively noted her significant contributions to Latin American literature and her high "level of recognition and importance usually barred to women."

Garro's obituary also added a few significant facts about her life overlooked in Charles Thomas' biographical sketch of her for the CIA: "Soon after marrying [Octavio Paz in 1937] she and Mr. Paz moved from Mexico City to Spain to write about the Spanish Civil War. They lived in Paris after World War II and became part of the literary group that included the Argentine poet Jorge Luis Borges and the surrealist Andre Breton. Later they lived in Japan before returning to Mexico. Their marriage dissolved in the early 1960s and they never spoke to each other again. In the late 1960s, Mexico, like many other countries, was immersed in protest and rebellion. The Mexican student movement had been fired in part by the country's intellectual elite. But Ms. Garro turned her back on the movement, at one point calling it a 'crazy adventure.' Her remarks stirred open hostility and brought about an almost complete break with Mexico's literary community. She moved to New York, and later to Paris, remaining in exile for 23 years before returning to Mexico in November 1991."

Garro's *Times* obituary makes no mention whatsoever of her 1963 encounter with Lee Harvey Oswald and his companions or of her subsequent experience with the CIA. Indeed, by all accounts of those who knew Elena Garro well, she had no desire to remember anything to do with Lee Harvey Oswald or the CIA. She told close friends that she felt that she and her daughter had been treated "shabbily" by the CIA and FBI, that she had been treated like a woman who had no clue what she was talking about or what she had witnessed. Garro, according to one friend, was especially incensed to learn years later, when she read FBI and CIA documents, that she had been referred to as a "housewife" by both American agencies. That it was a time (the 1960s) when women were easily dismissed as being "crazy" or "hysterics" – and CIA officials, like Winston Scott, without any rational reason, were expert in practicing such slanderous dismissals – simply did not sit well with Garro. (One can only wonder what would have occurred in the story of JFK's murder had a Latin American male, or any male for that matter, made the initial report about Oswald that Garro did. Sadly, women whistle-blowers are often still treated the same way today by the American Government.)

Dr. Rhina Toruno-Haensly, a professor and graduate head of Spanish at the University of Texas, was one of the last people who spent time with Elena Garro shortly before Garro's death. Dr. Toruno-Haensly, in 2011, published an insightful book on Elena Garro's life, *Encounter with Memory*. In her book, Dr. Toruno-Haensly only briefly mentions what she terms Garro's "incident of international magnitude," when Elena and her daughter "attended a party organized by her cousin Rafael Duran and his wife, who was secretary at the Cuban Embassy in Mexico [with whom Lee Harvey Oswald also met]."

Dr. Toruno-Haensly in the same section of her book reveals that, before returning to Mexico "from abroad" (as described by Charles Thomas' December 10, 1965 report) Elena Garro in 1959 "was forced to abandon Mexico by a mandate from the president of the Republic of Mexico." Garro had spent the years 1953-1959 writing about the plight of Mexico's large poor and landless population and had strongly supported their efforts for agrarian reform and having their land, seized by large landowners and agricultural interests, given back to them.

According to Garro's own words, supported by numerous historical accounts, as well as CIA documents that reveal the Agency was backing large landowners and corporate interests, "Once the peasants from Ahuatepac, from the state of Morelos, became aware that I wrote for the newspapers about the ownership of the land controlled by a few landowners, while the majority was not able to own anything, they asked me to represent and defend them at the tribunal courts. Well, I made a lot of noise, to a point that the president of the republic (Adolph Lopez Mateos, 1958-1964) asked Octavio to send me out of the country because I created too much noise, and he wanted me to abandon the problems created by the Agrarian Reform (that happened in 1959)."

Dr. Toruno-Haensly's book then goes on and briefly mentions the Oswald incident as such:

Elena did not have anything to do with [Oswald's] presence at the party, but in December 1965, Garro related the incident to her friend (Charles William Thomas), who was an attaché at the U.S. Embassy in Mexico, without knowing that he worked for the intelligence services. Such a statement is found in seven documents classified as secret and declassified in 1978, published in the Appendices, Volume III, of the House of Representatives Investigation. The majority of the documents were written in 1965 and were CLASSIFIED, Grade 3, subject to be declassified in 36 years.

When they were declassified in the second investigation of Kennedy's assassination, the State Department deleted some lines, and reserved [censored] a few complete paragraphs that could "jeopardize the relationship between the United States and Latin America, or reveal confidential sources or methods, which are part of the operation of our Embassy in Mexico," the State Department explained in its letter. The CIA declined to open to the public the archives about Garro, although it allowed some documents to be reviewed by the Congressional Investigators (C. Puig, Proceso, 803, 23 March 1992). As the title of the article reads, in the Sixties, the objective of the American Embassy in Mexico was to monitor the intellectual life of Mexico, and Elena Garro already was a public and political figure. Her biography, written by her so-called friend Charles William Thomas, became part of the CIA's documents. In that biography, Garro was portrayed as "an active participant in the Confederacion Nacional de Campesinos (CNC) [National Confederation of Peasants], it also informs that in 1965 Elena Garro paid a hotel in the city, for charges incurred by one hundred peasants who were in the city to resolve problems.

The experience from the interviews at the American Embassy, along with the "expulsion from the country" just because she defended the agrarian reform, adding to this the Tlatelolco massacre, permeated Elena Garro's personality, who became "hunted" after 1968.

Not long before she passed away, Elena Garro said, "We told the truth about the man Oswald. He was there at the party. We told the truth because we thought it right. There were people who did not want the truth known. But we told the truth."

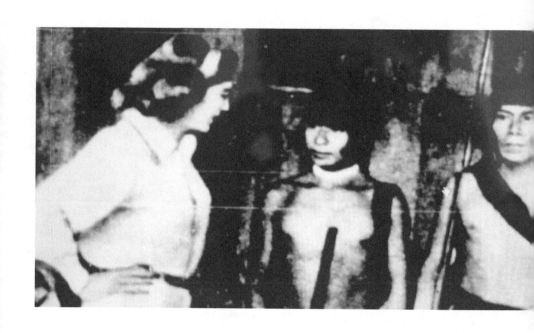

Chapter Eleven

Femme Fatale Enigma:
Viola June Cobb

I feel a basic distrust for everything mechanical and mathematical, you know.

—June Cobb, 1960

Most people knowledgeable about the assassination of President Kennedy know nothing about June Cobb. Even most serious assassination researchers are unaware of June Cobb's role in the annals of Kennedy's murder. June Cobb's story is at once fascinating and incredibly revealing of the ways the United States intelligence community works. Cobb's story is also a remarkably serendipitous tale of an iconoclastic woman whose life just happened to intersect the lives of numerous minor and major players in the assassination in highly unusual, strange, and poorly understood ways. This, most significantly, includes Lee Harvey Oswald. This chapter seeks to shine a light on Cobb's long overlooked role.

MAY 24, 1960 – 9:20 P.M. – HAVANA, CUBA.

Harry Hermsdorf was impressed with the woman sitting across from him. She was very attractive, tall with the slender figure of a film star, long blond hair, sparkling blue eyes, and classic features, marred only by a small scar on her forehead. He knew that she was thirty-three years of age, that she shared Hermsdorf's refined tastes for fine food and wine and had traveled the world extensively. She was well read and spoke several languages, yet there was an edge to her demeanor that made her allure appear deliciously dangerous and forbidden. People who knew June Cobb well spoke of her sultry mannerisms, her husky Lauren Bacall-type voice, and demure sex appeal that could quickly melt into troubling vulnerability or hard, brooding anger. In New York City, where she had lived before coming to Cuba to work for Fidel Castro, she had frequented many of the same jazz clubs and restaurants that Hermsdorf favored. Harry, often referred to as a "bon vivant" by those who knew him well, enjoyed meeting someone whose tastes were similar to his.

Hermsdorf, a tall and robust former OSS officer and now seasoned CIA official, had made his distinctive mark on the OSS – and a real name for himself – when he had become involved in assisting Fritz Kolbe, a turncoat Nazi who had smuggled thousands of secret Third Reich documents to American intelligence officials in Switzerland. Allen Dulles, who was Kolbe's handler, called the risks Kolbe took "incalculable." Following the war, Hermsdorf became a close friend to Kolbe and helped the former spy secure employment with a private company in the United Sates.

Hermsdorf, who was also very close to CIA director Allen Dulles, having served with him in Berne, Switzerland during the Second World War, considered himself an excellent judge of character. Based on all of his pre-meeting advance work, he felt strongly that the blond-haired woman sitting across from him could be a major asset to the CIA.

The woman, whose full name was Viola June Cobb, also shared several friends with Hermsdorf, including at least four Federal Bureau of Narcotics agents, three of whom also worked covertly for the CIA. Years earlier, Cobb had acted as a confidential informant to former OSS officials and now narcotic agents George Hunter White, Charles Siragusa, Garland Williams, and later to FBN branch supervisor George Gaffney.

In 1952, as noted before, George White and Charles Siragusa were central players in establishing the CIA's Greenwich Village safe house where surreptitious drug experiments were conducted under the auspices of the Agency's infamous MK/ULTRA program. Experiments with LSD and other mind-expanding drugs were conducted on unsuspecting and unwitting underworld figures, confidential informers, as well as politicians, prostitutes and other targeted individuals. The Greenwich Village safe house was closed down a few months after Dr. Frank Olson's November 1953 murder, and a new safe house was established in San Francisco, but not before Cobb began occasionally socializing with George White and his wife Albertine.

In the years immediately following the JFK assassination, the CIA conducted a thorough review of Cobb's extensive Agency file (estimated at over 2,500 pages) and quickly moved to mark "secret" all of the documents within it that related to her work with the Federal Bureau of Narcotics, but from a few remaining documents found elsewhere and in two CIA Office of Security interviews with Cobb, we are able to reconstruct the genesis of that relationship and some of its highlights.

June Cobb's long-term relationship with the Federal Bureau of Narcotics began in early 1952, about four years after she had fallen hopelessly in love with Rafael Herran Olozaga, a young man from an elite, wealthy and politically prominent Colombian family. Rafael's great grandfather, Pedro Alcantara Herran, and great-great grandfather, Tomas Cipriano de Mosquera, had both served as Presidents of Colombia during the nineteenth century.

In 1948, 20-year-old June Cobb had traveled to Colombia with then-fiancé Rafael and his twin brother Tomas. The two young men had grandiose plans for a base in Colombia from which to cultivate, process and traffic in opium. Said June a decade later: "They were two boys looking for adventure, but they had no idea about the dark world they were seeking to enter. They trusted people far too easily. I was young, naïve in some ways, and blindly in love, but I wasn't innocent to what was going on."

In late December 1956, the twins Rafael and Tomas were arrested in Havana for possession and distribution of a large shipment of heroin. The arrest was carried out by Cuban law enforcement authorities assisted by agents of the United States Federal Bureau of Narcotics from the Bureau's New York City branch office. June would recount four years later that her fiancé and his brother were apprehended 24-hours after she had conveniently departed Cuba for Coral Gables, Florida "to visit a girl friend." June had traveled to Havana with the Herran twins to help them unload several ounces of cocaine, as well as several grams of heroin. Cobb explained that when the three of them, along with several people working with them, arrived in Cuba, Rafael and Tomas "discovered the realities of life": that at the time, there was no extensive or lucrative market for heroin in Cuba.

Following their 1956 arrest, the Herran twins were quickly released due to their family's diplomatic, political and business connections. They were again arrested in February 1957 in Medellin, Colombia for operating a clandestine cocaine laboratory on the edge of their parent's palatial estate. This second arrest came as a result of a joint law enforcement operation mounted by the Colombian Intelligence Service and the U.S. Federal Bureau of Narcotics, led by Bureau agent George Gaffney.

Decades later, Gaffney told writer Douglas Valentine that the raid originated "in New Orleans when a woman with CIA connections offered information to [Narcotics] agent Arthur Doll." Gaffney did not provide the woman's name to tenacious researcher Valentine, but it was June Cobb. Agent Doll would even later guardedly tell this writer that the woman, whom he refused to identify, had "very strong ties to the CIA." How did Doll know this? "Because," he said, "agents [George] White and [Garland] Williams had dealt with her in Cuba months earlier." In 1960, during Cobb's first CIA interrogation for full-time employment, she said: "I visited the Federal Narcotics Bureau in New Orleans, and I told them about my ex-fiancé's laboratory."

The details and extent of what Cobb told FBN agent Doll, and eventually other agents, is still largely classified, but we are able to extract a few names from Narcotics Bureau files cited in FBI files related to the JFK assassination. Chief among these names are ones quite familiar to assassination researchers: Santo Trafficante, Jr.; Carlos Marcello; Jack Ruby; and Sam Giancana; and a few not so familiar names, like John Roland Jones (sometimes identified in FBI documents as "John Paul Jones"); Morris Melton; Lewis McWillie; and Ronald Dante, better known as Dr. Dante, a hypnotist, stage magician and frequent visitor to Mexico City and Cuba, who, in 1969, married actress Lana Turner, his seventh wife and her eighth husband. [See Notes for this chapter for more on Dante's amazing story.] Also rubbing an occasional elbow with June Cobb and her fiancé was a former U.S. Marine Corps veteran named Henry Saavedra, who worked for Trafficante at his Capri Casino in Havana and who was known to have associated with Sylvia Duran, who worked at the Cuban Embassy in Mexico City. Saavedra also sometimes worked with John Roland Jones, who in tandem with Maurice Melton, a Chicago-based trafficker, and Jack Ruby, occasionally smuggled a load of opium from Mexico to Dallas, Houston, and Chicago.

In her rambling and sometimes near incoherent responses to her 1960 interrogation by the CIA, Cobb described the early drug activities of the Herran brothers:

At any rate, from 1948, when we went into the jungle …[Rafael] and his brother wanted to plant opium…. Anyway, they wanted to plant opium in a certain part of the jungle that's in the… that's a river basin in Ecuador. Well, it was completely far-fetched. They are not practical boys. They're the type of blue-blooded Spaniard that belongs to 300 years ago, you know. So it was completely impractical in the first place. And they were from a highly respected family and their mother is a very re-vered woman, and so forth. At any rate, they tried to plant in the jungle; it didn't work. It was a perfectly crazy idea.

And then they came out and tried to prepare to plant opium in Columbia in the mountains … work still on the preparation for a plantation and during a terrible period in Columbia while it was involved in political persecution. They discovered by ac-cident, for numerous reasons coca leaves would produce there. So it was like taking three or four boats to New Castle, so they switched and decided it would make more sense to buy the coca leaves then cut them. So they began and for seven years they never made a dime, you know, because this is work for – ev-erything is work for a professional, you know. I never saw such confusion to get involved in … I mean if they're not involved in underground work…. They were not the type, you know. You should be born in the Lower East Side if you want to be pos-sessed of narcotics. You should not be born in … and anyway, it's no joke, really.

But they didn't make any money and they kept borrowing money from their mother, seeking more and more money all the time and didn't get a damn thing. So they had a laboratory in the Middle East and, as a matter of fact, one of the brothers [Tomas] had to work as a pilot … for enough salary to support the labora-tory … because they were always being deceived by the under-world, you know. They would deliver a kilo of cocaine and the un-derworld would just say, you know, we don't decide to pay. What are they going to do, you know. Well anyway, they were cross but, it became an obsession practically with Rafael…. And Rafael can't speak English so he couldn't speak to them himself. So he didn't know, you know, he had no reason to react to anything.

So anyway – in fact, their mother got involved, and they owed their mother a lot of money. They thought the only way they would ever be able to pay her back would be ... so 1949, this time they were always just producing cocaine and taking it up [to Cuba].... They were once or twice deceived by the underworld, but the customers they had that paid were doctors in Havana. However, the money they received from ... and cocaine, they simply reinvested it back into the business, you know, to try to improve their facilities, whether it was transportation or whatever, you know, it was still needed on a big scale, you know. So, they did sell a few shipments but they certainly didn't produce money. Well, as I said, they sold it to doctors in Havana."

The story of the Herran brothers' excursion into drug trafficking and other illicit enterprises is one near completely forgotten. While there can be no doubt that June Cobb was knowingly complicit in the drug trafficking operations of the Herran brothers, there is considerable information left out of her supposed frank and honest confession to the Narcotics Bureau. For example, what was June Cobb doing in New Orleans in 1960?

The second trafficking case brought against the Herran brothers in 1957 was also quickly quashed through their family's extensive diplomatic connections, but not before federal narcotics investigators tripped over several additional ties between the twins' dealings and other traffickers in Cuba and the United States. Some of these traffickers were strongly tied to the Florida-based criminal operations of Santo Trafficante Jr., Chicago-based Sam Giancana, and New Orleans Mafia Chief, Carlos Marcello. Said former FBN agent Arthur Doll: "The Herran brothers, despite all their visions of becoming drug kingpins, were essentially pampered rich boys who didn't have the guts or know-how to maneuver around or deal with guys like Marcello in New Orleans. They were over their heads, way over their heads ... they were lucky to have this woman [Cobb] with them to bestow some sanity to the situation, but the elements around them [the brothers], different story all together."

On at least two of her trips in the mid-1950s to Cuba with the Herran brothers, she and the twins encountered representatives of notorious Corsican drug trafficker Paul Damien Mondolini, including New York-based trafficker Milton Abramson. (Cobb, while in Mexico in 1965-66, helped set up Abramson and a few others, including Adela Castillo, for arrest stateside by the FBI.) Mondolini, for at least nine years, dominated trafficking in Havana, but primarily used the island as a transport stepping-stone to the United States. Especially interesting to underscore here is the connection between Adela Castillo and a man named Jesse Gregory, who reported having met a man in Mexico City in September 1963 who he thought may have been Lee Harvey Oswald. [See Notes for this chapter for Gregory's account, as investigated by the FBI in 1963.]

Sitting across from Harry Hermsdorf in Havana, June Cobb was a long way from home. Cobb, who never used the name Viola, had been born in 1927 in Ponca City, Oklahoma, a small oil town near the Kansas border. After graduating from high school and attending the University of Oklahoma for one year, during which she barely attended classes, she worked in Ponca City at a radio station and then as a courthouse reporter for a local newspaper.

In 1947, irrepressibly bored with life in Oklahoma, June struck out for Latin America and Mexico. In Mexico City, she enrolled in classes at the University of Mexico, but attended few after she began spending most of her time with love interest Rafael Herran Olozaga. Cobb later said, "Rafael was irresistible. Confident, curious, adventurous, intelligent and fiercely loyal, he was everything I had dreamed of in a man. I was hopelessly smitten from the start.... It took months for reality to cloud in."

By 1949, June Cobb and the Herran twins were deep in the jungle of Ecuador where they were conducting their cocaine business in earnest. In 1951, Cobb was forced to return to the United States, having contracted a rare tropical blood disorder that caused her to be hospitalized for several months at Mount Sinai Hospital in New York City. Following her recovery, June was employed by the hospital for about five months as an administrative assistant, and then she went to work for *Time* magazine in the letters department in the summer of 1952. In March 1953, Cobb traveled to Chicago where she was employed by Cook County Hospital as a secretary to the director of medical education, the same physician she had worked for in New York.

In late 1953, Cobb moved back to New York City, working as a translator and interpreter for clients referred to her by "a good friend" named Warren Broglie. A gregarious, multi-lingual Swiss-national, Broglie was the manager of the Waldorf Astoria hotel. He also served undercover as an asset and confidential informer to the FBI, FBN, and CIA. Over a twenty-year period, beginning in mid-1952, Broglie, as revealed in one long and once deeply buried CIA file, is identified as a "most reliable asset whose loyalties are unquestioned." That he ostensibly worked under the cover of being a widely respected "hotelier," or hotel manager, is well established through diligently researching the history of a number of the world's most glamorous and expensive international hotels, where Broglie could be almost exclusively found.

In late-1955, after departing New York City, the CIA assisted Broglie in his hiring as the general manager of the Nile Hilton in Cairo, Egypt. Like CIA director Dulles, Broglie was close to Hilton International owner, Conrad Hilton, and his assignment to Egypt put him in a key position. Egyptian president Nasser had just nationalized the Suez Canal provoking England, France, and Israel to join forces to invade Egypt in order to regain control of the canal. Naturally, the CIA was most concerned with the success of the invasion.

How Broglie was first introduced to the world of intelligence work is unknown, but there is evidence that he came into contact with OSS official Allen Dulles sometime during the Second World War in Basle, Switzerland. Additionally, both men, as well as Conrad Hilton, and several other high ranking CIA officials, were directors in the Knights of Malta, a long-standing Roman Catholic lay order founded at the time of the Crusades, that today counts among its members some of the richest and most influential men in the world, including many former and current high-ranking CIA officials. (Warren Broglie first appeared publicly in Kennedy assassination-related literature as a minor, yet intriguingly mysterious, figure in the JFK assassination story when author Dick Russell mentioned Broglie in his masterful book, *The Man Who Knew Too Much*.)

In 1960, when June Cobb filled out a background form for the CIA's Western Hemisphere Division, she listed Broglie on an addendum sheet as an associate. His name was misspelled "BROGLEY," and he was thus described: "BROGLEY, Warren: head of the Foreign Department ; Swiss; office at the Waldorf. Former manager of Hilton Hotel in Mexico City; more recently manager of the Hilton Nile in Cairo." Within a few weeks, Broglie would be consulted in the process of Cobb's being cleared by CIA security officers.

As we shall learn, Broglie would play a strong role in June Cobb's work in Mexico City in 1963 and beyond, where under the supervision of CIA official David Atlee Phillips, she served as a CIA asset for the CIA Station there, often feeding information to Station chief Winston Scott passed on to her by Broglie, who at the time was manager of Mexico City's Hotel Luma. Winston Scott by all accounts was well-acquainted with Broglie, and Scott frequently employed the facilities at the Hotel Luma for both personal and Agency functions. Here it in interesting to consider that June Cobb briefly mentioned Broglie's name in 1962 when she testified before a U.S. Senate subcommittee. [See Notes for more on Hotel Luma.]

June Cobb Testifies Before Senate Subcommittee

In mid-March 1962, June Cobb – following her formally being hired by the CIA and then being assigned to Mexico City – was requested to appear before an executive session of the U.S. Senate Subcommittee to Investigate the Administration of the Internal Security Act and Other Internal Security Laws. Cobb appeared before the subcommittee on the morning of March 30, 1962. The subcommittee apparently had no knowledge that Cobb was working for the CIA at the time of her appearance, nor did Cobb reveal anything about her dealings with the Agency. It is also interesting to note how Cobb explained her days in Colombia and brushed over the time she spent there and elsewhere in Latin America. Below follows selected sections of her testimony:

> **Mr. A.G. Sourwine** [chief counsel for the Subcommittee]: You were in South America?
> **Miss Cobb:** I was in the jungle in Ecuador. I went with a fiancé of mine on an expedition. I was there for about six months. I was in the jungle. Six months following that I was in Colombia, a kind of abandoned region of Colombia. Also not employed. That brings me up to 1950, 1950 I returned to Oklahoma, where I was also not employed. I spent about ten months with

my father. I might have been employed for a few weeks temporarily with the Continental Oil Co. or something like that, but in general, not. I returned to Colombia in 1951, the winter of 1951. I became very ill with a tropical fever, and spent the best part of the next year in the hospital. Which brings me up to 1953. In 1952, I was employed at Mount Sinai Hospital in New York City.

Senator [John] McClellan: In New York City?

Miss Cobb: Yes, as secretary to the director of medical education, who had just cured me of the tropical fever I had had.

Senator Dodd: Where were you hospitalized with the tropical fever?

Miss Cobb: First in Colombia, then in Mount Sinai, in New York City. After that I worked at Mount Sinai Hospital for some several months. I was employed by *Time*, in the letters department, briefly, in the summer of 1952.

I was, early in 1953 and the end of 1952, I was employed at Cook County Hospital in Chicago, also as secretary to the director of medical education, who had transferred from Mount Sinai to Cook County Hospital in Chicago.

In 1953, later in the year, I was back in New York City, where I did some translating, interpreting, minor public relations, for clients recommended by the manager of the foreign department of the Waldorf Astoria, Mr. Warren Broglie. He is no longer there. He is manager of a hotel in Mexico City now. [Emphasis added.]

The end of 1953, I was employed briefly by a construction company. I can't think of the name, but a construction company that was building a refinery in Colombia. It is one of the largest construction companies. I can't think of the name of it. Foster Wheeler. I think it is Foster Wheeler. That was the end of 1953. In 1954, I again did some – back in New York City, the same kind of work, through the Waldorf Astoria, and other clients, but temporary, very temporary. In 1955, I was traveling in Latin America, not working.

In 1956, I was in Colombia, where the only paid employment that I had was for the Colombian-American Culture Foundation, Centro Colombo-Americano, which operates through the State Department, in Medellin, Columbia, and the American school, where I taught very briefly.

In 1957, I was in Oklahoma, with my father. I was employed by the county seat of Kay County, in Oklahoma, was secretary to the county attorney, briefly, a few months, while I was there.

In New York City, I was later that same year, I was employed by RCA Victor distributor ... as secretary to the sales manager, also for a matter of a couple of months. I did some temporary secretarial translating work that year. I was then employed by MD Medical News magazine as secretary to the managing editor, or editorial assistant, I am not sure of the title. The magazine is in New York City – for part of 1957 and part of 1958.

In 1959, I was employed in some editing with the same doctor for whom I had worked a few years before, editing of medical textbooks.

In the spring of 1959, I went to Havana, on the invitation of the Prime Minister, Fidel Castro, and his private secretary, Celia Sanchez, where I was in charge of English publications of the Prime Minister's office on behalf of the revolutionary government. This invitation was a result of voluntary activities in New York City, early in 1959, where I published an edition of Fidel Castro's defense plea after the Moncada attack, and certain other activities with the 26th of July.

Incidentally, this publication has been reprinted in private editions since that time, and one of them, the most recent, to my knowledge, was brought out by Lyle Stuart on behalf of the Fair Play for Cuba Committee a few months ago, a year ago, as a matter of fact, advertising another of his books.

In 1959, I was employed in Havana, most of 1960, about. I returned to the United States in October of 1960 on a leave of absence I had declared for myself, and I simply did not return.

Since the fall of 1960, I have had no formal employment. I have had income from writing, teaching, and certain limited income from "The Shark and the Sardines." [Emphasis added.]

Mr. Sourwine: When did you meet Celia Sanchez?

Miss Cobb: April 1959.

Mr. Sourwine: In New York City?

Miss Cobb: In New York City, where I was introduced to her, as also to Fidel Castro ...

Mr. Sourwine: Had you met him before that time?

Miss Cobb: ... by Luis Conte Aguero, well known leader of the Cuban counterrevolution at the present time.

Mr. Sourwine: Had you met Fidel Castro before that time?

Miss Cobb: No, I had not.

Mr. Sourwine: You had joined the 26th of July movement earlier?

Miss Cobb: No, I think I finally did join it, but after I was in Havana.

Mr. Sourwine: You had worked with the 26th of July movement?

Miss Cobb: No, excuse me. I will explain. In February of 1959, I had made a very brief visit to Havana out of curiosity, to see if the advertised changes there were taking place – in other words, the changes in vice and so forth. I spoke with the Minister of Health, Fidel Castro's Minister of Health at that time, about cooperation between the revolutionary government and certain Peruvian, Bolivian, and Colombian doctors who were interested in combating the use of coca leaves, and, therefore, the use of cocaine, as part of their declared campaign against vice.

While I was there, in February of 1959, I was given a copy of Fidel Castro's famous defense plea. I was greatly impressed by it, and returned to the United States to translate and publish it, so that it might be available to the newspaper editors who had invited him [Castro] here for a conference in April 1959.... When Luis Conte Aguero, at the time, a close friend and counselor of Fidel Castro, learned, through a friend of mine, about the publication of this speech in English, he visited me in New York City, contributed to the cost of printing, and wrote a prolog, and introduced me to Fidel Castro.

Mr. Sourwine: Now, did you live in Cuba for a time during the Batista regime?

Miss Cobb: Actually, I didn't live there. I visited Cuba a few times.

Mr. Sourwine: You were helpful to one of the services of the U.S. Government during the latter period of the Batista regime in a certain matter, were you not?

Miss Cobb: Yes, I was.

Mr. Sourwine: Is there any reason why that couldn't be brought out in the record, as far as you know?

Miss Cobb: If it is pertinent, Mr. Sourwine. If it is not pertinent, I should prefer that it would not be.

Mr. Sourwine: *May we go off the record for a moment.* [Emphasis added.]
Senator Dodd: Yes.

[Discussion off the record.]

Senator Dodd: On the record.
Mr. Sourwine: You had, then, prior to the end of the Batista regime been of some assistance to the U.S. [Federal] Bureau of Narcotics?
Miss Cobb: Yes, that is right.
Mr. Sourwine: Now, do you have information respecting communists' connections with the narcotics trade or the narcotics racket in Cuba or elsewhere in Latin America?
Miss Cobb: Not at all, Mr. Sourwine. After all, during the Batista regime, the communists were not running the Government in Cuba, and the narcotics operations with which I might have had some – of which I might have had some knowledge in Latin America, also were in countries where there was certainly no influence of the Communist Party in the government. In other words, it was a dictatorship of Rojas Pinilla in Colombia, and in Ecuador I don't know who was the President, but certainly no communists or pro-communist regime.
Mr. Sourwine: You have no knowledge of any communist connections with the narcotics traffic in Latin America?
Miss Cobb: Only what I read in the newspapers.
Mr. Sourwine: For instance, there is a report in the newspapers this morning from Miami, with a UPI dateline, that FBI agents have seized half a million dollars worth of cocaine believed smuggled from Cuba. They got 4 1/2 pounds of cocaine and seized four men and one woman, all Cuban born. There have been similar news reports. You have no knowledge of anything of this sort going on in Cuba?
Miss Cobb: I only have read it in the newspapers, that is right.
Mr. Sourwine: You have never used any name other than your own, have you, Miss Cobb?
Miss Cobb: No ...
Mr. Sourwine: Do you know ...
Miss Cobb: Well, off hand I can't think that I ever have.

Prior to June Cobb's appearance before the Senate subcommittee on Internal Security, word of her pending Capitol Hill testimony understandably set off some alarm bells at CIA headquarters, as well as within the Agency's ever-expanding JM/WAVE covert operations station in Miami, Florida. Its ultra-secret Task Force W, or TFW, as it was commonly referred to, was the CIA's unit dedicated to Operation Mongoose, a lethal program to overthrow Castro's government.

Several top-secret CIA memoranda regarding concerns about Cobb's pending testimony culminated in a very telling March 29, 1962 memorandum that gave broad hints at what Cobb's activities were at the time. The document, simply titled "June Sharp Cobb (201-278,841)" (Cobb's 201 file designation) was written by Cobb's Agency handler Jean T. Pierson, identified in the document as an "intelligence researcher" for Task Force W.

Pierson leads off by stating that she had been telephoned by Jerry Droller, Chief, WH/POA [Western Hemisphere/Political Affairs Office; Droller's aliases were Frank Bender and Don Federico] to inform her that June Cobb "was arriving in Washington to appear before the Senate Subcommittee on Internal Security, at their request." German-born Droller, a former OSS officer, had been a central organizer in the CIA's violent overthrow of Jacobo Arbenz in 1954 in Guatemala, and in 1960 and 1961 he oversaw the establishment of a network of paramilitary training camps for Cuban exiles and others in Florida, Panama, and Guatemala, where he first encountered June Cobb. Pierson continued and stated that Droller explained that, as far as he knew, Cobb was being asked to testify "on her connections with the Cuban Government and her knowledge of Juan Arevalo, former President of Guatemala and author of the book, *The Shark & The Sardines*, which Subject [Cobb] translated into English."

Continued Pierson: "Mr. Droller intends to contact Lt. Col. Albert Davies, C/TFW/INTEL, to request permission for the undersigned [Pierson] to contact [June Cobb] if this is deemed necessary and is in the best interests of the Agency." Pierson went on and explained that she had discussed the matter in detail with Droller, and as a result had reactivated "a sterile phone number formerly used by Cobb, "in the event she should attempt to contact Pierson." Pierson also stated that Droller had put her in touch with George Carey, CIA Legal Counsel, who, she wrote, "is interested in the case." Wrote Pierson: "Mr. Carey stated that had we been notified earlier of Cobb's invitation by the Subcommittee, it would have been possible to have had the appearance before the Subcommittee cancelled."

Pierson concluded her memorandum by writing: "Lt. Col. Davies has been informed of the above, and of the background of the case by me, and will in turn advise Mr. [William] Harvey, C/TFW, of the situation." Lt. Col. Albert C. Davies was a military officer assigned to Task Force W as its chief of intelligence. As some readers are aware, William K. Harvey was the director of Task Force W, and also the CIA's lead official of assassination matters, including its infamous QJ/WIN program.

Lt. Col. Davies and Harvey, assisted by David Sanchez Morales, at this same time were busy assembling alias and backstopping documentation for June Cobb, as well as a number of other Task Force W employees, including Anthony Sforza, Frank J. Belsito, and Rene E. Dubois, all men deeply enmeshed in the CIA's more unsavory operations. The fact that June Cobb was working closely with Sforza and others, well known for their skills in "wet affairs" or assassinations, is significant in terms of her duties in Mexico City, which have consistently been downplayed by some writers, as well as former CIA officials, as mostly administrative and cultural-liaison related tasks.

After returning to New York from Chicago, June enjoyed life in Manhattan. On occasion, she would socialize with Federal Narcotics agent and covert CIA contractor George White and his wife Albertine at their city apartment. The White's parties were notorious for their hijinks and gaiety. At least once, Warren Broglie was there for the fun. At least twice, June met George and Albertine White at the Bronx Zoo, where they strolled through the exhibits and then had lunch together. Might they have passed by a tough youth in a black leather jacket named Lee Harvey Oswald?

In 1955, June traveled back to Latin America where she rejoined her fiancé, Rafael. In early 1956, she briefly worked for the Colombian-American Culture Foundation, which operated through the U.S. State Department. In 1957, following the arrest of Rafael and Tomas in Cuba, June returned to the United States, staying with her father in Oklahoma for about eight months, sometimes traveling to Norman, Oklahoma to visit friends there. In 1959, she was back in New York City and was employed doing secretarial duties and some editing of medical textbooks for the same physician she had previously worked for at Mount Sinai Hospital and in Chicago. The physician was now back in New York doing research connected with the Rockefeller Foundation.

In the spring of 1959, June traveled to Havana, Cuba at the invitation of Fidel Castro and his private secretary Celia Sanchez. As Cobb would later explain in 1962 before a U.S. Senate subcommittee meeting in executive session to question her about her time in Cuba, as well as the Fair Play for Cuba Committee: "This invitation was a result of voluntary activities in New York City, early in 1959, where I published an edition of Fidel Castro's defense plan after the Moncada attack, and certain other activities with the 26th of July Movement." In Havana, June had been employed by the Castro regime from 1959 through most of 1960, at which point she requested a leave of absence and traveled back to the United States to meet with a man she knew as 'Heinrich Heubner.'

Harry Hermsdorf, traveling under a fake Austrian passport issued to "Heinrich Heubner," had briefly encountered Cobb a few weeks earlier while using the same CIA alias and meeting with Jorge Losada, editor of the Latin American magazine *Vision*. While having coffee with Losada in the Havana Hilton hotel coffee shop, Cobb had stopped to greet Losada, and the editor had introduced her to Harry – whom Losada also knew only as Heinrich Heubner, a visiting European journalist.

After a brief conversation that day, June offered to assist Heinrich by setting up appointments with various Cuban officials for both him and Claus Jacobi, a German correspondent for *Der Spiegel*. Harry Hermsdorf would later write, "We met again several times during my stay in Havana and I found her a woman with many contacts among leaders of the Revolutionary movement." It may be fair to say that Hermsdorf came away from his encounter with June Cobb a bit smitten by the young woman.

Before departing Cuba, Hermsdorf took June to dinner. Harry's chief purpose for sitting down with Cobb was "to evaluate whether or not her services could be useful to this Agency [CIA] and if so, steps are to be taken for her recruitment." Following additional meetings with Cobb over the next two days, Harry discretely inquired if Cobb could possibly "accept an invitation from me to come somewhere outside of Cuba" where he could discuss an employment opportunity with her. Cobb seized on the request and told Heinrich "the only place she would like to go would be New York City."

She told Harry, whom she still thought to be Heinrich Heubner, she "had a legitimate excuse for going there." Previously, she explained, she had undergone treatment at Mount Sinai hospital for what she said was "anemia." Harry responded that this would work fine and that he would make all the necessary arrangements and that June should inform Castro's secretary, Celia Sanchez, that she would be departing for New York City on June 3. Harry told her that once she landed in New York, she should proceed directly to her hotel, where he would meet with her that evening at 7:00 P.M.

"Contact absolutely nobody before that time," Harry instructed June.

In his subsequent report covering his May meetings with Cobb, Harry wrote: "I should add that in my dealings with Miss Cobb, it was obvious that she has had some conspiratorial experience by the way in which she handled my presence in her apartment and also by the manner in which she had me pay for her fare."

Harry also wrote: "At no time in my discussions with [Cobb] was CIA named or inferred." Harry stated he only "talked to her about her 'future' and coming to New York to discuss an employment possibility which would make use of her talents."

"What would I have to do?" June had asked.

"Well, some reporting and writing, and possibly some public relations activity," Harry had replied, deliberately being vague.

When June agreed, Harry handed her $180 cash to purchase her plane tickets. Days later, Harry would be informed by CIA Security Office officials that Cobb had only purchased a one-way ticket to New York and had used the remaining money to pay off some personal debts.

June Cobb arrived in New York City on June 3 and went by taxi to the Drake Hotel on Park Avenue, where Hermsdorf had made reservations for her. Over the following two days, June met several times with Harry. During these meetings Harry "gradually indoctrinated [Cobb] to the fact that my interests in her were of an intelligence nature."

Wrote Harry, in a report to CIA WH/4 Branch chief Jack Esterline, dated the same weekend: "CIA was never mentioned in our discussions, yet at one point she said she suspected I must be from CIA because no other government agency operates outside of the United States and her past experiences with the FBI was of a nature to indicate that they always ask her to visit them at their offices."

Hermsdorf remained determined to recruit Cobb as a paid Agency asset, but he had adopted a more cautious approach given the concerns of others within the WH/4 branch, especially Jean T. Pierson, who was slated to become Cobb's case officer when and if she was hired.

Wrote Harry in the same report: "While in New York discussing her [Cobb's] potential with her, it was obvious that her complex background, present activities, vast circle of friends and her unstable character would call for a more thorough debriefing."

Hermsdorf suggested that June travel with him to Washington, D.C. to "see and talk to a friend for a technical evaluation of her ability to act securely." June agreed.

On June 6, Harry Hermsdorf and June Cobb flew to the nation's capital, where June checked into the modest Hotel Blackstone at 1016 Seventeenth Street, NW, under the name "Annabelle Wilson." That evening, Cobb was taken to the stately Hotel Raleigh at Twelfth Street and Pennsylvania Avenue – a hotel frequently used by the CIA – specially outfitted by the Agency for surreptitious surveillance and technical evaluation. (See chapter on Adele Edisen.)

At the Raleigh Hotel, as previously arranged by Hermsdorf, June Cobb was interrogated and subjected to a lie detector session for over five hours. Unbeknownst to June, the room she was in was being electronically monitored and observed from an adjoining room, and her polygraph session was being recorded in its entirety. At the same time that Cobb was at the Hotel Raleigh, CIA Office of Security agents, under orders from Security Office official and future Watergate burglar, James McCord, were awaiting the go-ahead to perform a "surreptitious entry" and "black bag job" on her hotel room. However, this action was postponed because the Agency's primary contact at the hotel was not on duty that evening.

Cobb returned to New York City the following morning, June 7, and on to Havana that evening. Prior to her departure, Harry told her "that if she was sincere in wanting to aid and assist [the CIA] in obtaining factual information about current activities in Cuba, she would have to be completely honest and subject herself to some control." Harry informed June she would be given "a few targets to concentrate on until our next meeting as an attempt to evaluate her ability along these lines."

Harry specifically requested that June obtain and pass along to the Agency the "names and contacts of Soviet and satellite citizens" dealing with the Cuban government. In addition, Harry requested that June go to see "the Chief of *Prensa Latina*," whom Cobb knew well and to monitor his activities. He also instructed her "to find a ruse to see Kung Mai, head of the Free China News Agency" in Havana and to monitor his activities closely.

Lastly, June was asked to try to determine what Nunez Jimenez had accomplished on his recent visit to the Soviet Union, and to keep her eyes and ears open to all matters pertaining to Cuban relations with the Red Chinese and the Soviets, as well as local Communist Party activities with the Cuban government.

In his June memorandum, Hermsdorf made it clear that, despite lingering reservations, the decision had been made to employ June Cobb as a CIA asset. Stated Harry: "If Miss Cobb can be controlled and accepts steering, it would perhaps *be desirable to mould her into a long-range asset by having her become very cozy with the communist leaders and become, overtly, ever more 'rabid' about the revolutionary movement. Later she could perhaps be used elsewhere in Latin America, probably among the rabid left wing youth groups that are becoming increasingly anti-American and more powerful in various areas.*" [Emphasis added.]

Harry added that June would be paid 200 Cuban pesos a month plus approved expenses. Additionally, he stated, "Miss Cobb's next visit to New York has already been laid on by her physician friend who will request her to visit the city for 'treatment' before the doctor departs for Europe on an extended trip."

June Cobb's "physician friend" was Dr. Isidore Snapper. June had first met Snapper in 1951 when she had been hospitalized at Mount Sinai Hospital in New York, where Snapper was medical director. Snapper was born in the Netherlands in 1889 and earned his medical degree from the University of Amsterdam. In 1939, he moved to China where he was appointed Professor of Medicine at the Rockefeller Foundation-funded Peiping Union Medical College, whose staff, including Snapper, was held prisoner by the Japanese for several war-torn years. Snapper came to the United States in 1944 and soon became Medical Director of Mount Sinai Hospital, New York. In 1952, he journeyed to Chicago where he became Director of Medical Education at Cook County Hospital. The following year he returned to New York to become Director of Medicine and Medical Education at the Brooklyn VA Hospital. Dr. Snapper also served as a consultant to the U.S. Army Surgeon General.

Following June Cobb's June 7 interrogation and polygraph session in Washington, CIA Security Office officials made the determination, after thorough review of her interrogation transcript, "that there were many present and future Security ramifications involving [Cobb] and that as much investigation and research as possible would be done and plans would be made for [Agency interrogator Ralph True] to re-interview and interrogate [Cobb]." These additional interrogation and polygraph sessions were conducted on October 11 and 12, 1960 at a covert location in Boston, Massachusetts.

COBB'S INTERROGATION IN BOSTON

June Cobb, accompanied by her case officer, Jean Pierson, flew to Boston by air on October 10, arriving at 9:50 P.M. While Cobb and Pierson were on the same flights, they made a point of not sitting together or conversing in any way, according to CIA Security files. At Boston airport, Cobb and Pierson took separate taxis across Mystic River into the city, where both were dropped off at the Hotel Touraine, a favorite CIA haunt in Boston.

Oddly, despite the strict travel precautions, Cobb and Pierson shared a double room that had been secured on October 5 by the CIA's Boston Field Office at the direction of CIA official Paul T. Auden, acting at the direction of Agency security official Fred Bacci. Auden had instructed the Boston office to "register this room in the names of June Corwin and Joan Price, both of New York City." Auden also requested that the field office "obtain an adjoining room whereby you [are] to install KING coverage before October 9." KING coverage refers to surreptitious physical surveillance as well as recorded audio coverage.

The next day, Cobb and Pierson traveled separately by taxi to the Hotel Bellevue, where Ralph True interviewed and polygraphed Cobb that day and the next, October 11 and 12, 1960. Ralph True was CIA Acting Chief of the Agency's Interrogation Research Division. He worked out of CIA headquarters and also managed the operation of two Agency-owned proprietary companies, Anderson Security Associates on the East Coast, and General Personnel Investigations, Inc. on the West Coast. According to a June 23, 1972 FBI report related to the Watergate break-in, True planned on going to work for the private investigation firm, McCord Associates, owned by "former" CIA official James McCord. The day before the Watergate burglary True had met with McCord about going to work for McCord Associates on June 16, 1972, at the offices of the Committee for the Re-Election of President Nixon.

Ralph True's subsequent report on the two-day session (dated October 17, 1960), began by noting that June Cobb was extremely concerned "about what she felt was a break of security regarding herself." Cobb explained to True that a woman named Diana Alexandria, who lived at 120 East 72nd Street, New York City, had contacted her "sometime during the end of [last] September." Alexandria, who had been referred to Cobb by Marita Lorenz's family met with June several times socially, and during one of these encounters informed Cobb that she [Diana] was dating a "male friend" who "works for the CIA."

This male friend, identified by Cobb as Dick Daniels, had informed Diana that "June Cobb was a very questionable person in the eyes of CIA and that if Diana should have contact with [her] she should be very careful of her." Diana went on and told Cobb that Daniels "was apparently in love with her [Diana] and that an intimate relationship was in progress."

Cobb told Ralph True that she was concerned, upset, and angry to hear all of this and had immediately contacted her case officer, Jean Pierson, whom Cobb only knew as "Aunt Elizabeth" or "Joan Price." Two days after contacting Pierson, Cobb saw Diana, who appeared quite upset. Diana told June that she had received a telephone call form Dick Daniels who accused Diana of "blabbing too much because he had received a telephone call from Washington reading the riot act to him for having told Diana about June Cobb."

After recounting this, Cobb smugly informed Ralph True that as a result of this incident, she had, as True wrote in his report, "confirmed in her own mind that she [Cobb] is in touch with CIA."

True remained silent on this issue, and Cobb went on and said that she had assumed all along that "it was CIA that was in contact with her." Wrote True, "[Cobb], in essence, stated that to her way of thinking, this was very poor Security on the part of CIA and she was amazed that such an incident as this could happen."

Further along in his interrogation of Cobb, True was startled to hear her relate that Diana Alexandria had also been the former "girlfriend" of Capt. Yanez Pellitier and that Diana was "still very much in love with him."

Jesus Yanez Pellitier was a high-ranking Cuban rebel who was close to Fidel Castro.

> **True:** Was she a girlfriend or mistress? Was she intimate with him or what?
>
> **Cobb:** Yeah. Well, uh, serious girlfriend.
>
> **True:** June, before we go any further, I am going to have you … I brought up some things for you to read and I want you to sign something. We will get to this in just a minute and while you are on this, I will go ahead and let you tell me all about it. As you know, I represent security. I want to tell you before you start telling me anything that it is very important that you keep to facts. Now, I'm not insinuating that you are not giving facts. I am just advising you to keep the facts and details as precise as you can. I want to be sure that when I'm through talking with you and giving you this interview …
>
> **Cobb:** That you understand me correctly.
>
> **True:** Yes. I understand you and I want to know your motives. I want to know everything about you. I want to be sure that nobody can make accusations against you. We want to protect you. Now this may seem strange to you but this is the way Uncle Sam works. When he wants somebody to help him, he wants to be fair to them. This is one way we have to be … We have to be completely honest with each other. Now, I'll …
>
> **Cobb:** And by the way …
>
> **True:** Now what I want you to understand is this – that when I ask questions of you, stay in that area of the question that I ask.
>
> **Cobb:** I will, and also if it's hearsay, I'll tell you that it's hearsay rather than estimate on my own knowledge.
>
> **True:** If it's hearsay, I want names of people, I want descriptions, I want identity because under the last setup that you and I had, we were pressed for time. It was not the type of conditions that I like at all. Now I have plenty of time here.

Cobb: Well, this is complicated, because you know everyone that I mention, they are behind the tale, you know.

True: Well, you see, they draw a picture for us that they don't draw for you.... Well, I just want you to be sure in your own mind that this only connects with the petty details. I don't want you to evaluate things in your mind. When I ask you something, I want you to give me what you know about that – no assumptions unless I ask "Well, what do you think this situation is?" or "What is your opinion as a result of this?" So now, going back to Diana.

Cobb: I said girlfriend and you said which way.

True: You told me that she was the former girlfriend of whom now?

Cobb: Captain Yanez Pellitier.

True: Captain Yanez Pellitier. That's the one in prison?

Cobb: Yes.

True: Would you call her a mistress?

Cobb: Well, I don't call girls who have love affairs with men mistresses.

True: Well, no. They are two distinct things. Was she being kept by him?

Cobb: No. As far as I'm concerned, I don't think I have ever known anyone who was anybody's mistress. I don't move in those circles.

True: Now, she was the former girlfriend of Yanez Pellitier during what period?

Cobb: From about last May until August.

True: May of '59 until August? In Cuba?

Cobb: In Cuba.

True: Now, she is from where?

Cobb: Uh, Diana lives in New York City. Her parents live in San Diego.

True: Do you know what her parents do?

Cobb: Her father is in business.

True: Well, what kind of business? If you don't know, that is all right, but if you do …

Cobb: A store, a couple of stores.

True: He owns two stores. You don't know what type of stores they are?

Cobb: Well, she is Jewish.

True: Stasia told you that Diana …

Cobb: That Diana Alexandria and Lorenz Stanley … and the FBI, all three told her …

True: Now top Lorenz's name …

Cobb: That's the girl of the Confidential article. Do you remember?

True: Maria?

Cobb: Marita, and her mother.

True: All right, Diana and Lorenz Stanley and …

Cobb: The FBI.

True: The FBI. Now she knows this was the FBI?

Cobb: No. She said when she was over at 69th Street and 3rd Avenue – and that's the FBI – that she was there for questioning.

True: When did she go there?

Cobb: In February for the first time and then she went once again after that.

True: Was that Sasha?

Cobb: Her real name is Estelle Sokolowska, but she uses the name Stasia.

True: All right, Estelle visited the FBI at 69th and 3rd.

Cobb: Through the course of the questioning and that …

True: Wait a minute now. First in February of this year, and second, some time thereafter. All right.

Cobb: All three have told me the same stories – that I was involved in narcotics traffic with Yanez Pellitier down in Cuba through this winter and that I was using her as a recent part …

True: Using Stasia?

Cobb: Stasia. In other words, what had happened was that in January when Mrs. Lorenz began to threaten that she was going to give this story about her daughter to the newspapers if she didn't get three thousand dollars. By telephone, telegraph, and all kinds of ways she was sending this threat down in Cuba.

On a more serious note, Cobb recounted to True what Speller had told her about Allen Dulles.

CIA official Ralph True undoubtedly felt that he had earned a few extra Agency merit badges after sitting with June Cobb for so long. The near Abbott and Costello banter between him and Cobb is certainly amusing, but one cannot overlook the importance of this long ignored information.

In his initial report regarding his October sessions with Cobb, True stated quite clearly that in his opinion, Cobb "has not and is not serving Soviet or Satellite Intelligence organizations; that she is not serving intelligence organizations of Cuba; and that she has not revealed her associations with members of the Agency to members of the Cuban Government or Intelligence Services."

COBB IS PSYCHOLOGICALLY ASSESSED FOR CIA JOB

On November 9, 1960, June Cobb's Agency handler, Jean Pierson – whose real name may have been Elizabeth Vetter (according to CIA operative Gerry Hemming) alerted Agency officials David Atlee Phillips and J.C. King that she and a CIA psychiatrist from the Agency's Medical Staff, Dr. Boyd L. Burris, had traveled to New York City two days earlier "to assess June Cobb's suitability for an operational assignment." Stated Pierson in a report about the trip: "It had been originally planned to send her [Cobb] back to her job in Habana; however, cancellation of her appointment necessitated a reevaluation of her potential use."

Dr. Burris and Pierson met with Cobb at the Statler-Hilton Hotel in New York, another hotel well wired electronically by the CIA, as well as well staffed with Agency operatives. (Frank Olson was murdered in the Statler Hotel in New York in 1953.) Dr. Burris conducted an assessment that lasted about five hours, and then Pierson met separately with Cobb. Wrote Pierson on their meeting: "Cobb appears to have accepted the fact that she cannot return to Cuba – doing so would be foolhardy and dangerous. The future possibilities for her in New York were discussed and she has decided to accept an offer from Lyle Stuart ... and to do some articles for him and possibly do some translations. She also has her connections with the Fair Play for Cuba Committee, if she wants to stay pro-Castro. However, she appears to want to stay middle-of-the-road till she sees which way the wind blows."

Pierson's report goes on to clearly indicate that Cobb was already feeding the CIA a substantial amount of information about the Fair Play for Cuba Committee. Indeed, Cobb was carrying on an extensive social, written and telephonic relationship with FPCC executive secretary Richard Gibson.

Pierson's report also reads: "In addition, she [Cobb] was instructed to do some entertaining."

Pierson's report concludes: "Cobb requested the undersigned [Pierson] to see her on Tuesday as she expected to have some additional information. She informed me that Jose Vasquez was not returning from Cuba after his marriage but was to be sent to Paris as Ambassador to France. Joachin Sanchez did not give up his job and leave for Los Angeles as he suggested to her he might do, but has been assigned to the permanent UN delegation. Olga Finlay has been hired by the New York Office of *Prensa Latina* as a teletype operator."

On December 8, 1960, CIA staff psychiatrist Dr. Boyd Burris formally submitted his brief report on June Cobb to Jean Pierson. Burris wrote: "Of great importance to the final evaluation was the Subject's [Cobb] long history of borderline anti-social behavior, her emotional lability and her definite trend toward depressive episodes. From the psychiatric standpoint she is considered to be an extremely poor candidate for use as an agent." For reasons not recorded on any declassified Agency documents, the CIA went ahead and hired June Cobb regardless of Dr. Burris' assessment.

Once the CIA made the decision to hire Cobb and give her a starting amount of $200 a month plus expenses, she was officially assigned to Agency case officer and Western Hemisphere Branch 4 official Jean T. Pierson. (Some recent books on the JFK assassination claim that "Jean Pierson" was an alias for Cobb, but this is not true.) Two of Cobb's CIA pseudonyms – Joan Price and Janette Post – were somewhat similar to the name of her CIA case officer Pierson, causing some confusion for historians. Cobb's other pseudonyms were Aunt Elizabeth and Clarinda E. Sharp. (Sharp was June Cobb's mother's maiden name, and not June's married name as has been often reported.) Jean Pierson was one of the few female Agency employees in the CIA's Western Hemisphere division.

Declassified Agency documents make it clear that Pierson had serious concerns about the wisdom of hiring Cobb, but her superiors, Harry Hermsdorf and J.C. King, both of whom were enamored with Cobb's good looks and tough veneer, overruled her. Cobb was formally hired in December 1960, and Jean Pierson, ever the loyal Agency employee, began training Cobb at a temporary safe house in Ponce City, Oklahoma. The location would be "natural" because

June traveled to Ponce City ostensibly to visit her father who lived there and who had been cleared by the CIA weeks earlier to receive June's monthly $200 stipend, plus expenses, for being a covert asset.

Pierson's concerns were based, in part, on reports that Cobb had previously suffered at least one nervous breakdown and had spent undisclosed time in a mental institution prior to traveling to Cuba. Pierson additionally suspected that Cobb may have also suffered a minor mental breakdown in Cuba and had needed to convalesce there for about 15 days. Lastly, it probably did not help their relationship at all that Cobb early on had told Pierson that she reminded her greatly of her mother and that she thought it was nice to have a mother-like figure back in her life.

The CIA was not the only U.S. intelligence-gathering agency interested in June Cobb. A month before Harry Hermsdorf first contacted her, an FBI report, dated April 15, 1960, claims that Cobb had served as a confidential informer to Jon Speller – son of Robert Speller the founding owner of the right-wing Robert Speller and Sons, Publisher, New York City. Jon Speller was a virulent anti-communist and personal secretary to Sergius M. Riis, a former American intelligence officer in Revolutionary Russia. Speller was also closely associated with a group of characters whom readers will encounter in the second volume of this work: Alexander Irving Rorke, Jr.; Haviv Schieber, a Polish-born Jew from Israel who was with the Anti-Communist International; Laureano Batista Falla, military leader of the Movimiento Democrata Cristiano, an anti-communist organization headquartered in Miami; Gerald Patrick Hemming, Jr., a soldier of fortune and CIA contractor who was head of the anti-Castro group Interpen headquartered in Florida; Frank Fiorini, also known as Frank Sturgis, an anti-Castro soldier of fortune and CIA contractor; Gifford Pinchot, an associate of Rorke's and Fiorini's who lived in New York City; and William Alexander Morgan, a former U.S. Marine who had been stationed in Japan at Atsugi Air Base, where Lee Harvey Oswald had also served while in the Marines, and who now lived in Havana, Cuba.

Jon Speller, according to the report, told the FBI that in mid-March 1960 he had received information "from three sources in Cuba to effect there is a cell of seven American communists in our

Embassy [in Cuba]." Speller identified the three sources as: Ruby Hart Phillips, a *New York Times* journalist covering Havana; Henry K. Ward, a retired U.S. Secret Service employee living in Cuba; and June Cobb, a "public relations employee" in Fidel Castro's office. Concerning June Cobb, the report reads:

> Cobb is native-born American who has been employed in Castro's office as translator and in public relations capacity since September 1959. She was interviewed by [the New York City FBI office] on December 2, 1959, at which time she expressed admiration for Castro, sympathy for aims of Cuban revolution, and conviction there is no communist influence in Castro regime. During the interview with Speller, he claimed Cobb has now become concerned about communist influence in Cuba and has organized a network of anti-communist Cubans in that country. According to Speller, Cobb feels State Department is pro-Castro and she has not furnished information to State since she fears it would get back to Castro and jeopardize her life.

The report continues:

> [Speller] on April 13, 1960 recontacted [*sic*] the FBI's New York City office and reiterated request that date not be disseminated. He said he was leaving that evening for Washington, D.C., where he would contact General Cushman and other "highly placed" individuals; that he had other information re activities of labor attaches in Central America which he planned to give FBI after checking certain facts during visit to Washington.

General Cushman was Major Gen. Robert Everton Cushman, Jr., a highly decorated Marine, who, in February 1957, was assigned to serve four years on the staff of then-Vice President Richard Nixon as Assistant to the Vice President for National Security Affairs.

At the conclusion of its report, the FBI requested that an inquiry be made "as to possibility Cobb will be available for interview in U.S. in near future."

An additional document connected with the FBI report on Speller is remarkable for its implications, as well as its brevity. It is a facsimile of a sheet of official letterhead from the White House,

Office of the Vice President that reads: "R.E. CUSHMAN, Room 361, Senate Office Bldg., Wash. 25 D.C. 2121." The typed caption at the bottom of the letterhead copy reads: "This document was passed to June Cobb by Jon P. Speller with instructions to show it to the Chief, INS, in the event she had any difficulties in entering the United States. She has been carrying it since receiving it. It has been in her possession in Cuba. (Received 6 June 1960)"

(Interesting to note about Speller is that Cobb in her first interrogation by the CIA remarked that Speller had confidentially informed her that Allen Dulles was a dedicated communist spy whose loyalties had been with the Soviets since World War II.)

> *Lend me your eyes poor lady,*
> *to wear like amber on my forehead*
> *so I can seek my demon*
> *just as the sun goes down.*
>
> -Cicely d'A. Angleton

> *Cheep cheep*
> *chit chat yes yes much violence in America.*
> *Ma si Mafia, anche in Italia. Strong resignation*
> *and fatigue engrave their faces. Etruscan tombs*
> *with-holding secrets from the curious.*
>
> -Cicely d'A. Angleton

"JANETTE WILL SEE YOU IN JULY." JUNE GOES TO MEXICO ...

On June 5, 1961, June Cobb's CIA case officer, Jean T. Pierson, reported to her superiors in the Agency's Western Hemisphere Branch 4, Covert Action Division, and Agency officials in the U.S. Embassy in Mexico, that Cobb had departed New York City on May 26 for Mexico City, Mexico.

"She is planning to remain until sometime in August," Pierson wrote. A few weeks later, she amended "sometime in August" to Cobb's staying in the Mexican capital for an "unidentified period of time."

According to Pierson, Cobb was staying at the expensive Hotel Regis, located on the Avenico Suarez. Pierson also noted that she had informed June Cobb to expect to be "contacted by an individual who will identify himself with the statement, "Janette will see you in July."

June Cobb's specific tasks for the CIA in Mexico are difficult to determine because the CIA still refuses to release the bulk of its files on Cobb's time in Mexico. From a handful of declassified documents we are able to glean a very partial sketch of Cobb's activities.

In an undated memorandum sent to Western Hemisphere chief J.C. King concerning a conversation between an unnamed CIA official – most likely David Atlee Phillips – and Cobb in Mexico City, we are able to glean the nature of some of her earliest work there. The memorandum reveals that she had been doing work in Mexico for the Association Escritores de Mexico and expresses the CIA's desire to have Cobb report on the "make up, influence and membership" of this writers' group.

One of the first contacts June made in Mexico City was with her old friend Warren Broglie, who was now the manager of the Hotel Luma, an upscale lodging facility located on Orizaba Street. Broglie had put in a good word to Winston Scott, CIA Chief of Station in Mexico City, about Cobb's arrival, although several CIA documents and cables from the time reveal that Jean Pierson had also notified Scott of Cobb's pending arrival. (Hotel Luma was often misidentified in documents by the CIA and FBI as the "Hotel Luna.")

As previously revealed herein, Broglie, a Swiss-national, had been a confidential informer and willing asset to the CIA (as well as to the Narcotics Bureau and FBI) for about ten years. Broglie was also quite close friends with Winston Scott as he was also with Scott's third wife, Janet Graham Leddy Scott. Indeed, Broglie was a special, head-table guest, along with David Atlee Phillips, another of his close friends, at Janet Scott's lavish 1963 birthday party reportedly held in a private room at the Hotel Luma. Janet Scott became Winston's wife not long after the strange death of his first wife Paula Scott on September 12, 1962, sixteen months after Cobb's arrival in Mexico.

On July 20, 1964, W. J. Kaufman – then chief of the CIA's Western Hemisphere Division One – requested that "the Operation Approval" for June Cobb "be amended to include authority for the Mexico City Station to utilize Cobb as an access asset against a Soviet Press Attaché and Soviet Information Bulletin Representative." It appears that this request, as well as the filing of Operational Approval Amendments, was a routine Agency bureaucratic process by which headquarters was better able to track the ongoing field duties of its assets. The same July 20 request noted that an earlier June 29 amendment of Cobb's operational authority "was not implemented since that target's visit to Mexico City never materialized."

Another of June Cobb's very first contacts in Mexico City was with an covert operative she first encountered in Havana, Cuba, Edward G. Tichborn. The alias "Tichborn" is a troublesome one as it is often confused as the title of an Agency operation or project, as in Project Tichborn, and because the alias "Edward Tichborn" was used on several occasions on the West Coast by dapper mobster Johnny Rosselli. Also well worth underscoring here is that "Edward G. Tichborn," a CIA covert asset who worked for several years in Mexico City, reported often to David Atlee Phillips, David Sanchez Morales, and Joseph Piccolo, Jr.

A draft CIA report on Edward G. Tichborn dated February 2, 1960 (written by CIA official Evalena S. Vidal) reveals that Tichborn traveled to Washington, D.C., before returning home to L.A., on January 31, 1960 to be debriefed on his time spent in Cuba as a covert asset. Among the information passed on to the CIA at his debriefing was his observation that Fidel Castro "is in no danger of loosing his grip or the devotion of his followers for some time to come" Said Tichborn on Castro: "He seems to become most upset and almost panicked by defections. Possessing a 'Messiah-type complex' he cannot bear the thought of someone leaving the fold."

June Cobb frequently meet with Tichborn, as well as another covert operative known as "Leopoldo," often with both men together. There is credible evidence, based on the CIA's obscure description of Leopoldo, that he was one of the men who paid the still controversial visit to Silvia Odio in September 1963.

A November 1961 memorandum sent to Mexico Chief of Station Winston Scott from WH Chief J.C. King and Jake Esterline intended to inform Scott of June Cobb's character and attributes reads: "According to the assessments made on June Cobb, it is believed that because of emotional vacillation and potential susceptibility to leftist indoctrination, she should be handled with caution. She can be provided with general requirements but should be kept unwitting of modus operandi. Cobb requires direction and guidance to insure specific information; failure results in receipt of varied and often interesting information, but not necessarily that which is desired. AMUPAS/1 [Cobb's newly granted code name] is an individual who needs a 'cause' – who apparently needs something or someone she can crusade for. In the past it has been a paramour, and the Cuban Revolution; at the present time it is assisting her country to combat the spread of communism; tomorrow it could be communism itself. It is therefore necessary to keep her motivation directed along lines of our interest so that she will not be tempted to look elsewhere. It is with the possibility in mind that she could espouse an alien cause (perhaps unwittingly) that contact with and direction of her, should not reveal modus operandi of a too-sensitive nature. Handled with the above restrictions in mind, Cobb can provide a wealth of information. To date she has not been told for whom she is working although she strongly suspects CIA; she has been given no training or SW system; at most, she would be able to describe possibly a half-dozen persons she has met under alias. It is therefore suggested that she be given specific requirements which she can fulfill in normal circles, or which she can acquire from contacts she makes through normal channels. The psychiatrist further suggests that she will probably respond to direction by a female case officer more effectively than to a male, since she is apparently under some strain to assure herself of her attractiveness in her associations with men."

June Cobb and CIA Official Bustos-Videla

Had Lee Harvey Oswald never traveled to Mexico City, we most likely would never have known the name Charlotte Bustos-Videla, despite that June Cobb's activities in Mexico City placed her in frequent contact with Ms. Bustos, who regularly monitored and assessed Cobb's work in Mexico City for the agency's Western Hemisphere Division. Bustos-Videla occupied the Mexico City desk at CIA headquarters in Langley, Virginia. Bustos was a long-time agency employee, having been on the job some twenty years at the time of the assassination. Some government documents identify Bustos as "Elsie Scaleti," a pseudonym created possibly by Congressional investigatory committees.

An hour after JFK was shot and Lee Harvey Oswald's name and image appeared on television screens worldwide, Bustos-Videla located at least one photograph of Lee Harvey Oswald that had earlier been forwarded to agency headquarters from Mexico City. Bustos apparently then forwarded a copy of the photo to her superiors along with copies to the FBI and the White House. Somewhere along the line, the photograph was shown to a CIA official named Joseph Stephen Piccolo, Jr., who was stationed in Mexico City from at least 1957 through 1968, although there is some question as to whether Piccolo was actually in Mexico City in 1963 when Oswald visited and when the assassination took place. Like Bustos, Piccolo worked on occasion with matters pertaining to June Cobb and on several occasions met with Cobb in Mexico and Guatemala. Piccolo, by his own admission, was periodically involved in a number of secret operations against Cuba and Fidel Castro from 1962 through to 1975. Piccolo also worked closely with defectors from Cuba's intelligence services and handled double-agents and covert assets for the CIA, one of whom was AMMUG/1.

WHO WAS JOSEPH PICCOLO, JR.?

Perhaps entirely by happenstance Joseph S. Piccolo Jr., another CIA employee who said he saw photos of Oswald taken In Mexico City, also, according to CIA records, worked closely with June Cobb while she was in Mexico. Heavily redacted Agency documents from 1961, 1962, and 1963 reveal that Piccolo interacted with Cobb, often through her handler Jean Pierson, sometimes in New York City, in Mexico, and in Guatemala, where Cobb frequently traveled from 1961 through to 1965. There are also numerous references in many of the Cobb-Piccolo related documents that Piccolo and Cobb's handler, Jean Pierson, were consistently reporting on Cobb's activities in Mexico to not only David Atlee Phillips but also to CIA counterintelligence chief, James Jesus Angleton.

Joseph Piccolo had been with the CIA since 1957, and was occasionally backstopped to positions with the U.S. Army and the Air Force. In a 1978 interview, Piccolo stated "that at the time of President Kennedy's assassination" he was "a support assistance analyst in the agency's Directorate of Operations." This is the CIA's branch that houses covert operations and paramilitary activities. Piccolo explained that his "responsibilities included maintenance of records, running traces, and Spanish language analysis for purposes of operational support." Piccolo also stated that he "served in the CIA's Mexico City Station from December 1957 to January 1960 and from August 1965 to January 1968," however, some heavily redacted Western Hemisphere Division documents appear to place him in Mexico City in the years 1961 to 1963. The same interview with Piccolo reads: "It was further ascertained that Mr. Piccolo was involved in some Agency operations directed against Cuba during the time periods 1962 to January 1968, January 1969 to January 1970, and a three month period during 1975."

Several CIA documents from the years 1963 through 1969 strongly indicate that Piccolo worked under the direction of David Atlee Phillips while engaged in activities directed at the Cuban government. Asked during the interview "if you are familiar with the cryptonym AMMUG/1," Piccolo responded affirmatively "and stated that [AMMUG/1] was the first Cuban intelligence Service (CUIS) defector from the then newly formed DGI, the CIA's Cuban counterpart for external security and counter-intelligence operations."

During the same 1978 interview, Piccolo was also asked if he "had ever seen any photographs of Lee Harvey Oswald resulting form the photographic surveillance operations conducted by the CIA Mexico City Station." Piccolo answered, "Yes, I have."

Piccolo, Paradise, the Mafia, and the French Connection

On October 22, 1966, a well-known mobster and narcotics trafficker named Joseph Paradise was gunned down in New York City. Paradise had been arrested earlier on June 6, 1966 by the Federal Bureau of Narcotics for drug trafficking. According to a Narcotics Bureau document concerning the murder dated December 19, 1966, sent to the CIA's Security Office immediately following Paradise's death, his brother William Paradise "assumed control of their illicit activities including traffic in narcotics." The document continues: "Joseph Paradise had, prior to his death, been negotiating for a large quantity of heroin with one Jean Aron, a famous narcotics trafficker of Paris, France." Neither the Narcotics Bureau document, nor any subsequent CIA reports, make any mention that Jean Aron had previously been reported as the same suspected "French trafficker engaged in the import-export business" who owned the "property located at 61 Barrow Street in New York City's Greenwich Village." This was the building used in 1951 through early 1954 by narcotics agent and CIA contract agent George Hunter White as a CIA safe house for LSD and other drug experiments.

The last sentence of the document reads: "The attached letter was found on Paradise's body and is forwarded for your information." The letter was addressed to Joseph Paradise and had been written and signed by CIA official Joseph Piccolo, Jr. Joseph and William Paradise were Piccolo's uncles.

Piccolo's letter to his mobster uncle Joseph was particularly upsetting for the CIA. Piccolo tells Paradise in the letter that he is "fed up with the old government service." He continues: "The past few months have really opened my eyes that I refused to open before." With that, Piccolo then asks his uncle to "keep your ears open for anyone that might be interested in taking on a 31-year-old former foreign service officer with ambitions to make nothing but money no matter how hard or long the hours and work are."

Adds Piccolo, "Contributing factors are that this semi-retired former foreign service officer has a knowledge of Mexico and Latin America in general, speaks fluent Spanish and knows how to do business/negotiate with Latins.

"I have a couple of ideas on places and areas to be invested in etc. that should bear some fruit within a few years. Also have a good potential for an inside line to some high level Nicaraguan's and have good contacts in Mexico for reasonable business ventures. I have had several offers to stay in Mexico from friends of mine, but I'm sort of tired of the overseas living as a permanent thing and want back into the U.S.A."

The CIA's Personnel Security Division and Office of Security summoned Piccolo to Washington, D.C. for an interview with special assistant William A. O'Donnell. The interview took place on January 12, 1967. Piccolo told O'Donnell that he knew that "his letter had been found on the uncle's body inasmuch as his parents had written to him in Mexico and told him of this." Piccolo informed O'Donnell "he first met" Joseph Paradise "about 1963 or 1964 when he visited him in New York." The report does not state why Piccolo visited his uncle at this time, but it does reveal that since about 1963 "he [Piccolo] has seen his uncle about six times." The report does not provide any specific dates, but states, "In April or May of 1966, Uncle Joe and his wife were on vacation in Mexico and Subject [Piccolo] went out with them the three nights that they were in Mexico City. During the visit, the uncle mentioned to Subject that

411

he had invested heavily in an air freight expediting company and had applied for an international license."

The report goes on: "Subsequent to the uncle's visit to Mexico, Subject [Piccolo] said things started to go down hill for him. He broke up with his fiancée and was passed over for a promotion. Against this background, Subject wrote the letter to the uncle expressing his dissatisfaction with his job and asking uncle if he could do anything for him. The undersigned [O'Donnell] asked Subject if there were any hidden or double meanings in the letter and this he denied categorically. He stated that he mentioned in his letter about contacts in Mexico and Nicaragua. Subject said he had in mind the uncle expanding the air freight business into Central and South America where Subject felt they could take advantage of the Central American Common Market."

One cannot help but note that Piccolo's attitude about his CIA job and lack of promotions is quite similar to those troubles that allegedly drove Charles William Thomas to suicide. The question to Piccolo about "hidden or double meanings in the letter" to his uncle appear quite appropriate given the missive's first statement: "What's new up there? Did my old buddy 'Juan' ever send the extra purse and shoes? If not I'll give him the word. If he did and they aren't right, then let me know and I'll give him the other word."

Apparently, the CIA concluded that Piccolo's activities with his uncle were nothing more than mere coincidence and had no nefarious purposes, however, the released agency files on Piccolo contain no mention or any information at all about the other known mobsters, who knew William and Joseph Paradise well, who were also in Mexico City during Piccolo's tenure there, as well as during his uncle's visits.

Here it should be noted that on November 14, 1957, the CIA's Office of Personnel Records and Services Division issued a memorandum regarding Joseph Stephan Piccolo requesting that all of Piccolo's records "be blocked from all outside inquiries from 16 October 1957 forward." The memo concerning this action reads: "Inasmuch as it has now been determined that Piccolo's entire association with the Agency must be denied." Piccolo continued to work for the CIA until about late 1975. He was one of only two people in the U.S. Embassy in Mexico City to state that he saw a photograph of Lee Harvey Oswald taken in at the Russian embassy in 1963.

> *When I call for myself, silent,*
> *and someone I'm not remembers me,*
> *weeping and bleeding at mid-height,*
> *over what is suspended*
> *discovered*
> *and recovered.*

-Eunice Odio

EUNICE ODIO: WHO WAS SHE AND HOW DID SHE DIE?

Very little has been written in English about Eunice Odio, other than that she was an extremely talented and beautiful poet from Costa Rica who died quite mysteriously when she was fifty-two years old. In the annals of the JFK assassination, we only know of Odio as a woman who somehow in 1963 knew June Cobb.

Eunice Odio

As some readers may be aware, oft-quoted CIA documents consistently state, "Shortly after the assassination, an American woman, June Cobb, came and spent several days in Elena's [Garro] house. She was sent by their mutual friend, Eunice Odio, a Costa Rican who is now June Cobb's roommate and who was formerly the mistress of Vasques Amoral [*sic*] when he was with Rockefeller Foundation, and Ernesto de la Pena."

"Vasques Amoral" was actually Jose Vazquez-Amaral, a highly respected writer, editor, and translator. He had earlier translated Ezra Pound's *Cantos* into Spanish. Pound, as some readers may be aware, was a strong supporter of Fascism, Benito Mussolini, and Adolph Hitler. Pound wrote for publications owned by Oswald Mosley, an infamous British Member of Parliament and staunch supporter of Fascism. (Pound was arrested for treason by American authorities in 1945, and was confined in St. Elizabeths psychiatric hospital in Washington, D.C., where he reportedly was subjected to a number of CIA Artichoke Project "interrogation sessions.") In 1953, Vazquez-Amaral received a Rockefeller Foundation grant to produce additional translations of important Latin American works.

The House Select Committee on Assassinations in its report on Oswald, the CIA, and Mexico City – commonly called the Lopez-Hardway Report – is even more abbreviated in its mention of Eunice Odio: "According to Elena [Garro], Ms. Cobb was sent to her house shortly after the assassination for a few days, by a mutual friend, a Costa Rican writer named Eunice Odio."

Eunice Odio was an intensely passionate, mystical, and private woman. "I detest biographies," she once wrote. "The affairs of my private life are the most private and, in general, no one knows them, except me." Therefore, with sincerest apologies to Eunice and with the thought that perhaps she would somehow appreciate the following account, we shall examine her life.

Eunice Odio was born Eunice Odio Infante in San Jose, Costa Rica in 1919. She read and wrote poetry from her earliest years as a child, and her first collection of poems, *Los Elementos Terrestres*, was published in Guatemala in 1947. Subsequently, she moved to Guatemala and became a citizen there, never returning to Costa Rica. She published additional collections in 1953 and 1957, one of which created "mythological characters to tell the story of the world's creation."

Odio moved to New York City in 1959, and stayed for over two years. While there, she wrote poems about the United States, the Statue of Liberty, the Hudson River, and an elegy for well-known jazz musician and singer, Louis Armstrong. "The United Sates scares me," she later wrote. A recent article on Odio reads: "Although a 'model of social justice' and a 'paradise of the proletariat', she concluded that the country was a 'highly-polished disaster'. She disliked, in particular, the Beats, Pop Art, and feminism. The latter comes as a surprise, given that she lived an independent life wholly dedicated to her art. A self-confessed 'reaccionario', she complained: 'In North America roles are inverted: she is he; he is she.'"

Upon leaving New York, Odio journeyed to Mexico City in 1961 and reportedly became a Mexican citizen in 1962. However, formerly classified CIA files state that she lived in Mexico "illegally."

CIA documents on Eunice Odio, although scant, readily reveal that the Agency was keenly interested in her presence in Guatemala. A declassified CIA cable, dated November 5, 1952, from an unknown Western Hemisphere Division official to the Director CIA reads:

> Files indicate Eunis [*sic*] Odio is a Costa Rican commie or sympathizer poet, winner of Guatemala Literary contest about

1947. Came to Guatemala following overthrow of Picado, and consorted with Guatemalan intellectuals. Advised American Charge of Affairs "confidentially" in August '50 of presence in Guatemala of Eudocio Ravines, who she called Peruvian commie. Ravines wrote "The Yenan Was [*sic*]"; nothing to confirm allegation [that Odio] was Arbenez mistress." Eudocio Ravines was a controversial figure with the CIA – sometimes a friend, sometimes a foe.

A November 14, 1952 declassified CIA dispatch from Western Hemisphere chief J.C. King and associate Scott Stiles, dated November 14, 1952, provides more detail on Eunice, much of it about Odio's physical appearance. Possibly it was produced by someone who had had personal contact with her.

Describing Odio's writing style as "distinctively Merudian," the memorandum states, "This is not strange, as she is a very active communist in Costa Rica, being a member of the famous communist literati cell – Eugenio Maria de Bostos– to which Corina Rodriguez also belongs."

The memorandum goes on: "Eunice Odio was described in 1947 as being about twenty-five years of age, white, with black hair and black eyes, about five feet five inches tall, and weighing approximately 118 pounds. She is of attractive appearances and wears her hair long, which extends half way to her waist. Her platform personality is pleasing, and her voice, which is the most attractive feature, easily captivates her audiences, because of its low soothing quality."

Politically, the document describes Odio as a fanatical advocate of communism in Costa Rica, and cites a 1947 letter addressed to Odio by Joaquin Gutierraz Mangel, the son of the Costa Rican Ambassador to the United States in which Gutierraz "spoke highly" of Corina Rodriguez, a "well known Costa Rican communist."

A brief follow-up November 21, 1952 CIA cable about Odio to Agency headquarters in Washington, D.C. requests the authority to try "to achieve her expulsion from country" [Guatemala] and stated "rumors persist she [is] mistress of Jose Quetglas, Presidential Press Secretary."

Eunice Odio died in 1972 at the age of 52 under very strange circumstances. She was discovered four days after her death in her bathtub. The medical examiner listed the cause of her death as being poisoned by her own hand, but few facts were provided in the official report, which seems to have been misplaced a few years after her death. It appears quite likely that given the passage of time and the deaths of many who were close to her, we may never know the full details surrounding her death.

LHO AND JUNE COBB'S BOOK TRANSLATION

In my investigation of June Cobb as a much overlooked player in the JFK assassination, I had several discussions with a former intelligence operative who had worked in Mexico City during the early 1960s. During one such conversation this person guardedly mentioned that Lee Harvey Oswald had met with Cobb and Eunice Odio in Mexico City during his infamous visit there in September-October 1963.

This operative initially remarked: There is also Oswald's meeting with Cobb and Odio.... Among other things, they talked about Guatemala. That's well worth looking at."

I replied, "You mean Sylvia Odio?"

"No," came the reply. "I mean with the Rosicrucian poet and Cobb. You should look at that."

"There's evidence of that?" I asked, thinking, Oh, no, here we go with the occult and Rosicrucians.

"Look more closely," came the reply.

I looked more closely. Sure enough, buried in the Warren Commission files, there was a reference to Oswald and the book that Cobb had translated for Juan Jose Arevalo. That reference is explained in detail below. I was also pleasantly surprised to discover a connection between Eunice Odio and the secret order of the Rosicrucians. According to several scholarly articles on Odio, sometime in the late 1950s she became actively involved with the Rosicrucian Order and rose to the rank of Second Grade Superior of the Temple. The Rosicrucian Order is a secret society from the early 1600s, with a modern group, the Ancient and Mystical Order Rosæ Crucis, founded in 1915. According to several reports to the CIA by June Cobb, Sylvia Odio and a number of other well-known Mexican and Latin American writers and artists were attracted to the philosophy and writings expressed by the Rosicrucian Order, which maintained at least two well-organized chapters in Mexico City, as well as Costa Rica.

On November 6, 1963, a little over two weeks before JFK was assassinated, Lee Harvey Oswald visited the Dallas Public Library's Oak Cliff branch and checked out a copy of the book by Juan Jose Arevalo, *The Shark and the Sardines*. June Cobb had translated this book along with Raul Osegueda. Cobb's name appears prominently on the book. June Cobb went to Mexico City towards the beginning of June 1961 and remained there until sometime in 1966. It appears from all the evidence gathered about Oswald's final weeks in Dallas that Arevalo's book was the very last that he read. The book was due to be returned on November 13, 1963, nine days before the assassination.

FBI correspondence, dated February 25, 1964, with Mrs. Lillian Bradshaw, the director of the Dallas Public Library, confirms that the book had been checked out by Oswald on November 6, 1963. Mrs. Bradshaw told the FBI that her records indicated "no other delinquencies for Oswald." Bradshaw provided FBI investigators with two copies of a delinquency notice addressed to Oswald at his 602 Elsbeth Street, Dallas address. Bradshaw also provided a brief publisher's review of the book, which read in part: "In your hands you hold a controversial book – a book that speaks out against your State Department's dealing with the peoples of Latin America during the Twentieth Century."

Years later in 1969, as noted earlier, writer Albert H. Newman would discover that the long-thought-lost book had indeed been returned to the Oak Cliff branch sometime after February 1964. Nobody has been able to determine who returned the book or how the return was accomplished. Reportedly, the returned copy bore no markings or notations made by Oswald.

Apparently, the CIA learned of Oswald's having checked out Arevalo's book slightly before the FBI. A January 28, 1964 memorandum by CIA Security Research Staff chief, Paul Gaynor, underscores the agency's position on the book and its publisher, Lyle Stuart. Wrote Gaynor, who was notorious at the agency for maintaining what many then called the agency's "Fag Files," a huge detailed list of American citizens who the CIA claimed were either "homosexuals or sexual deviates":

For a number of years, the publisher of *The Shark and the Sardines*, Lyle Stuart of New York City, has engaged in the

417

publication of various types of books, mainly anti-religious material, material highly critical of the United States, and books best classified as pornographic.... The publication in November 1961 of Arevalo's book, originally written in Spanish but translated for him into English by one June Cobb, coincided approximately with an ad published on 21 November 1961 in the *New York Times* which immediately created widespread reaction, particularly with the United States business interests having connections with Latin and South American countries. The book itself is strongly anti-American and anti-American business and is a succession of smears on American business interests throughout Latin America and the United States Government and its Latin American policies. The author of the book, J.J. Arevalo, has not been established as a communist but definitely is an extreme Leftist and radical and anti-American in action and certainly in his writings. The translator of the book, June Cobb, has definitely been shown to have been a salaried employee of Fidel Castro and was arrested as a courier in November 1961 in Guatemala while carrying Soviet and Cuban propaganda....

Gaynor's memorandum is noteworthy for what it did not reveal about June Cobb, and for its deliberately slanderous material on Stuart, some of it untrue. It is also interesting that Gaynor's memorandum made no mention of Lee Harvey Oswald.

Why did Oswald hold onto the book past its due date? Is it possible that Oswald met Cobb in Mexico City? As we know, Cobb's principle assignment with the CIA in Mexico City was to work as a paid asset for the Agency's station within the U.S. Embassy in Mexico.

COBB MEETS ROBERT BUICK AND OSWALD IN MEXICO CITY

Any discussion about Oswald in Mexico City must first take into account the ill-supported theories that Oswald was never there. Our concern here is with Oswald's September-October 1963 visit to Mexico. Several prominent conspiracy theorists, best exampled most recently by attorney Mark Lane, staunchly maintain that Oswald was never in Mexico, despite overwhelming evidence that he was there for at least three visits. Lane, of course, is wrong, as any serious student of the assassination knows. Acting to cement his false claim is the account of Robert Clayton Buick, who, as chance would have it, met Lee Harvey Oswald in Mexico City in late September 1963, and a note typed by June Cobb in October 1963 [the note bears no specific day-date] and is addressed to "DP." The note reads: *The day after LO in Comercio, encountered Buick, the American bullfighter, at H. Luma. Warren [Broglie] says Buick is drawing attention here.*" [Emphasis added.]

LEE HARVEY OSWALD: "YOU THE BULLFIGHTER?"

On April 20, 1966, Robert Clayton Buick was indicted by a Federal Grand Jury in Los Angeles, California for violation of the Federal Bank Robbery Statute. According to numerous FBI documents and reports generated from 1963 through 1976, Buick committed armed robbery at twenty-two Federally insured banks in Southern California between July 1961 and February 1966.

Hundreds of FBI pages regarding Buick's various bank heists going back to 1963 reveal that Robert Clayton Buick "had lived in various cities in Mexico, including Mexico City, Nogales, Juarez, and in San Juan, Puerto Rico." In all of these cities, Buick, according to FBI investigators, "has fought in the bull ring as a bullfighter." Buick also "owned and operated a marble importing business in Mexico City and San Diego, California."

Robert Buick

Before his trial, Buick wrote several letters to the United States Attorney at Los Angeles asking that he be allowed a conference "to discuss an issue which he said 'pertains to Dallas,'" stated one Department of Justice report. Buick wrote the U.S. Attorney that by not meeting with him the attorney might force Buick to "create utter international chaos."

In response, an Assistant U.S. Attorney, joined by Buick's attorney, attempted to hold a discussion with the serial bank robber, but Buick flatly refused to talk to the Assistant Attorney, stating that he would only sit down with the U.S. Attorney, a Federal judge, or U.S. Supreme Court Chief Justice Earl Warren. Federal officials declined to forward Buick's request to anyone other than the U.S. Attorney, who still declined to meet at all with Buick.

Following Buick's trial, during which he was found guilty, Robert Buick wrote a series of additional letters to the U.S. Attorney. After receiving a telephone call from Buick, and after consulting with Buick's attorney, Assistant U.S. Attorney Richard M. Coleman agreed to meet with Buick. Reads an FBI report: "Coleman had received information that Buick, in a letter to his wife, made reference to the 'news from New Orleans' saying 'it adds perfectly well' with what he has."

Coleman and a U.S. Secret Service agent met with Buick on March 23, 1967, but Coleman stated at the start of the meeting that he was only there to "discuss matters pertaining to [Buick's] trial." The FBI report states, "Attorney Coleman refused stating they were present to discuss information Buick claimed to have concerning the assassination." Again, Buick refused to discuss his trial if the assassination could not also be included in any discussion. The meeting ended on this note.

On March 24, 1967, Buick telephoned Coleman to tell him that he was "writing to the President of the United States with copies for the Attorney General, the Director of the FBI, and others. Buick asked Coleman if the jail where he was being held would censor the letters. Coleman told Buick "that the FBI had no control over jail regulations."

An FBI report written about Buick's problems with Coleman reads: "Review of psychiatric reports on Buick disclose that Buick in these interviews also indicated he had information concerning the assassination. One psychiatrist reported "this defendant is playing a very skillful game of trying to convey the impression that he has valuable information but is unable to divulge it except to such people as the Chief Justice of the United States. He has the typical effrontery of the sociopath."

A February 2, 1972 FBI report provides more details about Robert Buick's ongoing case. The report reveals that on February 1, 1972 a man named August Ricard von Kleist, who lived in New Mexico, contacted the FBI and advised the Bureau that he had "certain information concerning a plot to assassinate President John Fitzgerald Kennedy. According to von Kleist, this information came to his attention from Robert Clayton Buick, a convicted bank robber on whom he was preparing a story for publication in *True* magazine; however, this story was not accepted by *True* magazine and remains unpublished to date. The story about Buick is not connected with the alleged assassination plot, but rather reports he was a bull-fighter in Mexico at the same time he was robbing banks in California." (Von Kliest was most likely unaware that True magazine maintained a very close relationship with both the FBI and CIA through its editor and several of its top feature writers.)

Von Kliest handed the FBI a two page, double spaced summary of what he understood had happened at the Hotel Luna [sic], Mexico City, July 1963. The summary read: "Parties included in the plot were Alex Hydell [sic], otherwise known as Lee Harvey Oswald; a female attorney who is well known communist in Los Angeles (blond, about 35 years age at that time); hotel headwaiter, Frity [sic], first name unknown, who owned a launch believed to be shuttling between Mexico and Cuba. Also believed to be involved – Warren Brogie [sic], hotel chain manager; and Richard Case Nagell, former Captain, U.S. Army, associated with Counter Intelligence in Japan in 1959. [This army intelligence officer would also be convicted of attempting to rob a bank.] Barbara Warren was involved with Alex Hydell and Brogie at the time scheme was planned.

"Nagell sent letter to J. Edgar Hoover warning him of plot against Kennedy and naming Alex Hydell as one of the assassins. Hydell was not known to Nagell as Lee Harvey Oswald. The copy of the letter Richard Case Nagell wrote to J. Edgar Hoover on August 13, 1963, informing him of Oswald's plan to kill Kennedy is being held by Nagell's sister, Eleanor Gambert, 82-25 Grand Ave, Long Island, N.Y. The letter contains information about Oswald, who was named and referred to as Alex Hydell, and advises Hoover that Kennedy would definitely be killed.

"The history of Richard Case Nagell is important. While a member of Counter Intelligence in Tokyo, he was dealing with a Soviet attaché officer stationed with Russian Embassy in Tokyo at that time. He was approached several times and was said to have dealt with said Russian officer as to vital information (classified). A year or so later Nagell, while working for California Alcohol Beverage Control, was shot through the right chest when involved with a Los Angeles police officer because of communistic implications. He survived gunshot wound and took off to Mexico or Cuba in launch owned by Frity of the Hotel Luna. All of this is and was known by J. Edgar Hoover and FBI. Nagell was later arrested in El Paso for bank robbery after discharging a firearm in an El Paso bank. He was in Leavenworth Federal Prison for 2 1/2 years and was later brought to El Paso for an appeal. Appeal was denied. From there he was sent to Springfield, Missouri (Federal Prison) and is believed to still be there (now listed as a mental patient?). Further information coming on Warren and a Dr. Fujiyam."

WHAT ROBERT BUICK KNOWS

There is no doubt whatsoever that Robert Buick lived in Mexico City in 1963 or that he was a world renowned American bullfighter, a rarity indeed, who many in Mexico greatly admired and called "El Ciclon del Norte," the Cyclone of the North. Numerous articles in Mexican newspapers praised his fearless style and ability in the bullring. Thousands of people attended his bullfights, perhaps even Lee Harvey Oswald, although Buick says confidently, "No, he never attended any of my bull fights." Buick, however, did meet and speak with Lee Harvey Oswald in September 1963 in Mexico City. Indeed, Buick and Oswald encountered one another at the Warren Broglie-managed Hotel Luma at 16 Orizaba Calle.

"Yes, says Buick, "I met Oswald in Mexico City. At the time, it was no big deal. I had no idea who he was and he initially made no impression on me at all."

Buick describes his encounter with Oswald in great detail in an intriguing book he published in 2006 entitled, *Tiger in the Rain*. The book also goes to great lengths to describe and explain Buick's other assassination-related experiences in Mexico City (all of which will be covered in Volume Two of this work).

It was late-morning in late September 1963 and Buick was at one of his favorite hangouts, the bar at the Hotel Luma. When he entered the bar, Warren Broglie's ever-present assistant and sometimes bartender Franz Waehauf was serving drinks to a packed house along with a young girl from the university.

Buick had joined a group of attractive young women sitting in a booth and in the middle of conversation with them, Buick writes, "I felt the presence of someone standing over me."

Buick turned and looked up at a young man he had noticed minute's earlier standing with Waehauf at the service bar.

"You the bullfighter?" the young man asked.

"Yeah, that's right," Buick replied.

"How's a guy get into that racket?" the man asked.

"Well, it helps to be a little crazy," Buick said.

At this point, Franz Waehauf arrived at the booth with a tray of drinks. Buick looked up again at the young man and asked, "Would you like a drink?"

"No, no thank you," the man said. "I've gotta leave for a while, but I want to talk to you about this bullfighting business. You going to be around later?"

Buick replied, "Yeah, I'll be here about eight, give or take ten minutes either way."

Buick then extended his right hand to the man and said, "By the way, I'm Bob Buick."

The young man shook Buick's hand and said, "I'm Alek Hidell."

"Alright Alex," Buick said standing, "I'll see you about eight."

"It's Alek," the young man said, placing emphasis on the "k." The young man then turned and left the bar. (As many readers know, Hidell is a name that Oswald used several times on various writings and documents, as well as in Russia.)

Robert Buick returned to the Hotel Luma that evening and a short while later watched Alek Hidell and Franz Waehauf come into the cocktail lounge. Hidell joined Buick at the bar and suggested that they take an empty booth at the rear of the lounge.

Waehauf asked Buick and Hidell if they wanted to order drinks, and Hidell said, "A beer, I'll just have a beer."

Hidell asked Buick, "You like it here in Mexico?"

"I love it here," Buick replied.

"Don't you like the States?"

"Not unless you're a multimillionaire," said Buick.

"What do you mean?"

"Here, the good life of political corruption is not simply reserved for the powerful politician or magistrate, as in the United States," Buick explained. "Everyone is on the take here, from the lonely beat cop, to the man in the presidential mansion."

Hidell asked, "What if you refuse to pay the bribe?"

"Then it would cost you anywhere from a thousand to twenty-five thousand pesos to bail yourself out of jail and to get your car out of impound."

Buick added, "Down here you play the game; it's the way of life, and it's been going on since the beginning of time."

"That's interesting, very interesting," Hidell said. "Do you think you'll ever go back to the United States?"

"I go back all the time," Buick replied.

"No, I mean permanently."

"Not if it doesn't get any better."

"What do you mean?"

Buick smiled and said, "Hey, you got total disorder up there, niggers burning and destroying cities, politicians running around with their heads up their ass ..."

Hidell fell silent for a while, and then explained to Buick that he "had similar thoughts and motives," Buick wrote.

Hidell then told Buick that he was of Russian heritage, and then "spoke a few words in that language."

Hidell said he was actually in the process of returning to "Russia by way of Cuba," Buick wrote.

"I asked by what form of transportation he would use to get to Cuba, stating that no commercial airline was available from Mexico or the States," Buick writes. "He grinned and ambiguously hinted that it would be by sea."

Hidell then told Buick that his real interest for wanting to talk was not bullfighting but was in how he could possibly remain in Mexico, if need be for some time, before going to Cuba and Russia.

Buick told Hidell that he "was curious as to the reason he wanted to go to Cuba, and that I sympathized with Castro, but that the Cuban people were in a sad state of affairs because of the many disastrous decisions Castro had made in the past."

Hidell said, "It's all Kennedy's fault!"

"No, my friend, you gotta go back in time and put the blame where it belongs," said Buick.

Hidell countered, "Would you call the Bay of Pigs invasion a reassuring gesture toward Castro and Cuba?"

"No, my friend, that one I could never understand," said Buick.

Hidell was again quiet for a moment, and then said, "Well, he's going to pay for that one."

"What do you mean? Buick cautiously asked.

"He's going to get hit!" said Hidell.

"Who's going to get hit?"

"Kennedy," Hidell replied. It's all set. The machinery is already in gear."

"That's awful heavy, pal, said Buick. "It's not what I would call a logical method by which to solve a problem; it merely creates a crisis."

Hidell laughed at Buick's words. He said, "You're shallow, man, that's the most logical solution."

"You call that logic?" asked Buick.

Said Hidell: "I have given the remedy much thought and have studied the solution as far back as to ancient times, and assassination is the most moral and logical course to follow, for violent revolution is not the answer, because with armed revolutions comes violence and destruction. The people gain nothing, only the burden of rebuilding what a violent revolt has destroyed. Governments are like large serpents and monsters; the ultimate morality is to remove the head of the creature and replace it with another."

As readers may well expect, Robert Buick, on the day of the assassination, recognized Alek Hidell as the alleged assassin of President Kennedy, however, that recognition was far from the end of Buick's account of his involvement with Lee Harvey Oswald and the assassination. Indeed, Buick's story, as will be revealed in Volume Two of this work, becomes even more intriguing and convoluted, and Federal authorities continue to do their best to ignore anything he has to say.

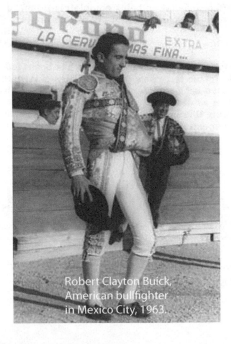

Robert Clayton Buick, American bullfighter in Mexico City, 1963.

UNITED STATES GOVERNMENT

Memorandum

TO : Mr. Mohr DATE: April 30, 1964

FROM : C. D. DeLoach

SUBJECT: ASSASSINATION OF THE PRESIDENT

Walter Jenkins, Special Assistant to the President, told me on 4/29/64 that a friend of his had just returned from Dallas, Texas. In Dallas Jenkins' friend had allegedly met with one of our Special Agents. This Agent had formerly been assigned to the New Orleans Office. The Agent told Jenkins' friend that he had been transferred from New Orleans as a result of getting into difficulty with a woman in the French quarter.

The alleged Agent also reportedly told Jenkins' friend that he assisted in the investigation of the Oswald case and that Oswald, prior to his murder, was definitely an FBI informant. The "Agent" stated that FBI files in Washington would prove this fact.

I told Jenkins that while I doubted very seriously that any of our Agents had furnished this fact to his "friend," that at the same time we, of course, would make a check and find out if the description given this "Agent" fitted any of our people. I asked Jenkins if he would mind letting us interview his friend. He stated that the information had been furnished him in confidence and he preferred not to reveal the identity of this fellow. He stated he wanted to let us know, however, that he had made it very clear to his friend that this was an old rumor that had arisen time and again, and that the FBI had branded it as being completely false. Jenkins stated there was no question in his mind regarding the falsity of this matter.

NOT RECORDED
139 MAY 15 1964

RECOMMENDATION:

Despite the fact that this matter has been tied down as being false, it is considered desirable to review personnel files of Agents in Dallas to find out if any of the Agents have been transferred there from New Orleans for a type of disciplinary problem as described above. If there is such an Agent he should be interviewed regarding this matter. It is, therefore, suggested this memorandum be forwarded to the Domestic Intelligence Division for appropriate action.

1 - Mr. Belmont
1 - Mr. Sullivan
1 - Mr. Rosen
1 - Mr. Jones

CDD:dgs (6)

5 9 MAY 19 1964

JY MAY 14 1964

PERS. REC. UNIT

An FBI Letterhead Memorandum discussing a report of an FBI Agent telling a friend that "Oswald ... was definitely an FBI informant."

NOTES

CHAPTER ONE

Delillo, Don, *LIBRA*, Penguin Books, New York, 1989; Letter to Robert Oswald from Lee Harvey Oswald, November 26, 1959, Warren Commission Exhibit 295, Volume. XVI, pages 815-822; Marrs, Jim, *Crossfire*, Basic Books, New York, February 1992, and January 1993; Additional material on Lee Oswald will appear in Volume Two of this work.

Dr. Henry K. Beecher: According to Dr. Louis Lasagna, Associate Dean, Tufts Medical School, Boston, Massachusetts, in an interview with Dr. David Healy, Beecher's last name was thought to be Unangst, "his paternal name." Lasagna worked closely with Beecher. See: *The Psychopharmacologists II* by Dr. David Healy, Arnold, Hodder Headline Group, London, 1998, pp. 138-139.

"Mental Study of Oswald at 13 Found Him Angry" by Martin Arnold, *New York Times*, December 4, 1963. A copy of this article can be found in the Mary Ferrell Foundation online archives. The same issue of the *New York Times* carried a separate brief article reporting that Marguerite Oswald was to receive an $863 life insurance payment from the National Life Insurance Company on a $1,000 policy she had taken out on Lee Oswald's life in 1945. The reduced amount to be paid was due to "failure to pay premiums after April, 1959."

Testimony of Dr. Renatus Hartogs, Warren Commission, April 16, 1964, at 7 East 86th Street, New York, NY, taken by Mr. Wesley J. Liebeler, assistant counsel to the President's Commission.

Albarelli, H.P., Jr., Draft monograph, "*Lee Harvey Oswald and The Manchurian Candidate*, 1959-1963," pp. 17-36, author's files.

"The Mind of Lee Oswald—His Psychiatrist's View" by Joseph Wershba, *New York Post*, December 15, 1963.

Reports of Social Work and Probation Officer: While at Youth House, young Oswald was also examined and interviewed in April 1953 by Evelyn Strickman, a social worker. Strickman's report may have been the most accurate observations of the youth. Wrote Strickman: "Lee is a seriously detached, withdrawn youngster of thirteen, remanded to Youth House for the first time on a charge of truancy. There is no previous court charge." Strickman wrote that Lee told her that he "never did like school." She observed, "apparently [he] never formed relationships with other people." "Lee was able to respond to expressions of understanding for his lonely situation, but he denied that he really felt lonely." Continued Strickman: "He [Oswald] acknowledged fantasies about being all powerful and being able to do anything that he wanted. When I asked [whether] this ever involved hurting or killing people, he said that id did sometimes but refused to elucidate on it."

After young Oswald appeared in juvenile court for truancy, he was assigned a Probation Officer named John Carro. Carro's detailed files on Oswald state that Lee, while attending P.S. #47 was "absent 48 whole days and two half days." Carro wrote in his report on Oswald: "The P.O. feels that we are dealing with a boy who feels a great deal of insecurity and the need for acceptance. As it does not seem that this can be done with the boy remaining at home but it was felt that perhaps placement in an institution where these needs can be met would be beneficial at this time. However, recommendation is being held in abeyance pending the receipt of the psychiatric examination.... This 13 year old well built boy has superior mental resources and functions only slightly below his capacity level in spite of chronic truancy from school which brought him into Youth House. No finding of neurological impairment or psychotic mental changes could be made. Lee had to be diagnosed as 'personality pattern disturbances with schizoid features and passive aggressive tendencies.' *Lee has to be seen as an emotionally, quite disturbed youngster who suffers the impact of really existing emotional isolation and deprivation, lack of affection absence of family and life and rejection by a self involved and conflicted mother. Although Lee denies that he is in need of any other form of help other than 'remedial' one, we gained the definite impression that Lee can be reached through contact with an understanding and very patient psychotherapist and if he could be drawn at the same time into group psychotherapy. We arrive therefore at the recommendation that he should be placed on probation under the condition that he seek help and guidance through contact with a child guidance clinic, where he should be treated preferably by a male psychiatrist who could substitute, to a certain degree at least, for the lack of a father figure. At the same time, his mother should be urged to book psychotherapeutic guidance through contact with a family agency."* [Emphasis added.] Of course, none of this went forward as Lee's mother soon packed up, without notifying the New York authorities, and took her son back to Louisiana.

Some of the additional information in Carro's reports is intriguing and provokes a number of serious issues and questions. Carro, in his initial report, dated April 21, 1953, identifies Lee Oswald's father as "Robert Lee Harvey." This seems hardly a mistake because, as Carro's report states, the information was provided to him by Lee's mother Marguerite in a face-to-face interview that day in Carro's office.

Renatus Hartogs: *Time* magazine, Monday, March 24, 1975, "The Sexes: Love Thy Analyst."

Hartogs, Renatus, M.D., Ph.D. and Freeman, Lucy, *The Two Assassins*, Thomas Y. Crowell Co., New York, 1965; Freeman, Lucy and Roy, Julie, *Betrayal*, Pocket Books, New York, 1977.

H.P. Albarelli Jr. & Dr. Jeffery S. Kaye, "The Hidden Tragedy of the CIA's Experiments on Children," Truthout.org Investigative Report, August 11, 2010; Malitz experiment: see West, Louis Jolyon M.D., editor, *Hallucinations*, Grune & Stratton Books, New York, 1962.

Bender, Lauretta, M.D., *Aggression, Hostility and Anxiety in Children*, Charles C. Thomas Publishers, Springfield, Illinois, 1953, pp. 10-39. See also: Bender, Lauretta, B.S., M.A., M.D., *Psychopathology of Children with Organic Brain Disorders,* Charles C. Thomas Publishers, Springfield, Illinois, 1956.

Drs. Joel Elkes & Abraham Wikler: Elkes, who would perform LSD and drug research and experiments for nearly twenty years, went out of his way to praise Wikler and in at least one extensive interview praised Dr. Wikler as the driving force behind LSD and psychochemical research at the federal facility in Lexington, Kentucky.

Shorter, Edward and Healy, David, *Shock Therapy: A History of Electroconvulsive Treatment in Mental Illness,* Rutgers University Press, New Brunswick, New Jersey, 2007.

Metrazol & Insulin Shock Therapy: Recently obtained CIA ARTICHOKE Project documents dated 1952, 1953, 1954, and 1956 reveal that CIA physicians acting as members of various ARTICHOKE Teams assigned to selected CIA foreign stations, including Japan, Germany, and France, employed Metrazol and insulin shock therapy as an instrument of torture in coercive interrogation sessions. Medical papers referred to in some of these documents include: "Effect of Metrazol Convulsions on Brain Metabolism" by Harold E. Himwich, Karl M. Bowman, Joseph F. Fazekas and Leo L. Orenstein, *Experimental Biological Medicine*, November 1937, Volume 37, Number 2, pp. 359-361; "Metabolism of the Brain During Insulin and Metrazol Treatments of Schizophrenia" by Harold E. Himwich, M.D., Karl M. Bowman, M.D., Joseph Wortis, M.D., Joseph F. Fazekas, Journal of American Medical Association, 1939, Vol. 112 (16), pp. 572-574; "A Study of the Central Action of Metrazol" by B. Libert, J.F. Fazekas, and Harold E. Himwich, *American Journal of Psychiatry*, 1940, Volume 97, pp. 366-371. The horrors patients experience with Metrazol shock therapy can be viewed on YouTube.com with various videos found there.

Project ARTICHOKE, Narco-hypnosis, and Special Interrogations: CIA Memorandum to Assistant Director/Scientific Intelligence from Chief, Medical Staff, subject: Special Interrogations, 19 May 1952, Copy No. 1, author's files; "Narco-Hypnosis and Children," a partial CIA Artichoke document dated June 1954, CIA-SRS, author's files.

"Oswald's 1959 Interview with UPI" by Aline Mosby, Paris, November 23, 1963 (UPI), UPI Archives; "Aline Mosby, 76, UPI Correspondent," *New York Times,* August 19, 1998; May 1978 Interview with Mosby; CIA 1958 cable on Mosby that reads: "We believe Mosby and [redacted name] unwitting Kubark [CIA] follow up. Our impression [redacted name] liked Mosby as a woman and discussed generalities with her while attempting make time since she attractive and had car. Assessed Mosby to be not very bright, not politically informed, she expressed pinkish views, but [redacted name] blames it on her ignorance rather than convictions. Knew Mosby only as free lance writer."

Priscilla Livingston Johnson: Johnson was the other reporter who interviewed Lee Harvey Oswald in Moscow, four days after Mosby's interview. Johnson was longtime friends with CIA official Cord Meyer and his wife Mary Meyer, who was murdered in Washington, D.C. Priscilla Johnson applied for employment with the CIA in 1952, but reportedly was denied a security clearance and not hired. In 1953, she worked for Sen. John F. Kennedy.

"*We Were Strangers*: Did it Trigger the JFK Assassination?" article by Ken Brooks, *FilmFax* magazine, Issue 115, July 2007.

"Frank Sinatra's Assassination Role: Telling It Like It Wasn't" by Martin Shackelford, *The Third Decade*, Vol. 1, Issue 6, November 1984-September 1985, pp.13-15.

Notes

I Led Three Lives and Robert Oswald: Oswald, Robert with Barbara and Myrick Land, *Lee: A Portrait of Lee Harvey Oswald by His Brother*, Coward-McCann, New York, 1967, p. 47.

Oswald, Robert L. with Myrick and Barbara Land, "He Was My Brother," *The News*, Mexico, D.F, Special Feature, Saturday, October 7, 1967. See this article on the Mary Ferrell Foundation web site.

Readers interested in possible further links between Lee Harvey Oswald and the films cited in this chapter should consult a slim book by author John Loken entitled, *Oswald's Trigger Films: The Manchurian Candidate, We Were Strangers, Suddenly,* Falcon Books, November 1, 2000. Loken's study examines the three films in their relation to Kennedy's murder and the attempt to kill Gen. Edwin Walker.

U.S. State Department, Memorandum of Conversation, Subject: Lee Oswald; Participants: Mrs. Oswald, PPT: Edward J. Hickey; SCS: Denman F. Stanfield; SOV: D.E. Boster, January 26, 1961; Letter from Richard E. Snyder, American Consul, to D.E. Boster, Officer in Charge, USSR Affairs, Department of State, Washington, D.C., October 28, 1959.

Oswald's "suicide" attempt: Readers wanting to learn more about Oswald's alleged suicide attempt should see the brilliant online analysis of this incident done by Peter Wronski: "Lee Harvey Oswald in Russia: An Unauthorized History from the Kennedy Assassination, Parts 1-4"; and Weberman, A.J., Nodule X5-Dispatched Defector, available on-line as part of Weberman's extensive JFK assassination site.

Memorandum from DDP Richard Helms to FBI Director J. Edgar Hoover, Subject: Assassination of President John F. Kennedy, February 17, 1964.

FBI Teletype to Director and SAC, New Orleans from SAC, Dallas, regarding information from J.C. Murdock to Dallas FBI office, November 25, 1963. According to this teletype, "Secret Service has been notified."

Pierre Lafitte: "The Gourmet Pirate," *Time* magazine, Friday, December 19, 1969; for much more on Pierre Lafitte see author's book on Frank Olson's murder, *A Terrible Mistake*; also see George Hunter White's private letters to Pierre and Rene Lafitte, 1961-1970; to Garland Williams, 1955-1964; and to Harry Anslinger, 1953-1963; see White Archives, Perham Electronics Museum, Sunnyvale, California (today at Stanford University), and additional letters and documents compliments of Albertine White, Sausalito, California.

"Warrant Out For Arrest of Lafitte," Boston AP wire story, *Lewiston* [Maine] *Evening Journal,* December 4, 1963. This brief article states that Lafitte "claims to be a descendant of the famous Louisiana pirate."

"Did Lee Harvey Oswald Drop Acid?" article by Martin A. Lee, Robert Ranftel, and Jeff Cohen, *Rolling Stone* magazine, March 1983. This article quotes an unidentified serviceman who reportedly served at Atsugi Naval Air Base in Japan around the same time as Oswald. The serviceman states that drugs, including LSD, were experimented with at Atsugi, but extensive military and Pentagon records, which reveal the names of military installations where LSD and other similar drugs were experimented with on unwitting servicemen, do not include the Atsugi base. Former CIA officials, including Dr. Sidney Gottlieb, have reported that LSD was "used [by the CIA] on a limited basis" for "interrogation objectives" at Atsugi and at another location in Manila, Philippines; other interviews with Edward G. Gillin, including, most importantly, that with Dick Russell. See Russell's, *The Man That Knew Too Much*, Carol & Graf, New York, 1992, pp.385-387. Researcher Greg Parker has pointed out that when the FBI searched Oswald's (Paine) residence after the assassination, a vial of "white powder" was found, but it has never been identified in any published documents. The *Rolling Stone* article recounts the CIA's early efforts with drugs, mind control, and interrogation, and then briefly returns to ADA Gillin's alleged Oswald encounter, pointing out that Gillin was "extremely nearsighted" -- implying that perhaps the young man had not seen Oswald. Interestingly, Gillin recalled that the young man who visited him referred to an author whose books on drugs described a new world. Gillin wrote down the author's names as "Hucksley." Obviously, this was Aldous Huxley, whose books we know Oswald did read, along with a list of science fiction books and Ian Fleming's James Bond novels. (Huxley, who took LSD a number of times, died on November 23, 1963, the same day JFK was murdered.)

Edward Gillin report: FBI Report by Special Agent Regis L. Kennedy, December 13, 1963, New Orleans, Louisiana, File number: 100-16601.

Newman, Albert H., *The Assassination of John F. Kennedy: The Reason Why*, Clarkson N. Potter, Inc., New York, 1970, First Edition.

Oswald's CAP membership: Marguerite Oswald testified before the Warren Commission about young Lee's membership in the New Orleans CAP branch run by David Ferrie. Marguerite said that she thought

Lee, at the age of 15, only attended CAP meetings for about a month, but being the fine mother that she was, she was not sure. Lee Oswald's boyhood friend, Edward Voebel, told New Orleans police in 1963 that Oswald may have attended at least one party at Ferrie's home. At least one of the young boys Ferrie molested, said [in 2009, off the record] that he "thought because Ferrie tried to molest Oswald, he [Oswald] left the CAP program." Voebel also testified that Oswald, who he said had purchased a CAP uniform, was only a CAP member for about a month.

"Negro with reddish hair": CIA Memorandum from Richard Helms, DDP to J. Lee Rankin, General Counsel, Warren Commission, Subject: Information Developed on the Activity of Lee Harvey Oswald in Mexico City, 4 June 1964.

Worth a reminder here is that serviceman Lee Harvey Oswald was also in the Philippines (in late 1957 and January 1958), yet nobody has ever made any connection between Oswald and the LSD stored there, as was also reported in Inspector General Kirkpatrick's memorandum on the Frank Olson case.

Intelligence-speak: "Distributive responsibility," according to a former CIA official, refers to "a product distributed directly from and by the CIA to another party outside the Agency." Under this definition, a drug such as LSD, sent by another party outside the Agency at the request of the CIA to a third party, would *not* fall under the definition of "distributive responsibility." Therefore, any drugs sent by the Sandoz or Lilly drug companies to a third party at the request of the CIA would not fall under this definition.

In 1953, as reflected in the same memo cited above, a number of other locations besides Atsugi and Manila had LSD. Indeed, a December 1, 1953 follow-up memo by CIA Inspector General Kirkpatrick lists "Grants in aid to Dr. Harold Abramson, 133 East 58th. Dr. Robert Hyde, Boston Psychopathic Hospital. U.S. Public Service Hospital, Lexington, Kentucky (Dr. Harris Isbell). Dr. Carl Pfeiffer, Department of Pharmacology, University of Illinois, School of Medicine, Chicago. Lilly has been trying to make it [LSD]. Another trying by radioactive to see what part of body it works on. These are top secret cleared."

CHAPTER TWO

In all, Melba Christian Marcades, born November 14, 1923, had at least 35 aliases that she used with varying frequency. These included: Zada Mary Gano; Zada Scars; Zada Lynn Garo; Patsy Garo; Zada Rodman; Zada Fitzgerald; Patsy Rodman; Rose Rodman; Melba Rodman; Christine Rodman; and at least an additional twenty-five more.

Many people today, including some writers and journalists, are certain that Rose was thrown from a car in Eunice, Louisiana. She was not. This image comes from the creative opening scenes of Oliver Stone's film, *JFK*.

Rose Cheramie [*sic*], Staff Report of the Select Committee on Assassinations, U.S. House of Representatives, Ninety-fifth Congress, Second Session, March 1979.

Dr. Louis Jolyon West: Dr. West bears the despicable distinction of having killed a 7,000-pound elephant by dosing it with a huge amount of LSD. The unfortunate mammal, named Tusko, after being injected with the drug, began having seizures within 5 minutes and died 45 minutes later. During his career, West treated Charles Manson, Jack Ruby, Sirhan Sirhan, and Patty Hearst.

Other confidential law enforcement reports shared with the FBI in 1967 and 1968 (and passed on to the CIA), reveal that Rose Cherami, at the time of her first car accident, may have been running drugs for two men named Willis Spencer and Alfred A. Courtiade. Indeed, in 1962 and 1963, Courtiade had had discussions in New Orleans with Thomas Eli Davis, III (see this book's section on Davis) concerning the filming and distribution of stag films. Davis and Courtiade discussed using women from Jack Ruby's Dallas clubs for the films, as well as "girls from some of the better Louisiana clubs." Courtiade was believed to be partially bankrolled by Carlos Marcello, and reportedly he and Marcello shared the same attorney, G. Wray Gill. Also, well worth noting here is that Courtiade reportedly did extensive business involving illicit prescription drugs with Silver Slipper owner Mac Manual. See: Confidential Report to FBI (with copies to CIA) on "A.A. Courtiade, aka Dickey Carter, and Wholesale Drug Distribution, 1962-1964," by William C. Gray, U.S. Pure Food and Drug Administration, HEW, New Orleans, LA. April 23, 1964.

Dr. Don Bowers: In 2002, in a letter to researcher Robert Dorff, Dr. Bowers denied Fruge's claims about him. Bowers wrote, "Dr. Weiss' statement [that I asked him to see Rose and that Rose had predicted the assassination before November 22, 1963 to me] is untrue. I was not at the hospital on Monday, November the 25th.... I never saw Rose Cherami and only found out about her allegations on Sunday, November the 24th, 1963 during a dove hunting engagement with Dr. Weiss. It was he who told me what she allegedly

Notes

told Weiss and possibly others. I was never contacted by anyone from the House Select Committee on Assassinations."

Interview of Jerry Moore by J. Gary Shaw, n.d.; interview with members of the Youngblood family who declined specific identification, and one of whom said, "We saw what happened to Rose and that's enough."

Rose Cheramie, Staff Report of the Select Committee on Assassinations, U.S. House of Representatives, 95th Congress, Second Session, March 1979, HSCA, Vol. X.

For more details on the Martin Billnitzer death and controversy, see: article by H.P. Albarelli, Jr., "Answers Demanded in Decades Old 'Suicide' Case," *World Net Daily,* September 8, 2002; also see draft article, "A Kettle Full of Snakes: The Murder of Martin Billnitzer," H.P. Albarelli's website.

Summers, Anthony, *Not In Your Lifetime,* Marlowe & Company, New York, 1998, pp. 433-434; Douglas, James W., *JFK and the Unspeakable,* Orbis Books, Maryknoll, New York, 2008, pp. 244-48, 441 n131; Waldron, Lamar with Hartman, Thom, *Ultimate Sacrifice: John and Robert Kennedy, the Plan for a Coup in Cuba, and the Murder of JFK,* Carroll & Graf, New York, 2006, pp. 728-30, 787, 796-97; Mellen, Joan, *A Farewell to Justice,* Potomac Books, Washington, D.C., pp. 206-208, 215, 260-61; Hurt, Henry, *Reasonable Doubt,* Henry Holt & Co., New York, pp. 411-12; Hancock, Larry, *Someone Would Have Talked,* JFK Lancer Productions and Publications, Texas, 2006.

Numerous letters and memos by Federal Bureau of Narcotics agent and CIA contractor George Hunter White, Perham Electronics Museum, Sunnyvale, California. The author spent a week going through this collection, since moved to Stanford University, California; George Hunter White Diaries, 1953, 1954, 1955, copies author's collection; George Hunter White letters and records provided the author by Albertine White, Sausalito, California, 1999-2001; Albertine was the first person to mention Billnitzer's death to this author; George Hunter White letters to Garland Williams, 1954-1962, author's files; Letters ands reports to Charles Siragusa and FBN director Harry Anslinger from George Hunter White, 1952-1963, author's files; George Hunter White letters to Jean Pierre Lafitte, 1954-1964, author's files; letters to Pierre Lafitte from James Phelan, 1960-1964, author's files; author's interviews with Dr. Aimee Phelan, California, 1999-2001; letters from Lafitte to wife, Rene, and to George White, author's files; author's interviews with Phen Lafitte, Miami 1999-2007; author's interviews with Charles Leblanc, Concord, New Hampshire 1999-2003.

Albarelli, H.P. Jr., *Midnight Climax: The Life and Times of George Hunter White, Federal Narcotics and CIA Agent Extraordinaire,* forthcoming 2014 from Trine Day Publishers, Oregon.

"Rose Cheramie: How She Predicted the JFK Assassination," article by Jim DiEugenio, *Probe* magazine, July-August 1999, Vol. 6, No. 5; "Rambling Rose," article by Chris Mills, 76 Main St., Burton Joyce, Nottingham NG14 5EH; for another odd twist to Rose's story see: "The Silver Slipper" article by Lisa Peace, *Probe* [CTKA], Vol. 6, No. 5, July-August 1999.

Memorandum to Jim Garrison, DA, from: Frank Meloche, Re: Rose Cherami, March 13, 1967; Report of Lt. F.L. Fruge, LA. State Police, Parish of St. Landry, City of Eunice, April 4, 1967.

"Woman Lying on Highway Fatally Hurt," *The Gilmer* [Texas] *Mirror,* September 9, 1965, page 1. This article also states: Jerry Don Moore "was absolved of any blame in the accident," and that Rose "died about 10:00 Saturday morning" having "never regained consciousness after she was brought to the hospital."

Oswald's address book: The address "1318 1/2 Garfield, Norman, Oklahoma" was found in Oswald's address book after his death. Intrepid JFK researcher A.J. Weberman reports, "Mae Logan, who owned this property from 1961 to 1967, was contacted in August 1993. She stated that several white teenagers along with one black lived in the top part of a rental unit she owned between 1962-1963: 'They quit payin' the rent, got into drugs and were arrested in Phoenix. There was lady who lived up there to begin with. She got cancer and went to the M.D. Anderson Hospital. Her father and mother had died of cancer two years ago.' Logan was never questioned by the FBI." Investigating the Garfield address, this author observed that another character linked to the JFK assassination, Thomas Eli Davis, Jr., also briefly lived in Norman, Oklahoma, before Kennedy's Dallas assassination. Compounding matters, and perhaps simply coincidentally, yet another assassination related character, Loran Eugene Hall, lived briefly in Norman, prior to the assassination. People that closely knew Tom Davis have stated that he and Hall together had gunrunning dealings with Jack Ruby in 1962 and 1963, but these same people have consistently refused to speak publicly about the Davis-Hall relationship, or about any possibility that both men were involved with the group that occupied the 1318 1/2 Garfield apartment in Norman. (See this book's sections on both Tom Davis and Loran Hall.) This author, however, has been able to confirm that at least one person who knew Lee Harvey Oswald did live at the Garfield address in 1963. This was Paul Gregory, who testified before the Warren Commission in 1964, and when asked for his address only mentioned the University of Oklahoma in Norman. Gregory's father, Peter Paul Gregory, a petroleum engineer, born in 1929 in Siberia, taught Russian at the Fort Worth, Texas library, where he was once approached by Oswald for help in possibly getting a job as a Russian translator or interpreter.

CHAPTER THREE

Telephone interviews with Adele Edisen, September 2010-December 2010; January-February, December 2011; Testimony of Adele Edisen, November 18, 1994 Hearing, Dallas, Texas, AARB; numerous e-mail messages between author and Adele Edisen, 2010, 2011, 2012.

Adele Edisen's papers [sampling list]: "Effects of Asphyxia and Repetitive Stimulation on Intramedullary Afferent Fibers," study supported by National Institute of Neurological Diseases and Blindness and the Commonwealth Fund, May 6, 1957; "Primary Afferent Fibers of Contralateral Origin in the Lower Spinal Cord of Cat," *Experimental Neurology* 18, pp. 38-48, 1967; "Synaptic Inhibition in the Spinal Cord," *Intern. J. Neuroscience*, 1970, Vol. 1, pp. 119-128, "Regional and Lateral Specificity of Acupuncture-Induced Action of Blood-Factor Effects Inhibiting Hindlimb Flexor Reflexes in the Rabbit," *Physiological Chemistry and Physics and Medical NMR*, 15, pp. 189-199, 1983.

Dr. Robert G. Heath: "Comparative Effects of the Administration of Taraxein, d-LSD, Mescaline, and Psilocybin to Human Volunteers," article by F. Silva, M.D., R. Johnson, M.D., and W. Johnson, M.D., *Comprehensive Psychiatry Journal*, Volume 1, 1960, p. 370-376 (LSD 879/PSI 55), author's file; Heath, R.G., "Pleasure and Brain Activity in Man: Deep and Surface Electroencephalograms During Orgasm," *Journal of Nervous and Mental Disease*, Volume 151, 1972, pp. 3-18. Also see: "The Search for an Endogenous Schizogen: The Strange Case of Taraxein" by Alan Baumeister, Psychology Dept., Louisiana State University, Baton Rouge, LA, *Journal of the History of the Neurosciences*, 20: pp.106-122, 2011.

Drs. C.E. Muan and R.G. Heath, "Septal Stimulation for the Initiation of Heterosexual Activity in a Homosexual Male," *Journal of Behavior Therapy and Experimental Psychiatry*, Volume 3, 1972, pp. 23-30.

Florence B. Strohmeyer: Strohmeyer, a research chemist who worked with Dr. Heath at Tulane University School of Medicine for several years, later expressed "serious reservations and concerns" about Dr. Heath's work and experiments. Interviewed in 2009 at her home in Chester, Vermont, she told this author that she "had no idea that the CIA or Pentagon were involved in Heath's experiments and that their objectives were counter to the well-being of the subjects involved."

Winston Russell de Monsabert, PhD: de Monsabert was born in New Orleans and was a cousin to King Louis of France. He received a B.S. in Chemistry from Loyola University, New Orleans in 1937; in 1945 received an MA in Education from Tulane University, New Orleans; and a PhD in Chemistry from Tulane in 1952. From 1948 to 1969, de Monsabert worked as Professor of Chemistry at Loyola University. From 1966 to 1969 he also served as Chief Chemist at the National Center for Disease Control, Department of Health and Human Services, Atlanta, and served as Chief Contract Liaison, National Center for Health Services Research from 1969 to 1973. He was Chief Extramural Programs, Bureau of Drugs, FDA from 1973 to 1979, and was Scientist Administrate, Office of the Commissioner, FDA from 1979-1983. He served as Chairman of the Georgia Chapter of the American Institute of Chemists in 1954. He died in 2009. (Robert Howard, JFK Assassination Debate Forum online, administrator John Simkins; and *The Times Picayune* newspaper, New Orleans, June 11, 2009.)

It has been reported that in November 1962, after "a CIA doctor," Dr. Edward Mansfield Gunn, approached him about doing research for the Agency, Heath became outraged that the CIA would try to involve him in intelligence matters. Heath made this revelation over thirteen years after the alleged approach took place and after indignation and outrage had been expressed by the American public following widespread media revelations about the CIA's use of mind-altering drugs. Dr. Gunn, who worked briefly with Jose Rivera at the Armed Forces Institute of Pathology, was posted for at least one year at a CIA medical facility in New Jersey to administer LSD to CIA employees so that they would become experienced firsthand with the effects of the drug. Gunn was first hired by the CIA in 1955, and remained in the Agency's employ until May 1971, when he resigned as Deputy Director of Medical Services. Shortly after his resignation he went to work for former CIA SRS officer and Watergate burglar James McCord. It has long been believed that McCord's business, McCord Associates, was a front company for the CIA. Also working for McCord's company were Ralph Orlando True, Jr. (whom readers shall meet in this book in connection with June Cobb and the Agency's Office of Security), and William Francis Shea, whose wife worked for McCord's company as an administrative assistant. Dr. Gunn, True, and Shea were also associated with McCord

Associates affiliated company, the Institute for Protection and Safety Studies, which was housed in the same space as McCord Associates. While it was not a central part of his CIA employment, Dr. Gunn was often consulted by the Agency on matters related to assassinations. In the late 1950s and throughout the 1960s, he was asked to quickly devise lethal compounds that could be used to kill targeted individuals, including Fidel Castro. Dr. Gunn was once consulted, while working for McCord, about the task of killing columnist Jack Anderson. Gunn was also consulted about dosing Anderson, and other media figures, with LSD and BZ. In July 1984, Watergate burglar Gordon Liddy testified in a court case involving former CIA official Howard Hunt who was employed by another CIA front company, Mullen and Associates. Liddy testified: "We discussed Dr. Gunn's suggestion of the use of an automobile to hit Mr. Anderson's automobile when it was in a turn; if you hit a car at just the right speed and angle, it will ... burn and kill the occupant.... But what I suggested is, we just kill him. And they both agreed that would be the way to go about it, and the task would be assigned to Cuban assets." Dr. Gunn, True, and Shea also worked often with former CIA and army intelligence officer Allan Hughes, who told this writer, "We used Cubans and Corsicans on a fairly regular basis to either seriously mess up or murder targeted individuals.... Far more in number than anyone would imagine ... Why? Because very few were high profile, and low profile wet jobs were basically off the radar screen ... and if the operative was creative enough the cause of death almost always came off as something in the regular medical lexicon ... heart attack, stroke, you name it." Lastly on Dr. Gunn: it is surprising to note the number of CIA documents concerning Lee Harvey Oswald that were generated after the assassination, from 1964 through 1967, that refer to Dr. Edward Gunn as having a role in any psychological assessment of Oswald. For example, this line from a March 1964 CIA memorandum: "The report of FBI special agent, Robert P. Gemberling, dated January 7, 1964, Dallas, Texas, (DBA 63708) contains an interesting exchange of letters from an individual in Dallas and a psychiatrist which speculates over Oswald's motivation in killing the President. This may be of general interest to Dr. Edward M. Gunn and Dr. Bernard Malloy of the (CIA) Medical Staff." (March 20, 1964 CI R&A [Counterintelligence Research Staff] Memorandum on Lee Harvey Oswald.)

Dr. Ichiji Tasaki: Tasaki, who died in 2009, was known and respected worldwide as a biophysicist and physician involved in research relating to the electrical impulses in the nervous system. He is credited with the discovery of the insulating function of the myelin sheath, which has resulted in a better understanding of diseases like multiple sclerosis. In the 1950s, Tasaki served as Chief of NINDB. Dr. Tasaki worked closely at NIH with Dr. Wade H. Marshall, whose laboratory work focused "on the function of the nervous system, specifically neural transmission and neuronal interactions, the cerebral cortex, and special senses, in an attempt to understand physiological phenomena occurring in the nervous system that would mediate behavior." In his work, Marshall experimented with LSD and the "effects of the blood-brain barrier." Tasaki also worked closely with Dr. John C. Lilly who conducted studies on "unanaesthetized monkeys aimed at creating a general map of spatial and temporal patterns of electrical activity on the surface of the cortex." Lilly also administered LSD to dolphins in attempts to communicate with the mammals. (See: Farreras, Ingrid; Hannaway, Caroline; Harden, Victoria, *Mind, Brain, Body and Behavior*, IOS Press, Netherlands, 2004.)

E-mail communication with William E. Kelly, Jr. March-May 2009; December 2010-February 2011.

"Jose Rivera: The Story That Will Not Die" by William E. Kelly, Jr., *The Fourth Decade*, Vol. 7, No. 1, November 1999, pp. 9-17.

University of Texas at San Antonio Archives and Special Collections, MS 200, Oral History Collection: Adele E.U. Edisen Transcript, March 23, 2009.

Dr. Carl Lamanna: Publications of the Naval Biological Laboratory, School of Public Health, University of California and Naval Medical Research Unit #1, Berkeley, California, 1942-1965, Director, Naval Biological Laboratory, Naval Supply Center, Oakland, California. This publication can be found online.

"*Effects of Extreme Heat and Cold on Human Skin III. Numerical Analysis and Pilot Experiments on Penetrating Flash Radiation Effects,"* article by Dr. Konrad Buettner, from the Department of Radiobiology, USAF School of Aviation Medicine, Randolph Field, Texas, Cold Spring harbor Symposium Quant. Biology, January 1, 1959.

"President's best friend" and suicide: Adele later came to believe that this was Edward Grant Stockdale. In March 1961, President Kennedy appointed Stockdale Ambassador to Ireland. Prior to this, Stockdale had been director of the Florida State Committee to Elect JFK. Following Kennedy's nomination, Stockdale actively campaigned for him in West Virginia, Oregon, and New York. Stockdale was also a member of the Democratic Party's National Finance Committee. During the 1962 investigation of Bobby Baker, a close friend of LBJ, some people raised the issue that Stockdale had business connections to Baker, who was reportedly tied to the Mafia and Sam Giancana. According to writer Seymour Hersh, at the beginning of November 1963, JFK asked Stockdale to raise $50,000 for his personal use. Stockdale told friends it had something to do with the Bobby Baker case. Following the assassination of JFK, Stockdale flew to Washington, D.C. and met with Bobby Kennedy and Ted Kennedy. On his return home, Stockdale told several friends that, "the world was closing in." On December 1, he spoke to his attorney William Frates who later recalled: "He started talking. It didn't make much sense. He said something about 'those guys' trying to get him. Then about the assassination." Stockdale died on December 2, 1963 when he fell (or was thrown) from his office on the thirteenth floor of the Dupont Building in Miami. He did not leave a suicide note. Many of his friends said he was not the type of person to kill himself.

Interviews with NIH personnel who declined to be named in this book; CIA MK/ULTRA Briefing Book, 1976, author's files; several conversations with Doug Horne, 2010-2011; see forthcoming book: Albarelli Jr., H.P., *Exploiting Evil: Project Paperclip, the Pentagon, CIA, and Human Experimentation*, to be released by Progressive Press, 2013.

A special thanks to James Richards, Steven Duffy, William Kelly, Steve Rosen, Robert Howard, Linda Minor and Greg Parker for the assiduous and superb research they have done on Adele Edisen's story and related subjects over the past two decades.

Jose Albert Rivera: Rivera was never a board member of NIH, as reported in at least two other books, nor is there any evidence that he ever suffered a nervous breakdown that caused him to be institutionalized, as reported in another book. Over the past two decades it has been sporadically reported that Rivera was in attendance at the autopsy of President Kennedy. As of this writing, this is unverifiable. Officials at Bethesda Naval Hospital state that he was "not present for the autopsy." Given his position at NIH at the time, it seems doubtful this is true. Additionally, while Rivera is often referred to as "Dr. Rivera," this author was not able to locate any evidence that he ever graduated from medical school.

CIA programs MK/ULTRA, ZR/ALERT, Armour Project, and Project ARTICHOKE: *CIA Briefing Book on Behavior Modification Projects, 1952-1963*, author's copy.

For more information on John Mulholland, Armour Research Foundation, see: Albarelli, H.P. Jr. *A Terrible Mistake: The Murder of Frank Olson and the CIA's Secret Cold War Experiments*, Trine Day Books, 2010; also see: Robinson, Ben, *The MagiCIAn: John Mulholland's Secret Life*, Lybrary.com Books, First Edition, 2008.

John Mulholland and CIA: Gottlieb did not mention that the CIA's Security Office, in the person of Paul Gaynor, and perhaps also Morse Allen, raised a number of concerns about Mulholland in the process of clearing the magician for Agency contractual work. Chief among Gaynor's concerns were Mulholland's "sexual proclivities" and his long-standing relationship with his personal assistant Dorothy Wolf. As noted earlier in this book, SRS chief Gaynor was expert in identifying and exploiting certain idiosyncrasies of targeted individuals. Mulholland had employed Ms. Wolf for about seven years before he married Pauline Nell Pierce, yet he had never ended his romantic entanglement with Wolf. Indeed, Mulholland's love for Wolf was so sincere and steadfast that he informed his wife-to-be that his relationship with Ms. Wolf would not end and that Pauline would have to accept it if they were to be married. Writes Mulholland biographer Ben Robinson, Pauline Mulholland would later remark, "Johnny was so much a man, one woman's love would not satisfy him." Mulholland's infatuation with and love for Wolf seemed very similar to that of Henry Murray's for Christiana Morgan, his lifelong love. Like Murray, Mulholland was way ahead of convention and the times when it came to sexual exploration and marriage.

Despite Gaynor's concerns, Mulholland was finally approved for work with the Agency, and he signed his security oath with the CIA on November 14, 1953, after it was hand-delivered to him in New York by Robert Lashbrook. Quimby had first suggested Mulholland for hire in early 1952, and Gottlieb had first met with Mulholland in mid-November 1952, and then again in early February 1953, to discuss the specifics of what TSS initially wanted the magician to do for the CIA. Understandably, Gottlieb had grown impatient with the security clearance process. That he spoke personally to Dulles about Mulholland is certain, and surely it weighed heavily in the magician's favor that the Rockefeller family, inclusive of Nelson, was quite fond of Mulholland, and that Pauline Mulholland was related to Barbara Bush, George H.W. Bush's wife, and a cousin of former U.S. President Franklin Pierce. Additionally, Pauline's family was quite wealthy, and her father, Arthur J. Pierce, was a Brigadier General in the U.S. Army.

Albarelli, H.P. Jr., *A Terrible Mistake: The Murder of Frank Olson and the CIA's Secret Cold War Experiments*, Trine Day, 2010, The Horace Mann School in New York City is alleged by some conspiracy theorists to have "connections with the CIA" through the wholly-fabricated "CIA-operated Project Monarch," long alleged to have been part of MK/ULTRA and having originated from Nazi mind-control programs. Some theorists claim the school was used by "CIA agents for operating homosexual and pedophilia programs." This author has seen absolutely no evidence of any such programs or activities.

Steven Duffy and Greg Parker research on William Bryan, Jr.: Hypnotist Bryan died under very strange circumstances in a motel room in Las Vegas. The details of his death vary and are quite unclear. Some reports assert that he died of a heart attack; others state he was shot to death, and still others claim he committed suicide after having a three-day party of sorts with two underage prostitutes. One additional report states that Bryan was killed by a prostitute after he told her he had hypnotized Sirhan Sirhan to murder Robert Kennedy. (Some readers may recall that in the past 25 years at least ten CIA employees have died under strange circumstances in various motels across the country.) Bryan was once charged in Nevada (his home state) for furnishing liquor to a young girl under the age of eighteen while he was attempting to convince her of the merits of "free love." In 1961, Bryan was extradited to California to face charges filed by District Attorney William Raggio, who was a close friend of Frank Sinatra. Reportedly, Bryan was also very close to Sinatra. Bryan told a number of people that Sinatra was responsible for his being hired as a consultant on the film, *The Manchurian Candidate*. Bryan lost his license to practice medicine in California. Bryan, like Dr. Renatus Hartogs before him, was once found guilty of sexual misconduct with four female patients. Reportedly, he paid another woman $50,000 to not file a sexual misconduct complaint against him. There are also claims that Bryan hypnotized and programmed would-be-assassin Arthur Bremer to kill Gov. George Wallace in Maryland. And last, but not least, Bryan was a close associate of David Ferrie, having taught Ferrie hypnosis. Bryan, like Ferrie, was a member of the Old Catholic Church.

"Pioneers in Psychopharmacology" by David Healy, Bangor, Wales, *International Journal of Neuropsychopharmacology*, 1998, pp. 191-194. Dr. Healy is, in this author's view, the world's foremost expert on the history of psychopharmacology.

Roberts, Andy, *Albion Dreaming*, Marshall Cavendish, Ltd., London, 2008, pp. 11-12, 14-15, 19-31, 33-35, 38-45; CIA/U.S. Army [Pentagon] Briefing Book, 1949-1969 on U.K. Linkages to U.S. Psychochemical Programs Funded by the U.S. Government, author's copy.

"Update for the UK and an Interview with Pioneering Psychedelic Psychiatrist Dr. Ronald Sandison," by Ben Sessa, Ph.D., MAPS, Vol. Xviii, No. 3, Winter 2008-09.

Albarelli Jr., H.P., *The Secret History of LSD and the CIA*, draft chapter 5, forthcoming book, Peredur Publications, Ltd., New York, London, 2014.

Dr. Seymour Solomon Kety: Kety was involved in experiments funded by the Scottish Rite, a Freemason's group, that drew the strong interest of HEW, NIH, and the CIA in their Scottish Rite (Freemason) Schizophrenia Research Committee, of which Kety was a member. Kety was a member of the Scottish Rite/Freemasons organization, and was also national director of the Society for the Study of Social Biology, formerly the American Eugenics Society. For decades now there have been credible reports that Kety's work with the Scottish Rite and Social Biology Society also employed physicians at the now-closed Lexington, Kentucky Federal Prison Farm. For more on Kety, see: Ross, Colin A., *The CIA Doctors*, Manitou Communications, Inc., 2006, pp. 133-134.

Truthout.org website see: "The CIA's Shocking Experiments on Children Exposed: Drugging, Electroshocks and Brainwashing" by H.P. Albarelli Jr. and Dr. Jeffrey S. Kaye, Truthout.org, August 12, 2010. This article reveals that Dr. Joel Elkes, one of the earliest physicians in Europe to experiment with LSD, was also closely associated with Dr. Abraham Wikler, who worked closely with Dr. Harris Isbell at the Lexington, Kentucky Federal Prison Farm. The article also details the abusive LSD psychotherapy conducted by British physicians Thomas M. Ling and John Buckman, and contains an interview with one of Buckman's unwitting subjects, who as a child was dosed by Buckman with LSD. Elkes' associations with physicians in the U.S. and Seymour Kety's work with the CIA are covered in great detail in the author's forthcoming book on LSD and the CIA, as well as in a forthcoming documentary film on the same subject.

In December 1976, Adele Edisen's attorney, Jack Peebles, wrote a letter (see pages 453-454) to the U.S. House of Representatives' Select Committee on Assassinations. There was no reply received to the letter.

CHAPTER FOUR

Dimitrov's story takes on added significance in light of recent revelations of the extensive torture, covert conspiracy and intelligence operations conducted by the American CIA and Department of Defense, in conjunction with their British counterparts and a host of other governments, including Israel, Jordan, Morocco, Pakistan, Poland, to name a few. After a series of exposures during the 1970s, many assumed that the worst excesses of the Cold War torture research and training programs, and their implementation in projects such as the CIA's Operation Phoenix in Vietnam, were fixtures of the past. However, subsequent revelations, e.g. the appearance of a US-sponsored torture manual for use in Latin America in the 1980s, and more recent documentation of torture by US forces in the immediate aftermath of 9/11 and the invasion of Afghanistan, demonstrate that a direct line exists between the torture and rendition programs of the past and the practices of the present day. Recently, articles have detailed how the 2006 rewrite of the Army Field Manual allowed for use of ongoing isolation, sleep deprivation, sensory deprivation, induction of fear and the use of drugs that cause temporary derangement of the senses, as well as use of water boarding, mutilation, sexual assaults and beatings.

The Binyam Mohamed story is unfortunately not unique, but it does demonstrate that the implementation of a SERE-derived (Survival, Evasion, Resistance, Escape) experimental torture program began months before it was given legal cover by the memos written by John Yoo and Jay Bybee in 2002. Other stories, for instance of "War on Terror" captives being drugged and tortured, have been related by the prisoners themselves, by their attorneys, and by US and international rights agencies, including the International Committee of the Red Cross, whose report on the torture of CIA "high-value detainees" was leaked to Mark Danner of the *New York Review of Books*.

While Binyam in many ways had a very different personal background than Dimitrov, like the Bulgarian political leader, he was transferred to a US foreign ally for torture. He was drugged. He was considered unreliable and a "disposal" problem for US leaders, who kept secret the actual treatment they inflicted. Both were victims of a torture program run by the CIA. Both were sent from their foreign torturer back to US custody, where they again endured intense psychological as well as physical torture.

Binyam Mohamed was arrested in Pakistan in April 2002, where his torture, as evidenced by the latest UK court release, was supervised by US agents. This torture was akin to the treatment meted out to Abu Zubaydah. Binyam was subsequently sent to Morocco in July 2002, where he was hideously tortured for 18 months, including a period where multiple scalpel cuts were made to his penis, and a hot stinging fluid poured on the wounds in an attempt to get him to confess to a false "dirty bomb" plot. (The US only dropped the bombing claims in October 2008.) At one point, a British informer was used to try to "turn" Mohamed into an informant for the US or Britain, just as the Artichoke treatment had been used to "re-orient" Dimitrov in a pro-US direction. Mohamed also indicated that he had been drugged repeatedly.

In January 2004, Binyam Mohamed was flown to a CIA "black" site in Afghanistan, the infamous "Dark Prison." Mohamed is one of five plaintiffs in an ACLU suit against Boeing subsidiary Jeppesen Data Plan Inc., which ran the aircraft for the CIA's "extraordinary rendition" program. According to an ACLU account:

> In US custody, Mohamed was fed meals of raw rice, beans and bread sparingly and irregularly. He was kept in almost complete darkness for 23 hours a day and made to stay awake for days at a time by loud music and other frightening and irritating recordings, including the sounds of "ghost laughter," thunder, aircraft taking off and the screams of women and children.

Interrogations took place on almost a daily basis. As part of the interrogation process, Binyam Mohamed was shown pictures of Afghanis and Pakistanis and was interrogated about the story behind each picture. Although Mohamed knew none of the persons pictured, he would invent stories about them so as to avoid further torture. In May 2004, Mohamed was allowed outside for five minutes. It was the first time he had seen the sun in two years.

Amazingly, this was not the end of Mohamed's ordeal. From the Dark Prison he was sent to Bagram prison, and later to Guantanamo. In August 2007, the British government petitioned the US for release of their subject. Eighteen months later, and after being subjected to more abuse at Guantanamo, he was finally able to leave US custody and return to Britain. (Many thanks to Dr. Jeff Kaye, who wrote an article with this author containing much of this information.)

Memorandum for the Record, to: File, from: Morse Allen, Subject: Kelly Case, January 25, 1952; Memorandum for the Record to: File, from: Morse Allen, Subject: Kelly Case, February 7, 1952; Office of Security File Summary: Dimitrov, Dimitre Adamov, Lyle O. Kelly, 46165; Office of Security Soft File: Kelly/Dimitrov, n.d.; Office of Security, SRS Report on Bluebird/Artichoke Overseas Activities, 1952-1963, December 1963. Office of Security, SRS Report on Artichoke Domestic Activities, 1952-1960,

December 1960; Office of Security, SRS Report on Artichoke Activities, 1953-1962, partial report, December 1962; Office of Security, Artichoke Team Case Listings, September 1962.

David Sanchez Morales: Morales was born in Phoenix, Arizona in 1925. As an enlisted man in the U.S. Army in 1949 he was with 7821st Composite Group, European Command in Germany, where he worked closely with the Counterintelligence Corps (CIA). His recruitment by the CIA began in late 1949, and he was approved for hire by Agency Security Chief Sheffield Edwards on January 18, 1950. The CIA was initially concerned about Morales' lack of schooling beyond high school and one year of college, but his fluent Spanish and superior service record overrode concerns. From his point of hire forward Morales exceeded expectations everywhere he went for the Agency. He retired from the CIA in 1975.

Political situation in Bulgaria in late 1940s and early 1950s: [from CIA report] "The political situation in Bulgaria has grown more critical as intensified efforts by the communist-dominated coalition Government to consolidate its control over the country have met with increasing resistance from the opposition. A Government campaign of intimidation and unprecedented violence is now under way, and the opposition is reported even to be preparing for possible armed resistance. Both groups have been impelled by the same factors: the anticipated general elections this fall, prospects of the withdrawal of Soviet troops when a peace treaty has been concluded, and the moral support given the opposition by the Western Powers." [Top Secret, "Political Tension in Bulgaria," Weekly Summary Excerpt 5 July 1946.]

Ganser, Daniele, *NATO's Secret Armies: Operation GLADIO and Terrorism in Western Europe* (Contemporary Security Studies), Routledge, UK, July 12, 2005; see also: Willan, Philip, *Puppetmaster: The Political Use of Terrorism in Italy*, iUniverse, October 7, 2002; Willan, Philip, *The Last Supper: The Mafia, the Masons, and the Killing of Roberto Calvi*, Robinson Publishing (April 12, 2007).

Letters by Dimitre Dimitrov [Donald A. Donaldson] to Francis Anne Loomis, 1964-1977; John Zolas, 1956-1962; Stella Pavlatos; and Marie Tosev, 1962-1976.

Draft article by Dimitrov for possible submission to *Argosy* or *Gallery* magazines concerning his time in Panama at Fort Clayton and Fort Gulick. Dimitrov writes in these pages that he was transported twice to Fort Gulick to discuss guerilla warfare techniques with U.S. Army officials.

Panama: Lindsay-Poland, John, *Emperors in the Jungle: The Hidden History of the U.S. in Panama*, Duke University Press, North Carolina, 2003; Musicant, Ivan, *The Banana Wars, A History of U.S. Military Intervention in Latin America From the Spanish-American War to the Invasion of Panama*, R.R. Donnelley & Sons Co., Indiana, 1990; Anderson, Scott, Anderson, Jon Lee, *Inside the League*, Dodd Mead & Co., Inc., New York, 1986.

Fort Gulick, Panama: Some military and CIA documents reveal that Fort Gulick served as a training center for handpicked paramilitary forces specializing in the proper handling and covert delivery of chemical and biological weapons. There is also evidence that several individuals who allegedly played prominent roles in the JFK assassination were trained at Fort Gulick, including Gilberto Alvarado, who made serious allegations about Lee Harvey Oswald's visit to Mexico City. Interviews with former Army CIC officers and "rough boys," and Artichoke team members: Dr. James L. Burch, Jr. and Miles P. Hunt. Dr. Burch, a retired psychologist, said that on several occasions in 1956 and 1957 Artichoke teams were dispatched to the air base in Atsugi, Japan, where the CIA kept a large station, to interrogate suspected double agents and at least one defector. CIA Artichoke reports support this claim. In all, it appears that, between the years 1952 and 1963, the CIA maintained about eight Artichoke Teams of upwards of five members each. Hunt states that at the close of World War II he, along with a team of CIC interrogators, moved into the I.G. Farben building at the same time that OSS officials "were moving huge wooden crates packed with corporate war files out of the facility into guarded trucks." He said, "In all, about 50 or more crates were loaded onto the trucks and then taken to waiting airplanes that transported them to a huge federal warehouse in Alexandria, Virginia."

Paul Gaynor, SRS, and Artichoke: Gaynor was notorious among CIA officials for having his staff maintain a systematic file on every homosexual, and suspected homosexual, among the ranks of Federal employees, as well as those who worked on Washington's Capitol Hill, including elected officials. Gaynor's secret listings eventually grew to include the names of employees and elected officials at State Government levels, as well, and even the siblings and relatives of those on Capitol Hill. In early January 1953, State Department employee John C. Montgomery, who handled considerable classified material, hanged himself in his Georgetown home after learning of his inclusion in Gaynor's list. In 1954, U.S. Senator Lester C. Hunt (D-WY) killed himself in his Senate office after he was threatened by Republicans, using information provided through Gaynor's staff, that they would publicly expose his son's homosexuality.

Gaynor's veiled and more despicable activities also extended to racial matters, a bigotry he seemed to share with many of the CIA's early leaders, as well as with some of the Pentagon's early ranking officials. According to one former CIA official, Gaynor was once informally cautioned by Allen Dulles concerning his overt support of former Congressman Hamilton Fish III, a strident Nazi sympathizer, and for associating, along with fellow CIA official Morse Allen, with John B. Trevor, Jr., an ardent racist, anti-Semite, pro-Nazi, who called for amnesty for Nazi war criminals. Before the CIA was formed, Gaynor was also associated with Trevor's father, John B. Trevor, Sr., a Harvard-educated attorney who worked with Army intelligence and who once strongly advocated arming a group of citizens with 6,000 rifles and machine guns to put down an anticipated Jewish uprising in Manhattan that only took shape in Trevor's twisted mind.

"Cries From the Past: Torture's Ugly Echoes" article by H.P. Albarelli Jr. and Dr. Jeff Kaye, Truthout. org, Sunday, May 23, 2010. "Black Psychiatry": According to the CIA, "the term refers to psychiatric methods used by trained and licensed physicians on human subjects. These methods may not be in the best interest of the subject's mental well being and health." The same official said: "There was no shortage of or problems recruiting psychologists in the 1950s and 1960s who would willfully, and sometimes enthusiastically, practice 'Black Psychiatry.'" The various methods of "Black Psychiatry" were provided in a training setting in the 1950s and beyond to at least the 1970s at the CIA's Butler Health Center facility in Rhode Island, where many physicians worked for the Agency. The Butler Center also served as the Agency's central site for exposing CIA officials to the effects of LSD and other drugs.

Author's interviews with Mose Hart, Miami, Florida, 2004, 2007; CIA-TSS official Walter Driscoll spent countless hours with White at the Greenwich Village safe house; for more on the CIC's "Rough Boys" see: McCoy, Alfred W., "Science in Dachau's Shadow: Hebb, Beecher, and the development of CIA Psychological Torture and Modern Medical Ethics," *Journal of the History of the Behavioral Sciences*, Vol. 43(4(, p. 401-417; H.P. Albarelli Jr., "Project Artichoke and the CIA's Development of Enhanced Interrogation Techniques," forthcoming article 2013; CIA Quarterly Reports, Artichoke Project, 1953-1961, CIA, Security Research Staff, Office of Security.

"The Missing General," by Willem Oltmans, *Gallery* magazine, April 1978, pp. 2-8. Article in Mary Ferrell Archives: 1993.08.11.17:4238:530039; JFK box 35.

Plausible denial: Plausible denial is a CIA term of art. In general, according to the doctrine of plausible denial, intelligence activities "that might cause embarrassment (because they violate international law or for some other reason) should be planned and executed in a way that allows the head of government [or the Agency itself] to deny that he had anything to do with the activities or even know they were occurring." Shulsky, Abram, *Silent Warfare: Understanding the World of Intelligence*, Brassey's (U.S.), New Jersey, 1991, pp. 132-134.

CIA Memorandum for Director, FBI, Attn: Intelligence Division, Subject: Assassination of President John Fitzgerald Kennedy – Willem Leonard Oltmans, Dimitur Adamov Dimitrov, November 11, 1977. This memorandum is heavily redacted and CIA declined to make censored, blackened sections available.

Memorandum for Anthony A. Lapham, CIA General Counsel from A.R. Cinquegrana, CIA's Office of General Counsel, Subject: Bluebird/Artichoke Soft File Review –"Kelly" – Dimitrov, D.A., October 7, 1977; partial pages from Bluebird/Artichoke Report, CIA Office of General Counsel, November 1977.

Hypnotism: See numerous CIA-SRS files from 1952-1961, Project Artichoke, author's FOIA files; see Beck, Melvin, *Secret Contenders*, Sheridan Square Publishers, New York, 1984. Well-known Israeli psychic Uri Geller reported that the CIA used him in Mexico City on a number of hypnosis-related missions in return for visa preferences and special treatment.

Rosselli: John Rosselli was well acquainted with David Sanchez Morales. It appears that Rosselli first encountered Morales in Florida in the early 1960s. Of all the Mafia figures that the CIA interacted with, Rosselli became the one most deeply involved in Agency assassination programs and closest to several top CIA officials, including Sheffield Edwards, CIA Office of Security chief. Sometimes Edwards would attend parties where Rosselli was present. To the extent that anyone became close to him, Rosselli was also quite close with Jean Pierre Lafitte [QJ/WIN], mostly due to his shared fondness for fine food and wine. Rosselli was introduced to Lafitte by George Hunter White, who had first encountered Rosselli in Chicago in the late 1940s. There is some evidence that Rosselli occasionally would pass information to White, either directly or through Lafitte who, on several occasions in the late 1960s and 1970s, met with Rosselli in Las Vegas. There is no evidence this author could find that Lafitte knew Morales, or that Rosselli knew Dimitrov.

Notes

Dorothy Mae Kilgallen: Kilgallen was a well known American journalist and television game show panelist, who died suddenly on November 8, 1965. She was very critical of the Warren Commission and other government entities. She was the only reporter to interview Jack Ruby, Oswald's killer. Reportedly, after her Ruby interview, she told several of her friends that she had information that would "blow the JFK case sky high." Kilgallen was adamant about never revealing her confidential sources to anyone and was known for anyways getting her "facts right." Kilgallen's death is controversial mainly because the medical examiner wrote "circumstances undetermined" on her death certificate. Another remarkable coincidence of many between the JFK story and the murder of Frank Olson is that New York medical examiner Dominick DiMaio signed Kilgallen's death certificate. In 1999, DiMaio told this author that he had "no recollection of ever signing Kilgallen's certificate" or of "ever having dealt with her death." At the same time, DiMaio told this author that he was cognizant that Frank Olson had been dosed with LSD nine days before his death in 1953, something he never revealed at the time of Olson's death or later in 1975 when it was revealed publicly that the CIA had dosed Olson with the drug. No autopsy was ever performed on Olson. Kilgallen's autopsy is reported to have revealed no evidence of homicide.

CHAPTER FIVE

"Oswald Told Untrue Story of His Soviet Stay, Says Man Who Aided Him on Return," by Peter Kihss [Khiss], *New York Times*, November 26, 1963, p.1A. Noteworthy here, is that *New York Times* reporter Peter Kihss [Khiss], who extensively covered the JFK assassination, eventually grew very skeptical about much of the information he was given about Lee Harvey Oswald from the Warren Commission, CIA, and FBI.

FBI Interview Report, November 27, 1963, taken by SA Wilfred Goodwin from Spas T. Rankin, Rio Grande, Ohio on 11/27/63, author's FOIA FBI files.

Nerin E. Gun: *The Red Roses of Dallas*, Frederick Muller Publisher, London, UK, 1964.

On Gun also see: Memorandum for the Director of Central Intelligence from Richard Helms, Deputy Director of Plans. Subject: "Plans of British and French Publishing Firms to Publish the Thomas Buchanan Articles on Assassination of President Kennedy," 20 April 1964. This Helms memo – without offering any supportive evidence to its claims that named people within it are communists or members of the Communist Part of the U.S. – reads in part: 'The Agency is aware that Thomas Gittings Buchanan, born in Baltimore, Maryland, 16 March 1919, was discharged as a reporter for The Washington Star in 1948, at which time he admitted he was a member of the Communist Party of the United States.... Concerning Nurin [sic] Gun, it has been reported that he was born in Rome on 22 February 1924 of Turkish parents. He has been a free lance journalist since 1946 and has placed articles in American and Western European publications. In 1956 he resided in Toronto, Canada and the Turkish Consulate in that city refused to grant him a passport to return to Turkey because he was considered by them to be a communist.'"

Gun and Marina Oswald: In an article from a French-language weekly newspaper, *MINUTE*, dated August 21, 1964, Issue No. 125, Marina Oswald told Nerin: "I had two husbands: Lee, the father of my children, an affectionate and kind man; and Harvey Oswald, the assassin of President Kennedy. I immensely pity Lee, my husband. But I do not feel anything with regard to Oswald, the assassin. That Oswald was a madman."

Epstein & Jones Harris: Epstein, Edward Jay, *Legend: the Secret World of Lee Harvey Oswald*, McGraw-Hill Book Company, New York, 1978, pp. 156 and 310.

FBI Urgent Teletype to FBI Director J. Edgar Hoover from Cincinnati office, Subject Interview Cleary F'Pierre/Lee Harvey Oswald, IS-R-Cuba, June 19, 1964.

Additional FBI Reports on those who had contact with Oswald in NYC: FBI report and teletype to FBI director J. Edgar Hoover: Subject: Lee Harvey Oswald, NYC, June 13-14, 1963.

CIA Memorandum from Foreign Documents Division, J. J. Bagnall, to Personnel Security Division, Attn. Mr. William E. Enott, Subject: Request for Clearance of Contract Personnel – Project USJPRS, August 13, 1957.

Memorandum from Chief, Foreign Documents Division to Chief, Personnel Security Division, Subject: RAIKIN, Spas T. #134669, signed by W.M. Knott.

FBI Memorandum, Subject: RAIKIN, Spas T., by SA [Special Agent] Joseph A.H., Headquarters Field Office, November 20, 1957.

CIA Memorandum for the Record, Subject: Spas Todorov Raikin by Donald M. Allen, CIA SRS, September 9, 1960.

CIA memorandum to Chief, FDP from Chief of Station Lloyd K. Desmond, Subject: Escape of Seven Bulgarian Refugees, November 29, 1951.

"Lee Harvey Oswald and New York City, June 1962: A Complete Investigation and Substantial Questions and Issues," Draft paper by H.P. Albarelli Jr., August 2012, author's files.

FBI Report, New York City, December 13, 1963 by John James O'Flaherty, 105-38431, Case: Lee Harvey Oswald, report dated 12/11/63, furnished to New Orleans Office, FBI.

Spas Raikin's anti-communist connections: A "Report to the Rockefeller Commission" by Ralph Schoeman dated March 26, 1975, reads: "And on their arrival back from the Soviet Union, the Oswalds were met by Spas T. Raikin, supposedly of the Travelers Aid Society, who helped them through customs [sic]. Raikin in fact was an official of the American Friends of the Anti-Bolshevik Nations, Inc., its secretary-general and he was in touch with the Central Committee of the Kuomintang in Taiwan. This extreme right-wing group was part of the World Anti-Communist Congress for Freedom and Liberation together with such as the former officer of the Abwehr in Riga and Lisbon from 1939 to 1945. The supposed communist, Lee Harvey Oswald, who would pretend to be a spokesman for a Fair Play for Cuba Committee was met by a man of the extreme neo-Nazi right with intelligence affiliations. But what was to prove important was that the World Anti-Communist League of Raikin had contact with Carlos Bringuier of the Cuban Revolutionary Council. The CRC was the organization of the CIA and E. Howard Hunt located at 544 Camp Street in New Orleans, the headquarters to be of Oswald's dummy Fair Play for Cuba Committee. Raikin thus was related to intelligence operations of Hunt and of the CIA supported Student Revolutionary Directorate (DRE) with whom Oswald was to have consistent contact. Oswald in Dallas was to have consistent contact as well with the right-wing émigré Russian community with oil, intelligence and military industry connections. George Bouhe was of Texas Instruments. Max Clark was security director of Convair and with General Dynamics, Paul Raigorodsky was director of the Tolstoy Foundation performing confidential missions for the U.S. government in Europe."

Peter Dale Scott writes: "Spas T. Raikin was also the Secretary-General of the American Friends of the Anti-Bolshevik Bloc of Nations, a small but vigorous group of right-wing revanchiste East Europeans in direct touch with the FBI [Author's Note: a reference to this group was most likely the redacted section of one of the 1964 FBI memorandums quoted above.] and Army Intelligence – and also with the Gehlen spy organization in West Germany, the Kuomintang in Taiwan, the mother of Madame Nhu, right-wing Cubans like Oswald's DRE contact Carlos Bringuier, and other elements of a shadowy 'World Anti-Communist League.' This WACL had contacts with U.S. anti-communists in New Orleans, in the building with the Camp St. address [Author's Note: also in the Balter building before this when E. Howard Hunt maintained a small office there] used by Oswald on his pro-Castro literature, and also by the CIA's Cuban Revolutionary Council of which Bringuier had once been press secretary. As I have indicated in my book, The War Conspiracy, Mr. Raikin's personal correspondents in Taiwan (the Asian Peoples' Anti-Communist League) were intelligence agents involved in the Kuomintang's narcotics traffic – a fact dramatically illustrated by the 1971 arrest in Paris of the Chief Laotian Delegate to the APACL, whose suitcase containing 60 kilos of high-grade heroin would have been worth $13.5 million on the streets of New York." See: The Assassinations: Dallas and Beyond, edited by Scott, Paul L. Hoch and Russell Stetler, Random House, New York, 1976. (For decades now there has been strong tightly-maintained intelligence chatter in several closed circles concerning that when Oswald in 1963, months before the assassination, visited the Habana Bar, New Orleans he may have been exposed to possible drug trafficking dealings connected to either DRE or CRC. Some people in these same circles wink and nod at related reports that accompanying Oswald on at least one of his visits to the Habana Bar was David Sanchez Morales.)

Not noted by Peter Dale Scott are Raikin's eventual connections through the World Anti-Communist League, formed in 1966, with other assassination-related persons and groups. Through this League connection, and many of the organizations Raikin was already aligned with, there exists the possibilities that he could have encountered Gen. Edwin Walker, H.L. Hunt, Edward Butler, Clay Shaw, David Ferrie and others. Indeed, several documents "withheld" from government and private researchers appear to indicate a possible link between Raikin and a 1962 plot to assassinate Fidel Castro. Volume Two of this work will completely explore these connections in detail.

Mae Brussell, "The Nazi Connection to the John F. Kennedy Assassination," The Rebel, January 1984. Appreciation to Andrea Skolnik for drawing my attention to this article found online at maebrussell.com/articles.

Notes

In 2001, Spas Raikin published a book entitled *Rebel With a Just Cause: Volume 2, A Political Journey Against the Winds of the 20ᵗʰ Century, Reminiscences 1922-1951*, Pensoft Publishers, Sofia, Bulgaria, 2001, First Edition, April 2001. In his book, which makes for some fascinating reading in parts, Raikin makes no mention whatsoever of his work in New York City with Travelers Aid, or of his encounter with Lee Harvey Oswald and Oswald's family.

In 2012, Spas T. Raikin, at 90 years of age, donated his papers to the Hoover Institution, Stamford University. The university released a detailed press release on January 20, 2012 about the donation headed: "Oswald's Bulgarian Connection: The Spas Raikin Papers." The release reads in part: "In New York, Raikin became a social worker who helped resettle Bulgarian refugees in the United States under a State Department Program, as well as a staff member in the Travelers Aid Society. It was in that capacity that he was directed to meet Lee Harvey Oswald upon his return from Russia. *Raikin found a hotel room for Oswald, his wife, and baby, and handed [Oswald] a check, that paid for their move to Forth Worth, Texas.*" [Emphasis added] Obviously, this public relations claim is less than truthful, unless, of course, the FBI and Travelers Aid Society of New York, as well as the New York City Welfare Department all lied to the Warren Commission and others. Raikin's biography, as detailed in the press release says nothing about his work for the CIA.

CHAPTER SIX

This chapter on David Sanchez Morales is not intended to be comprehensive in nature and has been edited down from a longer, more detailed work written in 2012 and still in progress in ample ways. There were many more fascinating personalities and intelligence officials that Morales had significant dealings with. Parts of this chapter were also drawn from a forthcoming article entitled, "An Unauthorized History of CIA Projects QJ/WIN and ZR/RIFLE," by H.P. Albarelli Jr. and Daniel MacCurdy.

Phillips, David Atlee, *The Carlos Contract*, Ballantine Books, New York, 1978, pp. 32, 130, 139.

Interview with Paco Gutierrez Dial, New Mexico, 2010; interview with a Morales relative who declined to be identified in this book; interviews with Carmen E. Rodriguez, Phoenix, Arizona; numerous, heavily redacted CIA and U.S. Army documents concerning David Morales, 1948-1970; interviews with former associates and family members of David Morales who declined identification in this book; various personal letters and diary entries by Viola June Cobb; unpublished 1968 interview with Geraldine Shamma; Bohning, Don, *The Castro Obsession*, Potomac Books, Dulles, Virginia, 2005, see pages 161-162 on Morales; Martino, John & Wylie, Nathaniel, *I Was Castro's Prisoner*, The Devin-Adair Company, New York, 1963, p. 47.

CIA Memorandum to Chief, CIA Research Division from Ermal P. Geiss, Personnel Security Branch, Subject: MORALES, David Sanchez-39418, 10 October 1949.

We are given a unique glimpse of some of the CIA's activities in Panama at the time Morales and Dimitrov were there by former CIA case officer, Balmes Nieves "Barney" Hidalgo, Jr. (In 1960, Cuban-born Hidalgo was a trainer at Miami's JM/WAVE station.) In 1950, Barney was dispatched to Panama for assignment at the CIA's covert station within Fort Amador, a U.S. Army installation whose military intelligence unit provided cover for the Agency. Hidalgo's initial responsibilities were to "set up a Travel Control system that would allow the [CIA] Station to monitor all arrivals, departures and transits, both legal and illegal, through the Republic of Panama." Among the many persons Barney monitored was a young Bulgarian named Dimitrov, who arrived in Panama by air and under heavy guard by a cadre of U.S. Army MPs and military intelligence officers. Dimitrov was taken to the Army's Fort Clayton. Hidalgo, following Dimitrov's eventual departure, apparently never dealt with him again. But, years later, in 1978, Barney was requested to appear before a closed session of a Congressional Assassination Sub-committee in Washington, D.C. He was asked "about certain operations in Mexico City and my opinion of how the death of the President might have been connected to these operations," Barney recounted in 1997. "I gave my opinion that the people who killed [Kennedy] were the ones who hated him. But who hated him? Many Cubans in the U. S. and Cuba hated him. The Mafia hated him. His Vice President, Johnson, surely disliked him as much as the Kennedy family disliked Johnson. In general, my opinion was then, and still is, that the killing was a conspiracy in spite of the 'findings' of the Warren Commission. In an attempt to put blame on a high CIA Case Officer, Dave Phillips (now dead), the committee asked me to identify a drawing of one Maurice Bishop as being identical with Phillips. This 'Bishop' was alleged to have had conversations with Lee Harvey Oswald in the US Embassy and had erased taped surveillance photos of Oswald entering the Embassy. I was asked if this composite drawing was Phillips. I said that it was not. While admitting that I had met a Maurice Bishop (more than one Agency Case Officer had used that alias) I never told the Committee who the person in the drawing was. He was a very good man who was already dead. He had been a very good friend and superior and I decided that I would not connect him with the affair unless specifically asked. I was not." Barney revealed, "Later I was called a 'former covert operative believed by the staff to have been used on assignments involving violence.' This I quote from … the book *Conspiracy* by Anthony Summers. Someone in the committee evidently leaked confidential information regarding my name, official alias, address and phone numbers. I soon started receiving death threats from an individual who called me by the name that was my official alias used during the Bay of Pigs and during my Miami operations against Castro. The Agency tried to make me recant my statements that I had met a Case Officer at headquarters by the name of Maurice Bishop."

Barney also revealed to the Subcommittee that from 1960 to 1964 he worked for the JM/WAVE Miami Station and in that role traveled on occasion to New York City, New Orleans, Mexico City, Guatemala, and El Salvador. Queried by the subcommittee on his visits to Mexico City, Barney said that he was sure he had been there in 1961 and 1962, and possibly 1963 but he could not recall. Barney testified that he worked in Mexico City under an alias and that he had contact with a number of CIA officials there, including one woman (unnamed, but believed by this author to be June Cobb) who, along with another unidentified CIA official, helped Hidalgo "in setting up what we called a safe house" in Mexico City.

See: Hidalgo, Barney, *Hey Spic!*, American Literary Press, Inc., Five Star Special Edition, Baltimore, Maryland, 1997; testimony of Barney Hidalgo, Thursday, August 10, 1978, House of Representatives, Subcommittee on the Assassination of President Kennedy, Washington, D.C.

Bohning, Don, *The Castro Obsession*, Potomac Books, Dulles, Virginia, 2005, see pages 161-162 on David Morales.

Hans Tofte: Weiner, Tim, *Legacy of Ashes: The History of the CIA*, Doubleday, New York, 2007, p. 56; Thomas, Evan, *The Very Best Men*, Simon and Schuster/Touchstone, New York, 1995, pp. 53, 187, 313; Haas, Michael E., *In the Devil's Shadow: UN Special Operations During the Korean War*, Naval Institute Press, Annapolis, Maryland, 2000, pp. 151, 178-80; Cullather, Nick, *Secret History, The CIA's Classified Account of Its Operations in Guatemala, 1952-1954*, Stanford University Press, California, 1996, 2006, pp. 39-41.

Charles F. Gilroy: I encountered Gilroy through my attempts to interview Grayson Lynch in Florida. Lynch lived not far away from where I did. I was never successful in getting Lynch to say anything more than what he had written in his book, but I was very fortunate through the process to learn of the existence of a group of retired Agency and military people who informally meet regularly at a restaurant near downtown Tampa.

Tofte: Hunt, E. Howard, *Undercover: Memoirs of an American Secret Agent*, Berkley Publishing Corporation, New York, 1974, p. 137. In this book, Hunt recalls that Tofte "alleged that the [CIA Security] agents not only entered his home illegally but stole a quantity of his wife's jewelry, and [Tofte] sued [Richard] Helms [and the CIA] over the incident."

Albert Haney: Weiner, Tim, *Legacy of Ashes, The History of the CIA*, Doubleday, New York, 2007, pp. 94-95.

Enno Hobbing and *Time* Magazine: *The Man Who Knew Too Much*: Interview Transcript, Thomas Bass and Bob Garfield, Friday, October 20, 2006, On the Media, WNYC, New York.

Henry Hecksher: Murphy, David E., Kondrashev, Sergi A., Bailey, George, *Battleground Berlin: CIA vs. KGB in the Cold War*, Yale University Press, New Haven, 1997, pp. 115, 122-124, 407-408.

Trento, Joseph J., *The Secret History of the CIA*, Forum, Random House, New York, 2001, pp. 125, 168.

Morales at the White House: Philips wrote that Nixon "asked a number of questions, concise and to the point, and demonstrated thorough knowledge of the Guatemalan political situation. He was impressive." When all was said and done, Phillips recalls, Eisenhower shook Allen Dulles' hand and said, "Thanks, Allen, and thanks to all of you. You've prevented a Soviet beachhead in our hemisphere."

Rip Robertson: "The Kennedy Vendetta" by Taylor Branch and George Crile, III, *Harpers* magazine, July 23, 1975; "CIA Plotted to Blast Cuba Refinery" article by Jack Anderson, *The Washington Post*, Sat., April 11, 1971, p. D15.

Earl Williamson: Williamson, following Cuba, was sent to Costa Rica to act as station chief. U.S. ambassador to Costa Rica, Clarence Boonstra objected to Williamson's assignment, later stating: "When he [Williamson] was proposed as station chief, I had objected unless Williamson would work under my orders and would not do what he was noted for, disrupting things with unnecessary covert action – monkey business."

LAD/JFK Task Force CIA document, Subject: Review of ZR/RIFLE File, October 1976, Job # 69-S-551. Author's files.

Lansdale and Valeriano: McClintock, Michael, *Instruments of Statecraft: U.S. Guerilla Warfare, Counterinsurgency, and Counterterrorism, 1940-1990*, Pantheon Books, New York, 1992.

CIA Memorandum for the Record, Subject: "Interview [by R.D. Shea, CIA] with Dave Morales, GS-14, Chief of CI Section, Miami Base, 25 May 1961," June 2, 1961.

Hunt, Linda, *Secret Agenda*, St Martin's Press, Thomas Dunne Books, New York, 1991.

Lucien E. Conein: "From Aiding French Resistance to Plotting in Vietnam, Conein Led a Life of 'Pulp Adventure,'" by Bethanne Kelly Patrick, see: Military.com. Also see: Spartacus Educational Biography of Conein at Spartacus.schoolnet.com.uk by British historian John Simkins; letters/diaries of Jean Pierre Lafitte, 1945-1954, private family collection shared with author; Memorandum for the Files from Pete Kinsey, Subject: Interview with Lucien Conein, January 21, 1975, author's files; "The Colonel's Secret Drug War" by George Crile III, *Washington Post*, Sunday, June 13, 1976, pp. C1-C5; Valentine, Douglas, *The Strength of the Wolf*, Verso Books, London, UK, 2004.

Gerry Hemming: In 1999 and 2000, I interviewed Hemming by telephone. Then in 2001, I interviewed Hemming in North Carolina. My primary interest in meeting with Hemming was an American soldier of fortune, Richard "Rex" Sanderlin, who had mysteriously died in 1963 in Cuba. Sanderlin, a former U.S. Marine who served in Korea, had been recruited to go to Cuba by Frank Sturgis. I also took the opportunity to ask Hemming about Lee Harvey Oswald. Hemming was a wealth of information on Oswald, Cuba, and many other subjects but recalled only meeting Sanderlin once briefly in Cuba. I had been referred to Hemming by two other former soldiers of fortune, Neill W. Macaulay and Donald Soldini, both of whom lived in Florida. Hemming spoke confidently about Oswald saying that he met with him twice in the United States and perhaps one additional time. I carried on an e-mail correspondence with Gerry for years after I met with him. I was saddened by his death in January 2008. He was one in a billion. Volume Two of this work will contain a full chapter on Hemming. Hemming was a central member of a group of anti-communist soldiers of fortune retained by cut-outs for CIA to train anti-Castro Cubans in the early 1960s at a secret compound on No Name Key, Florida, 25 miles north of Key West. Hemming consistently said over the past two decades that he was never a CIA employee. Hemming, who knew David Morales, but thought "Morales lacked the hard-earned skills to train certain Cubans in counterinsurgency techniques," told this writer that the JFK assassination was acted out by "three teams" consisting of "two shooters" and "one spotter." "Each team was unmindful of the others," he explained. Hemming identified Cuban Nestor Izquierdo as one of the spotters in the assassination. "Nestor was close to Morales and Rosselli," Hemming said, "in a school-boy sort of way. He thought Morales was the cat's pajamas," Hemming said sarcastically. "He admired Rosselli because of his amorous skills with the women he always brought around, I guess." [More on Hemming in Volume Two of this work.]

Currey, Cecil B., *Edward Lansdale: The Unquiet American*, Brassey's, Washington, D.C. and London, 1998.

June Cobb in Guatemala: Classified Message to Winston Scott, CIA Station Chief, Mexico City, November 15, 1961. Interviews with Cobb's close friends Connie McMurphy and Sylvia Hogarth, New York City and California, 2010-2011.

CIA Memorandum for the Record, Subject: "Conversation 21 June 1972 with Dave Morales re: AMCLATTER-1" by WH/COG/OS official Chris Hopkins, 21 June 1972.

Nicholas Deak: See the excellent Salon.com article: "Amazing Investigation: How a Real Life James Bond Got Whacked by a Bag Lady Assassin," by Mark Ames and Alexander Zaitchiki, also found at Alternet. org.

Corn, David, *Blond Ghost: Ted Shackley and the CIA's Crusades*, Simon & Schuster, New York, 1994.

Ayers, Bradley, *The Zenith Secret*, Vox Pop/Drench Kiss Media Corporation, New York, May, 2006.

Astorga, Luis, Drug Trafficking in Mexico: A First General Assessment, Management of Social Transformations (MOST), Discussion Paper No. 36, www.unesco.org/astorga, n.d.

Mahoney, Richard D., *Sons and Brothers: The Days of Jack and Bobby Kennedy*, Arcade Publishing, New York, 1999.

Hancock, Larry, *Someone Would Have Talked*, JFK Lancer Productions and Publications, Southlake, Texas, 2006.

Undated CIA Memorandum for the Record, David S. Morales: Recommendation for the Intelligence Medal of Merit, and Citation of Award, probably written in 1977-1978.

Fonzi, Gaeton, *The Last Investigation*, Thunder Mouth Press, New York, 1993.

Twyman, Noel, *Bloody Treason: The Assassination of John F. Kennedy*, Laurel Publishing, Rancho Sante Fe, California, 1997.

Horne, Douglas P., *Inside the Assassination Records Review Board*, Volume Five of Five, Douglas P. Horne, 2009.

Some writers believe that David Morales was also in LA at the time of RFK's assassination.

CHAPTER SEVEN

Oswald, Robert with Land, Myrick and Barbara, "He Was My Brother," newspaper article, *The News*, Mexico, D.F., World News, October 3, 1967.

FBI Special Agent report by Jack B. Peden, DL 100-10461, December 24, 1963. Basye's letter to Dr. Milton H. Erickson is included in Peden's report, as is Dr. Erickson's letter of reply to Basye.

E-mail correspondence with children's book author and writer, Dale E. Basye, Jr., January 2012. Dale Jr. says his father "started out at the *Dallas Morning News* as a junior editor in the early 1960s. He then moved to the oil industry, working for the Oil and Gas Journal, and ultimately Chevron as their communications person." He added, "I have never, ever heard my father mention hypnotism one way or the other. My dad was in the Navy for a bit, graduated from Texas Tech. He loved marathon running." The elder Dale Basye died in 2005. There appears to be no record of his doing any follow-up to his 1963 efforts on Oswald and hypnotism. We know of no reaction, if any, on his part to the 1975-1978 Rockefeller Commission revelations about the CIA's Project Artichoke and MK/ULTRA hypnosis experiments.

FBI Report DL 44-1639 on Ira Jefferson "Jack" Beers by Special Agent James C. Kennedy and Will Hayden Griffin, December 4, 1963.

FBI Report DL 44-1639 on Dale E. Basye by Special Agent Jack B. Peden, December 18, 1963.

Condon, Richard, *The Manchurian Candidate*, McGraw-Hill Book Company, New York, 1959. First feature film released in 1962; the second released in 2004.

Hypnosis and CIA: Albarelli Jr., H.P., *A Terrible Mistake: The Murder of Frank Olson and the CIA's Secret Cold War Experiments,* Trine Day Publishers, Oregon, 2010.

Kathy Kay: a British woman, Kay was a regular and popular stripper at Ruby's club. The policeman with Kay that evening was probably Harry Olsen, who married Kay following the assassination. At the time of Basye's meeting with Ruby, Kay and Olsen were married to other people.

Jack Beers: Ira Jefferson "Jack" Beers recalled that Ruby's "shot was a dull, muffled explosion, indicating the gun was very close to Oswald's body." Beers also told the FBI that on November 23, 1963, when Oswald "had been brought downstairs from the jail to appear before representatives of the press and television … Oswald had what he would consider a 'smirk' on his face. Beers said that while Oswald was being brought down the hall for this appearance, he [Oswald] seemed to be searching for a microphone in which to make some statement."

Letter from J. Lee Rankin, General Counsel, President's Commission on the Assassination of President Kennedy, to Richard Helms, Deputy Director for Plans, CIA, May 19, 1964.

Very interesting to note is that one of DDP's Helms' written responses to Rankin, which was stamped 'SECRET" and never released publicly by the Warren Commission, contains references to the Soviet Union's work with "psychogenic agents such as LSD," which Helms stated was "receiving some overt attention with, possibly, applications in mind for individual behavior control under clandestine conditions." Helms also wrote in a July 19, 1964 memorandum to the Commission: "Soviet research on the pharmacological agents producing behavioral effects has consistently lagged about five years behind Western research. They have been interested in such research, however, and are now pursuing research on such chemicals as LSD-25, amphetamines, tranquillizers, hypnotics, and similar materials." This memorandum to the Warren Commission may have been the Agency's very first tacit acknowledgement that it, too, was working with LSD and other similar drugs.

TSD Report on Brainwashing: "Communist Control Techniques," TSD Technical Report, CIA Technical Services Division, Behavioral Activities Branch, April 2, 1956, author's files.

Estabrooks, G.H. and Lockridge, Richard, *Death of the Mind,* E.P. Dutton & Company, New York, 1945; "Hypnotism Comes of Age" by G.H. Estabrooks, *Science Digest,* April 1971, pp. 44-50.

In addition to Dale Basye, at least one other person in late 1963 alerted the FBI to the possibility that Oswald may have been a subject of hypnotic suggestion. This was a person initially identified as informant BU T-1, whom this author has identified as Wilton J. Lutwack. Lutwack offered his theory to the FBI on December 5, 1963. Lutwack, the founder and president of a multi-million dollar book-cover corporation, advised the FBI that while he was in college at the University of Iowa, and many years since, he had studied hypnotism. He told the FBI he was "aware that the U.S. Army is experimenting in the use of post-hypnotic suggestion," and that he was of the opinion that during Oswald's three-years in Russia, he was prepared "for the assassination of Kennedy through mistreatment and brainwashing, followed by post-hypnotic suggestion." Lutwack told the FBI that "facts supporting his theory" could be found in a book by George H. Estabrooks, *Hypnotism.* Interestingly, Lutwack's cousin was Justice Marc J. Robinson, one of the presiding judges at the Nuremberg War Crimes trials.

CHAPTER EIGHT

Letter from Director J. Edgar Hoover, FBI, U.S. Department of Justice, to Honorable J. Lee Rankin, General Counsel, President's Commission on the Assassination of President Kennedy, January 17, 1964 [Commission No. 295.]

Airtel Message to: SAC, New York, From: Director, FBI (105-82555), Subject: Lee Harvey Oswald, IS-CUBA, "Personal Attention," January 28, 1964.

Airtel to Director, FBI from SAC, New York (97-1791), Subject: Robert B. Taber – RA CUBA, January 31, 1964.

Memorandum to Chief, CIA Personnel Security Division from Leo J. Dunn, Special Assistant, Subject: Robert B. Taber [351511 (O); 54547 (C)], March 13, 1964.

DePalma, Anthony, *The Man Who Invented Fidel,* Public Affairs, Perseus Books Group, 2006. A well-sourced and credible account.

"Change of Disguise" by Herminio Portell-Vila, Bohemia Internacional, February 2, 1965, pp. 16-17, 53. This article states, "During his speech of November 27, 1963, at the University of Havana, when Castro said 'the first time Oswald was in Cuba,' his tongue was under the influence of Peralta cognac, and he revealed something very important."

In September 2010, Robert Taber's son Peter wrote: "The issue of whether Robert Taber knew Lee Harvey Oswald is a red herring, which in the present-day inaccessibility of archival records should only be of interest to diehard conspiracy speculators. As his son, I can state with complete assurance he never knew the man accused of assassinating John F. Kennedy. Furthermore, he despised the sort of prankster schoolboy incompetents who made up the CIA and would never have affiliated himself with them. Certainly Robert Taber was sympathetic to the Cuban Revolution, both in the romantic sense and as it promised to be, both politically and culturally, before the United States of the Dulles brothers' mindset foolishly drove Cuba into the Soviet orbit. The Fair Play for Cuba Committee was founded by my father and fellow former CBS reporter Richard Gibson in an attempt to bring public attention to this tragically short-sighted vision of the U.S. policymakers of the time. Sadly, it was ultimately unsuccessful and almost half a century later we have all paid and continue to pay a stiff price for not learning the lessons that might have been learned. Incidentally, by the time Kennedy was assassinated and Oswald was briefly linked to a shadowy New Orleans chapter of FPCC, the national organization had been thoroughly infiltrated by a motley assortment of government agents and the expected collection of half-baked malcontents which, together with the by-then confirmed direction of American foreign policy, rendered its original purpose moot. By the time Kennedy was shot my father had long disassociated himself from the group and gone back to Cuba for a couple of years to work directly on behalf of the revolution. That included taking up arms against U.S.-supported mercenaries parachuted into Oriente Province. He also participated with the defending forces at Playa Giron (Bay of Pigs) where he was gravely wounded. He returned to the United States to rejoin his family the following year and was vilified by the scurrilous likes of Senators Thomas Dodd and James Eastland before settling back into an honorable and otherwise ordinary enough life as a journalist and freelance writer. He died in 1995."

Taber, Robert B., *M-26, The Biography of a Revolution*, Lyle Stuart, New York, 1961; and *The War of the Flea: A Study of Guerrilla Warfare Theory and Practice*, Citadel Press, New York, 1970.

U.S. Department of State cable from Tangier re T. E. Davis, Jr., Action: Secretary of State, 59 Priority, Info: Rabat 33, December 9, 1963, 12:00 noon.

J. Edgar Hoover, FBI Director, letter of appreciation to [National Bank of Detroit teller] Raymond J. Van Hoeck, June 27, 1958.

CIA Briefing Manual on Project MK/ULTRA; Author's Project Artichoke, 1952-1964 files; Project ARTICHOKE Briefing Paper, CIA-SRS, Morse Allen, 1955.

Dr. E.D. Luby: see Cohen, B.D., E.D. Luby G. Rosenbaum and J. S. Gottlieb. *Combined Sernyl and Sensory Deprivation*. Comparative Psychiatry, 1, pp. 345-348, 1960.

Reporter Seth Kantor accompanied President Kennedy on his fatal visit to Dallas, and reported that on that same day, he encountered Jack Ruby at Lakeland Hospital. "Ruby Role in Guns Studied," article by Earl Golz, *Dallas Morning News*, Dallas, Texas, July 10, 1976, p. 7A.

"Dallas: An Unfinished Drama," article by Seth Kantor, *Detroit News*, November 11, 1977, p. 3. Kantor's article provided no details, sources or evidence backing up why he dubbed Davis a CIA operative. This author could not locate any CIA comment on the claims Kantor made in this article, but was informed that the Agency has a hefty 201 file on Davis, which the CIA formally refused to release in any fashion.

Kantor, Seth, *The Ruby Cover-Up*, Kensington Publishing Company, Zebra Books, New York, 1980.

Department of State Priority Incoming Telegram, from: Madrid to: Secretary of State, Subject: Thomas Eli Davis, Jr., Control 19195, No: WIROM 1335, December 30, 1963, 1:00 p.m.; Department of State Incoming Telegram, from Madrid, Subject: Victor Oswald, -2- 1335, December 30, 1:00 p.m.

FBI Memorandum to J. Edgar Hoover from SAC, LA (105-14523), Subject: Thomas Eli Davis, Jr. Neutrality Matters; IS-Haiti, June 7, 1963; see also FBI Memorandum to J. Edgar Hoover, Director FBI, from: SAC, Los Angeles (105-14523) (P) Subject: Thomas Eli Davis, Neutrality Matters; IS-Haiti, June 6, 1963.

Interview with T.E. Davis, Jr., 1018 Bangor Lane, Ventura, California, June 7, 1963, by SA John J. Schmitz, Los Angeles 105-14523: JMF, June 6, 1963.

Paul V. McNutt: Perhaps entirely coincidentally, on November 25, 1963, three days after the JFK assassination, FBI director J. Edgar Hoover received a somewhat odd letter from an Indiana attorney named Jesse H. Williamson. Williamson recounted to Hoover that during World War II, he had sat at a restaurant table across from Hoover "with Paul V. McNutt's daughter and my own daughter, then a translator in secret work in Washington." See: Letter from attorney Jesse H. Williamson to FBI director J. Edgar Hoover, November 25, 1963, Mary Ferrell Archive.

FBI Interview of William Henry Wade on May 28, 1963, Gardner, California by SA Richard J. Dorers and SA James H. Hoose, Jr., LA 105-14523, May 28, 1963.

Personal letter from "Charlie" Siragusa, June 12, 1963, to Albertine and George Hunter White in Sausalito, California.

Eladio del Valle: Kaiser, David, *The Road to Dallas: The Assassination of John F. Kennedy*, Belknap Press of Harvard University Press, Massachusetts, 2008, pp. 402-403.

Letter from Director J. Edgar Hoover, FBI, U.S. Department of Justice, to Honorable J. Lee Rankin, General Counsel, President's Commission on the Assassination of President Kennedy, January 17, 1964 [Commission No. 295].

Airtel Message to: SAC, New York, From: Director, FBI (105-82555), Subject: Lee Harvey Oswald, IS-CUBA, "Personal Attention," January 28, 1964.

Airtel to Director, FBI from SAC, New York (97-1791), Subject: Robert B. Taber – RA CUBA, January 31, 1964.

Memorandum to Chief, CIA Personnel Security Division from Leo J. Dunn, Special Assistant, Subject: Robert B. Taber [351511 (O); 54547 (C)], March 13, 1964.

Leslie Norman Bradley: FBI Reports to Director on Leslie Norman Bradley from Minneapolis and New Orleans via Airtel, December 28, 1967 and December 29, 1967.

Press Release, Wednesday, July 3, 1963, From the Senate Internal Security Subcommittee, Robert Taber Testimony Released; Memorandum to Mr. Mohr, from C.D. DeLoach, Subject: Robert Taber's "Return Engagement" Testimony, July 1, 1963.

Robert Taber testimony, Fair Play for Cuba Committee, Hearings Before the Subcommittee to Investigate the Administration of the Internal Security Act and other Internal Security Laws of the Committee on the Judiciary, U.S. Senate, 87th Congress, First Session, Part 3, June 15, 1961.

Robert Taber testimony, Castro's Network in the United States, Hearing Before the Subcommittee to Investigate the Administration of the Internal Security Act, U.S. Senate, 88th Congress, First Session, Part 3, April 10, 1962.

Gosse, Van, *Where the Boys Are: Cuba, Cold War America & the Making of a New Left,* Verso Books, U.K., 1996.

Williams, Robert F., *Negroes with Guns,* Marzani & Munsell, Publishers, New York, 1962.

"Castro Arrests Ex-Aide for 'Double Cross'," *Miami Herald,* Herald Wire Services, October 22, 1960, p. 1.

Robert F. Williams testimony, Hearing Before the Subcommittee to Investigate the Administration of Internal Security Act, U.S. Senate, February 16, 1970.

U.S. Department of State cable from Tangier re T. E. Davis, Jr., Action: Secretary of State, 59 Priority, Info: Rabat 33, December 9, 1963, 12:00 noon.

J. Edgar Hoover, FBI director letter of appreciation to [National Bank of Detroit teller] Raymond J. Van Hoeck, June 27, 1958.

FBI Reports on Thomas Eli Davis' Attempted Bank Robbery, 1958, 1959.

CIA Briefing Manual on Project MK/ULTRA, 1976; author's Project Artichoke, 1952-1964 files; Project ARTICHOKE Briefing Paper, CIA-SRS, Morse Allen, 1955. Dr. E.D. Luby: see Cohen, B. D., E. D. Luby, G. Rosenbaum and J. S. Gottlieb, op. cit.

"Ruby Role in Guns Studied," article by Earl Golz, *Dallas Morning News,* Dallas, Texas, July 10, 1976, p. 7A.

Kantor, Seth, *Who Was Jack Ruby?* Everest House Publishers, New York, 1978;

CHAPTER NINE

Eric Ritzek often refers to himself in his alleged diary as "the Master Craftsman." Readers familiar with Freemasonry will note that in the formal Masonic Education Program there is an attained ranking referred to as the Master Craftsman. Additionally, the European guild system allowed only "master craftsmen" as guild members.

Report of the FBI Laboratory, Washington, D.C., Re: Lee Harvey Oswald, aka IS-R-CUBA, September 18, 1964, Lab. No. D-457801 AX, FBI File No. 105-82555.

"The Diary of Eric Ritzek" – CIA Office of Security copies, file number 201-289248, DL 100-10461, Document Number: DBA-82152, September 19, 1964 [copy of actual black colored, bound notebook diary].

FBI Memorandum/Airtel to Director, FBI (105-825550, from SAC, Dallas (100-10461), RE: Lee Harvey Oswald, aka IS-R-CUBA, August 31, 1964. In this report the FBI noted that following its laboratory studies of the diary it planned no additional studies of the document.

Enoch hynauch: These appear to be ancient Welsh words. The word *hynauch* is also said to have come from an ancient encryption system from the Middle East called Atbash.

CHAPTER TEN

The sections of this chapter concerning Charles William Thomas, Elena Garro, Winston Scott, David Atlee Phillips, Lee Harvey Oswald, and June Cobb are drawn from a much longer article by this author and Daniel MacCurdy, which will be published in 2013. Please note, this chapter focuses primarily on the Charles William Thomas-Elena Garro story as it unfolded in Mexico City. The writers (Albarelli and Daniel MacCurdy) are not unmindful about other characters and incidents directly and indirectly related to Elena Garro's story. Volume Two of this work will deal with all of those related accounts.

Letter from Charles William Thomas to Honorable William P. Rogers, Secretary of State, July 25, 1969, with memorandum and four attachments.

"A Guantanamo Connection? Documents Show CIA Stockpiled Anti-malarial Drugs as 'Incapacitating Agents'" by Dr. Jeffery Kaye, Truthout.org report, June 2012.

Charles R. Norberg: See this author's article co-written with Daniel MacCurdy, *The Genesis of the CIA's Fund for Human Ecology*, forthcoming, 2013.

Deep appreciation goes from this author to writer and assiduous researcher Bruce Campbell Adamson for his findings and information concerning Charles R. Norberg. As previously noted, Volume Two of this work will feature a lengthy chapter on Adamson's findings.

Mellen, Joan, *Our Man in Haiti: George de Mohrenschildt and the CIA in the Nightmare Republic*, Trine Day LLC, Walterville, Oregon, 2012, pp. 259-260. Mellen writes, "de Mohrenschildt hired a Washington, D.C. lawyer named Charles R. Norberg. From 1946 to 1951, Bruce Adamson discovered, Norberg had been employed by CIA. Norberg's assignment now for de Mohrenschildt was to enlist foreign service officers on his behalf. Norberg learned from Haitian officials that de Mohrenschildt had been dealing with 'one Haitian government worker who had a personal stake' in his sisal enterprise."

Attachment to Thomas' letter to Secretary of State Rogers, Subject: "Investigation of Lee Harvey Oswald in Mexico," July 25, 1969.

"Lee Harvey Oswald & Kennedy Assassination," REFERENCED: Memorandum of Conversation, December 10, 1965, Elena Garro de Paz, Mexican Writer, From: Charles Wm. Thomas, Political Officer, December 25, 1965. Un-redacted FOIA copy; author's files.

CIA Memorandum for the Record, Mexico City CIA Station, from COS [Chief of Station] Winston Scott, to CIA Headquarters, Subject: Visit by Three Staff Representatives of Warren Commission [William Coleman, W. David Slawson and Howard P. Willens], 11 April 1964. All three commission representatives were attorneys; Willens was an assistant attorney general, DoJ.

Top Secret Memorandum for the Record, From: W. David Slawson, To: Warren Commission, Subject: Trip to Mexico City, April 22, 1964.

Winston Scott & Warren Commission: Because Warren Commission attorney William Coleman was African-American, Jefferson Morley writes in his book, *Our Man in Mexico*, that Winston Scott's "personal politics," according to Anne Goodpasture, his longtime CIA assistant, were "to the right of George Wallace" the "populist Alabama governor who championed racial segregation." One can only speculate about how Scott felt about Mexicans, or brown people. Former associates of Scott's, who declined to go on the record in this book, report that he was "occasionally prone to off color jokes about Mexicans." Morley's book is well worth reading for anyone interested in Oswald's Mexico City time. This author's conclusion from reading it was that Scott really knew little about what was going on with Oswald, the CIA outside of Mexico City, and most likely was a bit too preoccupied with his personal and social affairs to concentrate on much else. This is not, however, to say he was not a good administrator. Perhaps he was too good at administration and delegation.

Thomas' "Suicide": "The State Department: Undiplomatic Reforms," *Time* magazine, Monday, November 15, 1971. Also: an undated CIA document outlining the history of Elena Garro's allegations about Oswald and the twist party, headed "EJL First Draft," bears the handwritten note: "Should also point out that HSCA investigated whether Thomas' 'selection out' was related to the investigation. Conclusion was that his dismissal was unrelated. Get statement from Mrs. Thomas."

Charles Thomas: An October 21, 1963 CIA memorandum on "Thomas, Charles William, 376 323" reads: On 16 October 1963, Mr. Walter JESSOP, Office of Security, advised that Charles William THOMAS received a security clearance on 12 February 1954 under provision of EO 1045 to handle material including 'Top Secret' in connection with his duties. Liaison contact further advised that SUBJECT [Thomas] has a background investigation completed in 1951."

CIA Memorandum for the Record from N.L. Ferris, Legal Attaché, to Mr. Winston Scott, Subject: LEE HARVEY OSWALD, 105-3702 (10-13-66), October 13, 1966.

Handwritten and typed notes by Joyce Pinchbeck/June Cobb on "Elena matter" dated 1964 and 1964, sent to "DP" and "HH," partial copies Lopez files and author's files; Pinchbeck notes on E. Odio and "Rosicrucian connections" with handwritten notes on Elena Garro and "occult influences France and Mexico."

Memorandum from Bert M. Bennington, Acting Chief, Division of Protective Security, Department of State, to Deputy Director of Plans, CIA, Subject: Charles W. Thomas, August 28, 1969. This memorandum marked attention: Miss Jane Roman.

FBI LHM for Director of the FBI, "Lee Harvey Oswald – Report that Subject Attended Party Given by Ruben and Silvia Duran in September-October 1963," December 11, 1964.

Dr. Toruno-Haensly, Rhina, *Encounter with Memory,* Palibrio, Bloomington, Indiana, First Edition, 2004.

FBI Interview Report with Elena Garro de Paz and Elenita Garro re: Lee Harvey Oswald, Mexico City, Mexico, December 11, 1964.

Charles Thomas/Sarah McClendon Article: FBI Memorandum from C.D. Brennan to W.A. Branigan, Subject: Assassination of JFK, November 22, 1963, May 6, 1971. Charles Thomas' name is redacted in all copies of this memo released to the public and researchers. McClendon's name is not redacted. There is no mention in the memo of Thomas working for the CIA.

Baker, Russ, *Family of Secrets,* Bloomsbury Press, 2009. Baker's book contains a great deal of vital information that adds to the George de Mohrenschildt story as can be related to Charles William Thomas.

Morley, Jefferson, *Our Man in Mexico: Winston Scott and the Hidden History of the CIA,* University Press of Kansas, 2008.

Newman, John, *Oswald and the CIA,* Skyhorse Publishing, 2008.

Obituary for Clarence A. Boonstra, *Washington Post,* Friday, April 14, 2006.

CIA Memorandum for the Files, from Willard C. Curtis, Subject: June COBB, 25 November 1964.

CHAPTER ELEVEN

Viola June Cobb, aka Clarinda E. Sharp, was born in 1927 in Ponca City, Oklahoma. Cobb's father's name was Jasper E. Cobb; her mother was Jesse Lois Sharp. June had two older brothers, Jasper E. Cobb, Jr. and Tom Arthur Cobb. June served as an adjunct of the Civil Air Patrol squadron of Norman, Oklahoma, at the rank of 2nd Class Lt., before she left Oklahoma for attending school in Mexico.

This chapter is drawn from the author's draft manuscript, *CIA Femme Fatale: The Secret Life of June Cobb,* 2011. Because this is work in progress, for privacy and confidential reasons, some of the FOIA and CIA documents, as well as private letters, diary entries and interviews used in this chapter are not specifically cited below. Volume Two of this work will contain a lengthier, more detailed chapter of June Cobb's CIA activities in New York, New Orleans, Cuba, Guatemala, and Mexico City, as well as Robert Clayton Buick's dealings with Oswald.

Contrary to Internet mythology, June Cobb did not have a twin sister (she did have two brothers) nor was she a trained aircraft pilot.

"Recruitment Plans for Viola June Cobb," report by Harry Hermsdorf, CIA Covert Action WH-4 Staff, not dated, most likely early June 1960.

Andres Lopez Restrepo and Alvaro Camacho Guizado, "From Smugglers to Warlords: Twentieth Century Columbian Drug Traffickers," *Canadian Journal of Latin American and Caribbean Studies,* Jan.-July, 2003.

Eduardo Saenz Rovner, *THE CUBAN CONNECTION: Drug Trafficking, Smuggling, and Gambling in Cuba from the 1920s to the Revolution,* University of North Carolina Press, Chapel Hill, 2008, translated by Russ Davidson.

Various Federal Bureau of Narcotics documents from 1948 through to 1963, Record Group 170, Drug Enforcement Administration [DEA], National Archives and Records Administration [NARA], College Park, Maryland; interview with former FBN and DEA official Arthur Eugene Doll, Colorado, 2010. Arthur Eugene Doll served in the U.S. Navy during World War II (Asiatic-Pacific Theatre) and in the U.S. Army during the post-war years through the Korean War, where he served in an intelligence unit. Discharged from the Army in 1956, Doll was recruited by the Federal Bureau of Narcotics, and served the Bureau into its DEA years, until 1977. From 1965-1971, Doll was stationed to Beirut, Lebanon. When I asked Doll if June Cobb was his source, he hesitated and then said, "I still can't tell you the woman's name. She was a confidential informant who had helped us on quite a few cases. Leave it at that."

George Hunter White Papers, Perham Foundation, Sunnyvale, California; private George Hunter White and Jean Pierre Lafitte letters and documents, compliments Albertine White, Sausalito, California, and Rene Mankel Lafitte, Miami; "Paul Mondolini and the Cuban Pipeline to the United States" article [in French, 2010] by Jeanette Mia Monti, Paris-based private research group, Combine Associates, Ltd.; Paul D. Bethel, who was the press officer at the U.S. Embassy in Havana during Castro's rise to power, revealed in his 1969 book entitled *The Losers* that William Morgan produced great consternation among U.S.

officials in 1959 when he began "keeping company with a very unwholesome American who lived at the Capri Hotel," whom others described as a "gangster." Federal Narcotics Bureau documents strongly suggest that this was an associate of Spiritto's who frequently stayed at the Capri Hotel using a false U.S. passport bearing the name Samuel Rowland. This was actually Paul Damien Mondolini, a former French intelligence agent turned international narcotics trafficker. Mondolini, who is also believed to have been an occasional CIA contractor, was a silent partner in the El Morocco Club in Camaguey, Cuba, which was also partly owned by Meyer Lansky and Isadore Shadletsky. Mondolini had been deported from Cuba to France in February 1957 to face criminal charges but quickly returned to Havana, where he often brokered heroin shipments using convicted New York City traffickers Adela Castillo and Milton Abramson.

Jesse Gregory, Lee Harvey Oswald, & Adela Castillo: Gregory advised the FBI on December 5, 1963, according to the Bureau's report of the same date, "that he believed he saw an individual in Mexico City who bore a striking resembalance to Lee Harvey Oswald." Gregory was a retired Civil Service Commission employee, who worked in Washington, D.C. until 1953. Beginning August 30, 1963, he took a two-month vacation to Mexico City. There he took a room for one month in an affordable boarding house located at 43 Varsobia. Gregory told the FBI that "on or about September 23, 1963 or September 24, 1963, "a young white male American, name unknown, about 20 to 25 years old, obtained a room at the same boarding house." Gregory soon talked with this young man for about an hour one day when they had breakfast together at the boarding house. The young man, who never introduced himself to Gregory, said that he "disliked the United States Government and the United States as a country." The man told Gregory that one of the main reasons he disliked the United States was "the racial situation." The FBI report states, "Gregory has the impression this suspect was not particularly anti-Negro, but was disturbed over the racial problem in the United States and felt nothing would be done in the United States to alleviate the racial problem under the current system of government." The young man told Gregory he was going to college in Mexico but that he had once lived in Washington, D.C. and Texas. Gregory also told the FBI that the young man may have been involved in distributing communist literature in Mexico with a group of Mexican students. Gregory also told the FBI that a woman named Adela Castillo also had a room at the boarding house and that she knew the young man he thought was Lee Harvey Oswald. Apparently, the FBI never again spoke with Gregory. Before his death, Gregory remarked on several occasions that he felt that the FBI did not really take his report seriously and most likely did no follow-up on it. Gregory also said that "the more I studied photos of Oswald" and "listened to tapes of him [Oswald] speaking, the more I was certain the man I sat down with was Lee Harvey Oswald."

Ronald Dante: Some readers may recall that Dante was also known as "Dr. Dante," a well known hypnotist and stage performer, whom Jack Ruby met with in New York City, prior to the assassination, in August 1963. Ruby apparently, according to Warren Commission documents and reports, knew Dr. Dante well. Dante was also known as Ronald Pellar, possibly his real name, although he employed numerous aliases, including Phillip Harris, Earl James Clevenger, Harold Ritchie, and Harold James Hood. A 1956 CIA SRS-OS memorandum reveals that the Agency in May of that year discussed requesting that CIA-contractor Dr. Louis West interview Ronald Pellar in order to assess his potential usefulness in matters related to Project Artichoke. Asked about his possible relationship to the CIA in 2006, an 87-year old Pellar said, "I've lived this long fairly well and hope to survive another decade or more, so no comment on that." In the mid-1970s, Pellar was convicted of attempting to murder a rival hypnotist, Michael Dean, a well-known California hypnotist Pellar had known for over 15 years. Pellar served about 4 years in prison for trying to hire a hit-man to kill Dean. People who knew Pellar well claim that he was "an extraordinary hypnotist who could induce a subject to do anything while in a trance state." After being released from prison, Pellar continued to perform and to teach hypnotism, and also created what he said was the very first "permanent-makeup business in the world." Said Pellar, "I made over $14 million doing permanent makeup." Pellar claimed that he was born in 1920 in Malaysia and, after his parents were murdered when he was 5 years old, grew up in a Chicago orphanage, until he was 11 years old, when he walked away from the orphanage and soon learned hypnotism. He also organized a number of business ventures. A number of Pellar's former associates claim that he visited Jack Ruby in prison on at least two occasions, but this author was unable to verify this. The Warren Commission reported Ruby's contacts with "Dr. Dante" in 1963, but apparently made no attempts to discover Dante's real name or any information about him.

FBI Memorandum for the Record from A.H. Belmont to S.B. Donahue, Subject: Foreign Political Matters – Cuba Internal Security- Cuba, April 15,1960.

Hotel Luma: A July 1969 Department of Justice memorandum reveals that the Hotel Luma was used by anti-Castro forces and individuals. The memo reads in part: "T-2 [informer] further advised that Dr.

Notes

VARONA, ARTIME, RASCO and CARRILLO were in Mexico City and held a press conference together at the Hotel Luma, Calle Orizaba #16, Mexico, D.F. to present the [anti-Castro] manifesto of the FRD." See: U.S. Department of Justice, FBI Memorandum titled: "ANTI-FIDEL CASTRO ACTIVITIES," July 19, 1960.

Testimony of Viola June Cobb, Hearings before the Subcommittee to Investigate the Administration of the Internal Security Act and other Internal Security Laws of the Committee on the Judiciary, United States Senate, Eighty-Ninth Congress, Second Session, March 30, 1962. See page three of her testimony for her mention of Warren Broglie.

CIA Memorandum: Meeting in New York City with June Cobb, Aide to Juan ORTA from Harry Hermsdorf to Chief CIA WH/4, June 3-5, 1960.

CIA Interviews with Viola June Cobb, Boston, Massachusetts and Washington, D.C., 1960, un-redacted copies, author's files.

CIA Memorandum to Chief, Security Support Division, Attn: Fred Bacci, From: Acting Chief, Interrogation Research Division [Ralph True], Subject: June Cobb, 17 October 1960.

Moncada: The July 26, 1953 attack on the Batista fortress called Moncada by Fidel Castro's rebels. The attack failed and more than half of Castro's rebels captured were slaughtered, with many brutally tortured before being murdered. See: Santamaria, Haydee, *MONCADA: Memories of the Attack That Launched the Cuban Revolution*, Lyle Stuart, Inc., New Jersey, 1980. Robert Taber, a founder of the Fair Play for Cuba Committee, wrote this book's introduction.

June Cobb's Interrogation: September 21, 1960, Room 1515, Governor Clinton Hotel, New York City. [Transcribed copy CIA.]

Jean Pierson/Elizabeth Vetter: E-mail message from Gerry Hemming: GPHEMMING to Malcolm Blunt, UK, Subject: JUNE COBB et al, August 16, 2004.

June Cobb's Second CIA Polygraph Session, October 11, 1960, Hotel Bellevue, Boston, Massachusetts, author's files.

Jean Pierson's notes on AMUPAS/1 Boston trip, 14 October 1960, Jean Pierson WH/4/CI/4448.

Charlotte Bustos-Videla: In February 1961, Ms. Charlotte L. Zehrung, employed by the CIA's WH Division, became engaged to Cesar Bustos-Videla, a U.S. citizen. The two were married on March 18, 1961 in Dayton, Ohio. See: Memorandum for Director of Security from Paul E. Arneson, Chief WH Support Division, 9 March 1961.

"ARRB Document Releasing History: Batch Three" by Joseph Backes. See: http://www.kenrahn.com/March/ARRB/arrb-docs.html.

Piccolo: HSCA Interview of Joseph Piccolo, Jr., 11 August 1978, Box 24, Folder 19, HSCA files, Washington, D.C.

Federal Bureau of Narcotics Memorandum from William J. Durkin to Winston M. Scott, Political Section, Federal Bureau of Narcotics (FBN), Subject: Joseph Paradise, December 19, 1966; also see FBN records on Jean Aron, William Paradise, Jean Jehan, and Alexander Schoenfeld, NARA; and for further information on William Paradise see: Valentine, Douglas, *The Strength of the Wolf*, Verso Books, London, UK, 2004.

Memorandum for the Record to Acting Chief, CIA Personnel Security Division, from Special Assistant, PSD William O'Donnell, Subject: Piccolo, Joseph S. #109-709.

Cobb travels to Mexico: Memorandum to: WH/3/Mexico from Jean Pierson, WH/4/CI, Subject: WH/4/CI Asset Traveling in Mexico, June 5, 1961.

Modern Poetry in Translation, Series 3, No. 1, 2004, *Eunice Odio* by Keith Ekiss and Mauricio Espinoza.

"James Jesus Angleton and the Kennedy Assassination" by Lisa Pease, *Probe*, CTKA, September-October 2000, Volume 7, No. 6.

Memorandum from W.J. Kaufman, Chief, WH/1, Subject: Amendment of the OA for LICOOKY-1 (201-278841), 20 July 1964, signed by J.C. Spencer for Kaufman.

FBI Investigative Report, Dallas, Texas, February 19, 1964, by Special Agent Raymond P. Yelchak, DL 100-10461; Newman, Albert H., *The Assassination of John F. Kennedy: The Reason Why*, C.N. Potter, Crown Publishers, 1970.

Gaynor CIA memorandum on Lyle Stuart: Memorandum for Curator, Historical Intelligence Collection/ OCR, from Paul F. Gaynor, Chief, Security Research Staff/OS, Subject: Lyle Stuart aka Lionel Simon & "The Shark and the Sardines," 28 January 1964. Some readers may be surprised to learn that the CIA still regularly produces intelligence on American book publishers as well as in-house reviews of books it deems germane to intelligence gathering purposes and national security. The CIA also, according to one of its former officials, owns in part or wholly through public and private investments "at least 100 publishing houses" worldwide. This author's own book on the murder of Dr. Frank Olson was subjected to review by the Agency, as was its publisher, and the CIA took the further step of publicly reviewing the Olson book on its website which, much like the above Lyle Stuart review, deliberately went out of its way to provide erroneous and slanderous information about the book.

Robert Clayton Buick: On September 1, 2011 Buick wrote one of his many e-mail messages to this author: "No, Lee Harvey Oswald never attended any of my bullfights. It has been so many years [Buick is in his 80s] that it is difficult for me to remember everyone I met and associated with at the Hotel Luma. I had (only) two or three conversations with Oswald and my interest was more directed to [Warren] Broglie and Fritz Waehauf [who] seemed to be more involved in the secretive activity than Oswald. Lee was more direct than they were. They were more secretive and clandestine whereby Oswald was seemingly more revealing (in a sense) trying to tell me (in reality) to stop this plot to kill the president and I truly believe this after I have reviewed this encounter over and over again and researched his specific intent throughout the many years. When you put it all in sequence, it all comes to one conclusion, JFK has to go or we in Texas are going down. Turn over the stones and what do you find??? Do you have the balls to do it, for I have already done it." Buick also wrote to this author on September 2, 2011, in response to a question about "what women you may have encountered at the Hotel Luma?," Buick wrote: "There were several Latin women in attendance at the Luma. I saw one from the Cuban Embassy pass a small brown package to Oswald …"

Buick, Robert Clayton, *Tiger in the Rain*, AuthorHouse, Bloomington, Indiana, February 14, 2006, First edition.

Notes

JACK PEEBLES

ATTORNEY AT LAW

305 BARONNE STREET - SUITE 1006

NEW ORLEANS, LA. 70112

TELEPHONE: 525-4361

December 13, 1976

000531

Rep. Thomas N. Downing
Select Committee on Assassinations
U.S. House of Representatives
Washington, D.C. 20515

Dear Representative Downing:

I represent a client in the New Orleans area who
may have information relevant to the inquiries of the
Select Committee on Assassinations.

My client is a professional person, who holds a
Ph D. degree in the biological sciences and is currently
teaching and doing research in the field. She advises
that during April, 1963 she became acquainted with one
Jose A. Rivera in Washington, D.C., who at the time
was connected with the National Institute of Health as
an administrator. My client believes that Mr. Rivera
may have had some connection with research activities
of the Central Intelligence Agency, and may have
conducted unauthorized experiments on her with drugs
during the spring of 1963. More interesting, she further
advises that at the time the same Mr. Rivera gave her a
message to give to Lee Harvey Oswald in New Orleans
upon her return, and in fact she did telephone a number
provided by Mr. Rivera and spoke to someone who identified
himself as Lee Harvey Oswald. She further advises that
she gave this information to the government immediately
after the assassination of President Kennedy, but no
further inquiries were made of her. She has recently
written the CIA and FBI and requested information under
the Freedom of Information Act, and these agencies have
replied that they have no records of significance
concerning her.

My client would like to provide you with any
information she can, if you feel that it may be helpful
to your investigation. She realizes that she cannot
produce independent verification for much of what she
states, and she does not want to be embarrassed by having
her name appear in your public records as having been a
person who makes sensational allegations. Therefore, she

The next two pages: In December 1976, Adele Edisen's attorney, Jack Peebles, wrote a
letter (see page 435) to the U.S. House of Representatives' Select Committee on Assassinations. There was no reply received to the letter.

453

has asked me to communicate with you and see if arrangements can be made so that, if she does provide a statement to you, the statement will remain confidential and her identity will remain confidential unless your investigation produces independent verification for her statements. Only in that event would she be willing to have her identity revealed.

I am not personally acquainted with this client, but I can assure you that she has produced sufficient evidence to me to establish her identity, the identity of Mr. Rivera, and I have noticed no contradictions or behavior on her part which would cause me to dismiss her statement out-of-hand.

If you wish to inquire further into this matter, let me know.

Thank you for your attention to the above.

Yours truly,

Jack Peebles

JP/cm